MW00335391

A Superpower Transformed

A Superpower Transformed

The Remaking of American Foreign Relations in the 1970s

DANIEL J. SARGENT

OXFORD
UNIVERSITY PRESS

OXFORD

UNIVERSITY PRESS

Oxford University Press is a department of the University of
Oxford. It furthers the University's objective of excellence in research,
scholarship, and education by publishing worldwide.

Oxford   New York
Auckland   Cape Town   Dar es Salaam   Hong Kong   Karachi
Kuala Lumpur   Madrid   Melbourne   Mexico City   Nairobi
New Delhi   Shanghai   Taipei   Toronto

With offices in
Argentina   Austria   Brazil   Chile   Czech Republic   France   Greece
Guatemala   Hungary   Italy   Japan   Poland   Portugal   Singapore
South Korea   Switzerland   Thailand   Turkey   Ukraine   Vietnam

Oxford is a registered trademark of Oxford University Press
in the UK and certain other countries.

Published in the United States of America by
Oxford University Press
198 Madison Avenue, New York, NY 10016

© Oxford University Press 2015

First issued as an Oxford University Press paperback, 2017

All rights reserved. No part of this publication may be reproduced, stored in
a retrieval system, or transmitted, in any form or by any means, without the prior
permission in writing of Oxford University Press, or as expressly permitted by law,
by license, or under terms agreed with the appropriate reproduction rights organization.
Inquiries concerning reproduction outside the scope of the above should be sent to the
Rights Department, Oxford University Press, at the address above.

You must not circulate this work in any other form
and you must impose this same condition on any acquirer.

Library of Congress Cataloging-in-Publication Data
Sargent, Daniel J.
A superpower transformed : the remaking of American foreign relations in the 1970s / Daniel J. Sargent.
pages cm
Includes bibliographical references and index.
ISBN 978-0-19-539547-1 (hardcover); 978-0-19-067216-4 (paperback)
1. United States— Foreign relations—1969-1974.   2. United States—Foreign relations—1974-1977.
3. United States—Foreign relations—1977-1981.   4. United States—Foreign relations—Decision
making.   5. Presidents—United States—History—20th century.   6. Statesmen—United
States—History—20th century.   7. Great powers—History—20th century.
8. Geopolitics—History—20th century.   9. Cold War.   10. World politics—1945-1989.
I. Title.
E855.S26 2015
327.73009047—dc23
2014013877

For Alethea

CONTENTS

ACKNOWLEDGMENTS

The year 1979 was pivotal in the making of this book. Culminating in the Soviet Union's invasion of Afghanistan, 1979 marked the end of the transformative phase that this book traverses. With rather less consequence, 1979 was also the year when the author began accumulating debts. This book does not discharge them, but I am glad to be able to acknowledge in print at least some of the obligations that I have accrued in the writing of it.

The research project that culminates in this book began at Harvard University, under the direction of Akira Iriye, who guided my graduate studies and gave me historical vantage on world politics. From Charles Maier, in effect a coequal adviser, I learned how to think about the past—and why the 1970s mattered. Ernest May taught me the history of the United States—and how to practice it. Niall Ferguson joined these mentors midway and brought new insight, energy, and enthusiasm. Others at Harvard from whom I learned include Sugata Bose, Liz Cohen, Erez Manela, and Kenneth Weisbrode, who was a peer in theory but a guide in practice. That I learned anything at Harvard depended on earlier mentors. At Cambridge University, Susan Bayly and David Reynolds taught me how to think, argue, and write like a historian. But I would never have made it to either Cambridge—Cambridgeshire or Massachusetts—without Paul Summers, Richard Wiles, and many other dedicated teachers, without whom the journey leading to this book would not have begun.

Various institutions facilitated the research that led to this book. At Harvard, the Department of History, the Charles Warren Center for American History, the Weatherhead Center for International Affairs, and the Graduate School of Arts and Sciences supported my career in various ways. Pre-doctoral fellowships at the Olin Institute for Strategic Studies, under the directorship of Steve Rosen, and at the Weatherhead Center provided sustenance and camaraderie, for which I remain most grateful. I am also indebted to Dunster House and Ann and Roger Porter, who offered lengthy hospitality and firsthand insight into the Ford administration. After Harvard, I spent a year—too little time—at International Security Studies at Yale University. I remain grateful to John Gaddis and Paul Kennedy for welcoming me to New Haven and, no less, for the superlative standards they have set for the field of international history.

It is at the University of California, Berkeley that this book emerged from the research project that spawned it. My colleagues at Berkeley have contributed much to the writing of it, from the standards they achieve in their work to their sustained engagement with my work. While the entire faculty participated in formal reviews, from which I learned much, I would like to mention those colleagues with whom I discussed the manuscript in person. These include Mark Brilliant, Richard Cándida-Smith, Cathryn Carson, Margaret Chowning, John Connelly, Alex Cook, Beshara Doumani, David Henkin, David Hollinger, Kerwin Klein, Yuri Slezkine, Jan De Vries, and James Vernon. Tom Laqueur, Mark Peterson, and Nick Tackett provided intellectual camaraderie not only in Dwinelle but also down hills. Neither Brian DeLay nor Robin Einhorn put themselves in such physical jeopardy, but both read this book in multiple drafts, and both gave crucial feedback on a late version that was 35,000 words longer than the final text. Brian has, moreover, been my closest collaborator at Berkeley; our being recruited together was, from my vantage, a double fortune. At Berkeley, Beth Berry and Ethan Shagan offered wise guidance in their roles as department chairs, while the magnificent staff in the Department of History supported my work in numerous ways. Generous funding from the Hellman Fellows Foundation enabled me to sustain an ongoing research agenda while completing the revisions on this book. Special acknowledgment is also owed to the University of California's Faculty Family Edge initiative, which made it possible to juggle a career and fatherhood.

The Institute of International Studies at Berkeley and its director Pradeep Chhibber supported my work in various ways, including sponsoring a 2010 manuscript conference that yielded much productive feedback. I remain indebted to all who participated in this conference, both to those who traveled from afar: Tim Borstelmann, Jeff Engel, Susan Ferber, Daniel Immerwahr, and Charles Maier, and to local colleagues, including Barry Eichengreeen and Nils Gilman, who made time in busy schedules to share deep insights. A number of graduate students joined the conversation and offered valuable feedback, including Anna Armentrout, Chris Casey, James Lin, Rhiannon Dowling-Fredericks, and especially Lynsay Skiba, whose research on human rights is making important contributions. To be able to work with scholars of their caliber is a great fortune. Two Berkeley graduate students also played key roles in the development of this book. Yana Skorobogatov provided invaluable research assistance, and Chris Casey assisted with technical revisions and designed the charts and maps.

Like any work of history grounded in the primary sources, this book could not have been written without the guidance of dedicated archivists too numerous to mention. For their assistance, from Ann Arbor to Yorba Linda, I am most grateful. The State Department's *Foreign Relations of the United States* book series also warrants acknowledgment. The *FRUS* series makes it possible for citizens and scholars to engage the historical documentation firsthand, and it sets high standards for accessibility and clarity. While I conducted most of the archival research in person, Leah Richier of the University of Georgia collected documents at the Jimmy Carter Presidential Library, and Martha Grant of Yale University visited the Minnesota Historical Society and interviewed former congressman Donald Fraser on my behalf. Acknowledgment is also due to those who shared documents with me: Barbara Keys, Victor MacFarland, Mike Morgan, and Lynsay Skiba. Conversations with retired officials enabled me to fill gaps in an emerging documentary record. Special thanks here are due to President Jimmy Carter and Dr. Zbigniew Brzezinski for conversing with me at length and with candor. I also acknowledge, with considerable gratitude, the support that the John Anson Kittredge Educational Fund and its chair, Philip Zelikow, lent to my research efforts.

Like most works of scholarship, this one has benefited from its author's engagement with other scholars. I am grateful for the opportunities I had to present parts of this project to receptive audiences and for the feedback that I received on such occasions. For these opportunities, I am grateful to Frank Gavin, Fabio Ghironi, Erez Manela, Andrew Preston, Jeremi Suri, and Stephen Wertheim. Thanks are also owed to friends and colleagues beyond Berkeley who engaged with the text at various stages. These include Mark Bradley, Hal Brands, Matt Connelly, Osamah Khalil, Bethany Moreton, Sam Moyn, and David Wight. Extra special thanks are due to Andrew Kinney, Mark Lawrence, and Mike Morgan, who read the manuscript at a late stage and provided much useful guidance. Meg McGavran Murray, my mother-in-law, read the final draft and excised from it diverse errors and infelicities of style. Susan Ferber at Oxford University Press has been my vital collaborator throughout: Susan brought this book under contract, guided its development, and worked with me through round and after round of revision. To work with Susan is a great privilege. Particular thanks are also due to everyone at OUP and Newgen who has shepherded this book into print, especially production editor Molly Morrison and copyeditor Ginny Faber. While I have received—and required—a great deal of help, it goes without saying that all errors, omissions, and surviving infelicities are my own.

That I was ever in a position to write this book owes to the companionship of friends and family too numerous to list but some of whom I would be remiss not to mention. I embarked on the journey that led to this book with Andrew Kinney and Kyle Harper, and they have had my back covered from Cambridge,

Massachusetts, to Plains, Georgia, and beyond. That I ever followed this path owes to the influence of Richard Davis. Himself a distinguished historian, Richard has been an exemplar of intellectual vigor, moral integrity, and personal courage; he defines the standards to which I aspire. I am grateful for all that he and Elisabeth Davis have done to support me. My parents, meanwhile, opened a world of opportunities and equipped me to pursue them. From my father, Jonathan Sargent, I acquired ceaseless curiosity and the conviction to pursue answers; he and my stepmother Paula Sargent have provided great support and sage counsel. From my mother, Judi Sargent, I learned the empathy on which historical writing depends; her support has been unconditional, and I am most grateful for it (and for all the help with child care). Neither my sister Amy Sargent nor my grandmother Mary Sargent had much to do with the writing of the book, but they had everything to do with the making of its author, and I would like to acknowledge them for that. Nor did my daughter, Corrina Mary Sargent, contribute much to the manuscript, beyond prodding at the keyboard and scattering papers on the floor. Yet, it is Corrina who makes the future count for so much more than the past. My wife, Alethea Sargent, encouraged me to keep these acknowledgments succinct. Accordingly, I will not attempt to express what I intend this book's dedication to convey.

ABBREVIATIONS

The following abbreviations recur throughout the text. Abbreviations that appear infrequently are defined as they appear. Abbreviations that appear only in the endnotes are defined in a separate list of abbreviations that appears in "Notes."

AFL-CIO	American Federation of Labor and Congress of Industrial Organizations
CIA	Central Intelligence Agency
CSCE	Conference on Security and Cooperation in Europe
EEC	European Economic Community
G-7	Group of Seven (industrialized countries)
G-77	Group of Seventy-Seven (developing countries)
ICBM	intercontinental ballistic missile
IMF	International Monetary Fund
NATO	North Atlantic Treaty Organization
NGO	nongovernmental organization
NIEO	New International Economic Order
NSC	National Security Council
OECD	Organization for Economic Cooperation and Development
OPEC	Organization of Petroleum Exporting Countries
SALT	Strategic Arms Limitation Talks

NOTE ON SOURCES AND PRICES

In the interest of concision, the endnotes follow a short-form system. Full citations to published sources appear in the bibliography section in "Sources." A list of abbreviations used in the endnotes to identify unpublished sources is included at the beginning of the section "Notes." Where historical documents are available in archival and published form (i.e., in the State Department's *Foreign Relations of the United States [FRUS]* series), the published—and most accessible—versions are cited wherever possible.

Prices are presented in nominal (i.e., current) US dollars, except when otherwise specified. Where prices are presented in real (i.e., adjusted for inflation) terms, they are presented in 2010 US dollars except when noted. Price conversions are based on the US Department of Labor's Consumer Price Index.

A Superpower Transformed

Introduction

History is a tale of efforts that failed, of aspirations that weren't realized, of wishes that were fulfilled and then turned out to be different from what one expected.

Henry Kissinger, 1974

A superpower is different. Unlike most other international actors, it operates on the world scale and even presumes responsibility for the international system as a whole. For William Fox, the political scientist who in 1944 distinguished the "super powers" from the rest, what made a superpower were military and geopolitical resources: armed forces and the far-flung bases from which they operate. Yet power, as Fox acknowledged, is relational; it involves the capacity to shape outcomes, to compel others to do what they would not do otherwise. Arms furnish power; but affluence coerces, ideas persuade, and culture entices. The resources on which power depends are myriad, and they are specific to context. As resources ebb and flow and the diverse contexts in which power is wielded evolve, superpowers rise and fall.[1]

Fox identified three superpowers in his times: Great Britain, the Soviet Union, and the United States. Yet, British superpower was a facade; it could not overcome material debilities and historical processes, especially decolonization, which dried the wellsprings of Britain's power. This left two. The Soviet Union was at the Second World War's end the world's vastest state, and its geographic expanse gave the Red Army proximity to the industrial heartlands of Europe and Northeast Asia. The war's end nonetheless found the Soviet Union in ruins and its leaders anxious to consolidate a defensive security. America's predicament stood in stark contrast. The United States bestrode the world in 1945, supreme in military capabilities, serene in geopolitical security, and unrivaled in economic productivity. Confident in their power, American leaders intended to remake the international order, expecting to assume "the responsibility which God Almighty intended," as President Truman put it, "for the welfare of the world."[2]

1

Estrangement between the United States and the Soviet Union transformed the postwar order into a bipolar settlement in which Washington assumed hegemonic responsibilities—not for the whole world, as Truman envisaged, but for the parts of it in which American influence and American arms predominated. The Cold War (or postwar) order that emerged from the 1940s endured for less than a quarter of a century. The postwar order collapsed in the 1970s, and a historical transformation in the superpower role of the United States ensued. This transformation proceeded across distinct arenas of international engagement; it redefined the sources of American power; and it wrought durable consequences, opening a new phase in America's career as a global superpower.

Until the 1970s, the United States superintended a rules-based international economic order in which tariffs and financial controls kept globalization at bay. With the implosion of the Cold War order, international trade and financial globalization resurged, reaching levels not seen since the late nineteenth century. The relationship of US economic power to the world economy also shifted. The United States in the era of the Cold War was a dynamo of production, an industrial hub, from which resources flowed outward to allies and clients. By the 1970s, this role could not be sustained. "Americans are moving into an era when we are going to be dependent on the outside world," explained one former official in 1973. "American self-sufficiency is over." In the 1970s, the US economy became dependent on external inputs, which made the United States a beneficiary of globalization, as it had been in the late nineteenth century. The United States in 1971 ran its first trade deficit since 1893. It became in the mid-1980s dependent on foreigners' savings to sustain domestic consumption and to finance what Fox defined as the superpower's hallmark—its worldwide military reach. The US government, meanwhile, began to cede the responsibility for managing the world economic order that it had exercised since the 1940s—not to foreign nation-states but to integrating markets.[3]

American military power did not retreat from the world in the 1970s, but the locus of its exercise shifted from Southeast Asia to the Middle East, which became a primary zone of US engagement, alongside Europe and Northeast Asia. Having delegated responsibility for regional security to allies and clients, the United States came in the late 1970s to accept a permanent military role in the Persian Gulf. This reorientation hinged on economic changes, which the oil crises of the 1970s made manifest. The world's dominant oil producer until the late 1960s, the United States became in the 1970s an oil importer. In 1977, Americans imported more than half the oil they consumed. In energy, as in other sectors, the advantages that once made the United States the powerhouse of the world economy were narrowing; as the margins of superiority closed, Americans imported more oil, more goods, and more capital, and the superpower became dependent upon the resources that an integrating world economy furnished.

If the United States was no longer the freestanding colossus it had been in the 1940s, new developments afforded its leaders opportunities to reinvent Washington's hegemonic role. A remaking of Cold War geopolitics centered on China. Until the late 1960s, Washington engaged the Communist world as a bloc and China as a foe. China and the United States nonetheless became tacit allies by the end of the seventies, and their realignment carried great significance. Developments beyond the realm of geopolitics opened up different kinds of opportunities. A mobilization for human rights flourished, not in the arena of interstate relations, but in a transnational realm of activism, engagement, and mobilization. The United States, like other governments, at first viewed human rights as an intrusion on the prerogatives of nation-states, but Washington came during the 1970s to align itself, at least rhetorically, with the new idiom of justice. Doing so marked the resurgence of a crusading style in US foreign policy and the end of a pragmatic Cold War phase, during which American leaders accepted ideological diversity as a reality of international life and a prerequisite for stability, even survival.[4]

The transformation of the American superpower in the 1970s was neither foreordained nor planned. Rather, it followed a series of adaptations to unexpected and confounding circumstances. This is not to say that American decision-makers in the 1970s did not pursue grand designs; they did, but these decision-makers mostly failed to achieve their intended purposes. Instead, they improvised in response to events that their strategies neither anticipated nor accommodated. Leaders thus participated in the remaking of America's superpower role, but they did not fabricate history on their own terms, as they themselves acknowledged. "History," Henry Kissinger reflected, "is a tale of efforts that failed, of aspirations that weren't realized, of wishes that were fulfilled and then turned out to be different from what one expected." Explaining how the seventies transformed America's world role and remade its superpower vocation, not according to a coherent design but in a chaotic pattern, is the central task of this book.[5]

⌀

"The postwar era is over," historian Fritz Stern declared in 1972. "Gone, too, are the simple—perhaps dangerously simple—certainties that went with it." The 1970s initiated a phase of uncertainty, and the unpredictability and improvisation that ensued recalled the disintegrations of earlier international orders. In 1815, the great powers reconstituted Europe's international order upon a crude equilibrium of interests and a shared commitment to containing revolutionary nationalism. Consecrated at the Congress of Vienna, the settlement of 1815 endured until the late 1840s, when the resurgence of revolutionary nationalism, combined with shifts in Europe's geopolitical balance, inaugurated a phase of decay that endured without cataclysm or resolution until the First World War. Statesmen in this late phase improvised, manipulating the forces of nationalism and the international system's geopolitical instabilities to serve their own purposes, none with more aptitude than Otto von Bismarck. Still, no statesman achieved the durable reconciliation between nationalism and international order that Giuseppe Mazzini, the great Italian nationalist, envisaged. The ascent of popular nationalism instead helped to precipitate the collapse of the nineteenth-century order, leading to the cataclysm of 1914.[6]

At the First World War's end, the victors worked to make a new settlement. The Peace of Paris proposed to reconcile nationalism to international order, establishing collective security and the consent of the governed as the dual tenets of world politics. The new architecture would not endure. After an interlude of stability in the mid-1920s, the settlement of 1919 faltered on its own omissions. The post-1919 order did not extend the prerogatives of national self-determination to the non-European world, which eroded its legitimacy, and collective security failed to contain German, Japanese, and Italian aggression in the 1930s, leading to its collapse. The Second World War devastated the international system's European core and left the flanking powers—Great Britain, the Soviet Union, and the United States—responsible for the remaking of world politics, resulting in another new international order, which cohered during the 1940s.[7]

The settlement of the 1940s was an achievement of design, an accommodation to circumstances, and an adaptation to events. The United States worked during the Second World War to construct a new architecture for collective security (the United Nations) and an economic regime that would permit international trade to coexist with new welfare states (Bretton Woods). American officials presumed that this new order would span the world, but the Soviet-American estrangement in 1945–46 cleaved the world in two. Thereafter the United States constructed a Pax Americana in its sphere of a divided planet. A hierarchical system of order, the Pax Americana was a hegemonic but consensual alliance within its transatlantic core, which Washington's leadership and the Soviet threat held together. The Soviet Union, for its part, came to construct its own hegemonic system, which was the East Bloc. These blocs were not equal, but the rough equipoise between them constituted a distinctive Cold War order, which stabilized in the early 1950s. The ideological and military competition between the Soviet and US-led blocs was intense, but both superpowers accepted division as the basis for stability, which made the Cold War an international order of sorts.[8]

Like international orders before it, the Cold War order was prone to decay; within twenty years, it would be buckling, straining, and fracturing. In the late 1960s, the postwar order broke down, and a new phase of disorder and improvisation ensued. Contemporaries grasped the fragmentation of the status quo.

"The postwar order of international relations—the configuration of power that emerged from the Second World War is gone," declared the Nixon administration in a 1971 report to Congress on US foreign policy. "The once seemingly rigid pattern established after World War II has by now obviously undergone a deluge of accelerating changes," concluded the Council on Foreign Relations. This bore consequences for the United States. "An era in American foreign policy, which began in the late 1940s, has ended," opined Samuel Huntington and Warren Manshel, cofounders of *Foreign Policy*, a journal intended to devise solutions for the dilemmas of a new era. The disjuncture that observers perceived in world affairs owed not only to the trauma of the Vietnam War but also—and more profoundly—to deep-rooted structural changes: the Cold War's ossification and globalization's resurgence.[9]

The ebbing of Cold War tensions became tangible in the 1960s. "The classic Cold War today is past," wrote political scientist Paul Seabury in 1966. That conflict's "original nature," Seabury argued, "has been obliterated by the passage of time and the intrusion of new problems." "The age of the superpowers," Henry Kissinger agreed, "is drawing to an end." By the mid-1970s, national leaders were ready to declare that "the Cold War is over." "It is now a relic of the past," exclaimed Senator Ted Kennedy of Masschusetts. The Cold War, in this view, had ended with neither victory nor reconciliation but with the obsolescence of the bipolar order. Stalemate had rendered the superpowers' military arsenals ineffectual, while the waning of East-West hostilities had unleashed centrifugal forces within the alliance systems. Cold War patterns, as a result, no longer defined international politics. Even George Kennan, a key shaper of the Cold War order in the 1940s, urged Americans in 1972 to "put aside the fixations and rigidities of the Cold War," to attend instead to "common dangers" threatening humanity, and to build an "organization of international life" equal to the challenges of an new era. Others were even blunter. "The concept of the superpower," one former official declared in 1973, "is obsolete."[10]

Globalization was foremost among the forces that changed world politics in the 1970s. Signifying the integration of markets in its narrowest definition and the expansion of social and economic processes to the planetary scale in its broadest sense, globalization stirred much debate. While the word *globalization* remained unfamiliar (becoming commonplace only in the 1990s), social scientists and policymakers in the 1970s marveled at the "reciprocal effects among countries" that transnational trade and investment produced. Talk of "interdependence" and discussion of its consequences proliferated, as the value of offshore financial holdings surged from 1.2 percent of world GDP in 1964 to 16.2 percent in 1980. World trade tripled over the same period, which indicated the capacity of containerized shipping, among other innovations, to reduce transaction costs. Globalization triggered diverse reactions. Skeptics, such as the economists Richard Barnett and Ronald Müller, lamented the erosion of the nation-state's capacity "to maintain economic and political stability." Others hailed borderless capitalism and mocked the nation-state's pretensions to economic sovereignty. "The nation-state," declared diplomat George Ball, "is a very old-fashioned idea and badly adapted to serve the needs of our present world."[11]

Globalization's consequences were at first sharpest in the developed countries, which together accounted for some 76 percent of world trade in 1970. The scope of late twentieth-century globalization nonetheless broadened quickly. The oil crises of 1973–74 and 1979 made the industrialized world's dependence on the Middle East evident, while China's choice to undertake economic reform at the end of the 1970s initiated the reintegration of the world's largest society to the globalizing world. The consequences, meanwhile, cut deep. The interdependencies—and vulnerabilities—that globalization produced inhibited the management of national economies, with adverse consequences for economic and even social stability. Some economists warned that countries might recoil from globalization, retreating into autarky as they had done in the 1930s. Others hoped that concerted international management of the world economy might tame globalization's disruptive effects. What transpired among the industrialized countries in the 1970s, however, was not the remaking of international economic governance but its rollback, as integrated markets began to trump the managerial capacities of existing political authorities.[12]

Within capitalist societies, globalization contributed to a transnational crisis of the public sector. This crisis halted—but did not necessarily reverse—a rise of the public sector, which accelerated during the Great Depression and continued through the Second World War. Made manifest in the welfare state, public mobilization seemed inexorable in the early postwar years as governments taxed, borrowed, and spent; provided for the economic needs of their citizens; and implemented the managerial economic policies that John Maynard Keynes commended. Yet in the 1970s, public mobilization and the welfare state faltered. "We used to think that you could spend your way out of a recession," Britain's prime minister, James Callaghan, admitted in 1976. "I tell you in all candor that that option no longer exists." The crisis of public mobilization owed to complex causes: globalization weakened the economic authority of nation-states, but policy choices and intellectual shifts contributed to the formation of new consensuses around market-oriented (or neoliberal) economic policies. Dwindling gains in industrial productivity, flagging economic growth, and surging price inflation all discredited the old order, eclipsing its earlier accomplishments.[13]

As public mobilization faltered, individuals asserted their prerogatives against governments. The resurgence of individualism was a predominantly Western development, and its political implications varied. In the United States, civil rights activists deployed the language of individual rights, but the opponents of school busing and the proponents of taxpayers' rights used similar language to oppose public efforts to redress economic and racial inequalities. In the global arena, the human rights movement of the 1970s assumed an individualistic, anti-statist cast. Proponents wielded human rights as an ideological weapon against the Soviet Union and other authoritarian regimes, from Argentina to South Korea. Human rights carried globalizing implications: advocates declared that rights attached to individuals, not communities; and they worked to turn their convictions into a universal reality. Challenging the prerogatives of nation-states, transnational orgnizations, such as Amnesty International and Human Rights Watch, proclaimed violations of individual rights within nation-states to be the world's business. Some proponents even contended that the individual human being must supplant the nation-state as the basic element—and primary concern—of international order. "In the long view," one wrote, "the ultimate goals of a worldwide community of man must center upon the individual."[14]

Reflecting on the dynamics of his era, political scientist Zbigniew Brzezinski discerned novel patterns. "Nation-states are losing their centrality," he wrote in 1974, "amidst a shift from traditional international politics to a new global process." The sensation of disjuncture in world affairs prompted some to contemplate the remaking of international order. "We have a historic opportunity," secretary of state Henry Kissinger declared in 1975, "to help construct a new political and economic world system." "The United States has no choice," concurred president-elect Jimmy Carter's advisers, who included Brzezinski, "but to be engaged in a protracted architectural process to reform and reshape the international system." Situating themselves in a phase of tumult, leaders in the 1970s perceived the end of the postwar era, the faltering of an international order inherited from the 1940s. Like Giuseppe Mazzini, who sought to reconcile the nineteenth-century international order to nationalism's ascent, policymakers and intellectuals in the 1970s asked how an international order constructed at a time when nation-states had predominated might be reconciled to new developments, especially globalization. As in the nineteenth century, what emerged from the collision between old structures and new forces would be instability and disorder, not a meaningful stabilization of international politics. The 1970s, it follows, opened a new era but not a new order.[15]

◕

This book focuses on American decision-makers at the pinnacles of power. Richard Nixon, Gerald Ford, and Jimmy Carter, occupants of the US presidency between 1969 and 1981, and Henry Kissinger and Zbigniew Brzezinski, the era's leading foreign-policy thinkers, are its central figures. This tight focus serves an analytical purpose. Presidents and those who advise them deal (or try to deal) with world politics in a holistic fashion. Lowlier bureaucrats are often more knowledgeable about particular issues and regions, and it is they who generate the options among which the top decision-makers choose. In this sense, the bureaucracy makes foreign policy, the myriad of actions and choices, of decisions and nondecisions that mediate relations with other international actors. It is, nonetheless, at the very highest levels that policies cohere and overarching strategic purposes emerge. Strategy, a central focus of this book, is what holds the policymaking enterprise together, imbuing disconnected actions (and inactions) with coherence, direction, and purpose. Strategic thinking makes assumptions about history that guide policy choices. Strategy interprets the present in relation to the past and the future. Strategy, at its most ambitious, may even envisage managing history itself.[16]

Making strategy is invariably fraught. Distilling complex events into legible processes requires prioritizing some phenomena over others, and it risks distortions, oversights, and omissions. American decision-makers in the early Cold War defined the rise of Soviet power as the predominant theme of their era and acted accordingly. Had they instead inferred that decolonization and anticolonial nationalism were the central developments of their times, they might have made different choices. So, too, did decision-makers in the 1970s prioritize certain historical processes and phenomena over others. Their prioritizations and omissions wrought durable effects. Strategic assumptions are consequential, but they can be difficult for outsiders—and historians—to grasp. "What appears to be of one piece to us," Zbigniew Brzezinski wrote, "is often seen by the public as a disconnected and incomprehensible pattern of events."[17]

The "underlying rationale" of foreign policy, as Brzezinski called it, does not necessarily become clearer with time. While declassification makes official documentation available, the briefs, memoranda, and transcripts that make up the documentary record are, as Henry Kissinger notes, "often silent about larger purposes or premises," being concerned mainly with "tactical or technical" problems. To gauge and comprehend the strategic assumptions guiding policy across three administrations, this book probes at the assumptions and beliefs that reside in a broad range of sources. Crucially, it draws on readings of entire archival series: series of documents that presidents read and/or annotated, series of memorandums of presidential conversations with foreign leaders and officials, and series of weekly reports on foreign policy. Reading such series facilitated the reconstruction of strategic assumptions, indicating how assumptions and priorities changed over time. Other kinds of sources—from the social-science literature of the day to the documents of international and nongovernmental organizations, such as Amnesty International and the International Monetary Fund (IMF)—illuminate the dynamic circumstances in which decision-makers operated.[18]

The results of this study are revealing and disorienting. Contrary to the common assumption, which some scholarship on US foreign relations still echoes, the Cold War was not the singular theme of postwar international history; it was, as a growing number of historians now agree, one of a number of major themes that shaped the international relations of the postwar era. Nor did American decision-makers adhere for forty years to a consistent strategy of anti-Soviet containment, as the myth of Cold War strategic continuity would have it. Nor even did they pursue diverse strategies of containment, although this comes much closer to the mark. Instead, decision-makers strove to comprehend historical forces at work in their times and improvised in response to unanticipated challenges, both domestic and global. By reconstructing the strategic outlooks and the tactical improvisations of US decision-makers, this book suggests an alternative vantage to the Cold War paradigm that still frames the international history of the 1970s. These were years of Soviet-American détente, but they were also years when the Cold War ceased to define world politics (if indeed it ever had done) and new challenges proliferated. The Cold War did not end in the seventies, but the decade confirmed the advent of a distinctive post–Cold War era, an era that took shape even as the formal estrangement between the superpowers endured.[19]

If diplomatic historians presume a basic continuity in international structures in the era of the Cold War, this book aligns more closely with scholars who see disruption and disjuncture in the 1970s. Buttressing contemporaneous research on interdependence, historians of globalization present the seventies as a crucible of late twentieth-century integration. Others explore the changing roles of the territorial nation-state, whose autonomy and authority globalization curtailed. Historians of the United States concur that the 1970s remade the postwar political-economic order, resulting in the ascent of the market, rise of the service sector, and widening social inequality. Scholars of ideas, law, and politics, meanwhile, characterize the 1970s as a phase when Americans (and others) were fixated on individual rights, even as a phase when a global human rights movement emerged. The seventies, as a result, are being reinvented as a phase of fracture and disruption, a decade when a settled postwar order (or orders) broke down, and invigorated social, intellectual, and political contestation ensued. This book seeks to integrate the history of American foreign policy, usually framed in terms of Cold War stabilization, to the insights that emerge from scholars who locate in the 1970s the demise of the postwar era and, as historian Philippe Chassaigne puts it, "the origins of our modernity."[20]

For its part, this book makes several contributions. It is among the first interpretations of US foreign relations in the 1970s to be based on an archival record that declassification has made available; but the chapters that follow offer more than new evidence. They offer a fresh, new vantage on the 1970s as a phase when

US decision-makers grappled with challenges beyond the Cold War, when the postwar international order fractured, and when a new phase in America's superpower career cohered. By rethinking the 1970s, this book evokes connections between the scholarship on globalization, which identifies the decade as a phase of breakthrough, and the scholarship on the US domestic experience. Bringing a global perspective to bear suggests, however, that the remaking of the capitalist order that turned on the 1970s was neither the result of a neoliberal counter-revolution nor the achievement of self-conscious design. Rather, globalization produced a disjuncture between territorial politics and transnational economics that empowered markets at the expense of government. For the American superpower, globalization conferred benefits, but it also left democracy diminished, curtailing the capacities of representative institutions. Globalization without governance also left open the question of how global dilemmas, such as climate change and financial crises, might be engaged, much less managed. The seventies thus opened dilemmas that would define a post–Cold War era, dilemmas whose persistence into the twenty-first century made manifest the failures of decision-makers during the 1970s to remake the international order in order to master the dilemmas of their own—and our own—times.[21]

Rethinking the 1970s also yields new perspectives on the decision-makers who populate this book. Richard Nixon, it argues, did not seek to transform America's world role; rather, the Nixon administration sought to bolster the sinews of American power within a conservative concept of Cold War politics. Nixon worked to stabilize the status quo, to the short-term advantage of the United States, but he failed to engage, much less master, new forces in world politics. Over time, those forces upended his efforts. The consequences of economic globalization, combined with the effects of Nixon's choices, collapsed the international monetary order in the early 1970s. The rise of transnational politics thwarted Nixon's calculation that national interests could be pursued with little regard to their humanitarian and ideological stakes. More than any other event, it was the oil crisis of 1973–74 that exposed the limitations of a foreign policy based upon the pursuit of conservative stability. The oil crisis coincided with Nixon's political disgrace in the Watergate scandal, which permitted new leaders to predominate. Thereafter, Henry Kissinger emerged as the dominant figure in the making of US foreign policy, and a more creative phase ensued.[22]

Henry Kissinger sought to preserve Nixon's accomplishments; as he did so, he embraced novel methods, achieving a transient mastery over the complex historical circumstances of his times. Like Bismarck in the 1860s and 1870s, Kissinger mobilized disruptive forces—nationalism in Bismarck's case; globalization in Kissinger's—on behalf of national interests and international stability. Recognizing the damage that the oil crisis was doing to core US alliances, Kissinger brokered cooperative solutions to the West's energy crisis, which soon expanded to encompass broader cooperation on dilemmas associated with new interdependencies. For historians, this Kissinger still remains an unfamiliar figure. Kissinger's engagement with new challenges in the mid-1970s did not resolve the myriad difficulties facing the United States and its allies, but Kissinger managed to hold the West together, and he established a basis on which global- ization might be managed in an ad hoc fashion. These achievements did not win re-election for Gerald Ford, the president Kissinger served. Instead, Kissinger's disinclination to accept human rights in foreign policy dismayed critics, confirm- ing for many Ford's inability to transcend the expedience of the Nixon years.[23]

After Kissinger, the Carter administration proposed to make the manage- ment of new global challenges the central purpose of its foreign policy. To this end, Carter devised what was, in effect, the nation's first post–Cold War strategy. Downgrading anti-Soviet containment, Carter instead prioritized the manage- ment of economic interdependencies among the industrialized countries and the worldwide promotion of human rights. This was a significant and construc- tive agenda, which historians have not always recognized as such. Still, Carter's agenda for "world order politics" did not endure. It faltered in the late 1970s, undone by economic difficulties that international policy coordination would not resolve, by the effects of the Iranian Revolution, and by the resurgence of Soviet-American hostilities, to which Carter's own preoccupation with human rights contributed. As a result, Carter after 1978 reverted to foreign-policy con- cepts associated with the high Cold War. Contrary to pervasive assumptions, what undid the Carter administration's bid for a new foreign policy was nei- ther internal discord nor the failure to formulate a coherent strategic concept so much as the inherent difficulties of imposing singular strategic concepts on complex and confounding realities.[24]

The chapters that follow present an analysis in three parts. Chapter 1 follows the consolidation of a distinctive international order—the postwar or Cold War settlement—in the 1940s and explains how that settlement became destabilized during the 1960s, creating the circumstances the decision-makers of the 1970s inherited. Part I, which comprises chapters 2 through 5, follows the Nixon administration's bid to stabilize the postwar order. Nixon, it explains, looked backward: he sought to sustain the postwar international order and to bolster the Pax Americana. Being fixated on political and military relations among the great powers, Nixon neglected transnational economic and political relations, the significance and urgency of which sharpened with globalization. Nixon's bid for stability faltered during the oil crisis of 1973–74. Thereafter, his successors stumbled forward, cognizant of the need to adapt America's superpower role to evolving global circumstances. Part II, comprising chapters 6 through 9, fol- lows their efforts and their improvisations. Henry Kissinger, it demonstrates, worked in 1974–76 to assimilate new priorities into US foreign policy; Jimmy

Carter attempted to reorient American grand strategy to meet new challenges. These efforts met with varying success, but Carter's bid for a new foreign policy faltered in the late 1970s, amid a resurgence of geopolitical rivalries, which climaxed in the Soviet Union's invasion of Afghanistan. Lacking the capacity to define their circumstances, American decision-makers adapted, and their adaptations marked the limits of their power.

Power, like strategy, is a central analytical concern of the book. Situated in relational context, as William Fox defined it, a superpower's power may appear vast, as it often is within bilateral relationships. In a more holistic, even global, context, the superpower's predicament assumes a more ironic guise. Its capacities may be vast in relation to less powerful nation-states, but a superpower's resources seldom give it the command of its own fortunes. The diversity and complexity of the issues with which decision-makers must deal and the contradictory demands that weigh upon them recurrently confound their efforts to manage change, dooming them to frustration and leaving them captives of history's caprice. None of this is to say that American choices and actions did not have consequences for the people who bore their brunt in the seventies—from Chile, to Iran, to Indochina. Instead, what decision-makers failed to master was the superpower's own destiny. The United States emerged from the 1970s a superpower transformed, but its transformation followed no coherent design or strategy.

Still, the absence of self-conscious design ought not imply the absence of historical logic. Rather, the breakdown of the postwar international order during the 1970s opened a new phase in the superpower career of the United States, a phase that the superpower's dependence on transnational resources, even on the dynamics of globalization, would define. Having been during the early Cold War the productive epicenter of the global economy, the United States began to run endemic trade deficits, financing them with borrowed money. Having forged multilateral institutions to structure the relations of sovereign nation-states, the United States began to align itself with transnational actors propounding ideological purposes, such as human rights, and to promote democracy as a universal norm. Having been, for a time, a bastion of stability in a world of nation-states, the United States began to play a more revolutionary role in the affairs of the world.

Situated in much broader historical context, the transformation that turned on the 1970s may appear a reversion to type for a republic whose relations to the international order, even to the notion of order, remained ambivalent until the Second World War. In the 1940s, however, the threats that American leaders perceived in world politics and the material advantages that the United States wielded compelled and enabled them to enact a self-conscious reordering of world politics. With the demise of the postwar order, opportunities abounded for a generation of decision-makers to remake the American superpower's relations to the larger world, a world now in the throes of globalization. These leaders sought the purposeful reordering of American foreign relations, but they did not realize their intended designs. Instead, the transformation of American superpower in the 1970s was a result of improvised responses amid dynamic circumstances, the consequences of which would reverberate into the twenty-first century.

1

Pax Americana

In our posture abroad, in our approach to the conduct of foreign relations, in our structure of alliances, in the terms in which we try to sell our ideas and our policies, America is succumbing to a creeping obsolescence.

Richard Nixon, "America in the World City," 1967

The United States in the late 1930s hovered aloof from the gales sweeping Eurasia. The Old World's crises nonetheless beckoned, and Americans debated what involvement they wished to have in its affairs. For some, engagement was irresistible. "What Rome was, what Great Britain has been," journalist Walter Lippmann proclaimed, "America is to be." The publisher Henry Luce called for an "American century," in which the United States would spread the "ideals of civilization throughout the world." Others chaffed at such ambition. Charles Beard, historian and isolationist, worried that international entanglements would erode American democracy. "America is not to be Rome or Britain," Beard retorted. "It is to be America."[1]

The world's wars prompted Americans to rethink old precepts. As Hitler bid for mastery, President Franklin Roosevelt became convinced that Europe's catastrophe imperiled the United States. The bomber and the aircraft carrier, he inferred, meant that the Western Hemisphere was a haven no longer from foreign strife. After France's fall, FDR began to ship arms to the British; when Hitler invaded the Soviet Union, he aided Moscow. Roosevelt acted because he presumed that "their liberty and our security" were entwined. This geopolitical insight marked a turning point in American strategic thought, but ideological commitments and material interests also embroiled the United States in foreign wars. In East Asia, Japan's bid to create a regional imperial system conflicted with American commitments to free trade. Both sides tried to avoid war, but their interests and their visions of East Asia's future proved irreconcilable, and so war came—in a preemptive Japanese assault on the US Pacific Fleet. Hitler seized

Pearl Harbor as an opportunity to declare war on the United States, and two wars became one, with the United States at the center.[2]

The Second World War ended with between forty and seventy million deaths and the defeat of the German-Japanese Axis. It took a grand coalition to win the war, but the outcome left no doubt as to which of the victors was the most victorious. The war devastated the Soviet Union, killing about 13 percent of its citizens. China lost almost as many lives and teetered on the brink of civil war. Western Europe suffered the horrors of occupation; Eastern Europe suffered far worse. Yet the war did not exhaust the United States, and bombs did not devastate its lands. Instead, America emerged from World War Two victorious and rich. Between 1938 and 1944, per capita GDP doubled. In 1945, the United States produced 60 percent of the industrialized world's output. The wartime development of nuclear weapons showcased America's technical mastery and compounded the military advantages that the world's largest navy and a far-flung network of bases bestowed. The United States in 1945 was not the first among equals. It was, as President Truman exclaimed, "the most powerful nation, perhaps, in all history."[3]

The ascent to primacy transformed the national debate about America's world role, but the question Henry Luce had posed still endured: "What internationalism have we Americans to offer?" For Luce in 1938, the American Century meant the outward projection of American achievements. It fell to the Americans, Luce believed, to share "with all peoples our Bill of Rights, our Declaration of Independence, our Constitution, our magnificent industrial products, our technical skills." Luce rode ahead of public opinion, but Americans came during the war to favor an active international role. As public opinion shifted, political leaders accepted the opportunity to rebuild the world. At Bretton Woods, the United States and its allies created institutions to sustain growth and promote trade. At Dumbarton Oaks, they drafted a blueprint for the United Nations, a collective security organization. Institutional frameworks, these architects of the future hoped, would hold the postwar world together and recast it in an American idiom.[4]

The world that emerged after 1945 was not the world that wartime planners foresaw. To the surprise of policymakers who fixated on the problems of the 1930s, estrangement between the United States and the Soviet Union transformed world politics and the prospects for American leadership. As Soviet-American tensions sharpened, the United States constructed a tight and integrated militarized system of military alliances and economic relationships—not an American Century but a Pax Americana. This system institutionalized Washington's leadership of the non-Communist world in the name of anti-Soviet containment. American leaders, as they made the Pax Americana, nonetheless accommodated their ambitions and their designs to circumstances.

Preeminent among the constraints that history imposed upon them, this chapter argues, were the ascent of economic planning and public mobilization, legacies of the Great Depression; the bipolar division of the postwar international order, a consequence of geopolitical realities; and the triumph of anticolonial nationalism, which confirmed the worldwide diffusion of the modern, territorial nation-state.[5]

Remaking the World Economic Order

The Great Depression's legacies defined the political-economic contours of the postwar world. Besides breaking the world economy apart, the Depression heralded the ascendancy of economic planning. The major capitalist countries isolated themselves from the world in the early 1930s and mobilized their economies in pursuit of recovery. The economist John Maynard Keynes offered a theoretical justification for macroeconomic management, arguing that prolonged economic downturns required public action. But policymakers embraced economic interventionism for diverse purposes. While German leaders in the 1930s favored military mobilization, British leaders in the 1940s committed themselves to building a welfare state. There were in practice as many varieties of economic nationalism as there were nation-states; the 1930s nonetheless heralded the rise of economic nationalism, a development that war mobilizations corroborated.[6]

The emergence of the United States as the world's dominant power thus coincided with a historic crisis of classical liberalism. This was in some ways ironic: Americans remained more committed than most peoples to liberal tenets and open markets, and their Constitution restrained the power of the federal government. The Great Depression and the war that followed nonetheless transformed the American political economy. Federal spending surged—from 3.4 percent of GDP in 1930 to 9.8 percent in 1940 and 35 percent in 1945. President Roosevelt heralded this expansion in the fiscal powers of the federal government as a welcome, even necessary, development. Should the democracies fail to assure their citizens' economic rights, Roosevelt warned, they would surely falter, and "dictatorships" would flourish. This was the lesson of the 1930s, and it affirmed that public mobilization was a strategic imperative. Government, as a result, became the guarantor in the 1930s and 1940s of citizens' economic well-being as well as of their physical security, and it did so throughout the capitalist world.[7]

This transformation of the nation-state's economic role conditioned the remaking of the international economic order. Activist states, theory and experience both decreed, required some autonomy from external forces, especially transnational capital flows, if they were to manage economic growth and bolster social welfare. Committed to welfarism, American policymakers in the mid-1940s sought to facilitate such public mobilization on a global scale. Far from imposing open-market solutions on foreign countries, US policymakers worked with their foreign counterparts to restrain globalization. What they sought, as they designed an international economic order for the postwar world, was a regime that would permit economic statism to coexist with international trade, a compromise between globalization and the welfare state. This agenda reflected both the lessons that officials drew from the Great Depression and the limitations of the international monetary order that had collapsed in the thirties: the gold exchange standard.[8]

Adopted in the late nineteenth century and restored, in modified form, after the First World War, the gold standard fixed the values of currencies in relation to gold, producing an international matrix of stable exchange rates. Monetary stability encouraged trade, which flourished. The gold standard also provided a solution to trade imbalances. If a country ran a trade deficit, it would use gold reserves to finance the shortfall. Insofar as governments depended on gold reserves to support their currencies, the loss of gold reserves would reduce the deficit country's money supply, thereby raising interest rates, deflating the economy, and reducing consumption. The ensuing economic contraction would increase the international competitiveness of the deficit country's exports, returning its balance of trade to equilibrium. Trade surpluses, by contrast, would lead to inflation—raising prices, making exports less competitive, and correcting the original payments surplus. The gold standard thus provided an efficient mechanism for achieving balance-of-payments adjustments. It nonetheless achieved international stability at the cost of persistent instability within national economies.[9]

Gold also brought adverse macroeconomic consequences, including a deflationary bias. Tethering currencies to a scarce metal kept interest rates high, subduing economic growth. This was William Jennings Bryan's complaint. "You shall not crucify mankind upon a cross of gold," Bryan declared in July 1896. Bryan advocated a bimetallic standard, under which silver, more plentiful than gold, would become a source of monetary growth. The Klondike Gold Rush rendered concerns about deflation moot for a time, but depending on prospectors to expand the world's money supply was no way to run the global economy. Keynes in 1924 declared gold a "barbarous relic," arguing that it constrained macroeconomic choice—a point that the Great Depression confirmed. Only after countries abandoned gold—as Britain did in 1931 and the United States did in 1933—were governments able to depreciate their currencies and reflate their economies. The demise of the gold standard in the early 1930s was a grand turning point. The economist Karl Polanyi hailed it as society's revolt against the market, declaring that the gold standard's demise subjected economics to the authority of politics.[10]

The financial experts who gathered at Bretton Woods in 1944 intended to remake the international monetary order. Forty-four countries participated in the United Nations Monetary and Financial Conference, but the Americans and the British dominated the conversation. Despite significant disagreements, the American and British delegations at the conference concurred that the postwar international monetary order would have to permit nation-states far more economic autonomy than the gold standard had done. They sought a stable monetary order within which trade could resume, but they also sought to protect welfare states and managed capitalism against the effects of untrammelled globalization. To this end, they created the International Monetary Fund (IMF).[11]

The IMF restored international monetary stability by establishing a system of fixed but adjustable exchange rates based upon the US dollar. Henceforth, countries would fix the values of their currencies to the dollar, while the dollar would remain convertible into gold at $35 per ounce. This gold-dollar linkage offered credibility, but governments remained free to adjust the values of their currencies as they saw fit. The IMF would lend money to countries running payments deficits, while other rules buttressed the macroeconomic autonomy of nation-states. The IMF would even permit governments to postpone currency convertibility until their economies recovered from the war and to impose restrictions on transnational finance thereafter. Besides making globalization safe for the welfare state, Bretton Woods aimed to resolve the gold standard's deflationary bias. Here, the dollar was crucial. The gold-dollar standard enabled foreign countries to hold US dollars as reserve assets on terms interchangeable with gold. This would allow the world's money supply to expand far faster than it had under the gold standard. If international stability had been the logic behind the gold standard, Bretton Woods prioritized domestic economic stability and national economic growth.

Bretton Woods was a multilateral settlement, but it was also an expression of American hegemonic power. The US dollar was central: it was the world's reserve currency, its numéraire (the unit of value in which other values are expressed), and a source of liquidity for the world. "We are the giant of the economic world," Harry Truman declared in 1947, and the architecture of world monetary order revealed the truth behind his boast. Bretton Woods affirmed the Pax Americana as the successor to the Pax Britannica, ending the interwar interregnum during which Britain had struggled to sustain the responsibilities of hegemony and Washington had disdained to share them. America-centered, the new order was to be global in scope. Soviet economic officials joined the Bretton Woods dialogue, and Washington expected that the USSR would participate in the new international economic order that the 1944 conference had established.[12]

Bretton Woods was a bold departure in international economic governance, but it left urgent questions unanswered. How would war-torn economies recover to the point at which they could sustain balanced trade relations? The IMF, it turned out, was unable to bridge the inequalities of economic power left by the war. Helping the vanquished recover would require direct intervention on a scale that Roosevelt had not contemplated. The United States, Roosevelt assumed, would be a preceptor of rules and institutions to the postwar world, not its Atlas. That is nonetheless the role the United States assumed, in the context of an intensifying Cold War.

The Cold War and the Pax Americana

Fission and fusion made the Cold War's geopolitics, as they did its nuclear weapons. The Soviet-American estrangement divided the postwar world, while the superpowers' mutual hostility animated the fusion of their alliances. The dynamics reinforced each other. As East-West rivalries intensified, the Pax Americana became more integrated, more hierarchical, and more militarized than anything wartime planners had anticipated. Still, the world's division did not necessitate confrontation and bloc consolidation. There was no inherent reason, as Walter Lippmann argued, why East and West could not coexist as worlds apart, not worlds opposed. The Cold War began in two phases: estrangement, then confrontation.[13]

Estrangement came fast. British prime minister Winston Churchill in 1944 traveled to Moscow and carved Europe into spheres. Roosevelt acknowledged the inevitability of a divided world, even as he conjured for the public a vision of an integrated global future. At Yalta in 1945, he conceded to Stalin that the USSR would dominate Eastern Europe. But Roosevelt did not communicate the concession to the American people or to the vice president who would soon succeed him. Instead, his heirs remained committed to an idealistic peace based on self-determination, international cooperation, and "the improvement of living conditions all over the world."[14]

This hopeful vision did not survive 1945. At year's end, the Soviet Union announced that it would not participate in the IMF. The decision was momentous. Nonparticipation meant isolation from what Soviet officials called "the major international project" of the postwar era, and it corroborated the views of diplomat George Kennan, who argued that Moscow was unalterably hostile to the outside world. Stalin confirmed the point in February 1946, when he proclaimed the likelihood that capitalism would spawn another world war. Kennan now drafted a "long telegram" assessing Soviet motives. His dispatch con-firmed the division of the postwar world. The next month, Winston Churchill announced, with President Truman sitting beside him, that an iron curtain had descended across Europe.[15]

Confrontation followed, and novel burdens accompanied it. In February 1947, Great Britain communicated to Washington that it could no longer afford to support the Greek government's war against an internal Communist insur-gency. Truman acted to aid Greece and broadcast his willingness to aid other "free peoples" resisting Communist forces. Truman moved next to rehabilitate the parts of Germany that American and British armies occupied. These efforts prompted the Soviet Union to sever the Western powers' access to West Berlin, an enclave of Western control within Soviet-occupied eastern Germany. The Berlin Crisis escalated the Cold War and prompted the creation, in 1949, of the North Atlantic Treaty Organization, an integrated military command under an American proconsul. NATO was in theory an alliance of sovereign states but was in practice a hierarchical structure, in which the United States predominated.[16]

Nuclear weapons conditioned NATO's evolution. The United States deto-nated the first atomic bomb in 1945. The USSR followed in 1949. Four years later, both powers were testing hydrogen bombs far more powerful than these early weapons. Whether delivered by bombers or atop ballistic missiles, nuclear arms had revolutionary consequences for international relations, negating the state's capacity to secure its citizens against violent death. Lacking nuclear weap-ons (Britain apart), Washington's European allies depended in the early Cold War on the United States to protect them against the Soviet Union. The chal-lenge for Washington was to make its commitment to use nuclear weapons on Europe's behalf credible, to convince its allies that it was willing to jeopardize American lives to deter a Soviet attack on Europe. To provide reassurance, Washington devolved operational responsibility for some nuclear forces to the West Europeans. Such concessions only confirmed that Europe's security depended on America's nuclear shield. Without "immediate use of atomic weap-ons," NATO concluded in 1954, "we could not successfully defend Europe." As the guarantor of the West's security, the United States assumed for the entire Atlantic Alliance a role customarily associated, at least in the modern era, with the prerogatives of sovereignty.[17]

Security was not all that the Pax Americana offered. As the Cold War intensi-fied, Washington extended economic support to its allies. The United States pro-vided loans to several European governments after the war, but these constituted neither a systematic nor a generous response to Europe's needs. As Cold War tensions rose in 1946–47, however, US observers began to fixate on the risks of social and economic collapse in a hungry and dejected Europe. To preempt this prospect, secretary of state George Marshall, in 1947, announced a program of financial assistance. Marshall Aid provided Europeans with nearly $13 billion, enabling them to import food, consumer durables, and industrial machinery from the United States. Stalin's refusal to permit Eastern Europe to participate in the program, meanwhile, confirmed Europe's division.[18]

Marshall Aid served Cold War purposes, but it did not remold Europe in an American image. West European governments resisted American entreaties to merge their economies into an integrated bloc, preferring instead to pursue national plans and projects. Some, like France, devised industrial policies; others, like Britain, nationalized industries and expanded welfare protections. This was not Washington's vision, but the United States ran with the tide of public mobilization in Europe, providing technical expertise as well as financial transfers to Western Europe's burgeoning welfare states.[19]

In its North Atlantic core, the Pax Americana was a curious hybrid. It was a hierarchical alliance in which Washington provided military security and defined the limits of political diversity; but it was also an association of free nation-states, which exercised considerable autonomy in their internal economic affairs. The whole edifice depended upon a Soviet threat that conditioned both Western Europe's acceptance of US military protection and America's acceptance of European economic nationalism. As transformative as the Cold War was for Europe, its advent was remarkably peaceful. In East Asia, the Cold War's coming was far bloodier.

Until the late 1940s, the Cold War left East Asia relatively unscathed. Moscow and Washington divided Korea, but Cold War tensions were less intense in Asia than in Europe until October 1949, when Mao Zedong declared victory in the Chinese Civil War. Next came the Sino-Soviet alliance, forged in the winter of 1949/50, and the Korean War. Truman interpreted North Korea's June 1950 invasion of South Korea as a Soviet-inspired act. In response, he sent a half million soldiers to Korea. They surged forward, retreated hastily, and battled to a stalemate. The Korean War nonetheless affirmed Washington's willingness to commit military power against Communist forces in far-flung locations, and it accelerated the military, strategic, and economic integration of the Pax Americana. As the offshore base for American forces, Japan was the war's unambiguous beneficiary. US military purchases catalyzed Japanese economic recovery, while the division of East Asia transformed Japan from a defeated adversary into something resembling a strategic partner.[20]

Korea also consecrated a doctrine for waging the Cold War: a strategy of containment. Kennan articulated the initial version in 1946–47, but Korea galvanized a containment strategy more sweeping and more militarized than Kennan's. In its mature version, containment traced a frontier around the Sino-Soviet bloc and committed the United States to resist further expansion of Communist power. Containment defined the East bloc as a morass of hostility, and it advocated rallying the West's resources for a long existential struggle. Laid forth in NSC-68, a top-secret memorandum, containment also envisaged high levels of military spending. Indeed, US defense expenditures averaged 10.4 percent of GDP per year in the 1950s, eclipsing social spending, which averaged 4 percent of GDP per year. The commitments were vast, but containment nonetheless remained a strategy of limits. Instead of pursuing Communist forces into China, as General Douglas MacArthur urged, the United States accepted a military stalemate along the 38th parallel and worked on its side of that frontier to construct a South Korean bulwark state, building in miniature a microcosm of a divided world.[21]

In just a few years after 1945, the United States assumed quasi-imperial responsibilities for foreign nation-states, especially for its closest allies. The debates between internationalists and isolationists that preceded Pearl Harbor were hardly a decade old, but by 1950, they seemed a lifetime earlier. International burdens changed the United States, much as the isolationists feared. A peacetime draft, introduced in 1948, evoked the militarization of American society, while red baiting, loyalty oaths, and espionage scandals defined the Cold War's politics. The clustering of defense industries in places like Northern Virginia, Southern California, and the Seattle-Tacoma conurbation made manifest the Cold War's transformative socio-economic consequences.[22]

Some Americans feared these changes and distrusted the relationships the Cold War brokered among the nation's military, economic, and political elites. President Eisenhower, who succeeded Truman in 1953, warned against the acquisition of "undue influence" by a "military-industrial complex," but he nonetheless struggled as president to do more than stabilize the militarization of American society. To limit the Cold War's costs, Eisenhower affirmed NATO's dependence on nuclear weapons. The moral implications of using these weapons were atrocious, as Eisenhower acknowledged, but nuclear weapons, once invented, were cost-effective, which permitted the stabilization by the mid-1950s of the Pax Americana's burdens.[23]

A World of Nation-States

The twentieth century saw the triumph of the territorial nation-state as the world's default unit of political order. Situated in broad historical context, this was a striking development. Until the modern era, most people lived either outside organized states or within hierarchical systems of political order—often called empires. As empires retreated in the nineteenth and twentieth centuries, nation-states flourished. In 1820, less than a quarter of human beings inhabited such polities. By 1970, virtually all people did. The end of this long transition from a world of empires to a world of nation-states coincided with the early post-war decades, and it shaped the choices available to US policymakers, beginning with the postwar settlement.[24]

In August 1941, Franklin Roosevelt and Winston Churchill concluded the Atlantic Charter, a declaration of common intent and a loose blueprint for the postwar international order. The Charter envisaged a society of nation-states, but it was ambiguous on the question of who would have the right to form self-governing communities. Churchill insisted that the clause of the Charter promising the return of "sovereign rights and self government to those who have been forcibly deprived of them" applied only to Hitler's victims; Roosevelt countered that it applied to all peoples, including the victims of British colonialism. Clarifying Washington's position, the State Department, in 1943, prepared a Declaration on National Independence. It affirmed that colonized peoples were citizens of the international community and endorsed their right to form nation-states of their own. This conclusion aligned the United States with anticolonial nationalism.[25]

Hindsight would give it the appearance of inevitability, but decolonization after 1945 did not realize a natural destiny. The creation of the United Nations animated the hopes of Third World nationalists, but some of the UN's firmest advocates believed that the new organization would affirm colonialism's mandate. Anticolonial forces mobilized in the UN General Assembly, but it was the Bandung Conference of 1955 that affirmed the historical arrival of postcolonial nationalism. The representatives of African and Asian countries who gathered at Bandung rallied against colonialism and affirmed the equality of nation-states and the right of all peoples to form them, articulating an egalitarian vision of international order. The General Assembly concurred in 1960, passing the Declaration on the Granting of Independence to Colonized Peoples and aligning the United Nations with anticolonial nationalism. The self-determining nation-state thus became the world's de facto unit of political organization. But its triumph left difficult dilemmas unanswered.[26]

Two questions in particular vexed the new order. First, who would—and who would not—form nation-states? The UN's 1960 declaration affirmed the right of colonized peoples to de-yoke themselves from colonialism, but it said nothing about minority populations within postcolonial nation-states. Their dilemmas would be fraught, for the political geography of postwar world politics mapped imperfectly onto the geographies of ethnicity and culture. In a world encompassing up to a thousand distinct ethnic groups, any international system comprising a hundred or so nation-states would, by necessity, include ethnic, cultural, and linguistic fault lines along which national projects might fracture. Basques, Bengalis, and Biafrans would contest the rule of nation-states after 1945, much as colonized elites once challenged the rule of empires. Over one-third of the states that became independent in the quarter century after World War II would fight civil wars before the twentieth century ended.[27]

A second dilemma was human rights, rooted in the assertion that all people enjoy specific rights by the simple virtue of being human. The idea was present at the dawn of the postwar era, Franklin Roosevelt having in 1941 identified "four essential human freedoms"—freedom of speech and of worship, freedom from want and from fear. Transforming aspirations into meaningful protections nonetheless proved difficult. The Nuremberg war crimes trials of 1945–46 affirmed that leaders could be held responsible for crimes against humanity, but Nuremberg's relevance to governments' violations of human rights in peacetime and inside their own borders was unclear. Less ambiguous was the United Nations' Universal Declaration of Human Rights, approved in 1948. The work of an international committee, chaired by FDR's widow, the Universal Declaration identified a range of rights applying to "all members of the human family." Eleanor Roosevelt hoped that the declaration would become "the international Magna Carta of all men everywhere." Enforcement, however, remained an open question. John Humphrey, one of the declaration's principal draftsmen, believed that realization of the Universal Declaration's "revolutionary" promise required some "supranational supervision of the relationship between the state and its citizens." This was bound to be contentious.[28]

Humphrey's point was not lost on national governments. Delegates from several countries attacked the Universal Declaration, calling it an affront to sovereignty. There was also pushback within the United States. The president of the American Bar Association dubbed "so-called human rights" a threat to the US Constitution—and to the racial order in the former Confederacy. His objections made sense. Upholding individuals' rights under international law would, by necessity, circumscribe the juridical autonomy of nation-states—and threaten the institutional framework of American racial segregation. As a practical matter, the defenders of sovereignty need not have worried. The Charter of the United Nations exalted territorial sovereignty and disavowed UN intervention in the domestic affairs of member states. "Nothing contained in the present Charter," stated Article 2.7, "shall authorize the United Nations to intervene in matters which are essentially within the jurisdiction of any state." This trumped human rights, at least for now.[29]

If states were sovereign in the postwar order, it did not follow that all nation-states were equal. The Security Council of the United Nations institutionalized inequality, giving the great powers (and the Republic of China) veto power over UN peacekeeping actions. In the Cold War era, moreover, two powers surpassed all the rest. Within a divided world, the United States and the Soviet Union constructed hierarchical alliances, between which resided a vast nonaligned zone. As the Cold War in Europe and Northeast Asia stabilized,

beginning in the mid-1950s, superpower tensions spilled over into this intermediary zone, the so-called Third World. Both superpowers intervened here, with
dismal consequences for Third World peoples.

The rise of Third World interventionism was lamentable, but it followed early
efforts to align postwar US foreign policy with decolonization. Washington
had pushed Britain to decolonize (and to abandon its imperial tariff) in the
mid-1940s, freed the Philippines in 1946, and coerced the Netherlands to
grant Indonesia its independence in 1948. As the Cold War intensified, geopolitical interests and ideological paranoia nonetheless trumped Washington's
commitment to self-determination. Truman's decision to back French colonialism in Vietnam marked the shift, and Eisenhower's decision to support a
British-instigated coup in Iran in 1953 confirmed it. The United States thereafter
intervened elsewhere—in Guatemala, the Dominican Republic, Cuba, Laos,
and Vietnam, and so on. Recalling older habits of US imperialism, these interventions often had catastrophic consequences, and they marked the difference
between wartime ideals and the Cold War realities that US decision-makers
inhabited—and made.[30]

Still, neocolonial meddling did not abrogate Washington's commitment to
nationalism as an organizational principle. Indeed, US policymakers recurrently
aligned themselves with, not against, nationalist forces. In the name of anti-Soviet
containment, they rallied foreign nation-states in formal alliances and assisted
nationalist projects in the Third World. The United States focused its assistance
on allies, such as South Korea and South Vietnam, but it also aided countries like
Egypt and India that resided between the Cold War blocs. The threat of violent
US intervention nonetheless remained, and it manifested itself with the greatest vigor where pro-American regimes seemed poised to defect—and in Latin
America. Cuba illustrated the pattern. Fidel Castro's 1959 revolution overthrew
a pro-American dictatorship and triggered a series of US retaliations, including a
failed invasion. These precipitated an East-West confrontation that brought the
superpowers close to war and prefigured fundamental change in the Cold War
order.[31]

The Cold War Ossifies

On October 14, 1962, an American spy plane captured images of Soviet missile
sites in Cuba. A thirteen-day standoff between Washington and Moscow ensued,
during which the United States blockaded Cuba and mobilized American military forces for action. The Soviet leader Nikita Khrushchev backed down in
late October, agreeing to remove Soviet missiles from the Caribbean island.
For President John F. Kennedy, the missile crisis confirmed the Cold War's

existential risks. Following the crisis, Kennedy acted to reduce Soviet-American tensions. Kennedy's June 1963 speech at American University, in which he called for a "real peace," evoked a new mood. The installation of a telegraphic link between the Pentagon and the Kremlin and the Limited Nuclear Test Ban Treaty of August 1963 prohibiting the atmospheric testing of nuclear weapons were more tangible steps toward the management, if not the diminution, of East-West hostilities.[32]

The missile crisis taught Soviet leaders different lessons. Khrushchev appears to have intended the installation of nuclear missiles on Cuba to serve multiple purposes. The weapons committed the Soviet Union to the defense of Cuba, ensuring that Castro would remain a loyal client, and they put North American cities within range of intermediate- and medium-range Soviet missiles, offsetting US advantages in intercontinental ballistics. The military gamble was bold, but it failed. Khrushchev's October retreat confirmed the Soviet Union's military inferiority and precipitated his ouster from its leadership in 1964. Khrushchev's departure left behind a troika of leaders—Brezhnev, Kosygin, and Podgorny—who learned from the missile crisis that the Soviet Union was a second-class superpower. To remedy this predicament, they embarked upon on a massive buildup of offensive forces, as figure 1.1. indicates.[33]

The arms race became a stalemate in the 1960s, but American leaders did not panic. As impressive as the Soviet Union's production of intercontinental ballistic missiles (ICBMs) was, the USSR's offensive forces lacked the tactical flexibility that America's triad of ICBMs, submarine-launched missiles (SLBMs), and nuclear-armed bombers provided. But what really mattered, defense secretary Robert McNamara reasoned, was that both superpowers by the mid-1960s possessed so many weapons that each could absorb a preemptive nuclear strike while retaining sufficient offensive capabilities to retaliate against the other. The predicament, McNamara contended, made nuclear war improbable. This was MAD (mutual assured destruction), and it rendered ineffectual the atomic arsenals that both superpowers had built. "The nuclear bomb is just like the Old Testament God," explained Britain's prime minister, Harold Macmillan, in 1967. "People don't believe in it anymore."[34]

MAD had diverse implications. One had to do with the size of the US nuclear arsenal. If mutual destruction were assured, McNamara argued, the United States need possess only enough nuclear weapons to retaliate against a Soviet attack. Sufficiency became the watchword of US nuclear policy, and the growth of Washington's nuclear arsenal stalled. Another of MAD's implications was that the two superpowers now shared a common interest in stabilizing the nuclear arms race—and in excluding new participants from it. For some, the proliferation of atomic weapons in the 1960s eclipsed the US-Soviet rivalry as a security threat, especially after China tested a nuclear weapon in 1964. The

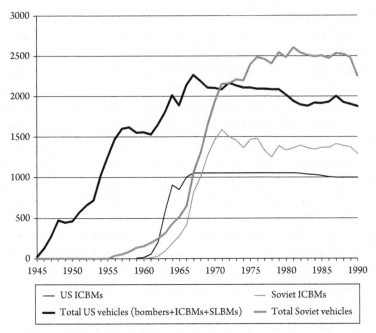

Figure 1.1 The strategic arms race, 1945–1990
Source: National Resources Defense Council, Archive of Nuclear Data. http://www.nrdc.org/
nuclear/nudb/datainx.asp.

two superpowers, in response, signed the Treaty on the Non-Proliferation of
Nuclear Weapons (NPT), committing them both (along with Great Britain)
to an agreement not to transfer nuclear technologies to non-nuclear countries
and to seek the "cessation of the nuclear arms race." France and China, the other
nuclear-weapons states, did not sign the NPT. Their reticence showcased rising
resistance to superpower leadership among the world's second-tier powers.[35]

European reactions to the NPT evoked a strained alliance. West German
leaders muttered about superpower "complicity" and worried that their own
"interests" would be "sacrificed" on the altar of the "Soviet-American partnership." The concern was not irrational. Since the late 1940s, Washington's allies
had depended on US nuclear forces to contain the Soviet Union, but in a MAD
world, it could not be presumed that an American president would risk nuclear
retaliation against the United States in order to defend Western Europe. Creating
independent deterrents was one solution, but the NPT prohibited the transfer of
nuclear weapons technologies to non-nuclear countries, which limited nuclear
sharing within NATO. Instead, the NPT affirmed a Soviet-American military
stalemate that eroded one of the Pax Americana's core assumptions—that the
United States was responsible for the security of its allies. This brought NATO's

role into question. Under President Johnson, US diplomats tried to rally the alliance around East-West "bridge building," but this was, at some level, paradoxical. Did NATO's cohesion not depend on the existence of an East Bloc threat? How could alliance unity and bridge building be reconciled?[36]

European actors exacerbated the strains on the Pax Americana, beginning with Charles de Gaulle. On his return to power in 1958, France's great wartime leader inquired whether Washington might be open to joining with Paris and London to forge a multilateral—but enduringly hierarchical—alternative to the Pax Americana, a tripartite directorate for the West. Rebuffed, he pursued an independent course, centered on the acquisition of an independent nuclear deterrent. France tested a nuclear bomb in 1960 and a thermonuclear warhead in 1968. Unlike Britain's smaller nuclear force, France's *force de frappe* (strike force) was not integrated within a transatlantic command structure. Instead, de Gaulle withdrew from NATO's military command in 1966 and evicted the NATO military staff from Paris. He also expanded relations with the Communist world. De Gaulle's normalization of relations with China in 1963–64 was stunning, but his opening to the Soviet Union reached further in its implications. The joint declaration that de Gaulle signed when he visited Moscow in 1966 conjured the prospect of a new, cooperative relationship between Europe's leading military powers, echoing the pre-1917 Franco-Russian entente. Politics as normal were resuming, it seemed, indicating the passage of the bipolar era.[37]

West Germany's challenge to bipolar strictures was subtler than de Gaulle's. Divided at the end of the Second World War, Germany 's relationship to the Cold War order was unique. West Germany's Basic Law did not acknowledge the nation's division, treating Soviet occupation of the East Germany as temporary. The Christian Democrats who dominated West German politics in the 1950s would not recognize East Germany or maintain diplomatic relations with any country that did, treating the Cold War as a durable schism. In the mid-1960s, however, new leaders began exploring new approaches. Willy Brandt, a Social Democrat who became West Germany's foreign minister in 1966 and its chancellor in 1969, worked to redefine relations with the East. Brandt traveled to Moscow and Warsaw, signing treaties affirming Germany's post-1945 borders. His most dramatic move came in 1972 with the Basic Treaty, which established formal relations between the two Germanys. Brandt's *Ostpolitik* (eastern policy) was a complex process, but what appeared to animate it, beyond German frustrations with the United States, was the prospect of surmounting division through the expansion of social, economic, and cultural ties—the transcendence, perhaps, of geopolitics.[38]

Even the British drifted away from the Pax Americana in the 1960s. Financial weakness prompted London, in 1968, to abandon its military role in the Indian

Ocean, forsaking what had been a significant British contribution to the West's worldwide security interests. Economic imperatives also pulled Great Britain toward the European Economic Community (EEC), which it finally joined in 1973. Meanwhile, Europe's economic resurgence, like de Gaulle's political assertiveness, called the Pax Americana into question. "The conditions that made America the leader and protector of Western Europe were temporary ones, and they are now passing," wrote historian Ronald Steel. Henry Kissinger concurred, perceiving an "emergence of political multipolarity" and the resurgence of "traditional political pressures" within the Western Alliance.[39]

Events within the East Bloc corroborated the crisis of the bipolar order. Unrest in Eastern Europe was not surprising: popular revolts had already shaken East Berlin in 1953 and Hungary in 1956. In Czechoslovakia, economic difficulties and popular disaffection prompted efforts to synthesize a reformed Communism in the 1960s. These gathered pace in 1968 under Alexander Dubček, a reformer who urged party colleagues to "overcome old thinking" and embrace a "new policy." As Dubček's reform agenda broadened and Czechoslovakians rallied in support of reform, Soviet leaders fretted. In August 1968, they acted to crush the Prague Spring. In September, Moscow articulated the Brezhnev Doctrine: a declaration that Moscow would intervene in Eastern Europe to correct deviations from socialist orthodoxy. This was naked imperialism, shorn of socialist fraternity; but it could not disguise the cracks within the bloc.[40]

It took the Sino-Soviet split, however, to break the Communist world in two. The schism unfolded over a decade, culminating in a military skirmish over the Ussuri River in early 1969. That clash did not lead to war, but it confirmed that the Communist world was not the monolith that American strategists had once presumed it to be. Prefiguring new alignments, the Sino-Soviet estrangement confirmed the sense among many observers of world politics in the late 1960s that Cold War patterns were passing. The two superpowers, Marshall Shulman wrote, had become "like two tired wrestlers whose ring is swirling with many spectators."[41]

Endogenous processes strained the Cold War order in the 1960s: the nuclear stalemate rendered the military power of the superpowers abstract, while the diminution of inter-bloc rivalries weakened inner-bloc cohesion. Exogenous developments also proved disruptive. Anticolonial movements rose in the Third World, often repudiating Cold War binaries in favor of North-South dichotomies. Globalization, meanwhile, began to challenge the prerogatives of nation-states, in world politics and in the international economic order. The settlement built in the 1940s began to crumble in the 1960s, and its crumbling was evident in the strains that manifested themselves within Bretton Woods, a central institutional pillar of the Pax Americana.

Bretton Woods Unravels

Bretton Woods institutionalized a predominant role—and commensurate responsibility—for the United States in the international monetary order, but the margins of American superiority closed in the decades after 1944. The US share of the industrialized world's economic output declined from 59 percent to 45 percent between 1945 and 1960, and America's share of world exports fell from 22 percent to 15 percent between 1948 and 1960. This decline was relative and natural, a consequence of Europe's and Japan's recoveries from the Second World War, not of American failures, but it combined with the effects of a resurgent financial globalization to destabilize Bretton Woods in the 1960s.[42]

The year 1958 brought a return to currency convertibility, as European governments lifted restrictions that they had mostly maintained since the war. With this, Bretton Woods became a full-fledged international monetary order; currencies could now circulate freely, making it possible to conduct trade on a multilateral basis. Yet the system was already becoming unstable, as outflows of dollars destabilized the US balance of payments. One consequence was a loss of US gold reserves in 1958–60, as foreign money holders converted dollars into gold, an indication of waning confidence. The dollar crises of the late 1950s ended only after US authorities intervened in the markets in 1960 to suppress the price of gold, which eased pressure on the dollar. The dollar's post-1958 difficulties nonetheless inaugurated a decade of monetary turmoil, during which policymakers struggled to mitigate and manage the disruptive effects of US payments deficits and an increasingly overvalued dollar on an international monetary order whose stability depended on the dollar's credibility.[43]

Dollar deficits were not novel. The United States had exported dollars from the outset of the postwar era—some via Marshall Aid, others to support US forces overseas; US corporations invested many more in Europe. The problem was that foreign central banks were by the late 1950s awash with dollars. This created a risky situation, as the economist Robert Triffin explained. The accumulation of dollars overseas, Triffin warned, brought into doubt the capacity of the US government to convert dollars into gold at the official rate of $35 per ounce. If enough dollar holders demanded that the United States convert their dollars into gold, the United States would have little choice but to devalue the dollar or break the gold-dollar linkage on which Bretton Woods depended. Triffin thereby articulated the central conundrum of Bretton Woods, that the accumulation of dollars overseas undermined the dollar's credibility. A significant threshold was crossed in 1964–65, as figure 1.2 indicates, when the total value of dollars circulating outside the United States surpassed the value of US gold reserves.[44]

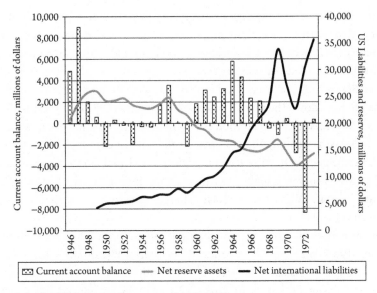

Figure 1.2 The US balance of payments, 1946–1973
Sources: IMF, International Financial Statistics; and White House, *Economic Report of the President* (1974).

Triffin favored a radical solution: create an artificial currency to buttress the dollar's role in the international monetary order. Systemic reform was, however, harder to achieve than ad hoc solutions, which US policymakers instead pursued in the 1960s. From the Eisenhower administration onward, US officials struggled to shore up the dollar and Bretton Woods. Washington worked to bolster US trade surpluses, which offset the balance of payments consequences of dollar outflows, and constructed ad hoc defenses against attacks on the dollar. Washington's allies were helpful, to a point. German officials agreed to make "offset payments" to mitigate the costs of US troop deployments, and they promised not to seek conversion of the Bundesbank's dollar reserves to gold. De Gaulle was less cooperative. In 1965 he denounced the dollar as a source of exorbitant privilege and demanded that the US Treasury convert some of France's dollar reserves into gold. While he advocated a return to the gold standard, de Gaulle said little about the gold standard's defects, which the experience of the 1930s had made clear. There were, in short, no easy fixes to the Bretton Woods dilemmas.[45]

De Gaulle apart, international monetary relations in the 1960s evinced cooperation as well as conflict. Public officials collaborated to protect Bretton Woods against a resurgence in transnational finance. Central bankers worked to offset short-term financial movements by intervening in the foreign exchange markets, an effort the Federal Reserve Bank of New York took a lead role in facilitating.

Besides cooperating to manage destabilizing financial flows, governments collaborated to buttress the architecture of the world monetary order. The General Agreement to Borrow of 1961 created an international credit line on which central banks could draw to support their exchange rates, while the gold pool the United States and its allies created in 1962 supplied bullion to the London gold market to hold down the market price of gold and thereby lower pressure on the dollar. The Johnson administration even embraced the creation of a new international reserve asset along the lines that Triffin advocated, which led to the 1967 creation of Special Drawing Rights (SDRs)—a virtual currency administered by the IMF. This was a high-water mark in the international effort to stabilize Bretton Woods. When these efforts faltered, governments turned instead to financial controls.[46]

For its part, the US government deployed capital controls to defend the dollar. In 1963, President Kennedy introduced the Interest Equalization Tax, intended to discourage the issuance of foreign bonds in the United States. To curtail the overseas transfer of American assets, LBJ in 1965 introduced the voluntary Foreign Credit Restraint Program. These initiatives varied in effectiveness, but their logic was to restrain transnational financial transactions to lessen pressure on the dollar and bolster Bretton Woods. It is nonetheless striking that the capital controls US officials constructed in the 1960s focused on long-term financial outflows, which exacerbated the strains on the dollar. Insofar as inflows of capital to the United States supported the balance of payments and the dollar, US officials did not attempt to circumscribe them. Rather than opposing financial globalization per se, American policymakers sought only to control transactions that eroded the US payments balance and the dollar's international position.[47]

Capital controls nonetheless had an ironic consequence: they spurred the growth of transnational finance. Located mainly in London, the so-called Euromarkets emerged in the 1960s as a market for funds mediated outside their territory of issue. The Euromarkets' origins reach back into the early 1950s, when resourceful London bankers, hidebound by postwar restrictions on the sterling's convertibility, courted business in dollars. The Euromarkets grew fast in the 1960s, and their growth was entwined with the expansion of US-based multinational enterprise in Europe. Multinational corporations turned to the offshore market to circumvent capital controls, and they plowed profits back into the Euromarkets, where deposits often earned higher interest rates than they did in domestic financial markets. The total value of dollar-denominated Eurodollar holdings quadrupled between 1966 and 1970, from about $16 billion (or 8.4 percent of the US money supply) to over $60 billion (32.2 percent of the US money supply). Financial globalization was stirring, especially from the late 1960s on.[48]

The consequences for Bretton Woods varied. In the short term, the Euromarkets may have mitigated the widening overhang between US gold reserves and dollar liabilities: the high interest rates available offshore likely encouraged dollar holders to hold on to their dollars for longer than they would otherwise have done. The Euromarkets nonetheless corroded the containment of transnational finance on which Bretton Woods depended. They facilitated the evasion of capital controls, encouraged currency speculation, and "complicated" the management of monetary policy, as Federal Reserve governor Andrew Brimmer saw it. Residing beyond the reach of US regulatory power, there was little the United States could do to control the Euromarkets—at least not without the cooperation of foreign monetary authorities.[49]

The first months of 1968 brought a major dollar crisis, prompting decisive action. To stabilize the dollar and calm inflation, the Johnson administration had in January adopted a package of emergency measures: mandatory capital controls, interest rate hikes, and tax increases. With these, Johnson reversed his prior refusal to subordinate domestic autonomy to external stability. As dramatic as they were, Johnson's measures did not halt the dollar's decline on the foreign exchange markets. As money holders clamored to convert dollars for gold, the US Treasury announced in early March that it would no longer convert privately owned dollars; henceforth, only central banks would be able to exchange dollars for gold. The curtailment of gold-dollar convertibility helped to achieve a respite of monetary stability in 1969–70, but it abrogated a foundational commitment and left the future of the international monetary order uncertain.[50]

Globalization and the Remaking of World Politics

Economic globalization in the 1960s carried implications for governance that were at odds with prevailing political trends. With the completion of decolonization in the mid-1970s, the nation-state became universal, the world's natural unit of political order. Nationalism in the postwar world was an economic phenomenon too; governments planned growth, promoted welfare, and regulated markets. The Bretton Woods institutions accommodated this mobilization of public sectors, as did the informal frameworks of the Pax Americana. By the late 1960s, however, new developments were complicating the management of national economies.

The economist Richard Cooper published *The Economics of Interdependence* in 1968. While he did not use the word *globalization*, Cooper argued that interdependence was upending an international economic order predicated on the assumption that nation-states were—and would remain—autonomous, self-governing entities. Since the 1940s, Cooper explained, tariff liberalization and falling transportation costs had lowered barriers to trade, while the widening "psychological horizons" of consumers had encouraged imports and foreign travel. Financial capital had evaded controls, integrating money markets. Transnational economic relations were making the advanced industrialized countries interdependent. Cooper presumed that the march of interdependence increased opportunities for productive specialization, improving aggregate welfare. He nonetheless grasped the dilemmas it created for governance.[51]

Among Cooper's central questions was whether interdependence allowed "freedom for each nation to pursue its legitimate economic objectives"? Cooper thought not and predicted a backlash against globalization in the near future. Raymond Vernon, a political scientist, shared this concern. Like Cooper, Vernon believed that innovations in the areas of transportation and communications were making the industrialized countries interdependent. The growth of cross-border trade, finance, and tourism had been "spectacular" in recent years, Vernon asserted, which posed "challenges of a new order to the nation-state." The multinational corporation, in particular, embodied both the promise and the costs of a transnational, globalizing capitalism. Politics, by contrast, remained national and territorial. The world's political and economic orders, Vernon concluded, constituted distinct realms. They were "two systems," he argued, whose purposes were sometimes complementary, and sometimes at odds.[52]

There would be no dramatic showdown between nation-states and transnational forces in the 1960s, but tensions between these realms emerged in an ideological crisis of the West's consensus politics; in the travails of postcolonial nationalism; in the rise of human rights; and in the perceptual innovations that made the "global village" a novel and pervasive concept. Globalization expanded the interdependence of societies, curtailing the autonomy of nation-states with disruptive implications for foreign policy. Their predecessors having built a Pax Americana in a world of nation-states, US policymakers in the 1960s and after would have to adapt their mental maps of world politics—the conceptual foundations of their strategic commitments—to processes of transnational integration that manifested themselves in a variety of guises but served, cumulatively, to transform world politics and the prospects for US leadership.

More dramatic than architectonic changes in the global economic order were the street protests that exploded throughout the West at the end of the 1960s. US government analysts discerned a threat to social order in the "world-wide" phenomenon of "restless youth," but the challenge that protestors posed to the nation-state was ideological in nature. What was being disputed in the United States and elsewhere was the legitimacy of the postwar status quo, of the national projects that the public mobilizations of the 1930s and 1940s had bequeathed. Welfare states had since 1945 fostered stability and prosperity, but disenchantment ran deep and broad. In the United States, protestors on the left decried the Vietnam War and the Cold War fusion of public and corporate interests. On the right, Ronald Reagan rejected President Eisenhower's accommodation with the New Deal and railed against "bureaucracy" in language that anticipated Mario Savio's assault on "the machine." The political center was not crumbling, but an ideological synthesis that had cohered around managed capitalism—a synthesis that Americans called New Deal or Cold War liberalism; a synthesis that European Christian Democrats and Social Democrats all embraced—was ceasing to command, much less inspire.[53]

Postcolonial nationalism was doing no better. By the end of the sixties, decolonization was nearly complete, but postcolonial development was faltering. India's per capita GDP increased, in real terms, from $1,040 in 1947 to just $1,350 in 1967. The average Ghanaian's income increased 8 percent in the first decade of independence—a miserly accomplishment over a decade when Italian per capita incomes rose by 65 percent. This was not the future of which Nehru and Nkrumah had dreamed. Still, India and Ghana at least stayed intact; other new nations waged civil wars. International conflicts also proved costly. Egypt and Syria suffered military humiliation at Israel's hands in 1967, and their defeats discredited President Gamal Abdul Nasser's secular Arab nationalism. More broadly, the travails of postcolonial nationalism had consequences for US decision makers, who had in the past aligned themselves with nation-building postcolonial elites. As the 1960s progressed, US foreign policy took a cynical turn. Lyndon Johnson's support for Brazil's 1964 coup contrasted with Kennedy's Alliance for Progress in Latin America. Spending on foreign assistance declined from 0.76 percent of GDP in 1962 to 0.45 percent in 1968, as Washington forsook postcolonial nation building for accommodations with Third World dictators and autocrats.[54]

As postcolonial nationalism lost its luster, the idea of universal human rights resurged. Leading the charge was Peter Benenson, a British lawyer who in May 1961 published a newspaper article describing the fates of six men who had been jailed in countries as far apart as Hungary, Angola, and the United States. International law had not protected the rights of these men, Benenson argued, but global opinion—"feelings of disgust all over the world"—might yet be able to do so. Benenson soon tested his hypothesis, collaborating with delegates from the United States, France, Belgium, Ireland, and Switzerland to found Amnesty International in 1962. Amnesty became a prominent NGO, whose members wrote letters to governments on behalf of the "prisoners of conscience" whom they adopted. The cause was selfless, but the politics of transnational human rights proved contentious. One Indian diplomat denounced the International League for the Rights of Man, another such NGO, as an "odious organization," a reaction that hinted at the radicalism of the human rights movement. What the

NGOs sought was an improbable reconfiguration of world politics that would vindicate the rights of individuals and subject nation-states to the writ of global justice.[55]

Amnesty International, the International League, and the other human rights NGOs were participants in what historian Akira Iriye calls a "global civil society" operating beyond the realm of nation-states. Like Vernon's realm of transnational economics, the maturation of transnational politics depended on technological innovations that lowered barriers and brokered connections, facilitating globalization. Telstar, the world's first communications satellite, launched in 1962, and an infrastructure for satellite broadcasting developed quickly thereafter. It was too soon to tell how this worldwide information grid would affect world politics, but Zbigniew Brzezinski, a political scientist, predicted the collapse of distinctions between domestic and foreign affairs. "Moral immunity to 'foreign' events," he argued, could not "be maintained" amid "the electronic infusion of global events into the home." This was, in effect, Benenson's gambit: that transnational opinion might be able to restrain the powers of sovereign governments.[56]

If flows of information broadened cognitive horizons, other innovations shrank physical space. The advent of the shipping container—a standardized metal box that could be stacked in the holds of vast container ships—slashed the real costs of seaborne transportation, while the Boeing 707 did much the same for passenger air travel. The real price of a round-trip air ticket from New York to London dropped from $5,970 in 1951 to $2,680 in 1966, while the maiden flight of the Boeing 747 in 1969 promised further economies of scale. In orbit, in the air, and upon the oceans, the mobilization of technology for the purposes of transportation and communications contracted distance and time in the 1960s, deepening the interdependence of societies.[57]

Marshall McLuhan called the world that interconnections were making a "global village." He intended the metaphor to connote fractiousness, not harmony, but McLuhan had little to say about globalization's implications for politics. On this point, a beloved leader of the Catholic Church offered greater insight. In 1963, Pope John XXIII issued *Pacem in Terris* ("peace on earth"), his final encyclical, in which he asserted the interdependence of the world's societies and the claims of human rights. The pope dissected the tragic predicament of a globalizing world: problems of "world-wide" scale loomed, but nation-states lacked the capacity to resolve them. The pope's point became commonplace in the 1960s, as did the calls for action. Global ecological degradation, humankind's demographic explosion, and the prospect of epidemic disease became the subjects of globalist jeremiads. Secular prophets like Lester Brown, Kenneth Boulding, and Buckminster Fuller invoked the metaphor of "spaceship earth" to evoke the singularity of the planet's predicament, the interdependence of its peoples, and the need for worldwide action to advance what Pope John called the "common good of all peoples."[58]

Even American politicians embraced the politics of globalism in the late 1960s. "The world is becoming one great city," one declared in 1967. "Distances are shrinking, time-spans are shortening." In the "world city," the speaker continued, "there is no retreat to the suburbs." Hunger, poverty, and overpopulation were the world's dilemmas, not just the problems of the poor, and they ought to concern the world's leading superpower. Yet the United States, the speaker warned, was failing to meet history's challenge. "The deficit in our balance of payments," he chided, "is matched by a mounting deficit in our balance of influence."[59]

The speaker was Richard Nixon, the former vice president and veteran candidate. As he prepared his 1968 presidential bid, Nixon spoke often on world affairs—fluidly, creatively, and without notes. At stake in the election, Nixon declared, was the future of American leadership in the world. The United States had failed to adapt to vast changes in the world: the "wave of decolonization" and the rise of the "global city." The Pax Americana of the 1940s had become brittle and outmoded, even irrelevant. "Our example has lost its fire," Nixon exclaimed; "our influence has lost its drive." Was the United States "succumbing to a creeping obsolescence," Nixon asked, condemned to be "an old nation in a new world"? Richard Nixon hoped not, but the capacity of the United States to adapt its leadership role to the relative decline of American power and to new patterns of globalization would depend upon choices, choices that the election's victor would make.

PART I

REACHING BACKWARD

2

In Pursuit of Primacy

This then is the overall image of the U.S. as a reluctant giant: seeking peace and reconciliation almost feverishly . . . tired of using its physical force, and firmly resolved to cut existing commitments.

Fritz Kraemer, "The Modern World," 1969

Richard Nixon's January 1969 inaugural surveyed the world as the astronauts saw it. Weeks earlier, the crew of Apollo VIII had taken a photograph that captured the planet, a semishadowed marble, lifting above the lunar horizon. "In that far perspective," Nixon exclaimed, "man's destiny on Earth is not divisible." The image, *Earthrise*, became a sensation: Lyndon Johnson, in the last days of his presidency, sent a copy of it to the leader of every nation on earth. The poet Archibald MacLeish penned a tribute. "To see the earth as it truly is," MacLeish reflected, "is to see ourselves as riders on the earth together." Nixon seemed to concur, addressing himself not only to his countrymen but also to his "fellow citizens of the world community."[1]

For Nixon, the astronauts' vista evoked historical disjuncture. Some moments in history "stand out as moments of beginning, in which courses are set that shape decades or centuries," the new president declared. "This could be such a moment." The prospect of epochal change captivated the new administration. "We are in a transitional period of international politics, in which the familiar structures of power . . . are eroding," wrote one official. Nixon's national security adviser discerned a "watershed." Outside observers buttressed the assumption that major change was underway in international affairs. Some discerned the passing of the Cold War. Others, like Stanley Hoffmann, another political scientist, called upon US decision-makers to transcend the axioms and assumptions of the past. "To be truly effective," Hoffmann wrote, "we must rid ourselves of irrelevant concepts and habits." The world, Hoffmann argued, had changed since the 1940s: new nations had emerged, and the superpowers no longer dominated world politics. The United States, it followed, needed to rethink such outmoded axioms as containment and anti-Communism and instead cultivate "a more complex and balanced system of world order."[2]

Plainly, the world of 1969 was not the world in which the Pax Americana was cast. Beyond the multiplication of nations and the ossification of alliances, thickening transnational relations and rising non-state actors were deepening the interdependence of societies. What most preoccupied the new president, however, was the specter of decline. Nixon believed that the United States had "lost the leadership position we held at the end of World War Two" and might spill further "down the drain as a great power." Others stirred and excited his fears. Fritz Kraemer, a Pentagon adviser, warned that the United States was becoming a "reluctant giant," retreating from the world and "seeking peace and reconciliation almost feverishly." "Sad but true," Nixon scrawled in the margins of Kraemer's memorandum. The president disagreed with Dean Acheson, an architect of the Pax Americana, and others who saw the relative decline as the result of "historical and natural processes," not as a cause for consternation. Decline, for Nixon, was a consequence of flagging will and purpose. Americans "want to put their heads in the sand," he lamented. The stakes, as the new president saw them, were momentous. "If America were to become a dropout," Nixon warned, "the world would live in terror."[3]

⸎

Fearing decline, Richard Nixon sought to stabilize a faltering Pax Americana amid unfavorable circumstances. The Vietnam War facilitated Nixon's election, but it divided the nation, making the restoration of a domestic consensus for internationalism improbable, and compounded the Pax Americana's fiscal burdens. Nixon grasped the prevailing economic and political constraints and worked to transcend them through the construction of a new international "structure of peace." This structure and Nixon's bid to realize it are the dual themes of this chapter. The chapter begins by establishing Nixon's dominance of the foreign policy process, his fixation with hegemonic decline, and his determination to restore US primacy. The narrative turns next to Vietnam. Believing the war's dissolution to be imperative, Nixon struggled to extricate the United States from Indochina and ended up escalating the war's violence. Nixon failed to achieve the "peace with honor" that he sought, but he defined in Vietnam a template for a broader retrenchment of US military commitments, the so-called Nixon Doctrine.[4]

The Nixon Doctrine aimed to sustain, not shed, the international commitments that the United States had assumed since the 1940s. A strategic reaction to adverse circumstances, the Nixon Doctrine served a conservative purpose, which was to sustain and preserve the Pax Americana. More dramatic, but no less conservative in intent, was Nixon's détente, which sought a new balance among the leading Cold War powers: the United States, the Soviet Union, and China. Nixon's boldest innovation thus seized advantage of the Sino-Soviet split to position the United States as the dominant element in this geopolitical triangle. Détente thereby substituted diplomatic daring for waning material strength. If the Soviet Union was approaching military coequality with the United States, and if American economic preeminence was faltering, the United States could still dominate the Cold War international system, the architects of détente gambled, through geopolitical manipulation. The gambit worked for a time, but it offered no new beginning of the kind that Nixon conjured on his the day of his inauguration.

Nixon in January 1969 evoked the challenges of a new era: new interconnections among societies, new human aspirations, and new demands on foreign policy. He would nonetheless fail to engage in a constructive way with the variety of issues that were proliferating beyond the arena of high geopolitics at the dawn of the 1970s. Radical as his diplomatic maneuvering would be, Nixon did not transcend the assumptions of the Cold War, which held that the superpowers and their competition were what mattered in world politics. While this chapter explains what Nixon sought to accomplish, the three chapters that follow explore areas of major omission: the rise of transnational humanitarianism, which blurred distinctions between foreign and domestic politics; the advent of financial globalization, which manifested its consequences in a crisis of the international monetary order; and the dilemmas of energy interdependence, which the 1973–74 oil crisis exposed. Nixon's failures in these areas indicate his inability to overcome his conditioning as a man of the Cold War, but they also suggest the limitations of grand strategy as a conceptual device for guiding foreign policy in a complex and dynamic world. The challenges of the 1970s proved too diffuse, too myriad in their sources and implications, to be subsumed within singular grand designs.

"We Can't Let the United States Be a Second-Rate Power"

Richard Nixon struggled to escape his roots until he returned to them in his last words as president. Exiting the White House in disgrace, Nixon would recall his "common" father and saintly mother, as if their prosaic virtues could absolve him. The experiences of a difficult childhood remained with Nixon: his ascent from the family gas station to Whittier College and Duke Law School informed his core beliefs about work, diligence, and meritocracy, and he would, as president, still brag about his "absolute discipline" and "stamina."[5]

Naval service during the Second World War was Nixon's education in internationalism, and it propelled him into public life. When the California Republican Party identified Nixon as a promising candidate for Congress in 1946, he seized the opportunity. As the Cold War descended, Richard Nixon established his reputation as an ideological warrior, winning celebrity for his dogged pursuit of Alger Hiss, a diplomat and Soviet spy. Catapulted to prominence, Nixon ran for the Senate in 1950. Lambasting the Truman administration as "soft" and his opponent as a "pink lady," he stormed to victory. When Dwight Eisenhower, a moderate, won the 1952 Republican presidential nomination, the general made the young senator his running mate. Nixon was ideological ballast with political sharp teeth, but he gained Eisenhower's trust and made a number of overseas trips as vice president. These travels provided encounters with foreign leaders from Caracas, where his car was pelted with rocks, to Moscow, where he and Nikita Khrushchev wrangled over the merits of Communism and capitalism in their "kitchen debate." The prize came when Nixon won the Republican Party's nomination for the presidency.[6]

By the summer of 1960, perhaps no American had done better out of the Cold War than Richard Nixon. That fall, the ascent stopped. Amid re-counts and allegations of vote fraud, Nixon lost the presidential election to John F. Kennedy of Massachusetts. Kennedy did not repudiate Cold War assumptions, but he welded them to a progressive liberalism that left Nixon looking outmoded. Next, in 1962, Nixon lost a race for the California governorship and, in defeat, swiped at the media. "You won't have Nixon to kick around anymore," he exclaimed. Although he was not yet fifty, Nixon was damaged goods, no longer the veteran with the shining future. On television, ABC did a postmortem on his career and invited Hiss to deliver the "political obituary." At this point, a less obstinate man might have turned his back on public life. But Richard Nixon moved to New York, practiced law, and plotted his resurrection. He traveled abroad and campaigned for Republican candidates in the 1966 midterm elections. Then in 1968, Nixon returned to again claim the party's presidential nomination. With the Democrats divided over Vietnam and civil rights, Nixon eked out a victory over Vice President Hubert Humphrey in the November ballot.[7]

Henry Kissinger, the man who became Nixon's associate in power, was no less a product of the Cold War than the new president. Born in Germany, Kissinger arrived in New York in 1938, a refugee from Nazi persecution. While Nixon climbed the ladder of politics, Kissinger's ladder was the Cold War University. He published several books, including influential analyses of the nuclear arms race and the NATO alliance. Although he won tenure at Harvard, Kissinger set his sights on a larger stage. He was a consultant for the Kennedy administration and in 1968 joined the presidential campaign of Nelson Rockefeller, a liberal Republican who trailed to defeat in the primaries. Kissinger lamented Rockefeller's loss, fearing that

Richard Nixon's "frozen" worldview and "cold war outlook" were inappropriate to the challenges of a changing world. These differences of perspective notwithstanding, Nixon reached out during the presidential transition and invited Kissinger, who ranked among the Republican Party's leading foreign-policy thinkers, to join his administration as his national security adviser.[8]

∞

New presidents bring their own priorities, and domestic issues often predominate. Even Eisenhower, unequaled in international experience, appears to have been concerned as president mainly with guarding American society against the political consequences of unwarranted militarism. Richard Nixon, unusually, gravitated toward foreign policy. The United States "could run itself domestically" without a president, Nixon explained. "The president makes foreign policy." Nixon told aides that he did not want to be bothered with domestic policy and delegated responsibility for it to an assistant, John Ehrlichman. Nixon would make foreign policy, and Henry Kissinger, as his assistant, would coordinate its implementation.[9]

In Nixon's first meeting with Kissinger, the president-elect articulated his desire to focus control of foreign policy in the White House by cutting the State Department and the Congress out of the policymaking process. Kissinger orchestrated this bureaucratic shake-up, a reorganization that "compounded the existing exclusion of the Congress and the public from foreign policy," in the words of one insider-critic, and put the office of the national security adviser at the heart of the foreign-policy apparatus. The national security adviser would chair a fortified National Security Council (NSC) and an array of interdepartmental groups dealing with issues from crisis response to strategic planning. By giving the NSC oversight of "middle and long-range policy issues" as well as "current crises and immediate operational problems," Kissinger's plan curtailed the State Department's influence. Chairing the key committees, Kissinger would himself control the flow of paperwork from the bureaucracy to the president, while Nixon would hover above the entire apparatus, the aloof arbiter of grand strategy.[10]

In the beginning, the only exception to this concentration of power in the National Security Council was Middle Eastern policy. The anomaly indicated Nixon's problematic views about Jewish Americans, which led him to presume that Kissinger could not be neutral on matters involving Israel, but it confirmed Nixon's determination to insulate diplomacy from domestic politics. Nixon allowed his secretary of state, William Rogers, to run Middle Eastern policy because he assumed that Rogers would be less susceptible to emotional bias and pro-Israel domestic lobbying than Kissinger. As the years passed, even this sphere of State Department ascendancy fell under the NSC's sway. Careful observers soon recognized that the State Department was "no longer in charge of the United States' foreign affairs." Senator Stuart Symington, a Missouri Democrat, accused the White House of violating a "fundamental premise on which our country was founded," namely, "representative democracy." Because the NSC is not an executive agency, it is not obliged to testify before Congress, and its activities were therefore effectively shielded from congressional oversight. For Nixon and Kissinger, this was one of the new system's advantages.[11]

Besides excluding the State Department from the formation of foreign policy, Nixon and Kissinger aimed to marginalize State's role in its execution. Naturally, Kissinger's small NSC staff could not replicate the functions of an agency employing 12,000 people, but the White House short-circuited State on matters of critical importance by establishing conduits—Kissinger called them "back channels"—to foreign governments and US ambassadors. The most important of these was opened early, when Nixon told Soviet ambassador Anatoli Dobrynin that he should communicate with Kissinger on matters of real importance. "The most sensitive business in U.S.-Soviet relations," Kissinger wrote, "came to be handled between Dobrynin and me." Similar channels were opened to China and to close West European allies. In addition, the White House received foreign ambassadors without State Department participation. From the president's perspective, marginalizing State was a prerequisite to the effective conduct of foreign policy. "There have been more back-channel games played in this administration than any in history," Nixon explained, "because we couldn't trust the God-damned State Department!"[12]

Nixon and Kissinger argued that their diplomacy depended on the circumvention of standard procedures; without secrecy, they insisted, the superpowers could not deal frankly and effectively with each other. There is some truth to the claim: secret diplomacy facilitated breakthroughs in East-West relations and the resolution of crises. When US intelligence revealed, in fall 1970, that Soviet forces were building a submarine base in Cuba, for example, secret diplomacy enabled the crisis to be resolved without loss of face. Still, secrecy entailed costs. One was the circumscription of internal debate. Another was the personalization of world politics, as Nixon's ardors and enmities afflicted diplomatic relationships. Most damaging, perhaps, was the toll that secrecy took on the domestic legitimacy of foreign policy, especially when it was broached. Given Nixon's ostensible commitment to rebuilding a domestic consensus for American internationalism, this was an ironic and regrettable consequence of practices and procedures that focused power at the very highest levels.[13]

⌒∞⌒

Decline and renewal were priorities for Nixon and Kissinger. Both men feared what Kissinger called "deterioration in the U.S. power position in the world," and both related the prospect to internal developments. Nixon believed that the

United States had entered a "revolutionary period." Kissinger concurred that Nixon faced "the most domestic pressures any president has had to face since the Civil War." The combination of domestic disenchantment and adverse global trends—including the rise of Soviet military power and the relative decline of US capacities—made America's retreat from internationalism possible, even likely. Nixon shuddered at the prospect. Should we "let go abroad," he warned, "we might destroy ourselves." For Nixon, as for the architects of Pax Americana, leadership was America's historical appointment. "Because of our economic and military position," he explained, "the fate of freedom and peace in the last third of this century will depend upon how we meet our responsibilities." Revealingly, Nixon described the British Empire as a model to emulate. "We are now in a position," he explained, "to give the world all the good things that Britain offered in her Empire without any of the disadvantages of nineteenth-century colonialism."[14]

Nixon's commitment to American leadership resembled that of Woodrow Wilson. Although Nixon cultivated the persona of a foreign-policy realist, at odds with Wilson's idealism, the two presidents shared a belief that international order was America's special providence. Fearful of German militarism, Wilson had argued that the United States could not prosper—or even survive—in a hostile world arena. Only America, in the Wilsonian formula, could create an international order in which democracy—and the United States—would be safe. Nixon, who called Wilson "our greatest president of this century," echoed this bleak outlook, which linked international security with American internationalism. "If we retreat from the world," Nixon asked, "who's left?" "With all our stupidity, with all our impetuousness," he continued, "what other nation in the world is more idealistic than the United States?"[15]

Henry Kissinger appeared less convinced than Nixon that the United States had a singular role to play in world politics. More cosmopolitan than the president, Kissinger cherished the "tolerance" and "personal freedom" that the United States offered, but his concept of international order lacked Nixon's emphasis on America's special destiny. Kissinger had in his scholarly work explored the European international settlements that Metternich and Bismarck brokered, and he would in his own career prove more eager than Nixon to share the responsibilities for sustaining international order with like-minded nation-states. Later, as Nixon's influence waned, Kissinger would reinvigorate America's relationships with its allies and even redirect American leadership to the management of challenges emanating from novel global interdependencies. Until then, Nixon remained the dominant influence on policy, and the arrest of America's decline remained his overriding preoccupation. "In the final analysis," Nixon insisted, "we can't let the United States be a second-rate power."[16]

This preoccupation with decline revealed the dominance of a "Cold War lens"—the cognitive and intellectual biases that led policymakers during the Cold War to prioritize high geopolitics and superpower relations at the expense of other international actors and issues, including transnational relations. Some officials grasped the oversight but struggled to reorient the White House away from its preoccupation with Cold War geopolitics. Robert Osgood, an NSC staffer, pointed out that "the scope and reach of American commercial, technical, and cultural influence" had "continued to expand" during the 1960s, even as the "direct influence of the US government" in the world had waned. This was a prescient insight, but its implications remained neglected. At the summit of the foreign-policy apparatus, the leaders with ultimate authority over US foreign policy sought not to devise creative alternatives to the hegemonic role that the United States had assumed in the late 1940s but, instead, to rescue the Pax Americana from the crisis into which it had fallen. Eager for renewal, they turned not to new global challenges but to the epicenter of the crisis, the war in Vietnam.[17]

From Vietnam to Guam: Rationalizing Burdens

By January 1969, some 36,000 Americans had died in the effort to sustain South Vietnam in its wars against Communist North Vietnam and the guerillas of the National Liberation Front. Vietnam was a civil war, a war for postcolonial succession, a Cold War proxy war, and a trial of American resolve. Washington decision-makers in the 1960s elevated the last two paradigms over the alternatives, rationalizing American intervention. The war effort peaked in 1968, when over 16,500 American soldiers fell in a single year. It was ironic that they—and hundreds of thousands of Vietnamese—died at a time when Moscow and Washington were moving toward cooperation on nuclear nonproliferation and other issues. Vietnam also manifested a crisis of superpower authority that called into question the Pax Americana's future. The United States remained the world's dominant superpower, but not even its reservoirs of economic strength and military force enabled it to defeat its adversaries in Vietnam.[18]

Back in 1953, Vice President Nixon had declared that defeating Communist forces in Vietnam was essential to the containment of Communism in Southeast Asia. Yet by 1969, the war had worldwide implications that eclipsed those regional stakes. "The real point of Viet-Nam," summarized one official, "is not Viet-Nam itself but our world-wide role." "I am utterly convinced," Nixon concurred, "that how we end this war will determine the future of the U.S. in the world." "If we yield," Kissinger exclaimed, "we're just inviting the Soviets into a confrontation." American defeat, Nixon foresaw, would encourage the Soviet Union such that the tentacles of Communist influence would soon appear "in the Middle East, in Berlin, eventually even in the Western Hemisphere." The stakes in Vietnam, then, were twofold. US military defeat would embolden Soviet adventurism, but abandoning the South Vietnamese would jeopardize the credibility of Washington's commitments elsewhere. "If our allies saw we were undependable to a small ally," Nixon worried, "big allies would lose confidence in us." To let go in Indochina would thus be to abdicate American leadership in the world. "What was at stake," Nixon insisted, was "the survival of the U.S. as a world power with the will to use this power."[19]

Still, the new administration could not ignore the war's fiscal and political consequences. Costing almost two billion dollars a month at its peak, Vietnam destabilized the US balance of payments and divided American citizens; the dollar crisis of March 1968 and the mayhem at the Chicago Democratic National Convention in August were both symptoms of the war's corrosive effect. While a thin plurality of Americans seemed to support the war, pollsters at the end of 1967 detected "a general weariness and overall disillusionment." Beneath the rancor, supporters and critics alike recognized that the war could not go on forever. The critics favored rapid extrication, but the incoming Nixon administration recognized that the war had become a threat to the preservation of the Pax Americana. Vietnam's paradox was this: keeping the war going eroded America's capacity for leadership, but its overhasty dissolution would, Nixon believed, be no less damaging for American power and influence.[20]

The paradox offered no easy resolution. Instead, the Nixon administration would attempt to sustain Washington's commitment to the defense of South Vietnam while trying to mitigate the war's costs. What Nixon would not do—at least not initially—was renege upon America's commitment to Saigon. Instead, he struggled to sustain the unsustainable until it could be sustained no longer. In the interim, Nixon and Kissinger searched in vain for a formula that would enable them to liberate American power from its long embroilment in Indochina while preserving South Vietnamese independence. They expanded and intensified the war's violence, but their tactical escalations achieved neither victory nor a political settlement. Only when Congress moved to cut war appropriations in 1972 would they accept defeat as the price of extrication.

∽

Nixon's Vietnam policy began with a neologism: *Vietnamization*. This was defense secretary Melvin Laird's concept for shifting the burdens of the war from American shoulders to Vietnamese ones while bolstering South Vietnam's military capacities. The drawdown of US troops proceeded quickly. In 1969, there were 535,500 US troops in Vietnam; by 1972, only 69,000 remained. The political benefits at home were obvious, which is why Nixon embraced Vietnamization. Kissinger nonetheless feared that Vietnamization was a synonym for defeat; as US forces withdrew, all the Communists needed to do was be patient. "We need a plan to end the war," Kissinger insisted, "not only to withdraw."[21]

Within the framework of Vietnamization, the Nixon administration faced multiple Vietnam wars. The first was the battlefield campaign, in which American forces made decent progress during 1969. The second, which Nixon called the "Saigon political war," was the struggle to make South Vietnam capable of defending itself. The third was the war on the home front. The fourth was the diplomatic struggle to extract peace terms from the North. Henry Kissinger waged this last war in a series of Paris meetings with North Vietnamese officials, beginning in August 1969 and continuing until the end of 1972. What made the diplomatic war so difficult was that it depended on the United States being "reasonably successful on [all] the other fronts." To exit Vietnam, Nixon and Kissinger would have to make it look like they were winning the other wars. Their pursuit of a multiplex settlement in Vietnam revealed characteristics that would define their foreign policy. These included Nixon's and Kissinger's tactical flexibility, their enthusiasm for military escalations, and their Cold War–centric image of world politics.[22]

Indeed, Nixon and Kissinger sought from the outset to use Cold War diplomacy to bring the war to an end. Conceptualizing a policy of linkage, Nixon and Kissinger contrasted their willingness to utilize superpower geopolitics on behalf of America's war in Vietnam with LBJ's disinclination to do so. Linkage failed to achieve its intended purposes. Competing with each other for Hanoi's favor, neither the Soviet Union nor China curtailed its support for North Vietnam and the National Liberation Front. Beijing and Moscow both interceded with North Vietnam on behalf of peace negotiations, but neither could control Hanoi with any more precision than Washington was able to control Saigon. In the end, Nixon and Kissinger's geopolitical efforts to transcend Vietnam's wars failed. Geopolitical acrobatics offered no easy solutions to the problem of extrication, which left the war on the ground in Indochina.[23]

Nixon and Kissinger resumed the bombing of North Vietnam and expanded the fighting into Cambodia. The objective was not to defeat the Vietnamese Communists on the battlefield but to batter Hanoi into making concessions and, by destroying Communist sanctuaries, to make Indochina safe for Vietnamization. Kissinger, in particular, favored using military methods to transform political realities, but he struggled to leverage military force into political advantage. Fearing that Vietnamization was eroding his negotiating position with Hanoi, Kissinger, in late summer 1969, proposed a new bombing campaign, code-named Duck Hook. On this occasion, Nixon shied away from escalation, arguing that the United States could not bear the domestic turmoil that would surely ensue. Public revulsion at the war's carnage thus restricted the waging of it.

Nixon nonetheless wanted his enemies to see him as a president who was "out of control," capable of stunning and irrational violence. Shortly after rejecting Duck Hook, Nixon launched a secret nuclear alert, which he hoped would encourage Moscow to put pressure on Hanoi. On this occasion, ambiguous atomic gesturing accomplished little except to confirm the difficulty of extracting political leverage from nuclear weapons. Thereafter, Nixon returned intermittently to what he called "madman" tactics. He sent troops into Cambodia in spring 1970 and supported South Vietnam's incursion into Laos the following year. In May 1972, Operation Linebacker unleashed an air armada in ostensible retaliation for Hanoi's invasion of the South. The human consequences of these tactical escalations were horrendous—and borne mainly by Vietnamese and Cambodians—but decision-makers hoped that increasing the war's violence would invigorate the stalled peace talks and facilitate extrication from Indochina.[24]

While the fighting played out in Indochina, Nixon's Vietnam War produced far more contentiousness at home than the (equally violent and equally expensive) Korean War had ever stirred. Part of the reason for this was the dishonesty that had permeated the Vietnam War from the outset. The Johnson administration opted for military engagement on the basis of flimsy evidence, and the Nixon administration hatched military escalations in secret. These choices bred distrust once revelations of secret bombings and official malfeasance leaked to the public. The ongoing stabilization of the Cold War, meanwhile, made the war's ultimate purpose all the more elusive, undercutting its initial geopolitical rationale. Then there were the US war deaths, which non-white and working-class Americans bore in disproportionate numbers. Nixon tried during the 1968 election to assuage concerns over the casualties by promising to end the military draft; he would do so, but not until 1973. In the meantime, Vietnamization reduced American deaths, but it did not mitigate the violence that the war inflicted upon Vietnam. On this subject, American reactions were more divided, reflecting both moral engagement and callous indifference.

To principled critics, the iniquity of the war was unambiguous. Telford Taylor, who had led the prosecutorial effort in the Nuremberg Trials, argued in a heartfelt 1970 essay that the United States was perpetrating the kinds of war crimes in Vietnam for which it had once prosecuted Nazis. Less pointedly, the New York-based League for the Rights of Man, a prominent NGO, accused all sides in the war of violating human rights—of engaging in torture and mutilation, perpetrating "systematic terror and assassination." The prominence of such concerns owed in part to the effects of McLuhan's global village, in which the distinctions between foreign wars and domestic politics were blurred. "Television," reflected Cyrus Vance, a policymaker who had participated in planning the escala-tion, "brought home the horrors of war in a way that the American people had not experienced since the Civil War." This was true, but the effect ought not be exag-gerated. Images of brutality animated the war's critics, but the media self-censored, and many Americans regarded the suffering of the Vietnamese with indifference. When the US Army put 2nd Lieutenant William Calley on trial for the horrific slaughter of hundreds of Vietnamese civilians at My Lai, many Americans objected to the prosecution, prompting numerous state governors to petition the White House on Calley's behalf. Nixon would, in time, issue him a tacit pardon.[25]

One lesson of the Calley trial was that the war's opponents did not comprise a clear majority. This point seemed to vindicate Nixon and Kissinger's efforts to mar-ginalize the war's critics through Vietnamization abroad and harassment at home, efforts predicated on a belief that a "great, silent majority" of the American people supported the war. The problem, Nixon reasoned, was that the war's critics were more vocal than its supporters. The antiwar movement for Nixon neither repre-sented the nation nor made a well-reasoned case. "They hate us, the country, them-selves, their wives, everything they do," Nixon exclaimed of the war's opponents. Kissinger explained the war's domestic politics in terms of elite fragmentation. "The collapse of our establishment is frightening," he lamented. The White House could overcome the elite's spinelessness, Nixon reasoned, if it mobilized ordinary Americans—the silent majority—and did a better job of selling the war. "We have not had a well-planned PR effort" was the president's rueful assessment. Still, even if a silent majority could be rallied, the public's toleration of the war would depend upon troop withdrawals, the logic of which was to make the war unwinnable.[26]

Under such constraints, it proved difficult to end the war. Saigon had little rea-son to accept a peace settlement that would leave it vulnerable to the North. The search for a peace formula acceptable to all sides thus continued, until the US Congress forced the issue. Late in 1972, Congress threatened to cut war appro-priations. The move precipitated the war's conclusion. In December, Kissinger and representatives from Hanoi concluded a peace treaty that provided for US troop withdrawals and made no guarantees as to the South's future security. In a bid to bring Saigon along, Nixon unleashed Linebacker II, a final, devastating aerial offensive. "We bombed the North Vietnamese into accepting our conces-sions" was one aide's verdict. Following the Paris Peace Accords in January 1973, American troops vacated Indochina, leaving Saigon in an uncertain predica-ment. This was not the peace with honor that Nixon had sought; the withdrawal nonetheless became a model for tactical retrenchments elsewhere and was a pre-condition for sustaining the worldwide containment strategy Washington had upheld since the late 1940s.[27]

⹀⹀

In July 1969, Richard Nixon visited Guam, the locus of US air power in the South Pacific. There, in response to a reporter's question, the president articulated a new strategic doctrine for using US military power in the world. The Nixon Doctrine affirmed that the United States would expect its allies to assume responsibility for defending themselves against internal enemies, such as the National Liberation Front. "The United States," Nixon explained, "has a right to expect that this problem will be increasingly handled [by] the Asian nations themselves." He thus applied the logic of Vietnamization to the entire Asian scene. As it developed, the Nixon Doctrine comprised three main tenets. These were that the United States would keep "all its treaty commitments"; that Washington would use nuclear weapons to defend its allies and other nations whose "survival we consider vital to our security" against attack by a nuclear superpower, which is to say the Soviet Union; and that in situations involving internal subversion, Washington would "furnish military and economic assistance" but would expect "the nation directly threatened" to provide "the manpower for its defense."[28]

Later articulations expanded the scope of the Nixon Doctrine to the entire world, but its meaning remained open to debate. "This is a formula for an American retreat," the *Washington Post* concluded, a view against which Nixon chafed. "Rather than being a device to get rid of America's world role," the president wrote, the Nixon Doctrine "is devised to make it possible for us to play a role—and play it better, more effectively than if we continued the policy of the past." The president's rationale was straightforward. In the face of political and economic constraints, Nixon proposed "to maintain our forces overseas" by getting "a decent effort from the countries supported." For NATO allies, this would involve increased financial contributions. Front-line allies in the Third World, such as South Vietnam, would have to expand their armed forces and tolerate higher levels of military casualties. In assessing the Nixon Doctrine, TASS, the Soviet news agency, came closer to the mark than did most Western commentators when it concluded that "the main aims and task of US policy remain unchanged."[29]

Indeed, the Nixon Doctrine aimed to reconcile long-standing commitments with changing circumstances. At home, Nixon feared that a "new spirit of isolationism" was consuming the country; he perceived himself to be "fighting" with an American public that "want[s] out of the world." The president disdained those whom he called "new isolationists," but, evidently doubtful of his own silent majority theory, he feared that resurgent isolationism might compel national retreat. NSC staffer Robert Osgood corroborated Nixon's concerns in a policy review drafted in the summer of 1969. "There is a widespread feeling that the nation is 'over-committed,'" Osgood wrote, "and that the familiar rationale of American involvement—containment, falling dominoes, the Munich analogy—no longer fits the facts." If Americans were wearying of international burdens, non-Americans, Nixon believed, shared the responsibility for their fatigue. The president worried that European discrimination against American exporters was alienating domestic support for NATO, and he feared that the spectacle of anti-Americanism overseas—"the temptation to kick the Yankee"— was lifting the isolationist "tide." The perception that Americans were turning away from an ungrateful world informed Nixon's efforts to reinvigorate US leadership, making the pursuit of the Nixon Doctrine's goals of retrenchment and international burden sharing imperative.[30]

Economic as well as political realities conditioned the Nixon Doctrine. Under Lyndon Johnson, the United States expanded welfare protections for the elderly and indigent, transforming the federal budget. In 1971, the United States, for the first time since 1949, spent more on human resources than on military purposes, as figure 2.1 indicates. Facing a Democratic majority in the Congress, Nixon was in no position to eviscerate the welfare state to sustain the warfare state. Instead, military spending found itself on the cutting block. International monetary instability provided another reason to reduce overseas military spending, as it had in 1968, when LBJ rejected General Westmoreland's request for another 250,000 troops in Vietnam in the context of a major dollar crisis. Since then, the balance of payments had deteriorated further. With government

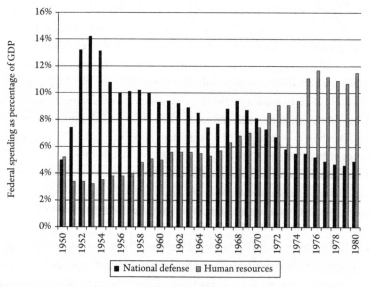

Figure 2.1 The welfare state and the warfare state: federal spending 1950–1980
Source: Office of Management and the Budget, *Budget of the US Government: Historical Tables,*
Washington DC, U.S. GPO, 1995.

outlays overseas ranking high among the factors draining the US payments balance, Nixon had little choice but to reduce military spending in Indochina and elsewhere. Reluctant to curtail war-fighting capabilities, he at first proposed draconian reductions in overseas State Department and CIA personnel. Such palliatives could not make the Pax Americana's burdens bearable, however, and the Nixon Doctrine instead demanded that allies shoulder responsibilities that the United States could no longer sustain alone.[31]

The Nixon administration thus acknowledged the encroachment of limits. The factors that weighed on and inhibited US Cold War commitments included the fragmentation of domestic support for internationalism, the relative decline of American economic power in the world, and the growth of domestic fiscal commitments that rivaled the defense budget. The limits on American power in the 1970s were political, economic, and even existential. In the face of such constraints, Nixon had little choice but to embrace military-burden sharing. For all their tactical boldness, Nixon and Kissinger proved more inclined to devise new methods for sustaining old commitments than to rethink the underlying purposes of the Pax Americana.

⌒∞⌒

Defining a sustainable defense policy was an early task. Among the flurry of presidential directives issued in the first weeks of 1969 was National Security Study Memorandum (NSSM) 3, which mandated a thoroughgoing review of "our military posture and the balance of power." The deputy secretary of defense, David Packard, a Silicon Valley pioneer, orchestrated the review. Under Packard's guidance, the review process was divided into two parts: one dealt with strategic (nuclear) forces, the other with general-purpose forces. While nuclear weapons were controversial, conventional forces were costly, consuming more than 60 percent of the national defense budget as opposed to less than 25 percent spent on nuclear forces. This made the the general-purpose-forces review the more significant part of the exercise. NSSM 3 produced five alternative scenarios for conventional force projection, but Kissinger excluded from consideration the two options that would have increased military commitments before the National Security Council even debated Packard's proposals. These excisions confirmed that the purpose of the exercise was cost-cutting.[32]

Of the three options that remained when the NSC convened in September 1969, none envisaged cutting troops from Western Europe. Only Asian commitments were open for debate. The most parsimonious of Packard's options was a proposal to reduce US forces such that the United States would depend entirely on local clients for war-fighting capabilities. The most expansive option would have maintained existing force levels (23⅔ divisions) in Asia, giving the US the ability to fight simultaneous wars against the Soviet Union and China plus one "regional" conflict, such as the Vietnam War. This was the so-called "two-and-a-half wars" posture. Nixon chose not to maintain it. He instead shifted US military planning to a "one-and-a-half wars" basis, opting for Packard's "Worldwide Strategy 2," which cut forces in Asia to fourteen and a half divisions and lopped $5 billion off the defense budget, a reduction of more than 6 percent from the previous year's spending. The president's end-of-year report to Congress hailed the "one-and-a-half war principle" as a formula that would provide "general purpose forces adequate for simultaneously meeting a major communist attack in either Europe or Asia," while requiring allies to assume an expanded share of the Pax Americana's collective military burdens.[33]

If the NSSM 3 exercise signaled a retreat from the "pay any price" rhetoric of the high Cold War, the Nixon administration aimed not to end Cold War commitments but to sustain them. The shift from "two-and-a-half" to "one-and-a-half wars" was rhetorically potent, but its substantive implications were minimal. The new formula would not permit the "simultaneous defense of NATO Europe and Asia," but with China and the Soviet Union having exchanged gunfire across the Ussuri River in early 1969, "the likelihood of a closely coordinated Soviet-Chinese attack" on American interests had "disappeared." Unless the administration preferred to spend $5 billion deterring a chimera, which is what the Communist monolith had become, the "one-and-a-half war" formula was the maximal strategy Nixon could have chosen. Situated in its political context, the NSSM 3 exercise was a preemptive move, conceived to preserve existing commitments. Congressional sentiment in the late 1960s, Kissinger writes, was such that "the cuts would probably have been far worse had not Nixon attempted to respond to the national mood by trimming the defense budget himself."[34]

In a significant innovation, Packard's review related defense spending to domestic spending. This allowed "the President to decide on a worldwide military strategy in the light of its implications for both defense and non-defense spending." After the NSSM 3 study was completed, the administration sought to institutionalize this methodology by creating the Defense Program Review Committee. Predictably, Kissinger complained that setting defense spending within an overarching fiscal framework was unfair so long as similar standards were not applied to domestic spending. The complaint obfuscated the real point (of which Kissinger was well aware) that the limits to American power in the Nixon years were as much political as economic. The United States could in theory have spent a larger fraction of its national income on military purposes than on social programs, had voters and their representatives been willing to do so. The problem was that the ebbing of Cold War tensions, the growth of competing fiscal claims, and the public's concern over militarism run amok had all contributed to a congressional reluctance to authorize defense appropriations on the scale of the recent past. NSSM 3 sought to preserve a maximal defense effort within the prevailing limits.[35]

Had anti-militarists in Congress interpreted Worldwide Strategy 2 as a high bid, they would have been mistaken. For Nixon, the force levels NSSM 3 projected were a bottom line, not an opening gambit. Crucially, the White House in 1969 proposed that Congress pass a "five year force and program plan," which Nixon intended to preempt the legislature's annual whittling down of defense appropriations. Despite the president's effort to preempt legislative cuts, Congress soon slashed an additional $2.1 billion from the White House's 1970 defense budget—a budget that had already reduced spending by $5 billion from the previous year.[36]

Indeed, the fight over the 1970 budget reveals the extent to which the Nixon Doctrine authors were struggling to hold their ground against the proponents of fiscal retrenchment. Kissinger believed that the new congressional cuts "nickeled and dimed" the military, reductions in naval spending, in particular, going "over the line" of fiscal prudence. "I think the Defense budget is below the tolerable level," he warned John Ehrlichman. As Nixon's assistant for domestic affairs, Ehrlichman held a different view: "Everyone knows that DOD has been getting too much." Still, the national security team would not back down. Confirming that the NSSM 3 guidelines were a bottom line, Nixon in October 1970 ordered that there would be "no withdrawal of US forces or personnel committed to NATO" and no withdrawals from South Korea beyond those already envisaged. Meanwhile, the NSC staff economist inveighed against the "absurdity" of reducing overseas commitments on balance-of-payments grounds. "What," C. Fred Bergsten asked, "would be the signal to the Soviets if we were to do so?" This aligned with the president's view. What was at stake in the defense budget, Nixon contended, was the "success or failure of our entire foreign policy."[37]

While the NSSM 3 exercise aimed to reconcile the tensions between the Pax Americana and what Nixon called "pet domestic projects," the conflict would not be easily resolved. Indeed, the Nixon administration struggled without success to reverse the sharp decline in the real value of US foreign assistance since the mid-1960s. At its 1964 peak, US development aid amounted to over 0.5 percent of GDP; by 1970, it had fallen to less than half of this amount. Security assistance followed a similar pattern. The waning of foreign assistance cut against the logic of the Nixon Doctrine, which proposed to cultivate "the self-sufficiency of recipient countries," but the administration could not overcome congressional parsimony. Instead it trimmed assistance budgets. The Nixon administration worked with foreign governments to relate military-assistance budgets to actual threats, and it introduced a new system of country-based budgeting that tied security assistance to development aid. More concerned about preserving military assistance than development aid, the administration sharpened the distinction between the two and promoted multilateral institutions and private investment as alternative sources of the latter. Despite these efforts, Congress continued to assail foreign aid, thwarting the purposes of the Nixon Doctrine.[38]

Tension between the Nixon administration and the Congress over military spending peaked in spring 1971 in the struggle over the Mansfield Amendment. Long concerned about cutting the costs of overseas military commitments, Senator Mike Mansfield, a Montana Democrat and Senate majority leader, introduced an amendment to the Selective Service Act proposing to slash US force commitments to Europe in half. Mansfield argued that burdens were inequitably distributed within NATO and that the European countries should bear more of the costs for Europe's defense. For the Nixon administration, the amendment was "absolutely unacceptable." Mansfield's success, officials believed, would "dismay our allies" and "strike at the heart of the military, political, and economic strategy" of anti-Soviet containment. The issue's politics were nonetheless tricky. While such pillars of Cold War internationalism as the American Federation of Labor and Congress of Industrial Organizations (AFL-CIO) joined the administration in opposing Mansfield, the senator enjoyed public support, and he drew succor from a dollar crisis that laid bare the disruptive consequences of financial globalization. The "tremendous growth of international business and banking," wrote one State Department official, was enabling "businessmen to shift huge quantities of dollars across national borders," precipitating, in summer 1971, a dollar crisis that bolstered Mansfield's crusade.[39]

The Nixon administration responded to Mansfield with vigor. Kissinger led the effort, convening an interdepartmental group to oppose the amendment. Nixon himself lobbied wavering senators, warning them that Mansfield's success could mean the dissolution of NATO. Even Dean Acheson lent his support. Manning the phones just months before his death, Truman's secretary of state assembled a coalition of high-ranking former officials, including Dean Rusk and Robert Lovett. For this group of veteran Cold Warriors, NATO was sacrosanct. Their alliance with Richard Nixon was nonetheless striking. Back in 1952, Nixon had lambasted Acheson as the dean of a "college of cowardly containment." They now stood shoulder-to-shoulder in defense of the institutional commitments that Acheson had forged and on which Pax Americana depended. "We never disagreed on NATO," Nixon would recall; "this was what united us." In the summer of 1971, the administration's lobbying effort proved successful, and the Senate voted down the Mansfield Amendment by 61 votes to 36. What Acheson called "the second battle of NATO" was won, and the victory confirmed the essential conservatism of Richard Nixon's strategic agenda.[40]

Richard Nixon did not orchestrate a major transformation of American grand strategy. He and Kissinger would dissolve the Vietnam War, but their willingness to shed this unbearable burden should not be construed as enthusiasm for a broader rethinking of America's world role. Fearful of national decline and wary of resurgent isolationism, they rationalized burdens in order to sustain them. By linking the future of the Pax Americana with the sustenance of anti-Soviet containment, Nixon and Kissinger even suggested that securing the future of American leadership in the world might depend on keeping the Cold War going.

Détente: The High Tide of Geopolitics

Like Nixon and Kissinger, Andrei Sakharov made his career in the Cold War. After graduating from Moscow State University, he became an atomic physicist and played a crucial role in the design of the USSR's fusion bomb. During the 1960s, Sakharov embraced arms control and critiqued ideological rigidity, hopeful that a transnational flow of ideas might transcend Cold War rivalries. In early 1968, Sakharov authored his famous essay, "Reflections on Progress, Peaceful Coexistence, and Intellectual Freedom." East-West cooperation on new global challenges, it predicted, might not be long in coming given the superpowers' mutual interest in arms control and the convergence of their social systems around a common technocratic humanism. Rebuffed at home, Sakharov's views received positive reception in the West, where some were pronouncing the Cold War over, and others were trumpeting the "convergence" of the capitalist and socialist systems. Even bilateral diplomacy inspired optimism about the future of superpower relations for a time in the late 1960s, especially Lyndon Johnson's congenial June 1967 summit with Alexi Kosygin in Glassboro, New Jersey.[41]

The spirit of Glassboro, as some called it, departed in August 1968. That month, Warsaw Pact forces invaded Czechoslovakia, crushing the Prague Spring. Dismayed, Sakharov retreated from public life to mourn his wife's death; when he returned, he would no longer be a critical insider but an unapologetic dissenter. Across the Atlantic, Lyndon Johnson refrained from confronting Moscow over Czechoslovakia, but the Soviet invasion crushed hopes that the Soviet Union might be reforming itself. Instead, it seemed that oscillation between optimism and disappointment would remain the pattern of the Cold War. For Henry Kissinger, still a Harvard professor, the ebb and flow of American hopes betrayed a misplaced preoccupation with Soviet motives. "There have been at least five periods of peaceful coexistence," he wrote. "Each was hailed in the West as ushering in a new era of reconciliation . . . each ended abruptly with a new period of intransigence." Kissinger argued that to break the pattern of hope and disappointment, Americans would do best to shed the "obsession with Soviet intentions" and construct their own "concrete idea of what we understand by peace," to act proactively instead of reactively.[42]

Kissinger was correct to argue that Cold War relations had long cycled between détente and confrontation. Stalin's death in 1953 ushered the first thaw; a heads-of-state summit in 1955 generated talk of a spirit of Geneva. Tensions resurged in the late 1950s, and the missile crisis brought the superpowers to the brink. The thaw resumed thereafter, but Khrushchev's ouster in 1964 seemed to augur another difficult turn. Hopes for détente nonetheless returned in 1967–68, only to fade with the Soviet invasion of Czechoslovakia. This was the cycle of hope and dismay that Kissinger intended to break. To do so, he and Nixon envisioned a strategy of détente distinct from the cycles of détente that the Cold War had long manifested. The distinction merits elaboration. In its generic meaning, the word *détente* suggests a relaxation of hostilities, an organic rapprochement. Under Nixon, it came to signify something different: a purposeful strategy for managing the Soviet-American rivalry. Americans had in earlier phases of détente invested hope in the Soviet Union's liberalization. Nixon and Kissinger did not. Skeptical that the USSR had the capacity to change, they sought accommodation, not reconciliation. Theirs would be a hardheaded diplomacy that aimed to serve US interests, not overcome the Cold War.

Complicating the quest for stability was a military balance of power that was, by the late 1960s, tilting against the United States. As American strategists in the 1960s were putting their faith in mutual assured destruction, their Soviet counterparts were pursuing a rapid buildup of forces. In 1966, the USSR commanded barely 400 ICBMs, a force less than half the size of the thousand-strong missile force that the US Strategic Air Command operated. By 1970, the Soviet Union boasted nearly 1,500 intercontinental missiles, while the US offensive force remained unchanged in size. The United States still retained important military advantages, but careful observers feared that they were waning. Some even argued that the United States was slipping behind. "While we have heretofore achieved a very high level of security from the danger of a Soviet attack because of an overwhelming nuclear retaliatory force," wrote John McCloy, the old Cold War hand, "we are now faced with a large expansion of Soviet nuclear capability." This was the reality with which détente's architects would have to deal. Admiral Elmo Zumwalt, then Chief of Naval Operations, recalled Kissinger telling him in 1970 that the United States had "passed its historic high point" and that "his job is to persuade the Russians to give us the best deal we can get."[43]

Kissinger disputed Zumwalt's recollections but the specter of relative military decline framed Nixon's strategy. For their part, Nixon and Kissinger sought to maintain America's military capabilities vis-à-vis the Soviet Union. Despite the practical obsolescence of nuclear weapons and the diffusion of power away from the superpowers, processes that Nixon and Kissinger grasped, the military balance still mattered to decision-makers who feared that further Soviet gains would encourage Moscow to seek political benefit from military advantage.

Kissinger described the paradox of a "world which is bipolar militarily but multi-polar politically," an observation that captured the perplexities of world politics at the turn of the 1970s. Until at least 1973, when new events—the end of the Vietnam War, the oil crisis, and Nixon's disgrace—prompted new strategic approaches, the administration fixated on the Cold War balance of power, above all the prospect that the USSR's military capacities were overtaking its own. The quest to surmount this relative decline became the central preoccupation of Nixon's strategy.[44]

The administration's Soviet centrism indicated a bleak conception of the USSR, not a belief that the Soviet Union and the United States were destined for reconciliation or convergence. Nixon had little faith in Moscow's capacity for reform, and he did not cease to believe that "the Soviets have a long-range strategy to subvert the free world." Certainly, he and Kissinger recognized that the Soviet Union lagged behind the United States in its economic capacities, and they understood the brittleness of its East European empire. "That the Soviets have used direct force . . . only against their allies and have brutally suppressed any flowering of intellectual dissent," Kissinger wrote, "is not an index of great power, but of fundamental weaknesses." In the arena of military power, however, the Soviet Union's capacities were growing fast. This impelled the Nixon administration to uphold the tested strategy of anti-Soviet containment even as they worked, through the Nixon Doctrine, to mitigate containment's economic and political burdens. Shadowed by the realities of rising Soviet military power, Nixon and Kissinger did not transcend the Pax Americana's intellectual inheritance. That is not to say that they did not innovate; but they did so within the Cold War's conceptual paradigm.[45]

The dual purposes of Nixon and Kissinger's détente were to halt the strategic arms race and to persuade Moscow to accept the geopolitical status quo, as it was at the end of the 1960s. Stabilization, however, was not an end in itself. Rather, it was connected to the preservation of American global power. The Pax Americana had, after all, emerged in a bipolar world, and Washington's leadership of the West still depended, in some fundamental sense, on the Cold War division of the world. The logic of détente thus aligned with the logic of the Nixon Doctrine. Whereas the Nixon Doctrine rationalized Cold War burdens in order to sustain them, détente aimed to preserve American international primacy through the construction of a geopolitical balance that would preserve—not resolve—the bipolar schism that had opened in the 1940s. Détente's architects would leverage the People's Republic of China, now estranged from Moscow, as an integral element of the Cold War balance of power. The Nixon administration nonetheless accepted that the Cold War was permanent—and even hailed the Cold War as a source of Washington's power over its allies and clients. As Nixon put it: "Our interests in the Middle East, Europe, [and] China require keeping the

Soviet Union going." Stabilization, not transcendence, was the purpose of détente.[46]

∽

Détente began in early 1969, when Nixon decided to seek a "limited adversary relationship" with the Soviet Union. The concept was to trade concessions for concessions, and the relationship evolved in the back channel, where Kissinger and the Soviet ambassador Anatoli Dobrynin developed a rapport. Progress on Vietnam was slow, but Dobrynin in late 1969 accepted an American proposal to seek controls on nuclear weapons in a dialogue that would become known as the Strategic Arms Limitation Talks (SALT). For the United States, arms control was a core objective: achieving it would freeze an arms race that was tipping toward Moscow. Talks began almost immediately, although negotiators stalled on the question of whether or not to include antimissile defense systems within an arms control agreement. That loggerhead was broken in the spring of 1971 when Dobrynin and Kissinger agreed to move forward with separate but simultaneous treaties, the Anti-Ballistic Missile Treaty (or the ABM Treaty) and the SALT Interim Agreement.[47]

SALT yielded a treaty limiting the deployment of anti-ballistic-missile systems and the so-called Interim Agreement, which imposed numerical ceilings on nuclear forces. Nixon and Brezhnev signed both agreements in May 1972, at their first bilateral summit meeting. The Interim Agreement capped the Soviet Union's offensive forces at 1,618 intercontinental ballistic missiles (ICBMs) and America's forces at 1,054 of these missiles. This numerical inequality did not mean that the United States came out second best. In fact, the United States still led the way in long-range bombers and sea-launched ballistic missiles (SLBMs), which offset the Soviet Union's advantage in ICBMs. Nor did the Interim Agreement prevent its signatories from upgrading their missiles with multiple warheads. Known as MIRV technology (for multiple independently targetable reentry vehicles), this was an avenue of development in which the United States led. Referring to this qualitative edge, the Nixon administration hailed SALT for preserving American strength and proclaimed that the agreement broke the "momentum" of Moscow's military buildup. While America's technological edge was likely to be temporary, since the Soviets were "bound to match" US mastery of MIRV systems, SALT stabilized the strategic balance for a time. Nixon's declaration that the treaty was "advantageous to the United States" was therefore accurate for now.[48]

For the men in the Kremlin, SALT affirmed the Soviet Union's status as a superpower equal to the United States. In addition to the arms control treaties, the 1972 Moscow summit produced an agreement between the two sides on basic principles that would guide their relations. The basic principles agreeement affirmed that the superpowers would conduct their relations on "principles of sovereignty, equality, [and] non-interference in internal affairs." Especially important, it established that "differences in ideology and in the social systems of the USA and the USSR" would not be "obstacles to the bilateral development of normal relations." The basic principles agreement attracted little attention in the United States, but its enunciation of superpower equality confirmed détente's conservative thrust. In their determination to bind the Soviet Union to "an international system based on mutual respect and self-restraint," Nixon and Kissinger appeared to be abandoning hope of changing Soviet society. The move toward détente thus suggested a pessimistic outlook somewhat at odds with the historical optimism that had long guided US Cold War policy. If containment in its classic guise aimed to ensure that Soviet military power would not preempt the inevitable victory of liberal institutions over Marxist-Leninist dogmas, Nixon and Kissinger's innovation, in a trough of national despair, was to transform containment into a strategy for indefinite coexistence.[49]

By making the moderation of Soviet diplomacy their goal, Nixon and Kissinger set themselves a considerable challenge. Their initial mechanism for inducing Soviet compliance was linkage: a formula for connecting heretofore disconnected issues in the web of relations between the two superpowers. "The Soviet leaders," Nixon explained, "should be brought to understand that they cannot expect to reap the benefits of cooperation in one area while seeking . . . tension or confrontation elsewhere." Linkage was the initial method of suasion, but Nixon and Kissinger also attempted, with more drama, to induce Soviet cooperation by recasting the Cold War as a triangular competition. In their boldest move, they attempted to forge a new American relationship with China and a new balance of power among the Cold War's superpowers. The 1971–72 "opening" of the People's Republic thus revealed both the audacity of the administration's diplomacy and the dominance of geopolitical assumptions within the strategic concept that guided its policy choices.[50]

That some kind of Sino-American rapprochement would occur in the 1970s was, as Kissinger conceded, "inherent in the world environment." The breakdown in relations between China and the Soviet Union became almost total during the 1960s. It was also implausible that Beijing could remain forever "outside the family of nations," as Richard Nixon put it. Acknowledging the inevitability of reengagement, the State Department worked from early 1969 to develop a new China policy, one predicated on the assumption that "not even a nation as large as mainland China can live forever in isolation from a world of interdependent states." At the same time, Nixon and Kissinger began to contemplate a new approach, which, in contrast to State's, would be less concerned with Sino-American rapprochement as such than with the worldwide balance of power. "If you have two enemies," Nixon remarked, "play them against each other." "It is better to align yourself with the weaker, not the stronger of two antagonistic partners," Kissinger concurred. These were distinct concepts of engagement: State pointing toward an organic opening, Nixon toward a more instrumental accommodation.[51]

With the first major steps, geopolitics came to the fore. In July 1971, Kissinger visited Beijing. The lack of State Department participation confirmed that China policy was now a White House exclusive. Kissinger's discussions with Premier Chou Enlai in Beijing coursed from philosophy to Vietnam, but the Soviet Union was a central theme. "They are deeply worried about the Soviet threat," Kissinger concluded, "and see in us a balancing force against the USSR." Appropriately, given the primacy of geopolitical motives, Nixon's visit to China took place three months before his summit with Brezhnev in Moscow. As Nixon and Kissinger had hoped, their China opening "improved Russian manners" and invigorated Soviet-American détente with new urgency. The Cold War's triangulation generated an atmosphere of competitive cooperation among Nixon, Mao, and Brezhnev, with the US president occupying the central role. What Nixon's triangular diplomacy had achieved by 1972 was stunning. Détente appeared to be drawing China and the Soviet Union into a geopolitical triangle that Washington would orchestrate. Nixon and Kissinger appeared to be succeeding in their bid to use diplomatic maneuvering to supplant America's waning material and military capacities.[52]

For its part, the administration presented détente as an exercise in hardheaded realism. Its public diplomacy evoked "mutual incentives," "concrete issues," and "authentic give-and-take." The reality proved more complicated. For all Nixon's and Kissinger's confidence that they could use concrete incentives to induce specific outcomes, the geopolitical rationale for triangular diplomacy became murkier as the years passed. As the dialogues with Moscow and Beijing continued, both openings—particularly the Soviet-American opening—assumed their own momentum, becoming less hardheaded and more far-reaching than their authors had intended. Détente, in fact, began to resemble the kind of organic rapprochement that Nixon and Kissinger initially disdained, as the shift toward East-West trade liberalization illustrates.[53]

Nixon and Kissinger did not at the outset favor expanding Soviet-American trade, but they encountered strong pressure from those who did. Within the administration, officials at the Council on International Economic Policy and at the Commerce Department argued that the Soviet Union was a large potential market. Access to the Soviet market, these officials pointed out, would secure export markets, improve the US balance of payments, and enhance the prospects for peace. Nixon nonetheless dismissed trade liberalization as "a fetish" of "business types." "We cannot give this away without having a quid-pro-quo," he declared, while Kissinger disparaged the "nonsense" that "increased trade leads to world peace." By early 1971, however, the White House was moving to support the expansion of Export-Import Bank financing for Soviet-American trade. The move prefigured a significant shift in trade policy during 1972, a reorientation that unfolded even as Moscow continued to ship arms to North Vietnam.[54]

In the summer of 1972, the administration accepted the normalization of US-Soviet trade relations as a vital element of détente. Soviet leaders, for their part, left no doubt about the issue's importance. "With a vast territory and enormous economic wealth," Brezhnev bragged, the Soviet Union "always has something to buy and sell." After the May 1972 summit, Nixon dispatched his treasury secretary, George Shultz, to Moscow to reassure Soviet leaders of the president's determination to expand trade relations. Before long, however, Nixon and Kissinger began to encounter resistance from critics who argued that economic opening without commensurate social and political engagement was symptomatic of a jaundiced détente that served Soviet interests without promoting change within the East Bloc. Caught between their initial vision for a geopolitical détente, which presumed the calibrated use of carrots and sticks, and a more capacious rapprochement, which détente became as it progressed, Nixon and Kissinger struggled to sustain their initial vision for an instrumental détente, geared to specific purposes.[55]

What Nixon and Kissinger achieved would be a partial détente that neither delivered all the benefits they sought nor achieved the wholesale opening that Andrei Sakharov envisaged, for which some in the West—especially in Europe—still yearned. Vietnam was an early indication of détente's limits. Here, Nixon's geopolitical diplomacy did not yield peace with honor and may, in fact, have encouraged the North Vietnamese to fight harder. The failures of linkage in Indochina foreshadowed détente's inability to inhibit the spillover of Cold War rivalries into other parts of the Third World. So far as the Cold War's axial rivalry was concerned, détente accepted bipolarity as the price of stability and renounced the notion of a transformed Soviet Union, a point that the Basic Principles agreement confirmed. This marked the distance from earlier approaches to Soviet-American rapprochement that had aimed, as political scientist Zbigniew Brzezinski argued, at "terminating the doctrinal abyss dividing mankind." Nixon, in Brzezinski's view, sought détente "for the purpose of structuring a special bilateral power balance, stabilizing existing divisions and spheres of influence." Sure enough, Nixon's disinclination to seek political change in the Soviet Bloc became a focal concern for détente's critics in the United States.[56]

Détente nonetheless served useful purposes. For its high-profile protagonists, the political and psychic payoffs were considerable. Summits awash in vodka and Maotai, hydrofoil rides on the Moskva River, excursions to the Forbidden City, and intimate audiences with Mao were among détente's rewards. And if the preservation of American primacy was détente's purpose, diminishing the risk of war ranked among its major dividends. Indeed, the Doomsday Clock that the *Bulletin of the Atomic Scientists* published identified the détente years as one of two Cold War phases when the risk of nuclear war was at its lowest (the other was 1963–68). When challenged at home, this was the high ground to which the architects of détente retreated. "We are trying to avert a disastrous nuclear conflict," Nixon explained. "The thermonuclear age," Kissinger argued, made it a moral imperative to "strive for coexistence." This was fair enough, but preserving peace was never détente's primary goal. Rather, Nixon and Kissinger aimed to calm what Kissinger called "near-civil war conditions" at home and to prevent the Cold War military balance from slipping further toward the Soviet Union. Fearing that the alternative to Soviet-American détente would be American retreat and the world "becoming entirely Communist," Nixon and Kissinger settled for a world that would "remain half-Communist."[57]

◌◑◌

In hindsight, détente's omissions and oversights appear glaring. Nixon's détente reified what one scholar calls a "Soviet-centric image of the international system," marginalizing alternative perspectives on world politics. Rendering the world in monochrome did not, of course, make it thus. Issues removed from Cold War geopolitics demanded the attention of decision-makers at the dawn of the 1970s. Such issues included the breakdown of the international economic order; the unfulfilled aspirations of the postcolonial countries for a more equitable world; and the disenchantment of foreign allies and Americans at home with the Pax Americana. Issues that lay beyond the traditional competencies of foreign policy also demanded attention. These included the management of globalization, increasingly a common concern for the industrialized countries; a new order of global threats, including ecological and demographic changes on the world scale; and the moral and political imperatives of promoting human rights, which transnational politics made urgent. While officials acknowledged this "new dimension of diplomacy," decision-makers remained fixated on the familiar tasks of the Cold War.[58]

The limits of Nixon's foreign policy reflected his own choices. Nixon and Kissinger grasped the fluidity of the moment they inhabited. They understood that postwar international structures were creaking and that America's superpower role required recalibration, if not rethinking. They sometimes even glimpsed new developments on the global scale. Nixon, on the cusp of his election, described a world transformed by new leaders, new ideas, new ideologies, and new nations. He perceived new interdependencies among societies and nations, even the stirrings of globalization. "For the next 25 years," Nixon explained to student protestors in 1970, "the world is going to get much smaller." Yet Nixon and Kissinger struggled—and failed—to convert glimpses of an integrating world society into workable solutions for foreign policy. Caught between the Cold War and an emerging order of global and transnational challenges, they prioritized geopolitics over alternative idioms of international engagement. Transnational issues remained "a missing ingredient in the articulation of our policy," as one insider put it.[59]

Within the paradigm of Cold War geopolitics, Nixon and Kissinger proved to be adept practitioners of superpower diplomacy. Their dependence on subterfuge and personal diplomacy made their détente a high-wire act, but they won deserved reputations as Cold War managers, even peacemakers. Yet the world of the 1970s was too complex for a grand strategy that was fixated on the Cold War. Had they looked beyond the arena of high geopolitics, Nixon and Kissinger might have steered a new course for US foreign policy. Lacking confidence in the domestic bases of American internationalism and fearful of rising Soviet power, they instead devoted themselves to preserving the status quo. Men of the Cold War, they set themselves against the currents of change and found themselves thrust back into the past.

3

Geopolitics and Humanitarianism

> We don't even pretend high-sounding morality on some of these issues,
> except in the deepest sense.
>
> Henry Kissinger, Meeting with Nixon, 1971

For the Third World, the mid-1960s initiated a phase of turmoil and violence as the wave of democratization that followed the Second World War retreated. Latin America had in the early 1960s been largely democratic; by the early 1970s, authoritarians ruled in Argentina, Brazil, Uruguay, and elsewhere. In Africa, authoritarianism came fast on the heels of decolonization. Ghana's democracy crumbled in the mid-1960s; Nigeria's in 1966. Elsewhere, military rulers seized power in Pakistan in 1958, in South Korea in 1961, and in Indonesia in 1965. Even Greece, in 1967, succumbed to a military coup. The dictators and autocrats who overthrew democracies invoked the specter of social destabilization, even revolution, to rationalize their seizure of power, their transgressions of constitutional orders, and the regimes of terror they built. Political scientists devised theories of "bureaucratic authoritarianism" to explain trajectories of political development that did not conform to liberal archetypes.[1]

The United States played a role in this worldwide retreat from democracy, and it did so for largely, but not wholly, geopolitical reasons. The Eisenhower administration acted to overthrow elected leaders in Iran in 1953 and Guatemala in 1954, with tragic consequences for fledgling democracies in both countries. (In the case of Guatemala, the influence of the United Fruit Company indicates that policymakers did not proceed from Cold War preoccupations alone.) Geopolitical fixations led the United States to collaborate in the construction of authoritarian regimes in South Korea and South Vietnam in the 1950s, while reliance on allies like Pakistan and Indonesia for Cold War purposes tilted civil-military relations within client states toward the generals. Support for coups in South Vietnam in 1963, in Brazil in 1964, and Indonesia in 1965 confirmed Washington's willingness to indulge illiberal forces in the Third World, a cynical habit that prefigured the Nixon administration and conditioned the options available to it.[2]

The Nixon Doctrine presumed that the United States should curtail its direct involvement in Third World conflicts and that the Third World remained an arena of urgent geopolitical contestation. To reconcile these presumptions, Nixon asked second-tier powers, such as Brazil, Iran, and Indonesia, to bear more responsibility for regional security. This mandated cooperation with authoritarian regimes, a tactical gambit that Nixon's prejudices corroborated. "Latin America's not any good at government," the president affirmed. Africans and Asians, Nixon believed, were also ill suited to democracy, which was in his view "hard to institute" and inappropriate to Third World circumstances. So far as US foreign policy was concerned, Nixon would happily "aid dictators if it is in our interest." Disavowing ideology, he undertook to deal with foreign governments as they were. "I won't lecture him on his internal structure," Nixon exclaimed of Ferdinand Marcos, the Filipino dictator. "Our concern is foreign policy."[3]

It was Nixon's misfortune to be a realistic president at a time when new forces in world politics were elevating the importance that domestic audiences attached to the internal character of countries with which the United States did business. Globalization propelled a politics of transnational humanitarianism in the 1960s, exposing domestic audiences to images of distant suffering and facilitating the work of transnational activists, who called on powerful governments to respond. Human rights, a theme of the 1970s, were not an inevitable outgrowth of transnational humanitarianism, but the two were closely related: globalizing in their implications, both challenged American decision-makers to transcend pragmatism and embrace a foreign policy more oriented to human beings and ideological commitments than to geopolitical interests and the sustenance of international stability.

⌒∞⌐

This chapter explores the rise of transnational humanitarianism and its consequences for US foreign policy through two crucial episodes: the Biafra War of 1967–70, which divided Nigeria, and the South Asian crisis of 1971, which cleaved Pakistan in two and birthed Bangladesh. The episodes ended on different terms, but their similarities were striking. In both, postcolonial nation-states fractured, and civil wars killed, maimed, and dislocated millions of people. Transnational activists alleged that genocides were taking place, as did the afflicted, challenging the world to respond. For sheer human devastation, these were epic catastrophes, bearing comparison to the Vietnam War, yet they remain marginal episodes in most histories of postwar world politics. Those who lived through them did not neglect these crises, however. On the contrary, ordinary citizens and political leaders in the United States and Europe mobilized on behalf of the perceived victims and clamored for action. The politics of humanitarianism thus made demands on foreign policy, demands that were unrelated to—and sometimes opposed to—US national interests as decision-makers in the Nixon administration construed them.[4]

In Biafra and Bangladesh, transnational mobilizations yielded divergent responses on the part of US decision-makers. In Biafra, the Nixon administration indulged humanitarian concerns, grasping the political dividends of doing so and perceiving no conflict with its larger geopolitical purposes. In South Asia, the Nixon White House rebuffed the activists and refused to condemn Pakistan, much less restrain its ally's actions. Instead, Washington supported Pakistan's military government, defying transnational opinion. The difference was that Nixon and Kissinger construed Cold War interests in South Asia but not in Nigeria. Contrasted, these episodes reveal the tension between Cold War commitments and ideological aspirations in US foreign policy, a tension that sharpened during the 1970s. More than this, the episodes evoke the widening schism between an international society of nation-states, which aligned with Nigeria and Pakistan, and a transnational society of nonstate actors and activists, which rallied in the name of humanitarian responsibility and against the prerogatives of territorial sovereignty.

The Specter of Genocide

Claiming from one to three million lives, the Biafra War was a civil war, but it reverberated in the transnational arena. No foreign government intervened to support Biafra's bid for independence from Nigeria, but nonstate actors provided the aid that kept Biafra alive. Nonstate activists shaped the politics of the war, while the international media catalyzed the war's internationalization. Biafra was one the first humanitarian crises to appear on television. Images of distended stomachs and disfigured corpses defined the war for global audiences, prompting some viewers to act. Bernard Kouchner, a French doctor, founded Médecins sans frontières (Doctors without Borders) to intervene in future humanitarian crises, seeing in Biafra the mandate for a new politics of humanitarian responsibility. For American decision-makers, the conflict in Biafra thrust international conventions and transnational politics against each other, with vexing consequences.[5]

The crisis in Nigeria began in the legacies of colonialism. In Nigeria as elsewhere, British administrators carved a nation-state out of complex materials: Hausa and Fulani tribal groups in the north, a Yoruba population in the southwest, and Igbos in the southeast, which became the Eastern Region.

Independence in 1960 made Nigeria Africa's largest country, but the federation began to fracture in January 1966, when a military coup brought John Aguiyi-Ironsi to power. An Igbo, Ironsi worked to centralize authority. His efforts were met with violent opposition in the north, where a rash of attacks against Igbos broke out. Six months later, another coup, this one led by northern officers, overthrew Ironsi and brought the urbane, British-educated General Yakubu Gowon to power in Lagos. Though he reversed Ironsi's centralization drive, Gowon could not arrest the interethnic violence that Nigeria's political instability had unleashed. Igbos fled the Northern Region for the Eastern Region, while northerners evacuated in the opposite direction. Some refugees bore gunshot and machete wounds. Others did not complete their journeys.

Nigeria's leaders could not hold the crumbling country together. The governor of the Eastern Region, Colonel Odumegwu Ojukwu, initially opposed secession, but he soon concluded that independence would achieve for the Igbos not only security but also control of Nigeria's offshore oil deposits. In May 1967, the Eastern Region declared itself the Republic of Biafra. War came in July. Great Britain continued to sell weapons to the Nigerian Federal Military Government, but the Johnson administration declared an arms embargo, angering Lagos. The fighting nonetheless turned against the rebels. By late 1967, the Biafrans were surrounded; their supply lines and communications were almost completely severed. Still, Nigerian forces struggled to overcome Biafra's dogged resistance, and the civil war settled into stalemate (see figure 3.1). The siege left between eight and fourteen million Biafrans vulnerable to famine, a population that expanded and contracted with the movement of the front lines.[6]

Civilian relief now became an urgent dilemma. The Federal Military Government would not permit aid to flow unimpeded to Biafra, insisting that cargoes undergo inspection. The Biafrans would not accept Nigerian scrutiny of deliveries. The International Committee of the Red Cross found itself caught in the impasse. By early 1968, NGOs active in Biafra were predicting catastrophe. In June, Oxfam warned that two million Biafrans could be dead by August. Children were especially vulnerable to death by protein deprivation, known in West Africa as *kwashiorkor*. Journalists soon wrote of "sad, misshapen creatures, their legs dangling like loose strings, their bellies bloated by malnutrition, their skin bleached by sores, their eyes wide and pleading." Frustrated by Nigeria's refusal to permit assistance to flow, the Red Cross, in August 1968, declared that it would fly relief missions into Biafra without Lagos's permission. Angered by this affront to its sovereignty, the Federal Military Government attacked a Red Cross relief camp. Tensions were sharpening between a Nigerian government that considered the Igbo rebellion a domestic affair and the foreign humanitarians who sought to assuage the war's savage consequences.[7]

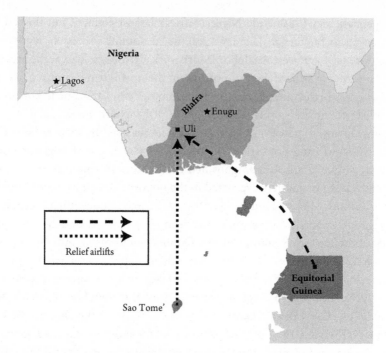

Figure 3.1 The Nigerian Civil War, 1967–1970
Source: GIS data is from www.naturalearthdata.com. Map design by Christopher Casey.

The Federal Military Government could not control the war's international reverberations. As 1968 progressed, missionaries, journalists, and aid workers sent news of Biafra's catastrophe out to the world. Religious groups played a crucial role. At the war's outset, there were about six hundred Catholic missionaries in Biafra; most stayed, and they became brokers of information as well as providers of aid. Missionaries mobilized church leaders, prompting the Vatican and the World Council of Churches to issue, in March 1968, a joint statement urging the cession of hostilities and a negotiated peace. Journalists continued to chronicle the war's barbarities. In July 1968, *Life* magazine plastered images of suffering Igbo children over newsstands. Later that month, television crews entered Biafra, and footage of starving infants began to appear on the evening news shows. Biafra's plight began to be debated in the British House of Commons. Prime Minister Harold Wilson, who favored Lagos, grumbled that "the purveyors of Biafran propaganda" had established "moral control over Western broadcasting systems." Indeed, the Nigerian Civil War captivated public opinion throughout the West. French citizens, according to one poll, ranked the Biafra War as the most urgent world issue in the summer of 1968. For foreign audiences, what mattered were not the political stakes—whether Biafra would win its independence or not—but the war's humanitarian consequences.[8]

In early 1968, religious NGOs, including the Catholic relief organization Caritas and a group of Scandinavian Protestants calling themselves
Nordchurchaid, began to airlift supplies to Biafra from the Portuguese colony of
Sao Tomé, just off the Nigerian coast. Operating without regard for legal niceties, the NGOs had to contend with Nigerian antiaircraft guns, which almost
shut down their operations in the summer of 1968. Then in August, a Swedish
nobleman swept into Biafra, carrying tons of food and medicine aboard a DC-7
that he flew at tree-top height to evade Nigerian air defenses. Count Carl Gustav
Von Rosen thus opened a new air corridor into Biafra. Soon, the NGOs that
had rallied to aid Biafra reconstituted their efforts into a new organization: Joint
Church Aid, or JCA (prompting some of the aviators who flew relief planes to
dub the operation Jesus Christ Airlines). These pilots ran what amounted to
a renegade Berlin Airlift. Their landing strip at Uli became Biafra's lifeline, the
gateway through which food and guns passed. The operation fed the Biafrans,
and it made the breakaway republic "a ward of the international community"— a
community not of nation-states but of a ragtag group of NGOs.[9]

Nongovernmental activists became central players in the war's transnational
politics. They fought to raise awareness, to engage Western audiences, and to
influence the foreign policies of the most powerful nation-states. Biafra activism attracted a motley collection of idealists. Some saw themselves as participants in a struggle to reorient world politics toward the claims of individual men
and women. "It is our opinion," wrote one American activist group, "that Biafra
is a test case to determine whether or not governments are capable of more
than paper commitments to human rights." Transnational activism blossomed
as the Biafran tragedy deepened. In 1968, two Americans who had served as
Peace Corps volunteers in Nigeria founded a clearing house, the Nigeria-Biafra
Information Clearing House, to collect and disseminate information about the
war. The American Committee to Keep Biafra Alive emerged later that year.
Activists in the United States created links to similar organizations in Europe
and coordinated with them, establishing networks of transnational advocacy.[10]

Biafrans and Nigerians participated in the shaping of world opinion. Shortly
after declaring independence, the Biafran government contracted with two
public relations agencies, Robert Goldstein Enterprises of Los Angeles and
Markpress of Geneva, to work on its behalf. Goldstein focused on film and television; Markpress dealt in print, issuing press releases and bombarding foreign
parliamentarians with mail. For his part, General Gowon acknowledged the
effectiveness of the Biafran propaganda. "World opinion thinks of me as a monster," Gowon conceded. For the Biafrans, it made excellent sense to confront
Federal Nigeria on the terrain of world opinion. Outgunned on the battlefield,
confined to a small pocket of territory, and dependent on airborne relief, the
Biafrans waged a propaganda offensive, recognizing that their survival depended

on it. They did so with aplomb. Biafra's propaganda was "brilliant" and "cynical" in the eyes of US diplomats. Nigeria's efforts to manipulate world opinion were less successful. Gowon was, in the *Economist's* view, "a Dunce at propaganda." The Nigerian government contracted with an agency and placed apologias masquerading as reportage in foreign newspapers. Lagos's propaganda efforts nonetheless lacked the sharpness of the Biafran campaign, which made the devastating claim that the Nigerian government was perpetrating genocide.[11]

As defined in the Genocide Convention of 1948, genocide involves the "intent to destroy" a national, ethnic, racial, or religious group. Biafra's internal cohesion and its propaganda outreach hinged upon the assertion that this was what Nigeria planned to do. Unless the Biafrans prevailed militarily, Ojukwu insisted, they faced extermination. This claim reverberated from the war's outset. A pamphlet titled *Pogrom*, for example, used eyewitness testimony, victim narratives, and grisly images to argue that the killings of 1966 had amounted to ethnic murder. As the war progressed, Ojukwu's strategy for survival came to depend on persuading the world that a "palpable genocide" was taking place. This required casting the famine not as a consequence of the military stalemate but as a deliberate effort to exterminate the Igbo people.[12]

Biafra's supporters embraced this interpretation of Nigerian motives. Tanzania, one of the few foreign governments to recognize Biafra, declared that the Biafrans had "suffered the same kind of rejection within their state that the Jews of Germany experienced." Among Biafra's supporters, this analogy took hold. The Committee to Keep Biafra Alive placed a full-page advertisement in the American news media featuring a grim photograph of Adolf Hitler under the bold-type words: "Welcome Back." Still, Biafra's supporters could hardly expect that the passion of their outrage and invocation of the Holocaust would transform the unfavorable military realities. Instead, Biafra's advocates would have to sway the great powers, above all the United States, to do something. If the mission as the American Committee to Keep Biafra Alive defined it was "to preserve the Biafran tribesman from genocide," the "education of the American people" appeared to many activists to be the best available weapon.[13]

With the United States embroiled in Vietnam, Biafra was a secondary priority for the Johnson administration in the summer of 1968. With Biafra on the front pages "almost constantly," officials nonetheless recognized the need to act. President Johnson put the case bluntly: send some aid, he implored aides, and "get those nigger babies off my TV set." The first command proved easier to fulfill than the second. By the end of the year, the United States had provided over half of all of the humanitarian aid delivered to Nigeria, though little of it reached Biafra. Where more vexing political questions were concerned, however, the administration deferred to the pro-Nigerian consensus within the international community of nation-states. Here, Great Britain, the former colonial power, adhered to its customary position that postcolonial borders were not subject to renegotiation, while the United Nations affirmed its commitment to the preservation of the Nigerian nation-state, insisting that humanitarian aid must pass through the offices of the International Red Cross. The Organization of African Unity was implacable in its support for Nigeria, reflecting the consensus position among the members that intervention in the affairs of postcolonial states was tantamount to neocolonialism.[14]

Few world leaders conceded that the Nigerian nation-state might have been a flawed project from the outset. Charles de Gaulle suggested in September 1968 that the unitary nation-state was not always a "very good or very practical" solution in the postcolonial context, but cynics suggested that the French president saw in Nigeria's dissolution an opportunity to circumscribe British influence in West Africa. Tanzania argued for the rights of Africans to revise "the boundaries we inherited from colonialism," but this was a minority position within the Organization of African Unity. More imaginative political solutions existed only in theory. One pro-Biafra advocate envisaged a pan-African confederation that would permit fluid configurations of governance at the regional and local levels, but this was improbable. What was in practice at stake was whether Biafra would become an independent nation-state or remain part of federal Nigeria.[15]

Aligning itself with the pro-Nigerian consensus among the world's governments, the Johnson administration demurred from supporting the NGOs that were aiding Biafra. This ensured that it did not alienate the Lagos-based government, for which helping the NGOs was tantamount to providing "aid and comfort to the enemy." Only in the administration's last weeks did this policy begin to change. Sympathetic to the Biafrans and aware of the "increasingly vocal concern" for them in US domestic politics, the NSC's Africa specialist Roger Morris persuaded national security adviser Walt Rostow to approve the sale of eight Globemaster airplanes: four to the Red Cross and four to the NGOs. The decision "outraged" the Nigerian government. It also marked the end of an American relief policy that recognized the Red Cross as the sole responsible agency of the international community. Public opinion was a crucial factor in the shift. "It is much easier to justify Globemasters" than to explain their denial "to Kennedy [and] McCormack," Morris wrote, referring to House Speaker John McCormack and Senator Edward Kennedy, two leading proponents of humanitarian engagement in Biafra's catastrophe.[16]

∽

Nixon's election generated enthusiasm within the pro-Biafra community. During the campaign, Nixon called for the United States to "act as the world's conscience" and to save those "who otherwise are doomed." He even described the starvation as "genocide," using a word most politicians avoided. As president, however, Nixon would not fulfill the hopes he inspired. Some speculate that he caved to Britain; others that he shifted his position in the hope of gaining access to Nigerian oil. In reality, Nixon did what he could but found himself caught between domestic, international, and transnational pressures. Under Nixon, the White House would prove to be more sensitive to public opinion than the foreign-policy bureaucracy, which adhered to the pro-Nigerian consensus among governments. The State Department policy, as William Rogers put it, was "to support states as they now exist." Yet the sympathies of domestic audiences were with Biafra: Americans who favored recognizing Biafra's independence outnumbered those who did not by more than four to one. With public opinion and diplomatic convention set against each other, Biafra revealed how the pressures of humanitarianism could, in an era of accelerating globalization, create vexing dilemmas for foreign policy and its makers.[17]

Pro-Biafra agitation mounted as Nixon took office. Difficulties with Equatorial Guinea, the main staging area for relief flights, led the Red Cross to suspend its relief operation there in January 1969, which left the religious relief agencies as Biafra's only source of sustenance and increased the pressure on Washington to act. Supporters of Biafra called on Nixon to aid Biafra or broker a ceasefire. Half the Senate signed a resolution demanding presidential action, prompting Nixon to comment: "It's time to spur State to get more action on this." In the United States, Biafra tugged at diverse heartstrings. One conservative radio host who traveled to Biafra proclaimed the Biafrans to be "deeply religious Christians." The American Jewish Committee took such intense interest in the crisis that it marked, in the Committee's words, "the first time that the American Jewish community as a whole organized for the support of sufferers who were not Jews." As the crisis resonated with Americans and others, it ceased to be, in the adminsitration's view, a "strictly international" conundrum.[18]

Nixon appeared to be sensitive to the humanitarian imperatives. "I want a program for Biafran relief," he ordered in January 1969. "The hell with State's opposition." A quick policy review soon devised a "two track policy." "High public impact actions" to aid Biafra would advertise the administration's "concern for the humanitarian plight of Biafra," while Washington would continue to favor "ultimate Nigerian victory" as the most stable long-term outcome. To bolster the relief effort, Nixon appointed C. Clyde Ferguson, a Rutgers law professor, to coordinate it. Ferguson soon announced a multi-million dollar increase in US support for the Red Cross and encouraged the international agency to resume relief flights into Biafra.[19]

Intelligence reports, meanwhile, indicated that Lagos was planning a spring offensive that might bring the war to an end. It did not. Despite early Nigerian gains, the Biafrans halted the assault in mid-May, preserving their independence—and the deadly military stalemate. While the war was, in essence, the cause of the Igbos' tragedy, many foreign sympathizers saluted Biafra's plucky resistance, including Richard Nixon. "I hope the Biafrans survive," the president commented in May. Unsuccessful on the battlefield, Nigeria turned against the relief operation once again, evidently determined to starve Biafra into submission. In June, Lagos declared nighttime flights into Biafra "illegal" and shot down a Red Cross plane. As activists protested, General Gowon demanded that the outside world "respect Nigeria's sovereignty" and desist from "violation of Nigerian air space."[20]

With relations between the Red Cross and the Nigerian government in disarray, political leaders in the United States urged the Nixon administration to act—either to impose a negotiated settlement or to compel Nigeria to permit relief. "The Congressional chorus on Nigeria-Biafra," Henry Kissinger warned, "may be rising again." As conditions in Biafra worsened, media coverage amplified the reverberations. In June 1969, CBS reported from Biafra, screening a special edition of *Sixty Minutes* on the crisis. Humanitarian pressures mounted during the summer. A series of state governors proclaimed Biafra Months, several of which offered sharp critiques of the society of nation-states. Governor Kirk of Florida lamented that "the world powers have seen fit not to intervene," while Governor Ogilvie of Illinois spoke of "genocide." Invoking the Holocaust, Governor McCall of Oregon warned that Biafra "seems destined to rival the carnage of Hitler's persecution of Europe's Jews." As Americans called for action, the globalization of the Nigerian Civil War demanded the attention of policymakers.[21]

"President Nixon," read one pro-Biafra advertisement in July 1969, "is the only man there is to turn to." The appeal caught Nixon's attention. "Henry," the president noted: "I agree with this." Nixon now concluded that he would "try to do something to conciliate the situation." Moving beyond the relief issue, he began to explore the possibility of negotiating a settlement. Doing this, Nixon believed, would require wresting control of US policy away from a State Department that had proven institutionally deferential to Nigerian sovereignty. Implementing this new approach, the NSC worked to initiate a "serious effort at mediation." Roger Morris met with Biafran representatives in New York in September. When State Department officials found out about Nixon's peace initiative, they tried to thwart it. In an attempt to salvage a coherent policy from this "bureaucratic guerilla war," Nixon instructed the State Department that all statements on Nigeria would henceforth require White House clearance. State ignored the directive, and Nixon failed to devise a peace proposal acceptable to either side, let alone both.[22]

As peace talks stumbled, the disputes over relief continued. In late 1969, Nigeria, Biafra, and the Red Cross abandoned talks over the reopening of relief corridors, meaning that the United States could no longer channel aid through the international agency. Decision-makers nonetheless recognized that "domestic public opinion would not permit disengagement." The only option, it appeared, was for Washington to throw its full weight behind Joint Church Aid. The Nixon administration did this, transferring to Joint Church Aid aircraft that it had lent to the Red Cross and expanding financial support for the religious NGOs. One historian concludes that the administration support "helped Joint Church Aid build up until it was flying in as much as JCA and [the Red Cross] together had been averaging." Washington's approach nonetheless antagonized Nigeria, which viewed the Joint Church Aid airlift as an illegal incursion on its sovereignty. Meanwhile, the situation in Biafra continued to deteriorate. Journalists reported that the Biafrans looked like they were "about to die in isolation," and US policymakers appeared unable to do much to aid their plight. The most that C. Clyde Ferguson could do at this point was to sponsor a public-health survey, which found that over a million Biafrans were at risk of dying from starvation.[23]

What resolved the impasse over relief was a series of rapid Nigerian military victories in late 1969. In late December, Nigerian forces severed Biafra into three parts, making the breakaway republic's capitulation inevitable. The war ended in early January when federal forces seized the Biafran capital and Ojukwu fled into exile, warning of probable genocide. In his victory declaration, General Gowon warned "the governments and organizations which sustained the rebellion" against further meddling in Nigeria's affairs. Getting relief to the defeated Biafrans now depended on Lagos permitting aid to flow, and foreign observers were not optimistic about the prospects for Nigerian magnanimity. Many expected that Nigeria would now exact vengeance from the Biafrans. Pope Paul warned of genocide. Even the NSC's Africa specialist feared that "the elimination of the Igbos as a tribe" might now be attempted.[24]

Domestic clamor continued to press upon Washington policymakers. Senator Kennedy demanded action "to prevent further tragedy" and worked to keep the plight of the Igbos at the forefront of public attention. The Nixon administration proposed making cargo planes available to the Nigerian Red Cross and offered Lagos millions of dollars in aid to fund relief efforts. With one eye fixed on domestic politics, the administration also pressed for an international airlift into Biafra. Internationalization of the relief effort, preferably under the auspices of UNICEF, now became the key objective for Biafra's former supporters. Recognizing the issue's political power in the United States, Henry Kissinger emphasized the need for a "strong political push" to "protect" the administration's position at home. The Department of State nonetheless continued to oppose actions that might offend Nigerian sensibilities, the Lagos embassy arguing that conditions inside the fallen territory were better than outsiders presumed. Diverging from the White House line, the State Department argued that the Nigerian Red Cross was competent to manage the humanitarian crisis. There was in the end no international airlift to relieve the Igbos; Lagos would not tolerate it. But the worst damage had already been done, and the Nigerian government did not perpetrate the genocide that Biafran propaganda had predicted and foreigners had feared.[25]

⁓

For outsiders, it was tempting to impose prefabricated analogies upon the Nigerian crisis. One stood out for its potency and the frequency of its invocation. "History is being repeated," exclaimed Gustav Von Rosen—among many others. "The Nigerians are the Nazis, and the Biafrans are the Jews." The implication was clear: the world must act to help the Biafrans, where it had failed to help Europe's Jews. Yet, for all the horrors the Biafrans endured, the analogy was inappropriate. There is scarce evidence to suggest that Nigeria sought to destroy the Igbos. After Biafra's fall, famine relief was slow and haphazard, and the starvation continued for months, but the Nigerian government extended an amnesty to those who had participated in the revolt and worked, slowly, to bind the nation's wounds. Gowon turned out not to be "the Hitler of Africa" as Ojukwu had dubbed him but an aspiring Lincoln. This is not to deny the war's costs. Between one and three million people, many of them infants and children, perished. Their deaths raise troubling questions. Did the humanitarians who rallied to Biafra's cause mitigate the war's consequences, or might they have made things worse? Did the Nixon administration, in its deference to domestic opinion and its tilt toward the humanitarian NGOs, do more harm than good?[26]

The conundrum has no easy answers. Nigerian acceptance of Biafran secession would have saved more human lives—and faster—than a Nigerian military victory could have done. Unlike Lincoln, Gowon accomplished no purpose beyond the preservation of a nation-state that colonial administrators had built. Still, the NGOs that rallied to Biafra's cause did not necessarily make outcomes better than they would otherwise have been. As historian Toyin Falola concludes, "international involvement in the Nigerian Civil War undoubtedly helped to prolong the conflict." Americans, who furnished half the material aid that made its way to Biafra, played a role in prolonging the crisis. For this, Washington paid a price in its relationship with Nigeria, whose leaders came to view the United States as "all but an enemy." Actions that embittered Lagos included Washington's embargo on arms exports, its support for Joint Church Aid, and its "tolerance" of Biafran propaganda within the United States. Nigeria remained "suspicious" of the United States after the war for having "given moral–if not material–support to the secessionists." Five years later, lingering "suspicions from Nigerian perceptions of the US role in the Nigerian civil war" remained an impediment to US-Nigerian relations.[27]

The consequences of the Nigerian Civil War reverberated far beyond diplomatic relationships. Non-state actors shifted the civil war out of the realm of interstate relations and into a realm in which transnational actors and forces shaped its narrative and its stakes. As they rallied for Biafra, the activists and the humanitarians eroded the barrier between foreign and domestic affairs that has traditionally structured the relations of nation-states. All this makes Biafra a revealing episode in the globalization of humanitarianism. As such, its legacy ought to be more cautionary than celebrated. The humanitarians got things wrong, including the allegations of genocidal intent. Meanwhile, juxtaposing Biafra against another African catastrophe just three years later suggests the fickleness of the humanitarian gaze. Whereas Biafra attracted worldwide scrutiny, the deaths of several hundred thousand Hutu at the hands of a Tutsi army in Burundi in 1972 attracted little attention.[28]

For the makers of American foreign policy, the pro-Biafran groundswell shaped the available options. Relatively insulated from political pressures, the State Department deferred to Nigerian sovereignty. Prominent congressional leaders took a quite different approach. In the White House, Nixon tried to navigate between the demands of diplomacy and of humanitarianism and ended up satisfying neither. It was crucially important that Cold War considerations were relatively absent. It was only because Nixon was not preoccupied with the Soviet Union in West Africa that he was able to tilt as far as he did in a humanitarian direction. While Nixon's policy lacked coherence, it was, at least, neither cynical nor self-interested. Kissinger later wrote that Nixon enjoyed "for once" being "on the humane side of an issue." That was more than could be said for American policy two years later, when another colonial legacy-state collapsed into a maelstrom of civil war, state violence, and ethnic murder, this time in South Asia.[29]

Geopolitics, Genocide, and the Tilt

The parallels were ominous. "It's just like Biafra," Richard Nixon exclaimed. As in West Africa, colonialism had left complex legacies in South Asia. While India had balanced democracy and diversity with relative success, Pakistan, carved in 1947 from British India's Muslim-majority provinces, lacked strong civil institutions, leaving its politics prone to military domination. Pakistan was, moreover, a geographical contortion. Until their separation in 1971, its two wings resided a thousand miles apart, separated by India (see figure 3.2). Relations between West Pakistan, where Punjabis dominated, and Bengali-majority East Pakistan revealed the strains of historical, cultural, and economic differences. West Pakistanis looked down on the Bengalis as recent converts to Islam, still tainted by Hindu practices, while many Bengalis saw themselves as victims of Punjabi colonialism. In material terms, East Pakistan was the poor relation; per capita income in the West was 61 percent higher at the end of the 1960s. The

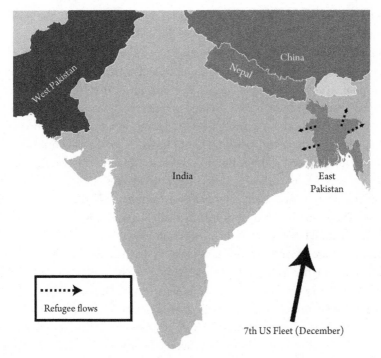

Figure 3.2 The South Asian crisis, 1971

Source: GIS data is from www.naturalearthdata.com. Map design by Christopher Casey.

cultural bonds of Bengali language, history, and literature, which spanned the international border with India, meanwhile, led West Pakistanis to suspect that their Bengali compatriots were disposed to pro-Indian intrigue.[30]

In November 1970, a colossal cyclone ripped into the deltas and barrier islands of East Pakistan, claiming a half million lives. A lackluster relief effort led many Bengalis to question anew their government's commitment to their welfare. After the flood came the landslide. In elections held in December 1970, the Bengali nationalist Awami League led by Sheikh Mujibur Rahman (Sheikh Mujib) took 167 of 169 seats in East Bengal, earning itself a slim majority in Pakistan's National Assembly. The elections marked Pakistan's return to democracy after a decade of military dictatorship. General Yahya Khan, Pakistan's military leader, had conceded this ballot ten months earlier amid pro-democracy protests, and he intended the elections to establish a new constitutional order. But Sheikh Mujib, now poised to form a government, was not committed to Pakistan. His Awami League maintained a quasi-secessionist agenda; its Six Points emphasized self-determination and envisaged only the flimsiest of connections between East Pakistan and the national government. Meanwhile, Zulfiqar Ali Bhutto, leader of the Pakistan People's Party, which dominated the ballot in the West, opposed devolving power from the federal to the provincial governments.[31]

Talks between Bhutto and Mujib failed to produce even the basis for a settlement. With separatist politics simmering in Dacca, East Pakistan's provincial capital, Yahya proclaimed martial law and postponed the opening of the National Assembly. Mujib now escalated his agenda, demanding in March 1971 that Pakistan's National Assembly be divided into separate bodies, one for the East and one for the West. Yahya was not himself opposed to compromise, but he would not proceed without Bhutto's consent, which Bhutto would not grant. Meanwhile, Bengalis waited at Karachi airport in West Pakistan to board the planes that would carry them home, as westerners made the same journey in reverse. These anxious repatriations recalled Nigeria's dissolution. American diplomats warned that a "blood bath" was imminent.[32]

Mujib declared March 23 Resistance Day. When it came, East Bengal erupted in demands for the independence of "Bangla Desh" ("Bengali land"). Yahya ordered a military crackdown, including the arrest of Mujib. In a bid to keep its campaign of suppression from foreign eyes, Pakistan's military corralled journalists into Dacca's Intercontinental Hotel at gunpoint. Doing so helped to veil events in Dacca, but several journalists avoided confinement, and news of what the *New York Times* called "one of the bloodiest slaughters of modern times" surfaced fast. Just days after the crackdown, British newspapers were describing savage butchery: "students dead in their beds . . . women and children roasted alive in their homes . . . Pakistanis of Hindu religion shot en masse." Wanton as it seemed, the violence appeared to follow a political logic. Participants in Mujib's nationalist movement, including students and faculty at the University of Dacca, were targeted for murder, as were Hindus. Some would-be victims found refuge in the homes of American expatriates. What relief they might get from the US government was less clear. But Washington would not be able to avoid taking a stand. As one NSC analyst warned, "the full horror of what is going on will come to light sooner or later."[33]

⟡

What interests did the Nixon administration perceive in an unraveling Pakistan? A member of both the Southeast Asian Treaty Organization (SEATO) and of the Baghdad Pact, Pakistan was a bulwark of Washington's Cold War interests. In line with the Nixon Doctrine, which advocated the delegation of responsibilities to regional allies, the Nixon administration favored Pakistan and eschewed the attempts by 1960s policymakers to devise a more balanced South Asia policy by expanding US relations with India. Islamabad also played a role in Nixon's China opening. The Pakistani government was an intermediary between Beijing and Washington, and when Henry Kissinger departed for China in July 1971, he did so from Pakistani soil. Nixon being Nixon, prejudice also shaped the administration's priorities. The president, Kissinger writes, preferred the "bluff, direct military chiefs of Pakistan" to India's "complex and apparently haughty" leaders. These preferences were, in part, a consequence of Nixon's travels to South Asia during the 1960s, during which Pakistan's leaders had received him graciously. In 1971, Nixon's "special feeling" for Pakistan corroborated his geopolitical instincts, which aligned US interests with those of Pakistan's government.[34]

Moved by a combination of self-interest and sentiment, Nixon indulged Pakistan from the beginning of his presidency. In 1969 he liberalized the arms embargo that Lyndon Johnson had imposed during the 1965 Indo-Pakistan War. When the cyclone hit East Pakistan in 1970, Nixon rejected domestic calls to internationalize the relief effort, deferring to Yahya, who insisted, despite plentiful evidence to the contrary, that Pakistan was capable of handling the disaster on its own. Even at this point, Nixon's prioritization of sovereign sensibilities over urgent human needs troubled Bob Haldeman, his White House Chief of Staff. "We have to look humanitarian," Haldeman implored. For Nixon, supporting a loyal ally who opposed the admission of international agencies into East Pakistan overruled the imperatives of "doing something."[35]

With Yahya's crackdown in March 1971, Nixon's dilemmas sharpened. Kissinger identified the stakes for the administration. Condemning Pakistan's brutality would be "humanitarian" and domestically advantageous, but even rhetorical interference would "harm our relationship" with Pakistan. Geopolitical considerations trumped humanitarian concerns, and the administration issued no statement denouncing the March atrocities. Off the record, Nixon expressed strong support for Yahya—"I wish him well"—and hoped that Pakistan might yet sustain a pseudo-imperial order in the East. "When you look over the history of nations," Nixon declared, "30,000 well-disciplined people can take 75 million any time." This disregard for human lives contrasted with Nixon's avowed sympathy for the Biafrans, even as he acknowledged the parallels. "I don't like it," he explained, "but I didn't like shooting starving Biafrans either." The difference was that Nixon had condemned Nigeria's war as "genocide" and sent aid to Biafra. Now he refused to even denounce the murder of civilians.[36]

Within the American government, Nixon's geopolitical calculus did not command universal support. The State Department this time took the humanitarian side of the crisis, reflecting both the perspective of the US consulate in Dacca, of which there had been no equivalent in Biafra, and State's exclusion from Nixon's China policy. "Our government has failed to denounce the suppression of democracy," the diplomats in Dacca telegraphed to Washington in early April. "Our government has failed to denounce atrocities." This missive became known as the Blood Telegram, named for Archer Blood, the consul who authorized it.

Unaware of Pakistan's role in Washington's opening to Beijing, the Dacca diplomats ascribed the Nixon administration's policy to the international convention of sovereign inviolability, not to hardheaded calculations of American
self-interest. "We have chosen not to intervene," the telegram declared, "on the
grounds that the crisis was an internal matter of a sovereign state." But could
even sovereign norms, let alone American interests, justify irresolution in the
face of barbarism? During 1971, the debate intensified, frustrating the formulation of US policy.[37]

⊂◊⊃

Strikingly, the Blood Telegram invoked "the overworked term genocide," declaring it "applicable" to the situation in East Pakistan. Dacca diplomats inferred
that the Yahya regime had decided to destroy Bengali nationalism, which made
its military campaign genocidal. Similar allegations reverberated in the public
sphere. American journalists and editorialists harped on Nixon's indulgent handling of Pakistan throughout the spring of 1971, but the outrage sharpened in
the summer, thanks to Anthony Mascerenhas, a senior journalist at Karachi's
Morning News. Mascerenhas visited East Pakistan in April 1971. Appalled
by what he saw, Mascerenhas fled to London, where he published a damning
exposé in the *Sunday Times* under the banner heading "GENOCIDE." While
Mascerenhas acknowledged the horrors that East Pakistan's Bengali militia were
inflicting on the province's small Bihari population, his central conclusion was
that the Pakistan military aimed to use genocidal methods to reestablish control of the East—namely, by eradicating Bengali nationalism. Pakistani policy,
he argued, proceeded from three assumptions: that the Bengalis would henceforth be ruled as colonial subjects; that religious reeducation in the East would
hold Pakistan together; and that property taken from East Pakistan's 7.5 million
Hindus—a minority targeted for expulsion or eradication—could be used to
win the East back into the nation-state. Mascerenhas's coolheaded diagnosis of
Pakistani motives was even more shocking than the descriptions of beatings,
shootings, and incinerations that accompanied his testimony.[38]

Waged for political ends, Pakistan's civil war had catastrophic consequences: ethnic cleansing, political murder, and, as the war dragged on, famine.
Mascerenhas had predicted much of this, warning in the spring that the breakdown of East Bengal's infrastructure would lead to massive starvation. Pakistani
officials seemed callous about the prospect. "Famine is the result of their sabotage," the head of Pakistan's Agricultural Development Bank told Mascerenhas.
"So let them die." In early June, World Bank officials corroborated Mascerenhas's
warning. In a report that the World Bank suppressed, a group of economists
who had "traveled extensively" in East Pakistan reported that infrastructural
destruction and government ineptitude augured a severe "food problem." "Even
if appropriate measures are introduced immediately," the economists concluded,

"it may be too late to prevent starvation." The World Bank report was unusually direct: Pakistani officials kept other international agencies out of East Pakistan, veiling the situation inside the province.

Still, Pakistan could not obscure the voices of those Bengalis whom hunger, violence, and desperation drove across the international border into India. By the time the US Senate convened its first hearings into the humanitarian crisis in late June, some five to seven million refugees had done just that. International and nongovernmental relief agencies assisted the refugees in India and, as in Biafra, focused transnational attention on their plight. The US Congress, once again, offered a political platform for the representatives of humanitarian organizations, including Catholic Relief Services, Oxfam, and the World Conference of Religion. Even rock stars clambered aboard the humanitarian cause. The Bengali musician Ravi Shankar collaborated with George Harrison, the former Beatle, to convene an August 1971 benefit concert. Featuring such luminaries as Bob Dylan, Eric Clapton, and Ringo Starr, Harrison's Concert for Bangladesh was both a revival of sixties idealism and a forbearer of future rock-star humanitarianism. Televised worldwide, the August 1971 event raised funds and awareness.[39]

Public clamor in the summer of 1971 created a difficult predicament for policymakers. What should the United States do now that its close ally Pakistan stood before the court of world opinion accused of genocide? US officials were realistic about Pakistan's political future, grasping from the outset that Pakistan would not be held together by force. "The concept of a united Pakistan is dead," a major NSC review concluded in April. So why not use American influence to encourage Yahya to leave East Pakistan to its fate? Washington controlled levers through which influence could be exerted. Military aid could be withheld; aggression could be condemned; and conditions could be attached to financial assistance. State Department officials favored using the available instruments to moderate Yahya's conduct, but the White House complained that the media was making a spectacle out of Pakistan's internal crisis. "The reporters there are missionaries," Kissinger complained. In a bid to quiet the critics, Kissinger nonetheless proposed deferring deliveries of "death-dealing" military equipment to Pakistan while permitting other forms of assistance to continue. Indulgent as this recommendation was, Nixon accepted it with reluctance, warning the foreign-policy bureaucracy: "Don't squeeze Yahya at this time."[40]

As in the Nigerian Civil War, the implosion in Pakistan pitched the claims of sovereignty against the force of humanitarian outrage. The neighbors, however, played rather different roles. Whereas the Organization of African Unity had aligned with Nigeria, India sided with the Bengalis, creating an ad hoc alliance between the activists and a powerful nation-state, whose leaders viewed Pakistan's disintegration with a mixture of apprehension and opportunism. For India, the refugee influx was the most immediate consequence of the crisis. By mid-April 1971, a half million people had already crossed the border; by the fall, nine million more had followed. These population flows created serious challenges: providing even rudimentary care for the refugees cost New Delhi 1 percent of its GDP for 1971, while the influx of refugees threatened to exacerbate latent instability in the province of West Bengal, already the scene of a Maoist insurgency.[41]

The refugee crisis drew India into Pakistan's catastrophe. Denouncing Pakistan's "genocide," Prime Minister Indira Gandhi worked to mobilize world opinion against her neighbor. To this end, she initiated a "massive diplomatic and publicity campaign," as one journalist called it, with the apparent purpose of forcing Yahya to abandon his efforts "to force millions of people to take refuge in our territory." Pakistan's implosion was not an internal matter, Gandhi insisted. Rather, "it is an Indian problem, it is a world-wide problem." This interpretation of events, which internationalized Pakistan's crisis and warranted external involvement to secure East Pakistan's independence, conflicted with Washington's preferred narrative, which made Pakistan's turmoil an internal matter and external meddling illegitimate.[42]

Yahya insisted that the war in the East was a domestic matter, and he denounced India's "open and constant intervention in our internal affairs." Despite the war's brutality, the support for this position in the international society of states remained durable. India apart, most foreign governments sided with Islamabad. Great Britain favored noninterference, as it had done in Nigeria, while a conference of Muslim nations affirmed support for Pakistan's "national unity and territorial integrity." Nonstate actors and activists meddled nonetheless; the Red Cross flew relief missions into the East in defiance of Pakistan's prohibition. Still, it was Indira Gandhi's intervention that proved decisive. Her government began to provide assistance to the guerilla forces of the Bangla Desh nationalist movement in July, and Gandhi herself guided Pakistan's fractious opposition parties into a united front in September. The White House, meanwhile, continued to side with Pakistan. "It is to no one's advantage to permit an internationalization of the situation," Nixon wrote. In private he reflected that asking Yahya Khan "to deal with the Awami Leaguers" was "like asking Abraham Lincoln to deal with Jefferson Davis."[43]

For Nixon and Kissinger, Gandhi's decision to sign a treaty of friendship and cooperation with the Soviet Union in August 1971 confirmed the wisdom of their pro-Pakistan tilt. Still, the geopolitical logic that projected Cold War alignments onto South Asia did not command a consensus within the United States. Military assistance to Pakistan became the focus of domestic consternation, especially once newspapers revealed that the administration was shipping ammunition to the Pakistanis, violating its own distinction between lethal and non-lethal assistance. As editorialists accused the administration of "underwriting" repression, the State Department argued for the suspension of deliveries. So concerned, in fact, did State Department diplomats become about US embroilment that they opened secret negotiations with Pakistan in a bid to close down the arms pipeline. When he heard about State's initiative, Kissinger was apoplectic. Still, the episode did not end the internal debate. "Almost to a person," one diplomat recalled, "the officials working on South Asia were convinced that the White House strategy would not work." Kissinger nonetheless insisted that the diplomats toe the White House line. "Why is it our business to tell the Pakistanis how to run their government," asked Kissinger. "State," he lamented, "is driving me to tears."[44]

While State Department officials chafed against the White House policy, critics in Congress lambasted the administration. Senator Kennedy of Massachusetts took the lead, emphasizing the humanitarian stakes of a "tragedy that has overwhelmed the moral sensibilities of people throughout the world." Kennedy held public hearings and traveled to India to inspect conditions in the refugee camps. "Whatever influence we have," he exclaimed, "we must use—not in aggravating the situation through the shipment of military supplies, or a policy of silence at the highest levels of our Government—but in truly working for peace and relief." Kennedy was, moreover, able to use his investigative powers as a Senate committee chair to reveal that the Nixon administration was supplying arms to Pakistan in defiance of formal restraints. The revelation prompted Congress to cut off further military assistance. Kennedy's successes indicated how alliances between transnational advocates—including the activists who testified at Senate hearings—and concerned legislators could circumscribe presidential control of foreign policy. Nixon himself acknowledged the point, warning Pakistani diplomats in May 1971 that the US Congress "could restrict our ability to help" in the coming months.[45]

The White House had little choice but to concede that domestic and transnational opinion aligned against its pro-Pakistan policy. "The political people—Democrat and Republican—are raising hell," the president conceded. "And they should from the standpoint of human suffering." Comparing the South Asian crisis to Biafra, Nixon nonetheless envisaged that a "massive" US aid program might be able to silence Pakistan's critics by separating the "relief" issue from the "political" dimensions of the crisis. This was most improbable: the United States could not presume to establish for itself a leading humanitarian role in South Asia even as it remained Pakistan's advocate and arms merchant. Instead, the administration would defy the force of transnational politics, elevating geopolitical interests, as it calculated them, over the conflict's humanitarian and political stakes. "We never yielded to public opinion," Kissinger bragged to the Soviet ambassador, but his intransigence on the point contrasted with the White House's courtship of world opinion during both the Nigerian and South Asian crises. The administration's pro-Pakistan tilt also positioned it on the losing side of the South Asian war that came at the year's end.[46]

∽

In early December, the tensions between India and Pakistan exploded into war. There had been border skirmishes in late November, but war did not come until Pakistan attacked Indian air bases in the west, one thousand miles from East Pakistan. In a two-front struggle, Indian troops made quick progress into East Bengal, reaching Dacca within a week. In the west, the front lines remained stable. That war had broken out did not surprise Nixon and Kissinger, who presumed that India sought Pakistan's destruction. Their evidence for this assumption was vague. When Indira Gandhi visited Washington in November, she had warned that the refugee problem constituted a threat to regional security, hinting at the use of force. Kissinger nonetheless inferred that New Delhi favored war not as a method to resolve the chaos on its border but because the schism in Pakistan was a geopolitical opportunity. "India will never again get the Paks in such a weak position," Kissinger reasoned. It would be perverse for India not to destroy Pakistan in its moment of weakness, he concluded, which led him to the idiosyncratic—and revealing—conclusion that what Indira Gandhi sought was Pakistan's defeat and dismemberment.[47]

Cold War assumptions defined the White House view of the third Indo-Pakistan war. "What we are seeing here," Kissinger commented, "is a Soviet-Indian power play to humiliate the Chinese and also somewhat us." The South Asian war, in this analysis, put in jeopardy the White House bid to triangulate the Cold War through its opening to China. With relations between Beijing and Washington still embryonic in the winter of 1971–72, the Soviet Union, Kissinger reasoned, was aiming to disrupt the Sino-American rapprochement via an underhanded attack on Pakistan, their matchmaker. Once the war began, Kissinger's geopolitical logic dictated a hard tilt toward Pakistan. Yet even Nixon was now questioning some of the assumptions on which US policy had been based. "The partition of Pakistan is a fact," the president now conceded. "You see those people welcoming the Indian troops?" "Why then," he asked, "are we going through all this agony?" Kissinger reminded him: to prevent Pakistan's destruction, to protect the China connection, and to preserve the worldwide balance of power. With so much at stake, it mattered not whether the Bengalis were welcoming the Indian troops as liberators.[48]

The White House thus cleaved, in public, to the idiosyncratic conclusion that Pakistan's catastrophe was India's doing, that Indira Gandhi sought to dismember Pakistan. "Cannibalize, that's the word," mused Nixon. "The connotation is savages." Neither Nixon nor Kissinger, however, really believed that Pakistan could be preserved intact; both, by December 1971, acknowledged the inevitability of division. "Autonomy [for the East] must be the answer," Kissinger had surmised in September; "there's no other way it can go." In private, the White House now urged Yahya to accept a settlement that would set East Pakistan free, even as the US ambassador to the United Nations denounced India's dismemberment of a sovereign state. Nixon and Kissinger thus rallied to Pakistan's side, cognizant that they could not save Pakistan but determined to intimidate India and—they presumed—the Soviet Union. The war's geopolitical stakes thereby dominated the administration's decision-making. The White House, accordingly, devised three initiatives to "scare off" the Indians. In the first, Washington sought to leverage its influence at the United Nations; in the second, it extended military aid to Pakistan; and in the third, it dispatched US naval forces into the Bay of Bengal in a bid to intimidate New Delhi.[49]

The administration's diplomatic offensive against India proceeded from the recognition that world opinion was not synonymous with transnational activism. If the court of global opinion had convicted Pakistan, the doctrine of territorial sovereignty still held sway in the UN General Assembly, where the United States maneuvered to brand India an aggressor. Indian diplomats recognized their vulnerability in the council of nation-states, and they fast retreated from their initial characterization of their war as a "humanitarian intervention." India's recourse to more traditional justifications for war—that Pakistan had attacked Indian air bases and, more creatively, that Pakistan had committed "refugee aggression"—marked the dissonance between the arena of transnational opinion, where Pakistan was guilty of genocide, and the international society of states, in which civil wars remained domestic matters, not grounds for intervention. The Soviet Union vetoed a US-backed Security Council resolution calling for an immediate ceasefire in South Asia, but George H. W. Bush, the US ambassador to the UN, scored a diplomatic coup when he took his ceasefire resolution to the General Assembly, where it passed by a wide margin. "It was a weird situation," Kissinger recalled. "Almost all the nonaligned [countries] were on our side. Yet the usual votaries of world opinion in our country were busy castigating the White House as if it stood irrationally against the decent opinion of mankind." The point was accurate, but drawing the distinction between the international and transnational realms of world politics did not resolve the predicament in which the White House found itself.[50]

Supplying weapons, meanwhile, bolstered Pakistan's military capacities, but doing so was illegal under US law, which prohibited the export of lethal military equipment to South Asia. The law contained a national-interest exception, which the White House could invoke with an executive declaration to the effect that exporting weapons served US national security. But the White House did not invoke this loophole, apparently fearing the political consequences of doing so. It instead concocted an elaborate, secretive, and illegal scheme to provide Pakistan with US military equipment currently in the possession of third countries. The White House tried at first to persuade Iran to transfer US-made warplanes to Pakistan, but the shah was unwilling to risk Soviet ire by doing so. The shah did, however, offer to send Iranian planes to Jordan, so that Jordanian fighter jets could be transferred to Pakistan. The White House approved this complex scheme and secured similar commitments from Saudi Arabia and Turkey. Kissinger bragged to Chinese diplomats about the administration's defiance of US law. All Nixon had to say about the scheme's illegality was "Hell, we've done worse." Still, the few warplanes that Yahya received as a result of these maneuverings made little difference to the war's outcome.[51]

A more dramatic transfer of American military hardware occurred when the White House dispatched the USS *Enterprise* to the Bay of Bengal. Presuming that US credibility was on the line, Nixon and Kissinger conceived of this gesture as a statement of solidarity not with Pakistan so much as with China. Fearing that India sought Pakistan's destruction, Nixon and Kissinger worried that China would be drawn into the South Asian crisis—and that the Soviet Union might use a regional war as an opportunity to attack China. To maintain a common front with Beijing, Kissinger proposed to diplomat Huang Hua that China and the United States cooperate to achieve "maximum intimidation" of India and the Soviet Union. Kissinger proposed that Beijing move troops to the Indian border and promised Huang that the United States would support Beijing in the event of a Sino-Soviet war. This commitment indicated the reach of the administration's geostrategic logic, which neglected both the plight of the long-suffering Bengali refugees and the political fractures within Pakistan, which had precipitated the crisis in the first place.[52]

Kissinger later claimed, without evidence, that India's declaration of a ceasefire that left West Pakistan intact was "a reluctant decision resulting from Soviet pressure, which in turn grew out of American insistence, including the fleet movement." In fact, New Delhi ended the South Asian war once its military objective—East Bengal's independence—was achieved. Few observers in the United States (or elsewhere) credited the administration with a triumph. More charged Nixon and Kissinger with an unforced error. When the columnist Jack Anderson printed secret transcripts of NSC meetings that revealed the hard-nosed logic behind the White House tilt toward Pakistan, a public uproar ensued. In the eyes of critics, the White House had backed both the wrong side and losing side. "It was by ignoring the moral realities, misjudging the power realities, and failing to heed the political realities," the *New York Times* commented "that Mr. Nixon put the United States on the slippery slope." Nixon now distanced himself from Kissinger, the principal architect of the tilt.[53]

Kissinger in the winter of 1971/72 came under sustained domestic fire, not least for sloppy security procedures at the NSC, where the Anderson leak originated. In the aftermath of the crisis, Kissinger found himself temporarily exiled from the White House, denied access to Nixon, and, as he put it, allowed to "twist slowly, slowly in the wind." For the national security adviser the experience was chastening. While the dynamics that it showcased did not lack for precedents, the South Asian crisis revealed the capacity of transnational politics to circumscribe the options available to policymakers and to exacerbate interstate conflicts like the one between India and Pakistan in 1971. "An increasingly interdependent world," concluded one congressional subcommittee, "means that disregard for human rights in one country can have repercussions in others." "The horrible atrocities of Nazi Germany and the tragic massacre in Bangladesh," it continued, "are examples of how gross violations of human rights precipitated bloody wars." These were realities with which policymakers—even self-construed realists—would have to contend.[54]

Humanitarianism, Human Rights, and Foreign Policy

Occurring just years apart, Biafra and Bangladesh revealed recurrent dynamics. In both episodes, postcolonial nation-states faced secessionist movements and responded with brutal force. Allegations of genocide abounded, emanating from the insurgents and amplified by transnational activists. Crucially, both crises exposed tensions between a transnational society of volunteers, activists, and opinion makers favoring humanitarian intervention and the international society of nation-states, which mostly concurred that the conflicts were internal affairs in which outsiders should not meddle. There were also crucial differences, however. In Nigeria, no external power played the role that India assumed as champion and vindicator of secession. The episodes ended differently. Biafra was reabsorbed into Nigeria. Bangladesh won its independence. In the United States, the two episodes produced divergent reactions. While domestic audiences and opposition leaders aligned with both the Biafrans and the Bangladeshis, the Nixon administration took different positions on the two crises, alternatively indulging and rebuking humanitarian demands.

For the White House, the Cold War made the difference. In Nigeria, Cold War concerns were largely absent; CIA analysts reassured decision-makers that the Nigerians and Biafrans alike viewed "Soviet ideology as irrelevant." While Lagos purchased Soviet weapons, it insisted on paying in cash so as to avoid dependence on Moscow. So marginal was the USSR's role that American analysts concluded that Moscow might prefer a negotiated settlement to a Nigerian victory. While US diplomats in Lagos sometimes warned of Soviet "visibility and presence," their warnings were jeremiads that revealed more about the State Department's pro-Nigerian bias than about actual Soviet involvement. In South

Asia, meanwhile, Nixon and Kissinger reasoned that India's victory over Pakistan would be a triumph for the Soviet Union and a humiliation for China and the United States. Their geopolitical instincts negated all other considerations.[55]

If the crises in Biafra and Bengal occurred in a bipolar world, the Cold War explains neither the origins nor the stakes of the episodes; these had much more to do with the contestation of postcolonial settlements than with East-West dynamics. Regardless, Cold War interests molded US reactions to Third World crises from the late 1940s onward. Situated more broadly, Nigeria was, in fact, an exception; and Pakistan, much closer to the rule; policymakers acted in South Asia as they had done in Guatemala, Iran, Cuba, the Congo, and Vietnam: they superimposed ideological binaries on political complexity. In South Asia, too, an exaggerated sense of the geopolitical stakes precipitated a muscular White House response. For Nixon and Kissinger, the Cold War still defined their era, even when events on its periphery moved to their own rhythms, not a bipolar beat. The Cold War's power as a narrative for interpreting the present, as a strategic prism through which complex events were filtered, influenced policymakers in the Nixon White House and led them astray.[56]

Situating the Biafra and Bangladesh episodes within the framework of globalization, in contrast, makes them harbingers of dilemmas that would define the post–Cold War era. Since the 1980s, after all, catastrophes in the developing world involving crises of political order, humanitarian emergencies, allegations of genocide, and questions of international responsibility have become urgent challenges for the American superpower—in the former Yugoslavia, in Rwanda, in Syria, and elsewhere. These post–Cold War dilemmas, as they sometimes seem, nonetheless antedated the end of the Cold War. In Nigeria and South Asia, transnational activists worked to bring global opinion to bear on humanitarian catastrophes, while television amplified the descriptions of suffering and misery, exposing audiences to what the writer Frederick Forsyth called "images of children reduced to stick insects" and "the constant low wailing of dying babies." Nonstate actors did more than stir outrage. In Nigeria, they provided much of the food that kept the Biafrans alive. Their engagement was less pronounced in South Asia, but it raised awareness of the human suffering in East Bengal and pressured decision-makers to act, much as the global dissemination of images of racial violence in the former Confederacy—police dogs and fire hoses unleashed on children—encouraged successive US presidents to act on behalf of civil rights at home.[57]

The emergence of celebrities like George Harrison as international actors suggested how world politics might be changing in the globalization era, but transnational humanitarianism did not lack for precedents. Non-state actors had mobilized against the slave trade in the late eighteenth century, in support of the Greek Revolt in the 1820s, and against the Bulgarian "horrors" of the 1870s.

Nineteenth-century US policymakers had also contended with domestic pressures for humanitarian engagement in foreign conflicts and encountered backlashes against their choices, as in the antiwar movement that accompanied the Mexican-American War. The dynamics that Biafra and Bangladesh manifested were not new, but the episodes suggested that an upsurge of transnational activism might be coinciding in the early 1970s with simultaneous developments—including the implosion of postcolonial projects in places like Pakistan and Nigeria—to bring humanitarian dilemmas to the fore of world politics.[58]

These were realities with which even the most powerful policymakers would have to grapple. Over Biafra, the administration aligned itself at least partially with the proponents of humanitarian engagement. "I want to be sure we take leadership on humanitarian problems," Nixon explained. In South Asia the White House took a different line, but that did not mean that it disregarded the power of "world opinion." Instead, Nixon and Kissinger tacked between the bravado of defiance and the delusion of control. Nixon hoped to turn "public opinion" against the Indians and wrote to Yahya offering advice. Could Islamabad not "package" its concessions, Nixon asked, in a single initiative that would transform global perceptions? Assuming that "the Indians are susceptible to this world public opinion crap," Nixon speculated that public opinion could be manipulated to support his policy. Even as the war ended on India's terms, Kissinger and Nixon reassured themselves that the votaries of conscience would soon turn against India. "In six months the liberals are going to look like jerks," they ruefully predicted, "because the Indian occupation of East Pakistan is going to make the Pakistani one look like child's play." They might have lamented it, but Nixon and Kissinger conceded the power of transnational opinion, which echoed in domestic politics, and they worked, with more or less success, to insulate their policies from it.[59]

While geopolitical calculations motivated their defiance of world opinion in South Asia, Nixon and Kissinger were nonetheless able to invoke an alternative language of legitimacy: the convention of national self-determination. It was regrettable, Kissinger later wrote, when regimes such as Yahya's pursued "shortsighted and repressive domestic policies." Yet if external powers intervened in matters that were essentially within the competence of sovereign states, "the international order" would "be deprived of all restraints." On this point, he and Secretary of State William Rogers concurred. "They are members of the United Nations," Rogers declared, "and we mean it when we say it, that we respect their sovereignty." This position enjoyed wide support in the community of nation-states, especially among Third World governments. The UN General Assembly and the British Commonwealth both concurred that the crises in Pakistan and Nigeria were internal affairs in which foreign powers should not meddle.[60]

One accusation nonetheless retained special power to pierce sovereignty's veil. Genocide was a unique crime under international law; according to the Genocide Convention of 1948, it mandated external intervention. In Biafra and Bangladesh, secessionist leaders and their supporters alleged that genocide was occurring, although the appropriateness of the allegation was in both cases unclear. In Nigeria, genocidal violence followed the 1966 coup that brought Gowon to power, claiming tens of thousands of lives. Thereafter, Nigeria waged a war for national unity that claimed hundreds of thousands more lives, while starvation pushed the death toll far higher. Still, there is scant evidence that Gowon sought to eliminate the Igbos; his restraint in victory, in particular, rebuts allegations of genocidal intent. In East Pakistan, the situation is murkier. Islamabad did not seek to exterminate the Bengalis, but it waged war against Bengali nationalism, fast-tracking intellectual, cultural, and political leaders for extermination. Of all Pakistan's actions, the ethnic cleansing of Hindus in East Pakistan came closest to meeting the definition of genocide, according to the International Commission of Jurists. Exaggerated in both cases, the accusations of genocide nonetheless stunned foreign observers. For the first time since the Second World War, large numbers of Westerners concluded that ethnic murder not dissimilar in scale from the Holocaust might be occurring. This conviction had significant repercussions.[61]

᳜

In the mid-1960s, the doctrine of sovereign inviolability came under pressure, as lawyers, politicians, and activists asked when violence within nation-states might mandate international action, even intervention. In the broad historical perspective, the proposition was not novel. Since Grotius, mainstream international thought permitted outside powers to intervene when events within states so shocked "the conscience of mankind" as to make nonintervention unconscionable. In 1945, however, the UN Charter enjoined its signatories to respect each other's sovereignty, a commitment that trumped the claims of human rights and humanitarian responsibility for a time, as the reaction of foreign governments to Biafra and Bangladesh indicated. These episodes nonetheless sparked a reevaluation of sovereignty, intervention, humanitarian responsibility, and the relationships between them. In the early 1970s, articles on humanitarian intervention began proliferating in the law journals, as lawyers and others worked to formulate recommendations for policymakers. In the Senate, Ted Kennedy proposed institutional reforms to improve upon Washington's "ambivalent and tardy" responses to events in Nigeria and Pakistan, even the creation of a new Bureau of Social and Humanitarian Services within the State Department. Among legal practitioners and in the US Congress, a quiet momentum was building.[62]

In both the Biafra and Bengal episodes, activists, protagonists, and lawyers deployed the language of human rights—if not interchangeably with the language of humanitarian responsibility, then in close relation to it—as Richard Lillich did when he advocated for humanitarian intervention "to protect human rights" and Michael Riesman did when he argued that international human rights commitments warranted action to save the Biafrans. The International Commission of Jurists concluded, similarly, that the "International Bill of Human Rights"—the Universal Declaration of 1948 and the UN Human Rights Covenants of 1966—mandated international intervention in East Pakistan. This is not to say that Biafra and Bangladesh *were* human rights causes; in both cases, the insurgents advanced collectivist agendas, framed in the language of national self-determination. In both cases, insurgents and advocates nonetheless invoked the language of human rights, as Ojukwu did when he argued that the Universal Declaration of 1948 offered justification for Biafra's revolt.[63]

In international relations and foreign policy, human rights and humanitarianism exist in tension with territorial sovereignty and sovereign inviolability. In both Biafra and Bangladesh, the responsible governments rebuffed well-intentioned meddlers, denouncing them as neocolonialists. Foreign governments rallied to support Lagos and Islamabad as nonstate activists rallied to support the rebels. The two episodes thereby shook the balance between international and transnational politics. Sovereignty still prevailed, but Biafra and Bangladesh prefigured future challenges to it. As the 1970s progressed, the challenge of transnational politics would increasingly take the form of mobilization for human rights, challenging policymakers to accommodate human rights in foreign policy, even to embrace the universalism of human rights commitments, something many decision-makers would eventually do.

"We don't even pretend high-sounding morality on some of these issues," Henry Kissinger commented, "except in the deepest sense." Foreign policy as Kissinger and Nixon construed it aimed to serve US national interests while sustaining the basic stability of the existing international order. The deeper morality Kissinger invoked presumably referred to the atrocious consequences that superpower conflict could produce in the thermonuclear age. For Kissinger, tilting toward Yahya bolstered American credibility and deterred the Soviet Union, thereby upholding the stability—and the peace—of a fractious bipolar world. Others found brittle and tenuous the logical chains that linked Cold War outcomes, much less the peace of the world, with events in South Asia. Whether Kissinger was correct or not, the pursuit of Cold War realpolitik would not become easier for US decision-makers in the years that followed.[64]

Inside America, a humanitarian backlash pressed on the makers of foreign policy at the dawn of the 1970s. The White House could not ignore moralism's clarion call, for which the Congress served as a vital echo chamber. In Biafra, the White House tried to accommodate activists' demands for a foreign policy responsive to humanitarian concerns. In Pakistan, it pushed back. The implications were clear enough: foreign policy could not be made as if transnational politics did not matter. Vietnam remained the most powerful illustration of this point, but Biafra and Bangladesh showed that unarmed opinion could alter the political stakes even of conflicts in which the United States was not directly involved. This both testified to the capacity of foreign events to penetrate the domestic sphere and hindered the execution of the Nixon administration's intricate grand strategy. The ethical aspects of foreign policy, it turned out, could not be ignored, as the forces of globalization encouraged Americans to rethink the balance between ideals and interests in foreign policy, curtailing the domestic constituency for Nixonian realpolitik.

Less than two years after the South Asian crisis, the Chilean military overthrew President Salvador Allende, on September 11, 1973. Air force jets bombed the presidential palace, and General Augusto Pinochet, head of Chile's armed forces, thrust aside Allende's Unidad Popular (Popular Unity) government, inaugurating a dictatorship that would last for decades. The coup culminated the personal tragedy of a Marxist who had sought social revolution using democratic methods, and it raised the specter of US involvement in Allende's downfall, the nature and extent of which would prove contentious.[65]

There is no question that Nixon and Kissinger had perceived Allende's September 1970 election to be a setback to US interests. "If we think that we can let the potential leaders in South America think they can move like Chile," Nixon reflected, "we will be in trouble." In the Western Hemisphere, where the assumptions of the Monroe Doctrine still applied, Nixon would broker no détente with the revolutionary left. Instead, his administration worked to destabilize and overthrow Allende. Under the guise of a "cool but correct" policy, Nixon had supported Allende's opponents, encouraged military officers to plot the coup, slashed bilateral aid, and blocked Chilean appeals to international financial institutions, ensuring that Allende would not be able to borrow his way out of disaster. But if they wished for it, fostered it, and aligned themselves with its perpetrators, it does not follow that Nixon and Kissinger orchestrated the coup that overthrew Chile's democracy; here the evidence is murkier. Regardless, the White House's intolerance of Allende was at odds with détente's realistic spirit and its tolerance of ideological diversity. Yet, in the minds of US decision-makers, the coup served détente's larger purpose of sustaining Washington's international primacy.[66]

If the geopolitical motives that animated US involvement in Chile were familiar, the domestic backlash that the events in Chile caused was striking. Americans had rallied in opposition to their government's meddling in Brazil in 1964 and in the Dominican Republic in 1965, but Chile proved a catalytic moment for the transnational politics of human rights. While activists had begun to deploy the language of human rights in other contexts—including during the civil wars in Nigeria and Pakistan—it was Chile that catalyzed the emergence of human rights as America's dominant idiom of international humanitarian engagement.[67]

Unlike the Vietnam antiwar movement, the mobilization against the Pinochet junta—and Washington's association with it—was mostly an elite movement, more active in law schools and in the halls of Congress than on college campuses. Frank Newman was representative of the participants. A law professor at the University of California, Berkeley, Newman was a pioneer who had introduced human rights to law-school curriculums. In November 1973, he led a mission to Santiago on behalf of Amnesty International. Newman's task was urgent: the International Committee of the Red Cross estimated that as many as fifteen thousand people had been arrested in the coup's aftermath, and concerns about torture and political murders abounded. To probe the allegations, Newman's team met with officials and prisoners alike. Shortly after his return home, Newman testified before the House Committee on Foreign Affairs, which had convened a hearing on human rights in Chile. Strikingly, Newman focused on rights, not politics. "We were concerned with the problems of prisoners, torture, and killing," Newman explained, "not with the problem of whether the junta should have taken over the government in Chile."[68]

The next year, Amnesty published the report of Newman's trip. It concluded that arrests after the coup had numbered up to forty thousand; that the junta had transformed Chile's National Stadium into a makeshift concentration camp; and that interrogators had used hoods, beating, electrocution, and rape as instruments of torture. Up to two thousand people had died at the junta's hands in the months after the coup, the report suggested. As grisly as the details were, the rapidity with which they were assimilated into a transnational discourse on human rights, international law, and the moral responsibilities of foreign policy was stunning. Activists, scholars, and parliamentarians from the United States and Europe participated in this discourse, which hinged upon the question: how could Chile's rulers be persuaded (or compelled) to respect individual rights under law?[69]

After the Chilean coup, the makers of American foreign policy had little choice but to grapple with this question. Human rights thus emerged in the 1970s as a central theme in domestic foreign-policy discourse, evoking purposes distinct from—and sometimes at odds with—those that Nixon's Cold War realism favored. In their essence, human rights were simple: proponents agreed that all people possess specific rights and that the international community bears some responsibility when governments violate the rights of individuals. Building on the wartime human rights mobilization of the 1940s, proponents in the 1970s worked to redefine the rights-bearing individual not only as a subject of the nation-state but also as a subject of the international community. This had direct consequences for US foreign policy. Critics began to assail Nixon's Cold War–centric policy on the grounds that it neglected human rights—not only in places like Chile and Pakistan, whose military rulers were aligned with Washington, but also in the Soviet Union, Washington's partner in détente but no paragon of human rights virtue. The politics of human rights thus challenged more than the diplomatic conventions of sovereign inviolability and self-determination; human rights challenged decision-makers to respond, to consider anew whether or not foreign policy's exclusive purpose was to serve the national interest.[70]

Where did this challenge originate? The human rights idea was present at the creation of the postwar order—articulated in wartime appeals for human rights, such as H. G. Wells's *The Rights of Man*; in FDR's rhetoric; and in the preamble to the UN Charter as well as in the Universal Declaration. Such declarations were ineffective in their time; nation-states after 1945 resisted external surveillance of their interior conditions, citing their sovereign prerogatives. When the United Nations convened an international conference on human rights in Tehran in 1968, the postcolonial world's hostility seemed to confirm the low repute into which human rights had fallen in world politics. Still, the seeds of a revival could also be discerned. Roy Wilkins, leader of the National Association of the Advancement of Colored People (NAACP), represented the United States in Tehran. He offered a valiant defense of human rights, invoking the achievements of civil rights at home as a model for global human rights. Wilkins's appearance in Tehran also suggested the liberating implications of domestic civil rights for US foreign policy; without desegregation at home, US entreaties for human rights abroad would have lacked even the patina of moral authority. Meanwhile, globalizing trends in world politics—including a "revolution in communications and technology"—would, Wilkins wagered, necessarily elevate human rights, empowering activists and curtailing sovereigns. "No state," he explained, "will be able to fence out ideas or fence in people."[71]

Globalization propelled the rise of a global human rights movement, facilitating transnational engagement and activism, much as Roy Wilkins foresaw. Still, if Biafra and Bangladesh clarified the connections between globalization and transnational mobilization, neither was, in essence, a human rights episode. It took more specific developments to transform the groundswell of mobilization these episodes manifested into a focused movement for human rights. Legal innovations during the 1960s, including the UN Human Rights Covenants of 1966, established a formal basis for human rights activism. Still, the rise of human rights in US politics was a consequence of the choices that policymakers made to align the United States with authoritarian and oppressive regimes, not only in Pakistan and Chile but also in Brazil, Greece, South Africa, and elsewhere. Decision-makers also chose to fight—and to continue—a war in Vietnam, which prompted some Americans to grapple with the destructive consequences of US actions for Third World peoples. Had American decision-makers considered more seriously the moral and even the domestic political stakes of foreign policy, as Nixon did in Biafra, the human rights insurgency of the mid-1970s might have been preempted. Instead, American decision-makers marginalized political considerations and ignored ethical concerns, encouraging the proponents of human rights to rally. The rise of human rights in the 1970s was not just a breakthrough; it was also a backlash.[72]

4

The Dollar and Decline

I think of what happened to Greece and to Rome ... What is left? Only
the pillars.

Richard Nixon, Remarks to Media Executives, 1971

"Henry doesn't know a damn thing about economics. What's worse, he doesn't know what he doesn't know." With this, Richard Nixon invited Peter Peterson to join his White House staff as director of the Council on International Economic Policy (CIEP), a position intended to parallel Kissinger's at the NSC. The council's purpose, as Nixon intended it, would be to transcend the bureaucratic struggles among the State, Commerce, and Treasury Departments and achieve "consistency" in US foreign economic policy. Nixon also hoped that the council would be able to "to look down the road 25 years" and guide the adaptation of policy to changing circumstances. As the the Pax Americana's burdens accumulated, the United States, Nixon believed, could no longer afford to be a benefactor to its allies; the time for a reconsideration of priorities and an adjustment of responsibilities had arrived. The pursuit of national economic interests would have to "play a far more important role in America's foreign policy" in the future.[1]

Taking stock was among Peterson's first tasks. Surveying Nixon's cabinet, he encountered a range of perspectives. The State Department saw no reason why wealth could not continue to lubricate foreign policy, as it had done since the Marshall Plan. Yet for the Commerce Department, the prospects for US industry appeared grave. "Unless we took strong action," explained Secretary of Commerce Maurice Stans, "we would soon become a nonmanufacturing economy." Business executives corroborated Stans's pessimism, including the Ford Motor Company's Lee Iacocca. "Ninety-one percent of all radios today in the U.S. are from Japan," Iacocca explained when he met Nixon and Peterson. The automobile industry faced similar pressures. "On the West Coast, twenty-seven percent of all cars are foreign." In some domestic markets, Japanese sales were already besting Detroit's.[2]

Peterson's analysis, published at the end of 1971, aligned with the prophets of decline. *The United States in a Changing World Economy*, or, more simply, the Peterson Report, made for grim reading. American growth rates had lagged behind West European and Japanese rates since the early 1950s, but the productivity gap had widened since the mid-1960s, which suggested that something more than postwar catch-up was going on: the Europeans and Japanese had caught up, and they were continuing to pull ahead. US manufacturers now accounted for just 31 percent of the world's automobile production, down from 76 percent in 1949–50. Far from being the "arsenal of democracy," as Franklin Roosevelt had envisaged, the United States was looking increasingly like a rentier superpower, Peterson concluded, "engaged largely in services, drawing income from foreign investments, and importing more goods than it exports."[3]

Peterson's conclusions caught the attention of a president who viewed the world economy as an arena for competition and struggle. Western Europe's resurgent economies were "tough, hard competitors," Nixon bemoaned, and Japan was an "economic giant" capable of "knocking us out of the box." Even the Soviet Union was beginning to compete in some markets, and China seemed poised to become "a major economic force." Looking forward, Nixon perceived a "five-fingered" world economy—the United States, Japan, China, Europe, and the USSR—in which American dominance could not be taken for granted. "Instead of being number one economically," Nixon warned, the United States might soon be "number two, three, or four." Much more than prosperity was at stake. "Unless we're number one economically," Nixon insisted, "we can't be number one politically." This was crucial. Committed to maintaining American primacy, Nixon viewed the rehabilitation of national prosperity as a strategic imperative of the highest order. "The future of the economy is in your hands," he implored his Productivity Commission in 1971, "but also the future of peace, the future of the world."[4]

⸎

Nixon's bid for national renewal and its consequences for the international monetary order are the two central themes of this chapter. They are related, for the Nixon administration concluded, early on, that national decline was a consequence of monetary arrangements that overvalued the dollar and disadvantaged US exporters. Accordingly, Nixon's bid for renewal hinged on the quest for a dollar devaluation, which would, US officials reasoned, reflect changes in the real economic capacities of the industrialized countries, restore America's competitive edge, and resolve the crises that had afflicted the international monetary system in recent years. To achieve this devaluation, Nixon proved willing to take drastic measures, even to sever the dollar's relationship to gold, which had anchored the Bretton Woods international monetary order since the mid-1940s.

He nonetheless underestimated the contentiousness that would accompany American unilateralism, and his actions divided the United States from its allies.

Remaking the international monetary order required not only renegotiating burdens among governments but also resolving the mounting tensions between nation-states and transnational economic forces. Offshore financial markets grew fast in the 1960s, and they posed serious challenges to governance. Central bankers were, by the early 1970s, complaining that "footloose funds," or "hot money," were complicating the making of national monetary policies and increasing the world economy's propensity to crisis. Fixated on national renewal, the Nixon administration was at first inattentive to the ways in which globalization was remaking the international economy. Nixon, contrary to some speculation, did not seek to unshackle financial globalization from the controls that had contained it under Bretton Woods. His bid for national renewal nonetheless damaged the international monetary order and international cooperation so as to make improbable the reestablishment by nation-states of collaborative international economic governance. Instead, governments ended up ceding their power to determine currency values to the financial markets. This outcome, mostly unsought, heralded the advent of a distinctive, and unstable, era of finance-led globalization.[5]

In Pursuit of National Renewal

Shortly after his inauguration, Richard Nixon established a working group on international monetary policy under Paul Volcker, Under Secretary of the Treasury for Monetary Affairs. Volcker confronted an unenviable inheritance. Bretton Woods still prevailed, but it was faltering, and its vulnerabilities centered on the US dollar. The dollar's predicament became especially serious in the mid-1960s, as the value of dollars circulating outside the United States surpassed the total value of the gold reserves available to the US government, creating a gold-dollar overhang. This made the dollar—and with it Bretton Woods—susceptible to a crisis of confidence, to a run on the dollar that would force the United States to suspend or abandon the gold-dollar linkage through which other currencies maintained indirect connections to gold. Nixon's predecessors had tried to buttress the Bretton Woods system, constructing ad hoc defenses to shore up an overvalued dollar, but the rise of transnational finance made the system more prone to crisis. Holders of offshore funds could easily shift assets from currency to currency, abandoning the dollar if it served their interests to do so.

At the root of the dollar dilemma was the US balance of payments. The balance of payments is a register of international transactions—private and public, financial and real. Trade surpluses are recorded as credits in the balance of payments, as are inflows of foreign capital (the balance of payments does not include future obligations to repay borrowed funds). Outflows, which include trade deficits and financial outflows (including the repayment of past debts), are recorded as debits. Figure 4.1 divides the balance of payments into four categories: the *military balance,* including US military expenditures overseas and revenues from foreign military sales; the *current account,* including trade in goods and services and income on US overseas investments; flows of *long-term or investment capital,* usually investments with maturities of more than one year; and flows of *short-term,* or *liquid, capital,* also known as "hot money."

In the Pax Americana's heyday, which endured into the early 1960s, annual current-account surpluses nearly balanced US military spending overseas and outflows of investment; regular emissions of monetary gold offset the small deficits that resulted. In the mid-1960s, this near-equilibrium started to unravel. The current-account surplus deteriorated beginning in 1964–65 (so precipitously, in fact, that the United States in 1971 ran its first trade deficit since 1893). US military spending overseas, meanwhile, remained a consistent drain on the payments balance. International flows of short-term capital became in the late 1960s the most dynamic element in the overall balance of payments. These flows masked—but did not resolve—the long-term deterioration in the US balance-of-payments position—the root cause of the monetary instability with

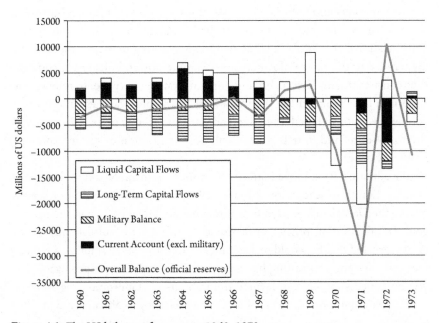

Figure 4.1 The US balance of payments, 1960–1973
Source: White House, *Economic Report of the President* (1974).

which the Nixon administration, and Paul Volcker in particular, would have to grapple.

In March 1969, Volcker envisaged two options. First, the United States could pursue a gradual reform agenda, the goals of which would include dollar devaluation to boost the US trade balance; rapid activation of IMF Special Drawing Rights (SDRs), the international reserve asset that the Johnson administration had hoped would ease the strain on the dollar; and achievement of "a more satisfactory NATO offset" to reimburse the costs of stationing military forces in Europe. Volcker's second, more radical idea envisaged slamming the gold window closed in order to relieve the United States of the burdens of dollar convertibility. Such a move would disrupt—if not forsake—the hegemonic responsibilities that the United States had exercised for a quarter century. For his part, Volcker recommended persevering with gradualism for another year or so. Thereafter, if the West Europeans and the Japanese remained unreceptive to US calls for dollar devaluation and other reforms to improve the US payments balance, the United States would have to "resign" itself to an inevitable "suspension of convertibility."[6]

However monetary reform was achieved, its purpose would be to shift the burdens of adjustment from the United States to its allies and trading partners. The parallels with the Nixon Doctrine were obvious, and dollar devaluation was the key to the whole concept. By reducing the value of the dollar, the Nixon administration would improve the competitiveness of American goods in world markets and increase the costs of foreign goods at home. Improving the US balance of trade promised to bring stability to international monetary relations, at least for a while, while invigorating domestic manufacturing, crucial to the future of American economic power. Volcker's agenda was thus consistent with Nixon's broader foreign strategic purpose: to reinvigorate American leadership within the framework of the postwar Pax Americana. If cooperative reform failed, the Nixon administration was prepared to collapse Bretton Woods and initiate a wholesale reconfiguration of the international monetary order.

The administration moved quickly to promote reform. Nixon took the lead, assuring European leaders on a March 1969 tour that he would not seek to restore the US balance of payments through a unilateral change in the price of gold. Devaluation, in other words, would be negotiated multilaterally. Nixon even suggested that he would make domestic adjustments to stabilize an unruly monetary system, contrasting his fiscal probity with Johnson's profligacy. This was no concession—Nixon favored domestic fiscal stabilization regardless of the international consequences—but it was a useful sop as Nixon urged his allies to join him in a push for rapid SDR activation, which would, US officials reasoned, ease the strains on the dollar.

Despite this early flurry of multilateralism, divergent national interests and systemic constraints circumscribed the opportunities for achieving multilateral monetary reform. West Germany and Japan, both beneficiaries of undervalued currencies, were reluctant to revalue, and the Bretton Woods system contained no incentives that could compel them to do so. The United States could close the gold window, but doing this might bring down the entire system. Having ruled that option out for the time being, American officials could only resort to the diplomacy of persuasion. But, even as the Nixon administration was urging reform, some of its actions were making that reform less plausible. More influenced by free-market ideology than its predecessor, the Nixon administration removed LBJ-era controls on foreign direct investment by American corporations. Absent a significant realignment of exchange rates, the relaxation of capital controls exacerbated the US balance of payments deficit, further diminishing confidence in the dollar. The administration's deeds, if not yet its words, suggested that the multilateralism of the 1960s, by which governments had collaborated to preserve Bretton Woods, was passing.[7]

Within months, the Nixon administration faced a speculative crisis that centered on the Deutschmark. In May 1969, short-term capital began to flee weaker European currencies, fearing devaluation in France (after de Gaulle's departure from the presidency) and scenting profit in the event of a Deutschmark revaluation. A rapid Deutschmark revaluation would have halted the influx—and achieved an effective devaluation of the dollar—but the United States could not command German action; even attempting to do so, Henry Kissinger warned, would have "highly sensitive foreign policy implications." Instead, US officials would have to accept Germany's refusal to revalue "as an accomplished fact for the time being." A devaluation of the franc in August would calm the crisis (for a few weeks), but the turmoil in May 1969 indicated both the inability of outsiders to compel revaluation and the urgency of monetary reform.[8]

It was in this context of mounting instability—as "the certainty of renewed crises" loomed—that Nixon's cabinet met in June to define an international monetary policy. Volcker's planning group now presented three options, two of which echoed his March recommendations. The first envisaged gradual reform aimed at a realignment of exchange rates. The second option was a unilateral suspension of dollar convertibility. This "would reduce gold losses, [and] stimulate favorable currency realignment." But it would also disrupt the world economy and spew toxic political fallout. The third option was, by Volcker's own admission, a nonstarter. It involved increasing the official price of gold, a technical move that would achieve nominal dollar devaluation. The problem with this approach was political. Devaluing the dollar against gold—as opposed to revaluing foreign currencies against the dollar—would punish those loyal allies who had held onto their dollar reserves, especially Japan, Canada, and West Germany, while rewarding those, namely France, that had converted dollars into gold. Reluctant to act preemptively, Nixon endorsed Volcker's original recommendation and adopted the gradualist approach that depended on foreign revaluations as administration policy.[9]

∽∾

Although the Nixon administration had committed itself to reform, it would not sacrifice rival objectives to stabilize the international monetary system. Even Volcker insisted that the balance of payments could not justify reductions in military spending. On the contrary, liberating "foreign policy from constraints imposed by weaknesses in the financial system" would be a "basic aim" of US monetary policy. Favoring regulatory liberalization, the Nixon administration also dismantled some of the deficit-control measures implemented by JFK and LBJ. Capital controls were relaxed further in the fall, and the expectation that recipients of development aid make purchases in the United States was abandoned. These steps were not taken without internal dissent. Pro-business officials argued that capital controls were "unpopular with our own business community," but the NSC and the State Department opposed their removal, arguing that dismantling capital controls would jeopardize the stability of the international monetary order and even of the Western Alliance. For the most part, the internationalists lost. With US policymakers unwilling to cede rival priorities to sustain the international monetary order, the framework of multilateral cooperation deteriorated.[10]

As the United States retreated from the collaborative maintenance of Bretton Woods, it became clear that the Nixon administration accepted Volcker's second option—the suspension of gold-dollar convertibility—as a plausible alternative to gradualist reform. After all, the administration's relaxation of controls suggested that, unless America's trading partners revalued their currencies, the United States would do nothing to prevent Bretton Woods from imploding. US policy under Nixon was from the outset less oriented to the preservation of the postwar international economic order than it had been under Kennedy and Johnson. The fate of Bretton Woods would, as a result, rest with America's allies. Still, it does not follow that the Nixon administration sought from the outset to demolish Bretton Woods and establish an alternative international monetary order. Rather, Nixon was fixated on renewing national prosperity and paid little regard to the consequences for the international monetary system.

In the fall of 1969, another speculative crisis demonstrated the fragility of existing institutional arrangements and the disruptive power of transnational finance. Again, West Germany was at the center of the storm; this time, the cause of the crisis was the politicization of the Deutschmark's exchange rate in the run-up to the September election. Foreign capital was flowing into West

Germany from investors anticipating quick profits if the Social Democrats, whose economics minister, Karl Schiller, favored revaluation, won the election. The Euromarkets facilitated this speculative assault, as the "avalanche effect" in the offshore markets increased "the flow of hot money." The financial influx was large enough to force the closure of the foreign exchanges, and it soon prompted even more radical experiments. After Willy Brandt led the Social Democrats to electoral victory, ensuring that Schiller would remain as the economics minister, Bonn floated the Deutschmark. West Germany thus abandoned its efforts to maintain the Deutschmark's exchange rate and instead permitted market forces to determine its value, at least on a temporary basis. The maneuver was intended to reestablish the Deutschmark at a new parity more in line with market pressures, and it produced a 6 percent revaluation. The episode came to what was, from the US standpoint, a salutary conclusion. But events in 1969 also affirmed the rising power of financial globalization.[11]

After September 1969, there were no major currency crises for eighteen months. Still, the respite resolved neither the underlying balance of payments problems facing the United States nor the question of how an international economic system organized around an overvalued dollar could endure. The calls for reform did not abate, however. Speaking to the IMF in the fall of 1970, French President Georges Pompidou set his sights on the dollar, calling for a concerted stabilization effort. "A currency that aims to play an international role," he declared, "must obviously be of a highly fixed nature." "None of you," Pompidou continued, "would agree to set his watch by a time that was out of order."[12]

The Nixon administration, meanwhile, fretted that the dollar's overvaluation was damaging not only US economic prospects but also the domestic political prospects of American internationalism. The travails of American industry, officials worried, were stirring trade protectionism in Congress. Should Congress pass restrictive trade legislation, the international repercussions could be catastrophic. "It would replicate the 1930s," exclaimed C. Fred Bergsten, the NSC staff economist. "We may be on the verge of a trade war with Europe and Japan," Henry Kissinger feared. Improving the terms of trade via dollar devaluation would at least assuage the protectionist menace in Congress. By reinvigorating the US economy and quieting the rising domestic clamor for trade protectionism, Nixon's economic nationalism—manifested in his quest for dollar devaluation—would serve internationalist purposes.[13]

Early in 1971, a personnel change within the administration prefigured this nationalist thrust in economic policy. That February, Nixon appointed John Connally as his new treasury secretary, replacing the self-effacing David Kennedy. Connally took the helm at Treasury as someone who knew "virtually nothing" about finance but who "understood that economics was political economics." A three-time Texas governor and protégé of Lyndon Johnson, Connally abandoned the Democratic Party to join the administration of Richard Nixon, with whom he developed a rapport so remarkable that White House staffers referred to it as "the president falling in love." Nixon conferred on Connally singular responsibility in international economics. "The Connally 1-man responsibility route is the best," Nixon wrote. "He should be the lead man."[14]

Connally's influence fast eclipsed that of Pete Peterson. An effective mediator, Peterson had worked to coordinate bureaucratic interests and had developed a good working relationship with Henry Kissinger. Connally, by contrast, aimed to focus control over international monetary policy within the Treasury Department, which marginalized alternative perspectives, especially those more attuned than his to diplomatic niceties. Connally was an economic nationalist, a man who did not believe the United States should sacrifice its commercial interests to its strategic alliances. "The philosophy of the Nixon Doctrine," he insisted, "has real meaning in economic terms too", or, more bluntly, "The foreigners are out to screw us. It's our job to screw them first."[15]

The End of Bretton Woods

The Nixon administration's choices had consequences, but large-scale historical changes conditioned the breakdown of Bretton Woods. Changes in the distribution of international economic power destabilized a monetary order configured around American predominance. Changes in the balance of power between nation-states and nonstate actors—banks, investors, and corporations—put pressure on the old structure, precipitating its collapse. Still, the end of Bretton Woods should not be understood as the result of structural changes in which human agents played no meaningful role. Experiences, beliefs, and interests shaped decision-makers' ideas about how the United States should respond to the crisis of the Bretton Woods system, determining their choices in the moment of upheaval.

Few, if any, policymakers saw beyond Bretton Woods. The transition during the 1970s from a world of capital controls and fixed exchange rates to a world of flexible exchange rates and financial deregulation did not mark a self-conscious choice; rather, the ascent of finance and the retreat of state power was the work of unintended consequences, not intelligent design. What Nixon and Connally sought in 1971 was not the liberation of financial markets from government control but a dollar devaluation that would improve the trade balance, put Americans back to work, and enhance Nixon's prospects for reelection. If Nixon played a decisive role in the historical ascent of financial globalization, his agency was less purposeful than ironic. Amid a crisis of the international monetary order, Nixon's economic nationalism may have foreclosed on opportunities to sustain

Bretton Woods through enhanced multilateral cooperation, ensuring that the dollar crisis of 1971–73 would be not a hiccup but a decisive rupture.

Still, the rise of transnational finance did not follow upon the collapse of the old fixed-exchange-rate regime. Instead, financial globalization antedated the end of Bretton Woods and contributed to its downfall—after a two-year phase in which transnational financial flows sustained the dollar and, with it, the faltering international monetary order. In March 1968, LBJ accepted the need for fiscal restraint and monetary tightening to calm an overheated economy and tame inflationary pressures. These decisions had important consequences for the dollar's international position. As US interest rates inched above those available to money holders in Western Europe, dollar-denominated securities became more attractive to investors. A westward movement of short-term funds across the Atlantic ensued, as figure 4.2 indicates, buttressing the US balance of payments and offsetting the outflows of long-term investment capital as well as the costs of American military spending overseas, especially in Vietnam.

Throughout 1969–70, high interest rates at home sustained an influx of short-term capital to the United States, subverting the logic of an international monetary system that had been designed to limit the destabilizing impact of transnational financial flows. But with London-based banks taking in billions of dollars in deposits and creating many billions more in credit, the US government no longer exercised full control over the dollar. Still, the influx was for now

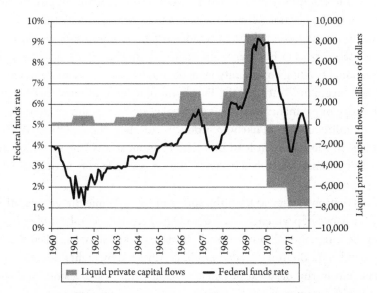

Figure 4.2 Interest rates and short-term financial flows, 1960–1972
Sources: IMF, *International Financial Statistics*; and White House, *Economic Report of the President* (1974).

beneficial. "Without the inflow of Eurodollars," concluded one analyst, "the United States would have had an enormous deficit on an official reserve basis."

The balance-of-payments data bear out the point. The scale of the Eurodollar influx can be gauged by comparing the official-reserves balance and the net-liquidity balance. These are alternative measures of the balance of payments: the first balance includes private short-term debts; the second balance does not. For 1969, the two positions revealed a $2.7 billion surplus and a $6.1 billion deficit. The difference was an influx of some $8.8 billion in mobile capital into the United States. As the source of these short-term funds, the Euromarkets enabled the United States to balance its international payments through international borrowing. The consequences of this capital influx into the United States showed up in the Euromarkets, where the rate on three-month funds increased from 7 percent to 11 percent during 1969. By March 1970, the Eurodollar liabilities of American banks approached $25 billion. This accumulation of short-term debt sustained the US balance of payments, but it contained disruptive potential. What would happen when the capital influx stopped? What if it reversed?[16]

The stability of the monetary system at the beginning of the Nixon era thus depended on American interest rates staying high and West European monetary policies running in the opposite direction. It was clear to Nixon's most perceptive advisers, however, that a "very precarious" US balance of payments position was being sustained by "an abnormal inflow of foreign capital." The unusual situation endured until early 1970, when Arthur Burns, Nixon's appointee as the chairman of the Federal Reserve Bank, began to relax the Fed's tight monetary stance. As Burns loosened credit, holders of short-term funds began to seek better interest rates in European currencies. By summer 1970, observers in the international banking community were beginning to warn of an imminent dollar crisis. Siegmund Warburg, the Eurobond pioneer, cautioned that persistent US balance of payments deficits, "exacerbated by that country's overseas military commitments," were likely to produce "currency uncertainties." What was "striking" in the eyes of at least one IMF economist was "the extent to which Euro-dollar transactions" had become "the key swing factor" in the US balance of payments.[17]

The situation worsened from the spring of 1971. While the deterioration in the US balance of payments over a decade had created a combustible situation, it was the international movement of short-term capital that sparked the crisis that would send Bretton Woods tumbling. Attracted by higher interest rates in Europe and fearful of dollar devaluation, dollar holders, investors, and speculators in the summer of 1971 presented dollars to European central banks for conversion into local currencies. As European central banks accumulated dollars they did not want to hold, White House analysts described a "tidal wave" of money fleeing the dollar. The dollar's free fall was not just an American dilemma; it fast became an international controversy.[18]

Interdependence cuts in multiple directions, and the strong-currency countries were no less affected by the dollar's tumult than the United States. As the major destination for short-term funds, West Germany was particularly vulnerable. To slow the influx of dollars—and to stem the inflationary consequences thereof—German leaders, in May 1971, abandoned their efforts to maintain a stable exchange mark for the Deutschmark and made recourse, once again, to floating. Other strong-currency countries followed suit. The Netherlands joined the German float, while Switzerland and Austria revalued their currencies in an effort to stave off the "tremendous inflow" of dollars. Ottmar Emminger, a Bundesbank vice-president, exclaimed that "the Eurodollar market has a lot to do with the undermining of monetary autonomy." US government analysts concurred. The "tremendous growth of international business and banking, with accompanying expansion of Eurodollar volume," one official wrote, "has provided a basis for businessmen to shift huge quantities of dollars across national borders very quickly."[19]

But if the Euromarkets provided the mechanism for transmitting disorder, they were not themselves the ultimate source of instability. Rather, financial-market integration was exposing what economist Maurice Obstfeld calls the "trilemma" of international monetary economics. This hypothesis holds that no monetary order can simultaneously accommodate open capital markets, fixed exchange rates, and national-policy autonomy. The most that any institutional solution can deliver is two of the three. Bretton Woods had sought to ensure fixed exchange rates and national-policy autonomy at the expense of open capital markets, but financial globalization made Bretton Woods ever-more unworkable, much as the trilemma predicts. In the moment of crisis, however, decision-makers on both sides of the Atlantic were less concerned with reestablishing monetary order on stable theoretical foundations than with muddling through, which they hoped a de facto dollar devaluation might allow them to do.[20]

The West European floats of May 1971 reduced the dollar's effective exchange rate by around 2.5 percent; but, with Japan unwilling to revalue the yen, this was not enough to reverse US trade deficits. With market forces unable to produce a sufficient dollar devaluation, Secretary Connally traveled to Europe to demand further redistribution of economic burdens. The problem, he explained to Valéry Giscard d'Estaing, France's minister of finance, was that the burden of responsibilities within the Western Alliance no longer followed the distribution of wealth and economic power. "Twenty years ago," Connally explained, "we were relatively rich in productive capacity and reserves, but this is no longer the case." "Basic trade adjustments," he continued, were now necessary to reduce the burdens on the United States. The entreaties failed to produce a French revaluation to accompany the Deutschmark float; Connelly had not cowed Giscard, who insisted that "the route of revaluation is closed."[21]

Meanwhile, the dollar's turmoil was attracting growing scrutiny inside the United States. Members of Congress called for a "full-scale investigation" of international monetary arrangements, even the formal adjustment of "parity relationships among currencies." In early August 1971, Henry Reuss, the chair of the House Subcommittee on International Payments, unleashed a firestorm when he suggested that the United States abrogate its commitment to convert dollars into gold at the $35 per ounce price. Reuss argued that orthodox balance-of-payments methods could no longer mitigate the fundamental overvaluation of the dollar. The United States, he concluded, would have to abandon gold in order to precipitate more far-reaching reform. It was a radical idea, but Reuss's objective was to strengthen the Bretton Woods system, not to explode it. Like Ottmar Emminger, Reuss argued that financial globalization—the "huge size" of the unregulated, offshore capital markets—was responsible for the present instability, and he favored "cooperation among monetary authorities to discourage or neutralize massive international transfers of liquid assets." Washington, the congressman proposed, should promote "cooperative monetary policy tools for managing Euro-dollar flows," and fixed exchange rates should remain, in principle, the foundation of international monetary order.[22]

Nor did Nixon's treasury secretary welcome the disruptive specter of massive, uncontrolled financial flows. "We do not like to see $50 billion in the Eurodollar market with no controls," Connally proclaimed. "Enormous short-term money flows," he warned, threatened "the system of fixed exchange rates and freely convertible currencies" that had nurtured postwar growth. Vigorous action was needed, Connally argued, to bring this "clear and present danger to our monetary system" under control. Connally favored keeping transnational capital subject to political discipline, as Bretton Woods had done, but the centerpiece of his reform agenda was rehabiliting America's wealth and economic power. Realigning exchange rates to devalue the dollar would bolster US industry and US exports, thereby easing the strains on the international monetary order. If unilateral closure of the gold window were necessary to achieve this adjustment, Connally was willing to countenance the unthinkable.[23]

⸎

On August 13, 1971, President Nixon and a group of cabinet officials, economic advisers, and political aides left the capital. Upon their arrival at Camp David, the presidential retreat, Nixon ushered his guests towards the visitors' book, indicating that they should sign their names to commemorate "the historic nature of the meeting," and he prohibited use of the telephone, lest it compromise the confidentiality of the discussions. Herbert Stein, representing the Council of

Economic Advisers, speculated, "This could be the most important weekend in the history of economics since 1933."[24]

The Camp David summit resulted in the approval of three emergency initiatives. First, the administration would impose a 10 percent surcharge on imports into the United States. Second, it would establish a system of formal wage-price controls to limit increases in consumer prices and workers' wages, thereby restraining inflation across the US economy. Third, it would slam the gold window shut, meaning that the dollar would no longer be convertible to gold. Together, these measures would create a new US policy, the New Economic Policy, an unintended nod to Lenin. Its public announcement on Sunday, August 15, would be "brutal and effective." Nixon compared his administration's New Economic Policy to its "opening" of China. (In Japan, these episodes would be memorialized as the Nixon *shokku* (shocks), a low point in postwar relations.)[25]

Nixon fancied himself a decisive president, but market circumstances had in fact determined the timing of the Camp David summit. The Treasury had announced on August 7 that the United States had recently sustained gold-reserve losses of more than $1 billion, news that increased the likelihood of further official gold conversions. Rumors in early August alleged that the Bank of England was asking the US Treasury to "cover" $3 billion of its dollar holdings. Whether true or not—British officials denied it—the United States faced an imminent dollar crisis. To thwart it, Nixon implemented his game plan and closed the gold window. Together with the import surcharge, this action promised to arrest the drain on US gold reserves and provide Washington with a lever—the import surcharge—to compel its trading partners to accept American demands. Nixon demonstrated little interest in the economic intricacies of the package, but he was aware of its political potency and its implications for the allies. "We have price freeze and some of that crap," Nixon told Henry Kissinger. "It will shake them." If the bullish defense of American economic interests reflected Nixon's priorities, credit for the emergency package went to the treasury secretary. "Connally was the big wheel on this," Nixon explained. "He did a hell of a job."[26]

Remarkably, the Camp David participants did not include a single foreign-policy specialist. Arthur Burns, one of the few orthodox internationalists in the room, trembled at the Nixon administration's contempt for diplomatic niceties. Since the late 1940s, after all, the United States had largely deferred its economic self-interests to those of its allies, accepting foreign protectionism and an overvalued dollar as the price that had to be paid for the cohesion of the Western Alliance. The New Economic Policy signaled a radical reversal in priorities. With Connally determined to "screw" the competition, "the major foreign policy implications" of Nixon's economic demarche, as the NSC put it, could not be disregarded.[27]

The European stock markets crashed on Nixon's announcement, and the dollar plummeted, increasing the price of European exports in the United States and giving US-made products a competitive edge in world markets. The overseas reaction was hostile. While foreign exporters lamented the import surcharge, friendly governments were aghast at the unilateral nature of the decision. Some denounced the administration's "big stick" diplomacy. Still, more sober analysts recognized the New Economic Policy as a temporary expedient with a diplomatic purpose. The British Cabinet Office staff concluded that US actions were "designed to shock the other countries" into accepting exchange-rate changes. Robert Hormats, Kissinger's staff economist, described the surcharge as "a bargaining lever to get other countries to revalue their currencies." Nixon corroborated this analysis, acknowledging, in private, that one purpose of the New Economic Policy was to force a reconfiguration of the economic relationship between the United States and its allies, in particular, Japan. "We have done everything for them and they have done nothing for us," he explained. "Now they will have to come to us for a few things."[28]

The purpose of the new policy was to bring about a dollar devaluation that would benefit American exporters and manufacturers. Yet the pursuit of monetary recalibration through unilateral action was closely linked to Nixon's broader agenda for reinvigorating American power. Only by ignoring the administration's larger foreign-policy agenda is it possible to see the New Economic Policy as a retreat from internationalism. The Nixon administration, moreover, remained committed to "an essentially free trade policy." What it sought in the summer of 1971 was the historical rejuvenation of US economic capabilities. Dollar devaluation, Nixon believed, could reverse the nation's relative economic decline. With a quick recalibration of exchange rates, exports and industrial production would be invigorated, and primacy sustained. The revitalization of national economic power and the sustenance of American leadership in the Cold War world were interwoven objectives.[29]

Beyond changing the terms of trade to benefit the United States, Nixon hoped to eliminate the recurrent balance-of-payments crises that had since the mid-1960s constrained the projection of US military power and irritated intra-alliance relations. Nixon was determined not to let monetary instability jeopardize his grand foreign-policy architecture. "I do not want to be bothered with international monetary affairs," he wrote in 1970. Yet the balance of payments could not be ignored; it exercised "constraints on both our domestic economic policy and our foreign policy." Determined to minimize the constraints, Nixon and his foreign-policy advisers understood the relationship between monetary economics and foreign policy as a negative linkage, in which currency crises sometimes intruded upon more important priorities.[30]

Nixon's response to the upheavals of Bretton Woods thus reflected both his commitment to Cold War internationalism and his belief that American vigor remained the bedrock of international order. What he sought through the instrument of his treasury secretary was a bold adjustment of currency parities that would make the dollar competitive and stabilize Bretton Woods. If Connally had to knock a few European heads in the process, neither he nor Nixon would be unduly concerned. Indeed, the treasury secretary relished the role of strongman. "I will plead guilty to speaking in plain words as directly as I can," Connally declared.[31]

Connally spoke for Nixon, but dissenting voices murmured. Outside government, business lobbyists urged the removal of remaining LBJ-era capital controls, even though such action would worsen the balance-of-payments situation. Neoliberal economists, meanwhile, argued for floating exchange rates as a permanent solution that would permit financial globalization to coexist with domestic monetary autonomy, allowing financial markets to determine the values of currencies on a permanent basis. Paul McCracken, the chair of the Council of Economic Advisers and an enthusiast of floating exchange rates, warned that "a system that combines rigidly fixed exchange rates with free trade and capital movements appears to be unworkable." He argued instead for a "system of greater flexibility." McCracken favored abandoning the Bretton Woods regulated currency system and adopting in its place a system of floating exchange rates that could facilitate the liberation of the capital markets from regulatory controls, something Milton Friedman, a leading neoliberal economist, had been advocating since the early 1950s.[32]

The influence of the neoliberals expanded under Nixon, who in 1968 had assured Friedman of his conviction that "the imposition of arbitrary controls is harmful to our Nation's long range interests." The avowal might suggest that the New Economic Policy emerged out of Nixon's distrust for regulated capitalism and his desire to explode existing arrangements in pursuit of market liberation. Such a verdict would, however, obscure divisions within the administration, blurring the distinction between Connally and the neoliberals. The treasury secretary preferred stable currencies and took "vigorous personal exception" to McCracken's advocacy of floating. While Connally embraced a temporary float to achieve dollar devaluation, he did not view exchange-rate flexibility as an acceptable long-term destination. To put it simply, Connally was reluctant to relinquish control over the monetary order to market forces. This position was substantively different from that of the neoliberals, who aimed to release global finance from the bondage of a state-centric monetary order. For now, Nixon sided with his treasury secretary.[33]

Nixon and Connally closed the gold window in summer 1971 in order to provoke a crisis in the Bretton Woods system that they believed would create the political leverage that would enable the United States to secure the dollar devaluation that its allies would not willingly grant. This was a profound tactical miscalculation. Already prone to instability, the Bretton Woods system could be preserved only through extensive international coordination to counteract the disruptive influence of short-term capital flows. As financial interdependence accelerated, monetary coordination among governments would have to expand in parallel if the monetary system was to be preserved. Yet, after the unilateralism of August 1971, Nixon and Connally could not expect their allies to collaborate with them in a thoroughgoing defense of the status quo. The Nixon Shock of August 1971, as the episode came to be called, thereby precipitated the breakdown of Bretton Woods.

⌒∞⌒

During the fall of 1971, the conditions under which Washington would restore fixed exchange rates and dollar convertibility became the key question in US foreign economic policy. The answer came to hinge on a struggle between Connally and the foreign-policy bureaucracy led by Henry Kissinger. Connally was determined to hold out for European and Japanese revaluations as large as he could get. He was also reluctant to devalue the dollar against gold as a quid pro quo. Kissinger, on the other hand, was concerned that a protracted struggle over exchange rates would inflict major damage on the Western Alliance. As Connally's dogged pursuit of national advantage ground into diplomatic stalemate, Kissinger worked to steer the administration's monetary diplomacy in more flexible directions. The future of the Bretton Woods system thus came to depend on the outcome of a bureaucratic turf war. The question was whether Washington would hold out for maximal national advantage, as Connally wanted, or seek a rapid and amicable return to the status quo, as Kissinger preferred.[34]

Administration officials made it clear that they sought to adjust, not abandon, Bretton Woods. Indeed, Paul Volcker quickly reassured his European counterparts that the United States remained committed to the "basic principle" of fixed parities. What the United States sought, Volcker explained, was a "fundamental strengthening of our position" that would help to restore "a stable sustainable system." To achieve this, Western Europe and Japan would need to allow the United States to enjoy "a period of surplus" in its international balance of payments. Still, international agreement on a new matrix of exchange rates was not forthcoming. The September 1971 meeting of the Group of Ten (G-10) advanced industrial nations failed to produce an agreement on dollar devaluation. European participants in the meeting argued that the Nixon administration's adjustment goals were too ambitious. They also demanded, as a precondition of any agreement, that the United States abandon the import surcharge and commit to devaluing the dollar against gold, concessions Nixon and Connally were not willing to grant, despite Kissinger's warnings that the impasse was wrecking damage on the alliance.[35]

The diplomats in the administration bristled at what they saw as Connally's obstructionism. At the NSC, Hormats warned that the "long-term retention of the surcharge can be extremely detrimental to our interests." Kissinger smarted at the treasury secretary's obstinacy, proclaiming to Pete Peterson that he would "take on Connally." Peterson, despite his own preoccupation with national economic renewal, nonetheless aligned with Kissinger on the issue. Kissinger even sought to enlist John McCloy, one of the early architects of the Atlantic Alliance, as a "counter to Connally." "We are heading for a catastrophe in Europe," Kissinger warned McCloy. "We can't throw away twenty-five years of what has been built up for Treasury reasons." Committed to Western unity, Kissinger maneuvered throughout the fall of 1971 to arrange a series of summits between Nixon and the West European heads of government, anticipating that personal diplomacy might resolve the crisis within the alliance. With France's "inflexible position" on dollar devaluation the "principal obstacle" to a settlement, Nixon's meeting with President Georges Pompidou in the Azores in December would be decisive.[36]

In late November, Nixon decided that the United States would have to make some change in the gold-dollar exchange rate as a concession to his negotiating partners. Devaluing the dollar against gold would reward France and other countries that had hoarded gold reserves, but Nixon recognized that without this concession, it would be impossible to secure a general revaluation against the dollar. Kissinger declared a quiet victory. "The political dimension has been put in," he explained. "Everyone understands basics now." At the Azores summit, Nixon and Kissinger met with Pompidou and agreed to devalue the dollar against gold in exchange for revaluation of the franc. The dollar's effective devaluation against a basket of European currencies would be about 9 percent. The two presidents assumed that their agreement would establish a basis for a larger multilateral settlement. "The extraordinary aspect of the encounter," Kissinger wrote, "was that France and the United States should have taken it upon themselves to work out the exchange rates for every one of the world's important currencies."[37]

Finance ministers from Europe, Japan, and North America met at the Smithsonian Institute in Washington at the end of December to ratify the deal Nixon and Pompidou had struck. Under the terms of the Smithsonian Agreement, the dollar was devalued against gold from $35 per ounce to $38—a devaluation of about 8 percent. Further relative devaluation was achieved through revaluations of the Deutschmark, the Japanese yen, the Swiss franc, and the Benelux currencies. The most dramatic change was in the value of the yen, which appreciated by almost 17 percent. In a minor but portentous victory for exchange-rate flexibility, the bands within which currency values were allowed to fluctuate were widened from 1 percent to 2.25 percent. The United States agreed to abolish the import surcharge.[38]

Nixon hailed the Smithsonian Agreement as "the most significant monetary agreement in the history of the world." This hyperbole oversold what had been an improvised settlement. But Nixon's satisfaction with the outcome confirms that his objectives had not included a fundamental reconfiguration of the international monetary order. Optimistic officials expected that a substantial devaluation of the dollar would stabilize the international monetary order, quell capital flight from the United States, and halt the recurrent balance-of-payments crises. Over the next fourteen months, however, the unraveling of the Smithsonian compromise would demonstrate that Nixon and Connally's elaborate game plan had failed. The dollar remained overvalued and prone to crisis. Moreover, the Smithsonian Agreement failed to insulate Bretton Woods from the increasingly disruptive effects of financial globalization.[39]

Into a New Era of Globalization

The Smithsonian Agreement affirmed that governments would continue to set the terms of the international monetary order, but the endurance of fixed exchange rates ought not to obscure the central role market forces played in the December 1971 adjustment. Once private money holders concluded that the United States was about to devalue the dollar, they converted their assets to other currencies. Foreign monetary authorities had had to absorb large dollar flows; several revalued to stave off the influxes—and the attendant inflationary consequences. As George Shultz, the secretary of labor, would point out, "U.S. officials had formed an alliance with the market itself to force a change in the behavior of foreign officials." Transnational finance thus proved a useful adjunct to national bargaining power. But hot money could not be called up, genie-like, and then forced back into the bottle. As the Euromarkets continued to grow, the capacity of short-term money flows to damage the Bretton Woods system increased. Financial globalization was transforming the international economic arena in ways that made the restoration of currency stability over the long-term improbable. Globalization—and how to deal with it—also became a topic of growing disagreement within the Nixon administration.[40]

As 1972 began, the divide between the proponents of national advantage and the partisans of liberalization widened. Neither camp mistook the Smithsonian Agreement for a final destination. The nationalists feared that the "trade policies of foreign countries may completely or partially negate the corrective influences of [Smithsonian] exchange rate changes." Led by Connally, they campaigned for the reduction of foreign tariff barriers. As one Treasury official saw it, "our ability to compete economically" would be "the determinant of whether the United States can continue to play an effective and constructive role in world political and economic progress." The liberalizers, meanwhile, contemplated more radical reforms. They argued that the "fundamental changes that have taken place in international monetary relationships" demanded an overhaul of the monetary system more far-reaching than the Smithsonian accord, and they favored floating exchange rates as a solution for the pervasive instability that Bretton Woods had manifested in recent years.[41]

In early spring, a personnel change at the Treasury created a more hospitable environment for the proponents of market-oriented solutions. Connally had always been something of an outlier in the administration in his willingness to leverage state power to coerce economic outcomes. His resignation in April 1972 created space for neoliberals to assert new influence. In June, George Shultz became the first economist with a PhD to serve as secretary of the treasury. In his academic career, Shultz had taught alongside Milton Friedman at the University of Chicago. Shultz's personal style was more subtle than Connally's, but his instincts were more radical. Even during the wrangling of 1971, Shultz had prevailed on Connally to endorse floating as "the basis for the new international monetary system."[42]

Upon his arrival at Treasury, Shultz was shocked to learn that no plan for thoroughgoing reform of the international monetary system existed, and he deputized Paul Volcker to create one. Shultz and Volcker devised a scheme, dubbed Plan X, which proposed to regularize adjustment by surplus countries and increase the flexibility of exchange values. Their "reserve indicator" plan would establish a range of permissible reserve levels for each country. If a country's reserve assets moved below the acceptable range, it would have to adjust, either through currency devaluation or deflation. Conversely, if a country's reserves moved above the normal range, adjustment would have to be made through revaluation or changes in domestic policy. Whereas the old fixed-rate system had used capital controls to limit the domestic consequences of monetary imbalances, Shultz preferred frequent—even perpetual—changes in exchange rates, believing that American interests would be best served by a system that "facilitated international trade and capital flows" and "involved a minimum of governmental restraints." Besides legalizing floating as a mechanism of adjustment, Plan X would neuter the ability of governments to intervene in the foreign-exchange markets to defend official currency values against currency speculators. Shultz, to put it succinctly, proposed to limit the control of national governments over exchange rates in order to pursue the integration of financial markets—a striking departure from the axioms that had guided Bretton Woods.[43]

The logic of the Connally years was being inverted. In summer 1971, the United States had acted unilaterally to seek national advantage within a stable concept of international monetary order. Just one year later, Shultz sought to build a multilateral consensus for reform. Plan X purported to maximize the autonomy of nation-states, and herein lay its seductive—and misleading—appeal. A reformed system, Shultz argued, would "impose fewer restraints on governments" than Bretton Woods had done. But if Plan X allowed governments to decide how to adjust, it removed the choice of whether to adjust. The power to determine exchange rates would, moreover, be vested in the financial markets. This was the plan's most radical departure. Since the late 1950s, rising industrial powers, such as Japan and West Germany, had used cheap currencies to give their exporters a competitive edge. By limiting governments' control over currencies, Shultz aimed to discourage such behavior. The Shultz plan, like the Connally bludgeon, would thus serve the economic interests of the United States.[44]

Unlike Connally, Shultz proposed transforming the international monetary system to accommodate the ascent of financial globalization. Insofar as international flows of short-term capital were already circumscribing national control over currency, Shultz was merely acknowledging the evolving realities. Indeed, as Plan X was being finalized, speculation against the dollar pushed up the market price of gold to $70 per ounce (almost twice the official Smithsonian rate of $38 per ounce), making another dollar devaluation likely, even inevitable. Over the next eight months, transnational finance would wreck both the Smithsonian compromise and Shultz's plan for a managed transition to expanded international monetary flexibility.[45]

The Smithsonian parities remained fairly stable through the first half of 1972. During this period, the nations of the European Economic Community (EEC) initiated the process that would lead to the eventual merging of their monetary sovereignties. In March, the EEC's six members announced that their currencies would be tethered within a narrower band than the Smithsonian Agreement required: 2.25 percent (+/−1.125 percent) as opposed to the 4.5 percent (+/−2.25 percent) band stipulated in the agreement. The EEC currencies would thus oscillate as a group within the Smithsonian band; hence, the colloquial description of the new arrangement as the "snake in the tunnel." In the short term, however, the European experiment with regional monetary coordination was no better able to curb volatility in the foreign-exchange markets than was the American flirtation with flexibility.[46]

The sterling crisis of June 1972 posed the first major challenge to the Smithsonian order. Its sources were impressionistic: a slight dip in the trade balance, the prospect that Britain's entrance into the EEC would disadvantage its industries, and the threat of a strike by public-sector unions. As confidence in the pound dwindled, money holders fled. In the third week of June, the Bank of

England lost about a third of its reserve assets. On June 23, London abandoned efforts to maintain its Smithsonian parity and allowed sterling to float. What was surprising was that speculative forces had rallied at a time "when Britain's current technical position in terms of reserves and balance of payments had been considered relatively strong." "The major culprit is short-term capital movement," concluded Kissinger's staff. The sterling crisis revealed the vulnerability of the Smithsonian parities to assault from speculators. Even the perception of overvaluation could produce a monetary avalanche that would make the original diagnosis a self-fulfilling prophecy. "This latest episode," Nixon wrote to Britain's prime minister, Edward Heath, "illustrates the need for fundamental changes in the monetary framework."[47]

Besides highlighting the need for reform, the 1972 sterling crisis raised the specter of a broader financial crisis. The influx of capital from Britain to continental Europe forced the closure of EEC currency markets on June 26. When the exchanges reopened, speculation resumed—this time against the dollar—as "massive flows of funds [moved] into various European countries and Japan," amounting to $6 billion in two weeks. EEC finance ministers contemplated a joint float against the dollar—a move that would have broken the fixed-exchange-rate regime. Neoliberals in the United States relished the prospect. But with French officials still attached to fixed rates, the snake outside the tunnel was a chimera. The movement of short-term capital into Germany continued, to the frustration of German officials, who lamented the "very bad internal effect" of international capital flows, especially for inflation. Absent floating, controls and barriers beckoned. Finance minister Helmut Schmidt warned Kissinger that unless the United States intervened in the foreign-exchange markets to defend the dollar's Smithsonian exchange rate, the Federal Republic would "immediately" shut down the influx of hot money by imposing strict restrictions on capital imports and trade.[48]

As they had in the fall of 1971, Kissinger and Arthur Burns lobbied for cooperation. Burns persuaded Shultz to allow the Federal Reserve to intervene in the money markets to support the dollar, which led to the reopening in July 1972 of the swap network that had closed in August 1971. Foreign-exchange operations quickly stabilized the dollar, and Kissinger and Burns commended Shultz's pragmatism. Both had feared that the economist would be "too doctrinaire." But if in the summer of 1972 the treasury secretary's pragmatism countermanded his preferences, Shultz would not commit to a permanent defense of the Smithsonian order. Following July's successful intervention, the chief market operator at the New York Federal Reserve Bank received a telephone call from Treasury ordering the bank to suspend "all further market operations." The dollar improved in August, but in the absence of a Treasury Department commitment to defend existing exchange rates, the long-term stability of the international monetary order remained contingent on "tranquility in money markets." Meanwhile, the long-term future of international monetary relations was being rewritten, under George Shultz's direction.[49]

Nixon, for his part, remained largely indifferent to his administration's monetary maneuverings. Preoccupied that summer with superpower summits and the quest for a settlement in Vietnam, the president's response had been curt when the Federal Reserve warned that the sterling float "could lead to speculation against the Italian lira." "I don't give a shit about the lira," Nixon retorted. Even after successfully negotiating the Smithsonian Agreement, Nixon remained uninterested in international economic policy. His overriding objectives remained consistent: national economic renewal and the eradication of monetary crises. But with the monetary system in crisis in summer 1972, it was clear to Nixon—and to Kissinger—that their political purposes now warranted monetary reform. "We can't afford a blow up in the monetary area," Kissinger warned in July. "Without reform there will be a blow up." When Shultz presented exchange-rate flexibility, even floating exchange rates, as a panacea for monetary disorder, the president joined the bandwagon.[50]

The president's opening remarks to the IMF and World Bank governors meeting in Washington in September 1972 dwelt on the relationship between international economic and political stability. "Unfair currency alignments and trading arrangements," Nixon declared, "put the workers of one nation at a disadvantage with workers of another nation." The US trade deficit, he argued, undermined the economic bases of American internationalism; balance-of-payments deficits rendered the United States unable to finance its expansive global military operations, while the closing of American factories and the loss of American jobs augured resurgent isolationism. These concerns underscored the basic continuity in Nixon's strategic purposes, transcending the transition from Connally to Shultz. The president's priority remained restoring America's global leadership. His purpose in seeking monetary reform, Nixon affirmed, was to ensure that the American people would be able—and willing—to bear the Pax Americana's costs into the future.[51]

If John Connally had been a blunt and brutal instrument in the quest for monetary adjustment, George Shultz was a conciliator whose understated style belied his radical agenda. In presenting Plan X to the world, Shultz explained that the United States was no longer interested in merely adjusting parities within the Bretton Woods paradigm. Rather, Washington sought a reevaluation of the balance between government and the market: "The new balance of which I speak does not confine itself to the concepts of a balance of trade or a balance of payments. The world needs a new balance between flexibility and stability." Shultz insisted that all nations shared a "mutual interest in encouraging the flow of capital to the places where it can contribute most to growth." This marked the departure from Bretton Woods, which had allowed states to maintain barriers to financial flows. Removing capital controls challenged the logic of regulated capitalism that had underwritten Bretton Woods, but this was precisely Shultz's purpose. To accommodate transnational finance, Shultz embraced exchange-rate flexibility.[52]

Shultz insisted on the need to transcend outdated institutions, but his was not the only conceivable reform agenda. Although the rise of integrated capital markets had eroded the stability of Bretton Woods since the mid-1960s, in 1972, many officials still believed that the old order of fixed exchange rates could be preserved. Charles Coombs at the Federal Reserve Bank of New York, for example, insisted that multilateral intervention in foreign-exchange markets could sustain the system of managed currencies, as coordinated intervention had done in the crisis of July 1972. Arthur Burns was skeptical of Shultz's plan to unfetter finance, and even Paul Volcker, the draftsman of Plan X, regarded Shultz's monetarist utopia with skepticism. Meanwhile, the IMF's Committee of Twenty (C-20), the body charged with reforming the monetary system, was already asking how multilateral surveillance of offshore capital markets might be expanded, an approach that pointed toward the reinforcement of the regulated international monetary order, not its abandonment.[53]

What Shultz's Plan X offered was an evolutionary roadmap to a radical destination. The treasury secretary acknowledged, crucially, that most countries wanted to maintain a "fixed point of reference" for their currencies in the short-term, even as he pointed toward flexibility as a long-term goal. His willingness to compromise was met with a palpable "sense of relief" on the part of foreign delegates, who were reassured that the United States had "decided to resume a position of leadership in monetary affairs." Of course, the viability of other nations' attempts to maintain fixed rates and exchange controls when the United States was committed to neither would be highly tenuous. But that was a concern for the future. For now, foreign officials hailed Shultz's resumption of the leadership role that Connally had abused. In late 1972, moreover, domestic economic growth and rising interest rates, which strengthened the dollar's international position, looked to be creating a propitious environment for a concerted reform effort in 1973.[54]

⁂

The dollar crisis of February 1973 began with several unrelated developments. In mid-January, the Nixon administration had announced the partial removal of the wage-price controls it had imposed in August 1971. With inflation mounting, the effect of the move was to "send a signal of indifference to both domestic and international audiences." Next, publication of official data revealed that the American trade deficit had "soared" to $6.4 billion in 1972. Meanwhile, from across the Atlantic, the lira returned to haunt Richard Nixon. In late January, the

Italian government had moved "to check its persistently large capital outflow" by introducing a floating financial lira alongside the fixed-rate lira that would still to be used for current account transactions. The move triggered an immediate deluge of funds into the Swiss franc. Fearing inflation, Switzerland floated the franc. Speculators moved next against the dollar. "Once again," observed one journalist, "the monetary storm clouds have gathered."[55]

The Bank for International Settlements (BIS) described the currency crisis of 1973 as "unfinished business left over from the upheaval of 1971." As the balance-of-payments data reveal (see figure 4.3) the Smithsonian recalibration had not reversed the underlying American trade deficit. Although intervention in the currency markets in June and domestic economic expansion had sustained confidence in the dollar throughout the second half of 1972, that confidence collapsed in early 1973, encouraging capital flight. As in the summer of 1971, transnational finance played a central role in the dollar crisis. One Treasury official explained that a net outflow of almost $6 billion in private transactions "was a major contributor to the official deficit" in the first quarter of 1973. It did not help that offshore money markets had grown since December 1971. The value of dollar deposits in the Euromarkets had increased by 37 percent during 1972, bringing total Eurodollar deposits to a staggering $98 billion—about seven-and-a-half times the total value of US reserve assets. When the dollar crisis struck, there was little that federal regulators could do to plug the levees. "We

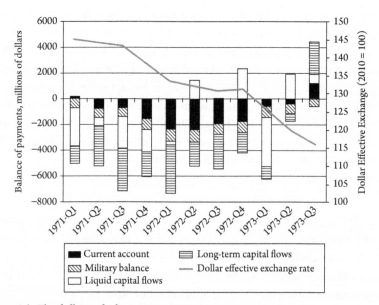

Figure 4.3 The dollar in decline, 1971–1973

Sources: BIS Statistics; and White House, *Economic Report of the President* (1974).

are reaching the point," Shultz quipped, "where aid recipients won't take aid in U.S. dollars anymore."[56]

Forced into action, the Nixon administration initiated a second dollar devaluation. Volcker departed on a 31,000-mile global odyssey, tasked with persuading West European and Japanese governments to accept another devaluation. In a series of meetings with his foreign counterparts, Volcker was able to negotiate multilateral support for another devaluation, this one even larger than the Smithsonian adjustment. His diplomacy won international plaudits and achieved rapid results. The West Europeans agreed to revalue their currencies so as to produce an effective dollar devaluation of about 10 percent, while Japan committed to floating the yen upward by 17 percent. Financial markets responded favorably to the Volcker devaluation. The dollar rose quickly to its new ceiling, and the Bundesbank was able to sell around $1 billion of the dollars it had accumulated during the February crisis.[57]

Volcker's efficient diplomacy notwithstanding, the February crisis had revealed the paucity of American commitments to defend fixed exchange rates. Shultz, in fact, used the crisis as an occasion to push the cause of financial liberalization with Nixon. When the secretary announced that the United States would seek an additional dollar devaluation, he added that Washington would remove all controls on international capital movements by "at the latest" December 31, 1974. This was a loud and unambiguous signal of indifference to exchange-rate stability. The momentum of events seemed to be with him, but Shultz's enthusiasm for financial liberalization remained distinctive, even anomalous. Most European finance ministers in early 1973 continued to endorse capital controls; many favored regulating the Euromarkets as the appropriate means to sustain "ordered relationships between exchange rates." The OECD, meanwhile, criticized floating as being destabilizing to international trade and even endorsed the creation of a European system of fixed exchange rates in the event of a breakdown in worldwide monetary stability. Nor did the administration cohere around a singular course of action. With policymakers simultaneously seeking a range of objectives—monetary reform, economic renewal, and political primacy—US policy remained contingent and contested.[58]

Volcker's devaluation lasted just over two weeks. Its effect on currency markets turned out to be "destabilizing rather than stabilizing," and speculation against the dollar resumed after a momentary interlude of calm. At the end of February, the dollar collapsed to its "lowest permissible level" under the new Volcker parities, as Frankfurt bankers received "heavy orders from all over the world to sell dollars." On March 1, the Bundesbank abandoned its efforts to maintain the Deutschmark's stable exchange rate against the dollar—after absorbing more than $2.5 billion in financial inflows. Other central banks followed suit. The new crisis indicated that speculators did not just distrust the dollar's current parity; they also lacked "faith in the monetary system itself." As Volcker saw it, "the markets showed no respect for the negotiating artistry" of nation-states and public officials.[59]

With the dollar flailing, West European governments contemplated a joint float against the "dollar peril." Willy Brandt, the architect of *Ostpolitik*, even dared to hope that he might transform the monetary crisis into a springboard for European unity. In early March, Brandt presented the Nixon administration with a stark choice: either accept the EEC's pursuit of regional monetary stability or resurrect the instruments of multilateral coordination and enforcement that the Nixon administration had discarded and foresworn—capital controls, foreign-exchange interventions, and domestic belt-tightening. Arrogant though his ultimatum was, Brandt called Washington's bluff. Unless the United States was prepared to return to the managerial macroeconomic policies of the 1960s, which Europeans leaders preferred but Shultz reviled, the West Europeans would consolidate their own monetary unity, an outcome that would thrust the Atlantic Alliance into escalated jeopardy. This was not what Nixon had intended when he closed the gold window.[60]

Unlike in August 1971, diplomatic concerns were central to the Nixon administration's crisis management throughout the upheaval of March 1973. With Nixon and Kissinger eager to minimize the political fallout, Shultz presented floating exchange rates as an irresistible solution to the "continuing thrashing around in these markets." The problem, as Shultz explained it to Kissinger, was straightforward. With the Deutschmark the destination of choice for speculators fleeing the dollar, successful dollar defense would require the Bundesbank's full cooperation. But with Bonn having demonstrated "a lack of conviction on the subject," Shultz explained, "the speculators would just murder the situation." Accurate in his analysis, the treasury secretary was nonetheless disingenuous in foisting responsibility for the failure of dollar defense on Bonn. After all, it was Shultz who had foreclosed on the Federal Reserve's foreign-exchange operations the previous summer, shutting down the mechanisms of central bank cooperation that had sustained Bretton Woods in the 1960s. Indeed, Helmut Schmidt called Kissinger from his hospital bed to lament Washington's refusal to defend the dollar on the currency markets. From Schmidt's vantage, the public perception that the United States "would not do anything in order to maintain the value of the dollar" was a central cause of the disturbances afflicting the world economy.[61]

Although Kissinger was fully engaged with the March 1973 crisis, he and Shultz were pursuing different objectives. Whereas Shultz sought to transform the international monetary order, Kissinger, like Nixon, aimed to preserve international political stability and thwart the consolidation of a European economic bloc that might hasten the fragmentation of the Atlantic Alliance. "My basic view," Kissinger explained, is that "we should not bring about any further European integration." "My reason," he continued, is "entirely political." Both geopolitical and domestic economic imperatives inveighed against further consolidation of the European project. European trade preferences would exacerbate the challenges facing American industry, while further political integration would, US officials feared, marginalize Washington's role in Europe. With Shultz determined to secure monetary flexibility, the optimal solution for Kissinger would have been a series of national floats that would have eradicated the recurrent monetary crises without consolidating the EEC monolith. This was almost—but not quite—what he got.[62]

When American, European, and Japanese finance ministers met as the Group of 10 (G-10) in Paris on the weekend of March 15–16, they reached an agreement that preserved only partial unity within the EEC, which had expanded its membership at the beginning of the year. Six of the nine EEC countries would fix their currencies in relation to each other. Great Britain and Italy would, like Canada and Japan, float against the dollar. This new G-10 accord confirmed the end of the gold-dollar exchange standard and marked the effective demise of Bretton Woods. Significantly, the G-10 did not mandate central bank interventions in the currency markets to stabilize exchange rates, although such intervention would be permitted. No longer obliged to defend the dollar, Washington would be free to abolish controls on international capital movements, a move that Shultz announced in January 1974, eleven months ahead of the schedule he had presented in February 1973. Disappointed with the EEC's joint float, Kissinger consoled himself in the belief that Shultz's disinclination to intervene in the foreign-exchange markets would "create conditions in which the Common float is as hard to work as possible." Bill Simon, chief negotiator in Paris, took a more positive view: "I think we got exactly what we wanted."[63]

Neoliberals welcomed the demise of Bretton Woods. For George Shultz, "the emergence of a market-based system" was "a great improvement over the inflexible gold-based system that preceded Camp David." Others were less sanguine. Paul Volcker acknowledged that most government officials in the United States and elsewhere viewed fixed rates as "more conducive to international rule consultation, international rule-making, [and] international enforcement than a floating rate system." But even the critics of market-based solutions to international monetary order had to recognize that the rise of transnational finance had, in the early 1970s, made the maintenance of a state-centric monetary system untenable. What happened in March 1973 was that speculative forces overwhelmed the old fixed-rate system, in a context in which state actors lacked the unity and the will to defend it. "The resort to floating in early 1973 was not taken out of any general conviction that it was a preferred system," wrote Volcker. "It was simply a last resort when . . . the effort to maintain par values of central rates seemed too difficult in the face of speculative movements of capital across the world's exchanges." This was a judicious verdict.[64]

༼∞༽

The events of 1973 pitted speculators against governments. "The balance of financial power," the *New York Times* explained, "has now tilted steeply in favor of speculators and against governments that try to maintain a specified official value for their currency." Indeed, the integration of financial markets had prefigured—and precipitated—the collapse of Bretton Woods. Technological and business innovation in the financial sector—"a panoply of dazzling new techniques and rituals" one Senate investigatory committee called it—encouraged the market upheavals of the early 1970s by facilitating the circumvention of capital controls. Emphasizing the inevitability of the transition, *Euromoney*, the trade journal of the offshore money market, described the shift from regulated to floating currencies as a transition from the rule of an oligarchy to a "dictatorship of the proletariat." The responsibility of governments for the sustenance of international economic order, now that the defenders of Bretton Woods had lowered the drawbridges to the hordes of speculators, remained opaque.[65]

Yet, for all the hyperbole in the financial press, transnational finance had not entirely dissolved the decision-making powers of government. Public officials, after all, made the key choices in 1971–73. Even Walter Wriston, a banker and a champion of deregulation, saluted Nixon's decision to float the dollar "as a key step" in the globalization of finance. In the spring of 1973, however, Nixon had little inkling that his monetary choices might produce such momentous consequences. He had scant interest in financial economics and no idea what might lie beyond Bretton Woods. What he sought was to bolster the American economy in order to sustain the Pax Americana and, secondarily, to fix the recurrent crises that had plagued Bretton Woods in recent years. Of all of the president's advisers, it was Shultz who had the clearest vision of the future. Yet the breakdown of Bretton Woods unfolded according to nobody's grand design; it was foisted on the Nixon administration by the markets' skepticism about the viability of the dollar at its fixed parity, by the administration's failure to achieve a sufficient devaluation of the dollar through diplomatic methods, and by the choices of American allies in early 1973.[66]

Foreign economic policy during Nixon's first term hardly reflected a coherent agenda, let alone a choice for globalization. Rather, policy emerged out of an array of competing outlooks and agendas. These included Nixon's preoccupation with national vigor, Connally's boisterous nationalism, Kissinger's Atlanticism, Shultz's urbane neoliberalism, and the engrained commitment to international consultation that officials from Arthur Burns to Paul Volcker shared. No single analytical framework—whether economic nationalism or ideological neoliberalism—can explain the complexities of policy development during these tumultuous years. Instead, the administration's actions show it groping for the exit door.

It is nonetheless difficult to see how the collapse of Bretton Woods could have been avoided. The resort to floating in March 1973 was a consequence not only of decisions already taken but also of structural changes in the global economy, over which decision makers had limited control. Could expanded multilateral surveillance have tamed the markets, as orthodox internationalists hoped it might? This was the alternative that Charles Coombs at the New York Fed favored. It is certainly the case that governments were, at times, able to come together to defend fixed exchange rates against speculative assault, as they did in the summer of 1972. Still, it is difficult to fathom how long costly multilateral surveillance of the markets could have been sustained. Nixon's gold-dollar demarche in 1971 had sapped foreign enthusiasm for a collaborative defense of the dollar. At the same time, the ongoing rise of international finance—made manifest in the growth of the Euromarkets—mandated a parallel expansion of multilateral surveillance if Bretton Woods were to be preserved. JFK's voluntary capital controls of 1963 had, after all, become mandatory controls in 1968; the intergovernmental gold market was barricaded against the market later that year. If fixed exchange rates were to survive, governments would have had to collaborate, vigorously, to contain transnational finance. Despite its experiments with domestic wage-price controls in the summer of 1971, the Nixon administration was never likely to have favored the expansion and consolidation of financial surveillance and regulation on the international scale.[67]

The direct political influence of bankers on policy choice in 1971–73 was remarkably limited. If this seems counterintuitive, it is important to recall that there was no consensus among international bankers as to the optimal constitution of an international monetary system. Walt Wriston, Wall Street's leading champion of market liberation, was an outlier in the early 1970s in his hostility to government regulation and his enthusiasm for floating exchange rates. For many more bankers, the end of Bretton Woods meant the disruption of a predictable business environment. David Rockefeller, a more mainstream figure than Wriston, tried in the fall of 1971 to present Nixon with recommendations for monetary reform. His sensible proposals aligned with the kind of multilateral, managed reforms that European governments favored, not with Wriston's market fundamentalism. (Nixon ignored Rockefeller's proposal.) The period of free floating in the fall of 1971 nonetheless exposed what Wriston called the "Chicken Little" mentality of monetary conservatives. "The world didn't come apart," Volcker observed, and bankers learned that they could profit from changes in exchange rates. Having grown accustomed to flexibility in the turmoil of 1971–72, bankers signaled their growing distrust of fixed exchange rates in the crisis of early 1973 by dumping the dollar.[68]

The consequences of Bretton Woods's disintegration were not immediately self-evident. Many observers, especially in Europe, interpreted the breakdown of fixed exchange rates as an interlude and expected that stability would soon be restored. But developments during 1973 consolidated the trend toward financial openness and monetary flexibility. The Euromarkets continued to grow, especially as oil exporters plowed revenues into the offshore money markets, from which oil importers borrowed. "Petrodollar recycling," as it became known, spurred the ongoing growth of the extraterritorial money markets and confirmed the international primacy of the dollar, in which oil exports were denominated. The IMF proposed establishing a formal international facility to recycle petrodollars, but US officials opposed the suggestion, insisting on the superior efficacy of private financial markets over international institutions.

In an indication of new policy directions, US policymakers after 1973 worked to establish New York as the world center for international financial intermediation. Besides helping US banks wrest offshore business away from London-based Eurodollar banks, Nixon's Treasury Department proceeded with the abolition of capital controls in January 1974. This, in the eyes of neoliberal reformers, was the administration's "most significant contribution" to the revival of "the United States as an international financial center." As globalization advanced, the consensus in Washington became that "interference by governments in an open world market system is counterproductive." Nixon affirmed in April 1974 that US policy was to minimize "governmental interference" in the money markets and place "maximum reliance on market forces to direct world trade and investment." US officials were by now embracing financial globalization, but this did not mean that they had worked proactively—and with a clear vision of the future—to overthrow the old international economic order. Through the years of Bretton Woods's breakdown, US policy had been far less cohesive than that. Nor did the end of Bretton Woods produce the utopia of international monetary stability that the neoliberals had predicted; the near future would, if anything, be more turbulent than the recent past.[69]

5

Oil Shocked

We are now living in a never-never land in which tiny, poor, and weak
nations can hold up for ransom some of the industrialized world.

Henry Kissinger, Staff Meeting, 1974

In October 1971, Mohammed Reza Pahlavi celebrated twenty-five centuries of Iranian monarchy. Prince Philip of Great Britain and President Nikolai
Podgorny of the Soviet Union as well as Yugoslavia's Josip Tito, and Ethiopia's
Haile Selassie were among the dignitaries who traveled to Persepolis to celebrate
with him. Lodging in a tent city constructed amid the ruined capital of the First
Persian Empire, they dined on truffles, quail eggs, and peacock crammed with
foie gras, all from Maxim's of Paris. The fireworks and the costumes also came
from France. For Pahlavi, the festivities declared to the world that "Iran is again
a nation equal to all the others—and much finer than many."[1]

Westerners sniffed at the shah's excesses, but they were, in effect, the ones
who were footing the bill—up to $100 million for the fête at Persepolis, some
estimated. Months earlier, the oil-producing governments of the Persian Gulf,
led by Iran, had concluded a landmark agreement with the multinational corporations that extracted and refined their oil. The Tehran agreement of 1971
raised the prices that the multinationals charged consumers for oil and gave
the producer governments an expanded share of the profits. For the first time,
more than half the sticker price on a barrel of Middle East crude would go
to the country from whose soil the oil was pumped. The Tehran agreement
challenged the neocolonial relationships that had long held the Middle East
in thrall to the interests of the West, and it gave Pahlavi an infusion of cash.[2]

The Tehran agreement was a turning point and a harbinger of future developments. Until the early 1970s, cheap and abundant oil had fueled growth and
lubricated social stability in the industrialized countries, whose citizens consumed a great deal of it. Between 1949 and 1970, US oil consumption increased
from 5.8 million to 16.4 million barrels per day; West European consumption,

from 970,000 to 14.1 million barrels per day; and Japanese consumption, from a few thousand to 4.4 million barrels per day. Worldwide demand for oil increased sixfold in the two decades after 1950, as oil displaced coal as the industrialized world's dominant fuel. Industrial plants and petrochemical industries devoured oil, but oil was also the lifeblood of postwar consumption. Britons owned 11.5 million cars in 1970, up from 2.5 million in 1950; the number of cars traveling Italy's roads increased from 342,000 to 10 million over the same period. For individuals, cars conferred autonomy and status, even freedom; for societies, mass car ownership meant dependence on oil and the international regime that kept it flowing.[3]

By the mid-1970s, gas-guzzling civilization was in crisis. In the United States, tail fins, drive-in diners, and V-8 engines gave way to gasoline lines, national speed limits, and fuel-efficient Japanese cars. For Bruce Springsteen in 1975, the automobile was a "suicide machine," chariot of a "runaway American dream." For a born-again Bob Dylan, oil shortages were a sign of God's wrath. "All that foreign oil controlling American soil," Dylan lamented, "it's just bound to make you embarrassed." More vulnerable to interruption of their energy supplies than most had imagined, Americans—and their allies—were oil shocked.[4]

⌁

Memorable manifestations of interdependence, the oil crises of the seventies were not the mere spillover of political events. Rather, oil shocks were, as this chapter explains, the result of economic changes and geological realities. The United States dominated world oil markets from the late nineteenth century to the late 1960s, but the end of America's oil ascendancy provided oil producers in the Third World with an opportunity to renegotiate the unequal terms on which Western corporations had long extracted, refined, and marketed their oil. Oil drew the United States into the Middle East, but so too did geopolitics. Decision-makers' efforts to disentangle and adjudicate their interests in the Middle East are this chapter's second theme. Prioritizing geopolitical purposes over economic interests, the Nixon administration did not oppose oil price hikes before 1973, reasoning that oil revenues would enable Iran and Saudi Arabia to purchase arms and furnish regional security, serving the purposes of the Nixon Doctrine. The administration thus subordinated the capitalist world's interest in cheap oil to the West's interest, as Nixon construed it, in the cultivation of client states in the Persian Gulf.

Developments in October 1973 prompted a reconsideration of priorities, which is this chapter's third theme. In early October, the Organization of the Petroleum Producing Countries (OPEC) orchestrated another major hike in oil prices. Days later, the Middle East found itself at war, as Egypt and Syria attacked Israel. Perceiving a Cold War proxy struggle, American leaders undertook to assist Israel. Doing so provoked a Saudi-led oil embargo. Together, the price hike and embargo quadrupled oil prices in a matter of months. The shock reverberated around the world, plunging the industrialized countries into the severest recession of the postwar era. As Washington's allies questioned US leadership, American decision-makers began to devise new strategic agendas. Lowering oil prices became an explicit priority for US foreign policy, as Henry Kissinger, now the dominant shaper of US foreign policy, worked to broker both a political settlement for the Middle East and economic solutions for the industrialized world. Kissinger remained committed to the preservation of the Pax Americana, but the oil crisis of 1973–74 prompted him to grapple, in a novel departure, with strategic challenges that interdependence made unavoidable.

The Rise of Oil Power

For oil exporters in the Third World, the 1950s and the 1960s were not golden years but decades of lost opportunity. The problem was that the supply of oil to the world market grew faster than did demand, which pushed prices downward. At the end of 1950, a barrel of Saudi light crude cost $14.70; by 1970, its price, in real terms, had fallen to $10.10 (see figure 5.1). This prompts two questions: where did the increases in production originate, and why did oil producers accept a production regime that depressed the value of their major asset? It was not the oil-producing nations of the West that were responsible for the

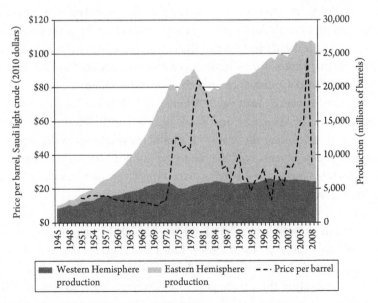

Figure 5.1 The world oil economy, 1945–2010

Source: DeGolyer and MacNaughton, *Twentieth Century Petroleum Statistics* (2009).

supply glut. The United States was in 1950 the world's greatest oil producer, but American production grew only slowly thereafter. Instead, it was the Middle East that accounted for the great postwar surge. But why did producers like Saudi Arabia acquiesce to a price regime that squandered their oil at bargain prices?

In most cases, Middle Eastern governments at the Second World War's end did not own title to the fossil fuels beneath their sands and shallow waters. Instead, multinational corporations such as the Arabian-American Oil Company (ARAMCO) and British Petroleum had, beginning in the early twentieth century, purchased concessionary rights to the region's oil deposits. The unequal terms of these early oil concessions invariably favored the multinational companies over the host countries, although the inequality often owed less to coercion than to the Middle East's political fragmentation and the desire of regional leaders to secure access to foreign currency. Once signed, producer governments could renegotiate the terms of oil concessions, but doing so might invite conflict. In 1953, the United States and Great Britain worked to orchestrate a coup against Mohammed Mossadegh, an Iranian reformer who proposed to seize British Petroleum's oilfields and use the proceeds to finance development. King Ibn Saud, on the other hand, secured an improved deal with ARAMCO in 1950 after threatening to nationalize. King Saud's new deal provided for a 50/50 split on the posted price of oil: half would go to Saudi Arabia and half would be retained by ARAMCO. The 50/50 split became the industry-wide standard.[5]

Even harder to surmount than unequal concessions was the competition between the producers to get oil to the market. Eager to convert their subterranean oil reservoirs into liquid capital, the governments of oil-rich states in the Middle East and North Africa pushed their multinational partners to increase production in the 1950s and 1960s. The competition drove down the price of oil. Recognizing this, some officials contemplated cartelization. Influenced by the Texas Railroad Commission, which enforced a minimum price for oil in the US domestic market, Juan Pablo Alfonzo and Abdullah Taraki, respectively, the oil ministers of Venezuela and Saudi Arabia, concluded that coordinating production levels among the major oil producers would serve their collective interests. If the producers could agree to cap oil production, they could raise oil's price while slowing the rate of its extraction. To promote cooperation along these lines, Taraki and Alfonso in 1960 created OPEC.[6]

The benefits of cartelization proved difficult to realize. During the 1960s, OPEC's attempts to bolster prices were waylaid by the ongoing expansion of production, especially in North Africa. Libya and Algeria opened vast new oil fields, which flooded the market with oil. The Soviet Union also sold oil to world markets, exacerbating the supply glut. The divergent interests and agendas of its members compounded OPEC's difficulties. Algeria and Iran were populous countries whose leaders increased oil production in order to finance economic and social development at home. Saudi Arabia, on the other hand, was sparsely inhabited and endowed with massive reserves. Its leaders could afford to be cautious and take the long view. The multinational companies did not make matters easier. While they and the producer governments shared a common interest in raising prices, the challenges of coordinating production targets among the nine OPEC countries (in 1967) and a similar number of multinational corporations were substantial. As a result, Alfonso and Taraki's project floundered.

Even war did not disrupt the cheap-oil regime. Israel and its Arab neighbors fought in 1948–49, 1956, and again in June 1967. The last of these conflicts, the Six-Day War of 1967, gave Israel control over the Sinai Desert, the Golan Heights, the West Bank, and the Gaza Strip and brought more than a million Palestinians under Israeli authority. The conflict also precipitated an Arab embargo on oil deliveries to the United States and Great Britain, which Saudi Arabia orchestrated in the hopes of loosening Washington's ties to Israel. The boycott proved ineffective. Iran refused to join the Saudi-led embargo, and the United States and Venezuela were able to step up production to offset the Arab shortfall. Ironically, the 1967 embargo intensified the supply glut when the boycotting countries resumed production.[7]

"It was ridiculous," Pahlavi commented at the time, "for any Arab to believe that the West could really be hurt by an Arab oil embargo." Other observers were less sanguine. Walter Levy, a consultant for the State Department, warned that an effective embargo would splinter the West and wreak chaos in the Middle East. This seemed improbable in 1967; but Levy was premature, not wrong, and the Arabs were less naïve than Pahlavi supposed. Had the United States and Venezuela been unable to make up the shortfall in Arab production, the embargo's consequences would have been serious. With demand rising and domestic supply finite, the United States would not be able to play the role of swing producer into perpetuity. In the world oil market, a historic shift had begun.[8]

⁓

Developments in the United States, in fact, proved more consequential for world oil than did the 1967 war. In the late 1960s, Americans experienced a transition from energy autonomy to energy interdependence, as a widening gap between consumption and production left the United States dependent upon imports, unable to be a swing producer for the world market. Economic trends and geological realities determined the advent of energy interdependence; as domestic oil consumption grew, finite natural endowments limited available supply. The geologist M. King Hubbert had predicted in the mid-1950s that US oil production would peak in the early 1970s, and his estimate turned out to be accurate. Acknowledging the point, the Texas Railroad Commission authorized all-out production in March 1972. It was not enough to reverse the trend lines. In 1950, about half of the world's oil had been extracted from American soil. By 1980, the United States would account for less than 15 percent of global oil output (see figure 5.2). This cession of dominance had significant consequences for the world economy.[9]

The relative detachment of the United States from the global oil market prior to the 1970s was the result of policy choices as well as nature's munificence. During the 1950s, a global supply glut produced a groundswell of oil protectionism in the United States, as domestic producers tried to bolster prices in the face of foreign competition. Leading the charge were the independents or minors—the firms that extracted, refined, and marketed oil within the United States. The majors, for their part, did much of their business outside the country and opposed trade protection. The minors outgunned the majors in Congress, and protectionist controls came during the 1950s in the form of oil import quotas. One result was that US consumers paid more for oil products than did non-Americans. Still, the separation of the domestic and world markets was never absolute; the quota system was riddled with loopholes, and it was liberalized somewhat in the 1960s. By 1971, imports were a quarter of domestic consumption—twice what they had been in 1950. Despite a policy regime that aimed to insulate the domestic market from external competition, Americans became dependent on foreign oil. As they did so, protectionism made less and less sense, which raised the question of whether the old quota system should be abandoned.[10]

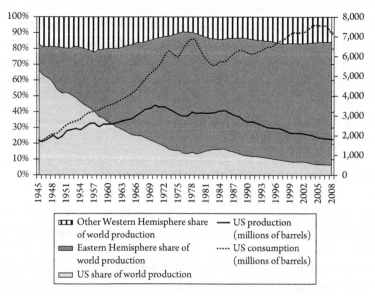

Figure 5.2 The US and the world oil economy, 1945–2010

Source: DeGolyer and MacNaughton, *Twentieth-Century Petroleum Statistics* (2009).

In 1969 Nixon established a cabinet-level task force to study the problem. The Task Force on Oil Import Controls identified the basic dilemma for energy policy: "domestic production has not been keeping pace with demand." There were two possible solutions. Either the price of oil—already 65 percent above world prices—could rise, or the United States could import more oil. George Shultz proposed replacing the import quota with a tariff. This would protect domestic producers while permitting imports to flow in expanded quantities. Shultz nonetheless accepted that some quota restrictions could be retained to guard against dependence on "insecure" Middle Eastern oil. Henry Kissinger opposed Shultz's distinction between Old World oil and New World oil, arguing that Europe's and Japan's reliance on Middle Eastern oil made the United States indirectly dependent on the region. Trying to insulate the United States from disruptions to Middle Eastern supply would, Kissinger warned, convey a lack of concern "about NATO's vulnerability." While Shultz focused on the interests of American consumers, and Kissinger on the interests of US allies, Nixon proved to be more sensitive to the interests of domestic oil producers. Faced with a difficult decision in which strategic, economic, and political purposes were entwined, Nixon rejected his own task force's conclusions and decided instead to retain the system of import quotas.[11]

So far as Washington's allies were concerned, Japan and Europe were more obviously dependent on the Middle East than the United States. Americans in 1971 imported just a quarter of their oil, while Japan imported 90 percent of the oil it consumed. Still, the United States was by no means immune to disruptions of Middle Eastern supply. Sustained interruption of oil supplies to Japan and Western Europe would strike at the cohesion of the Western Alliance, the maintenance of which was a core national interest. US dependence on Middle Eastern oil was, moreover, greater than the import ledger indicated. Five of the seven multinationals that dominated the Middle East oil economy—the so-called Seven Sisters—were US-based, and their profits, once repatriated, helped to stabilize the international balance of payments. "The contribution of the international oil industry to our balance of payments," one State Department study concluded, "is about as great as that of all other investments abroad combined." For financial as well as diplomatic interests, the United States could not be indifferent to the oil economy of the Middle East.[12]

Looking to the future, policymakers recognized that America's direct dependence on Middle Eastern oil was destined to increase. Despite the administration's failure to devise an alternative to the import quota system, the relationship between the domestic oil market and the world oil economy was, in the early 1970s, in the throes of transformation. Experts projected that the United States would be importing half of its oil from the Middle East before the decade was out. Conservation might mitigate America's reliance on foreign oil but could not prevent it. The fundamental problem was that domestic production had passed its peak. With the United States now producing less than 20 percent of the world's oil, and OPEC more than half of it, US oil producers were unable to meet domestic demand, let alone set the balance between global supply and demand. The failed embargo of 1967, as it turned out, marked the dusk of an era of abundant oil drilled and vended on the West's terms. The balance of oil power was shifting to the Middle East. Nowhere was this clearer than in the tumultuous case of Libya.

⌛

When the military officer and left-leaning nationalist Muammar al-Qaddafi overthrew the pro-Western government of King Idris in 1969, Libya was already a significant oil producer—the third or fourth largest in OPEC. After the Qaddafi coup, foreign observers feared a replay of the events that unfolded in Iraq in 1958, when a group of nationalist military officers overthrew the pro-Western monarchy and nationalized most of the Iraq Petroleum Company concessions. Indeed, Qaddafi opened negotiations with Occidental Oil, a leading concessionaire, in early 1970. After tense discussions, Qaddafi forced Occidental to accept an increase in the rate at which Libya taxed production, from 50 percent to 55 percent of the posted price. The ramifications were massive. Qaddafi had shattered the 50/50 compromise that had prevailed since the early 1950s.[13]

In the months that followed Qaddafi's breakthrough, other producer governments presented their own multinational partners with demands for a larger share of revenues. Shah Pahlavi secured a 55 percent deal in the fall of 1970; Venezuela imposed a 60 percent tax shortly thereafter. Soon OPEC presented the oil companies with a demand for an OPEC-wide minimum tax rate of 55 percent. The cartel also demanded that the multinationals give its governments an expanded role in the price-setting process that determined oil's posted price at market, a move that could have a revolutionary effect on the world market, empowering the producer governments at the expense of oil consumers in the advanced industrialized countries. The ensuing discussions between OPEC ministers and the oil multinationals soon broke into two separate negotiations, producing the Tehran and Tripoli settlements of 1971.[14]

Concluded in February 1971, the Tehran agreement increased the posted price of oil by 35 cents per barrel and confirmed a 55 percent share for the Persian Gulf governments. The Tripoli agreement, concluded in April, went even further, increasing the price of Mediterranean oil by 90 cents. Both agreements gave the producer governments a leading role in the price-setting process, marking what Walter Levy called the triumph of "oil power." "We are going to be dictating prices," said Sheikh al-Yamani, Saudi Arabia's oil minister, "and we are going to be very rich." From Tehran and Tripoli to the pageantry at Persepolis, then, 1971 was the turning point that marked oil power's rise. The Libyan coup had precipitated the reckoning, but changes in the world oil economy were ulti-mately responsible for the shift. What was happening was simple enough: the West's insatiable thirst for oil was outpacing non-OPEC sources of supply, which empowered OPEC. "By far the most important thing that happened," writes oil industry insider Francisco Parra, "was not a specific event but a sharp change in perceptions of future supply and demand for oil."[15]

In due course, rising oil prices would incentivize economic adjustment, driv-ing up the cost of energy-intensive production and encouraging alternative forms of economic activity. In the near term, the financial consequences of oil power proved disruptive. International monetary relations were already unstable in the early 1970s; by increasing oil prices, the Tehran and Tripoli agreements exacer-bated the strains on the Bretton Woods system. Estimates in 1972–73 suggested that Iran and Saudi Arabia would triple their export earnings over the next four years. "With the possible exception of Croesus," wrote one analyst, "the world will never have seen anything quite like the wealth which is flowing into the Persian Gulf." Anwar Ali, head of Saudi Arabia's central bank, complained that he was "sinking under a sea of billions of dollars."[16]

Speculation about what the oil exporters might do with the money abounded. They could, one British official argued, use their surpluses to sponsor infrastruc-tural development, women's education, and development aid for Africa. Others were more cynical. "It means they can all afford more wives," joked an American official. Geopolitical analysts worried that petrodollars would enhance the polit-ical influence of the oil exporters in the developing world. In practice, the priori-ties of the oil exporters varied. The more populous countries, such as Iran and Algeria, used their oil windfalls for domestic development; the less populous exporters, such as Saudi Arabia, Kuwait, and the Gulf emirates, struggled to find profitable outlets for their oil surpluses at home and sought investment opportu-nities elsewhere. Analysts feared that in the absence of overseas investment out-lets, the oil exporters might opt to "keep their assets in the ground," driving the price of oil even higher. The oil consumers thus faced two related problems: how to finance their own oil imports while assuring the exporters attractive outlets for investing their surpluses.[17]

The solution that presented itself was irresistible. Why could the Saudi Arabians and the other oil exporters not lend the importers funds to finance their growing trade deficits? This was, after all, the solution the United States had devised to accommodate Europe's trade deficits in the late 1940s, when Marshall Aid provided European countries with dollars to buy American goods. George Shultz made this point in a June 1973 speech to the American Bankers Association. This solution was practical, but it marked a profound shift in the economic foundations of the Pax Americana. A quarter-century before, it was the Americans who had the money and their allies who were borrowing it. Now, the capitalist countries would depend on regular influxes of capital from the oil exporters of the Middle East. The sums involved were substantial. The OECD estimated that the West's oil deficits could, by the end of the 1970s, be as much as $25 billion per year—over ten times the US trade deficit in 1971. With the oil importers struggling to finance their trade deficits, the most practical solution was for the oil exporters to lend them the money.[18]

Petrodollar recycling was nonetheless controversial. Some policymakers worried that the flows of hot money from the oil exporters to the oil importers would exacerbate "the problems caused by short-term money" in the international financial system. Evidence that "some of the oil producers had contributed to the run on the dollar" that brought down Bretton Woods in early 1973 corroborated fears that petrodollars would further unsettle international monetary relations. Accordingly, policymakers in 1973 debated how petrodollar recycling might be made more stable. West European officials favored creating an official facility for recycling petrodollars, presumably under the auspices of the IMF. Their US counterparts preferred to let markets do the heavy lifting. In pitting public-sector against private-sector solutions, the debate over petrodollar recycling exposed the central dilemma of the post–Bretton Woods era: would governments establish a multilateral framework for governing an interdependent world economy, or would they let the markets manage themselves? In early 1973, the Nixon administration was beginning to stand out among governments in its enthusiasm for market-based solutions.[19]

Enthusiasm for laissez-faire solutions did not, however, amount to a coherent energy policy. Spanning the arenas of foreign and domestic policy and implicating the interests of powerful constituents, energy flummoxed policymakers. Still, it was clear enough that action could not be deferred forever. By late 1972, State Department officials were describing an "impending energy crisis." The department's energy analyst James Akins went public in April 1973 with a dramatic warning that "the vulnerability of the advanced countries" to oil-supply shocks "is about to extend to the United States." He proposed a crash program to reduce energy consumption and develop alternative fuel sources. Akins argued that an effective program could deprive oil of its "predominance as a fuel." Others doubted government's capacity to devise solutions. The Treasury Department countered that "past action by the Federal government" had been "one of the primary causes of the energy problem." Unable to establish a clear agenda, the Nixon administration chased hypotheses. There were few proactive steps. Nixon did establish a new Energy Policy Office in 1973 and delivered a landmark energy statementthat April. Finally taking Shultz's advice, he announced that import quotas would be replaced with a system of tariffs. Nixon had little to say about conservation, however, and most of the measures that he proposed to expand production would require congressional action. Without a conservation plan, additional domestic supply, or alternative fuels, removing import quotas could only increase American imports of foreign oil, which is, in sum, what Nixon's energy policy accomplished.[20]

In late 1973, Nixon had been president for four years. During that time, economic growth and geological realities had made the United States dependent on the global oil market, the cockpit of which was the Middle East. "The main causes" of American vulnerability, the NSC concluded, were "the need for an increasing amount of oil imports and the dependence on a single, unstable, area of the world for most of our future energy imports." The geopolitical and the economic implications were unpalatable; yet policymakers at the highest levels had so far struggled to focus on the sources of energy interdependence—let alone to address its consequences. In part this was because they were preoccupied with the simultaneous imperatives of anti-Soviet containment in the Middle East. The region, as it turned out, was not only the crossroads of the world oil economy but also a vital fulcrum of Cold War geopolitics.[21]

Making the Twin Pillars

From the late nineteenth century, Great Britain controlled Egypt, Palestine, Jordan, Iraq, and an array of territories ringing the coast of Arabia, dominating the Middle East through the Second World War. The initial British engagement in the region owed less to geology than to geography, above all to Britain's interest in securing sea lanes between Europe and India. With the discovery of Arab oil fields, the Middle East itself became the prize, and the great powers scrambled for control in Arabia. The United States did not formally engage in colonialism, but ARAMCO built an informal empire on the Saudi oil frontier in the 1940s and 1950s. Still, ARAMCO's resource imperialism did not make the United States responsible for regional security, and US policymakers in the early Cold War preferred to delegate "primary responsibility" for Middle East security to the British. By the late 1960s, however, Britain's ability to sustain its regional responsibilities was dwindling.[22]

Here, as elsewhere, international monetary instability had geopolitical consequences. The British pound was the weakest link in the international monetary order, and in the winter of 1967/8, it snapped. In January, a balance-of-payments crisis prompted Prime Minister Harold Wilson to announce that he would withdraw British military forces from East Asia and the Persian Gulf. Coming just months after British forces evacuated Aden, a port and naval base on the entrance to the Red Sea, Wilson's announcement confirmed that Great Britain would no longer shoulder responsibility for military security in the Persian Gulf. For the Johnson administration, this was "profoundly damaging news," but it was Nixon who inherited the consequences. Britain's departure, US officials recognized, meant the end of a "system" that had "played a major political and security role for the West for a century and a half."[23]

Washington strategists feared that the retreat of British power might tempt the Soviets to make forays into the region. Russia had, after all, "historically sought to play a significant role in the Gulf," and oil only magnified the region's strategic value. The Six-Day War, meanwhile, had bolstered Soviet influence in the eastern Mediterranean and driven the Cold War wedge deeper into the Middle East. Bruised by their defeat, Egypt, Syria, and Iraq became increasingly dependent on Soviet military assistance. In the first months of 1970, about ten thousand Soviet advisers arrived in Egypt. For the United States, the rise of Soviet influence after 1967 was a serious setback. "Russian interdiction" from an Egyptian base might, after all, be able to accomplish the "sustained cut-off" of oil deliveries to the West. Egypt was the preeminent concern, but the Nixon administration saw Soviet threats elsewhere—in Iraq, Syria, and among the Palestinians who crowded after 1967 into Jordanian refugee camps. Nixon and Kissinger saw Soviet influence as the major threat to US interests in the Middle East; the Cold War, not the rise of oil power, was the strategic and historical challenge they aimed to meet.[24]

The question of how to engage Soviet power nonetheless divided US officials. For some diplomats, the Arab-Israeli conflict was an area in which the superpowers might usefully cooperate to try to bring about a resolution. In November 1967, after all, the UN Security Council had passed a unanimous resolution— Resolution 242—calling on Israel to withdraw from the territories it occupied at the end of the Six-Day War. For once, the Soviet Union and the United States found themselves on the same side of a major international issue. Eager to leverage superpower cooperation, the State Department in 1970 proposed four-power talks in which the Soviet Union and the United States would participate with Egypt and Israel. Kissinger distrusted this approach, which became known as the Rogers Plan. For Kissinger, no solution to the Arab-Israeli conflict should be attempted so long as the Soviet Union retained influence in the Middle East. By no means indifferent to Arab-Israeli peace, Kissinger anticipated that the United States would in time be able to broker a settlement on its own, after the front-line Arab states turned away from Moscow. In his view, American policy should aspire to expel Soviet influence from the region, establish the United States as the sole Middle East peace broker, and assure the security of the Persian Gulf. The challenge, in straitened times, was how to accomplish all this on the cheap.[25]

With Israel entrenched as Washington's primary ally in the Levant, the major dilemmas for regional security in the Middle East hinged on the Persian Gulf. Here, the options were limited. One approach would have been for the United States to assume the military responsibilities that Great Britain was vacating, but this solution was improbable. Although the small Arab states that hosted British forces would have welcomed the American troops, policymakers feared that stationing US forces in the Persian Gulf would provoke regional ire and a Soviet reaction. Expanding American military burdens overseas would, moreover, have been incompatible with Nixon's larger agenda for military and fiscal retrenchment. The Nixon Doctrine sought, after all, to uphold the framework of the Pax Americana by getting subordinate powers to carry more of the costs of anti-Soviet containment. In the Persian Gulf, the logic of the Nixon Doctrine led, inevitably, to the bolstering of existing security relationships with Iran and Saudi Arabia. Long-standing US clients, the two regional powers became the "twin pillars" of the Nixon administration's security concept for the Persian Gulf.[26]

The implementation of the twin pillars concept, however, revealed cracks in the administration's strategic agenda. As Nixon and Kissinger worked to exclude the Soviet Union from the Middle East, the realities of energy interdependence and the rise of oil power were transforming the arena in which they operated. Before long, the contradictions inherent among the myriad interests and commitments that the United States maintained—to Cold War security, to cheap oil, and to Israel—would expose the West's vulnerability to oil shocks.

∽

The central figure in Iranian-American relations was Iran's shah, Mohammed Reza Pahlavi, whose grandiose sense of self emerged from the shadow of an overbearing father. The son owed his kingdom to the Western-backed coup in 1953 that overthrew Mossadegh and transformed Iran's democracy into an authoritarian monarchy. Flush with petrodollars, the shah marshaled the power of the state in pursuit of modernity. He had in the early 1960s introduced a top-down reform project, which he called the White Revolution. Land redistribution transferred some absentee landholdings to the peasants who tilled them, and the government pushed health and literacy initiatives in the countryside. Women's rights were a priority. There was little room, however, for human rights, which Pahlavi lambasted as a Western conceit inappropriate to the Third World's needs. At home, the shah relied on torture and preemptive detention to stifle his critics. Repression did not command allegiance, however, and, as early as 1972, Iranian students were staging anti-regime demonstrations that shut down major universities. Still, to the makers of US foreign policy, Pahlavi looked to be Iran's vital man.[27]

In foreign policy, Pahlavi sought to avoid domination by the great powers while dominating the neighborhood. Great Britain's retreat from empire gave him the opportunity to press his ambitious agenda. In 1971, he established military bases on Abu Musa and the Greater and Lesser Tunbs, islands in the Strait of Hormuz. Pahlavi stockpiled vast quantities of military hardware—laser-guided bombs, F-4E Phantom and F-14 Tomcat Jets, Chinook helicopters, and the world's largest fleet of military hovercraft. As stunning as the shah's military buildup was, it aligned with regional patterns. Iran, Libya, and Syria were the world's top arms importers in the 1970s. The militarization of the Middle East was to some extent a consequence of Cold War dynamics. Soviet arms deliveries to Syria and Egypt encouraged the United States to increase American arms shipments to Israel, and vice versa, but the regional arms race was also a function of oil power, as Iran's experience indicates (see figure 5.3).[28]

Oil fueled Iran's transformation into a regional superpower. The problem was selling enough of it to finance the shah's military buildup. Here, Iran ran up against OPEC quotas that limited the amount of oil that cartel members could produce. These limits prompted Iranian rancor. It was unfair, Pahlavi complained, that Gulf sheikhdoms that maintained no significant military forces were rolling in cash, while Iran carried the burdens of regional defense. To circumvent the OPEC quotas, Pahlavi in 1969 proposed a secret barter with the United States whereby Iran would provide oil in exchange for military hardware.

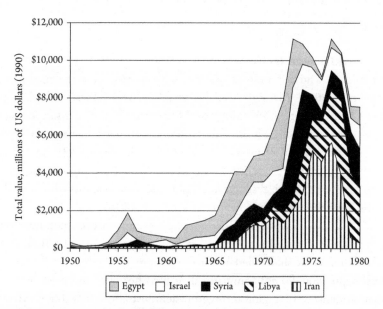

Figure 5.3 Arms imports to the Middle East, 1950–1980
Source: Stockholm International Peace Research Institute, Arms Transfers Database.

The scheme became an obsession for Pahlavi. Nixon was sympathetic, but the oil quotas that restricted imports to the United States made it impossible for the White House to make a special exception for Iran. As a result, no deal was forthcoming; the most that Nixon could do was extend military-sales credits to Iran.[29]

Unable to circumvent the US import quotas, Pahlavi pushed the multinational corporations that extracted and marketed Iran's oil to increase production and raise prices. As he did so, Pahlavi linked the price of oil to regional security, which was a shrewd move. When the oil companies asked the Nixon administration to intercede with Iran on their behalf, it refused to do so. Nixon, in fact, retorted that "American security" countermanded consumers' interests in cheap oil. The implication was clear: higher oil prices were a price that Washington would accept if it meant that Iran would bear the military responsibilities the Nixon Doctrine demanded of it. Still, simply ratcheting prices upward did not resolve the shah's financial troubles. His appetite for arms was so great that Iran began borrowing to finance its military imports. Nixon did not help matters when he abandoned long-standing requirements that US diplomats screen arms sales to Iran on the basis of military necessity and economic impact. When Nixon visited Tehran in late May 1972, he promised the shah that he would henceforth be able to purchase any non-nuclear weapons system he desired. Shortsighted as it may have been, Nixon's decision corroborated Iran's role as the dominant pillar in Washington's regional security system for the Persian Gulf.[30]

The other pillar was the Kingdom of Saudi Arabia, a vast and desolate land occupying most of the Arabian Peninsula, whose political cohesion derived from the House of Al Saud, the family that had unified the kingdom in the 1920s. Saudi Arabia in the early 1970s remained a traditional, conservative society in many respects, although oil and the transnational contacts it brokered were forces for social and political change. In the areas most affected by the oil economy, a Saudi "middle class" was emerging, oriented toward what US diplomats called "the outside and more sophisticated world." Navigating the social changes precipitated by oil wealth would be a challenge for the Saudi royals, much as it would be for the shah. About Saudi Arabia's natural wealth, however, there could be little doubt. In 1972, the Saudis exported about 6 million barrels of oil per day, and US analysts expected that output to leap to 23 million daily barrels by 1985—twice what Iran would then be capable of producing.[31]

Since World War II, the guiding principles of Saudi statecraft had been regional stability and partnership with Washington. The Riyadh monarchy was a loyal if unenthusiastic member of the West's Cold War camp: anti-Communist but dismayed by US support for Israel. Despite its antipathy for Israel, Saudi Arabia did not embrace Egypt, Syria, and Iraq, Israel's main antagonists. The Saudi royals loathed Gamal Abdul Nasser's secular, leftist nationalism and feared that his example might spread and afflict their own kingdom. Riyadh was nonetheless a financial sponsor of the front-line Arab republics. Indeed, money was a vital instrument of Saudi statecraft. Religion was another. As the guardian of Islam's holiest sites, the Saudi king exercised a leadership role in the larger Muslim community, while abundant petrodollars enabled Riyadh to finance global proselytization, including via organs like the Muslim World League, a Saudi creation. Thanks in part to Saudi sponsorship, a fundamentalist version of Islam constituted itself in the 1970s (and after) as a vibrant and transnational ideological system, a rival in some contexts to liberalism. Saudi Arabia was an epicenter of Islamic religious revivalism, a society that reacted against the modernity that the United States embodied and disseminated. This made Saudi Arabia's partnership with Washington incongruous, but the alliance affirmed the capacity of common interests to overcome the absence of real affinities.[32]

Besides being a major exporter of oil, Saudi Arabia was hostile to Communism, fearful of change, and preoccupied with stability, both domestic and international. Indeed, King Faisal's own Cold War outlook was so rigid that Nixon's 1972 trips to Beijing and Moscow prompted him to demand reaffirmation of Washington's commitment to its "traditional friends." That summer Riyadh made a formal bid for "closer cooperation" in military affairs. Faisal and Nixon, it turned out, were thinking in parallel. Besides designating Saudi Arabia as one of the pillars of its regional security concept for the Persian Gulf, the Nixon administration promoted defense cooperation between Iran and Saudi Arabia. The two countries conducted a joint planning exercise in 1970, and Faisal supported Iran's intervention in Oman. For US policymakers, Saudi-Iranian cooperation was vital. These "two key countries" would serve as the guarantors of regional security—and the West's access to oil. Their ability to play this role depended, of course, on military resources. Like Iran, Saudi Arabia stockpiled arms in the early 1970s. Petrodollars made the kingdom, previously a beneficiary of US military assistance, into a cash buyer. Saudi military purchases, adjusted for inflation, increased from $90 million in 1970 to almost $0.6 billion in 1974. This hardly compared to the sums Pahlavi was spending, but it signaled Riyadh's willingness to play a role in regional military affairs.[33]

As the price of oil rose, Iran and Saudi Arabia bought more weapons from the United States, ensuring that they would be able to defend the Persian Gulf against the Soviet Union. Oil, the source of the West's attraction to the Middle East, was also the solution to the strategic vulnerabilities that energy interdependence wrought. The circle was neat, but there were obstacles to its turning, none trickier than the relationship between Washington and Israel.

∽

"When you really study it," Henry Kissinger explained, "the nightmare of it is that no one caused World War I." Kissinger saw troubling analogies between pre-1914 Europe and the Middle East. Small Middle Eastern powers, engaged in struggles of their own, were connected by alliances to the great powers, in this case the United States and the Soviet Union. For the Israelis and the front-line Arabs against which Israel recurrently clashed, it was not the Cold War but the "local issues" that were paramount. Neither side was especially concerned with preserving peace. If the Arabs and the Israelis fought, Kissinger explained, there was a risk that the superpowers would be drawn into a conflict that Moscow and Washington "did not necessarily want" but that would nonetheless be "very difficult to arrest."[34]

Neither the United States nor the Soviet Union intended to take sides in the Arab-Israeli dispute; the superpowers were the first foreign countries to recognize Israel in 1948, and they both tried to maintain good relations with the Arab countries. Regional geopolitics nonetheless became polarized in the 1960s, with the Soviet Union lining up behind the front-line Arab states and the United States behind Israel. US domestic politics played a role in this realignment, but how significant a role is contestable. Political leaders beginning with Harry Truman understood that there were more Jewish votes than Arab votes in the United States; yet Stalin, who did not worry about votes, also calculated that recognizing Israel served Soviet interests. Nor did US domestic politics inhibit Eisenhower from siding with Egypt during the Suez Crisis of 1956.[35]

In the 1960s, the makers of American foreign policy ceased trying to straddle the Arab-Israeli conflict after trying for almost two decades to maintain amicable relations with both sides. Kennedy's 1962 decision to supply Israel with high-tech missiles owed something to affinity, but it was also a hardheaded move intended to dissuade Israel from building a nuclear bomb. Whereas JFK had worked to balance commitments to Israel with support for Egypt, LBJ had struggled to see beyond Nasser's anti-Western bluster. Johnson canceled aid programs to Egypt and aligned the United States more closely with Israel. Domestic politics facilitated Washington's shift towards Israel but so did bureaucratic politics as the NSC eclipsed the pro-Arab State Department. The Soviet Union, for its part, edged closer to Egypt during the 1960s, not only in reaction to American moves but also because it was eager to establish bases in the Mediterranean. As elsewhere, the process of Cold War division developed its own momentum. What Nixon and Kissinger inherited in 1969 was a Middle East divided into Cold War camps and a close US alignment with Israel. The room to maneuver, in other words, was limited by prior choices and the circumstances they bequeathed.[36]

On the face of things, Richard Nixon was an unlikely champion of Israel. Personal "ambivalences" (as Kissinger put it) clouded his attitude toward Jews, while Nixon had in 1968 secured just 10 percent of the Jewish vote. For geopolitical reasons, he nonetheless embraced Israel more tightly than any of his predecessors. "We are for Israel," Nixon explained, "because Israel is the only state in the Middle East which is pro-freedom and an effective opponent to

Soviet expansion." Kissinger, for his part, only reinforced Nixon's inclination to view the Arab-Israeli conflict through the Cold War lens, which had filtered Kissinger's own approach to the region beginning with the Black September crisis in Jordan in 1970–71. Having inherited a strategic predicament in which the United States had grown estranged from Arab nationalism and dependent on Israel, Nixon and Kissinger reinforced the status quo.[37]

Although Nixon was committed to a two-pillar strategy in the Persian Gulf, what he built in the Levant was a one-pillar strategy that produced an unstable configuration of regional partnerships. The problem was, in part, Saudi Arabia's unremitting hostility toward Israel. For Riyadh, Washington's relationship with Israel was a serious obstacle to closer Saudi-American relations. When John Connally met in late 1972 with Faisal, the Saudi king assured him that "the future course of US-Saudi relations would be adversely affected" if the United States failed to "bring about progress" on the "Arab-Israeli dispute." Before the year was out, Faisal committed himself to a "new posture of aggressiveness" that would "utilize the emerging and growing economic power of Saudi Arabia" in order to resolve the Arab-Israeli conflict to the satisfaction of the Arabs. By comparison, Iran's relations with Israel were warm. Although Iran did not maintain diplomatic relations with Jerusalem, informal ties between the two countries were close, and the shah supplied Israel with oil. Pahlavi recognized that his association with Israel strained Iran's relations with the Arab world and tarnished his domestic legitimacy; but from Washington's vantage, Iran's partnership with Israel was one of the useful services that Pahlavi provided to the West.[38]

As the rise of oil power transformed the Middle East, the bilateral relationships that Washington maintained in the region began to conflict with each other. Ensuring Israel's survival and "assuring the unimpeded flow of oil" were the basic priorities, and the tensions between them were obvious. For the journalist Cyrus Sulzberger, what confounded American policy was a timeless conflict between interests and ideals, "between our philosophical and political sympathies for Israel and our material and strategic hopes in the Arab world." In reality, the ideals were sparse, but the interests arrayed on all sides. In the eastern Mediterranean, where the Soviet Union was probing strategic opportunities, Washington depended on an Israeli client of whose military capacities American policymakers were confident. Although geopolitical priorities aligned the United States with Iran, the economic interests of the capitalist world diverged from those of the Shah, who was determined to squeeze oil consumers to finance his military ambitions. Saudi Arabia was more cooperative than Tehran when it came to oil prices, but Riyadh's interest in the Arab-Israeli conflict was a source of tension with the United States.[39]

Kissinger was right to warn that alliances between local belligerents and their superpower patrons could escalate a local conflict into a larger one. At the same time, a parallel set of relationships—economic rather than geopolitical—created interdependencies that cut across Cold War alignments and entwined the West's interests with those of the Arab oil producers. If another Arab-Israeli war broke out, the economic implications for the industrialized countries were, by the early 1970s, likely to be severe. There were risks in this predicament for the West, for European and Japanese leaders were likely, in the event of a crisis, to prioritize access to oil over support for Israel. Still more attuned to geopolitics than to economic interdependence, American decision-makers at the highest levels did not yet grasp the vulnerability of their position.

October and After

In September 1970, Gamal Abdel Nasser died. While the Six-Day War of 1967 had damaged Nasser's reputation, his death left Egypt and the broader Arab world bereft of leadership, bequeathing a vacuum of authority that his heir appeared unequipped to fill. To many Western eyes, Anwar Sadat seemed an improbable successor: an "impulsive and deeply religious man" who appeared to be a "bitter foe of Israel and one of the most outspoken critics of the United States." Still, Donald Bergus, the chief American diplomat in Cairo, concluded that Sadat might in practice be more flexible than his critics feared. "With plenty of patience," reported Bergus, "we can do business with this guy." The insight was prescient. Sadat, recalling Dwight Eisenhower's intervention on Egypt's behalf during the Suez Crisis, declared that Nasser "had treated the United States unfairly," and hoped to repair a relationship that had deteriorated sharply since 1956, when Washington had sided with Egypt against Israel, Britain, and France.[40]

The Arab-Israeli conflict remained the central dilemma in US-Egyptian relations. Sadat ended the "war of attrition" that had simmered since the ceasefire of 1967; but he also believed that the regional balance of power was not conducive to peace. Determined to enhance Egypt's position, Sadat at first urged the Americans to put the Israelis under "real pressure," something Washington was unwilling and unable to do. Unable to alter political realities through this outreach to the American superpower, Sadat pursued a more radical course. He distanced himself from the Soviet Union, expelling Soviet military advisers in July 1972, and made a bold move toward Saudi Arabia, reaching out to mend a relationship that Nasser had strained. Having broadened his diplomatic options, Sadat began in 1973 to intimate a renewal of Egyptian-Israeli hostilities. Neither Jerusalem nor Washington took his saber rattling seriously, but they did not perceive that Sadat's objectives were psychological, not territorial. Egypt lacked the capacity to regain the Sinai Desert by force; Sadat did not seek to recapture the territories Egypt lost in 1967, however, but to provoke what Kissinger later called "a crisis that would alter the attitudes into which the parties were frozen—and thereby open the way for negotiations."[41]

On Yom Kippur, October 6, 1973, Syria and Egypt launched coordinated attacks in the Golan Heights and across the Sinai Desert. Israel's leaders appealed for American support. Concerned with preserving the appearance of even-handedness, Kissinger at first rebuffed Israel's request that the United States resupply the Israeli Defense Forces with weaponary. US officials tried instead to assemble a fleet of charter jets to carry arms to Israel. News of a Soviet airlift to Syria, however, soon convinced Kissinger that the East-West balance was at stake, prompting him to abandon the restrictions he had initially imposed on American assistance and to initiate an arms airlift to Israel using US Air Force jets. Kissinger also appealed to Congress for up to $3 billion in military assistance for Israel. Cognizant that this show of support for Israel would alienate the Arab world, Kissinger worked to conciliate Saudi Arabia, emphasizing that his purpose was to contain Soviet power, not to determine the outcome of the Arab-Israeli war. The intervention nonetheless helped to tip the military balance in Israel's favor.[42]

The Israeli Defense Forces pushed the Egyptian forces back across the Sinai Desert and toward the Suez Canal. With the fighting swinging in Israel's favor, Kissinger flew to Moscow on October 20 to negotiate the framework for a ceasefire with Brezhnev. More quietly, he encouraged the Israelis to push Egyptian forces back as far as possible across the Sinai Desert before the truce took effect. By the time the ceasefire was approved by the UN Security Council on October 22, the Egyptian Third Army was lodged precariously on the east side of the Suez canal, surrounded by Israeli troops.[43]

Within hours of the ceasefire, it was clear that Israel had taken advantage of the lull in the fighting to encircle Egyptian forces, to the Soviet Union's chagrin. Although Cairo had distanced itself from Moscow, Egypt remained a Soviet client, and Brezhnev would not permit its humiliation at Israel's hands. The Soviet leader proposed that "decisive measures" be taken to stop Israeli violation of the ceasefire. After another round of Soviet-American negotiations, the UN Security Council passed a second ceasefire resolution on October 23. The next evening, a surprising—and threatening—message from Moscow arrived in Washington proposing joint US-Soviet military action to enforce the ceasefire. Superficially consistent with the spirit of détente, Brezhnev's proposal contained a veiled threat. "If you should find it impossible to act jointly with us," Brezhnev warned, the Soviet Union would consider "taking appropriate steps unilaterally." In response, Kissinger decided to put US forces worldwide on an elevated level of preparedness for nuclear war and cautioned Brezhnev not to intervene.

Brezhnev soon dismissed Kissinger's suggestion of unilateral action—either because the nuclear alert intimated him or because he had not intended to make a threat in the first place.[44]

The crisis of October 1973 marked the beginning of a new phase in US foreign policy. Incapacitated by stress and scandal, Nixon was a marginal figure throughout; in his stead, Kissinger stepped in, filling a role akin to that of acting president. The origins of this unusual situation lay in the Watergate scandal. Bob Haldeman and John Ehrlichman, Nixon's chief lieutenants, had resigned in April 1973, and the Senate opened hearings into Nixon's abuses of power in May. By June, Nixon was speculating that he might be forced to resign. At the height of the October War, Nixon fired the special prosecutor whom the attorney general had appointed to investigate the affair, prompting calls for impeachment. Amid all of this, Nixon, in September, appointed Kissinger to be his secretary of state. While Nixon did not want to elevate Kissinger, he worried about the toll that Watergate was taking on foreign policy, and he believed that Kissinger would provide continuity of leadership. In effect, Kissinger would be the head-of-state for foreign policy.[45]

Kissinger's views diverged from Nixon's in some respects, including over the Middle East. Even more disposed than Nixon to view the region as an arena of geopolitical competition, Kissinger ranked among Israel's staunchest supporters before the October War. This attachment did not derive from Kissinger's Jewish background, as Nixon suspected, so much as from geopolitical logic. Insofar as Israel remained Washington's core ally in the Middle East, Kissinger would not stand by to see Israel defeated by a Soviet client—which Egypt, in theory, remained. Kissinger's strategic purpose throughout the crisis remained ridding the Middle East of Soviet influence. On this point, he was more adamant than Nixon, who was relatively eager to countenance Soviet-American collaboration of the kind that Brezhnev proposed. When Nixon suggested that a Middle East peace brokered by the superpowers could be "one of the brightest stars" in the "galaxy for peace stemming from the Nixon–Brezhnev relationship," Kissinger proclaimed himself "shocked." Once unshackled from Nixon, Kissinger would attempt to entrench the United States as the dominant power in the Middle East. This would entail making the United States both the orchestrator of regional security, on which access to oil depended, and the architect of a political settlement that would extricate the front-line Arab states from their alliance with the USSR.[46]

∞

Throughout the October 1973 crisis, Henry Kissinger prioritized Cold War geopolitics, but doing so limited his vantage on events. There were other interests at stake in the fall of 1973—for the Arabs, for the Israelis, and for the United States.

Sadat's purpose, after all, was to escape the Cold War's vise, not to tighten it. The primacy of regional politics was also clear to West European observers who took the October War to be an "Arab-Israeli thing, not an East-West blow-up." Then, of course, there were the economic interests of the capitalist world.[47]

For the United States and its allies, oil was a source of vulnerability in October 1973. Led by Saudi Arabia, the Arab oil exporters deployed oil as a weapon, withholding supplies and raising prices, much as they had in 1967. This time, the weapon worked. It traumatized the capitalist world, divided NATO, and called into question America's leadership of the West. The irony of the 1973–74 oil crisis was that Kissinger's efforts to bolster the frontiers of anti-Soviet containment in the Middle East weakened US leadership within the Pax Americana's transatlantic core. While the West's economic vulnerabilities ought to have been clear to American strategists, their prioritization of Cold War geopolitics over other registers of international power and influence obfuscated the threat, ensuring that the deployment of the oil weapon brought panic and disarray.

Well before October 1973, careful observers in Washington perceived that a new international oil order was taking shape. "The past few years have seen a decisive shift in the balance of power in favor of the producing states," wrote one analyst in July 1972. Oil was now "a weapon for coercion or blackmail." Evolving economic realities emboldened Saudi Arabia's Faisal. After telling emissaries in late 1972 that he would curtail economic ties unless the United States abandoned its support for Israel, King Faisal went public in the summer of 1973. Speaking to the *Washington Post*, Faisal warned that American support for Israel was imperiling relations between Saudi Arabia and the United States. He soon made a fateful commitment. When Anwar Sadat traveled to Riyadh in August 1973, Faisal agreed to use "oil as a weapon" to support Egypt's impending war against Israel. Doing so entwined politics with parallel purposes.[48]

Raising oil prices and leveraging oil for political ends were distinct agendas. While Faisal sought to influence US foreign policy, others aimed to maximize oil's economic value, none more determinedly than Iran's Pahlavi. The move to initiate another price hike in fact began in mid-September, well before the outbreak of the war. Led by Iran, the OPEC governments demanded a 100 percent increase in posted oil prices; with the oil companies reluctant to concede more than 15 percent, talks collapsed. Days later, OPEC announced a unilateral 70 percent price increase. Only thereafter did Kissinger's decision to aid Israel prompt Faisal to use oil for political purposes. On October 17, the Arab states within OPEC (but not the non-Arab producers) announced a series of "rolling" cutbacks that would reduce Arab oil production by 5 percent every month until "the total evacuation of Israeli forces from all Arab territory" was achieved. They also threatened to embargo oil exports to countries that aided Israel. The threat did not vex Kissinger. Believing that the OPEC price hikes had more to do with economics than politics, Kissinger presumed that Saudi Arabia would not orchestrate an anti-US embargo. He was wrong. On October 19, Nixon proposed a $2.2 billion military appropriation for Israel. The Arabs rolled out a total embargo against the United States, with Faisal proclaiming a "jihad." Even after the fighting ended, the embargo remained.[49]

As it was, the embargo was not so severe as it might have been. Had the Saudis wished to inflict maximum economic pain, they could have embargoed Washington's allies as well as the United States. Still, the embargo was not the singular, or even the primary, cause of the oil crisis. Rather, the OPEC price increase, the Saudi-led production cutbacks, and the embargo combined to slash supply and drive prices upward. The price of oil at the end of 1973 was, as a result, about four to five times what it had been a year earlier. When OPEC acted to stabilize prices at around $12 per barrel at the year's end, a new status quo was ratified, quadrupling the price of oil. This price revolution was a consequence of the Arab-Israel War and—more profoundly—of long-term economic changes that had left the West dependent upon oil imports. As Shah Pahlavi put it at the year's end, "the industrial world will have to realize that the era of their terrific progress and even more terrific income based on cheap oil is finished."[50]

The economic consequences reverberated fast and hard. With oil providing more than half of the industrial world's energy inputs in 1973, a rapid quadrupling of its price was bound to have adverse effects. The United States entered a protracted recession, as did Great Britain. Oil prices dragged growth down throughout the capitalist world. After growing by 6.3 percent in 1973, the OECD countries as a whole grew by 1 percent in 1974 and just 0.4 percent the following year. In the United States, gasoline lines were a tangible symbol of the economic disarray. As the industrial world struggled, stock markets slumped. The Dow Jones Industrial Average lost a third of its value after October 1973; it would not recover to pre-crisis levels until 1976. The economic consequences of the oil crisis may be grasped through the misery index, a metric that adds the inflation and unemployment rates. For the OECD countries, as figure 5.4 indicates, the oil crisis marked the transition from a long era of postwar prosperity to a phase of instability and stagnation that would endure into the 1980s. The oil crisis was not the sole cause of the protracted economic downturn, but it nonetheless triggered an economic crisis on a transnational scale.[51]

"The world," the *Economist* exclaimed in December 1973, "has now spun into a simultaneous crisis of leadership, economics, and energy." Leadership at the highest levels of the US government was not absent so much as distracted. Henry Kissinger prioritized geopolitical over economic interests during the October crisis, but in the lower reaches of the policy bureaucracy, others had been more attuned to the economic risks. Indeed, the NSC had warned Kissinger in the early fall of 1973 that the West's dependence on Middle Eastern oil risked "much

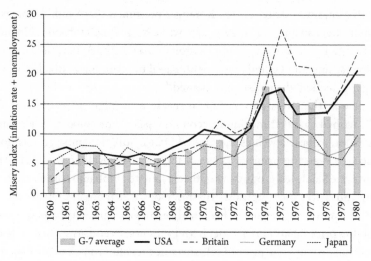

Figure 5.4 Economy misery among the G-7, 1960–1980
Source: OECD, iLibrary.

damage to us, our Allies, and our Alliances." Unwilling to see Israel defeated, Kissinger decided to resupply the Israeli Defense Forces. He did not expect an embargo, but Kissinger's expectation that anti-Communism would keep Saudi Arabia in line proved too hopeful. No longer so fearful of Arab radicalism as they had once been, Saudi Arabia's leaders declined to play the role of America's "good little boy" in the Middle East (as Kissinger put it). They instead decided to use oil power as an instrument of coercion. For the United States, the spectacle was humiliating.[52]

A century earlier, Kissinger observed, dealing with the embargo would have been a straightforward matter. The Western powers "would have landed, they would have divided up the oil fields, and they would have solved the problem." In a postcolonial age, however, military solutions were improbable. Washington's European allies opposed military intervention; British officials feared "total alienation of the Arabs and the risks of a third world war." Military intervention would, moreover, have invited a Soviet reaction, thwarting Kissinger's efforts to exclude the Soviet Union from the Middle East. The United States, in any case, lacked bases from which military action might be launched. This is not to say that contingency plans were nonexistent. Nixon apparently told Shah Pahlavi that he would support an Iranian invasion of Saudi Arabia should radicals over-throw the conservative House of Al Saud. Kissinger proposed devising at least "a plan for grabbing some Middle East oil" and speculated that the United States might have to intervene in the future "to protect access to raw materials." Still, the reality, for now, was that the United States would not act to bring the oil crisis to a violent resolution.[53]

Bereft of plausible options, Kissinger could only bemoan the asymmetries of economic and military power that the oil crisis juxtaposed. "It is ridiculous that the civilized world is held up by eight million savages," he complained. "We are now living in a never-never land in which tiny, poor, and weak nations can hold up for ransom some of the industrialized world." The fact nonetheless remained that US military power could no more readily end the oil crisis than win the Vietnam War. Energy interdependence gave the oil producers a powerful lever against consumers. Still, interdependence made the producers dependent too, above all on the revenues that oil generated. Should Faisal's embargo endure too long, the producer governments would lose revenues and suffer the consequences thereof. By the same logic, a global recession would not serve OPEC's interests: rather, it would contract world demand for oil. That the crisis would have to be resolved so as to restore transnational flows of oil was a reality that all parties to the dispute grasped. But the question remained: how to transcend the impasse?[54]

∽

The oil crisis exposed Western vulnerabilities, but the episode also afforded the United States opportunities to redefine its leadership of the West and to consolidate its influence in the Middle East. Once the fighting settled into a stalemate, Kissinger positioned the United States as the broker of peace between Israel and its neighbors. Shuttling in search of a settlement, he massaged Egypt's defection from Moscow's Cold War camp to Washington's. The fourfold increase in oil prices, meanwhile, served the purposes of Nixon's twin pillars strategy, enabling Saudi Arabia and Iran to finance imports of military hardware from the United States. So neatly did the fiscal consequences of the oil crisis mesh with US strategic purposes, in fact, that some critics have speculated that Washington orchestrated the price hikes in order to finance the delegation of military responsibilities to Riyadh and Tehran. Evidence for this claim is sparse, but the October War and the oil crisis served the geopolitical purposes of the United States, facilitating the exclusion of Soviet influence from Egypt and subsidizing the Nixon Doctrine in the Persian Gulf. The episode nonetheless did damage elsewhere, especially within the transatlantic core of the Pax Americana.[55]

For the West, the oil crisis pushed strained relations toward rupture. Since 1969, Washington had preoccupied itself with geopolitical balancing between Moscow and Beijing. Successful as it was, détente's high-wire act did not salve divisions within the Atlantic Alliance; instead, it raised the specter of a superpower "condominium" from which the Europeans would be excluded. The lessening of Cold War tensions, meanwhile, loosened the existential fears that had bound the West together for a generation. It was in this context that European integration lurched forward in early 1973 when Denmark, Ireland, and Great

Britain joined the EEC. US diplomats, for their part, worried that the West had entered a "transitional stage" in which pressures from détente, European integration, and the end of Bretton Woods might break the alliance apart.[56]

Recognizing the strains that historical changes and policy choices had inflicted on core relationships, Henry Kissinger had in April 1973 committed the Nixon administration to what he called the Year of Europe. The initiative was a dud. The Europeans resisted Kissinger's entreaties to devise "a new Atlantic Charter," and they disdained his proposal for engaging different kinds of international issues—military, monetary, trade, energy, and so on—within a "comprehensive" framework. Despite recurrent efforts to rehabilitate it, the Year of Europe concept petered out during 1973, a failure that Kissinger attributed to the effects of Watergate.[57]

Within the alliance, interests diverged over the crisis in the Middle East. Washington put Cold War purposes ahead of economic needs. Far more dependent on Middle Eastern oil, Europe and Japan did the reverse. For the British government, the imperative during the October War was to "do or say nothing to offend the Arabs." Portugal apart, the other NATO countries adhered to this line, denying US forces the use of airbases to resupply Israel. European behavior during the October War, Kissinger lamented, "was a total disgrace." Kissinger's mood did not improve when the EEC countries met in November and committed themselves to a Middle Eastern peace based upon UN Security Council Resolution 242, which mandated a settlement along the pre-1967 borders. The problem was that Europe's conception of its interests was anchored in economic realities, Washington's in geopolitical ones; this divergence pushed the Europeans toward the Arabs and the United States toward Israel. "One cannot avoid the perhaps melancholy conclusion," Kissinger complained, "that some of our European allies saw their interests so different from those of the US that they were prepared to break ranks with the US on a matter of very grave international consequence."[58]

For the oil consumers, there were at least three distinct issues at stake: the oil embargo, the production cutbacks, and the price hikes. The Arab embargo targeted only the United States, the Netherlands, and Portugal, but the rolling production cutbacks and the OPEC-wide price hikes afflicted all oil consumers. Mitigating the consequences became a common priority of the oil-consuming nations, yet, for many of these governments, bilateral deals with producer states offered an obvious means to secure access to oil. As 1973 passed into 1974 and energy use surged across the northern hemisphere, European and Japanese ministers paraded through the Middle East in search of bilateral arrangements. The British and the French had weapons and military experience to barter, and they traded both in Riyadh and Tehran. France, Germany, and Japan negotiated to build oil refineries in exchange for oil. "It would be irresponsible," explained the

British foreign minister, "not to do all we can to seek to increase available supplies." "Europe and Japan," concluded a US National Intelligence Estimate, "see
no realistic short-term alternative to making the best possible deals they can get
with the Arab oil producers to get through the new few months."[59]

The energy crisis exposed the nations of the West to the realities of interdependence, and they scattered in defense of their interests. Unable to satiate their
needs for oil from domestic resources, the consumer governments of Western
Europe and Japan sought special deals with the oil producers. The United States
found itself in a somewhat different situation. No longer the swing producer to
the world market, it remained a major oil producer in its own right. The United
States produced two-thirds of the oil Americans consumed in 1973, and most
of the rest came from the Western Hemisphere. This meant that the United
States was in a position to protect itself through a bold reach for autonomy.
Doing so was the logic of Project Independence, the energy program that
Richard Nixon unveiled in November. Lamenting America's slide into interdependence, Nixon pledged that the United States would, by 1980, be able to
meet its "energy needs" from its "own energy resources." Exhorting Americans
to achieve energy independence through conservation, exploration, and conversion, Nixon summoned the ghosts of past triumphs, above all the Manhattan
Project and the Apollo Project. Underlying this heroic ambition was the same
impulse that animated the Euro-Japanese rush for bilateral deals: the thrust
for economic security amid the march of interdependence. For some critics,
including within the administration, the implications of Project Independence
were troubling.[60]

Back in the fall of 1971, the transatlantic wrangling that followed the end
of dollar-gold convertibility exposed differences within the Nixon administration. Whereas Nixon sought national advantage, Kissinger strove to preserve
international cooperation. The oil crisis revealed a similar divergence. As Nixon
embraced Project Independence, Kissinger struggled to hold the West together.
Distressed as he was with European choices during and after the October War,
the secretary of state remained nostalgic for the transatlantic cooperation of
the early Cold War. What was now at stake, he reasoned, was the future of the
West. "The whole postwar system," as Kissinger put it, depended on breaking
"the regional autarky concept" and getting the Atlantic Alliance back to "some
of the more cooperative conceptions that underlay our policy at earlier periods." The West's unity was in peril, but the oil crisis presented an opportunity. If
Washington could bring its allies "towards cooperation across the energy front,"
the United States might reassert—and even redefine—its role as the leader of
the West.[61]

Kissinger made his pitch on a visit to London in December 1973. Speaking
to the Pilgrims Society, the secretary of state conceded that the Western Alliance

was at risk of "gradual erosion." He linked its difficulties to larger processes of historical change, including the resurgence of European strength, the arrival of Soviet-American nuclear parity, and the lessening of East-West confrontation. "A new international system," Kissinger explained, "is replacing the structure of the immediate postwar years." Unlike in the early Cold War, the West now had to grapple with the "fact" of economic interdependence. "We must resolve the paradox," he continued, "of growing mutual dependence and burgeoning national and regional identities." The energy crisis would be Kissinger's test case for cooperation, his bid to rescue strategic purpose from disadvantageous circumstances.[62]

Orchestrating a coordinated response to the energy crisis, Kissinger figured, might "get some political benefits for the United States" and even rehabilitate the alliance bonds that the October War had strained. Consumer solidarity would be the mantra of Kissinger's emerging energy policy, and, for the United States, this meant embracing interdependence. Kissinger thus rejected the view that energy was a domestic issue, to be solved by "domestic action." He insisted instead that energy was an international issue and had to be engaged as such. To this end, Kissinger visited Europe and Japan to make the case for international coordination. In his next move, the United States extended formal invitations to the other industrialized countries to participate in a conference that would coordinate Western policies and end the scramble for bilateral oil deals. The Washington Energy Conference, which convened in February 1974, marked the beginning of Kissinger's effort to invigorate the West by reorienting the alliance toward challenges defined not by the Cold War but by economic interdependence. The secretary of state did not necessarily expect success, but he now saw such cooperation as the West's best hope.[63]

Even as he worked to rally the West, Kissinger worked to disarm the Arabs' oil weapon. This would require establishing at least the framework for a peace settlement between Israel and its Arab neighbors. Progress would depend on Egypt's Anwar Sadat and Israel's Golda Meier. Sadat was easy. The Egyptian president had gone to war to make peace, and he had signaled to Washington his desire for peace before, during, and after the October War. The initial challenge for Kissinger would thus be to persuade Golda Meir's government to withdraw its forces far enough to permit a durable ceasefire. Mediating between Cairo and Jerusalem, Kissinger finalized a disengagement agreement that provided for the return of the Suez Canal to Egypt and laid the foundations for future negotiations. Peace remained a distant goal, but Kissinger had established the United States as its prospective mediator. While four-power peace talks including the USSR proceeded in parallel, it was Kissinger's hands-on diplomacy that secured an Egyptian-Israeli disengagement agreement in January 1974. The accomplishment did not lead Saudi Arabia to lift the oil embargo, but it left the secretary of state in a triumphal mood. "The moral force of the US in the world," Kissinger exclaimed, "is overwhelming."[64]

With Saudi Arabia recalcitrant, the Washington Energy Conference opened in mid-February with the oil embargo still in place. Yet the basic challenge for the West, as Kissinger now construed it, was economic, not political. The problem, as he put it at the conference, was that an "explosion of demand" for oil had "outstripped the incentives of producers to increase production." No nation could escape the predicament alone. To dampen demand and diminish oil prices, collaborative action would be required. Kissinger proposed a multipoint program including the promotion of energy conservation, the expansion of non-Arab oil supplies, the development of alternative energy sources, and the creation of emergency oil-sharing procedures. The substance of Kissinger's agenda built on Project Independence; what was striking and original was its scope. Projecting energy policy on a transnational scale, Kissinger envisaged a new "Project Interdependence" to solve the West's travails. "The energy crisis," he exclaimed, "indicates the birth pains of global interdependence." This demanded cooperative solutions. "Will we consume ourselves in nationalistic rivalry?" Kissinger asked, "or will we acknowledge our interdependence and shape cooperative solutions?" Whether the governments of the West could cooperate to slake their thirst for oil would be a crucial test of whether they could sustain a cooperative international system.[65]

The Washington Conference led to the creation of the International Energy Agency in November 1974. This fulfilled Kissinger's goal of establishing an international framework for cooperation on energy. The agency would in time undertake important work, including the creation of a coordinated international system of oil reserves. Energy politics nonetheless remained contentious within the West, nowhere more so than between France and the United States. Having opposed the Washington Conference on the grounds that it would antagonize OPEC, Foreign Minister Jobert refused to sign the final conference communiqué, instead issuing a unilateral dissent opposing the creation of a formal consumers' organization. Others were more willing to follow Washington's lead. Having concluded after months of prevarication that "the Americans are right and the French are wrong," British officials, like their Japanese counterparts, now accepted Kissinger's multilateral strategy. For his part, Kissinger situated cooperation on energy "in the tradition of Atlantic cooperation." Yet what Kissinger was attempting was to shift the alliance onto new terrain, where the management of economic interdependence—not the containment of Soviet power—would be what held the West together.[66]

Improvised amid crisis, Kissinger's quest for energy cooperation was bold, even creative. He was nonetheless phlegmatic about the prospects for success. "We are putting a Band-Aid on a cancer," the secretary of state lamented on the eve of the conference. What was malignant, in Kissinger's eyes, was the zeal that America's allies had shown for autonomous action during and after the October War. It was not without some hypocrisy, then, that the United States made its own bilateral outreach to Saudi Arabia in the early months of 1974. Visiting Riyadh in March, Kissinger envisaged a wholesale expansion of Saudi-American relations "in the military field, in the economic field, and in the scientific field." Still, the purpose of US-Saudi bilateralism was not just to secure privileged access to oil. Rather, US diplomats reasoned that the expansion of US-Saudi relations across a variety of fronts would enhance Washington's leverage over Riyadh, enabling the United States to exercise a moderating influence on oil prices. Thus construed, the purposes of Saudi-US bilateralism were compatible with Kissinger's multilateral energy agenda. The juxtaposition was nonetheless jarring, as it also was when American officials worked to bolster bilateral ties with Iran.[67]

Whether bilateral or multilateral in method, US energy policy from 1974 onward aimed to moderate oil prices. Here, the embargo was only part of the problem—and not the major part of it. It was, after all, Pahlavi who had both kept the oil flowing during the October War and who was the leading advocate of price increases within OPEC. The Arab embargo was as much an embarrassment as an economic burden, but US officials were nonetheless determined to end it. King Faisal told the United States in early February that the embargo would not be removed until the United States secured a disengagement agreement between Israel and Syria. Policymakers struggled to break this link, cajoling Faisal with promises of future diplomatic breakthroughs. Amid Kissinger's effort to expand US-Saudi relations, King Faisal soon agreed to lift the embargo in exchange for "progress toward disengagement" on the Israeli-Syrian front. Faisal finally lifted the embargo in mid-March, and Kissinger continued to push for a disengagement agreement between Syria and Israel. In May, after months of diplomacy, Kissinger orchestrated a Syrian-Israeli agreement to withdraw forces from the Golan Heights.[68]

The Egyptian and Syrian disengagement agreements were steps toward an unspecified peace whose shape remained inchoate and whose participants, Sadat apart, were reluctant. Kissinger offered no roadmap, but the Syria-Israel agreement nonetheless found him jubilant. "We are moving the Soviet Union out of the Middle East," Kissinger exclaimed. Establishing the United States as the sole broker of Arab-Israeli peace served what Henry Kissinger had long defined as the largest purpose of his regional policy—marginalizing Moscow's influence. Set within a Cold War frame, the crisis of 1973–74 had indeed benefited the United States, and Egypt's defection from the Moscow camp was the major prize. Yet, even as Kissinger worked to exclude the Soviet Union from the Middle East, he was beginning to transcend the geopolitical preoccupations that captivated the Nixon administration's foreign policy from the outset.

The experiments in collaborative energy policy that Kissinger proposed during the oil crisis were an indication of evolving priorities. In April 1974, Kissinger addressed the UN General Assembly and called upon its members "to come to grips with the fact of our interdependence."[69]

∞

The years between 1967 and 1973 transformed global oil markets. Its domestic production flagging, the United States ceded its position as the world's swing oil producer. This made the difference between the ineffectual boycott of 1967 and the effective embargo of 1973. In energy, as in other arenas of power, the sinews of the Pax Americana were fraying. The oil crisis nonetheless precipitated a surprising shift in the strategic assumptions—and purposes—of American foreign policy. After struggling for years to stabilize the Pax Americana through détente and the Nixon Doctrine, Henry Kissinger began experimenting with new approaches. The Washington Energy Conference, as political scientist Robert Keohane argues, proposed to substitute multilateral cooperation for hegemony, to achieve together what the United States had once done alone, which was to assure the availability of oil to the world at reasonable prices. Whether such cooperation could succeed was unclear. The attempt to orchestrate it nonetheless became a central priority for American diplomacy in 1974.[70]

The rise of oil power, meanwhile, did not necessarily give the oil producers control over their own destinies. For Iran, in particular, the victory of 1973–74 would be a Pyrrhic one. The whip of inflation and the economic inequalities that petrodollars exacerbated were already undermining the shah's regime. Saudi Arabia proved to be a more stable partner than Iran, but its stability depended upon domestic repression and the regime's embrace of a stifling religious conservatism. The effects of energy interdependence, it turned out, cut in multiple directions. A transitional episode, the oil crisis of 1973–74 revealed both the imprint of Cold War geopolitics on US foreign policy and the limits of geopolitical concepts, something Henry Kissinger began in 1974 to acknowledge, as he turned in new strategic directions. Devising new purposes for American foreign policy amid growing economic interdependencies and enduring Cold War realities now became a challenge not for the future but for the present.

PART II

STUMBLING FORWARD

6

Managing Interdependence

All of us—allies and adversaries, new nations and old, rich and poor–
are part of a world community. Our interdependence on this planet is
becoming the central fact of our diplomacy.

Henry Kissinger, Milwaukee 1975

On July 4, 1976, the United States celebrated its two-hundredth birthday. Firecrackers, tall ships, and rodeos marked the occasion, but fiscal difficulties constrained the festivities. The unfurling of the world's largest flag from the Verrazano-Narrows Bridge in New York Harbor evoked the nation's chastened mood. The banner unraveled on release, leaving ribbons of red, white, and blue fluttering in the breeze. But as a moment for introspection as well as celebration, the bicentennial encouraged some to contemplate America's relations with the world. "On this day of independence," the *New York Times* proclaimed, Americans were "ever more aware" of their "interdependence with the other industrial nations in economics and with the Soviet Union in nuclear stability." Independence Day could thus be reinvented as "Interdependence Day."[1]

The wordplay was trite, but the point resonated. To mark the bicentennial, historian Henry Steele Commager drafted the "Declaration of Interdependence." "All people are part of one global community," it proclaimed. Calling upon humankind to "free itself from the limitations of national prejudice," Commager declared the arrival of "a new era in human history." The nation-state was becoming obsolete; humankind's political institutions would have to be reinvented to manage social and economic processes of transnational scope. For critics, this was outlandish: "mush-headed nonsense" said Pat Buchanan. Commager's future-oriented globalism nonetheless commanded attention, even support. One-third of the members of US Congress signed his declaration. Minnesota's legislature endorsed the document and decreed that the UN flag would henceforth fly over the state capitol in St. Paul.[2]

The flurry of interdependence talk around the bicentennial was no fluke. By the mid-1970s, awareness of what the political scientist Joseph Nye called "complex interdependence" was shaping public perceptions of the world and of the tasks for US foreign policy within it. In 1974–75, the Chicago Council of Foreign Relations found that 70 percent of Americans agreed that "fostering international coordination to solve common problems such as food, inflation, and energy" should be a "very important foreign policy goal." Just 36 percent believed, meanwhile, that "defending our allies" should be a national priority, and fewer still endorsed "protecting weaker nations against foreign aggression." Defending allies and protecting weaker countries against Communism had been core American commitments since the early Cold War, but the public, it seemed, was turning away from priorities that NATO and the Truman Doctrine had enshrined and toward issues associated with interdependence.[3]

The nation's elites followed a similar trajectory. According to the Chicago survey, 86 percent of them believed that "fostering international cooperation to solve common problems, such as food, inflation, and energy" should be a "very important" goal. Interdependence thus loomed large on the foreign-policy horizon. The category nonetheless encompassed diverse issues. Some, such as restoring international monetary order after the collapse of the Bretton Woods system and assuring energy security after the oil crisis, involved cooperation among governments. Others blurred distinctions between foreign and domestic policies. Some dilemmas implicated the advanced industrial societies. Others involved the Global South. Of these, world food supply and population growth became especially urgent concerns in the 1970s because of the imbalances between the two that demographers were projecting. Indeed, US policymakers concluded as early as 1974 that the possibility of resource wars made global population growth a national security dilemma. The sources of international danger and instability thus appeared to be shifting from Cold War geopolitics to the challenges of a globalizing world.[4]

∽∾

Entering the White House in August 1974, Gerald Ford inherited the presidency at an opportune juncture. For five and a half years, Nixon and Kissinger had worked to uphold the Pax Americana. To this end, they worked to extricate US forces from Vietnam, triangulate the Cold War, and bolster domestic support for American internationalism. Their détente tore away the ideological blinkers that had long constrained US foreign policy. Cold War preoccupations had nonetheless limited their creativity. Nixon and Kissinger hailed Brezhnev and Mao as fellow realists but continued to see international relations as a game that superpowers played. This at times led them to stumble, for example, when they misconstrued Third World crises as Cold War trials. There were also omissions, including of interdependence issues. The oil crisis made manifest the shortcomings of Nixon's geopolitical approach to the world, and Henry Kissinger began in its aftermath to rethink the strategic foundations of American foreign policy.

The Ford administration, this chapter contends, proved to be a creative phase. Forced to confront novel dilemmas, Ford and Kissinger worked to reorient US foreign policy toward challenges that would define a post–Cold War world. Important strands of continuity between Nixon and Ford nonetheless endured. Human rights remained an oversight, especially for Kissinger, and Soviet-American détente remained a central strategic commitment. At a still more fundamental level, the Ford administration remained committed to sustaining the postwar international order, an essentially conservative goal. What changed were the methods used to achieve these ends. Nixon had sought a tryst with adversaries; determined to remake the Pax Americana in a more multilateral guise, Ford and Kissinger worked to cultivate cooperative relationships with core allies on a variety of issues, including the management of common economic dilemmas. As a consequence, decision-makers moved in directions that paralleled the national debate on foreign policy: away from a Cold War concept and toward interdependence issues.[5]

The emergence of a distinctive interdependence discourse outside government in the mid-1970s is the first theme of this chapter. The narrative turns thereafter to the so-called New International Economic Order (NIEO), which representatives of the Global South proposed in April 1974. Engagement with North-South economic relations, the chapter argues, was one constructive dimension of the Ford administration's policy. The chapter concludes with the Ford administration's handling of interdependence relationships among the advanced industrialized countries. Here, the administration's institutionalization of a dialogue on policy coordination was a key achievement, formalized in the annual G-7 summits. Still, if the Ford years shaped a framework in which policy coordination could proceed, they produced little consensus about what the purposes of international coordination should be. Tensions soon emerged between the increasingly neoliberal agendas of many (but not all) US officials and the enduringly Keynesian preferences of some (but not all) European governments. For all the oversights and inconsistencies, what unfolded in the mid-1970s was nonetheless an impressive reorientation toward a new order of global dilemmas and challenges, which interdependence increasingly defined.

Interdependence in Theory

The interdependence discourse that blossomed in the mid-1970s began with the work of economists. Richard Cooper was a pioneer, arguing in *The Economics of Interdependence* (1968) that economic globalization was curtailing the effectiveness of national economic policy. Though he favored coordination among governments to manage interdependence, Cooper thought it likelier that nation-states would seek autonomy through controls and tariffs. Charles Kindleberger, another economist, concluded in *Power and Money* (1970) that the rise of the multinational corporation was leaving "less room for the independent, idiosyncratic, law-unto-itself state." Raymond Vernon, a political scientist, pushed this theme further in a 1971 book whose title encapsulated its bold hypothesis: *Sovereignty at Bay*. Like Cooper and Kindleberger, Vernon argued that tension between territorial nation-states and transnational capitalism was sharpening. Governments, he anticipated, would soon fight back. Identifying a structural tension between interdependence and governance, these early analyses suggested that social scientists were beginning, at the turn of the 1970s, to view economic interdependence as a phenomenon requiring at least the attention, if not the hands-on management, of policymakers.[6]

The economists and political scientists who reflected on interdependence inquired into substantive but subtle change. More strident were the wonderers, speculators, and futurists who argued that global integration was remaking world politics. "A unified global society," the ecologist Lester Brown concluded, is "the inevitable reality towards which we must move." His 1972 book *World without Borders* contended that globalization was sweeping aside the pretensions of nation-states. "Cherished though it is," Brown argued, "national sovereignty is being gradually but steadily sacrificed for affluence." These were forceful conclusions, but Brown was an influential thinker; even the State Department's Policy Planning Staff consulted his work. If Brown was focused on the world he saw coming into being, others addressed the tumult of transition. Alvin Toffler's *Future Shock* (1970) argued that the emergence of a "worldwide super-industrial society" was the source of widespread psychological disruption that manifested itself in feelings of individual helplessness and disarray. Toffler's focus on the individual psyche was unusual. Futurist musings in the early 1970s tended to focus on the world as a whole—and the catastrophes that might afflict it. Here, the Club of Rome led the way.[7]

Created in 1968 as a council of self-appointed luminaries, the Club of Rome concerned itself with dilemmas affecting the whole world, with what it called "the predicament of mankind." Population growth became the most notorious such issue, especially after Paul Ehrlich, a Stanford University demographer, published *The Population Bomb* (1968). Unbridled by caution, Ehrlich warned that demographic expansion might produce "global ecological catastrophe," "global pestilence," and even "global thermonuclear war." The Club of Rome echoed his claims in its 1972 report, "The Limits to Growth," which used econometric techniques to project population growth into the future. Based on a computer simulation, the report concluded that the world's resources would not sustain current growth rates, and it called for global solutions. There were serious flaws in the Club's analysis, including the omission of monetary variables from its model. These helped explain some of the problems that the Club of Rome identified, including the surging agricultural prices of the early 1970s, but the Club's crude model saw only a fundamental disequilibrium in supply and demand, mandating drastic measures.[8]

Another problem with the globalist approach, besides its tendency to over-simplify, was its disdain for the reality that political authority in the 1970s remained territorial, vested in nation-states. For Alfred Sauvy, a French demographer, this was a serious defect with analyses like the Club of Rome's, which operated at a planetary scale and did not differentiate between national circumstances. Did it really make sense, Sauvy asked, to see all nations as heirs to a common demographic dilemma when their circumstances were so different? As significant as transnational relations were becoming in the 1970s, they obliterated neither territorial sovereignty nor national politics. The practical challenges of relating new patterns of transnational relations to existing international political circumstances thus escaped many of the globalists.[9]

Setting themselves against the globalists (or "modernists"), who argued that everything was changing, and the "traditionalists," who countered that nothing was, Robert Keohane and Joseph Nye collaborated to formalize a theory of international relations under conditions of complex interdependence. Their key statement was *Power and Interdependence* (1977), which sought to modify—but not abandon—the "state-centric" or "realist" paradigm that takes nation-states as the basic element of world politics and presumes them to be autonomous and self-interested. This old paradigm, they contended, offered an increasingly "inadequate basis for the study of changing world politics." Keohane and Nye proposed a new theory of "complex interdependence." It held that societies were becoming connected to each other in new ways: transnational relations were thickening, and governments were interacting across an expanding array of policy arenas. Whereas realists still took military competition as the sine qua non of international relations, Keohane and Nye argued that interstate relations were becoming concerned with a broad range of issues—agriculture, economics, labor issues, public health, and so on—among which there was no clear hierarchy. Where interdependence relationships predominated, they argued, military force became obsolete. This sketch of complex interdependence was not offered as a literal description of world affairs but as a hypothesis. The world of the mid-1970s, Keohane and Nye argued, existed on a continuum between realist and interdependence concepts: in some arenas, such as Soviet-American relations, realist assumptions prevailed. When it came to relations among the advanced industrial countries, complex interdependence provided a better guide. What Keohane and Nye offered, then, was a model that could be juxta-posed against the realist concept of world politics.[10]

Keohane and Nye were concerned with theory, but others focused on its application. By the mid-1970s, policy-oriented intellectuals, such as Zbigniew Brzezinski and Miriam Camps, were asking how interdependence might affect foreign policy. The question even prompted the creation of a novel transnational body, the Trilateral Commission. The rethinking of world politics and the adap-tion of policy to conditions of thickening interdependence proceeded in parallel, stimulated by intellectual cross-fertilization and real-world developments: the shortcomings of the Nixon years and, above all, the shock of the 1973–74 oil crisis.

∞

The story of the Trilateral Commission begins with Zbigniew Brzezinski. Like Henry Kissinger, Brzezinski came to North America in the late 1930s. The son of a Polish diplomat, he found himself twice a refugee: first from the German invasion of Poland, then from Stalinism. Like Kissinger, he acquired a PhD at Harvard, where he taught before accepting a professorship at Columbia. A spe-cialist on Communist Europe, Brzezinski argued that the Soviet bloc was vul-nerable to the pressures of resurgent nationalism and urged the United States to build bridges to the East, expecting that US engagement would hasten the East Bloc's fragmentation. While the Communist world remained his specialty, Brzezinski became interested in large-scale historical change during the 1960s. He concluded that the United States was moving beyond industrial modernity, into what he called a "technetronic age." The concept emphasized the role of electronic technologies in the formation of postindustrial realities.[11]

After the 1968 election, in which he advised Hubert Humphrey, Brzezinski traveled to Japan, where he spent a year. He also wrote two books that shaped the next stage of his career. Published in 1970, *Between Two Ages* elaborated Brzezinski's earlier reflections on the technetronic age. Working in broad strokes, Brzezinski contended that technology was shrinking physical distances, trans-forming societies, and producing a "global city," which he defined as "a nervous, agitated, tense, and fragmented web of interdependent relations." The realties of perforated sovereignty and diminished autonomy, Brzezinski argued, made it imprudent to conduct foreign policy as though the international system still comprised autonomous nation-states. His analysis echoed the conclusions of globalists like Lester Brown. Unlike them, Brzezinski focused on the implica-tions for foreign policy. The industrialized countries would do best, Brzezinski concluded, if they coordinated their domestic policies and worked to manage interdependence. His next book, *The Fragile Blossom*, argued that Japan must be considered a coequal member of the community of advanced industrial nations.

On his return home, Brzezinski talked to friends, including David Rockefeller, about how to promote cooperation among the industrialized democracies. Rockefeller had for some months been promoting the idea of an "International Commission for Peace and Prosperity." In July 1972, he convened a meeting to develop the concept.[12]

At the family estate in Pocantico Hills, Rockefeller gathered a small group of internationalists from the United States, Western Europe, and Japan. The meeting took place one year after the Nixon Shock of August 1971, and Rockefeller described his fear that the advanced industrial countries would "drift aimlessly" into policies that might "inflict harm upon each other." To promote cooperation across the frontiers of sovereignty, the Pocantico group decided to establish the Trilateral Commission. An elite, nongovernmental think tank, the Trilateral Commission would be small, with a membership of around 180. Its executive committee would comprise thirty-four delegates: fourteen from the EEC, nine from Japan, nine from the United States, and two from Canada, a distribution reflecting Rockefeller's and Brzezinski's belief that an era of overbearing American dominance was over. Americans would nonetheless exercise a guiding influence on the commission through Brzezinski, whom the group appointed to be the executive director. "For the first time in the history of mankind," Brzezinski explained in a 1973 statement of the commission's purpose, "a global political process is surfacing, a process that is still quite shapeless." The Trilateral Commission would strive to give it form by cultivating "among concerned Americans, Japanese, and Europeans the habit of working together." The ultimate goal would be "to arrive at agreed and workable trilateral policies designed not only to enhance closer trilateral cooperation but also to progress toward a more just global community."[13]

Set against its grand objectives, the Trilateral Commission's methods were modest. Beginning in 1973, it hosted meetings and commissioned studies, its Task Force Reports. The first study, coauthored by Motoo Kaji, Richard Cooper, and Claudio Segré, considered the future of international monetary relations after Bretton Woods. It made a series of practical recommendations, which included creating a new IMF facility for short-term lending and establishing machinery within the IMF to encourage the coordination of national economic policies. The second task force report, less focused and more conceptual, considered the capacity of existing international institutions to accommodate "growing interdependence." Its verdict was discouraging. The mutual suspicion that existed among the industrialized countries after the breakdown of Bretton Woods, it concluded, imperiled cooperation. The trilateral countries needed to do better. "A world which has reached current levels of interdependence," the report's authors concluded, "must devise new forms of common management." Hence the need, presumably, for the Trilateral Commission.[14]

Over its first three years, the Trilateral Commission published a dozen reports. Several addressed energy. Others considered trade, international institutions, and the Third World. These reports constituted the most visible face of the Trilateral Commission's work. The Trilateralists also worked to build connections to government officials. Such approaches were easy to make; many of the Trilateralists had worked in government. Brzezinski cultivated political leaders, sending them encouraging notes, often attaching his own articles. He wrote to Senator Henry Jackson and Henry Kissinger, sending copies of task force reports. Gerard Smith, the Commission's US chairman, met in the spring of 1973 with the treasury secretary George Shultz, who seemed enthusiastic but turned down an invitation to join the commission. Kissinger addressed the Trilateral Commission in December 1974, hosting its members at the State Department. Of all the relationships the Commission forged, the most important turned out to be with Jimmy Carter, the Governor of Georgia, who joined the group in 1973. Carter would later describe his participation as "profoundly important" in his development as a foreign-policy thinker.[15]

The Trilateral Commission fast became an object of suspicion among fringe critics who saw it as a conspiracy to establish a world government—heir to the Bilderberg Group, the Freemasons, and the Bavarian Illuminati. More revealing were reactions within the political mainstream. Conservatives distrusted the commission's supra-nationalism and its willingness to indulge Third World aspirations for a more equitable international order. Progressives called it a "rich man's club" and argued, with some justification, that its purpose was "to preserve the existing structure of Western power and predominance." Most troubling, perhaps, was the concern that elite governance permitted little scope for democracy.[16]

Indeed, the appearance of a 1975 Task Force Report on the "crisis of democracy" stirred concerns that the commission was hostile to democratic processes. Authored by Samuel Huntington, Michel Crozier, and Joji Watanuki, the report concluded that democracies were prone to "parochialism in international affairs" and ill equipped to manage an interdependent world society. This was a diagnosis, but it could easily be mistaken for an endorsement of authoritarianism. There was something inherently undemocratic about the Trilateral Commission's concept for achieving stability through elite collaboration, as political scientist Karl Kaiser had warned in 1971. Because territorial nation-states were the only institutions capable of effecting self-government on a large scale, binding them into communities of common purpose would, by necessity, diminish the scope of democratic accountability. Rule by technocratic elites, which the commission favored, might have been a solution to the dilemmas of a globalizing world, but its compatibility with democratic consent was not obvious.[17]

As controversial as it was, the Trilateral Commission became the most prominent organization to espouse solutions for the management of complex interdependence. That the commission was itself a transnational entity made it unusual. Its program, however, was not especially distinctive. By the mid-1970s, talk of managing interdependence and promoting "world order" was becoming common in the United States and elsewhere. As early as 1967, for example, a group of prominent American internationalists had created a journal titled *Interplay of European/American Affairs,* which explored transnational issues, ranging from the regulation of international financial markets to the waves of student protest that swept the advanced democracies in the late 1960s. *Interplay* proved short lived, but it prefigured the Trilateral Commission's work. It also stood as an early marker of the attention that policy intellectuals would soon shower upon interdependence and its implications for foreign policy.[18]

∽

Founded in 1922, the Council on Foreign Relations (CFR) remained in the 1970s the nation's most prominent organization devoted to international affairs and foreign policy. From its offices in New York, it published the journal *Foreign Affairs* and worked to foster interactions between scholars and policymakers. Since the late 1940s, the CFR had been aligned with—and had worked to sustain—the Cold War consensus in Washington. Within the CFR membership, however, that consensus did not survive the Vietnam War. The 1970s found the council grasping for direction under new leadership. In 1970, David Rockefeller replaced John McCloy, a Cold War wise man, at the head of the CFR's board. Two years later, Rockefeller selected Bayless Manning, dean of the Stanford Law School, to serve as the council's president. Meanwhile, Hamilton Fish Armstrong, who had for a quarter century personified the close relationship between the CFR and Cold War foreign policy, retired from the editorship of *Foreign Affairs* in 1972, to be replaced by William Bundy. These personnel changes prefigured new intellectual directions.[19]

For Manning, evolving circumstances demanded new approaches to the world. "The traditional conceptual and theoretical framework of international affairs," he proposed in 1973, had "come unstuck." If the council intended to preserve its role as an intellectual adjunct to US foreign policy, it would have "to achieve a new basic understanding of what is happening in the world about us" and "work out a new synthesis of policies that will move us in the right directions." To this end, Manning announced a major project, the so-called 1980s Project. Its mission would be to explain how international relations were changing and devise appropriate solutions for US foreign policy. The 1980s Project, Manning explained, would be the largest initiative that the council had undertaken since the War and Peace Studies of the 1940s. The comparison was revealing. Manning and his colleagues proceeded from the belief that the 1940s had produced a stable international settlement that was now crumbling because of "the emergence of strong non-governmental but transnational forces." Undertaken at a moment of historical flux, the 1980s Project aimed to retool American leadership for evolving conditions.[20]

Within the US government, at least some officials concurred with Manning that the present moment demanded novel solutions. Concerned that the energy crisis had exposed national vulnerabilities, the chief of naval operations, Elmo Zumwalt, convened a weekend seminar in March 1974 on the topic of "economic interdependence and the nation's future." The seminar assembled a group of high-powered participants, who included George Shultz, defense secretary James Schlesinger, Cold War strategist Paul Nitze, and Senator Henry Jackson. Kissinger did not attend; Helmut Sonnenfeldt represented the State Department. Zumwalt opened with a warning that US foreign policy had not kept abreast of changes in the international environment. "Over the last six or seven years, while the United States has been preoccupied with Southeast Asia," he explained, "major changes have been taking place within the world's economic structure." The consequences could not be ignored, not after the oil crisis. "The time has come," Zumwalt continued, "to take a look at the growing economic interdependence of nations and the impact which this interdependence is likely to have upon US policy."[21]

The participants in the Zumwalt seminar agreed that "economic interdependence" was now an "established fact" of international life. Managing it would be difficult. Bountiful natural endowments had given Americans a "self-perception of independence" that would inhibit their acceptance of "the type of international cooperation which will be necessary if there is to be true international economic interdependence." It would be hard to persuade Americans to use less gasoline, for example, or to accept monetary discipline in order to stabilize the international balance of payments. Nor was their government well configured to apply the "discipline" at home that would be necessary to preserve American leadership in an interdependent world. Domestic policy and foreign policy were still being conducted as if they were separate and noncontiguous areas of responsibility. "It must be realized," one participant commented, "that in a world of economic interdependence domestic policy is foreign policy." There was, however, little discussion of concrete steps that might be taken to improve the situation. The dialogue at the Zumwalt seminar remained conceptual, degrees removed from specific policy issues, such as energy or international monetary relations.

All the participants nonetheless agreed that the stakes were high. "Either there will be progress toward international cooperation," concluded one discussion paper, or else there would be "a continuation of destabilizing national ad hoc measures to deal with symptoms and exploit asymmetries." If the industrialized countries could not come together to resolve their common problems, in other words, the economic, social, and political costs of thickening interdependence might push them apart. The accomplishments of the Pax Americana seemed at the end of the Nixon years to be in jeopardy, threatened not only by Nixon's neglect of core US allies but also by the rise of domestic isolationist forces that the costs of managing interdependence seemed likely to exacerbate. The tasks of renovation would, however, fall to a new president.

Kissinger's Southern Strategy

Gerald Ford was an anomalous president; he had never won election to anything larger than Michigan's Fifth District. An effective, affable legislator, the congress-man led the Republican minority in the House from 1965 until late 1973, when the Senate confirmed him as vice president, replacing Spiro Agnew, who had resigned over a financial scandal. Within a year, Ford would replace Nixon, who resigned over Watergate in August 1974. Ford lacked Nixon's sense of history and his geopolitical instincts, but he brought assets of his own to the White House, including a quick grasp of detail and formal training in both law and econom-ics. These attributes made Gerald Ford a different kind of foreign-policy presi-dent—a leader better suited, in many respects, to the challenges of the emerging post–Cold War world. His background equipped him to engage technical issues, such as monetary policy and energy, while his collegiality engendered effective relationships with foreign leaders, including Valéry Giscard d'Estaing, Helmut Schmidt, and James Callaghan. Ford made the management of interdependence a priority. "We need new approaches to international cooperation to respond effectively to the problems that we face," he declared in the second month of his presidency.[22]

The international circumstances that the Ford administration faced were not propitious. Superpower relations were at least stable, so much so that American and Soviet leaders spoke of the Cold War in the past tense. Beyond the stability of high geopolitics, however, instability and uncertainty raged. The international monetary system remained broken, its future a source of dissension. Absent the discipline the gold-dollar standard had provided, inflation roared. Economic growth had stilled across the capitalist world, and unemployment was soaring. Rocketing food and energy prices exacerbated the disarray, especially for the nations of the Third World, whose citizens spent larger fractions of their income on food and energy than did Westerners. The future of the postwar international order looked uncertain. "The international system," the Trilateral Commission opined, "is undergoing a drastic transformation through a number of crises." Geoffrey Barraclough, an astute commentator on historical trends, perceived "the breakdown of the industrial system built up in the West since 1950 and of the international order it created." "If we do not get a recognition of our interdependence," Kissinger explained in October 1974, "the Western civilization that we now have is almost certain to disintegrate."[23]

Kissinger began after 1973 to embrace the management of interdependence as a priority for US foreign policy. Hinging on the oil crisis, this evolution antedated Nixon's departure, but the presidential transition confirmed it. Still, an underlying continuity girded the shift: the sustenance of international stability remained his purpose throughout. What had evolved was his sense of the immediate moment and its challenges. Kissinger's first gamble, in which Richard Nixon had been the senior partner, was that détente would stabilize the Cold War and the Pax Americana. His second, of which he was the principal architect, was that reorienting the West toward the management of interdependence would preserve the framework of international order inherited from the 1940s. This led him, ironically, to embrace policies not so far removed from those that critics like Zbigniew Brzezinski advocated as alternatives to the geopolitical "acrobatics" of the Nixon-Kissinger years. This final act proved to be a creative phase in Kissinger's career, the oversights and omissions notwithstanding.[24]

⁂

For the nations of the Global South, disenchantment with existing international institutions ran deep. The marginalization of the Third World was especially acute at the IMF and the World Bank, where voting rights were allocated in proportion to financial contributions, leaving the rich dominant. In the UN General Assembly, on the other hand, numbers offered leverage, and a Third World caucus emerged over time, which in 1964 became known as the Group of 77, or G-77. Besides collaborating at the UN, the developing countries had built international organizations of their own. The 1955 Bandung Conference had proclaimed their common purpose, and it prefigured the Non-Aligned Movement, born in 1961. Solidarity against the superpowers was easier to accomplish, however, than the reform of international economic institutions. In 1964, the developing nations convened the United Nations Conference on Trade and Development (UNCTAD), which proposed replacing the liberal economic order with one more oriented to the G-77's needs. The effort struggled. Raúl Prebisch, the Argentine economist who served as UNCTAD's first secretary-general, grew frustrated with bureaucratic infighting and UNCTAD's general ineffectiveness. The complaints against the postwar status quo that had animated UNCTAD's creation did not subside, however, and the Third World activism of the 1960s prefigured a more powerful assault on the international economic order in the 1970s.[25]

The oil crisis triggered the Third World's new insurgency. Economic growth slumped after 1973; after growing by an average 4.9 percent per year since 1950, world GDP grew by just 2.3 percent in 1974 and 1.5 percent in 1975. For the world's poor, sluggish growth mattered less than surging food prices. Price infla-tion exacerbated the problem, but it was a supply crunch that flung the world into a food crisis. In 1972, world food production declined for the first time in decades. By the fall of 1974, food prices adjusted for inflation were three times what they had been in 1970, causing distress and social strain. In some places, including middle-income countries, political tumult followed: popular unrest prompted dictatorial clampdowns in Greece and the Philippines; Indians suf-fered the curtailment of civil rights during Indira Gandhi's two-year Emergency. In Portugal, economic dislocation stirred a democratic revolution. While its consequences varied, the tumult of the mid-1970s reinforced a palpable sense of crisis. The future appeared more malleable than it had in 1964, when UNCTAD had first made the case for a new international economic order.[26]

In April 1974, Houari Boumedienne addressed the UN. Speaking for the G-77, the Algerian president proclaimed a "decisive turning-point in the course of international relations." The Third World could not develop, he exclaimed, without the transformation of world economic structures. It was not domestic institutions or natural endowments but the international economic order that was "standing in the way of any hope of development and progress." Drawing on dependency theory, which postulates a causal relationship between the prosper-ity of rich countries and the poverty of poor countries, Boumedienne divided the world into exploiters and exploited—"the forces of liberation" and "the powers of domination"—and called upon the General Assembly to remake the global order.[27]

In Boumedienne's New International Economic Order (NIEO), develop-ing countries would seize control of their natural resources, expropriating the property of foreign multinationals; international institutions would support the price of commodities; the international monetary system would be reformed to accommodate the developing world's needs; and the United Nations would create a "special fund" to serve the world's most desperate people. The oil cri-sis animated the NIEO concept. OPEC's example should be a "source of hope" to poor countries that did not produce oil, declared the leader of one that did. The initiative's anti-Westernism was palpable. So too was its statism. What the NIEO sought was the transformation of relations not only between the North and the South but also between the state and the market. Indeed, the first con-crete step that the G-77 took to realize the NIEO was the passage by the General Assembly eight months later of the Charter of Economic Rights and Duties of States, an anti-liberal manifesto that affirmed the absolute power of govern-ments over economic activity, including private property, within their borders. Multinational corporations and international trade might have been spinning webs of transnational interdependence in the mid-1970s, but some nation-states were determined to fight back.[28]

Five days later, Kissinger responded in a UN speech of his own, using the idea of interdependence to rebuke Boumedienne. Thanks to the oil crisis, he argued: "the notion of the northern rich and the southern poor has been shattered." The problem that the world faced, he continued, was not inequality as such but the awareness of inequality that globalization bred. "Global communication," Kissinger declared, "insures that the thrust of human aspirations becomes universal." Fortunately, technology also held out the "possibility to escape," through the development of cures for poverty and disease. Kissinger's outlook contrasted with the G-77's. Whereas the NIEO's proponents advocated redistribution, Kissinger favored growth. "The developing nations," he insisted, "can meet the aspirations of their peoples only in an open, expanding world economy." Anxious to reconcile the Global South to the liberal status quo, Kissinger made concessions. Although he had in the past resisted consumer-producer talks on energy, Kissinger now indicated his willingness "to countenance such a dialogue" and to extend it to include other commodities—bauxite, tin, copper, and so on. He would even consider creating international mechanisms to stabilize commodity prices, a core NIEO demand. His boldest commitments were reserved for food, where Kissinger pledged to expand US food production and to provide more help for the world's poorest people. The speech met with a positive reaction.[29]

Over the next eighteen months, Kissinger worked to devise a strategy for managing the North-South dialogue that the NIEO declaration had opened. In private, he was frank about his purposes. "I don't want to accept a New Economic Order," he told President Ford, "but I don't want to confront Boumedienne." Instead, Kissinger sought to stabilize the existing international economic order. This was a crucial distinction. As in the past, Kissinger subordinated economics to politics, insisting that the preservation of American ascendancy and international stability should trump "theology about the merits of the free market economy." If concessions had to be made, he was willing to make them. To this end, Kissinger advocated progressive accommodation with the NIEO's proponents. This was a surprising turn in a career that had thus far neglected the Third World. The underlying continuity resided in Kissinger's commitment to the stability of the international status quo. Appeasing the NIEO served two purposes. It promised to divide the developing countries and to hold the West together. With Britain, France, and others sympathetic to aspects of the NIEO, Kissinger recognized that taking an adversarial line risked alienating the United States from its allies. Kissinger's attentiveness to the global scale was nonetheless a novel departure, for modernization as US policymakers had long espoused it was framed and pursued within nation-states. As creative as it was, Kissinger's southern strategy, as this chapter calls it, provoked opposition within the US government, stirring a backlash that limited its effectiveness.[30]

Skeptics contested Kissinger's southern strategy on ideological and political grounds. This backlash was in some ways surprising, since US foreign economic policy had for a quarter century been pragmatic, open to experimentation and tolerant of diverse approaches. In pursuit of an anti-Soviet front, the United States had supported European social democrats, Third World socialists, and even Yugoslavian Communists. By the mid-1970s, however, the forces of free-market orthodoxy were rising. The failure of Keynesian economists to correct the recession of 1974–75 emboldened proponents of market-oriented liberalism. Several free-market liberals had served the Nixon administration, including George Shultz. Under Ford, their influence mounted. Alan Greenspan chaired Ford's Council of Economic Advisers. A disciple of Ayn Rand, he cleaved to market-based solutions. So too did Bill Simon, a bond trader from Salomon Brothers whom Ford named his secretary of the treasury. Simon saw himself as a defender of capitalism against the "dominant socialist-statist-collectivist orthodoxy" of the era; he was a fierce partisan of the market. The Ford administration also contained pragmatists who favored workable solutions over ideological purity. Defense secretary James Schlesinger was one, although he clashed bitterly with Kissinger. The president himself, while sympathizing with the free-marketeers, sided more often with the pragmatic Kissinger. Still, this neoliberal shift would constrain the options for foreign policy, as did the domestic political costs that attached to interdependence. Whether the goal was reducing energy imports or expanding food exports, accommodating interdependence often imposed costs on domestic constituencies, which led Ford's domestic political and economic advisers to express recurrent skepticism. Kissinger's efforts to reorient foreign policy toward "the challenge of interdependence" thus proved fractious, often isolating the State Department within the US government.[31]

∞

Food was an area in which the United States was well positioned to appease the G-77. The world's greatest producer of wheat, corn, and soybeans, the United States in 1974 exported some $22.5 billion in food products—more than the world's next three food exporters combined. Even as the NIEO was being formulated, NSC officials had recognized that expanding food aid could serve the purposes of foreign policy. A review completed in the fall of 1973 argued for the creation of an international food bank to release reserves in times of scarcity, ensuring that "those with the least ability to pay will not be the first to suffer."[32]

A year later, Kissinger participated in the World Food Conference in Rome, where he traced the outlines of a world food policy. Expanding production was the key. To this end, he advocated sharing agricultural technologies and techniques. If the world could surmount its food crisis, Kissinger argued, "global cooperation in food" would be "a model for our response to other challenges of an interdependent world: energy, inflation, population, protection of the environment." The United States, he said, would expand its overseas food aid programs and help build an international food bank. Famine, Kissinger declared, was a universal concern "now [that] our consciousness is global." In private, national interests still came first. "I don't give a damn about Bangladesh or humanitarian grounds," Kissinger reassured his cabinet colleagues. "I want it for foreign policy." Food, he continued, "is useful in weaning India away from the Soviet Union." This distinction between foreign policy and humanitarian purposes attested to Kissinger's ulterior purposes, but these now aligned with progressive, globalist engagement.[33]

Kissinger's effort to orchestrate a world food policy encountered difficulties at home, which was unsurprising given that his program aligned with neither the interests of American farmers nor with those of American consumers. Expanding production would lower agricultural prices, to the detriment of farm interests. Exporting more food could set domestic consumers against foreign buyers, as recent experience had taught. In 1972, a botched Soviet-American trade agreement resulted in the USSR purchasing large quantities of US grain at subsidized rates and driving up domestic food prices—an episode memorialized as the "Great Grain Robbery." Chastened, Nixon had in 1973 introduced a program of export controls to hold down domestic food prices; despite its deleterious effects abroad, the scheme was popular at home. Some worried that the additional spending on food aid would exacerbate inflation. Others were simply defending bureaucratic turf. "If Henry needs it," growled agriculture secretary Earl Butz, "let the money come out of his budget." "We are isolated within the government," warned the NSC staff economist. After the Rome conference, Kissinger nonetheless won Ford's approval to create an interdepartmental working group to develop his world food concept. Created in late 1974, the International Food Review Group was a State Department vehicle; Kissinger chaired it, and the assistant secretary for economic and business affairs, Thomas Enders, did the intellectual heavy lifting. The internal opposition continued.[34]

Free-market commitments did not always align against the kind of globalist food agenda Kissinger was now pursuing. Secretary Butz illustrated this point when he stopped requiring that farmers "set-aside" land in the interests of higher prices. Although Butz's decision benefited agribusiness at the expense of small farmers, it had a salutary effect on world food markets, increasing supply and bringing down prices. Kissinger could thus salute the removal of "government restrictions on production" as a conscientious move. On the other hand, Butz and other cabinet officials opposed State Department plans to create an international food reserve, a concept that Enders developed during the winter and Kissinger unveiled in May 1975. Their blueprint, which aimed to guard against food scarcity and to stabilize prices, called for reserves to be established at the national level, with "international rules or guidelines" to encourage the accumulation of reserves and to supervise their release. "In times of shortage," Kissinger explained, "there must be special provision to meet the needs of the poorest developing countries." This seemed reasonable, but Earl Butz, Alan Greenspan, Ford's economic adviser Bill Seidman, and Bill Simon all opposed State's proposal.[35]

Two weeks later, Ford's Economic Policy Board fired a broadside. Kissinger's willingness to indulge Third World demands, board officials complained, was both reckless and unprincipled. "We are in danger of compromising our basic commitment to the free enterprise system," wrote Simon and Seidman on the board's behalf. The State Department, they alleged, was prepared to "acquiesce in, or compromise with" a "new international economic order based on socialist principles." The United States, they countered, would do better to stand firm in defense of "free markets and free enterprise" than to "compromise" its "basic system." This was ideological posturing, but it showcased the influence of a faction that opposed even engagement with the G-77. This stance not only foreclosed on dialogue with the Global South but also threatened transatlantic comity. Just months earlier, the European Economic Community had signed an agreement to extend development aid and trade privileges to some forty-six developing countries. The Lomé Convention included provisions to stabilize commodity prices, signaling Europe's willingness to accommodate Third World demands for a more equitable economic order. Confront the Third World, as Simon and Seidman urged, and Washington risked alienating its allies. This was the State Department's point.[36]

Defending his approach, Kissinger disclaimed expertise in economics: "I am not reliable on economic matters," he told President Ford. Yet the issues at hand, he continued, "are not basically economic." What was at stake was the legitimacy of American world leadership. In the fall of 1971, Kissinger had identified Connally's economic nationalism as a threat to geopolitical objectives and worked to thwart it. Now it was the neoliberals who were putting American international leadership in jeopardy. Talking a few days later with Daniel Patrick Moynihan, the newly appointed ambassador to the United Nations, Kissinger was explicit about his purposes. "Our basic strategy must be to hold the industrialized powers behind us and to split the Third World," he explained. "We can only do that if we start with a lofty tone and a forthcoming stance." Prying the non-oil-exporting Third World countries away from "their OPEC brethren" required real concessions, Kissinger insisted, not neoliberal hectoring. Whereas Bill Simon saw opposition to commodity agreements as "an issue of principle," Kissinger worried that the United States would be "beaten back" if it got drawn into "a theological fight between free market[s] and regulated market[s]." Turn the struggle into an ideological contest, he argued, and "the Europeans won't support us. Nobody will support us." It was thus imperative "to avoid an international dispute where the Americans say the existing system is great, and the L[ess] D[eveloped] C[ountrie]s call for a new economic order." Putting pragmatism ahead of ideology, Ford sided with Kissinger.[37]

Kissinger's response to the NIEO was both constructive and cynical; it engaged the Third World in order to divide it and stabilize the status quo. To achieve these ends, Kissinger deployed a mixture of threats and concessions. He rebuked the G-77's tactics in a July 1975 speech that promised "concrete and constructive proposals for action across a broad spectrum of international economic activities." The specifics came in his opening presentation to the Seventh Special Session of the General Assembly in September. In the address he committed the United States to working with the developing countries to stabilize their export earnings—not through an international commodities organization, as the G-77 had demanded, but through stabilization agreements negotiated on a "case by case basis." Building on his speech to the World Food Conference, Kissinger urged the rapid creation of a world food reserve system and pledged $200 million to support agricultural development in the Third World. While he did not accept the G-77's call for a Special Fund to be created under UN auspices to aid the poorest countries, he endorsed the creation of a similar facility within the IMF. The message was that the United States, while it did not share their goals, would engage with the NIEO's proponents in a serious dialogue.[38]

Kissinger thus made the United States a participant in the North-South dialogue that the NIEO had opened. Indeed, the United States would soon participate in the Conference on International Economic Cooperation, a forum of twenty-seven countries that France hosted to address energy, commodities, and other contentious issues. In 1976, Kissinger traveled to Nairobi to address the fourth UNCTAD conference, where he debuted a proposal for an international resources bank. Although that initiative floundered, his participation in the conference underscored the significance that he attached to North-South relations. Moreover, Kissinger's southern strategy of 1974–75 served one of its chief purposes, which was to prevent the NIEO from becoming a source of explosive contention among the advanced industrial countries. After all, holding the West together while sustaining the achievements of the Soviet-American détente that he and Nixon had built was, in the aftermath of the oil crisis, where Kissinger's priorities lay.[39]

Holding the West Together

Détente prevailed in the mid-1970s, but the Cold War still endured, which made the West's turmoil the East's opportunity. The Communist Party of the

Soviet Union made this point in a *Pravda* editorial that itemized the symptoms of a "deepening crisis" in the capitalist world. These included inflation, energy, unemployment, and widening "contradictions" among the United States, Europe, and Japan. Marxist ideology attuned its followers to await capitalism's crisis, but now non-Marxists were also questioning the durability of Western institutions. German chancellor Helmut Schmidt lamented the "fragility of this elaborate system of economic relations among the nations of the world." With inflation rampant, growth slumping, and a rash of banking failures, comparisons to the 1930s abounded. Newspapers warned of a "world economic catastrophe as fraught with danger to political stability and peace as was the Great Depression." Whether the international economy could be restabilized was perhaps the West's most urgent dilemma.[40]

For a generation after 1945, Cold War fears were the adhesive holding the Pax Americana together. In the 1960s, however, the West's unity had loosened. The Middle East war of 1973 exacerbated transatlantic differences. But it also prompted a reorientation in Washington. Having heretofore focused on America's Cold War adversaries, Kissinger began to shift his sights toward Western Europe and Japan. As he did so, he worked to move the Western Alliance onto a new footing in which cooperation to manage common economic dilemmas would supplant containment of the Soviet threat as the source of cohesion among the nation-states of the West.

Rather than pursue a grand structure like Bretton Woods, Kissinger's tactics now called for incremental progress. Rebuilding common purpose through cooperation on tangible, technical issues would be his method—an approach that resembled his conduct of Soviet-American détente and Arab-Israeli peace negotiations. That it was a piecemeal process ought not to obscure the boldness of Kissinger's bid to reorient US foreign policy toward the sustenance of economic stability and reinvigorated prosperity among the industrialized countries. "The trick in the world now," he explained in 1975, "is to use economics to build a world political structure." Although they were not wholly successful, Kissinger's exertions nonetheless helped to sustain the West's unity through the treacherous conditions of the mid-1970s and contributed to the construction of a consultative framework in which national governments could manage their interdependent economic relations. Kissinger's efforts began with progress on two thorny, substantive issues—energy and international monetary reform—and proceeded to the promotion of policy coordination in general.[41]

⁂

The question of how to pay for oil imports ranked among the most urgent of the dilemmas facing the West after the oil crisis. Rough-and-ready estimates put the oil exporters' windfall in the last quarter of 1973 at somewhere between $65 and

$90 billion dollars. To put these numbers in perspective, the costs of the oil crisis would be similar to the US defense budget and would be borne, in the main, by the industrialized countries. The consequence for international monetary relations, as IMF Director Johannes Witteveen put it, was "an overall disequilibrium in trade accounts of unprecedented magnitude."[42]

To restore balance, as George Shultz had proposed back in early 1973, when the disequilibria had been smaller, the oil exporters' profits would have to be lent or "recycled" to the oil importers. The question of whether private banks or the IMF would do the work of petrodollar recycling still endured in early 1974, but the contentiousness around the issue lessened as the sums ballooned. Saudi Arabia still favored an IMF facility, but West European enthusiasm for recycling petrodollars via the IMF was waning. By the time of the Washington Energy Conference in February 1974, a consensus was emerging among the industrialized countries that "existing market and other financial mechanisms" would have to handle the task of petrodollar recycling. US opposition to an IMF-based facility aligned with neoliberal preferences for market-based solutions, but the real stakes involved politics and prices. Establishing an OPEC-financed facility under the IMF's auspices, US officials reasoned, would institutionalize OPEC's power, lock high prices in for perpetuity, and likely require the "indexation" of oil prices to inflation, a technical maneuver that would preclude inflating away the oil exporters' gains. Despite US and growing European opposition, the IMF established a small fund to assist countries struggling to pay for their oil imports in June 1974. Many more petrodollars would, however, be recycled via private banks, boosting the growth of offshore banking.[43]

Petrodollar recycling bridged payments imbalances, but it did not mitigate the economic damage that expensive oil inflicted. High prices exacerbated inflation, diverted capital from investment, and strained pocketbooks, jeopardizing the West's postwar prosperity. The price of oil, Ford exclaimed, was "probably the most serious problem in the Alliance and worldwide." Defining high prices as a threat to national security and international stability, the United States ranged itself against them. This was a turnaround from the Nixon years, when Washington had tolerated—and even encouraged—price increases that enhanced Iran's and Saudi Arabia's capacities to serve as guarantors of Cold War security interests. Now, restoring the West's economic vitality took precedence, and forcing oil prices downward became an urgent priority. Seeing the price hikes as an expression of political grievances, Washington sought at first to lower prices through political means, both conciliatory and belligerent.[44]

The geopolitical dividends from an Egyptian-Israeli settlement remained tantalizing, but the economic interests of the West also helped to draw the United States into the peace process. "The United States," Kissinger explained, "has an interest in the survival of Israel, but we of course have an interest in the 130 million Arabs that sit athwart the world's oil supplies." For Washington, peace promised not only to prevent another war—and the renewed oil shock that would likely accompany it—but also to appease and encourage so-called moderate forces in the Arab world. The linkage between peace and oil was a subtext of the Kissinger-led diplomatic process that culminated in the Sinai Interim Agreement in September 1975. Known as Sinai II, this Israeli-Egyptian agreement demilitarized the desert buffer between the two countries and committed both sides to reconciling disputes by peaceful means.[45]

Although it brought accolades, the peace process was often frustrating for the secretary of state, who conducted much of it in person. Having adopted an incremental approach to peace, Kissinger encountered criticism from the proponents of a "comprehensive" peace that would involve the USSR in the negotiations and the Palestinians in the settlement. Conversely, his efforts to broker Israeli withdrawal from its positions in the Sinai Desert encountered resistance from pro-Israel constituencies at home. Transnational politics thus appeared to be set against US economic interests—or so it seemed to Israel's staunchest supporters. "American Jews," explained Senator Jacob Javits of New York, "fear that our interest in the Arabs will lead us to ask Israel to make concessions." In practice, the trade-off between oil and Israel that Javits feared was not so easy to make. Sinai II was a major accomplishment, but within a month OPEC orchestrated another price hike. The peace process diminished the probability of renewed war, but it did not solve the dilemmas of supply and demand that precipitated the 1973–74 oil shocks.[46]

Besides reconciling Israel and Egypt, US officials worked to intimidate the oil producers. Frustrated with OPEC's recalcitrance on prices, high-ranking officials mulled the possibilities for a military response. In the event of a renewed oil embargo, Kissinger mused, the United States "may have to take some oil fields." This notion surfaced intermittently in public. In private, administration officials weighed the costs and benefits of military intervention and even discussed possible targets. "I'm not saying we have to take over Saudi Arabia," Kissinger suggested in January 1975. "How about Abu Dhabi, or Libya?" In reality, the obstacles to armed intervention were substantial and the risks of such an approach grave. The talk of war nonetheless served a psychological purpose, which was to breed uncertainty in the minds of OPEC leaders; whether this engendered flexibility remains unclear. Other tactical maneuvers aimed to divide the cartel. The Joint Economic Commissions that Washington created with Iran and Saudi Arabia would, US officials hoped, strengthen bilateral relationships and weaken OPEC unity. An oil deal that the United States pursued with Iran during 1975 and 1976 followed similar logic. "A major crack in the solid OPEC front," officials hoped, "could lead to a break in OPEC prices."[47]

What British diplomats called the "velvet glove and mailed fist" approach failed to bring oil prices down. For two years, neither Saudi Arabia nor Iran cooperated. Only at the end of 1976, amid entreaties and warnings, did Saudi Arabia exert decisive moderation, choosing a 5 percent increase in posted prices instead of the 15 percent hike that other OPEC countries favored. That US officials hailed this "split decision," which did not lower oil prices, as a victory attests to just how difficult it was to produce cheap energy through political means. It was hardly easier, however, to orchestrate what Kissinger called "the objective conditions necessary to bring about lower oil prices." The attempt to do so nonetheless constituted the second thrust of US energy policy during the Ford years. If the industrial countries could reduce their demand for oil, American officials reasoned, the loss of earnings would put OPEC under pressure, perhaps breaking the cartel. Thus construed, consumer cooperation was a creative response to the West's predicament. Indeed, the pursuit of cooperation among the industrialized countries contributed to the institutionalization of consultative relationships on interdependence issues more generally. It did not, however, do much to reduce oil prices.[48]

When finance and foreign ministers from France, Germany, Japan, and the United Kingdom met with Kissinger and Simon to discuss energy in September 1974, major issues still divided them. France questioned Washington's pursuit of consumer solidarity, preferring to negotiate with the oil producers. Britain favored establishing procedures for sharing oil among the consumer countries in emergencies but feared a confrontation with the producers. Kissinger nonetheless remained adamant that "oil prices must come down" and that consumer solidarity was the means to this end. He unveiled a substantive agenda in mid-November. Summoning the ghosts of the 1940s, Kissinger called for another "act of lasting creativity" by the West. Proclaiming energy cooperation a strategic imperative, he argued that collaborative conservation and alternative fuel sources could shift market conditions so as to improve the West's energy security. Days later, the International Energy Agency that Kissinger had proposed back in February 1974 came into being, with France still refusing to join. The pieces of Kissinger's consumer cooperation strategy were in place, but the prospects remained unclear.[49]

Just weeks earlier, Valéry Giscard d'Estaing had unveiled an alternative approach, inviting world leaders to attend a producer-consumer conference in Paris. What divided the French president and Kissinger was the question of whether the industrialized countries should negotiate with the oil producers forthwith or try first to reduce their demand for OPEC oil. The disagreement irked Kissinger, who complained about "French sabotage," but it reflected differences of circumstance. Although the United States was unable to meet domestic demand from domestic supply, it imported far less of its oil than did Western

Europe, which made confronting OPEC easier for Washington to contemplate. As it was, the spat resolved itself. Following Giscard's demarche, London fell in line behind Washington. In December, Ford and Kissinger met with Giscard in Martinique and finalized a compromise. The United States would participate in Giscard's producer-consumer conference, while France offered tacit cooperation—on "parallel paths"—with the International Energy Agency on conservation and alternative fuels.[50]

By the end of 1974, a rapid restoration of the pre-1973 cheap-oil regime appeared improbable; OPEC was noncompliant, and the realities of the West's dependence were too stark for conservation to overcome. Kissinger conceded this point, assuring Giscard that the real purpose of his consumer-solidarity strategy was to reverse what he called "the moral and political disintegration of the West." Thus construed, transatlantic cooperation on energy served a psychological as much as an economic function; it promised to "give the consumer nations a sense of control over their destiny." In this light, the restoration of Franco-American amity was an important success, making energy the focus of transatlantic cooperation, not conflict. Shortly thereafter, George Shultz represented the United States at a meeting with technical experts from France, Germany, Japan, and Great Britain in Kronberg, Germany. The meeting would mark an important step toward the institutionalization of a consultative dialogue among the advanced industrialized countries on economic matters of common concern.[51]

Dialogue remained easier to effect than results. The fundamental problem with energy, which recurred across other interdependence issues, was that progress mandated sacrifices, which domestic constituencies were reluctant to make. To promote conservation and alternative fuels, Kissinger favored raising—not reducing—the prices American consumers paid for gasoline. He even wanted a "floor price," beneath which the price of domestic oil would not be permitted to fall. This was a sensible approach and a repudiation of Nixon's energy policy, which had deployed price controls to insulate American consumers against world prices. Unlike Nixon, President Ford was prepared to make changes at home. The energy strategy that the president unveiled in his 1975 State of the Union address proposed to curtail energy use through price decontrol and the introduction of a new "fee" on imported oil. This aligned with Kissinger's strategy, which embraced conservation and alternative fuel sources as solutions to the West's oil dependence. Still, the international stakes mattered little to domestic critics. Some legislators fixated on the inflationary effects of Ford's program; others on the costs to ordinary Americans. Ford's energy plan stalled in the face of congressional objections, prompting the president to gripe that: "the Congress has done nothing positive to end our energy dependence."[52]

For industrialized societies, the energy crisis raised hard questions. "Do governments have the political will to face the truth?", the Trilateral Commission asked. "Will their people give them the power to act?" For Trilateralists, interdependence mandated sacrifices. "All our countries," concluded its December 1974 report on energy, "will have to get along with less energy." This was an insight that the Ford administration shared. Having previously neglected it, the executive branch came after the October War to embrace energy security as a priority, an issue implicating both the long-term prospects of American world leadership and the cohesion of the West. Eager to remake the market conditions that had precipitated the oil crisis, the Ford administration from 1974 embraced conservation and the development of alternative fuels, acknowledging that the United States, the capitalist world's most profligate consumer of energy, had the greatest distance to travel.[53]

By the summer of 1976, however, administration officials could only rue the West's vulnerability to oil shocks as a stubborn reality that they were powerless to alter. "The sorry state of US domestic energy policy," the NSC staff economist concluded, left Washington with few options besides chiding OPEC to produce more oil. This was not the coherent, emancipatory energy strategy that Kissinger sought. The failures of energy policy illustrated the point that the Trilateral Commission made in its report on the "crisis of democracy": that the democracies lacked the capacity for self-discipline that interdependence demanded of them. Energy revealed sharp conflicts between the imperatives of maintaining autonomy and managing interdependence, but the tension would be no more easily resolved across the variety of other global issues with which the United States was coming to grapple in the mid-1970s.[54]

⬥

When it came to international monetary reform, major questions remained open. Should fixed exchange rates be restored, or should the IMF sanction floating as a formal alternative to exchange rate stability? Should gold endure as an international reserve asset, or should it be phased out of world monetary relations? In its absence, what were the alternatives, if any, to a de facto dollar standard? Technical as these questions were, national interests and the future of the world economy hinged upon the answers. Giving floating exchange rates formal sanction would ratify the abandonment of fixed currencies, confirming market determination of currency values. Preserving gold's monetary role would benefit countries like France that possessed the largest reserves of it. At the same time, monetary instability was a source of uncertainty and inflation for the entire world economy, which gave governments a common interest in resolving it.

When Ford took office, there was already a consensus within the US government that floating exchange rates were here to stay. The long-term future of the international monetary system nonetheless remained inchoate, even as the United States seized opportunities that the end of fixed exchange rates presented. No longer obligated to defend the dollar's parity, the Nixon administration had liberalized financial controls, aiming to make New York a rival to London for offshore banking. The IMF's Committee of Twenty (C-20) worked, meanwhile, to devise a restored international monetary order that would provide at least a baseline of exchange-rate stability. The oil crisis interrupted the committee's work, disrupting the prospects of a return to exchange-rate stability. The C-20 dissolved itself in mid-1974 without having made specific proposals for reforming the international monetary order. The C-20's failure resolved the debate over future of the monetary system in favor of floating exchange rates.[55]

Setting aside the dilemma of stability left gold's role in the monetary system the major source of international contention. France sought US agreement to resume gold's use in international settlements. US officials, however, saw gold as a source of volatility and an obstacle to reform. Marginalizing gold was also an American interest for the simple reason that the Europeans now held the greater part of the world's gold stocks. From the European perspective, abandoning gold would leave few alternatives to dollar hegemony. Resolution of the controversy required concessions, which both sides offered. In Paris, the May 1974 election of Valéry Giscard d'Estaing installed an outward-looking president who was eager to rehabilitate Franco-American relations after the drift of the late Pompidou years. In Washington, treasury secretary Bill Simon likewise favored a pragmatic approach. Eager to resolve the gold controversy, Simon, in the summer of 1974 proposed amending IMF rules to permit governments to buy and sell gold—a compromise that would enable the United States to sell monetary gold to private citizens while permitting others to use gold in intergovernmental transactions (though not in official settlements). In return, France would agree to abolish the IMF's official price for gold and to sell some of the Fund's gold reserves. This would marginalize gold without shunting it out of the monetary system entirely, as US officials would have preferred.[56]

As in the fall of 1971, when Nixon and Pompidou renegotiated fixed exchange rates, the French and American presidents came together in December 1974 to catalyze resolution of a monetary impasse. When Ford and Giscard met in Martinique to discuss energy issues, they also agreed that the leading industrialized countries would determine the monetary system's future. "Twenty is perfectly useless," explained Giscard, "except to permit a meeting of the Five." The political implications of this move were consequential. With it, Giscard and Ford seized the debate on international monetary reform from the IMF, affirming that France and the United States would instead serve, along with Great Britain, Japan, and West Germany, as an informal directorate for the world economy.

Neither the smaller West European nations nor the developing countries would be invited to participate. The IMF would be diminished: its role would be to enforce, but not to make, the rules of international economic order. Ford and Giscard's decision thus had important consequences. Prefiguring the economic summit that convened the following year at Rambouillet, the Martinique meeting affirmed that informal cooperation among the most powerful countries would, in the future, substitute for the rules-based approach to international monetary order that had existed under Bretton Woods.[57]

∽∞∾

Loose concepts became tangible plans in the summer of 1975, as French and German leaders developed the idea of an international economic summit. Troubled by "deteriorating economic conditions in France and Europe," Giscard concluded in July that "joint action with the United States is required to turn the situation around." To this end, he mooted the idea of an economic summit. Schmidt endorsed the proposal in a "private memorandum" that argued for taking "concrete steps to stabilize the world economic situation."[58]

For Bill Simon, this was unpalatable. Giscard's summit, Simon reasoned, was a ruse to get the dollar back on a fixed exchange rate. Neoliberals also worried about the institutionalization of economic managerialism. "The basic philosophy underlying our approach to international economic problems," one official maintained, is that "interference by governments in the operation of an open world market system is counterproductive." Although neoliberals would in time come to see economic summitry as a vehicle for advancing market-oriented reform, their initial reaction was to fear that it would embroil the United States in an international stimulus program. "Stimulation is not the whole answer," insisted Bill Seidman. "We should emphasize what we are trying to do structurally to revitalize the private sector, through deregulation, etc."[59]

Despite these misgivings, President Ford embraced the summit concept. On a visit to Helsinki for the Conference on Security and Cooperation in Europe (CSCE) in August 1975, he accepted Giscard and Schmidt's suggestion that the leaders of the largest industrial economies convene to consider their common problems. Upon his return to Washington, Ford solicited Japan's involvement and dispatched George Shultz, former treasury secretary, to represent the United States in preparatory talks. Proceeding outside official channels was a priority for Ford and Kissinger, who feared that Secretary Simon would be excessively rigid.[60]

Henry Kissinger hailed the summit concept; although Giscard and Schmidt had initiated it, the proposal jibed with his own strategy for reorienting the West toward the management of interdependence. Kissinger chided the neoliberals at Treasury for their fixation with economic "theology." The summit's real purpose, he insisted, was to rally and bolster the West. This set Kissinger apart from other cabinet-level officials. "There is no doubt," Helmut Sonnenfeldt warned him, "that other senior people remain opposed to the summit operation altogether." The internal discord that the NIEO produced was recurring: Kissinger embraced economic cooperation as an opportunity to restore American leadership; others saw it as a threat. Fortunately for Kissinger, Ford embraced his view that the summit would transcend "purely economic matters" and reinvigorate the West with renewed purpose.[61]

Economic summitry reoriented Cold War alliances to new purposes, but its origins were hardly removed from geopolitics. Policy coordination promised to bolster economic and social stability at a time when Communist prospects in Europe were strengthening, especially around the Mediterranean. No less disturbing than the Portuguese Revolution, which overthrew the authoritarian Estado Novo in April 1974, was the resurgence of moderate Communist parties in Spain, France, and above all, Italy, where the Partito Comunista Italiano (PCI) took a third of the vote in elections in 1975 and 1976. The PCI committed itself to a *compromesso storico* (historical compromise) with the Christian Democrats, but Kissinger drew a hard line, warning that no government that included Communists could remain within NATO. As in the 1940s, the United States channeled funds to anti-Communists. The nature of the threat, however, was evolving. Inspired by the PCI, other Communist parties distanced themselves from Moscow, as "Eurocommunism" emerged in the mid-1970s as a distinct ideological strand.[62]

Kissinger's response may look like an overreaction, but West European interlocutors informed and reinforced US analyses. "The threat," Giscard warned, "is real." There was, moreover, a constructive dimension to Kissinger's response. While covert aid and verbal ultimatums recalled past Cold War interventions, the United States also worked to bolster Europe through policy coordination intended to stabilize the world economy. The strategic implications of economic summitry thus recalled George Kennan's early containment concept, which aimed to bolster the West, not to confront the East. This was more or less what Kissinger intended. Whereas the United States had in the past furnished resources, policy coordination implied that Washington would conduct its domestic policies with a view to the stability of an interdependent West. As in the high Cold War, American leadership was the result of invitation more than imposition. "Your strong leadership," Helmut Schmidt implored, "is needed."[63]

Plans came together fast. Through informal consultations that began in September 1975, the concept of an "intimate and serious discussion" emerged. There was some controversy over who would participate in the summit. Valéry Giscard d'Estaing, the host, invited Italy, transforming the G-5 into the G-6. Ford lobbied on behalf of Canadian participation, but Giscard remained opposed.

It was the bitterest disagreement in a preparatory process that otherwise proceeded smoothly and generated an agenda that left little to chance. Following a survey of economic conditions in Britain, France, Germany, Italy, Japan, and the United States, the summiteers would proceed through predefined topics: trade, monetary relations, energy, North-South relations, and East-West relations. If the agenda seemed scripted, the effect was deliberate; the summit's purpose would be to permit the exchange of views, not collective decision-making.[64]

President Ford, for his part, traveled to Rambouillet determined "to place the summit in a political framework" emphasizing "the enormous interdependence among our societies." It nonetheless fell to Kissinger to develop a historical rationale, which he aired in Pittsburgh, days before the summit convened. Rambouillet's task, Kissinger explained, was "to confirm and consolidate allied cooperation" at a time when postwar structures were fragmenting. Practical challenges including inflation and energy required collaborative action, but what was really at stake, he argued, was the vitality of the liberal democracies, the legitimacy of their democratic systems, and their leading role in the international system.[65]

Located on the outskirts of Paris, Rambouillet Castle provided a cramped venue for the summit that convened on the weekend of November 15–16. Having construed the event as an "intensive seminar on international economic affairs" for heads of government, the French hosts included other ministers only "grudgingly." The three sessions proceeded smoothly, beginning with a gush of hortatory language. "Rambouillet," Helmut Schmidt roused, "can send a message of interdependence and cooperation." When it came to the substance, the tensions were predictable: on monetary affairs, Giscard emphasized stability, while Ford invoked "market realities"; on Third World development, Great Britain favored a "Marshall Plan type initiative," while Ford espoused free trade; on energy, Schmidt was optimistic about the prospects for producer-consumer dialogue, while the Americans were not. Underlying these disagreements was an emerging philosophical divergence: where the West Europeans favored collaborative management of the world economy, the Americans were more inclined to leave it to the markets. For his part, Japan's Prime Minister Miki did not take strong positions, keeping a profile so low that Simon at one point passed Kissinger a note that read: "I think Miki has just died."[66]

Set against the soaring rhetoric, the results of the summit were inconclusive. Its final communiqué contained no breakthroughs. Still, lamenting its shortcomings missed the point of the summit. The purpose of the Rambouillet meeting had been psychological: restore the West's collective self-confidence. This was Ford and Kissinger's goal, and they declared themselves satisfied with the results. "Interdependence," Kissinger exclaimed, "makes isolated solutions impossible." By affirming that point in a dramatic manner, Rambouillet had served the purposes of a strategist for whom holding the West together was now the highest of purposes.[67]

Rambouillet's major substantive achievement occurred offstage. In a series of talks with French officials, the treasury undersecretary, Edwin ("Tim") Yeo, reached an agreement to modify the IMF Articles of Agreement so as to formalize floating exchange rates. This was a technical issue, but it closed a contentious debate. Building on the Martinique summit, the deal traded a US pledge to maintain orderly exchange rates for a French commitment to outlaw currency manipulation. The agreement redefined the role of the IMF, which would henceforth be tasked with adjudicating what constituted acceptable and unacceptable intervention in the currency markets. Gold's role in the international monetary system would be diminished but not eliminated: some of the IMF's gold would be retained, some would be sold, and some would be restituted to IMF members. The agreement, which traded US acceptance of gold's enduring monetary role in exchange for French concessions on exchange rate flexibility, was ratified in the first week of 1976 at the Jamaica meeting of the Interim Committee of the IMF. Bill Simon called the Jamaica Agreement "the first sweeping revision of our international monetary arrangements since the Bretton Woods Conference." Subsequent analyses have echoed his verdict, the official IMF historian calling the reform "an early embodiment at the international level" of a new economic dogma favoring "free markets and private enterprise rather than government regulation."[68]

The Jamaica Agreement ended the impasse on international monetary reform, but its achievements fell short of what some experts had hoped might be accomplished. When the State Department hosted a colloquium of economists in the fall of 1975, they expressed concern about "the uncontrolled growth of international liquidity" and argued that the world needed "to move quickly to an SDR-based international monetary system." That did not happen, which meant that the dollar continued to serve as the world's default currency. This outcome preserved the structural benefits that Bretton Woods had conferred on the United States: American debts to foreigners would still be denominated in dollars, and accumulations of dollars in foreign central banks would still, in effect, be interest-free loans of indefinite duration. Still, these benefits resulted more from the failures of reform than a deliberate bid on the part of US officials to preserve the advantages of hegemony. The experience of 1971–73 had, after all, revealed the dollar's role in the monetary system to be a source of vulnerability as well as strength, and US officials had pushed thereafter to rebuild the monetary system around the SDR. Their failure to do so owed to the necessity of compromise between French hopes for a restored Bretton Woods system and American preferences for floating exchange rates. Given this conceptual divergence, the "non-system" that emerged from Jamaica was a tolerable compromise.

So far as the politics of international order were concerned, Jamaica substituted collaboration among the major economic powers for the rules-based approach that prevailed until 1971. As the onward march of globalization made economic stability within nation-states ever more dependent upon external conditions, it became increasingly difficult, it seemed, for governments to entrust the management of the world economy to the IMF.[69]

⤜⤐

After Rambouillet, economic summits became a regular feature of the international landscape. This was not foreordained. Rambouillet's communiqué made no mention of future meetings, intimating that the summit was a one-time event. As it turned out, the subsequent institutionalization of summitry followed not upon Rambouillet's successes but its failures, specifically the summit's inability to resolve the malaise in which the industrial countries remained stuck. Within months of Rambouillet, US officials were dismayed, once again, by deteriorating economic conditions in Western Europe. Britain and Italy remained the most serious cases: with tax revenues lagging behind public spending, both governments resorted to borrowing, driving up inflation. Inflation exerted downward pressure on the sterling and the lira, which disrupted other European currencies and raised the prospect of trade controls. Alan Greenspan now emerged as a leading proponent of multilateral coordination, presumably in a second economic summit.

Greenspan's purpose was, however, distinct from Kissinger's. Whereas the secretary of state expected summitry to serve political ends, Greenspan advocated using multilateral mechanisms to discipline "the sick countries." This approach won strong support from the Treasury, where Bill Simon favored using financial assistance to force Italy to implement "strong domestic restraint measures." With this, the formerly close alignment between economic and political purposes in US policy loosened. The State Department, having been the leading proponent of summitry, expressed skepticism. One risk of imposing economic discipline from the outside, Helmut Sonnenfeldt warned, was that it could provide electoral openings for Communists. Kissinger shared this concern, but he nonetheless favored a "Rambouillet II," as did presidents Ford and Giscard, who met in Washington in mid-May and agreed that stabilization depended on taking responsible—not punitive—action to bolster Italy's economy and keep the Communist Party out of government.[70]

Summit II also began with informal consultations among the key heads of state: Ford, Giscard, and Schmidt. This time, the United States took the lead, and Italy loomed large. Rome's travails were a problem for the West and an illustration, US officials warned, of what other governments risked if they surrendered to demands for public spending without commensurate taxation. A goal for the summit, then, would be to build an international consensus around what

American officials called "non-inflationary" growth. Thus construed, Summit II aimed to recapitulate center-right solutions at the transnational scale. Kissinger worried that economic purposes were predominating. "We need more political rhetoric," he complained. "This is the moral foundation for these meetings." Still, Kissinger did not oppose the use of international pressure to force probity on wayward governments. On the contrary, he agreed with his counterparts at Treasury that external pressure could serve a useful purpose, especially where foreign governments recognized the need for restraint but lacked the will to impose it. "If the British are smart," Kissinger commented, "it could be in their interest to be pressured into agreement on conditions, so that they can say that the only reason they imposed stringent conditions on the British economy is because of those American SOBs." Disciplining wayward governments thus became a central objective for Summit II.[71]

President Ford went to Puerto Rico in June 1976 prepared to argue that "the enormous interdependence among our societies" mandated "common efforts" and that national governments would make the most effective contributions to international stability if they trimmed public spending and balanced their budgets. As host, Ford was able to include Canada, which he did, transforming the G-6 into the G-7. The president also set the tone for the summit, blaming welfare states for the world economy's travails. "The global inflationary climate resulted," Ford argued, "because governments overcommitted themselves to ameliorate social inequalities at home and abroad." The challenge for the future was to set more "realistic goals." Britain's James Callaghan contested the point. Rebuking Helmut Schmidt, who was aligned with Ford's disciplinary agenda, Callaghan declared that "we place as much emphasis on lowering unemployment as Helmut does on reducing inflation." With unemployment rates far above postwar standards—5.6 percent in Britain, 6.7 percent in Italy, 7.7 percent in the United States—the case for stimulus, Callaghan insisted, remained substantial. Waylaid by such basic disagreements on macroeconomic priorities, Puerto Rico produced no breakthroughs. As the second summit, it lacked Rambouillet's novelty. Ford and Kissinger nonetheless declared themselves satisfied. Measured against Kissinger's political and strategic objectives, their satisfaction was justifiable. The summits were sustaining a dialogue among the G-7 countries, even if major policy questions remained unsettled.[72]

The tension between stimulators and stabilizers that Puerto Rico showcased endured in late 1976, with Great Britain moving to center stage. In September, the pound plummeted, as labor unions planned strikes. After decades of stagnation, Britain seemed to have reached its breaking point. "It is a country," mused one European official, "that simply doesn't work very well." With bond yields rising, James Callaghan recognized that change could not be forestalled. "Britain," he exclaimed, "has lived for too long on borrowed time, borrowed money, borrowed ideas." After delivering a message of tough reform to the Labour Party conference, Callaghan appealed for help to the United States, West Germany, and the IMF. Finding succor in neither Washington nor Bonn, he concluded a $3.9 billion IMF bailout in December 1976. The loan's terms committed Britain to major cuts in public spending. With this, US foreign economic policy had, in effect, turned full circle. Back in 1946, Washington used the Anglo-American loan to compel British acceptance of liberalization. With the Cold War's advent, this coercive approach was superseded by the Marshall Plan, of which Britain was the largest beneficiary. Thirty years later, with Britain on the ropes, the United States insisted, once again, that London must accept severe conditions in exchange for financial assistance.[73]

Still, key officials within the British government accepted the need for change. For British reformers, external conditions served a useful purpose; policy conditionality mandated adjustments that powerful domestic constituencies, including labor unions, opposed. Similar dynamics recurred in Italy, which engaged in protracted negotiations with the IMF over the terms of a standby loan. Conditionality thus provided an answer to the question that the Trilateral Commission had posed: how were democracies to discipline themselves? One answer that emerged from Britain's experience was that external pressure might embolden public officials to wield restraint that they would not otherwise have mustered. In any event, the alternatives were sparse. Great Britain, as Callaghan acknowledged, could not continue borrowing in order to consume. Perhaps the reform process that had begun with the December 1976 IMF crisis could have been avoided, but this would have meant Britain's detaching itself from the world economy through trade and currency controls. This was an alternative that the Labour Party contemplated when Michael Foot, a hard-line left-winger, challenged Callaghan for the party leadership in early 1976. Consolidating a socialist welfare state through a turn to autarky would, however, have been a rupture with the status quo far more radical than the one that Britain made at year's end. So long as Britain remained part of the international economy, its dependence on foreign markets and foreign capital would circumscribe the range of the possible, as Callaghan acknowledged.[74]

Great Britain's was a severe case, but its predicament was more general. As it intensified, economic interdependence limited the scope for both economic autonomy and expansive public sectors. The United States was, in fact, somewhat less beholden to the realities of interdependence than were the other advanced capitalist countries. International trade and investment counted for less in relation to US GDP than they did for other G-7 countries, and North America remained a vast internal market. The Ford administration nonetheless embraced the management of economic interdependence as an urgent strategic priority, acknowledging in the aftermath of the oil crisis that the United States was not immune to international economic disruptions. Support for policy coordination in the United States after 1973 was broad. Internationalists supported it as a matter of conviction, and neoliberals came around once they realized that the opportunities for imposing reform abroad were riper than the risk of becoming embroiled in an international stimulus. Ford supported it, and so did Jimmy Carter, his opponent in the 1976 election. Carter was such an enthusiastic proponent of economic summitry, in fact, that Kissinger joked that if the Ford administration wanted uplifting language to adorn the Puerto Rico communiqué it could lift some from the Democratic Party platform.[75]

Kissinger, in his loftier moments, pronounced summitry a response to changing historical conditions. In numerous speeches, he explained that he saw cooperation among the advanced industrial countries not only as a response to advancing globalization but also as the basis for a renovated international order. For all the novelty, however, there were continuities between the new methods of economic summitry and the old commitments to Western Europe and Japan that the United States had shouldered since the late 1940s. The Ford administration embraced the management of interdependence as a strategic goal because it complemented—and did not jeopardize—the sustenance of the Cold War equilibrium that had been the purpose of Nixon and Kissinger's détente. The same could not be said of another challenge that came to the fore in the mid-1970s: the breakthrough of an international movement for human rights.

Human Rights and Détente

It would be easy for me to say we'll have nothing to do with them until
they change their internal system. But then we would have a massive
arms race. . . . Détente is the only chance for a live-and-let live world.
Richard Nixon, Cabinet Meeting, 1974

In early 1975, Daniel Patrick Moynihan returned from India, charmed but wary.
A Harvard sociologist who had advised Nixon on domestic policy, Moynihan
had just spent two years as the US ambassador in New Delhi. From this vantage,
he inferred that the postcolonial countries were the captives of a socialistic ideology that was illiberal, anticapitalist, and anti-American. Nowhere was the rise
of Third World illiberalism more tangible, Moynihan argued, than in the UN
General Assembly, a theater of anti-Americanism. Because of decolonization,
the countries of the Third World now dominated this forum, especially when
they aligned and voted with the Soviet Union, which they often did. The United
States could neither conciliate nor appease the UN majority, Moynihan believed.
Instead, American diplomats should accept, even embrace, an adversarial role at
the United Nations. Although outnumbered, the United States could nonetheless champion its "libertarian ideology" and "constitutional heritage of individual liberty" against the illiberal, statist, and redistributive concepts that the new
UN majority favored, as the G-77's proposal for a New International Economic
Order exemplified.[1]

Moynihan presented his conclusions in a March 1975 article titled "The United
States in Opposition." The essay stirred debate and caught Henry Kissinger's eye.
In a moment when US foreign policy was at low ebb, and Congress continued
to rebuff appeals for funds to help South Vietnam, Moynihan's call for a "tough"
line impressed the secretary of state. Grasping the domestic political benefits of
Moynihan's combativeness, Ford and Kissinger agreed to appoint the sociologist
as their ambassador to the United Nations. Moynihan's assertiveness, Ford presumed, "will delight the Congress." Indeed, the appointment was one of several

steps the administration took in 1975 to nurture domestic support for US foreign policy. Kissinger even barnstormed Middle America himself, speaking on such themes as the "moral foundations of foreign policy." But if Moynihan's appointment served political ends, it also generated conflict between foreign policy's domestic needs and its international purposes. Whereas Kissinger sought stability in a world of sovereign states and diverse ideologies, Moynihan exalted "the claims of the individual against those of the state" and became fixated on human rights, which he hoped might prove a "secret weapon" of US foreign policy. Their collision would not be long in coming.[2]

In October 1975, Idi Amin addressed the UN General Assembly, lambasting colonialism, Israel, human rights, and Amnesty International. The Ugandan dictator's speech generated little controversy, but Moynihan's rejoinder did. Speaking at an AFL-CIO dinner, Moynihan called the Ugandan president a "racist murderer" and rebuked his exaltation of the postcolonial state. "Ours is a culture based on the primacy of the individual," Moynihan declared, setting human rights against postcolonial sovereignty. Moynihan's intervention triggered strong reactions. The Organization of African Unity denounced his "deliberate act of provocation," but many American commentators hailed the US ambassador for standing up to the Third World.[3]

The Amin spat prefigured a sharper confrontation in November, when a group of Third World countries introduced UN General Assembly Resolution 3379, which declared Zionism to be "a form of racism and racial discrimination." Moynihan struck back, arguing that the resolution singled out Jewish nationalism and misappropriated the language of human rights. "The damage we do . . . to the idea of human rights," he warned, "could well be irreversible." Andrei Sakharov, a leading Soviet dissident, joined Moynihan in opposing the resolution, but the General Assembly passed it in mid-November. Moynihan reacted by introducing a resolution of his own proposing a global amnesty for political prisoners. His purpose was to expose the hypocrisy of countries like Cuba, Uganda, and the USSR, which wielded the language of human rights against Israel and the West but abused their own citizens. Kissinger did not endorse Moynihan's counteroffensive. Cut off from the State Department, Moynihan turned to Freedom House, the New York–based NGO. Drawing on its resources, he "challenged the UN to create a universal standard" for human rights and denounced the "selective morality" that "threatens the integrity" of human rights. The proposal did not make it out of the UN committee process.[4]

Kissinger worried that Moynihan was becoming a "laughing stock" and a diplomatic "disaster." When the British ambassador to the UN suggested in November that the North-South conflict at the UN was Moynihan's invention, some inferred that Kissinger had colluded with Britain to dress down his ambassador. Moynihan, his critics suggested, could not accept diversity as a fact of international life and had instead embarked on an ideological crusade, targeting allies and adversaries alike. "Now he is starting a brawl with South Africa on apartheid," Kissinger exclaimed, and "he says the UN has 130 dictators." At the end of 1975, Kissinger recanted on the appointment. A memorandum from Moynihan criticizing the State Department was leaked to the press. Next, a journalist who was close to Kissinger wrote of the secretary's disdain for Moynihan. The ambassador resigned the next day.[5]

⌒◯⌒

Moynihan moved on, and so did Kissinger. But their dissension evokes a larger tension between realistic purposes and ideological commitments in foreign policy, a tension that came to hinge in the mid-1970s on human rights. Defined as rights that all individuals possess without regard to citizenship, human rights and their implications for US foreign policy proved contentious. The origins of the human rights movement were complex: domestic civil rights were a foundation, as was the Vietnam War, which led some Americans to seek alternatives to cynical realpolitik. Human rights also built on the work of transnational activists who worked to subject national sovereignties to universal rights aspirations. The rise of human rights was thus both a consequence of recent events and a globalizing development. Like other global changes in the 1970s, the ascent of the human rights movement posed challenges for the makers of US foreign policy. The proponents of human rights assailed Washington's alliances with Third World authoritarians, but human rights also had consequences, as this chapter explains, for US-Soviet détente.[6]

To its critics, détente was imprudent and immoral: an "accommodation" with "totalitarian Communism," Moynihan called it. Kissinger nonetheless insisted that détente served American interests, and he was not prepared to sacrifice its accomplishments on the altar of ideological purity. The successes of détente nonetheless complicated its defense. It was "easy to posture against the Soviets," Kissinger remarked, "because we have them all quieted down." The stability that détente had achieved, in other words, catalyzed the backlash against it. Kissinger did not agree that the struggle over human rights in foreign policy was a conflict between values and interests, between morality and its negation. Superpower dialogue, he insisted, was its own "moral imperative." "We have an historic obligation," Kissinger argued, "to engage the Soviet Union and to push back the shadow of nuclear catastrophe." Few could disagree. But the proponents of human rights were not proposing to take the world to the brink of nuclear war; rather, they presumed that a mature superpower relationship could withstand some advocacy on behalf of ideological commitments. For Kissinger, however, invoking the specter of nuclear holocaust offered legitimation for policies that he believed served geopolitical interests.[7]

This chapter first situates the human rights moment of the 1970s at the intersection of domestic and transnational politics, where lawmakers and NGOs collaborated. It turns next to the consequences for Soviet-American détente. Critics on both the left and the right argued that détente neglected human rights, and the charge exacerbated the parallel complaint that détente consigned the United States to military coequality with, if not inferiority to, the Soviet Union. The ensuing crisis of détente is the chapter's final theme. While foreign policy does not explain the outcome of the 1976 election, the election results indicated how contentious the issue of détente had become. The backlash was ironic. Détente's architects gambled the Soviet Union might be enticed to behave as what Kissinger once called a "status quo" power, accepting "the framework of the international order as it exists." In this respect, détente achieved considerable success; but détente's achievements did not reconcile Americans to the Cold War status quo. Rather, Americans in the mid-1970s demanded a foreign policy more consistent with their self-image as an idealistic, crusading people. They, not the Soviets, proved the more insatiable revolutionaries.[8]

The Rise of Human Rights

In the early 1970s, critics accused Congress of being dominated by isolationists; the "spearhead of retreat," one called it. Congress had, after all, threatened to cut funding for the Vietnam War in the winter of 1972/3, forcing Nixon to conclude a peace settlement, and then in 1973 it passed the War Powers Resolution, limiting the president's capacity to deploy military forces. Progressive legislators railed against the foreign policies of the Pax Americana, but it was not isolationism that they offered as antidote; instead, they proposed an internationalism of their own. These new internationalists formed a caucus, which they called Members of Congress for Peace through Law (MCPL). Signature issues included revitalizing the International Court of Justice; promoting cooperation on transnational issues, such as narcotics, hijacking, and environmental protection; and increasing American support for the United Nations. Emphasizing international law, global cooperation, and transnational dilemmas, the MCPL program was the prototype of a foreign policy for an interdependent world. When the 94th Congress ended in 1976, the MCPL had 175 members—about one-third of the legislature.[9]

The new internationalists embraced human rights, none more vigorously than Donald Fraser, a Democrat from Minneapolis and a MCPL member, who chaired the House Subcommittee on International Organizations and Movements. In the summer of 1973 Fraser convened what became the first congressional hearings to consider human rights as a general issue in US foreign policy, outside any regional context. Members of the NGO community testified at the hearings, including Niall McDermott of the International Commission of Jurists and Martin Ennals of Amnesty International. Other witnesses included State Department officials, legal scholars, and Senator Ted Kennedy. Kennedy put the issue directly: what was America's responsibility "when millions of people are faced with the violation of their human rights?" His own view was strident: "The cause of mankind is the cause of America." The representatives of the NGOs were comparatively restrained. McDermott acknowledged that conflict between human rights and national sovereignty was inevitable. He argued that the NGOs would do the most good if they focused their efforts on mobilizing "public opinion," not on assailing the international system. As the hearings progressed, witnesses agreed on two points: that public concern for human rights was a function of growing interdependence and that nation-states were not only the chief violators of human rights but also the actors most capable of vindicating them. Influencing the foreign policy of the United States thus presented one plausible means by which the NGOs could elevate the protection of human rights in the international arena.[10]

After fifteen hearings and testimony from forty-three witnesses, the committee issued its report, in March 1974. The document proposed making human rights "a regular part of U.S. foreign policy decision-making." To this end, Fraser proposed creating an office for human rights within the State Department. What Fraser emphasized above all was the reordering of foreign-policy priorities so as to elevate the promotion of human rights above the pursuit of geopolitical interests. He favored using military assistance and economic aid as instruments of coercive human rights diplomacy. While Fraser took a tough line when it came to Cold War allies, he was no less critical of the Soviet Union. Indeed, he warned that East-West détente "must not extend to the point of collaboration in maintaining a police state." Fraser's conclusions proved controversial. Two Republicans and one Democrat on his subcommittee disclaimed the report, charging that human rights defied the established international norms of sovereign self-determination and nonintervention. The cause nonetheless had momentum. By early 1974, State Department officials were describing "increasing criticism on the Hill" over the human rights issue. Fraser, it seemed, was "not a lone Indian." On the contrary, it was Kissinger who increasingly seemed to be out of step with public opinion.[11]

The congressional embrace of human rights followed international developments. In September 1973, Salvador Allende of Chile fell in a coup that elicited suspicion of CIA complicity and captivated domestic audiences. Yet Chile was just one disturbing case among many. Across the Pacific, conditions in South Korea seemed to be worsening after Park Chung Hee issued the dictatorial Yushin Constitution. Intimations of a government crackdown in Greece in late 1973, meanwhile, attracted what State Department officials called an "inordinate amount of public and congressional attention." The mere existence of authoritarian regimes did not provoke the human rights mobilization unfolding in Congress, however. What motivated Fraser and other critics of US policy was Washington's association with abusive regimes. Such associations were hardly unprecedented, but they became harder to excuse in the context of Soviet-American détente. If Washington could deal with Communists in Moscow and Beijing, critics asked, why support a violent coup d'état against Allende in in Santiago? Kissinger argued that détente's effectiveness depended on containing Communism in the Third World and preserving anti-Communist alliances, but he struggled to persuade his critics. Détente thus opened space for human rights to flourish.[12]

Transnational politics propelled the ascent of the human rights movement, including in the US Congress. NGOs, such as Amnesty International, produced vital knowledge, dispatching study missions to Chile, Greece, and South Korea. The reports that ensued were disseminated in Congress and cited in the news media. Still, the NGOs brought more than information to the crusade. With Amnesty International in the lead, NGO activists testified in congressional hearings and even collaborated with Fraser and others to draft legislation; they thus played an active role in developing the legal framework that would guide human rights policy for the world's most powerful nation-state.[13]

Prompted by events and spurred by transnational activism, Congress pursued legislative initiatives on several fronts. One approach targeted specific violators, such as Chile and the Soviet Union. In the case of Chile, Congress in 1974 imposed a $25 million ceiling on US aid to the country and a ban on military assistance. Confronted with country-specific legislation that curtailed aid and trade, State Department officials could only lament the circumscription of choice. "The ability of the U.S. Government to normalize its trade relations with the Soviet Union, or to provide military and economic aid to South Vietnam or South Korea," the State Department concluded, "has been seriously affected by the critical views in Congress of official US policy toward human rights in those countries." There seemed to be no political logic behind the legislative insurgency save the elevation of human rights issues themselves. Far from serving a Cold War agenda, the human rights activists in Congress attacked allies and adversaries with equal vigor. This did not mollify the policymakers whose work the insurgents assailed. "We face massive domestic problems," Kissinger explained to Augusto Pinochet, the dictator who ousted Allende, "in all branches of the government over the issue of human rights."[14]

If one approach to human rights focused on particular violators, another aimed to promote human rights in general. The first such effort came in December 1973, when the House of Representatives called on the president to "deny any economic or military assistance" to any foreign country practicing "the internment or imprisonment of that country's citizens for political purposes." This was a nonbinding resolution, but the House acted thereafter to formally link the provision of American assistance and the human rights practices of the recipient countries. In late 1975, Tom Harkin, a young Iowa Democrat, proposed amending the International Development and Food Assistance Act of 1975 to establish that "no assistance may be provided [to] any country which engages in a consistent pattern of violation of internationally recognized human rights." As the first statute to bind foreign policy in the name of human rights, the Harkin Amendment was a breakthrough. It focused on development aid, but military assistance was no less appealing a target. Human rights enthusiasts inserted Section 502B into the 1974 Foreign Assistance Act, encouraging the White House to cancel military assistance to human rights abusers. Initially a recommendation, Section 502B was upgraded to a formal requirement in 1976, although it included an exception for "extraordinary circumstances" when the "national interest of the United States" warranted the provision of aid to human rights violators, which the executive branch would determine.[15]

Besides restricting material assistance, Congress required the State Department to submit regular reports on the human rights conditions in foreign countries receiving American aid. By mandating disclosure, these requirements made human rights a permanent element of the nation's foreign-policy discourse. Donald Fraser considered the requirement "the best thing we have done." The key legislation included the Security Assistance Act of 1976, which obligated the State Department to submit reports on countries receiving US military aid, and the Harkin Amendment. These laws prompted the State Department to hire someone to monitor the procedures: the Coordinator for Human Rights and Humanitarian Affairs would oversee compliance with the new human rights legislation and take responsibility for the reports that would have to be produced. Crucially, Congress commanded the State Department to incorporate "the relevant findings of appropriate international organizations, including non-governmental organizations," in its reports. This confirmed the linkage between the NGOs that dominated the production and dissemination of human rights knowledge and US foreign policy.[16]

Despite significant loopholes, the legislative breakthroughs of 1973–76 enshrined human rights promotion as a foreign-policy objective and committed the United States to cooperate with NGOs to censure human rights violators. There would be shortcomings in implementation, especially so long as the State Department—and the secretary of state in particular—resisted the congressional mandate. The new requirements nonetheless marked a point of departure for subsequent US human rights policy.

⌘

The cause of human rights attracted a diverse set of adherents. Among them were the globalists, who construed human rights as an ethical and legal foundation for an interdependent, integrating world. Idealists, for their part, presumed human rights to be a long-standing American commitment, from which Nixon and Kissinger had strayed, and, in some cases, a basis for a post–Cold War foreign policy. Neoconservatives, meanwhile, took human rights for a fluid battlefront in an enduring Cold War. Distinguishing among these distinct approaches or tendencies suggests the ideological complexity of the human rights project as it emerged and offers clues as to its subsequent development.

Richard Falk, an international lawyer who testified at the Fraser hearings, exemplified the globalist approach, as did Richard Gardner, a lawyer and diplomat. Falk described human rights as a consequence of a new social interdependence, as the expression of an integrating global community. The unshackling of empathy from the nation-state was, Falk argued, generating something akin to "public opinion on the world level," with effects that undermined "traditional notions of territorial sovereignty." "We are no longer so separated from the conditions and plight of peoples elsewhere," Falk explained. In terms of practical outcomes, Gardner recognized that "it would be utopian to ask for a world judiciary and a world police force"; he nonetheless favored international action to enforce universal human rights standards. For these "planetary humanists," as Zbigniew Brzezinski called them, human rights were one pillar of an agenda that emphasized other transnational issues, such as environmental protection, population control, and economic management. "Peace and security, economic and social development, and human rights," Gardner affirmed, "are three interrelated and essential elements in the triangle of world order." While the globalists agreed that human rights should be a commitment for US foreign policy, they also favored making multilateral institutions their ultimate arbiters.[17]

For the idealists, human rights were a legacy of the Enlightenment, an inheritance of the American Revolution, and the traditional basis of US foreign policy. They were also a standard that recent policy choices had dishonored. Ted Kennedy represented this approach. The senator from Massachusetts became a prominent spokesperson for human rights in the mid-1970s, and he expressed his commitment in the language of national ideals. Human rights, Kennedy avowed, were rooted in America's "historic" traditions, being an integral part of "our heritage as a people of compassion." Donald Fraser concurred. Declaring that human rights were "fundamental to our own national tradition," Fraser's 1974 report emphasized the congruence between the US Constitution and international human rights treaties. Kennedy and Fraser shared the globalist insight that interdependence was reordering world affairs, but they privileged national values as the fount of human rights commitments. The two idealists also put somewhat more emphasis on Washington's special responsibility to

defend human rights in the world than did the globalists, and they were conversely somewhat less inclined to exalt the role of the United Nations.[18]

Neoconservatives, on the other hand, situated human rights firmly within a
Cold War framework. The neoconservatives did not dominate the human rights
moment of the 1970s, but they played a crucial role in the making of it. An intellectual movement more than a political one, neoconservatism's signature traits
included the renunciation of youthful radicalism, the exaltation of American
power, and the conception of the world as a hostile arena. The neoconservatives
spanned the political spectrum: some, such as Irving Kristol, the movement's
godfather, tilted rightward; others, such as Senator Henry M. Jackson, were progressive in domestic politics. As capacious as their movement could be, however,
the neoconservatives rallied around a commitment to individual rights, to the
claims of "sovereign individuals," as Norman Podhoretz put it. "Ours is a culture
based on the claims of the individual against the state," explained Podhoretz,
the editor of *Commentary* and one of neoconservatism's intellectual dynamos.
Neoconservatism's anti-statism sometimes jarred with its commitment to
national power. Indeed, the neoconservatives' enthusiasm for human rights was
fused to a hawkish commitment to defense spending. They were also fixated on
the Soviet Union, sometimes overlooking the sins of other illiberal regimes. Still,
the globalists, idealists, and neocons all agreed that the internal conduct of foreign nation-states was a concern for the international community and for US
foreign policy, a position that set them apart from Kissinger.[19]

∽

Henry Kissinger did not accept that human rights in other countries were
America's business. His outlook reflected both a weary pessimism (some said
cynicism) and a conviction that "foreign policy must begin with the understanding that it involves relationships between sovereign countries." The purpose
of statecraft, Kissinger maintained, was to avoid major wars while advancing
national interests. The secretary of state characterized the preservation of peace
as a moral purpose, and he pursued it with conviction and vigor—at least among
the superpowers. The congressional offensive on human rights was for Kissinger
a misbegotten crusade. "What I believe," Kissinger explained, "is that there are
certain national interests of the United States which transcend the domestic
structure of the countries involved." Indulging the "sentimental nonsense" of
human rights carried risks. If squeamishness drove Washington to cancel assistance programs to friendly dictatorships, for example, hostile powers might
fill the vacuum that America's principled renunciation created. "In the name
of human rights," Kissinger declared about the issue's most ardent enthusiasts,
"they will undermine national security."[20]

Kissinger's convictions remained consistent, but his engagement increased in
the last years of his public career. According to one estimate, Kissinger used the

words "human rights" in 5.5 percent of his public statements in 1974, 13.2 percent in 1975, and 39.6 percent in 1976. This last year was an election year, and
Kissinger's recurrent invocation of human rights during the campaign attests to
the appeal of the issue in the arena of domestic politics. Even when invoking
human rights, however, Kissinger emphasized the issue's complexity and intrac-
tability. He did not dismiss human rights in public, as he sometimes did in private; he simply stressed the countervailing claims of territorial sovereignty. In his
speech to the United Nations in September 1975, he described "the realization
of fundamental human rights" as a challenge for a nascent "global community"
but also acknowledged "the triumph of the principle of self-determination and
national independence" as a practical reality, which statecraft must accommodate. This deference to sovereign norms set Kissinger against the human rights
crusaders, but it aligned him with the anti-interventionist consensus that prevailed among most of the world's governments, especially those of the Third
Word. Ambivalent, even hostile, to the idea of universal human rights, Kissinger
found himself the subject of countervailing pressures: he operated in an international arena that reinforced his misgivings; but he remained subject to domestic
politics, which refracted, concentrated, and magnified a transnational mobilization for human rights.[21]

The State Department had little choice but to address the human rights issue,
the Policy Planning Staff doing much of the early work. Led by Winston Lord,
the Planning Staff in 1974 produced a sixty-page paper acknowledging that "violations of human rights abroad" were "becoming an increasingly urgent problem
for the United States." Human rights, Lord's analysis concluded, created difficulties for practical diplomacy. Besides circumscribing options for decision-makers,
revelations of Washington's support for abusive regimes were tarnishing the
image of the United States. Domestically, Lord warned, the human rights mobilization was inhibiting the formation of the political consensus around American
internationalism that Kissinger hoped to cultivate. The "charge" that the administration was insensitive to human rights, Lord cautioned, "has tended to alienate
significant elements in the Congress, the media, the universities"—the "natural
foreign affairs constituency." Costly at home, the mobilization of transnational
politics on behalf of human rights was also not enhancing the reputation of the
United States in the world. If America's image "as the supporter of freedom" had
been "an undeniable asset" in decades past, including in the early Cold War, this
positive image was being supplanted by a rival image of the United States as "the
special friend and protector of tyrannical regimes."[22]

Given the reputational costs—and opportunities—why did the State
Department not embrace human rights promotion? The answer lay in part in
the tensions between transnational and international politics that Kissinger
often highlighted. On this point, Lord's study made an important distinction

between law and politics. International law, especially the human rights covenants of 1966, made human rights a "proper subject of concern to other countries." Deference to sovereignty, however, remained customary in diplomatic practice. "Most governments," Lord explained, "still regard statements" on "the human rights of their citizens as interference in their internal affairs."[23]

Still, tension between sovereign norms and universal aspirations was not all that arrayed against human rights. Policymakers from Kissinger on down continued to argue that cooperating with authoritarian and abusive regimes sometimes served national interests. Some abusive regimes, for example, were close allies. South Korea, Indonesia, and the Philippines were pillars of US military strength in East Asia. Iran was not only a military ally but also an exporter of oil. The Communist superpowers, meanwhile, posed special dilemmas. "Few countries in the world," Lord's study acknowledged, "violate the rights of the individual on as vast and intensive a scale as does Communist China." Still, China's insulation from transnational politics limited its exposure to global human rights currents. The transnational human rights mobilization of the 1970s was far more attentive to the plight of human rights in the Soviet Union. Even here, however, the idealists did not find Kissinger eager to assimilate human rights into the purposes of Cold War policy.[24]

Skeptical of the substantive agenda of the human rights movement but cognizant of its growing political momentum, the secretary of state brokered an uneasy compromise. Under pressure from Congress, the State Department appointed the career diplomat James Wilson to serve as its in-house coordinator for human rights, and Kissinger paid the issue rhetorical attention. But no major policy initiatives were forthcoming. The most that can be said for the record of the Kissinger years is that American diplomats, beginning with Kissinger himself, made quiet appeals to human rights violators, urging them to mend their ways or at least to make a show of releasing political prisoners. Such requests were typically accompanied by apologetic warnings that the Congress would create difficulties for the foreign government if contrition and penance were not forthcoming.[25]

Kissinger, as was often the case, tried to use his charm and charisma to reconcile the irreconcilable. He met with Donald Fraser, assuring him that quiet diplomacy was the most effective—if least spectacular—way to improve the treatment of political prisoners and other victims of human rights abuses. The argument was not without merit. Kissinger claimed to have freed 200 Chilean political prisoners through private entreaties. He argued as well that his own subtle encouragements had persuaded Moscow to increase the quotas for Jewish emigration, a cause dear to neoconservative hearts, from just 400 exit visas in 1969 to 35,000 in 1974. In private, the secretary of state chafed at his critics. He insisted that his own record on human rights was "very good" in terms of its concrete accomplishments, but he insisted that he would not "play" the activists' "self-serving game."[26]

Under Kissinger, the United States would not devise a human rights policy that extended beyond quiet entreaties and rhetorical flourishes. "We have to put human rights in perspective," the secretary of state complained. "We can't have a doctrine of intervention into virtually every country." From a certain perspective, Kissinger was right: human rights posed a radical, even revolutionary challenge to the long-standing international norm that governments demur from meddling in the domestic affairs of foreign countries—and expect the same in return. Kissinger was nonetheless out of step with historical changes that were blurring the boundaries between nation-states and exposing even closed and cloistered societies to the scrutiny of transnational activism and the assertions of universal human rights. This mobilization proved disruptive to Kissinger's strategic purposes, especially when it came to détente.[27]

The Helsinki Paradox

Allegations of ideological bias hounded Amnesty International in the 1970s, as critics asked whether the NGO was not more attentive to the sins of right-wing regimes than to those of left-wing governments. Within Amnesty, some conceded that the critics might have a point. Eager to correct the bias, or at least redress the perception of it, Amnesty International USA (AI USA) offered a 1975 resolution urging the International Secretariat to prioritize "areas of neglect" in the Communist world. The resolution passed Amnesty's International Council. Correcting biases proved difficult to accomplish, however. "Purely practical" considerations, as one AI USA official put it, made it easier to monitor human rights in authoritarian regimes like Chile and Uruguay than in quasi-totalitarian societies like China and Cuba. Culture also mattered. When it came to China, "the political and cultural differences" were "too big to be neglected or put on one side," wrote one Amnesty activist. Cambodia, North Korea, and Vietnam were also areas of prominent omission. Yet if Communist regimes in the Third World received less scrutiny than their authoritarian counterparts, few countries were more exposed to the scrutiny of transnational human rights activism than the Soviet Union.[28]

Nowhere did the human rights mobilization of the 1970s have greater impact than upon Soviet-American relations. Kissinger would in time acknowledge this, claiming in his memoirs that the introduction of human rights into détente had been, in fact, a purposeful effort to undermine the Soviet Union by nurturing internal dissent. This is not what the historical record shows. Kissinger remained committed to Cold War stability, saw human rights as an unwelcome intrusion, and worked to exclude ideological claims from superpower diplomacy. Only in the face of sustained pressure from US allies and domestic proponents did he concede space for human rights in East-West relations. Even as he worked to manage economic interdependencies, Kissinger cleaved to a conception of world politics in which domestic affairs were domestic and even well-intentioned meddling was inappropriate. Human rights thus marked the limits of his willingness—even his capacity—to assimilate the dilemmas of a globalizing world into his foreign policy outlook. The politics of human rights nonetheless became a central preoccupation in the mid-1970s, as actors and forces outside the State Department—from the Soviet dissidents who mobilized the language of human rights to the transnational organizations that facilitated their work and the American politicians who embraced their cause—exerted their influence upon US foreign policy and, through it, on the détente relationship that Nixon and Kissinger had built.[29]

The year 1972 was a high-water mark for détente but a bleak time for human rights in the Soviet Union. Three months after visiting China, Richard Nixon became the first sitting president to visit Moscow. After meetings with Kremlin leaders, he spoke to the Soviet people, hailing "a new road of cooperation." Nixon's vision of détente, however, offered Soviet citizens little besides peace. Rebuking universalism, Nixon affirmed "the right of each nation to choose its own system" and disavowed any intent to "impose" liberty on the East Bloc. Subsequent summits confirmed the impression that détente meant bonhomie among the Cold War's elites. Having welcomed détente at the outset, Andrei Sakharov concluded that the superpowers' engagement was rigged in favor of the Kremlin. What Nixon sought, Sakharov declared in 1973, was "rapprochement without democratization." By accepting the Soviet Union's "right to choose its own system," Sakharov argued, Nixon had endorsed an oppressive regime. Not only would Soviet citizens suffer, this geopolitical entente might also "contaminate the whole world with the antidemocratic peculiarities of Soviet society."[30]

The dissident movement of which Sakharov was a prominent member emerged during the Khrushchev era. Nikita Khrushchev was no liberal; yet he had relaxed the state's grip upon society, permitting the 1962 publication of Alexsandr Solzhenitsyn's *One Day in the Life of Ivan Denisovich*. That fictionalized account of Solzhenitsyn's experiences as a political prisoner spurred others to speak out and write. During the 1960s, a critical literature blossomed in self-published, or *samizdat*, form. Among the most important of the *samizdat* journals was the *Chronicle of Current Events*, the mouthpiece of the Moscow Human Rights Committee, which Sakharov had created with Valery Chalidze, a young physicist and pro-democracy activist. Founded in 1970, the Moscow Committee attracted international attention, and foreign media outlets aided its work by broadcasting news of its activities back into the Soviet Union. As the political edge of Soviet dissent sharpened after the Prague Spring, the party-state resorted to tough punitive measures. Sakharov found some protection as an academician; others, however, encountered harsh reprisals. In the fall of 1972, Chalidze was stripped of his citizenship after accepting an invitation to lecture in the United States. Later that year, the authorities shut down the *Chronicle of Current Events*. Soon, the secret police subjected Sakharov to unprecedented harassment.[31]

Embattled at home, the Soviet human rights movement blossomed in the larger world. Exiled from Moscow, Chalidze founded an English-language version of the *Chronicle of Current Events*, based in New York. The reinvention of Soviet dissent as a transnational cause depended on the resources of Western NGOs. KGB agents had observed "clandestine contacts" between Moscow dissidents and transnational human rights organizations as early as 1970; such contacts flourished thereafter. The International League for the Rights of Man granted formal affiliation to the Moscow Human Rights Committee in June 1971. Under pressure from AI USA, Amnesty's International Secretariat even permitted Soviet citizens, including Sakharov, to found their own section in 1974. Amnesty provided other kinds of assistance, including with the publication of translated versions of the *Chronicle of Current Events*, which would be cited in dozens of congressional hearings. Rejecting the Kremlin's theory of sovereign inviolability, the Soviet dissidents and their supporters in the arena of transnational politics clamored for intervention in the Soviet Union's internal affairs. Alexander Solzhenitsyn, perhaps the most famous dissident of all, put it bluntly. "Interfere as much as you can," he told an American audience in 1975. "We beg you to come and interfere."[32]

The plight of the "refuseniks" attracted particular attention in the larger world. These were Soviet citizens, mostly but not always Jews, who sought to emigrate—often to Israel, where Soviet Jews could claim residency and citizenship rights—but whom the authorities denied permission to leave or subjected to stringent exit taxes. To their defenders in the West, the Soviet mistreatment of the refuseniks revealed the country's harsh anti-Semitism, even genocidal intent. The realities were more complex. Jews had played an outsized role in the Soviet project, but the Soviet Union had also embraced the politics of anti-Semitism, which had peaked in the anti-Jewish campaigns of the early 1950s and receded thereafter. By the 1960s, Jews were both the subjects of ethnic discrimination and overrepresented in the Soviet intelligentsia and technical elite, a predicament that created a particular sensation of alienation. In the late 1960s, the strains increased, in part because of the Six-Day War.[33]

Israel's 1967 victory animated a resurgent Jewish nationalism and created practical dilemmas for Soviet officials. Permitting Jews to depart for Israel in large numbers risked alienating Moscow's Arab allies, but restraining Jewish emigration stirred a transnational backlash. The reaction was especially fierce in the United States, where Jacob Birnbaum created the Student Struggle for Soviet Jewry, and other NGOs assembled as the "Inter-Religious Task Force on Soviet Jewry." Prominent national leaders lent support, Martin Luther King declaring that Soviet Jews faced "a kind of spiritual and cultural genocide." The death sentences (later commuted) handed out to two would-be emigrés who had attempted to hijack an airliner only galvanized Moscow's critics. The United States had done nothing for Germany's Jews in the 1930s, declared Rabbi Avraham Weiss in 1971. What, he asked, would Americans do now for the Jews of the Soviet Union?[34]

"We will be able to secure an improvement in the lot of Soviet Jewry," Henry Kissinger wrote, "only if we can somehow convince the Soviets that an improvement will be in their own national interest." This prompted the question of what—if anything—American decision-makers might do to encourage their Soviet counterparts to ease up on the refuseniks. As they built détente, Nixon and Kissinger presumed that separate issues in the complex web of Soviet-American relations could be linked to create a web of incentives that would produce outcomes favorable to the United States. Human rights might, in theory, have been incorporated into this linkage concept, but neither Nixon's administration nor Ford's was inclined to include them. Self-conscious realists, US decision makers prioritized tangible interests like arms control over ideological purposes; pragmatic in their evaluations of the Soviet Union, these decision-makers also understood that the barriers to progress were great. Détente nonetheless created opportunities for actors outside the executive branch—in the Congress, in particular—to connect human rights to the web of incentives that détente's architects had weaved.[35]

Nixon and Brezhnev agreed in May 1972 to purse the normalization of Soviet-American trade relations, a vaunted goal for the Politburo. Requiring congressional action, the agreement provided the activists with an opportunity to act. When legislation granting most-favored-nation (MFN) status to the Soviet Union appeared in the Senate in early 1973, Washington's senator Henry M. Jackson, a human rights enthusiast and hawkish anti-Communist, introduced an amendment making the normalization of trade relations with nonmarket (i.e., Communist) countries conditional on those countries permitting unrestricted emigration. The measure became known as the Jackson-Vanik Amendment, for Jackson and Charles Vanik, its cosponsor in the House. Henry Kissinger rebuked the measure as a challenge to the authority of the executive branch. Kissinger also questioned its wisdom. Subtle entreaties were more effective with Soviet authorities than flamboyant protests, the secretary of state insisted. Jackson-Vanik nonetheless became a rallying point for détente's critics. The emigration issue was especially salient to Americans concerned about the welfare of Soviet Jews, but Jackson-Vanik transcended the interests of particular ethno-religious communities. The intervention even won the support of Andrei Sakharov, who urged the US Congress to uphold the amendment.[36]

Being "a defense of international law," Sakharov insisted, the Jackson-Vanik amendment did not constitute "interference in the internal affairs of socialist countries." Nixon disagreed, insisting: "We cannot gear our foreign policy to transformation of other societies." Jackson plowed on regardless. Recognizing that Jackson commanded the votes, Kissinger and Ford tried to strike a deal. In October 1974, Jackson agreed to withdraw his opposition in exchange for a Soviet commitment, to be communicated via Kissinger, to a "benchmark" figure of 60,000 emigrants per year. To Kissinger's chagrin, Jackson made the deal public, proclaiming a "great victory for human rights." He also publicized the specific numerical target—60,000 emigrants—which Kissinger had mooted, but which the Soviets had not yet accepted. Kissinger struggled to mollify the Kremlin. "I'm as angry as you are," he told Brezhnev. The White House, Kissinger explained, would be able to impose its will on Congress in the New Year. This was insufficient assurance for Soviet leaders, who presented Kissinger with a communiqué rebuking the notion that there had been any private assurance. Unaware of the démarche, Jackson pushed on. In December 1974 he inserted into the Trade Act of 1974 language making the normalization of trade relations with "non-market economies" conditional on free emigration. Moscow withdrew its request for US trade credits and MFN status. A pillar of détente had crumbled.[37]

Had Jackson not emerged as the leader of the anti-détente forces, Kissinger later argued, the US-Soviet trade agreement would have endured—and with it détente. Yet the Jackson-Vanik amendment was just one in a series of congressional initiatives that sought to tether US policy to human rights commitments. Since 1969, Nixon and Kissinger had gambled that foreign policy could be isolated from domestic politics so as to permit the construction of a Soviet-American settlement on terms favorable to the United States. Transnational relations had intruded to thwart the gamble that open and closed societies might coexist in an accommodation perched atop a delicate balance of interests. By the early 1970s, the International League for Human Rights was holding regular telephone calls with the Moscow Human Rights Committee. These and other contacts—from mainstream journalism to the information brokering of the NGOs and from the establishment of an Amnesty International affiliate in Moscow to the decision of the Norwegian Nobel Committee to award the 1975 Peace Prize to Andrei Sakharov—provided Soviet dissidents with a link to the outside world and an entrée into US politics, where they could confront the power of the party-state. Transnational contacts transformed the politics of American foreign policy, complicating the pursuit of détente. Soviet-American détente endured after the Jackson insurgency of 1973–74, but its capacity for creative accomplishment was exhausted.[38]

⟋∽⟍

The debate over the Jackson-Vanik amendment showcased one of the two major complaints that critics in the mid-1970s leveled against détente—that it was amoral. The other—that it was weak—hinged on the military balance of power. The Interim Agreement that Nixon had signed in 1972 as part of the SALT dialogue attracted particular ire. The Interim Agreement's "unequal aggregates" approach had allowed the USSR to maintain a somewhat larger fleet of ICBMs than the US strategic force had. For SALT's supporters, this was no disadvantage: the Soviet Union's numerical edge did not equal, let alone best, the technical advantages of American missilery, which included superior accuracy and the capacity to convey multiple warheads atop a single intercontinental missile.

Critics, including Senator Jackson, nonetheless insisted that SALT I formalized American inferiority. The complaint constrained policymakers as they negotiated a permanent arms control treaty to replace the Interim Agreement of 1972. When Kissinger and Ford traveled to Vladivostok in late 1974 to negotiate with Brezhnev, they acknowledged at the outset that only numerical parity between the superpowers—an "equal aggregates" approach—would meet with domestic approval and Senate ratification. That they pursued this approach despite Kissinger's conviction that an alternative, asymmetric approach would be militarily advantageous attested to the ways in which domestic politics were constraining the scope for choice in foreign policy. Like Jackson-Vanik, Vladivostok intimated that the détente moment was passing. Kissinger nonetheless remained committed to détente, arguing that it had won considerable benefits for the United States, stabilizing US leadership in the world and the Cold War balance of power.[39]

"We have made foreign policy look so easy," Kissinger lamented upon his return to the United States. "The American people think you just go to Vladivostok and make a deal. They don't know the work behind it, the precariousness of it." This was détente's irony; the stability it won catalyzed the backlash against it, and the critics had little concept of how fragile the whole enterprise was. The secretary of state knew that the United States had derived most of the benefits from détente and that the Soviet Union had offered the bulk of the concessions, and he worried that getting tougher with Moscow—as Senator Jackson proposed doing—risked jeopardizing it all. The Soviet leadership, Kissinger argued, had thus far proven to be remarkably cooperative. Brezhnev had overlooked the United States bombing of North Vietnam "to smithereens," and had tolerated Kissinger's efforts to muscle Soviet power out of the Middle East. For this, the Kremlin had received little in return, save for "ratification of the existing situation." Kissinger—and Ford—now worried that if détente tilted much further in Washington's direction Brezhnev might fall under attack from Soviet hard-liners, precipitating a return to the rivalry of the high Cold War. "They have a military-industrial complex, too," Ford emphasized.[40]

Soviet expectations in 1975 hinged on the Conference on Security and Cooperation talks in Europe. Europe's international borders were fixed and durable for all practical purposes, but Soviet leaders had still long favored convening a conference that would ratify international borders, confirm "the results of the Second World War," and formalize the USSR's role in Eastern Europe. The Warsaw Pact had first proposed a European security conference as far back as 1954, and the Brezhnev Politburo revived the initiative in 1969. At this point, Nixon and Kissinger had accepted the Soviet proposal, but they saw the initiative mainly as a lever they could use to achieve a mutual reduction in conventional force levels in Europe, reducing the fiscal burdens of Washington's commitments to Western Europe.[41]

As the preparatory process proceeded, the security conference concept became entwined with a different set of strategic purposes, ones more associated with Willy Brandt's *Ostpolitik* than with Nixon and Kissinger's détente. For the countries of the EEC, the security conference presented an opportunity to open Eastern Europe to the West's liberalizing influence. Hopeful that they might "spread the contagion of liberty" to the East, West European diplomats worked to establish "the freedom of movement, information, and cultural contacts" across the Cold War frontiers as priorities of the CSCE talks. The expectations of the CSCE participants thus diverged: the Soviet Union sought to "confirm the political and ideological division of Europe"; the Nixon administration saw an opportunity to trade a symbolic concession for substantive gains elsewhere; and some (but not all) West European leaders perceived an opportunity to transcend the Cold War entirely.[42]

Involving thirty-five nations, the CSCE negotiations began in late 1972 with preparatory talks and proceeded through two phases before culminating in the summer of 1975 in a conference in Helsinki, at which heads of state and governments signed the Helsinki Final Act. Early in the preparatory process, negotiators agreed to collect issues in three separate baskets. These dealt with political and security matters (Basket I); economic relations and scientific and technological cooperation (Basket II); and human contacts, cultural relations, and information flows (Basket III). Basket I affirmed the "inviolability" (but not the immutability) of borders and the "territorial integrity of states," commitments that affirmed the Cold War status quo (but did not preclude its peaceful adjustment), while Basket III envisaged the expansion of human, cultural, and intellectual contacts between East and West. The CSCE thereby ratified and subverted the Cold War international order, at the same time, a paradox that was manifested within the baskets as well as between them. The inclusion in Basket I of a clause affirming "respect for human rights and fundamental freedoms" generated a great deal of controversy during the preparatory process, the Soviet Union opposing it as ardently as some West Europeans rallied behind it.[43]

Kissinger's views on CSCE remained consistent until late in the process. He disparaged the initiative—"we never wanted it"—and questioned Basket III's legitimacy. Early in the CSCE process, he favored accepting a Soviet request for a commitment that "nothing [in the agreement] will affect the domestic legislation of the countries concerned." Kissinger's willingness to concede the point followed his view that CSCE was, in essence, a sop to Moscow—a Soviet desideratum that could be fulfilled in exchange for substantive concessions elsewhere—but it also confirmed his belief that international relations are conducted between sovereign nation-states and his skepticism that Basket III would produce durable change in the East. "I don't believe that a bunch of revolutionaries who manage to cling to power for fifty years are going to be euchred out of it by the sort of people we have got negotiating at the European Security Conference," Kissinger declared. "Being able to buy the *New York Times* in Moscow won't change the Soviet system." The "hang-up" on human rights and transnational contacts in CSCE, he explained to Ford, was "just a grandstand play to the left." Thus, the secretary of state was more or less sincere when he reassured Brezhnev that he did not "think the Soviet system will be changed by the opening of a Dutch cabaret in Moscow"—the kind of cultural interaction across the Iron Curtain that Basket III presumably warranted.[44]

As it matured, the Helsinki process struggled to reconcile two divergent concepts of international order. The first proceeded from Cold War hierarchical assumptions, according to which the superpowers would continue to exercise special prerogatives within their blocs. The second was more progressive, envisaging the diminution of geopolitical barriers, even national borders, and perhaps the East Bloc's eventual absorption into the West's interdependent world-civilization. There was no question about which view Soviet leaders held. "If you clear away the rubbish," Foreign Minister Andrei Gromyko avowed, the CSCE "boils down to three items: borders; respect for sovereignty, noninterference; and military détente." The historical irony here was that the Soviet Union had become, at least in Europe, a champion of international stability. Soviet conduct in the Third World would reveal the endurance of revolutionary instincts, but in Europe the Soviet Union embraced a conservative conception of international order. Not wholly unsympathetic to Moscow's view of the CSCE, Kissinger had acquiesced to it for tactical purposes. Indeed, Kissinger sometimes struggled to disguise his cynicism, giving foreign diplomats the impression that he saw Helsinki as "a matter of intergovernmental accommodation." By the mid-1970s, however, Cold War stability was coming under assault on multiple fronts—from the proponents of human rights in the arena of trans-national politics and, increasingly, from Washington's European allies.[45]

Kissinger found himself in a Helsinki paradox, trapped between those West European countries that rallied around a transformative conception of the CSCE and a Soviet Union that sought ratification of the Cold War status quo. Kissinger seems to have shared Moscow's skepticism about the appropriateness of includ-ing human rights commitments in the CSCE; he ended up siding with his allies against his adversary, however, confirming the reorientation that hinged on the oil crisis. The secretary of state might have ridiculed the Europeans' commit-ment to Basket III in private, but he also believed that "we can't jeopardize our relations with Western Europe over [it]." Other officials shared the concern and helped to cajole Kissinger into reaching this conclusion. Arthur Hartman, the assistant secretary of state for European Affairs, and Winston Lord had warned him in early 1974 not to underestimate the strength of West European feelings on the issue of human contacts. If Kissinger sided with the Soviet Union on this issue, they warned, he would incur "sharp resentment among all of our more important allies."[46]

Nixon proved the point in July when he and Brezhnev issued a joint appeal for rapid resolution of the CSCE process. This had a "dispiriting effect on the mem-bers of the Nine"—the nine countries of the European Economic Community, which negotiated together in the preparatory talks. More cognizant than Nixon of the damage that the CSCE negotiations were inflicting upon the West, Kissinger tried to reassure James Callaghan, Britain's foreign secretary, that he did not want the West Europeans to feel "raped" by the Soviets. Such diplomatic niceties could not bridge the substantive disagreements. Differences over Basket III had, by early 1975, stalled the CSCE talks, leaving the Soviet Union and the West Europeans at odds and Washington in an impasse. At this point, Kissinger tilted decisively toward the West Europeans, galvanized in part by US negotia-tors in Europe who characterized Basket III as a potential "asset for the West." From the bottom of the policymaking apparatus, Washington moved toward a progressive conception of détente. The NSC staff in May 1975 made a decisive recommendation, telling Kissinger that he should, when he met with the Soviet foreign minister, "impress upon Gromyko the need for the USSR to take a more reasonable position on issues of importance to the West." A tougher line on Basket III would, in particular, be "very much in our interests."[47]

When Kissinger traveled to Vienna to meet with Gromyko, he was less inclined to conciliate than he had been at the beginning of the year, when the Jackson-Vanik amendment impaled the Soviet-American trade deal. The fall of Saigon in April had dismayed Kissinger, chilling relations. "When the American position in some part of the world is overthrown by Soviet arms," the secretary complained, "that is a historical fact." Soviet leaders, for their part, chafed at a speech that Kissinger gave in May, in which he described "the expansion of Soviet military power" as a "heavy mortgage on détente." In a line pregnant with implications for the CSCE, Kissinger had reminded his audience that he considered "our allies and friends our first priority."[48]

In Vienna, Kissinger acted on these words. Following the advice of the American delegation to the CSCE, Kissinger played on the Kremlin's desire for an early conclusion to the conference. His tactic was to make Soviet concessions on human contacts the price Moscow would have to pay for a heads-of-state-and-government summit in summer 1975. Throughout the two-day summit, Kissinger took a hard line, blaming Moscow for the lack of progress and warning Gromyko that he was not optimistic about the prospects for a summit in 1975. The Soviet foreign minister, for his part, mocked the West Europeans' desire to include "principles" within the Helsinki Final Act. "That's a new one in international practice," he complained. Tellingly, Gromyko implied that control over information flows was an existential issue for the USSR. "We'd never accept broadcasting that undermined our system," he avowed, intimating that the regime that Lenin and Stalin had built depended for its survival on the barriers that separated it from the outside world.[49]

Kissinger's new steadfastness reaped results. The Soviet Union soon offered "significant concessions" on Basket III, which opened the way to a Final Act that traded Western recognition of postwar borders for Soviet promises to abide by universal norms, including human rights. Albert Sherer, the lead US negotiator, considered the bargain not "such a bad one." The Helsinki Final Act nonetheless met with disdain in the United States. Critics pointed out that it was the Soviet Union that had wanted the security conference in the first place and that Moscow had "won most of its goals," notably the affirmation of postwar borders and the enshrining of sovereign inviolability as a basic principle of European international relations. The hostility was especially sharp among Americans of East European descent, many of whom viewed the initiative as a "Super Yalta," as William Safire put it: a Faustian pact that conceded Western recognition of Soviet domination of Eastern Europe in exchange for superficial gains. The point was not lost on Kissinger, who acknowledged: "we will take some flak with the ethnics." The mainstream media also rallied in opposition, major news outlets opposing President Ford's participation in the conference that would conclude the Helsinki process. "Jerry Don't Go," the *Wall Street Journal* declared. Domestic audiences, it seemed, grasped the Soviet conception of Helsinki as a ratification of the Cold War status quo but not the possibility that the Final Act might serve a transformative purpose.[50]

Divisions over the meanings and possibilities of Helsinki manifested themselves not only between allies and adversaries and officials and pundits but also within the executive branch. Addressing the conference in August 1975, Gerald

Ford voiced surprising confidence in the potential of the Final Act to be a vehicle for human rights. Staring at Brezhnev, Ford declared: "It is important that you recognize the deep devotion of the American people and their Government to human rights and fundamental freedoms." This was not the speech that Kissinger's diplomats had prepared. Unhappy with State's "diplomatic gobbledygook," Ford had instructed his speechwriters to revise the a text to reflect a more progressive conception of the Helsinki Final Act. But if Ford's revised speech exalted human rights, its obeisance to "nonintervention, sovereign equality, territorial integrity, and inviolability of borders" tempered its idealism. Caught between the strictures of détente and a broader yearning for change, the president's speech captured the paradox of the Helsinki Final Act. Even as it articulated a role for human rights, the CSCE presumed a stable international order of nation-states, divided into Cold War blocs.[51]

Helsinki proved the high-water mark of a détente strategy that was by 1975 coming under heavy fire at home and abroad. As contentious as détente became, policymakers maintained that it served US interests and doubted the alternatives to it. Peace remained its moral underpinning, and this, for its supporters, trumped the claims of the Soviet dissidents. "We are trying," Nixon had exclaimed, "to avert a disastrous nuclear conflict." And if détente exalted stability, it did not foreclose on the possibility of change. "The one thing a totalitarian system must fear," Nixon believed, "is the friendship of free nations." This was nonetheless as far as they would go. Unlike Senator Jackson, the architects of détente would not assist reformist forces in the East Bloc. To do so, they presumed, would be to violate its precepts, jeopardize its stability, and risk its accomplishments. Despite Kissinger's accommodation of his West European allies over Basket III, the prioritization of stability over the promotion of human rights endured until the end of the Ford administration. Only thereafter would American policymakers work to assimilate human rights promotion into the détente relationship. The results would prove more destabilizing than transformative.[52]

Having begun as a bid for stability, the Helsinki Final Act after 1975 assumed a new identity as a rallying point for the transnational politics of human rights. Aided by supporters in the West, dissidents, such as Václav Havel in Czechoslovakia, wielded the Final Act as an ideological weapon against the East Bloc's party-states. A transnational movement for human rights appropriated Helsinki to its own purposes, building on the efforts of diplomats—Henry Kissinger included—to embed human rights commitments in the Final Act. The Ford administration did not, however, play an active role in Helsinki's post-1975 rebirth. On the contrary, Ford and Kissinger opposed the creation by Congress of a commission to monitor East European compliance with the Final Act. When Congress created the Commission on Security and Cooperation in Europe— the US Helsinki Commission, as it would be colloquially known—Kissinger questioned its "constitutionality." His initial conception of Helsinki as a superfi-cial concession to a vainglorious Soviet elite endured even as East European dis-sidents and their Western supporters—including such congressional advocates as Clifford Case, Dante Fascell, and Millicent Fenwick—worked to transform Helsinki into an instrument for promoting political change in the East. That Helsinki ended up serving a liberalizing role—hastening the end of the Cold War in the view of at least one historian—would owe more to good fortune and the fortitude of others than to the design and foresight of Nixon and Kissinger's grand strategy.[53]

The Eclipse of Détente

By the winter of 1975/6, then, détente was coming apart, as the controversy over the CSCE and Moynihan's theatrics at the United Nations indicated. These episodes showcased a rising disenchantment that transnational poli-tics stirred. Events in Africa, meanwhile, cast doubt on détente's capacity to restrain superpower rivalries in the Third World. Controversies over foreign policy would not decide the outcome of the 1976 election; "the overriding issue," as the victor put it, "was the restoration of faith in our government." Nixon's shadow still loomed, and Ford's decision to pardon his predeces-sor ensured that he would not escape it. Détente's politicization nonetheless indicated how the resurgence of American zeal for human rights, a domestic development that transnational politics energized, could diminish the scope of choice in US foreign policy.[54]

The Angolan Civil War followed the Portuguese Revolution of 1974, which had focused the attention of US policymakers on the prospect of Communist participation in Portugal's government. In early 1975, Lisbon announced that Portuguese forces in Angola would soon leave, sparking invigorated conflict among the colony's nationalist leaders. External sponsors aided rival factions. Holden Roberto, leader of the National Liberation Front of Angola (FLNA), received CIA support, while Agostinho Neto, leader of the People's Movement for the Liberation of Angola (MPLA), was close to the Soviet Union. As the major provider of military assistance to Neto's MPLA, Cuba was, perhaps, the most influential external actor in Angola. US policymakers for their part con-structed Angola's civil war as a proxy struggle between the superpowers. Still inhabiting the assumptions of the high Cold War, Ford worried that "if we do nothing, we will lose southern Africa." What ensued was a cycle of escalation in which the superpowers goaded each other to commit ever-more resources, such that the original diagnosis that Angola was a Cold War contest became a self-fulfilling prophecy.[55]

For Kissinger, what was happening in Angola was a "Soviet effort to tilt the political balance of Africa." Should the United States fail to thwart this Soviet bid, it was anybody's guess "to what measures" Moscow "might be tempted" in the future. This analysis persuaded Ford but not the foreign-policy bureaucracy. The State Department's Africa Bureau, in particular, took a different view. "We have no irrevocable commitment of U.S. power and prestige in Angola," the Africa Bureau advised, cautioning against US intervention. Eschewing its advice, Ford and Kissinger initiated a program of CIA assistance to Roberto and encouraged South Africa to intervene on the FNLA's behalf, which Pretoria did in the fall. When news of US involvement broke in the media, influential legislators challenged the policy. Some feared that the White House was wading into another Vietnam. Congress soon acted, amending the Defense Appropriations Act in December to prohibit public expenditures on Angola, a move that prompted South Africa to curtail its intervention, and led, soon enough, to Neto's and the MPLA's triumph. Although Neto turned out not to be the Soviet proxy that Kissinger had feared, the secretary of state lamented that domestic politics had thwarted the effective containment of Soviet influence. "We are living in a nihilistic nightmare," he exclaimed.[56]

Angola exposed the vulnerability of Ford and Kissinger's foreign policy to the pressures of domestic politics, even as it marked the limits of détente's ability to restrain conflict in the Third World. The notion that American and Soviet officials entertained divergent images of détente—and recoiled when their discordant expectations jarred—is a familiar theme in explanations of its demise. Washington, the historian Raymond Garthoff explains, expected Soviet leaders to exercise restraint throughout the world; whereas Soviet leaders perceived in détente an opportunity to press for revolutionary change in the Third World. What Angola revealed, beyond divergent expectations, was that détente's mechanisms of leverage would not allow the United States to dispel the Soviet assumption that a Third World revolution could be advanced under the cover of détente. Angola thus brought into question the efficacy of linkage. Ford and Kissinger might, in theory, have canceled Kissinger's January 1976 visit to Moscow over Angola; they might even have linked grain exports or SALT II to Soviet restraint in southwest Africa. But they recognized that the costs of such sanctions would be mutual. There was, in sum, little left to link.

In the absence of specific sanctions, Kissinger pressed the case for restraint in Moscow, to little avail. Far from enabling the United States to restrain the exercise of Soviet power in the Third World, détente had established a differentiation between the core of the Cold War system, where mutual restraint prevailed, and its Third World periphery, where it did not. Here, both superpowers pressed for parochial benefits. The Soviet Union sought advantage in southern Africa, but the United States had done much the same in the Middle East, while Nixon and Kissinger, in détente's early years, had worked to delink their escalations in Vietnam from the emerging structure of superpower peace. Their differentiation between Third World developments and core Cold War relationships had helped to assure détente's early successes, but it now became a source of misunderstanding and a rallying-point for domestic critics.[57]

In Henry Kissinger's verdict, Washington's inability to confront Soviet power in Angola owed not to détente's inner contradictions but to discord on the home front. The Ford administration, he writes, was caught between "liberals" who wanted "the United States to withdraw from the world and tend to our domestic improvement" and "conservatives" who clamored for an "ideological crusade" against the Soviet Union. Attributing détente's struggles to domestic politics downplays the dissonance between Soviet and American expectations, but it was in the arena of US domestic politics where détente imploded, as Soviet officials concurred at the time. Still, if Kissinger is right to conclude that American politics in the mid-1970s undercut Soviet-American détente, he oversimplifies the nature of the domestic backlash.[58]

Détente's dilemma was not being caught between internationalism and a resurgent isolationism but between rival internationalisms. These included a globalist vision of a foreign policy for interdependence, a post–Cold War outlook oriented toward international law and institutions; a neoconservative thrust for an invigorated Cold War policy, muscular and confrontational in its approach to the Soviet Union; and an idealist yearning for a restoration of libertarian values and ideological commitments in US foreign policy. Each of these approaches jibed, in different ways, with broader political currents: Americans in the mid-1970s, according to one opinion poll, lamented "what is seen as a weakening U.S. role in the world" and wanted "to be number one again"; but they also manifested "growing acceptance of an interrelated world" and recognized that "the traditional dividing line between foreign and domestic issues ha[d] become blurred." These were distinctive agendas, but the language of human rights offered terrain on which they could meet, as they did during the election year 1976.[59]

⧼◌⧽

Moynihan's accomplishment at the United Nations had been to fuse diverse ideological strands into a template for a crusading, idealistic foreign policy. That he accomplished this while working for Henry Kissinger was remarkable, but the Moynihan episode showed that the human rights debate could permeate the executive branch, as it did in Helsinki when White House and State Department officials clashed over Ford's speech. After Helsinki, some of Ford's domestic advisers concluded that Kissinger's realism was becoming a political liability, and they argued for realigning American foreign policy with the new moral idiom of human rights. Moynihan's collaborator Leonard Garment made a similar proposal in the summer of 1976, suggesting that Washington make human rights the central theme of its public diplomacy at the UN. Neither proposal came to fruition. Ford curtailed Kissinger's bureaucratic powers in November 1975, stripping his secretary of state of the national security adviser role. But Ford kept faith with Kissinger's strategy, insisting that "we have a damned good foreign policy."[60]

NGO activists, meanwhile, worked to drive the human rights bandwagon forward. Early in 1976, Amnesty International USA opened a branch in the American capital, the Washington National Office, in a bid to formalize the link between state power and transnational activism that ad hoc collaboration with legislators like Donald Fraser had forged. Acknowledging—but disclaiming—the "risks of co-option," the AI USA board was fixated on the "great potential for achieving our human rights aims" by working with the US government. Amnesty engaged in diverse collaborations—contributing to State Department reports on the human rights records of foreign countries, cultivating congressional staffers, and dispatching speakers to "educate" US diplomats. Some activists worried that embroilment with the US government threatened the integrity of Amnesty's mission. Others saw the opportunity to achieve grander results than lobbying could deliver. The rewards were also psychological. The burgeoning interest in human rights "in Washington and in the world" was gratifying to Amnesty's leaders. What was clear from the experience of the Washington office was AI USA's determination to cement its political influence, to leverage US foreign policy on behalf of its agenda, even to propel the globalization of human rights using the clout of the American superpower.[61]

The collaboration with the US government did not ease the concerns of those within Amnesty who worried that Third World governments viewed the NGO as "a Western-based organization promoting a Western cause." This point was contestable, but the anti-statism of human rights brought proponents into conflict with postcolonial nationalism. In contrast to anticolonial nationalists, who worked to build states of their own, human rights activists of the 1970s rejected the "special value of the nation-state," as Richard Ullman wrote for the Council on Foreign Relations, and prioritized instead "the human individual." Human rights, Patrick Moynihan and Norman Podhoretz concurred, embraced "the claims of the individual against those of the state." The point resonated in a moment when transnational activism was facilitating engagement with the experiences of individuals—Sakharov, Solzhenitsyn, and so on—across borders and distances. Ranged against the state, the ascent of human rights paralleled other globalizing developments of the era—the integration of capital markets, for example—that curtailed the nation's states capacities for self-determination and self-governance.[62]

Presenting a disruptive, even revolutionary, challenge, human rights proved difficult to reconcile with the practical management of world politics. Tensions were especially sharp in the postcolonial world, where self-determination and sovereignty had been hard won and would not willingly be compromised, and in the Soviet Union, whose leaders opposed admitting human rights to the arena of diplomatic relations. "We live in a world of 150 sovereign states, profound ideological differences, and nuclear weapons," Kissinger explained. Yet this was evidently not a world most Americans wished to inhabit—at least not those who rallied behind the human rights cause. They yearned instead for a restoration of idealism, for a globalization of their ideological commitments. Opinion polls taken during 1976, an election year, indicated that many "Americans found something seriously wrong in the way our foreign policy was being managed." Human rights promised a revival of moral purpose and, for the aspirants to Ford's job, became political terrain on which the administration's record could be outflanked.[63]

On his right, Gerald Ford faced an insurgent campaign for his party's nomination. Ronald Reagan, an actor turned California governor, was a severe anti-Communist who likened détente to "appeasement." Under the cover of détente, Reagan alleged, Moscow had stockpiled its forces, subverted the Third World, and consolidated its own totalitarian order. The litany of such complaints from Reagan and others prompted Kissinger to remark: "I think the Soviets are getting a bum rap." "Except for Angola," the secretary of state continued, "I don't believe they have massively increased their forces."[64]

Besides claiming that the United States had fallen behind the Soviet Union in military preparedness, Reagan lamented détente's failure to produce political change in the Soviet Union, and he hailed Solzhenitsyn as "the world's foremost symbol of man's age-old struggle against tyranny and oppression." Détente had won nothing for American values, Reagan declared, only "the right to sell Pepsi-Cola in Siberia." For Reagan, foreign policy was one signature issue among several, but détente proved to be a vulnerable spot for the Ford administration. As Reagan pushed the president in the New Hampshire primary and stormed to victory in North Carolina, Ford's advisers acknowledged that foreign policy was costing them votes. Ford defended Kissinger, but he repudiated the word "détente," telling journalists in March 1976 that the term was no longer "applicable to the situation." Some on Ford's team even toyed with the idea of putting Kissinger out to pasture. Rogers Morton, chair of Ford's campaign committee, suggested in April that the secretary of state's time might be up. The president would not renounce Kissinger, but Reagan's challenge and the murmurs within the Ford camp suggested that détente and Henry Kissinger were becoming political liabilities.[65]

Détente was not the only foreign policy issue to drive a wedge between Ford and the right wing of the Republican Party. Ford's willingness to countenance returning the Panama Canal to the Panamanians outraged the right, as did his policy in sub-Saharan Africa, where Kissinger traveled in April. In Lusaka, the capital of Zambia, the secretary of state committed the United States to supporting black-majority rule throughout Africa. The new policy applied to South Africa, where apartheid was well-entrenched; but it focused on Rhodesia, where the struggle between nationalist forces and Ian Smith's white-minority regime seemed poised to become a full-scale "race war." Kissinger worried that Moscow was hitching its interests to black nationalism, much as it had done in Angola, and he concluded that a peaceful transition to majority rule would avoid bloodshed and preempt Soviet gains. In Lusaka, Kissinger announced that the United States favored an immediate transition to majority rule in Rhodesia and a more gradual transition in South Africa. This shift in US policy, which had for decades aligned with the country's white-minority regimes, brought tears to the eyes of Kissinger's Zambian host. "We could not believe this was a Secretary of State from Washington, D.C.," Kenneth Kaunda exclaimed.[66]

Reorienting US policy towards the anticolonial aspirations of Africa's black majorities, Kissinger's Lusaka speech was a constructive departure, and it established the parameters of a peace process that led over the next three years to Rhodesia's peaceful transition to black-majority rule. Back in the United States, Kissinger's new thrust proved contentious. Days after the Lusaka announcement, Ford suffered a humiliating defeat in the Texas primary, which pundits and some in the president's campaign attributed to Kissinger's African policy. "Americans don't like blacks," the secretary of state commented. As counterintuitive as the point may seem, the political dynamics of the Rhodesian episode in some ways resembled those that human rights produced.

Kissinger acted in Africa, as he did elsewhere, for hard-nosed reasons. Prioritizing US national interests, he aligned his policy with self-determination and postcolonial sovereignty—the only practical basis, in his eyes, for conducting foreign policy. He did so in recognition of the likelihood that white Rhodesians would suffer as a consequence. Kissinger was himself able to empathize with Rhodesia's white minority, which faced what he later called an "imminent collapse of its way of life." "I am with the whites," he confided to President Ford. Kissinger nonetheless chose to bring American policy in line with the aspirations of southern Africa's black majorities, convinced that doing so served the national interests of the United States. Reagan took a different view, declaring that he would dispatch American troops to protect white Rhodesians. Such pandering did not win Reagan the Republican Party nomination, but his campaign took a toll on Ford, for whom victory was a release. "Now that we have gotten rid of that son-of-a-bitch Reagan," Ford exclaimed, "we can just do what is right."[67]

⤙⥈⤚

What was "right" remained contestable. While Kissinger and Ford continued to identify it with the clear-sighted pursuit of national interests, others pushed for a renewal of idealism in foreign policy. Despite Reagan's defeat, his supporters managed to insert a commitment to "morality in foreign policy" into the Republican platform. "We must face the world with no illusions about the nature of tyranny," it proclaimed. The measure implicated Kissinger; the assault on an incumbent secretary of state within his own party was remarkable. Ford's campaign staff even feared that Reagan's supporters would try to oust Kissinger from the cabinet. For his own part, the secretary of state concluded that he would resign after the election, whatever its outcome. In public he continued to defend détente. "In an age when nuclear cataclysm threatens mankind's very survival," Kissinger told voters on the election's eve, was peace among nation-states not "the first and fundamental moral imperative" of statecraft? His own waning popularity suggests not—at least not in the eyes of the American public.[68]

Having devoted himself to the pursuit of stability in a bipolar world, Kissinger struggled to adapt his foreign policy to the changes that pressed upon the world in which he operated, straining established assumptions about the purposes of foreign policy. Kissinger managed after the oil crisis to reorient US foreign policy toward the collaborative management of economic interdependence, but he did not assimilate the rise of human rights into his strategic concept. Here the countervailing claims of national interest and territorial sovereignty proved too rigid for a compromise to be struck, and disenchantment with Kissinger increased. His approval ratings dropped from the (extraordinarily high) 75 to 85 percent range in 1974 to the 50 percent range in 1976; his negative ratings in November 1976 were far higher than those of either presidential candidate. For all his successes—and for all the historical perspective he brought to public life—Henry Kissinger struggled to adapt to the upheavals of his own times. Transnational politics were, by the late phase of his career, animating a resurgent American idealism, calling into question realistic conceptions of the national interest, and thwarting the Cold War rationalizations that US officials had deployed for a quarter century. The time for Soviet-American détente and the time for Henry Kissinger appeared to be passing.[69]

Ford's opponent in the fall presidential election was a progressive and a Democrat, but he echoed notes that Reagan had struck. Détente had been a fine idea, Jimmy Carter concurred; the problem was that the United States in practice came "second" too often. Like Reagan, Carter accused Ford of delegating excessive responsibility to Kissinger, whom he dubbed a practitioner of "lone ranger" diplomacy. When it came to human rights, Carter went even further than Reagan. He reached out to the NGO community, stressing his "strong concern for human rights, particularly in the Soviet Union." Transcendent mantras—integrity, leadership, and trust—were the campaign's central themes, not policy specifics, but Carter spoke unapologetically of the United States as a model for the world. Whereas Kissinger had emphasized the reconciliation of interests and the toleration of diversity as diplomacy's guiding purposes, Carter envisaged "an international framework of peace within which our ideals gradually become a global reality." Carter linked the promotion of human rights to cooperation among the industrialized democracies. "We and our allies," he proposed, "can take the lead in establishing and promoting basic global standards of human rights." Despite the congruence between Carter's goals and Kissinger's record across a variety of specific issues, novel assumptions about the world and America's role in it animated Carter. His would be a foreign policy for a world converging around an interdependent, technocratic modernity. This was not a world that Henry Kissinger spent much time contemplating. Carter, Kissinger grumbled, "must deal with the world as it is."[70]

After the Democratic Convention in July, human rights became a prominent theme for Carter. He proposed "more vigorous support" for both "public and private international bodies" dealing with human rights, called international organizations "the conscience of the world community," and impugned the record of the Ford administration. "The question," Carter asked, "is whether in recent years our high officials have been too pragmatic, even cynical." Such talk infuriated Kissinger. Tensions climaxed in October's foreign-policy debate, a sparring match between Ford and Carter in which Kissinger and détente were prominent themes. Little was said that was memorable until Ford proclaimed, in response to a question about the Helsinki Final Act: "There is no Soviet domination of Eastern Europe." The clip of his response haunted the president in the campaign's last weeks. Although Ford had intended to say that the Helsinki Final Act did not recognize Soviet domination of Eastern Europe, the effect was contrary to his intent. Ford's poll numbers dropped, and analysts characterized his comments as evidence of indifference to Eastern Europe's captivity and to human rights more broadly. It was an unfortunate faux pas, exacerbated by Ford's reluctance to describe it as such. The real cost of the gaffe, however, was its implication that, despite talk of a "new Ford foreign policy," the strategic assumptions of the Nixon years still prevailed. There had in fact been much evolution, but Ford and Kissinger struggled to communicate the point. Foreign policy did not decide the election, but it did not help Gerald Ford.[71]

Ford's defeat marked the end of his and Henry Kissinger's public careers. In a little more than two years, they had built on the geopolitical stabilization Nixon accomplished, correcting some of the shortcomings of the Nixon years. The institutionalization of a cooperative dialogue on policy coordination among the advanced industrialized countries was a legacy on which the Carter administration would build. Oversights nonetheless remained, none more glaring than the Ford administration's failure to assimilate human rights within its strategic concept. Whether Jimmy Carter would be able to strike a more durable balance between stability and change, between the claims of interests and those of ideals, and between the prerogatives of nation-states and those of individual human beings remained to be seen.

World Order Politics

> If my people shall humble themselves, and pray, and seek my face, and turn from their wicked ways; then will I hear from heaven, and will forgive their sin, and will heal their land.
>
> II Chronicles 7:14

For a quarter century, Cold War bombast defined the presidential inaugural. Harry Truman in 1949 devoted his to repudiating the "false philosophy" of Communism. Eisenhower, in 1953, pitted "freedom . . . against slavery; lightness against the dark." Yet, whereas John F. Kennedy promised to "bear any burden" on liberty's behalf, Jimmy Carter admitted only a "clear-cut preference" for societies that shared American values. Carter's inaugural characterized the Cold War not as an existential struggle but in terms of technical challenges: how to control the "massive armaments race" and achieve "the elimination of nuclear weapons." "Not so many years ago," one Carter adviser wrote, "things were much simpler." "The enemy was World Communism," and "the rest of the countries of the world were put in two categories—either for us or against us." By the late 1970s, the bipolar dichotomies were wearing thin, and the United States faced "a more complex world" without the clarity that the Cold War once provided.[1]

Still, the Cold War's ideological clarity looked, in retrospect, to have produced murky outcomes, at least in the eyes of the new president. His predecessors had erred in the world, Carter acknowledged, and their errors had embroiled the United States in quagmires, notably Vietnam. In the future, Carter promised, "we will not behave in foreign lands so as to violate our rules and standards." A religious man, Carter had planned to include in his address a blunt scriptural passage, II Chronicles 7:14. His political instincts countermanding his spiritual ones, he ended up using verses from Micah emphasizing guidance and mercy, not contrition and repentance. Humility was nonetheless the inauguration's motif. Carter's decision to forsake the presidential limousine and walk from the Capitol to the White House marked his desire to reduce what he called "the imperial status of the president." In symbolic and substantive ways, Carter sought to curtail an imperial presidency that was, in key respects, a Cold War creation.[2]

Locating himself in a moment of change, Carter evoked a vague but constructive agenda for a world that "a new spirit" was awakening. Drawing from Zbigniew Brzezinski, he made human rights a guiding principle and a concomitant of vast historical changes. "Peoples more numerous and . . . politically aware," Carter declared, were "craving" and "demanding" their "basic human rights." As a nation dedicated to liberty, the United States had a particular responsibility to "shape" a world order hospitable to human freedom. What Carter meant by this was not what Cold Warriors meant when they juxtaposed American freedom against Soviet slavery. Their version of freedom was a line in the geopolitical sands; his was an ideal to which the United States must aspire. Human rights would be his lodestar. But Carter did not declare an ideological crusade to impose human rights on recalcitrant regimes; on the contrary, he committed himself to seek a "mature perspective on the problems of the world."[3]

Beyond exercising restraint, the United States, the new president insisted, would have to engage the challenges of an integrating, interdependent world. In a parallel inaugural address broadcast via satellite to a global audience, Carter identified some of these. Human rights promotion, nuclear nonproliferation, and global environmental stewardship, Carter explained, were priorities for changing circumstances. "We Americans," he declared, "have concluded one chapter in our nation's history and are beginning to work on another." What Carter evoked was, in essence, the need to formulate a post–Cold War foreign policy for a post–Cold War world.[4]

◘

The Carter administration, as one aide put it, committed itself to making "the world safe for interdependence." The only Democrat to occupy the White House between 1969 and 1993, Carter embraced a conception of "world order politics" that enjoyed wide support in his party and drew upon his experiences with the Trilateral Commission. What Carter attempted as president was novel in relation to his Cold War forebears but exemplary of contemporary ideas. Trilateralism, one observer wrote, was by the mid-1970s "almost the consensus position" among the foreign-policy elite. Still, if Carter proceeded from assumptions quite different from those that had animated his predecessors eight years earlier, he built upon their legacies, especially in international economic cooperation. He would, moreover, end up adapting his initial strategic priorities to circumstances more complex than he initially perceived, much as they had done after the shock of the oil crisis.[5]

This chapter first follows the evolution of Carter's post–Cold War foreign policy. While Carter often struggled to articulate it, his administration followed a more coherent strategy than historians have often allowed, one deriving from assumptions about history as well as from ethical commitments. Carter and his advisers, this chapter explains, coalesced around world order politics, in which human rights were a central tenet. After defining the premises of Carter's foreign policy, the chapter moves to the implementation, beginning with the administration's efforts to invigorate a sluggish but interdependent global economy through international policy coordination. These efforts culminated in the Bonn Economic Summit of 1978, a landmark in policy coordination that failed to resolve the structural challenges facing the industrialized countries. Last, this chapter turns to Carter's efforts to assimilate human rights into US diplomacy. Reconciling human rights to competing priorities proved challenging, more so in some contexts than in others. Iran, it concludes, was an especially difficult case.[6]

After 1978, Carter's post–Cold War strategy unraveled. Coordination among the industrialized countries failed to overcome the structural obstacles to international economic governance, while the predicament of the global economy worsened as the world descended into a second energy crisis that hinged on events in Iran. Meanwhile, tensions with the Soviet Union resurged, a consequence in part of the administration's schizoid East-West policy, prompting Carter to resurrect older notions of anti-Soviet containment. Still, the subsequent retreat from world order politics, toward a looser strategic mélange, should obscure neither the originality nor the coherence of what Carter attempted at the outset.

"To Make the World Safe for Interdependence"

The thirty-seventh president of the United States was born outside Plains, Georgia, in 1924. His rural upbringing gave him scant introduction to public affairs, but Jimmy Carter acquired in his youth a strong religious commitment and a dislike for racial oppression. His education at the US Naval Academy in Annapolis, Maryland, and his subsequent naval service offered experience of the world and an exhibition of presidential power, when Harry Truman in 1948 desegregated the US military and the submarine on which Carter served. Truman's example left an impression, but after leaving the Navy in 1953, Carter returned to Plains, where he and his wife Rosalynn took over the family business, a peanut farm and warehouse and a store. He became active in state politics in the 1960s, winning an improbable 1970 bid for the Georgia governorship.[7]

As governor, Carter personified the aspirations of the New South. He traveled abroad and solicited international opportunities for Georgia businesses. Carter's intellectual depth, internationalist orientation, and political gifts brought him to the attention of the Trilateral Commission. The responsibilities of the Georgia governorship, meanwhile, drove him to contemplate the impact that external events were having on American society. In the wake of the 1973–74 oil crisis, Carter studied energy issues with particular care. Influenced by such thinkers as Alvin Toffler and Robert Theobald, he became convinced that long-term energy security depended on conservation and international policy coordination. Writing to Zbigniew Brzezinski in 1973, he urged the application of "our trilateral approach to the energy question." Unlike Nixon and Kissinger, whose worldviews were forged in the high Cold War, Carter began thinking about international relations at a time when the problems of an interdependent world loomed large. This formative experience would shape his agenda as president.[8]

When Carter became president, no candidate from the Deep South had won election since Reconstruction, and no governor had become president since FDR. In the era of the Cold War, the American people looked to the Senate for leadership, believing that senators alone possessed the "knowledge and experience in foreign affairs" that equipped them to lead. This was the conclusion of Hamilton Jordan, one of Carter's closest aides. Jordan was nonetheless upbeat in his assessment of Carter's prospects. "In choosing a president," Jordan wrote in 1972, "we are no longer looking for a man to lead the Free World in its fight against international Communism." Carter could run as an outsider who would restore integrity, not as a seasoned Cold Warrior. Carter's victories in the early primaries enabled him to prevail against his rivals for the Democratic nomination, and he achieved a modest victory over Gerald Ford in November 1976.[9]

As president, Carter surrounded himself with aides from his home state. Jordan led the White House Staff. Jody Powell, another young Georgian, served as press secretary. Critics sniped that the White House staff was "plucked from the Georgia backwoods." The national security team, on the other hand, showed the imprint of Trilateral Commission. Zbigniew Brzezinski became national security adviser. Cyrus Vance, who had served at Defense under Lyndon Johnson, became the secretary of state. To lead the Department of Defense, Carter selected Harold Brown, the president of Caltech. Michael Blumenthal, a businessman with a PhD in economics, became the secretary of the treasury. Beneath them, the foreign policy bureaucracy bulged with talent. One future secretary of state, Warren Christopher, served under Vance; another, Madeline Albright, went to work for Brzezinski. International economics was a particular strength, with Richard Cooper and C. Fred Bergsten serving at the State Department. Joseph Nye, the theorist of interdependence, went to the Defense Department, while political scientist Samuel Huntington consulted for the

NSC. Experienced diplomats, including Richard Holbrooke and Tony Lake, also joined the administration.[10]

∽∾

The formulation of a foreign policy agenda preceded the election. Early strategic concepts bore the imprint of Carter's main campaign advisers: Brzezinski, Richard Gardner, and Henry Owen, all of whom were enthusiastic Trilateralists. It was Gardner, an international lawyer, who declared making "the world safe for interdependence" to be the task of US foreign policy. Attentive to North-South issues as well as to relations among the industrial countries, Gardner called for a phase of institutional construction to renovate the machinery of international order. Others offered similar perspectives. Henry Owen, an economist and diplomat, joined Carter's NSC, where he assumed special responsibility for the G-7 summits. For Owen, the imperatives of international policy coordination marked the historical obsolescence of economic sovereignty. "The modern nation-state," Owen wrote in 1973, "is not adequate to the needs of the day." With Brzezinski, Gardner, and Owen drafted the blueprint for the new administration's strategic concept. "The depth, extent, and pace of global change," they wrote, "is ushering us into a new era of either global cooperation or fragmentation."[11]

Locating themselves in the cusp of change, Carter and his advisers presumed that the postwar era in international relations was ending. Carter made this point in a landmark campaign speech to the Chicago Council on Foreign Relations. America's "old postwar monopolies of economic resource[s] and industrial power," he explained in March 1976, "have been swept aside." The Pax Americana, in other words, was over, and the Cold War order was receding. Accordingly, a bipolar concept of the international system would no longer suffice to guide American foreign policy. It was time, Brzezinski, Gardner, and Owen advised, to "initiate a new phase in U.S. foreign policy going beyond the Atlanticist / East-West Cold War framework of the years 1945–1976." "Balance of power politics," Carter declared on the campaign, "must be supplemented by world order politics."[12]

World order politics proceeded from the assumptions that technological modernization was contracting space and time; that transnational relations were rendering nation-states interdependent, if not obsolete; and that mass literacy and mass media were globalizing human aspirations, producing what Brzezinski called a "global political awakening." "Our point of departure," Brzezinski explained, "is the view that we are living in a time in which the world is experiencing the most extensive and the most intensive transformation in its entire history." The challenge for the United States, still *primus inter pares* among nation-states, was to orchestrate an international order in which "the entire international community," North, South, East, and West could participate. Doing this required embracing interdependence. First came the enhancement and deepening of "our collaboration with our friends in the industrial world." This would facilitate a second objective, which was to expand opportunities "for the new emerging states to enhance, through self-reliance, their own internal progress." In a third purpose, the Carter administration would involve the Communist countries in its world order concept. "We shall seek cooperation with the communist countries, while striving to reduce areas of conflict."[13]

Cold Warriors divided the globe into East and West; dependency theorists, into a core and a periphery; Mao Zedong into First, Second, and Third. The Carter administration, for its part, recognized just one world, an outlook that aligned it with the teleological assumptions of what would in the 1980s become known as globalization. The Trilateralists hoped to reconcile the USSR to their one-world concept, but deciding what to do about détente was a dilemma. Détente had quieted Cold War tensions, enabling post–Cold War issues to stake their claim on the foreign-policy agenda, but when critics assailed détente's weakness and immorality it proved hard, as Kissinger had found, to defend its accomplishments. During the election campaign, Carter declared that he favored détente in principle but not the compromises necessary to sustain it. As president, it would be harder to have it both ways, especially while downgrading superpower relations relative to other priorities. Carter sought to move US foreign policy beyond the Cold War–centrism of recent decades, but Soviet-American relations could not be disregarded, especially since some of Carter's world order objectives involved the Soviet Union.

The road to progress on nuclear arms control passed through Moscow. Whereas Kissinger had stabilized the arms race for geopolitical purposes, reducing nuclear arsenals was for Carter a moral commitment—and a defining preoccupation. "We had to do everything possible to stop this mad race," he explained. Carter declared his desire to abolish nuclear weapons when he announced his candidacy for president, when he accepted the Democratic Party's nomination, and in his inaugural address. Whereas nuclear arms had in the high Cold War been sentinels of the West's security, Carter designated the weapons themselves the threat and invited the Soviet Union to join with Washington to control them. Acknowledging that it had been "a major theme" of the campaign, Carter's transition team made nuclear arms control a high priority. Ted Sorensen, an informal adviser to the new president, urged Carter to pursue global nuclear disarmament, holding out the prospect of a Nobel Peace Prize. Carter did not need the encouragement; his own instincts made nonproliferation an overarching objective and arms control a priority for East-West relations.[14]

⚭

Human rights, another issue deriving from ethical commitments, became the most distinctive, acclaimed, and contentious of the administration's early priorities. Not a major theme in the early phase of Carter's presidential campaign, human rights became a central focus in 1976. As Carter framed them, human rights were the centerpiece of the American historical project and a transcendent idea toward which the United States must strive. Human rights were the birthright of all peoples, but Americans had a "special responsibility" to promote them. Thus convinced, Carter was himself the central figure in his administration's pursuit of human rights. "It is the President's personal feelings that form the core of our 'policy,'" wrote one NSC staffer. As speechwriter Jim Fallows saw it, Carter's motives were "not particularly complicated." The president believed in human rights "very strongly" and sought to advance their cause, at home and in the world.[15]

A self-described born-again Baptist, Carter maintained a wall of separation between his own religious convictions and the work of government. But if religion shaped Carter's ethics, which animated his human rights commitments, direct connections between Carter's religiosity and his human rights policy are difficult to trace. More directly influential were his experiences as a racial liberal in the Jim Crow South. The achievements of the civil rights movement had taught Carter that federal power could achieve progressive change where local authorities resisted it. Desegregation, he explained, was "something that had to be forced on us from outside." The analogy suggested that the international community might have to impose human rights on nation-states, much as the federal government had imposed civil rights on the South. The appointment of Patricia Derian, a former civil rights activist, as the assistant secretary of state for human rights made the connection between civil rights and human rights implicit. Speaking at the University of Georgia, Cyrus Vance made it unambiguous. "In the early years of our civil rights movement, many Americans treated the issue as a 'Southern' problem," Vance explained. "Now as a nation we must not make a comparable mistake. Protection of human rights is a challenge for all countries."[16]

If human rights built upon national accomplishments, they also offered a kind of absolution after the sins of Vietnam. Indeed, "human rights" and "morality in foreign policy" were substantially overlapping categories for Jimmy Carter. This had implications for the practice of human rights diplomacy. But, as laudable as the ends might be, the means mattered to the new president. A follower of Reinhold Niebuhr who nonetheless rejected Niebuhr's differentiation between the moralities of statecraft and of ordinary life, Carter heeded the philosopher's caution that moral zealousness should not precipitate unrighteous action.[17]

Zbigniew Brzezinski considered Carter's human rights to be "more embedded in morality and religion than in geopolitics and strategy." For Brzezinski, the reverse was true. Brzezinski perceived that historical changes were making human beings more politically engaged, more sensitive to inequality and injustice, and more aware of their position in the global order. "Throughout the world," he explained, "because of higher literacy, better communications and a closer sense of interdependence, people are demanding and asserting their basic rights." Human rights were an answer to this worldwide political awakening; by embracing them, the United States would align itself with historical change and seize a new leadership role in an integrating world. This is not to say that Brzezinski's embrace of human rights was cynical; he joined Amnesty International USA in its fledgling days and maintained close connections with Freedom House, the New York–based NGO. But if Carter's human rights were a transcendent idea residing beyond history, Brzezinski's existed within an auspicious historical moment. "An idea whose historic time has come," Brzezinski declared, human rights were "the genuine historical inevitability of our time." This conviction fused with Carter's ethical commitments to make human rights the master key to the administration's initial strategic project.[18]

❧

Issue by issue, the continuities between the Ford and the Carter administrations' foreign policies were clearer than the differences. When it came to the Soviet Union, the Carter administration talked human rights but sought to uphold détente. China policy remained stable, in the limbo it had been in since 1972. Renewing cooperation among the industrialized countries was a central focus, but here the new administration built on Ford's legacy. The differences between the administrations resided in the grand design, not the details.

Although Carter proceeded from a coherent strategic outlook, he struggled to communicate his guiding vision to the American people. Two months into his presidency, Brzezinski advised Carter that public support for particular foreign-policy initiatives was high. There was "considerable appreciation" for Carter's commitment to arms control and "remarkably widespread support" for human rights. But Americans were missing the big picture. "I do not believe," Brzezinski wrote, "that at this stage the larger design of what you wish to accomplish has emerged with sufficiently sharp relief." To remedy the problem, he urged Carter to articulate "a more coherent vision of his grand strategy." Carter decided to give a major speech outlining his agenda and priorities. It was appropriate, given the centrality of human rights in Carter's strategic outlook, that the speech chosen for this purpose had been slated to deal with that issue alone. Carter now requested from his speechwriter a broader statement of strategic purposes, which is what he delivered to the Notre Dame class of 1977.[19]

At Notre Dame, Carter declared that the Soviet Union was no longer a "unifying threat." Instead, the United States would have to align its policy with the new reality of globalization. "We must respond to the new reality of a politically awakening world," he explained. Having gestured at the big picture, Carter itemized his objectives. He would pursue arms control with the Soviet Union and nuclear nonproliferation on a global scale; he would expand cooperation with Western Europe and Japan; and he would reintegrate China into the world, while seeking majority rule in South Africa. The priorities were diverse, but a conceptual thread stitched the patchwork together. His strategic purpose, Carter explained, was "to create a wider framework of international cooperation suited to the new and rapidly changing historical circumstances." With this, the Trilateralists assumed for themselves the responsibility of governance and, with it, the opportunity to refashion American foreign policy according to their own design.[20]

Reactions were mixed. The *New York Times* applauded Carter's commitment to an enlightened foreign policy but expressed concern about how he would translate his lofty aspirations into practical solutions. "His diagnosis of our posture was splendid," the paper's editorialists wrote. "His prescription for our conduct remains to be defined."[21]

Indeed, what Carter formulated at Notre Dame was a conceptual framework, not an outline of workable policy solutions. Carter's shortcomings were not those of his predecessor's. Eight years earlier, Nixon and Kissinger had devised a concept for stabilizing the Cold War and, with it, the Pax Americana, but their grand strategy did not account for the ways in which forces exogenous to the realm of geopolitics were transforming world politics. Carter and Brzezinski devised a looser strategy, and it proceeded from the assumption that the strategist must accommodate history, not the reverse. Still, moving from conceptualization to implementation proved to be tricky. Tensions between domestic and international purposes would thwart the administration's efforts to manage economic interdependence, while divergences of interest stymied cooperation within the G-7. When it came to human rights, domestic audiences were enthusiastic, but the crusade elicited strong reactions abroad. The Carter administration struggled to balance its idealism with a broad portfolio of interests, which included the sustenance of détente. It nonetheless cleaved for eighteen months to its initial vision of a post–Cold War politics, only shifting its priorities as the difficulties mounted.

Trilateralism in Practice

On its surface, the economic outlook for 1977 was not so dire as Jimmy Carter had suggested on the campaign trail when he accused the Ford administration of owning "the worst economic record since the Depression." The US economy had, in fact, performed reasonably well after Ford pirouetted in early 1975 from fighting inflation to stimulating growth. GDP grew by over 5 percent in 1976. Still, growth slowed during the year, and unemployment remained high, reaching 7.6 percent in the fourth quarter. In most other industrialized countries, prospects looked worse. By 1977, talk of a "pause" in the post-1974 recovery was widespread. More serious than the short-term outlook were the structural challenges that the capitalist world confronted. Governments appeared unable to manage their economies as they had in the 1950s and 1960s; they now struggled to produce growth and full employment, dual commitments for the West's welfare states. Stimulus initiatives in the mid-1970s were exacerbating inflation without reducing unemployment, to the chagrin of Keynesian economists who had long presumed a negative correlation between these evil twins of macroeconomics.[22]

Interdependence was part of the problem. Formulated within a bounded concept of national economic space, Keynesian theory held that stimulating demand through tax cuts, public spending, and cheap money would correct cyclical downturns and bolster employment. By the 1970s, however, transnational economic relations had become so thick that most advanced industrial countries were no longer economies unto themselves. This made economic governance more challenging—and less predictable—than Keynesian theory presumed. In a globalizing world, economic stimulus in one country but not elsewhere could lead to disruptive and destabilizing capital flows. Yet the dilemmas for economic governance in the 1970s were also a consequence of structural changes deep within the West's capitalist economies.[23]

Beneath the drama of the oil crisis, waning economic productivity and falling rates of profit made a return to high postwar growth rates improbable. After 1973, US labor productivity increased by 1.7 percent per year, half what its growth averaged between 1948 and 1966. The causes of this slowdown were complex: the oil shocks set productivity back, but declining capital investment, diminishing returns on innovation, and the service sector's ascent all contributed to the slippage as well. Meanwhile, the pool of surplus agricultural labor that had long nourished economic growth was running dry; "since the late 1960s," the Council of Economic Advisers warned, the "shift out of agriculture has slowed, and productivity growth from this source has been much reduced." If postwar growth had been extensive, based upon the addition of factors within a stable techno-industrial paradigm, future gains would have to be intensive, which meant making existing factors of production more productive. Economic growth would, as a result, be slower in the future than it had been in the past, and it would have to come from improvements in productivity now that the abundant inputs of energy and labor that had sustained high rates of extensive growth in the 1950s and 1960s were expiring.[24]

The ebbing of recovery in the last quarter of 1976 made restoring growth both a political priority and a transcendent challenge. In its absence loomed distributive struggles and even political instability; for postwar policymakers, it was axiomatic that growth salved the social conflicts that had plagued prewar capitalism. Now that growth had ebbed, policymakers agreed on the imperative of restoring it but not how to achieve its restoration. Ford and his advisers had gambled that price stability, deregulation, and government austerity would restore private-sector productivity. These solutions prefigured Reaganomics in the 1980s, but in general market-oriented solutions did not dominate the policy arena. Democrats in the Congress and in the Carter administration, entertained rather different ideas about how to rejuvenate growth.[25]

While the neoliberals advocated rolling back the state, some Democrats favored expanding the federal government's economic role to include the micro-economic management of industries. In 1975, Hubert Humphrey and Jacob Javits, two powerful US senators with strong ties to organized labor, proposed creating a national planning board. The initiative won the support of progressive economists, such as John Kenneth Galbraith and Wassily Leontief, who argued that restoring growth required government involvement in planning and alloca-tion as well as restrictions on the international movement of trade and capital. Microeconomic managerialism, sometimes characterized as "industrial policy," commanded enthusiasm on the Democratic Party's left.[26]

Although Carter saluted Humphrey and Javits on the campaign trail, the pres-ident's instincts led him to favor deregulation, not industrial policies. The tariffs and controls on which industrial policies would depend were, moreover, diffi-cult to square with Carter's Trilateralist commitments to keep the world econ-omy open. "Tariffs, export subsidies, industrial policy, privileged treatment," concluded a Trilateral Commission report, "threaten the systems of interaction and interdependence which are a source of prosperity in the industrial world." Committed to internationalizing economic governance and to keeping world markets open, the Carter administration rejected both the left's microeconom-ics of managerialism and the right's microeconomics of the market. It persevered instead with the macroeconomic solutions that US policymakers had favored since the 1950s. An early stimulus package aimed to promote growth through tax cuts and grants to local government. Framed domestically, the stimulus was a predictable move. More innovative was its projection upon a transnational scale.[27]

Having assumed office inclined to Trilateralist cooperation and macroeco-nomic stimulus, the Carter administration found in the G-7 summits a vehicle for policy coordination. As before, the initiative emerged elsewhere. It was Valéry Giscard d'Estaing who, in late 1976, proposed the next summit, point-ing to the "developing division" between the strong and the weak economies within the G-7 as a "concrete" problem that the group should address. Britain, Italy, and France were flagging at the end of 1976, while Japan, Germany, and the United States were doing rather better. British officials had long advocated an international stimulus program, but their appeals had swayed neither Bonn nor Washington. Attitudes now looked to be changing. The Brookings Institution put out a report in late 1976 calling for a coordinated international stimulus. The logic of the proposal was that the strong countries would stimulate their economies and lift global demand, while the weaker countries would hold firm against price inflation. Known as the "locomotive theory," it gave Germany, Japan, and the United States special responsibility for pulling the industrialized world into recovery.[28]

The Carter administration embraced the locomotive. When Secretary Blumenthal went to Congress to defend the Carter domestic stimulus package, he linked it to international objectives, urging legislators to help the White House to foster "a better international economic climate." Vice President Mondale traveled to Europe to build support for the initiative, finding the British enthusiastic but the Germans wary. Helmut Schmidt acknowledged the utility of an "internationally concerted economic policy" but declared that his priority was fighting inflation, which in 1977 averaged almost 10 percent across the G-7 economies. Stimulus, the chancellor feared, would only exacerbate rising prices. Still, with the United States now leading the stimulus camp, Schmidt had cause to feel isolated. When the G-7 had last convened, Ford had sided with Schmidt, but the change in administrations, along with mounting concerns about the US balance of payments, led Washington to switch sides.[29]

Crucially, getting Germany and Japan to stimulate their economies would enable the Carter administration to pursue expansionary domestic policies without exacerbating the US balance of payments deficit. The locomotive nonetheless followed a grand strategic logic. Echoing Kissinger, the Trilateralists warned that "bleak economic prospects" in Europe and Japan would breed protectionism and instability. Restoring growth would secure social and political stability and keep the world economy open. Success nonetheless required collective action. Convinced that "economic interdependence has become a fact of international life," the Carter administration presumed that effective economic stimulus had to be coordinated; if the industrialized countries pursued divergent policies, they would fail in tandem. This made the next G-7 summit the administration's "most important foreign policy action," in Brzezinski's assessment. After "a protracted period of political stagnation and economic decline," a successful summit, Brzezinski predicted, could be the historical "turning point" that restored the West's confidence, prosperity, and purpose.[30]

The planning began months before the G-7 convened in London. Seeing the summit not as an informal seminar, as Giscard had construed the Rambouillet summit, but as an exercise in collaborative decision-making, US officials focused on the communiqué that would conclude the summit. Henry Owen represented Carter in the preparatory talks, working to steer them toward favored US goals. Besides coordinating stimulus efforts, these goals included expanding the IMF's lending resources and recommitting the G-7 to trade liberalization. Achieving shared commitments to nuclear nonproliferation, energy conservation, and Third World aid were also US priorities. Germany cautioned against inflation and trade imbalances, concerns that reflected its dependence on exports. North-South relations were another priority for Helmut Schmidt, who favored supporting the export earnings of the poorest countries but opposed creating an international system to bolster commodity prices, which would hurt countries, like Germany, that imported primary commodities and did not produce them.[31]

If national positions followed national interests, lofty purposes nonetheless enveloped the pre-summit dialogue. Amid the shock of interdependence, summitry would restore "leadership and purpose" to the West, marking the transition from the hierarchical Pax Americana to a "more mature" order in which the United States would practice "shared leadership with other nations." This was Brzezinski's view, and it echoed the Trilateralists' pre-1977 prognoses. But if the Pax Americana were to be recapitulated in multilateral guise, the United States would remain the orchestrator of world order. "There is a great desire in the Western world for a restoration of confidence," Jimmy Carter confided in his diary, "and I believe that unless that confidence is derived from the strength of our country it won't be coming from any other source."[32]

Confident in US primacy, Jimmy Carter undercut his negotiating position one month before the summit convened. Citing improved economic conditions, Carter in April 1977 asked Congress to rescind the personal tax rebate that had been a central component of the domestic stimulus package he had proposed in January. The move canceled one-third of Carter's $31 billion stimulus, to the chagrin of American taxpayers and the delight of Helmut Schmidt, who could now use Carter's words and deeds against him. Retracting the rebate may have been sensible in the domestic context, but it was a misstep on the international stage. Prime Minister Fukuda of Japan asked, pointedly, what Carter's retreat from stimulus signaled for US leadership. Carter rebuffed Fukuda's suggestion that the United States had taken "a step backwards." But the issue lingered. With Schmidt holding the line for price stability, the summit achieved only an uneasy compromise between stimulatory and anti-inflationary priorities, which was the same awkward balance Carter was struggling to maintain at home. Even with the support of Britain's James Callaghan, Carter could not persuade Schmidt and Fukuda to specify formal growth targets in the summit communiqué. Instead, the leaders agreed to informal growth targets: 5 percent for Germany; 6.7 percent for Japan; and 6 percent for the United States.[33]

Macroeconomic coordination was not the only contentious issue in London. Carter took a strident lead on nuclear nonproliferation, advocating the creation of an international framework to restrict the sale of uranium and the distribution of nuclear technologies to non-nuclear countries. Schmidt pushed back, expressing concern that Carter's proposals would engender "feeling[s] of discrimination" in the Third World. More than principles were at stake. Back in 1975, Germany had struck a deal with Brazil to develop enrichment and reprocessing facilities in Brazil in return for deliveries of uranium to Germany. The United States objected to the deal, not only because it might facilitate Brazil's nuclear weapons aspirations, but also because it circumscribed opportunities for US exporters and assured Germany a supply of uranium from non-US sources. Both sides, however, adopted the language of ideals: Schmidt invoked the prerogatives of sovereignty and Carter spoke for world order, illustrating how global and national purposes could be set against each other. Similar dynamics recurred over human rights, about which Carter was also strident, making "no apology for his espousal of the cause of human rights." Others, including Schmidt, preferred softer approaches and disavowed any interest in overthrowing illiberal regimes.[34]

Despite the fractiousness, Jimmy Carter declared himself satisfied with the results of the London summit and of the two other summits timed to coincide with it: the NATO summit and the Quadripartite summit (of the four powers with interests in West Berlin) that convened in London in May 1977. "They were very productive, far beyond anything I had anticipated," he wrote. Schmidt excepted, the president struck up effective relationships with the other heads of government. "I've gotten to know the other leaders," Carter continued, "and I think we have a good relationship." Henry Owen echoed Carter's verdict. In the G-7, the Trilateralists found a framework in which world order politics could be pursued. If the Carter administration could build on the achievements at the London summit, Henry Owen believed, it would forge "a new international institution—one that brings Japan, as well as Europe and North America, more closely together in common decision and common action."[35]

The initial exuberance soon faded. Administration officials concluded during the fall of 1977 that the London compromise was falling apart. Their concerns hinged on the macroeconomic locomotive. With Schmidt reluctant to stimulate, German growth looked to be lagging far behind its 5 percent goal. Japan appeared to be closer to its target, but exports, not domestic demand, were driving Japanese growth. This undercut the logic of the locomotive theory, which presumed that demand in the strongest countries would sustain export-led growth elsewhere. Of the strong countries, the United States was the only one "likely to meet both the numerical target and the spirit of the [London] communiqué," the only country, in other words, serving as a consumer of last resort. This had repercussions for the US balance of payments, which plunged during 1977. It also augured disruptive policy choices in the weak countries. Through late 1977, Britain, France, and Italy "roughly" adhered to the stabilization policies that were their part of the London bargain. Without an effective international locomotive, US officials feared, the weaker countries might adopt stimulus packages of their own, worsening price inflation worldwide and exacerbating international monetary instability.[36]

The Keynesians in the administration blamed "differential rates of growth" among the G-7 economies, but there was no disguising the fact that international trade and monetary imbalances hinged on the United States and the dollar. By the end of 1977, the US current account deficit, at $18 billion, was three times larger than the previous year's deficit and about half the total deficits of all the OECD countries. Not since the 1850s had the balance of trade run so hard against the United States. Until the fall, US officials had remained sanguine about the balance of payments, even as their European counterparts warned that the dollar's decline augured "a crisis of considerable proportions." The dwindling dollar, Schmidt argued, exacerbated inflation in Europe and encouraged oil exporters, who denominated their exports in dollars, to raise prices again. These were valid concerns, but there was minimal enthusiasm in Washington for raising domestic interest rates or restraining domestic demand to strengthen the dollar. Even for the Trilateralists, who proclaimed that global interdependence mandated national discipline, applying the macroeconomic brakes at home was harder than pushing the accelerator, which is what the locomotive concept prescribed.[37]

Still, the dollar's difficulties could not be wished away. US officials, including Blumenthal, began to seriously engage the dollar situation in late 1977, and Carter, in early 1978, conceded a point that the European leaders had been making for months: US trade deficits and the imploding dollar had much to do with "our heavy dependence on imported oil." He thereby linked monetary stabilization with another issue that transcended distinctions between foreign and domestic affairs, namely, energy.[38]

⟨∞⟩

In energy policy, Carter inherited an unenviable situation. The vulnerabilities that the oil crisis of 1973–74 manifested had not abated; instead, the United States had become more depenendent on foreign supply in the intervening years. Americans imported half the oil they consumed in 1977, up from 22 percent at the beginning of the 1970s. Domestic consumption was a major part of the problem. In 1977, Americans burned 18 million barrels of oil per day, almost half the oil burned by all the OECD countries combined and a third of total world oil consumption. They thus shared with OPEC special responsibility for driving the price of oil upward—from $10, in real terms, per barrel of Saudi light crude in 1970 to $45 in 1977. Like Gerald Ford, Carter recognized that reducing domestic demand for oil was an international imperative; unless American consumption slackened, world prices would remain high. "The success of your energy policy in reducing U.S. dependence," Brzezinski affirmed to Carter, "will have a significant effect on our relationship with Europe and on Europe's internal well-being."[39]

Because of the decline in domestic oil production, there were no easy answers to the dilemma of energy interdependence. Some industrialized countries, such as Japan and France, had embraced nuclear energy. But Carter, who had trained as a nuclear engineer, worried about accidents and the misuse of civilian technologies for military purposes, which ensured that he would not embrace the atom as a panacea. Indeed, Carter's eagerness to restrict the international sale of uranium and reprocessing equipment became a source of rancor within the G-7, especially with Japan. For Prime Minister Fukuda, ensuring the continuity of uranium supplies was a "life or death" issue. The controversy faded only when Carter approved the reprocessing of US-sourced uranium at Japan's Tokai plant. A setback for nonproliferation, the spat showcased Carter's determination to limit the spread of civilian technologies that could facilitate nuclear weapons programs, as had happened in India, which tested a fission bomb in 1974. The Tokai episode showed that world order objectives might conflict with each other—and with geopolitical goals. Restricting the spread of nuclear technologies cut against the administration's commitment to reducing the industrialized world's dependence on OPEC oil, raising questions about where Carter's priorities lay.[40]

Carter's attempts to manage international energy interdependence also bred friction at home. Jim Schlesinger, Ford's secretary of defense, whom Carter appointed as a special adviser on energy, was tasked with devising an energy program capable of mitigating international vulnerabilities. In April 1977, Carter unveiled the National Energy Plan. Borrowing a phrase from William James, the president called energy conservation the "moral equivalent of war." Failure to act, Carter warned, "could endanger our freedom as a sovereign nation." Two days later, Carter elaborated the plan before Congress. Besides promoting conservation, he would expand domestic oil production and, where possible, substitute alternative energy sources for oil. The key to the whole concept was pricing. Energy markets in the United States remained tightly regulated, and price controls kept the prices of domestic oil and natural gas below world levels. Raising the price of fossil fuels, Carter hoped, would leverage the market to "stimulate conservation" and make alternative fuels viable. This had been the thrust of Ford's energy policy, too, although Carter was less willing to countenance the outright removal of price controls. While he favored higher prices, Carter was loath to let energy companies keep the profits that decontrol would reap. He instead advocated a complex system of staggered price increases that would bring domestic oil prices up to world levels in combination with a windfall tax on corporate profits that would fund relief for poor consumers. Equitable distribution of the economic pain, Carter's team hoped, would enable the National Energy Plan to secure congressional support.[41]

The Democratic Party enjoyed a sizable majority in Congress, but the Carter energy plan ran into opposition in the Senate, where legislators debated the plan as a package of separate bills. In the House of Representatives, Speaker Tip O'Neill constituted a special committee to consider the plan as a single package, which the House approved in the summer of 1977. The Senate's convoluted process empowered lobbyists for the energy industry, leading Carter to remark, privately, that the "influence of the oil and gas industry" in the chamber was "unbelievable." Some progressive Democrats, meanwhile, objected to price increases on the grounds that they would hurt the Americans who could least afford it. Even the administration's rather skeptical willingness to explore nuclear power became contentious, being unpopular with environmentalists. All Congress could agree to do in 1977 was to establish a cabinet-level department, the Department of Energy, to oversee federal energy policy.[42]

Creating the Department of Energy was an accomplishment, but Carter's core goals in energy policy remained unfulfilled. Raising oil prices remained deeply unpopular among both Republicans and Democrats in Congress. Their recalcitrance hampered foreign policy. Insofar as the United States had done "very little to limit the growth in oil demand" at home, it was difficult for US diplomats, Brzezinski warned, to pressure OPEC "to hold down prices." Meanwhile, excessive US imports of foreign oil were destabilizing the international economy, pulling down the dollar, and exacerbating price inflation; one likely result, Blumenthal warned in early 1978, would be a serious dollar crisis. "Our nation's inability to deal with so crucial a question," Carter recalled, "was becoming an international embarrassment."[43]

⌘

The experience of 1977 exposed obstacles to the enactment of the Trilateralists' goals: informal commitments were easily forgotten; simultaneous purposes collided, as they had done on energy and nonproliferation; and domestic constituencies resisted making the sacrifices that international cooperation mandated. Meanwhile, international monetary instability and the prospect of a renewed global recession loomed. The two perils were not unrelated. The buoyancy of the US economy amid slowing foreign growth exacerbated the current account deficit, contributing to a striking decline in the dollar's effective exchange rate during 1977–78, as figure 8.1 illustrates. After the stability of the mid-1970s, it looked as if a dollar devaluation similar in magnitude to the one Nixon orchestrated in 1971–73 was unfolding. Some foreign officials suspected that the United States was trying to weaken the dollar to benefit domestic exporters, much as Nixon

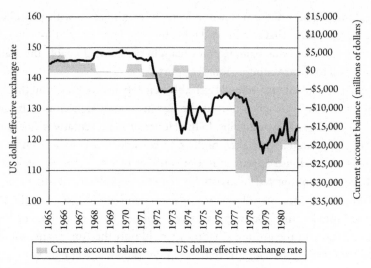

Figure 8.1 The balance of payments and the dollar, 1965–1980

Sources: BIS, Statistics; and US Bureau of the Census, Foreign Trade Statistics.

had done. This overstated the case. US officials were nonchalant about the dollar's slide throughout most of 1977, but they were taking it seriously by the year's end. In early 1978, Carter asked his advisers to keep him personally "informed and involved" with the "dollar problem."[44]

For US officials, the risks of a declining dollar included another OPEC price hike, the discrediting of US economic leadership, and even "a major international financial crisis." Saudi Arabia clarified the risks when it warned the United States in early 1978 that it might begin denominating its oil exports against a basket of foreign currencies, a move that would dethrone the dollar from its dominant role in the oil trade. For treasury secretary Michael Blumenthal, whom critics had accused of "talking down the dollar" in the summer of 1977, it was now clear that "the dollar problem involves serious risks to our national security." This recognition sparked action. In the new year, the Carter administration heeded calls from Europe and initiated a program of joint intervention with the Bundesbank to support the dollar on the foreign exchange markets. It nonetheless rejected James Callaghan's proposal for a concerted effort to restore international currency stability. The British prime minister's approach, Blumenthal warned, would set the world on "a road back toward fixed exchange rates." Unwilling to impose such a "strait jacket on US domestic economic policy," the Carter administration preferred to recommit to macroeconomic coordination, arguing that faster economic growth in Europe and Japan would correct the disequilibria responsible for the dollar's slide.[45]

Blumenthal and other US officials distrusted Callaghan's enthusiasm for monetary stabilization. But it was the British prime minister who in March 1978 proposed "a new act of collective leadership in the management of the world economy." Callaghan envisaged a grand bargain in which the G-7 powers would trade varied policy commitments, the result being a plan for collaborative action "across a broad front of economic policy." The priorities that Callaghan identified—macroeconomic stimulus, trade liberalization, monetary stability, and so on—were predictable, but putting them in a political framework, in which concessions would be traded, was an innovative move.[46]

Since Japan had agreed in winter 1977/8 to adopt new growth targets, the central obstacle would be Germany. To overcome "the difficulty of persuading the Federal German Republic to take further action on growth," Callaghan suggested that Carter agree to reduce US oil imports in exchange for Schmidt's commitment to achieving specific growth targets. That the next G-7 summit was scheduled to convene in Bonn in July 1978 only enhanced the opportunities to extract commitments from Schmidt. Henry Owen had, in fact, already used the implicit (and improbable) threat of US nonparticipation in the summit to encourage German concessions. It also mattered that support for a change of direction in economic policy was building within Schmidt's Social Democratic Party (SPD). Organized labor and the left wing of the SPD favored pro-growth policies, which aligned them with the Anglo-American quest for stimulus.[47]

Throughout the preparatory process that preceded the summit, the Carter administration defined clear goals. The centerpiece of the meeting would be "a three-way deal": the United States would act "to limit oil imports and control inflation"; Germany and Japan would implement "additional measures to stimulate domestic demand"; and all the G-7 countries would pursue "freer trade policies." Helmut Schmidt would not define a GDP growth target in advance of the summit, but he and Carter did establish the parameters of a deal. American "energy action" would be a "quid-pro-quo" for Germany "taking simulative action." This made it imperative that Congress take action to raise domestic oil prices. "Unless you are in a position to demonstrate forceful action on energy," Carter's foreign policy advisers told him, "the forthcoming Summit will be branded a failure." However, decontrolling oil prices was not a consensual commitment within the Carter administration. High-ranking advisers, including Stuart Eizenstat, the president's lead adviser on domestic affairs, opposed decontrol on the grounds that higher energy prices would be a political liability for Carter and a burden on ordinary Americans. Within the Congress, opposition to decontrol was strong. The Trilateralists nonetheless gambled that Carter's committing himself abroad would pressure the Congress into passing the domestic energy bill that represented Washington's end of the Bonn bargain.[48]

"We're getting boxed in," Carter worried as the summit approached. "Expectations," he feared, were "too high." The president was correct; expectations for the Bonn summit grew so high that the media ended up registering disappointment with its results. When it came to the substance, however, the Bonn summit met the administration's goals. The carefully prepared oil-for-stimulus deal fostered an easy and productive working atmosphere. "We feel like members of a fraternity," Carter wrote; "we share problems and political analyses, try to understand different national perspectives, and cooperate." This did not make authoritative global governance the summit's purpose; rather, the G-7 sought to negotiate and, where possible, to reconcile the divergent national priorities that threatened the stability of the international economic order and the prosperity of the advanced industrial countries.[49]

Evaluated in these terms, the Bonn summit was a success. Carter struck a conciliatory pose, as did his foreign interlocutors. Although Carter insisted that the weak US dollar was a consequence of anemic growth elsewhere in the world, he emphasized his commitment to fighting inflation and curbing energy consumption at home. This was enough to extract from Schmidt a commitment to pursue "additional and quantitatively substantial" stimulus measures worth about 1 percent of GNP. As he had done in London, Takeo Fukuda offered eloquent entreaties to common purpose, summoning his colleagues to transcend their "age of uncertainty." Substantively, the Japanese prime minister's decision to pursue 1978 growth targets that were 1.5 percent higher than the previous year's helped to catalyze agreement, focusing pressure on Schmidt.[50]

The weaker G-7 economies also played their parts: France, Italy, and Britain agreed to fight inflation and conclude the Tokyo Round of trade talks within six months. Canada reaffirmed its determination to fight inflation, and Prime Minister Trudeau provided one of the summit's most perceptive historical analyses, inquiring whether the G-7's predicament might not reflect the exhaustion of "the potential of the second industrial revolution." In the summit communiqué, Carter committed the United States to reducing oil imports by approximately 2.5 million barrels per day by 1985 and to increase the domestic price of oil to world levels by the end of 1980. Schmidt, meanwhile, pledged to stimulate demand. Overall, the Bonn declaration of the G-7 was a landmark in international economic relations; having arrived through political bargaining at a "package deal," the advanced industrial countries agreed to coordinate domestic policies in pursuit of shared prosperity and common stability.

In the short term, the participants mostly honored their commitments. The German Bundestag in fall 1978 approved a stimulus package that raised the Federal Republic's annualized growth rate to about 4 percent. This was, as Henry Owen testified to Congress, "a substantial advantage for the countries that trade with Germany." Japan did not quite meet its Bonn target, but it made what Owen called "a good faith effort," including adopting "an additional stimulus bud-get." Insofar as Carter had agreed to prioritize the fight against inflation, sub-sequent US decisions to tighten monetary policy, Owen believed, represented "a satisfactory fulfillment of that commitment." In the energy arena, however, Carter's record was patchier. After Bonn, Carter wrangled much of his domes-tic energy program through the Congress, but the legislative package of 1978 did nothing to raise oil prices, and the issue festered into 1979. Carter would in time implement price decontrol by executive fiat, not legislative assent, in circumstances that the Iranian Revolution transformed. Honoring his Bonn pledge would prove to be politically bruising for the American president, illus-trating a point Carter had made on the campaign trail. "Interdependence," he declared back in 1975, "means mutual sacrifice."[51]

The London and Bonn summits represent outstanding examples of inter-national policy coordination. Confronting an economic crisis of transnational scope, a group of leaders hailing from the political center and center-left worked to reconcile national interests and common purposes under circum-stances of interdependence and turmoil. Policy coordination, they gambled, would enable them to bolster growth and employment through the re-creation on a transnational scale of the Keynesian solutions that policymakers in the industrialized countries had followed since the Second World War. Yet they did not achieve their goals, for another oil crisis soon transformed the inter-national economic landscape. Some critics, including Helmut Schmidt, later argued that the Anglo-American crusade for an international stimulus in 1977–78 exacerbated the West's malaise. This is debatable. What is clear is that the summiteers were committed to preserving an open world economic order. Mindful of the 1930s, the G-7 leaders sought to keep the industrial-ized countries together through the cooperative production of growth. Their agenda was nostalgic in looking to restore the bountiful growth of the 1950s and 1960s, yet innovative in its bid to retool Keynesian policies for the circum-stances of interdependence.[52]

There were, of course, omissions. The summiteers at London and Bonn dealt with their own problems, not the whole world's. Accounting for half of world trade, the G-7 countries had in common a shared industrial modernity, lofty expectations for growth and welfare, and their interdependence. Together with the other advanced economies, they consumed 73 percent of the world's imports and produced 72 percent of its exports. Their position in the world economy was dominant, but dominance did not make the advanced economies a world unto themselves. The G-7 was "closely interdependent" with the Third World, as Valéry Giscard d'Estaing observed at Bonn. The summiteers, Giscard argued, "should not just pay lip service to relations with developing countries." In fact, this is what they did, offering platitudes but little else.[53]

The Bonn declaration affirmed the G-7's "shared responsibility" for international development and denounced the Communist bloc for its failure to do more for the world's poor. But Bonn produced few commitments beyond Japan's pledge to double development aid over the next two years. James Callaghan, whose concern with the Third World distinguished him within the G-7, rued that the summiteers looked "like a group of rich industrialized countries who at the end of their deliberations said that they must have a few paragraphs about the developing countries in their communiqué." This was an accurate assessment. The communiqué, however, reflected political realities within the summit countries. There was little support within the G-7 countries for increasing developmental aid, liberalizing the tariff barriers that shut Third World exporters out of the West's agricultural markets, and international schemes that would guarantee the export incomes of commodity-producing countries, such as the NIEO proposed. In the First World's parsimony toward the Third, the 1970s was truly a decade of limits.[54]

Disadvantageous circumstances thus doomed Carter's North-South policy. The administration entered office in 1977 insisting that the amelioration of global inequalities was a strategic imperative, not just an ethical concern. Brzezinski argued that "the emerging political consciousness of mankind" made it incumbent on the United States to seek "social justice between peoples, individuals, and even states." "North-South relations," he proclaimed, "are the long-run problem in international politics." Here, however, advances would not come without costs— or, to be more specific, without transfers. As Cyrus Vance pointed out, foreign aid was "the single most important" thing the United States could do to improve its relations with the Third World, but congressional parsimony proved insurmountable. No matter how badly the United States needed "a comprehensive and long-term North-South strategy," there was little enthusiasm in the Congress— or elsewhere—for expanding the foreign-aid budget. Indeed, Brzezinski concluded in mid-1977 that the administration would do better to focus on political outreach to the Third World South than on economic assistance. "North-South policy," one official observed, "was an idea whose time had not yet come." In its absence, Carter's outreach hinged on engagement with individual countries, such as Panama, whose grievances over the Canal Zone he tried to resolve, and on his oftenstated but contentious commitment to human rights.[55]

Making Human Rights Policy

A concern with human rights in foreign policy marked the difference between the Carter administration and its predecessors, but the old obstacles still endured. Reconciling universal aspirations to the stubborn realities of territorial sovereignty remained a particular dilemma. The administration recognized that embracing human rights might lead some to conclude "that we are embarked on a crusade to drastically alter or topple 100-odd governments." Carter none-theless repudiated Kissinger's prioritization of international order over univer-sal justice. When the president addressed the United Nations in March 1977, he neither uttered the word "sovereignty" nor intimated it as a significant pri-ority. Instead, he reified human rights promotion as a purpose for the United Nations—and for US foreign policy. The United States, Carter announced, would meddle in the internal affairs of foreign countries if human rights con-cerns warranted it doing so. This was a bold commitment and a striking depar-ture from Washington's previous diplomatic practice.[56]

As malleable as human rights are, defining them ranked among the most urgent tasks of the administration. One approach defined human rights in terms of core civil and political rights—the "negative" rights that individuals retain against states (and that Moynihan made the centerpiece of his UN crusade). The UN's Universal Declaration of Human Rights of 1948, however, included not only political and civil rights but also social and economic rights, "includ-ing food, clothing, housing and medical care." Unlike Moynihan, the Carter administration favored defining human rights in the "broadest sense." "The point to stress," Brzezinski noted, "is that human rights is a broad concept." The "universal appeal" of human rights depended upon their encompassing "basic minimum standards of social and economic existence." Thus, the administration adopted a capacious definition. Following the Universal Declaration, it included social and economic rights in its agenda, figuring that excluding them "would not only be inconsistent with our humanitarian ideals and efforts, but would also be unacceptable in the Third World." "Our policy," Cyrus Vance explained, "is to promote all these rights."[57]

Seeing themselves as the heirs to the natural rights revolution of Hobbes, Locke, and Jefferson, it was easy for American leaders to presume that the nation had a special relationship to the idea of human rights. The United States was not, however, on the cutting edge of international human rights law. In particular, the two UN human rights covenants of 1966—the International Covenant on Civil and Political Rights and the International Covenant on Economic, Social and Cultural Rights—still lacked American signatures. Envisaged as early as 1948, the covenants promised to transform the Universal Declaration's aspira-tions into binding international law. Carter, in October 1977, signed both doc-uments. In doing so, he aimed to transcend Cold War controversies over the meaning of human rights and to commit the United States to multilateral human rights enforcement. He nonetheless lacked the power to affix more than his own signature, for ratification of the treaties required the Senate's assent. Amnesty International, the International Commission of Jurists, and the International

League for Human Rights urged Congress to approve the treaties—and the White House to push hard for ratification—describing the two covenants as "essential to progress in protecting human rights." Louis Henkin, an eminent human rights lawyer, wrote that Senate ratification "would move the United States into the mainstream of the international human rights movement." The treaties nonetheless languished in committee.[58]

Without Senate ratification of the 1966 covenants, human rights would remain in the arena of foreign policy, as distinct from the realm of international law. Here, human rights would have to be balanced against parallel priorities, but Carter worked from the outset to elevate their prioritization. Besides appointing Patricia Derian to coordinate human rights policy at the State Department, the administration hired Jessica Tuchman Mathews to lead an NSC staff cluster dealing "with human rights and the range of problems that cut across traditional foreign policy areas." Beyond staff appointments, the Carter administration established machinery to coordinate human rights policy across the foreign-policy bureaucracies. Overseas embassies were required to designate "human rights officers" who would have "frank discussions" with foreign officials and meet with the victims of human rights abuses. At Brzezinski's suggestion, an interagency human rights group was established in the spring of 1977 under the chairmanship of Warren Christopher, Vance's deputy. The primary task of the Christopher committee would be to vet the allocation of US development aid, multilateral as well as bilateral, on human rights grounds.[59]

Though its purpose was to regularize policy across the regional bureaus, the Christopher committee proceeded on an ad hoc basis, which was not conducive to defining overarching standards. One NSC staffer reported feeling "uneasy" about the absence of clear guidelines for denying aid on human rights grounds. Nor did the interagency committee resolve the bureaucratic turf wars: by mid-1978, Jessica Matthews was complaining that Christopher was "making all the decisions himself." There were also limits to the committee's reach. It did not, for the most part, evaluate military assistance programs; these were determined at higher levels. Still, the bureaucratic innovations of 1977 were a marker of shifting priorities. Whereas Kissinger's State Department had resisted congressional efforts to inject human rights into foreign policy, Carter's embraced human rights as its own cause.[60]

The executive branch's conversion to human rights did not end the skirmishes with the Congress. In early 1977, Tom Harkin, an Iowa Democrat, slipped a human rights amendment into a piece of House legislation appropriating funds for the Inter-American Development Bank. It required the executive branch to vote against loan applicants whenever the prospective borrowers were proven abusers of human rights. After this success, Herman Badillo, a Harkin ally from New York, introduced legislation in April that would make US votes in international financial institutions (IFIs) contingent upon borrowers not engaging in persistent human rights violations. This was a bold move. Badillo believed that tying financial aid to human rights would establish a structural check on human rights abuses, to be applied worldwide and without discretion. Some of Badillo's detractors accused him of leveraging a source of structural power in the world economy to promote an ideological agenda; others condemned his encroachment on executive prerogatives. Fearing that Badillo's amendment would provoke adverse reactions in the Third World and recognizing that it obliterated the president's "negotiating flexibility," the Carter administration opposed the initiative and supported an alternative Senate bill that preserved diplomatic flexibility. Badillo and his allies nonetheless succeeded, and the IFI legislation became "the high-water mark of legislative initiative to require human rights tests on all forms of foreign aid." Tasked with implementing the law, the Carter administration struggled to preserve flexibility amid rigid mandates.[61]

From the administration's perspective, rigid sanctions were unsuited to a world in which sovereign prerogatives precluded universal law, and even close NATO allies distrusted Carter's human rights commitments. Flexibility, moreover, enabled the White House to promise rewards—such as IFI loans—to encourage foreign governments to improve their human rights standards. "We should be alert," administration officials noted, "to the potential benefits of using the 'carrot' as well as the 'stick.'" Still, the utility of flexibility did not obviate the need for overarching standards. Administration diplomats complained during 1977 about the absence of clear guidance about what constituted human rights violations and, more fundamentally, as to what Carter's policy was. In the absence of presidential instructions, Cyrus Vance's April 1977 speech on human rights to the University of Georgia Law School became the de facto reference point. Meanwhile, the Carter administration worked to formulate a set of general precepts, which became the first comprehensive executive-branch statement on human rights.[62]

In May 1977, the White House issued a presidential review memorandum (PRM) on human rights in foreign policy. The Christopher committee coordinated the drafting of the eighty-five-page paper, known as PRM-28, which provided the basis for a subsequent presidential directive (PD) on human rights, PD-30, in early 1978. These documents, which Carter edited himself, presumed a capacious, threefold definition of human rights, including "basic economic and social rights," bodily "integrity," and "civil and political liberties." To promote these rights in the international arena, PD-30 proposed using "the full range" of "diplomatic tools" from discrete bilateral suasion to public denunciation of violators.[63]

Whereas the congressional enthusiasts favored sanctions, Carter envisaged making use of "positive inducements" to reward countries that improved upon tawdry records. Doing so, the administration hoped, might enable it to steer social and political development in foreign countries in a positive direction. Indeed, PD-30 avowed that the "primary emphasis" of US policy would be on "longer term trends," not specific manifestations of brutality. The Carter directives thus suggested that the most useful role the United States could play would be to massage progressive historical change rather than express principled outrage wherever the specter of abuse appeared. If the agenda seemed cautious, even conservative, it reflected both Zbigniew Brzezinski's preoccupation with large-scale historical processes and Carter's wariness of blanket assertions of moral superiority. "Our own ideals in the area of human rights," Carter admitted at the United Nations, "have not always been attained in the United States."[64]

As vexing as defining human rights could be, the cause was popular. Congress embraced Carter's human rights commitments, the skirmishes over the IFI issue notwithstanding. Some fifty-seven senators co-signed a letter saluting Carter's stand, while Donald Fraser defended Carter against the charge that his policy constituted "interference" in the affairs of foreign nations. Public opinion was also supportive. One poll conducted in late May 1977 found overwhelming support, even when human rights were set against other important goals, such as nuclear arms control. "Particularly striking," the pollster concluded, was the fact that support for Carter's human rights policy "was broad-based, cutting across all traditional lines of party, age, region, and social class." Another survey, conducted by the pollster Pat Caddell, reported that voters defined human rights as their number one priority in foreign policy—24 percent calling human rights their top priority, as compared with 18 percent for US–Soviet relations. Surveys in other industrial democracies also revealed broad support. In France, Japan, Britain, Canada, and West Germany, the United States Information Agency reported, "the President's statements on human rights have struck a responsive chord among the more informed public." "The human rights policy," diplomat Anthony Lake concluded in January 1978, "may be the best thing this Administration has going for it."[65]

Still, it was easier to embrace human rights in the abstract than to advance the cause in specific contexts, where human rights might conflict with other goals and purposes. Many of the non-Communist governments that NGOs targeted were regimes the United States had nurtured. Indonesia, Iran, and South Korea were proven violators, but they were also close allies in rough neighborhoods. The People's Republic of China had a woeful human rights record (which the NGOs did little to excavate). China, however, remained a pivot point on which Cold War geopolitics turned. In these cases, human rights faced uphill struggles. The principles might be noble, but American diplomats, unlike the NGOs, would have to weigh human rights against other priorities. Thus, while Carter wanted to strike a balance that was quite different from Kissinger's, the tradeoffs between human rights and competing priorities endured, as did the countervailing claims of sovereignty.

⁓

In Latin America, the 1970s were a bleak time for human rights. Right-wing authoritarianism was ascendant, and Cold War polarization and the ideological claims of "national security doctrine" propelled the region's antidemocratic trends. With Washington's support, the governments of Argentina, Bolivia, Brazil, Paraguay, and Uruguay had in 1975 initiated Operation Condor, a transnational campaign of repression against the left. While the Soviet Union and Cuba provided succor to Latin America's revolutionary forces, it was the counter-revolutionaries who institutionalized state terror. Still, Latin America's military regimes chased order, not isolation, and their interest in preserving ties to the international community made them more susceptible to human rights activism than were closed societies like Cambodia and North Korea. For NGOs like Amnesty International and for human rights proponents in the US Congress, Latin America became a focus of inquiry and activism. Latin Americans were themselves active participants in the politics of human rights. Few nation-states were more supportive of human rights than Costa Rica, which championed the idea of a UN Commissioner for Human Rights, while antiregime activists in Argentina embraced international human rights as a tactic for resisting the junta in Buenos Aires. All this made Latin America a central priority for the Carter administration's human rights policy.[66]

Even as he prioritized human rights, Carter sought broad improvement in US relations with Latin America. Repudiating the Monroe Doctrine as an "imperialistic legacy," the administration sought to put relations "on a more normal footing." The days of "regional policy," were over, the administration declared; Washington would henceforth treat Latin America's republics as sovereign states with diverse interests, not as imperial protectorates. Central to this approach were the Panama Canal treaties of 1977, which committed the United States to restoring Panamanian sovereignty over the Canal Zone, a US overseas territory since 1903. Returning the Canal Zone was for Carter an ethical imperative; the president believed that Washington had "cheated the Panamanians out of their canal" in the first place. With the support of Ford, Kissinger, and other luminaries, Carter negotiated two treaties with Omar Torrijos of Panama that returned the Canal Zone to Panama, and then expended a great deal of political capital pushing them through Congress. Doing so attested to Carter's seriousness about improving US-Latin American relations, which meant working with the leaders of existing regimes, to whom Carter signaled his "high regard" for sovereignty. These leaders were not, by and large, a liberal group. Torrijos was by Carter's own admission a "military dictator," but Carter did not use the canal treaties as an opportunity to force human rights on him. Returning the Canal was a triumph, but the episode suggested that diplomatic engagement and human rights were not synonymous objectives; one entailed working with existing regimes, the other against them.[67]

Similar tensions manifested in the Southern Cone, where the Carter administration distanced itself from Kissinger's policy, which had condoned the repression of anti-regime forces. Since the 1973 coup that brought it to power, the Pinochet regime in Chile had become proficient in the practices of arbitrary detention, torture, and political murder. In the scale of its political violence, however, Argentina far eclipsed Chile. Thanks to Amnesty International and other NGOs, the misdeeds of the Argentine junta that seized power in March 1976 were widely publicized in the United States.[68]

Eager to take a stand, Cyrus Vance, at the June 1977 meeting of the OAS (Organization of American States), introduced a resolution declaring that "there are no circumstances which justify torture, summary executions, or prolonged detention without trial." A host of Caribbean and Central American nations sided with Washington, as the Southern Cone fought back, rallying behind the banner of sovereignty and turning the OAS meeting in Grenada into "a battleground for the US human rights policy." The debate became more heated as Carter escalated from gestures to actions. Within a few months of taking office, he prohibited the delivery of diverse military items to Argentina and Uruguay. Similar restrictions would later be imposed on Brazil, Paraguay, and several Central American countries. The value of US military sales and grants to Chile fell from $347 million in 1976 to just $18 million in 1980. Deliveries to Argentina fell from $294 million to $125 million over the same period. This was consequential, if incremental, change.[69]

Evaluating the impact of Carter's human rights policy in Latin America, the CIA in 1978 found "encouraging signs of progress," especially in Chile, but acknowledged wide disparities. There would, however, be no victory to declare. The most that could be said was that the scale of human rights violations diminished between 1977 and 1981. How much of this improvement owed to US influence was hard to say; even the State Department would not hazard a guess. Nor was it clear what costs the United States had paid for pushing human rights. "We cannot know," concluded the State Department's Tony Lake, "what price we might one day pay for the deterioration in our once close military relationships with Brazil and Argentina." What was clear was that Latin America was the principal "theater" for Carter's human rights policy. By January 1978, the United States had opposed on human rights grounds twenty-two IFI loans to Latin America, seven to Africa, and only four to East Asia. This did not mean the plight of human rights was worse in Latin America than elsewhere. Rather, it implied that abuses were more legible to US policymakers here than in other contexts and that the countervailing costs "to other American interests" were calculated to be lower than elsewhere.[70]

Across the Pacific, South Korea was a vexing case. A ward of US military power since the Korean War, South Korea's human rights record took a turn for the worse after Park Chung Hee imposed martial law in 1972 and persecuted the pro-democracy activists who clustered in South Korea's labor movement and in its Christian churches. Nixon and Kissinger had sided with the state, but others rallied behind South Korea's civil society. An Amnesty International mission to Seoul in 1975 indicted the regime's torture of political opponents and its harassment of lawyers. The US Congress held hearings on human rights in South Korea in 1975. Korea looked like an ideal case for the application of Carter's human rights policy, and the Carter administration voted against IFI loans on human rights grounds and made quiet appeals to South Korean officials, which helped to secure improvement in the treatment of dissidents.[71]

There were, however, limits to Carter's activism in Korea. He would not denounce Seoul in public, evidently for fear of destabilizing the regime. When Carter met with Park Chung Hee in the summer of 1979 the major issue between them was the prospect of US troop withdrawals, which Carter was seeking for fiscal and military reasons. The US president nonetheless seized the opportunity to press the case for human rights, advising Park that he attached "extreme importance" to the issue and intimating that US public opinion would not support military commitments unless Seoul improved its human rights record. But Carter established no formal linkage between human rights and military assistance, and the United States kept troops in South Korea even as the human rights situation deteriorated after the October 1979 assassination of President Park. When Park's successor, Chun Doo Hwan, launched a bloody assault on pro-democracy demonstrators in Kwangju in May 1980, the Carter administration refused to mediate, signaling tacit approval. When the stability of a pro-American regime was at stake, human rights would have to take a back seat, especially as Cold War tensions resurged in the last years of the 1970s.[72]

Iran also ranked among the "most difficult" human rights cases. In 1977, it was the world's second largest oil exporter and the dominant pillar of Washington's security strategy in the Persian Gulf. Mohammed Reza Pahlavi, Iran's shah, was a top-down modernizer and a voracious consumer of US military exports. At home, he ran a one-party state, which relied on its secret police, the SAVAK, to suppress opponents—secular liberals, revolutionary leftists, and a growing Islamist movement. Iran's human rights record became in the mid-1970s the focus of broad international concern. The International Commission of Jurists dispatched a mission to study Iran's legal system, and other NGOs worked to publicize Tehran's abuses. Western newspapers were fixated on the SAVAK and its grisly methods. Testifying to the US Congress, the poet and dissident Reza Baraheni described rape, kidnapping, and executions. "In exceptional cases,"

Baraheni recalled, "a hot iron rod is put into one side of the face to force its way to the other side."[73]

Still, the shah was a close ally, and US decision-makers had long declined to poke at his regime's underbelly. The Carter administration could not demur so easily; at stake was the legitimacy of its human rights policy. "Allies such as Korea, Iran, and the Philippines," Carter's PRM-28 exercise concluded in 1977, "cannot be immune from some applicability of the policy without endangering the integrity of our policy." Still, the shah's economic power and military clout ensured that the opportunities for imposing human rights on Tehran would be limited.[74]

The administration tried to nudge the shah but refrained from using the kinds of pressure that it applied to Latin America's juntas. A complex man who craved foreign approbation, Pahlavi had in fact initiated a liberalization process before Carter's inauguration. He may have hoped that reform would stabilize his regime; he may also have sought to preempt Carter's criticism. Regardless, the reproaches came fast after Carter's inauguration. Echoing the human rights NGOs, the Carter administration tried "to remonstrate with the shah concerning his human rights derelictions." When Cyrus Vance visited Tehran in May 1977, he emphasized the importance that the president attached to the issue. From the shah's perspective, however, it appeared that Carter's human rights policy was limited to entreaties. There was no suggestion of making military sales conditional upon reforms, as Washington did elsewhere. When Pahlavi proposed purchasing seven AWACS planes equipped with state-of-the art surveillance and communications equipment, the administration rallied behind his request. In Iran, unlike in Latin America, the geopolitical stakes were too high for human rights to be an overriding consideration. Carter broached the human rights issue himself, but Pahlavi told him that Iran's harsh political laws were "designed to combat communism." While Pahlavi's regime had been in key respects Washington's creation, the shah proved oblivious to Carter's entreaties on human rights.[75]

For all the difficulties, there were modest improvements in Iran's human rights record during 1977, for which the administration quietly claimed credit. That the shah had released political prisoners, opened trials to the public, and permitted the Red Cross to visit his jails owed in part, US officials concluded, to pressure from Washington. The claim would be difficult to substantiate; what is clear is that the shah oscillated between reform and repression, unsure which would assure the survival of his embattled regime. Despite its limited influence, the Carter administration became popularly associated in Iran with the cause of reform. Presuming that "the more liberal approach" that Pahlavi followed in 1977 had been "forced on the shah by US pressure," the shah's secular opponents stepped up their protests. Carter's human rights crusade may thus have exacerbated Iran's political crisis, which intensified during 1977 and 1978. Despite the absence of direct sanctions, such as restrictions on military sales, Carter's rhetorical attentiveness to human rights, combined with the engagement of NGOs, such as Amnesty International and the International Commission of Jurists, helped to persuade the shah's more liberal critics that the United States was on their side.[76]

When Pahlavi visited Carter in November 1977, crowds of demonstrators, many of them Iranian students, surrounded the White House, prompting the police to deploy tear gas. The Iranian opposition was rising. Underlying the shah's demise were the economic inequalities that oil wealth, economic modernization, and enduring poverty produced; an Islamist opposition that rallied around Ruhollah Khomeini, a Shi'a cleric whom Pahlavi had exiled in 1964; and the fundamental illegitimacy of a regime that originated in a coup d'état and relied thereafter on violent repression to sustain itself. The Iranian Revolution nonetheless unfolded in the context of globalization: petrodollars had exacerbated income inequality and social instability in Iran, while the Ayatollah Khomeini utilized modern media, especially cassette tapes, to disseminate his sermons and his anti-Pahlavi message. With Khomeini leading the revolution from Paris, it gained momentum in the last months of 1978. Popular demonstrations clogged Iran's streets in November and December, as millions of Iranians mobilized in opposition to the shah's rule.[77]

Watching the unfolding events with discomfort, Carter's foreign policy advisers were bemused and divided. Cyrus Vance argued that the United States should persuade the shah to persevere with reform. Brzezinski, believing that the opportunity for reform had passed, favored encouraging the shah to impose military rule. Carter worried that the shah was prevaricating. "He is not a strong leader," the US president wrote, being "very doubtful and unsure of himself." Much the same could have been said, in that moment, of the makers of US foreign policy. In contrast to the events of 1953, US officials were spectators to the regime change of 1978–79. His reign now untenable, the shah decided in mid-January to abandon Iran, leaving the civilian government of Shapour Bakhtiar to persevere as best it could. Two weeks later, Khomeini returned to the country. Bakhtiar soon departed, to be replaced by Mehdi Bazargan, a liberal but for now a Khomeini ally. On April 1, 1979, Iran declared itself an Islamic Republic. This sealed the fate of the Iranian monarchy. The effects of its demise would reverberate all over the world.[78]

Although Henry Kissinger blamed Carter's "vocal policy" for "developments in Iran," the diplomacy of human rights does not explain the Iranian Revolution. Carter's policy neither determined nor sealed the shah's fate, but it shaped events, as Pahlavi would himself argue in the bitter memoir that he wrote from exile. Conditioned by the 1953 coup to emphasize—and exaggerate—foreign influences on national politics, the Iranian opposition perceived, in the revolution's early stages, that the Carter administration was pushing the shah to reform before concluding, in its last months, that Washington was encouraging the shah to repress. The effect was to encourage the revolution and then to estrange the revolutionaries from the United States. Iran thus bore out a point that foreign policy analyst Earl Ravenal made: "If we are serious about the principle of human rights, we have to expect some nasty policy consequences." This was a fair point, even if specifying the downside costs was an exercise in speculative conjecture.[79]

Others were more charitable. David Hawk, a former executive director of AI USA, credited Carter's policy with bringing about improvements in a number of countries, including Argentina and Chile, and with making "the world more aware of human rights." A pragmatist, Hawk recognized that human rights vied with rival priorities in the making of foreign policy, but he conceded that this jockeying was "better than having it as not a factor at all." The International League for Human Rights credited Carter with making human rights "a subject of national policy debate in many countries [and] the focus for discussion in international organizations." These were judicious verdicts: they lauded Carter for raising the profile of human rights but acknowledged that he led the world's dominant superpower—not an NGO with nuclear missiles.[80]

The lack of consistency was nonetheless vexing. The administration tried to ensure "that human rights were based on principle," but making human rights "applicable to all nations" was easier said than done, as the cases of Iran and South Korea indicate. Other blind spots included East Timor, where the administration disregarded Indonesia's suppression of the Timorese nationalist movement even as it worked to secure the release of Indonesian political prisoners, and Cambodia, where Carter criticized the genocidal Pol Pot regime but would not go so far as to impose sanctions upon it. Making human rights an element of foreign policy mandated the accommodation of ideals to reality, which circumscribed their application. This made it hard to sustain human rights as the lodestar of foreign policy, as they were in the administration's initial strategic concept. Not the "soul of our foreign policy" as Carter intended, human rights became an ethical accoutrement, more relevant in some cases than others. Then there was the case of the Soviet Union.[81]

9

The Revenge of Geopolitics

> We did not wish the world to be this complex; but we must deal with
> it in all of its complexity, even if it means having a foreign policy which
> cannot be reduced to a single and simplistic slogan.
>
> Zbigniew Brzezinski, Bonn, October 1977

On January 23, 1980, Jimmy Carter addressed Congress. "It has never been more clear," an unsmiling president explained, "that the state of our Union depends on the state of the world." Carter remained an internationalist, but there was little mention now of interdependence and the global future. Carter instead situated himself in a line of presidents who had confronted and contained Soviet power. After an interlude of peaceful coexistence, he suggested, the Cold War was resuming. Less than a month earlier, Soviet tanks had rolled into Afghanistan. Carter called the invasion "the most serious threat to the peace since the Second World War." Pledging to make Moscow "pay a concrete price," Carter enunciated a doctrine. Any attempt by an outside power to gain control of the Persian Gulf region would be an assault on vital US interests, to be repelled "by any means necessary, including military force."[1]

The Carter Doctrine followed a series of retaliatory moves by the president. Besides curtailing exports of grain and high-technology goods, Carter canceled cultural exchanges, delayed the opening of new consulates in Kiev and New York, and warned that the United States would reconsider participating in the 1980 Moscow Olympics. More quietly, he initiated a program of military assistance to anti-Soviet guerillas in Afghanistan—"to send them weapons they could use in the mountains." This reaction was sharp, but the Soviet invasion of Afghanistan had dismayed US officials. His own "opinion of the Russians," Carter explained at the end of 1979, "has changed more drastically in the last week than even the previous two-and-a-half years."[2]

The Carter Doctrine was both a departure and a reversion. After its initial preoccupation with world order politics, the Carter administration embraced foreign policy concepts modeled on their Cold War forebears, especially the Truman Doctrine. Some policy intellectuals exhaled: Carter had at last devised a coherent strategy. Stanley Hoffman welcomed the Carter Doctrine as a "useful restatement of containment." The public seemed to agree; Carter's approval ratings surged in the winter of 1979–80. The skeptics included George Kennan, the intellectual progenitor of Cold War containment. Kennan considered the Soviet invasion "bizarre" and "ill-considered," but he lamented Carter's "militarization of thought and discourse." Senator Ted Kennedy, meanwhile, seized the opportunity to relaunch his bid to wrest the Democratic Party's presidential nomination from Carter, disavowing the president's "helter-skelter militarism."[3]

⌘

The Carter administration's shift toward a hawkish, anti-Soviet stance was a significant development in American strategic thought, but neither geopolitics nor domestic politics provides sufficient explanation for it. Like Kissinger's embrace of interdependence after 1973, Carter's strategic reorientation of 1979–80 demonstrates the inability of overarching strategic concepts to reduce history to legible narratives and actionable formulae. The point reflects not the failure of Carter's initial world order concept so much as the general limitations of grand strategic thinking as a tool for apprehending—and mastering—historical complexity.[4]

The Carter administration sought at the outset to transcend the "East-West / Cold War framework" and to initiate what it called "a new phase in US foreign policy." The United States, unfortunately, did not inhabit a post–Cold War world. For all the novel forces that the Trilateralists perceived in the world of the mid-1970s, the Soviet Union remained a serious rival, especially in military affairs. Zbigniew Brzezinski grasped this, and he cautioned against one-dimensional strategies. "A concentrated foreign policy," he advised, "must give way to a complex foreign policy, no longer focused on a single, dramatic task—such as the defense of the West." Still, orchestrating such a policy proved difficult, for strategy demands simplification as the price of coherence. Having prioritized world order politics, the Carter administration had to diversify its strategy to accommodate issues that its initial concept had marginalized. This required adapting a post–Cold War worldview to the enduring realities of Soviet power. Reacting to events in the Middle East and East Asia as well as to the Soviet Union's invasion of Afghanistan, the Carter administration revised, diversified, and expanded its strategic conception over several years. The process mirrored Henry Kissinger's rethinking of American priorities in the mid-1970s, except that Kissinger moved away from a strategic concept centered on the containment of Soviet power; and the Carter administration toward one.[5]

What the Carter administration achieved was a synthesis, not a reversal. The initial emphases on human rights, economic interdependence, and Trilateralist cooperation faded but did not vanish. Meanwhile, the administration assimilated priorities that its initial strategy neglected. This chapter follows that adaptation, turning first to US-Soviet relations and pointing to contradictions in the Carter administration's initial policy, which sought to preserve détente's gains while promoting human rights. The chapter turns next to international economic relations after the Bonn summit. Here the administration encountered endemic inflation, another energy crisis, and a free-falling dollar. The chapter concludes with the achievement in 1979–80 of a new strategic synthesis, hinging on the Persian Gulf, which proposed to confront Soviet power while assuring the energy security of the West. The resumption of Cold War hostilities in 1979–80 nonetheless marked the end of the 1970s as a distinctive interlude in which US policymakers tried first to stabilize the Cold War and then to transcend it.

Jimmy Carter's Cold War

"Being confident of our own future," Jimmy Carter declared at Notre Dame in 1977, "we are now free of that inordinate fear of communism which once led us to embrace any dictator who joined us in that fear." "Fear of Communism is no longer the glue that holds our foreign policy together," Zbigniew Brzezinski concurred. These declarations did not mean that Soviet power could be disregarded. The point was that anti-Soviet containment no longer offered a rationale for foreign policy.[6]

"In the past," Brzezinski explained, "US-Soviet relations dominated everything." "Other priorities in international relations," he now asserted, "are equally or more important." The Carter administration thus deprioritized the Cold War, acting on historical assumptions that inverted Kissinger's. Unsure of the West's prospects, Kissinger had tried to stabilize the status quo. More optimistic about the future, the Carter administration assumed that the Soviet Union was on the wrong side of history and that Soviet leaders would have to choose between obsolescence and interdependence. "We are challenging the Soviets to cooperate with us or run the risk of becoming historically irrelevant," Brzezinski asserted. The insight had implications for policy. "The objective," Brzezinski explained, was "to assimilate East-West relations into a broader framework of cooperation, rather than to concentrate on East-West relations as the decisive and dominant concern of our times." The Carter administration thereby presumed that it could push the Soviet Union harder on issues like human rights while preserving détente's gains. Brzezinski called this a "historically optimistic" détente, in contrast to Kissinger's alleged pessimism. Its practical viability remained to be tested.[7]

Two priorities defined Carter's Soviet policy in 1977: arms control and human rights. Committed to controlling nuclear weapons, Carter sought to reinvent SALT II as an exercise in disarmament. The framework that Ford and Brezhnev had finalized in November 1974 limited both sides to 2,400 nuclear delivery vehicles, a threshold that capped—but did not reduce—the superpowers' arsenals. Carter, for his part, preferred "deep reduction[s] in the strategic arms of both sides." Going beyond arms control, Carter was fixated on "the deprivation of human rights in the Soviet Union." His aides reached out to high-profile Soviet dissidents, and Carter himself received Vladimir Bukovsky, a prominent dissident, at the White House in March 1977. Carter also exchanged open letters with Andrei Sakharov. The Soviet dissident had initiated the exchange, but Leonid Brezhnev still fumed: "The Soviet Union must not be dealt with like that."[8]

The problem was that incompatible concepts of détente were colliding. Brezhnev articulated his in a speech at Tula in January 1977. "Détente," he explained, depended on "a certain trust and ability to take into account the legitimate interests of one another." The "equality" of the superpowers and "non-interference" in internal affairs were détente's foundational principles, Brezhnev wrote, referring Carter to the 1972 Basic Principles Agreement. This was not the détente that Carter sought. The new president retained the word "détente," but what he meant by it was a broad relaxation in tensions, not the framework of peace based upon mutual restraint and formal equality that Nixon and Brezhnev had built. Committed to making the Soviet-American relationship "more comprehensive" and "more reciprocal," Carter believed that he could extract more from Moscow without making the concessions that his predecessors had made. He presumed that Soviet leaders would be "willing to cooperate" with his ambitious arms control proposals even as he, by emphasizing human rights in the USSR, withdrew the legitimation that Nixon's détente had conferred.[9]

⌘

Compounding the conceptual contradictions were geopolitical circumstances less propitious to détente than those of the early 1970s. The first SALT agreement stabilized an asymmetric equilibrium between the American and Soviet arsenals, but the crude military balance did not endure. Soviet technological breakthroughs, especially involving the placement of multiple warheads atop a single rocket, made Moscow's heavy-duty missiles more useful than in the past. Innovations in missile accuracy further increased the prospects for success should the USSR launch a preemptive strike against the United States. Meanwhile, the USSR began in 1976 to deploy the SS-20, a medium-range missile not included within the SALT framework. The SS-20 left Europe vulnerable to Soviet military coercion, a point that Helmut Schmidt made in a famous October 1977 speech.

By the time Carter became president, the military balance had shifted toward the USSR. Whether it left the United States preeminent, gave the Soviets the edge, or constituted a rough equilibrium was difficult to ascertain.[10]

Ascertaining Soviet motives, meanwhile, remained a matter of conjecture. The most troubling assessment came from Team B, a group of outside experts whom CIA director George H. W. Bush in 1976 invited to review the official estimates of Soviet motives and capabilities. Led by the historian Richard Pipes, the members of Team B rejected the CIA's assumption that Soviet leaders accepted mutual deterrence as the basis of geopolitical stability, concluding instead that the Soviet Union sought "the maximum possible measure of strategic superiority over the U.S." The leaking of the report to the media exacerbated public concerns that America's military position had deteriorated in recent years. The concern that détente had consigned the United States to be "second best," as Carter himself had put it on the campaign trail, combined with concerns about Moscow's neglect of human rights to create a political headwind against which détente's proponents struggled.[11]

With the White House under pressure from the Committee on the Present Danger and other hawkish lobbies, it was Cyrus Vance who worked hardest to preserve détente's gains. While Brzezinski preferred to subsume US-Soviet relations to a post–Cold War strategic concept, Vance believed that East-West relations remained the "main problem" for US foreign policy. More solicitous of the Soviet leadership than Brzezinski, Vance was also more cautious when it came to injecting human rights into Soviet-American relations. Vance assumed primary responsibility for arms control, which he pursued through a series of bilateral meetings. The secretary of state visited Moscow in March 1977 seeking "deep cuts" in nuclear arsenals, but the Soviet leadership rejected this formula as an unserious propaganda exercise, and Vance returned home empty-handed.[12]

Critics who harped that Carter's insistence on deep cuts and his outspokenness on human rights had ensured Vance's failure had a point. While deep cuts would have been difficult to achieve under the best of circumstances, it was imprudent for Carter to assume that he could enlist Soviet leaders in a crusade to roll back the arms race while he was hectoring them on human rights. Carter was more realistic about American domestic politics. After Team B's revelations, a SALT II treaty based upon Ford's Vladivostok formula would have encountered stiff opposition in the Senate. A treaty based on Carter's deep cuts formula would have been likelier to secure Senate ratification, as Carter himself reasoned in deciding to pursue the more ambitious approach. Hereafter, Vance remained the point man for arms control, and he over two years inched toward the completion of a SALT II framework based upon the stabilization of nuclear arsenals, not radical cuts.[13]

The administration, in the interim, initiated a review of the East-West balance of power. The so-called PRM-10 study was conducted in two parts: one,
organized by the Defense Department, analyzed the balance of military forces
between the superpowers; the other, which Samuel Huntington conducted for
the NSC, considered broader trends in "political, diplomatic, economic, technological, and military capabilities." Conclusions were mixed. In nonmilitary arenas of competition, Huntington reported, the West enjoyed myriad advantages
and was surpassing the East Bloc. For Brzezinski, this confirmed the wisdom
of an "optimistic" détente. When it came to the military balance, the conclusions of PRM-10 were less reassuring. NATO would struggle in a conventional
war against the Warsaw Pact, the study's authors warned, while the ability of the
United States "to prevail against Soviet forces outside of Europe" was "uncertain." This conclusion prompted the Carter administration to initiate a modest
buildup of conventional forces, a decision consecrated in PD-18, Carter's August
1977 directive that committed the United States to increase military spending
by 3 percent per year above inflation.[14]

Carter achieved identical commitments from his NATO allies, who agreed
during the London summit of May 1977 to increase military spending by 3 percent per year above inflation. When it came to nuclear weapons, however, the
Carter administration sought stability, not enhanced capabilities. PRM-10 presumed that there could be no winner in a nuclear war and that the balance of terror would endure into the future. Recalling the defense policies of the Kennedy
administration, the Carter administration initially aimed to enhance NATO's
conventional capabilities while keeping nuclear weapons marginal except as
instruments of deterrence. This approach jibed with Carter's broader interest in
invigorating transatlantic relationships; it also left room for making deep cuts
in the size of the Soviet and US nuclear arsenals, corroborating one of Carter's
world order objectives. Human rights, in contrast, would prove harder to reconcile with détente.[15]

Unlike Kissinger, Carter assumed that he could advance human rights while
making progress in other areas of Soviet-American relations. It was "not his
intention," Carter reassured the Soviet ambassador to the United States, Anatoly
Dobrynin, "to interfere in the internal affairs of the Soviet Union." Yet this
was how Soviet leaders construed Carter's entreaties on behalf of Soviet dissidents. "We will not allow interference in our internal affairs," Brezhnev insisted,
"no matter what kind of pseudo-humane pretense is used." Talking about
human rights nonetheless remained the essence of Carter's interference. After
Bukovsky's White House visit, the president issued statements criticizing the
USSR's human rights record and supporting Anatoly Shcharansky (later "Natan
Sharansky"), a dissident whose 1977 arrest and incarceration in a Soviet prison
attracted particular attention in the West. By the fall, détente was in a rut, with

SALT II stalled and human rights the source of contention. Concerned about the lack of progress, Brzezinski urged Carter to reemphasize human rights.[16]

Beyond the bilateral jabs, the Carter administration's efforts to inject human rights into Cold War relations focused on the East-West dialogue that the CSCE initiated, especially the Belgrade follow-up meeting of October 1978. Over the opposition of Cyrus Vance, Carter appointed Arthur Goldberg, a former Supreme Court justice, to represent him in Belgrade. The hope was that Goldberg would consolidate the gains achieved for human rights two years earlier at the Helsinki Conference. True to expectations, Goldberg was outspoken, and historians credit him with keeping the flame of human rights alive within the CSCE process. Still, Goldberg's exertions produced no breakthroughs and generated friction with East Bloc diplomats, who debated US entreaties on behalf of human rights, dredging up the case of Sacco and Vanzetti from the 1920s as evidence of Washington's "unfitness to criticize." In the end, the final Belgrade communiqué omitted all mention of human rights, indicating the absence of common ground. Belgrade confirmed that human rights had become a dividing line between East and West and that the United States stood with the activists and dissidents who railed against Soviet rule. The implications for détente were discouraging. Even Amnesty International officials worried in private that Carter's policy had "degenerated" into "anti-Soviet slogans." Human rights were, however, one factor among several in the unraveling of détente.[17]

⌒∞⌒

Détente did not resolve Cold War rivalries; it stabilized them and displaced their violence to the Third World. The exile was temporary, and the escalation of Third World rivalries contributed to the deterioration of Soviet-American relations. This had not been Carter's intent. The president was an anti-interventionist, skeptical of American meddling in the Global South. "For years," Carter observed, "our policies have either ignored the developing countries or treated them as pawns in the big power chess game." Carter sought instead to treat developing countries as international actors with interests distinct from those of the United States, as his Latin American policy made explicit. The Carter administration nonetheless struggled to prevent Cold War rivalries from resurging in the Third World, including in the Americas. Geopolitical tensions led, in turn, to renewed superpower meddling and the re-escalation of the Cold War.[18]

Africa was a theater of anxieties, despite the administration's attempt to set Cold War preoccupations aside when forming its regional policy. Following Kissinger, Carter distanced himself from the white minority regimes in South Africa and Rhodesia. Cooperating with Great Britain, the Carter administration worked to build a framework for black majority rule in Rhodesia, later Zimbabwe. This was a laudable accomplishment. More vexing was the Horn of Africa, where a conflict between Somalia and Ethiopia over the Ogaden desert became entangled in East-West rivalries. Somalia had been a Soviet client, but Moscow in 1976–77 switched its support to Ethiopia, prompting Somalia to appeal to the United States. Washington made encouraging noises, embolden- ing Somalia, and then wavered. Cuban troops and Soviet equipment, meanwhile, flooded into Ethiopia. By February 1978, there were 18,000 Cubans in Ethiopia, and the war was turning against Somalia. For Zbigniew Brzezinski, who favored a tough policy, Soviet influence in the Horn of Africa was both cause and symp- tom of a "strategic deterioration" in America's global position. Brzezinski pushed for action, including the dispatch of a carrier group to offer "some deterrent to the Soviets and the Cubans," and publicly proposed linking progress on SALT to the exercise of Soviet restraint in Africa.[19]

Divisions within the administration widened over Africa. Brzezinski specu- lated that Soviet involvement in the Horn followed a "larger design." Vance assumed that Soviet leaders were merely exploiting "targets of opportunity." Rather than engage in a proxy war, the United States, Vance argued, should try to contain the war's consequences. Vance took particular umbrage at Brzezinski's suggestion that the United States should expand "consultations and even cooper- ation" with China. Playing Brzezinski's "China card," Vance warned, would jeop- ardize SALT II's prospects. Vance prevailed; Carter opted for a policy of restraint on the Horn of Africa, but the secretary of state nonetheless held US policies partially responsible for the deterioration in US-Soviet relations. Fearing "a new Cold War," Vance drafted a personal letter in April 1978, in which he encouraged Carter to reprioritize SALT II and warned against linking arms control to Soviet behavior in the Third World. Competition was a fact of superpower life, Vance argued, and the United States should manage it as it had in the past: by keeping its defenses and alliances strong.[20]

With his advisers pulling in different directions, Jimmy Carter wrestled with the ambiguities of his policy, ambiguities that resided within his own mind as much as between his counselors. Committed to peace, Carter sought arms control. Enamored with toughness, he was disinclined to compromise, includ- ing on human rights. Conceding the need for clarification, Carter used a June 1978 commencement speech to the US Naval Academy to clarify his position on the Soviet Union. Contrary to rumor, the president did not staple together memos from Vance and Brzezinski to produce his speech; the text was his own. Originality did not equal coherence, however, and what Carter articulated was a wavering policy, framed within an ambiguous strategic concept. Carter called for progress on arms control, which he hailed as a moral imperative. He also sounded tough words—lambasting the Soviet Union's "totalitarian and repressive" government, belittling its economic performance, and accusing it of seeking unilateral advantages under the cover of détente. Unguarded in his contempt, Carter seemed to be asserting both the Soviet Union's irrelevance to an emerging post–Cold War world and the indispensability of Soviet-American cooperation in the present moment. Both points could be debated, but predicating foreign policy on the contradictory insights that the Soviet Union was an ossified superpower, irrelevant to an emerging global future, and a still-awesome adversary, on which world peace depended, proved difficult.[21]

Journalists pointed to rivalry between Brzezinski and Vance as the source of the confusion. The tension was undeniable, but what was unfolding was a disagreement about whether the administration should locate itself in an enduring Cold War or reach instead to transcend the bipolar paradigm. The Carter administration, Brzezinski wrote, was torn between "two alternative models." The first accepted the Cold War as its historical framework and defined the preservation of détente as the major priority for foreign policy. The second involved "putting primary emphasis on our allies, downgrading the relationship with the Soviets . . . upgrading our relationship with China . . . [and] solving the Middle East problem but without Soviet participation." What was at stake, then, was whether the administration would pursue a Soviet-centric foreign policy or persevere with its effort to situate foreign policy in a new strategic framework based upon a more capacious concept of historical change.[22]

Brzezinski took the larger view. Convinced that the USSR was floundering for relevance at the dawn of a "technetronic age," Brzezinski saw no reason to exalt the Soviet-American relationship as the axis on which world politics turned. Unlike the hawks at the Committee on Present Danger, Brzezinski was animated by contempt, not fear. Pushed hard, the USSR, he assumed, would assimilate itself into the new world the Carter administration sought. The president was sympathetic to this approach. Disinclined to see the Soviets as "enormous ogres who were poised to take over the world," Carter nonetheless believed that "the Soviet Union was rotten to the core" and hoped that engaging it on arms control, while ratcheting up the pressure on human rights, would expose the rot. Vance, a diplomat who spent more time talking to Soviet officials than Brzezinski, presumed that the sustenance of détente remained the overarching purpose of US foreign policy. He favored human rights in principle, but grasped more clearly than Carter and Brzezinski that making progress on arms control depended on engaging Soviet officials as nominal equals, as Nixon and Kissinger had done. American policy toward the USSR was thus caught between irreconcilable assumptions.[23]

∽

Already fraying, Soviet-American relations finally unraveled in the spring of 1978. Addressing the Politburo in June, Leonid Brezhnev decried what he called "a serious deterioration." Carter, he claimed, was seeking reelection "under the banner of anti-Soviet policy and a return to the 'cold war.'" In fact, Carter's instincts were to do what he thought was right, not what seemed expedient, and the president remained committed, in principle, to "peace" and "better friend-ship" with the Soviet Union. The problem was the conceptual dissonance, which events and choices during 1978 exacerbated, not necessarily by design.[24]

Human rights remained a contentious issue, as a flurry of dissident trials in mid-1978 prompted Carter to cancel official visits to the USSR and slap restric-tions on Soviet-American trade. "We have here," *Pravda* snorted in reaction, "the very same designs to undermine the socialist system that our people have been compelled to counter in one form or another ever since 1917." As the differences over human rights festered, rivalries in the Third World sharpened. Carter in May upbraided Andrei Gromyko over central Africa, claiming that Cuba was sup-porting an invasion of Zaire's Katanga province by Katangese exiles and that this implicated the Soviet Union. Gromyko rebuked Carter, who exaggerated both Cuba's role in the incursion and Moscow's influence over Havana. Washington nonetheless encouraged France to create a military mission to help Zaire, which shaded the Katanga crisis in Cold War colors. Other dilemmas assumed simi-lar hues. Concluded in September 1978, the Camp David Accords were a step toward Egyptian-Israeli peace, but the negotiations reneged on Carter's commit-ment to involve the USSR in the peace process, and the backtracking dismayed Soviet officials. If setbacks in Africa and the Middle East were unhelpful, it was, however, in the Cold War's core geopolitical relationships where the develop-ments most disruptive to détente occurred.[25]

US-China relations at the end of the Ford years languished in an impasse: Nixon and Mao had transformed the Cold War, but the normalization of relations that the 1972 Shanghai Communiqué envisaged had not yet been accomplished. Mao died in September 1976, leaving China's future uncertain. For its part, the Carter administration decided at the outset to pursue normal-ization, but an early trip by Vance to Beijing foundered, thanks in part to the secretary of state's disinclination to dissolve security ties to Taiwan. Thereafter, Brzezinski wrested control of China policy away from the State Department. Eager to leverage Beijing against Moscow, Brzezinski advocated a rapid expan-sion of Sino-American ties. He found a like-minded partner in Vice Premier Deng Xiaoping, who emerged in 1977 as China's dominant leader. Deng calculated that normalizing relations with Washington would advance China's reintegra-tion into the world economy while consecrating a strategic partnership against the USSR. Deng's choices, more than Carter's, catalyzed new departures.[26]

In early 1978, Brzezinski "badgered" Carter for permission to lead a trip to Beijing, invoking Soviet actions in Africa as a rationale for cultivating China. Vance opposed him, fearing the consequences for Soviet-American détente. The secretary of state was right to worry. When Brzezinski visited China in May 1978, he and his hosts coalesced around a shared antipathy for the Soviet "polar bear." Members of the NSC staff briefed their Chinese counterparts and mooted cooperation in technological exchange and intelligence. These conversations produced "agreement that the overriding need was for unity among Japan, China, Western Europe, and the U.S." For China, the turnaround was stunning, and it paralleled Deng's embrace of economic reforms. Deng visited Japan and Singapore in 1978, proclaiming to his hosts his desire to emulate their modernity, while Chinese officials explored ventures with Western businesses and sought investment funds on the Eurodollar markets. It was in this context that Deng initiated talks with the United States to define the terms of a formal normalization of relations. Taiwan remained an obstacle, but negotiators in late 1978 struck a compromise whereby the United States would sever formal relations with Taiwan, and Beijing and Washington would agree to disagree on Taiwan's future. This formula enabled Carter to announce, in mid-December, the imminent normalization of Sino-American diplomatic relations and to confirm that Vice Premier Deng would visit the United States the following month.[27]

The trip was a blockbuster. Deng charmed American audiences, toured factories and laboratories, and talked strategy with Carter and Brzezinski. In private and in public, he disparaged the "polar bear," urging the United States to abandon détente and join China "to oppose the Soviet Union." Besides catalyzing a Sino-American entente, Deng's seduction of America gave the impression that Carter had approved the invasion of Vietnam that Deng launched two weeks after returning to China. The truth was more ambiguous: Carter had tried to dissuade Deng from invading Vietnam but had also shared military intelligence with him. But Carter spoke no words condemning the attack, in contrast to his moralistic response to Moscow's invasion of Afghanistan ten months later. The context made this non-reaction striking. What precipitated Deng's war was Vietnam's assault in December 1978 on Cambodia, then known as Democratic Kampuchea. The Vietnamese attack culminated years of border skirmishes, and it overthrew Cambodia's genocidal, pro-Chinese Khmer Rouge government. Deng dubbed Vietnam "the Cuba of the East," a threat to regional stability. Vietnamese diplomats cited the barbarities of the Pol Pot regime among the justifications for their invasion.[28]

The motives of the Vietnamese leadership can be debated, but for Washington to align itself indirectly with the Khmer Rouge, one of the twentieth century's most evil regimes, was an affront to Carter's human rights commitments. Carter had called the Khmer Rouge the "worst violator of human rights in the world today" and had supported the admission of Cambodian refugees to the United States, but he took no particular stand against a regime that had murdered up to two million people. When the deposed Khmer Rouge, now exiled to Beijing, contested the disposition of Cambodia's UN seat with the country's new Vietnam-backed government in 1979, the Carter administration sided with the Khmer Rouge. Nor did administration officials make particular mention of human rights in China. The omission echoed the disengagement of the human rights NGOs from the People's Republic, but it also followed hard-headed calculations. When it came to China, "other considerations"—namely geopolitics—took precedence. Thus when thousands of demonstrators filled Tiananmen Square in January 1979, demanding "human rights and democracy," the United States ignored them. For the time being, China remained an excep-tion to Washington's human rights policy. Rather than liberalizing China, the major consequence of the Sino-American rapprochement of 1978–79 would be to exacerbate the deterioration in US-Soviet relations.[29]

That Cyrus Vance managed to conclude SALT II in this context attested to the diligence of his efforts and the modesty of his goals. Vance and Gromyko made progress on arms control throughout the summer of 1978, even as US-Soviet relations trended downward. Technical issues involving the encryption of mis-sile telemetry thwarted completion of negotiations, however, and Moscow's umbrage at the Sino-American rapprochement deferred progress until spring 1979. Carter's role in the SALT process varied. Oscillating between the rhetoric of confrontation and talk of cooperation, the president continued to espouse arms control. "The possibility of mutual annihilation," he explained in April 1979, gave the two superpowers "a common interest in survival." Resolution came fast thereafter. In a final round of talks in April and May, Vance and Gromyko resolved their outstanding differences, agreeing to limit both super-powers to 2,250 (initially 2,400) delivery vehicles, while sublimits would restrict particular categories of weapons, including heavy ICBMs, and separate agree-ments would limit the deployment of cruise missiles and tactical bombers. This was a pragmatic sequel to the Interim Agreement of 1972 but no more than that. Back in the United States, critics were already rallying to defeat SALT II in the Senate.[30]

The stiff bonhomie that Brezhnev and Carter mustered when they met in Vienna to sign Vance and Gromyko's treaty belied the rut into which détente had fallen. This was neither superpower's design. Carter sought détente with sin-cerity, and Brezhnev reciprocated his interest. Soviet adventurism in the Third World had strained relations, though tactical opportunism and each side's exag-gerated perceptions of the other's perfidy made Third World issues more disrup-tive than they needed to be. The human rights issue also engendered mistrust. Carter's policy derived from principled commitments, and he applied it (selec-tively) to non-Communist as well as Communist regimes. The Soviet leadership nonetheless construed human rights as an ideological offensive, and détente suffered. Other actors contributed to the estrangement: Cuba intervened in the Horn, making an African war into a Cold War struggle, and Deng Xiaoping coaxed a divided administration into a tacit alliance against Moscow. Still, there was considerable inconsistency in Carter's policy toward the Soviet Union. He swung between alternative strategic concepts, one that prioritized détente and another that downgraded it.

The Carter administration's Soviet policy contrasted with its predecessor's approach—and so would its record. For Nixon, Ford, and Kissinger, the Cold War had been the central problem for US foreign policy, and its stabilization was their priority. The results were sometimes uninspiring, but stable and cooperative relations between the superpowers were preserved, often to the advantage of the United States. Carter and Brzezinski, for their part, made a brave effort to shift the strategic underpinnings of foreign policy away from the thirty-year old preoccupation with the Cold War, but as they did so they strained the structure of peace that their predecessors had built. Détente's achievements by early 1979 were primed for implosion. Meanwhile Carter's efforts to mobilize the industrialized countries around the collaborative management of economic interdependence were faltering.

Malaise and Trilateralism

One month after accompanying her husband to the Bonn summit, Rosalynn Carter reflected on the first eighteen months of his presidency. An active First Lady, Carter involved herself in varied policy arenas. What now struck her, as she reflected on the place of the United States in the world, was America's interdependence with other nations. "Now I know if we use too much energy, gas, oil, there is an impact elsewhere," she wrote. "We are much more interdependent than I had thought."[31]

Rosalynn Carter's words proved prescient. Although it prioritized the management of interdependence, the Carter administration was itself confounded after 1978 by transnational economic problems that international coordination would not resolve—at least not without the kind of domestic adjustments that decision-makers had so far resisted. Shocked by the realities of interdependence, US officials nonetheless began to adjust domestic policies to external conditions. This meant abandoning the international Keynesianism of 1977–78 and adopting policies that prioritized monetary stability and fiscal restraint. This disciplinary shift emerged more out of the exasperation of the administration's initial Trilateralist strategy than from self-conscious choice, but it marked the end of the 1970s as a transitional phase, during which US policymakers worked to manage globalization while avoiding the kinds of adjustments they urged on other countries, and the advent of a new phase, in which global economic realities defined the options available to economic decision makers within the United States.

∽

The dollar's crisis sharpened in the summer of 1978 amid international discord over the future of world monetary relations. Although the Jamaica agreement of 1976 made floating currencies permissible under IMF rules, the United States and its European allies continued to disagree as to how international monetary relations should be organized. American leaders coalesced around floating exchange rates, arguing that "sound underlying economic and financial policies in individual countries" would maintain international stability, as Treasury Secretary Blumenthal put it. More inclined to restore stable exchange rates, European leaders in July 1978 unveiled the European Monetary System (EMS) in July 1978. Reestablishing fixed exchange rates within the EEC, the initiative underscored transatlantic differences. Helmut Schmidt called the EMS a step toward "the goal of greater monetary stability throughout the world," while Blumenthal presumed the permanence of the "new system" that had emerged from the crisis of 1971–73.[32]

Floating exchange rates did not in practice produce the stability that their advocates promised: Germany and Japan ran endemic trade surpluses in 1977–78, and US trade deficits deepened, exacerbating the dollar's decline on the international currency markets. Carter's response was to encourage Japan and Germany to stimulate their economies, but policy coordination did not correct the US deficits. When the United States took a different tack and intervened directly in the currency markets to support the dollar in early 1978, it managed to halt the dollar's slide, achieving a respite of international monetary stability. The stabilization of early 1978 did not endure, however, and the dollar's decline resumed within a matter of months.

Currency markets in the summer of 1978 were turbulent. Between June and August, the dollar's effective exchange rate fell by almost 5 percent (see figure 9.1), prompting the *Wall Street Journal* to prophesy doom. "The United States is well on its way toward wrecking the international monetary system for the second time in a decade," it editorialized. There was consternation in Europe, but policymakers in Washington were not indifferent to the dollar's slippage. The dollar topped the agenda at a mid-August NSC meeting, in which Carter linked monetary stability to the realization of his Bonn commitment to curb oil imports. When international finance ministers and leading bankers convened in Washington for the annual meeting of the IMF in September, they remained skeptical about Washington's commitment to the dollar. "There are still serious doubts," Blumenthal reported, "about our willpower and ability to succeed." This pointed to the imperatives of confidence, the dwindling of which led dollar holders to sell dollars in the fall of 1978, driving the currency down on the foreign exchange markets. The dollar's crisis had serious implications for the international monetary order, but there were domestic ramifications too, none more troubling than inflation.[33]

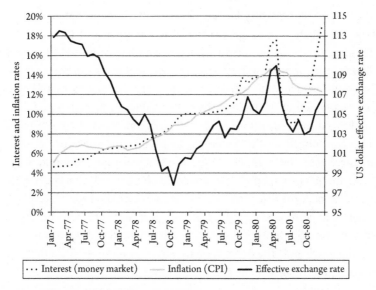

Figure 9.1 Dilemmas of the dollar, 1977–1980
Sources: BIS, Statistics; and IMF, International Financial Statistics.

Inflation still dominates Americans' memories of the 1970s, with good reason. Prices increased by an average 7.1 percent per year in the seventies, having risen by an average of about 2 percent per year during the 1950s and 1960s. Still, the rate of inflation waxed and waned in the 1970s. Carter became president at a moment when inflation, running at 5.2 percent, was not the overriding preoccupation that it had been in 1974–75, when inflation reached double-digit rates. The waning of inflation in 1976 seemed to allow for economic expansion, and Carter duly prioritized growth over price stability. The Federal Reserve obliged, keeping money cheap, and the economy grew fast in 1977–78. Inflation soon resurged, however, reaching an annualized 8 percent in fall 1978.

The White House blamed labor unions and businesses for the rise in price inflation, but waning productivity and increases in food costs contributed to the problem, while monetarist economists indicted the Federal Reserve's loose monetary policies. The causes of inflation remain debatable, but for the Carter administration, its consequences were unavoidable. "The corrosive effects of inflation," Carter worried, "eat away at the ties that bind us together as a people." Carter, in response, unveiled a new anti-inflation package in October 1978. Prioritizing fiscal tools over monetary policy, it combined curbs on federal spending with a commitment to pursue deregulation. Carter also urged business and labor leaders to accept informal wage-price guidelines. The president's announcement was dramatic, but the response to it was disappointing.[34]

"The dollar," the Treasury Department reported, "depreciated sharply" after Carter's anti-inflation message, reaching "new lows against the German mark and Japanese yen." The problem was that Carter had promised future restraint but offered little support for the dollar in the present moment. For market actors, his "woefully inadequate" anti-inflation package confirmed that Washington was not serious about the making the dollar stable. Bankers dumped the dollar, which plunged to its lowest value since the Second World War. On November 1, Carter announced another emergency package, this one aimed at saving the dollar. There were two main elements. The first was intervention in the foreign exchange markets to support the dollar. In the second, the Federal Reserve undertook to raise the discount rate, the rate at which the Federal Reserve banks lend money to commercial banks, from 8.5 percent to 9.5 percent. This action pulled commercial interest rates upward; money market rates averaged 10 percent by the year's end. The dollar rebounded fast, gaining 10 percent against the mark and 7 percent against the yen.[35]

The dollar rescue of November 1 subjected US domestic economic policy to monetary discipline, which Carter had previously resisted doing. In late October 1978, Carter had eschewed monetary tightening, calling it a burden on businesses and consumers. Faced with an imploding dollar, he accepted its necessity. Allan Meltzer, the Federal Reserve's leading historian, remarks that: "international concerns got the Federal Reserve to respond to inflation in a way that domestic factors did not." This was true, but the action was no less striking for it. Back in 1971, Richard Nixon had subordinated international monetary stability to domestic economic expansion. Eight years later, Carter reversed Nixon's priorities. Leaving multilateral Keynesianism behind, Carter embraced the politics of adjustment—much as Great Britain had done during the IMF crisis of 1976. External circumstances now defined the parameters of domestic macroeconomic choice, even for the United States.[36]

Globalization made external circumstances in the late 1970s quite different from what they had been in the heyday of the Pax Americana. With more than a half-trillion dollars of dollar-denominated assets now owned by foreigners, financial interdependence defined the terms of domestic choice. Markets were so integrated, in fact, that rumor and panic could spur a crisis, leading investors in fall 1978 to dump the dollar, even as the US balance of trade was improving. Michael Blumenthal expounded on this point. "Technology made this possible," he explained. "There were days in which a drop in the dollar occurred because of rumor," he continued, "which would be magnified several times as it traveled around the world." As in 1971–73, market disruption prompted a government reaction. This time, the dollar crisis did not bring down the international monetary order. Instead, the November crisis debunked the assumption that floating currencies would permit the United States to pursue a domestic economic policy without regard to its external consequences. Committed to keeping financial markets open, the Carter administration sacrificed economic expansion on the altar of international stability. Subsequent choices confirmed it, but on November 1, 1978 the trajectory was set.[37]

᠁

In the fall of 1978, the trading desks of London, Frankfurt, and New York had magnified currency imbalances, creating the dollar crisis. The global turmoil of 1979–80, by contrast, sprang from the streets of Abadan, Qom, and Tehran. Iran's revolution was, in part, a consequence of the instability that petrodollars had unleashed upon Iran. The revolution, in return, plunged the world economy into another oil crisis. This second oil crisis began with a supply shock. In November 1978, workers occupied the massive oil refinery at Abadan, causing Iran's oil production to atrophy. Iran's oil production in 1979 was less than half of what it had been in 1977; in 1980, production would be less than a third of the 1977 level. Events in Iran reduced the world's oil supply by between 4 percent and 5 percent. This was a setback, for sure, but it need not have driven nominal prices up from about $12 per barrel in 1978 to almost $40 in late 1979. Buoyed by rising non-OPEC production in Alaska, Mexico, and Europe's North Sea, the oil market could have withstood the shock of the Iranian Revolution better than it did. Market failures ensured that it did not. Traders and speculators played a catalytic role in the 1979–80 oil crisis, driving up prices and presenting OPEC's price hawks with an opportunity to seize.[38]

How did the second oil crisis unfold? In 1979 most oil was still priced according to contracts between the producer governments and the multinational corporations that refined and marketed it. Only a small fraction was sold in the spot markets, where prices fluctuated according to the interplay of supply and demand. This open market, interconnected via electronic terminals, nonetheless pulled prices upward during 1979. The oil companies played a crucial role in the price surge. Bereft of Iranian oil, they panicked, reneged on contracts, competed to safeguard supplies, and bid up prices in the spot markets. They also expanded their inventories, hoarding oil in unused depots, abandoned refineries, and oil tankers. Motorists did much the same, keeping their tanks full as a hedge against price increases and fuel shortages. Such behavior was understandable, but it increased overall demand for oil, exacerbating the pressure on prices. By May, oil was trading on the spot markets at more than $34 per barrel.

As buyers panicked, sellers gouged. OPEC orchestrated a 14.5 percent price increase in December 1978 and a further 9 percent increase in March 1979. Even more striking was OPEC's announcement, at the conclusion of this second "consultative meeting," that its members would henceforth impose whatever premiums and surcharges "they deem justifiable" on top of official oil prices. The cartel had, in effect, become a free-for-all. Dismayed, Saudi Arabia's Sheikh

Yamani pressed a lonely case for price moderation, fearing a global recession that would bring down demand and send prices tumbling. Yamani would be proved right, but not until official prices had caught up to spot market prices. In the meantime, the oil crisis revealed not only how integrated the world economy had become but also how volatile market-led globalization could be.[39]

For the Carter administration, the timing was disastrous. Congress passed the National Energy Act in October 1978, realizing elements of the National Economic Plan that Carter had debuted in April 1977. This legislative package established incentives to conserve, including tax credits, and it deregulated interstate restrictions on the sale of natural gas. It did not raise domestic oil prices to world levels—the objective to which Carter had committed himself at Bonn. Americans paid world prices for imported oil, which comprised 43 percent of the oil they consumed in 1978, but domestic oil remained subject to price controls that varied depending on when and where it had been discovered. Removing these controls would raise US oil prices, reduce imports, ease pressure on the dollar, and satisfy foreign leaders who saw American consumption as a leading cause of the world's energy woes. Higher prices would also incentivize conservation and alternative fuels, which was why Jimmy Carter favored them.[40]

There would also be costs. Decontrol promised to exacerbate inflation, burden ordinary Americans, and engorge corporate profits. Carter nonetheless decided in April 1979 to decontrol oil prices by fiat. He called simultaneously on Congress to institute a windfall profits tax that would recoup for the Treasury some of the profits that decontrol generated for the oil companies. Carter acted under authority deriving from the Energy Policy and Conservation Act of 1975, and he phased the rollback of price controls so as to "minimize sudden economic shock." This ensured that domestic oil prices would tail the upward trajectory of world prices through the summer of 1979 (see figure 9.2). Carter's choice of price decontrol helped to bring down imports from 43 percent of consumption in 1979 to just 28 percent in 1982, reaping long-term benefits. But if market mechanisms were a sensible means to allocate scarce resources under normal conditions, world oil markets that summer were misfiring, as crude oil prices surged to record highs, and consumers found themselves waiting in gasoline lines.[41]

The 1979 oil crisis confirmed the dependence of the industrial countries on Saudi Arabia, the only producer with the capacity to define market conditions on its own terms. As the crisis deepened, Washington pushed Riyadh to raise its production from 8.5 to 12 million barrels of oil per day. Despite Yamani's cautiousness on price gouging, Saudi Arabia was disinclined to cooperate, a reticence that US officials attributed to resentment of the Egyptian-Israeli peace that Jimmy Carter had brokered. Only under duress would Saudi Arabia, in early July 1979, increase production to 9.5 million barrels per day. This did not solve

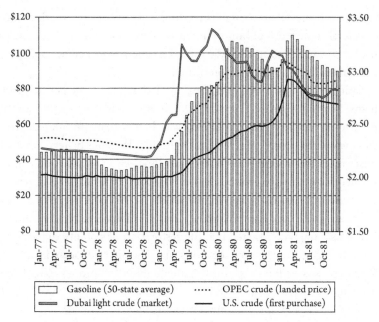

Figure 9.2 The Oil Crisis of 1979
Sources: Global Financial Data; and US Energy Information Administration.

the price crunch, but it corroborated the belief of US officials that Saudi Arabia was America's indispensable partner in the Persian Gulf.[42]

Henry Owen called Saudi Arabia's decision to raise production "a result" of Jimmy Carter's "success" at the Tokyo summit that convened in late June. The commitment by the G-7 countries at Tokyo to curb oil imports and expand oil production was, Owen argued, what prompted Riyadh's concession. Owen's verdict on the accomplishments at Tokyo was generous; Carter's was less sanguine. "The first day of the economic summit," he wrote, "was one of the worst days of my diplomatic life." Oil dominated the Tokyo dialogue, transforming the summit into a circus of recrimination. Carter's pursuit of an Egyptian-Israeli peace, Helmut Schmidt declared, "had caused problems with oil all over the world." Energy was the summit's focus; its communiqué declared that reducing oil consumption and hastening "the development of other fuel sources" were the G-7's "most urgent tasks."[43]

The dilemmas of reducing oil consumption revealed widening ideological divisions within the G-7. Having taken steps to curb US imports through price decontrol, Carter proposed that the summit countries establish quantitative national ceilings on oil imports. Doing so, he argued, would translate the International Energy Agency's goal of a 5 percent reduction in overall demand for oil into "understandable and credible" commitments. His approach aligned with a French proposal for reestablishing authority over the oil markets through a multilateral framework of import and price controls. This approach met with opposition from Schmidt and Margaret Thatcher, who had won election as Britain's prime minister the previous month.[44]

Declaring that "the price mechanism" had reduced oil consumption in Germany, Schmidt opposed "pressing the Summit participants into a straight-jacket." Doing nothing, he counseled, was better than misguided activism. Thatcher was even more adamant. Like Schmidt, Thatcher believed that letting "the price mechanism work" was "the most telling way of reducing demand," and she seemed disinclined to even discuss energy conservation. More urgent in her view was the fight against inflation, for which she blamed "Keynesian policies with their emphasis on deficit financing." This prompted a rejoinder from Valéry Giscard d'Estaing, who insisted that the restoration of stability did not require the kind of harsh, deflationary solutions that Thatcher advocated. Underlying the argument was a more basic disagreement about the proper role of government in the management of markets, an argument that was unfolding at the international level and, increasingly, within the G-7 nation-states.

When it came to oil, Thatcher and Schmidt insisted that markets manage themselves; Carter and Giscard contemplated building an international framework to restrain demand and stabilize prices. Amid this discord, Prime Minister Ohira managed to negotiate a compromise whereby Canada, Japan, and the United States would commit to specific import ceilings for 1980, and the four European countries would abide by a limit of 10 million barrels per day for the EEC, to be buttressed through the subsequent enumeration of specific national targets. In relation to actual imports, however, the Tokyo targets were generous and thus not an effective mechanism of restraint. As the oil crisis continued, the Carter administration debated the possibility of lowering import ceilings to restrain demand. Carter was impressed by France's successes with this approach. Divisions among the advanced industrial countries nonetheless made it improbable that there would be an institutionalization of quantitative restraints on oil consumption on an international scale. The Trilateralist project was foundering on the shock of the second oil crisis and more fundamental disagreements as to the proper role of governance in an integrating world. The achievements of the previous year's Bonn summit were receding, as the utility of economic governance itself became the subject of contentious debate.[45]

⸎

After Tokyo, Carter cut short a Hawaiian vacation to return to a nation in crisis. "Since you left for Japan," his chief domestic policy adviser warned him in July, "the domestic energy problem has continued to worsen." Gasoline lines were "spreading," and there was "sporadic violence" at the pumps. Inflation was soaring, and recession loomed. "This would appear," Stuart Eizenstat lamented, "to be the worst of times." Opinion polls compounded the sense of crisis. Just 28 percent of Americans in late June approved of Carter's job performance. The president's aides urged him to assail OPEC, citing the political advantages of doing so. Carter agreed—and then changed his mind. Delivering another speech on energy would be superfluous. Rosalynn Carter concurred. "Nobody wants to hear it," she declared after reading a draft. Carter instead decided to engage the nation's "broader and deeper" problems.[46]

Carter's decision perplexed White House aides, but it reflected the influence of pollster Pat Caddell, an adviser who was prone to "sweeping sociology." Caddell had recently drafted for the president a lengthy memorandum, "Of Crisis and Opportunity," which diagnosed a "crisis of confidence" imperiling the nation and Carter's presidency. Americans, Caddell concluded, had abandoned their faith in the future. Their "malaise" followed the breakdown of long-held beliefs. Americans once believed that their country fought only just wars, victoriously. Then came Vietnam. Americans once believed in the integrity of their leaders. Then came Richard Nixon. Americans once believed in natural abundance and in their government's ability to manage growth. Then came the oil shocks and stagflation. Americans once "believed themselves exempt from the processes of history," Caddell concluded. "Sadly, events ended that myth." If Carter could resolve the nation's existential crisis, Caddell inveigled, he would transform a teetering presidency into a great presidency and himself into "a great President on the order of a Lincoln, a Wilson, and a Franklin Roosevelt."[47]

Other aides warned that Caddell was leading the president down the rabbit-hole, but Carter proceeded nonetheless. To gauge the mood of a fretful nation, he convened a long series of meetings—with economists and energy experts; with academics and religious leaders; with elected officials and ordinary citizens. Carter sat through these conclaves, taking careful, longhand notes. "The Great Society days are over," he reflected: "the problems of the nation can't be solved with massive spending programs, public works, et cetera." After two weeks, the president emerged to give a speech quite different from the energy speech his advisers had proposed. Instead of blaming OPEC for America's woes, Carter turned his focus toward "our Nation's underlying problems." While he alluded to his own failures, Carter focused his remarks on the deterioration of democracy: doubt and disunity gripped the nation's citizens, he warned, and lobbyists swayed its Congress. The government had grown "isolated from the mainstream of our nation's life." Adrift, Americans had lost their confidence in the future, and their pessimism was "threatening to destroy the social and the political fabric." This was stern stuff, but Carter had a solution: let energy policy be the dynamo of renewal. If the United States could overcome its "intolerable dependence on foreign oil," it might also transcend its crisis of the spirit.[48]

As he peered into the nation's soul, Carter said little about the global circumstances that enveloped its fate. This was surprising. The president's economic advisers agreed that "the world oil crisis" was "at the core of our economic problem," and Carter had himself made the collaborative management of interdependence a priority from the outset. The predicament that Carter described—in which public institutions were crumbling, an "erosion of confidence in the future" was tearing at the social fabric, and "self-indulgence and consumption" were supplanting "close-knit families" and "faith in God"—could, moreover, have described much of the advanced industrial world. Unemployment and inflation were soaring across the industrialized world, and Western youth culture evoked a spirit of nihilism. The 1970s ended not in a revolt of righteous optimism, as the 1960s had done, but in a cacophony of resentment that juxtaposed the anger of punk and the irony of disco. "There's no future," snarled the British punk band the Sex Pistols, "in England's dreaming." "This is not just a US condition," Henry Owen advised. Underlying Carter's crisis of confidence, Owen explained, were structural realities, and these were generalizable. "Like other industrial societies," the United States could "no longer achieve all its important goals." Americans, like the citizens of other industrialized societies, would have to choose between fighting inflation and bolstering growth. Even Owen now doubted that governments could cooperate to transcend constraints. Carter, for his part, was retreating from Trilateralism; his efforts to rehabilitate growth through international policy coordination had reached their endpoint.[49]

If Carter's speech surprised Americans, his next move confounded them. It was a serious error to follow the address with a government reshuffle, which began with the president demanding that his cabinet resign en masse—a Nixonian move—so that he could choose whom to discard and whom to retain. Several heavyweights departed, including Jim Schlesinger, the architect of Carter's energy program, and Michael Blumenthal, his treasury secretary. The ensuing political cacophony stifled the more profound questions that Carter had raised, and it shifted the media's attention back to the executive branch. Most consequential, however, was the personnel change that Carter's reshuffle produced at the top of the nation's financial system. The president decided to replace Blumenthal with William Miller, a businessman who had led the Federal Reserve since January 1978. Although Miller had participated in the making of the November 1978 dollar rescue, he had declined thereafter to take a robust stance against inflation. Miller's move to the Treasury created a vacancy at the head of the Federal Reserve System.

To fill it, Carter tapped Paul Volcker, the president of the New York Federal Reserve Bank. If Volcker's instincts as Nixon's assistant secretary of the Treasury had been inscrutable, there could be little doubt now about his purposes. On a Federal Reserve Board divided between austerity and growth, Volcker inclined toward austerity; he worried about inflation, and he fixated on the international credibility of the dollar. Recognizing Volcker's disciplinary bent, some in the Carter camp inveighed against his appointment. Bert Lance called from Atlanta to warn that Carter "should not appoint Paul Volcker." Do so, Lance continued, and Carter would "be mortgaging his reelection to the Federal Reserve." Carter nonetheless proceeded, convinced that Volcker was "committed to controlling inflation and preserving the value of the dollar." The appointment was a purposeful choice by a president who understood its likely consequences. What Carter wanted was "the strongest possible effort to control inflation."[50]

Volcker's appointment was no panacea. Markets reacted favorably at first, but inflation continued to rise, the dollar dwindled, and gold prices soared. Volcker was, for his part, frank about the challenges. "The most pressing economic concern of the American people today," he acknowledged in September, "is the persistent and rapid rise of prices." Rising prices diverted resources into unproductive speculation; they created uncertainty; and they exacerbated the "weakness of the dollar in foreign exchange markets." Amid West European clamoring for intervention to support the dollar and "extreme nervousness" on the currency markets, Volcker opted for action. After traveling to Belgrade for the September 1979 meeting of the IMF and the World Bank, he convened an early October meeting of the Federal Open Market Committee (FOMC).[51]

The FOMC controls open-market operations, which involve the purchase and sale of US government securities on the open market. Through these, the FOMC manipulates commercial interest rates, usually targeting an index rate known as the Federal Funds Rate—an aggregate of the interest rates that banks charge each other on very short-term loans. Insofar as the Federal Funds Rate affects interest rates on mortgages, car loans, and bank deposits, it has vital consequences for the economy. As he grappled with inflation, Paul Volcker contemplated a change in the FOMC's procedures that would, if enacted, have significant consequences for interest rates and economic growth. As in August 1971, Volcker entered the decisive meeting with his game plan prepared. He acted now as he had done then, in response to "feverish" market pressures. "We wouldn't be here today," Volcker explained to the FOMC, "if we didn't have a problem."[52]

Volcker's plan was the result of careful deliberations. For several years, the FOMC had toyed with the idea of adopting a new method of monetary targeting aimed not at the Federal Funds Rate, but at the overall money supply. The distinction was technical, even arcane, but the stakes were great and the implications far-reaching. Believing that inflation was a consequence of too many dollars chasing too few goods, monetarists argued that getting control of the money supply was essential if inflation were to be conquered. The trouble with their prognosis was that targeting the money supply would produce dramatic fluctuations in interest rates and, most likely, economic contraction. Volcker was not a monetarist. He presumed that it was the anticipation of future price increases that had driven prices upward in recent years, not the money supply as such. "When I look at the past year or two I am impressed," he reflected, "by the degree to which inflationary psychology has really changed."[53]

Tightening the money supply could, Volcker nonetheless reasoned, serve a psychological purpose and assuage market actors' expectations of future price increases. The FOMC concurred, and the Federal Reserve announced on October 6 that it would henceforth target the money supply, not interest rates. This was the key shift, but two additional measures bolstered Volcker's choice for monetary rigor. The Fed also increased the discount rate and tightened the reserve requirements on commercial banks, restraining their ability to create credit. Overall, the October 6 package signaled to market actors the Fed's long-term commitment to price stability. Paul Volcker had made a decisive choice for discipline over growth and expansion.[54]

Volcker did not succeed, at least not in the short-term, but his October 6 package was a crucial turning point. After the Carter administration's 1977–78 experiments in international Keynesianism, the Volcker shift of 1979 was an acknowledgment of limits, and it confirmed the logic of the November 1978 dollar rescue package. To contain inflation and bolster the dollar, Volcker reasoned, the United States would have to accept discipline at home—and its attendant macroeconomic consequences. His choice contrasted with Nixon's in August 1971, when the United States wrecked Bretton Woods in a bid to restore domestic growth. In October 1979, Volcker invoked international imperatives—the stabilization of the dollar on international financial markets—and the persistent bugbear of inflation as rationale for a sharp, disciplinary shift. Americans would now have to swallow the bitter medicine that the United States had urged on Great Britain in late 1976. Implementing monetary discipline would nonetheless be more tortuous and the consequences less predictable than Volcker imagined.[55]

Adopting monetary targeting was a radical move, but it did not succeed in quenching price inflation. Inflation rose into 1980, and gold prices continued to soar. Frustrated, the Carter administration in March proposed establishing controls on consumer credit, to be administered by the Fed. Volcker distrusted the initiative, preferring to let his monetarist experiment run its course, but he was reluctant to oppose an administration that had given him free reign in October 1979. The administration's controls produced a sharp credit crunch, and the economy stumbled into a sharp recession. GDP contracted by 7.9 percent in the second quarter of 1980. Demand for money diminished, leading interest rates to fall. Volcker worried that the dip (see figure 9.3) would thwart the psychological purposes of his monetarist move. After the removal of controls in July

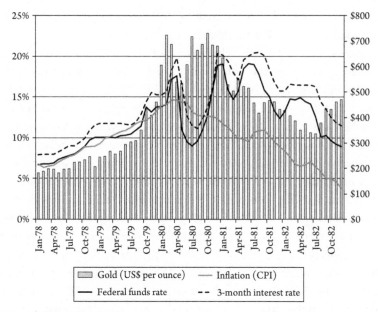

Figure 9.3 The Volcker Shock
Sources: Federal Reserve System, Historical Data; IMF, International Financial Statistics.

1980, higher interest rates returned, and Volcker's experiment proceeded. The sustenance of high interest rates into the early 1980s would restrain the growth of consumer prices, slaying the great inflation of the 1970s. The victory nonetheless came at considerable cost; the US economy rebounded in late 1980, but it entered a protracted recession in 1981 that saw unemployment rise to its highest levels since the 1930s. The Keynesian ascendancy that Bretton Woods had corroborated was over.[56]

The End of the 1970s

Already strained, Soviet-American relations descended into acrimony at the end of the 1970s, burying détente and Carter's bid to devise a post–Cold War strategy. Like the second oil crisis, this geopolitical disjuncture hinged upon the Persian Gulf. "The economic health and well-being of the United States, Western Europe, and Japan," Carter affirmed, "depend upon continued access to oil from the Persian Gulf." Here, the ties of economic interdependence were so legible that the point was a truism. More intriguing was the question of how American policymakers would assure energy security. Carter, like Ford and Kissinger, sought at first to mitigate vulnerability through the development of long-range energy policies to reduce the West's consumption of Middle East oil and promote alternative fuels. The oil crisis of 1979–80 exposed the insufficiency of this approach, precipitating alternatives.[57]

As energy secretary, James Schlesinger had made conservation and domestic production the centerpieces of the nation's first federal energy policy, but he concluded in the summer of 1979 that the West's "heavy and alarming dependence on Middle East oil" mandated more robust policies. Schlesinger left the cabinet in Carter's July 1979 reshuffle, and he seized the opportunity of his departure to advocate bold action. In a private memo to the president and in public speeches, Schlesinger warned of future disruptions to oil supplies. The risks included renewal of the Arab-Israeli conflict; the escalation of enmities between Iran and Iraq into war; the overthrow of Saudi Arabia's monarchy; and, "most significant," the intrusion of "growing Soviet power" into the region. America's capacities to meet these threats were so limited, Schlesinger warned, that the energy security of the West rested on little more than "the protection of Allah." Carter, Schlesinger urged, should take uncertain fate into his own hands and project American military power directly into the Middle East. The solution was dramatic, but the stakes as Schlesinger saw them could not have been higher. "Without access to Middle East oil," he warned, "the Free World, as we have known it since 1945, will collapse."[58]

For the Carter administration, the Middle East was not an overarching priority at the outset. Focused on the construction of a new architecture of cooperation among the industrialized countries, administration officials saw the Arab-Israeli peace process as their major challenge in the region. Carter favored a comprehensive settlement including the Palestinians but reverted to a bilateral approach focused on Israel and Egypt after Anwar Sadat made a stunning visit to Jerusalem in the fall of 1977. Sadat's bid for peace initiated a "new phase" in US policy and led to the Camp David Accords of September 1978 and the bilateral Egyptian-Israeli Peace Treaty of March 1979. The treaty was a breakthrough, but it did not yield the benefits that Sadat and Carter sought for the Palestinians, and Arab leaders rushed to denounce it. For strategic interests of the kind that Schlesinger prioritized, the utility of the Egyptian-Israeli settlement was unclear. Bilateral peace diminished the probability of regional war, but Carter's failure to secure what the Camp David Accords called the "legitimate rights" of the Palestinian people left a sore festering in American relations with the Islamic world.[59]

Zbigniew Brzezinski's role in the Arab-Israeli peace process was peripheral, but the national security adviser was not disengaged from the Middle East. Far from it, he became in 1979 the architect of a strategic reorientation that turned on events in Iran. In late 1978, Brzezinski adopted the idea that an "arc of crisis" spanning from Aden to Chittagong—a crescent atop the Indian Ocean—was the source of "our greatest vulnerability." In this arc, Brzezinski explained, a "political vacuum" arising from "fragile social and political structures" might "be filled with elements more sympathetic to the Soviet Union." Eager to preempt that eventuality, Brzezinski began to envisage a "consultative security framework" for the region. It would involve consolidating alliances with Egypt, Israel, and Turkey and an enhanced "special" relationship with Saudi Arabia. Brzezinski proposed developmental assistance, invoking the Marshall Plan, but his regional framework presumed a hard defensive shell. "We shall have to augment our military presence," Brzezinski wrote. He envisaged the permanent deployment of US forces, even the establishment of "an East-of-Suez Command entity of some sort." Now that the shah had dropped the responsibilities for regional security that Britain had forsaken in the late 1960s, the United States, Brzezinski implied, would have to assume that hegemonic role itself.[60]

The obstacles were considerable. Washington's support for Israel was contentious, and few, if any, Arab leaders wanted to host US military bases. The problem, as Carter put it, was that "we want a closer relationship with them than any of them want." The administration nonetheless proceeded during 1979 to elaborate a regional security framework. A series of high-level meetings confirmed the Middle East's strategic centrality but revealed divergent priorities within the foreign policy bureaucracy: Defense and the NSC pushed for military commitments, while State prioritized completion of "a just and comprehensive peace" between Israel and the Palestinians. By fall 1979, the hawks were winning the argument.[61]

Brzezinski in the summer of 1979 reinvigorated a 1977 proposal to create a "deployment force of light divisions with strategic mobility," which he now recast as a "contingency" force for the Middle East. This became the Rapid Deployment Force, which would in the early 1980s evolve into the United States Central Command, or CENTCOM—the military proconsulate that oversees the Middle East and Central Asia. Additionally, the White House decided in December 1979 to establish a military base in Oman. Besides making military plans, the administration cultivated allies. Officials envisaged "a new security relationship with Riyadh" and encouraged Saudi Arabia to build a base structure that US forces could inhabit if necessary. Egypt was another focus. Officials agreed that Carter should seek a "major program" of military assistance to Cairo, while Carter and Sadat discussed the possibility of a coordinated, "two-pronged" assault upon Iran by US and Egyptian forces.[62]

Overall, the effect of this strategic reorientation redefined the Middle East as a strategic priority of the first rank: "a vital U.S. interest on a par with Europe and Northeast Asia," as Brzezinski put it. The rush to build and bolster military relationships in the Middle East was a departure from the administration's earlier efforts to prioritize the promotion of human rights and the management of interdependence relationships. Strategic continuities nonetheless underpinned the ostensible discontinuities. The Carter administration elevated the Middle East as a strategic priority because policymakers recognized the West's unalterable and inextricable dependence on the region's oil. "Instability in the Middle East," Brzezinski wrote, "interacts closely with U.S., Western European, and Japanese economic conditions." Carter's pursuit of a prudent energy policy continued, but the security framework that the administration devised during 1979 indicated that making the world safe for interdependence might mandate military methods, not just architectures of cooperation.[63]

On November 4, 1979, a group of Shi'i radicals overran the US embassy in Tehran, taking sixty-three Americans captive. Carter's decision to admit the ousted shah to the United States to receive medical treatment had strained US ties with Iran's leaders, but the hostage crisis brought relations to their nadir. Within days, the secular government of Mehdi Bazargan collapsed, leaving Khomeini and the Council of the Islamic Revolution predominant in Iran. Two weeks later, violence convulsed Saudi Arabia, when a band of religious militants seized control of Mecca's Grand Mosque, taking hundreds of pilgrims hostage. Khomeini took to the airwaves to blame "American imperialism and international Zionism" for the assault, and the Islamic world from Turkey to the Philippines erupted in anti-American protests. In Islamabad, crowds stormed the US embassy, setting it ablaze. Back in Mecca, Saudi security forces regained control of the Grand Mosque, killing several hundred people. NSC analysts had recently downplayed the potential of political Islam, concluding in early 1979 that: "Islamic revivalist movements are not sweeping the Middle East, and are not likely to be the wave of the future." New developments mocked these sanguine conclusions. Then, in late December, the Soviet Union invaded Afghanistan.[64]

In response, Carter asked the Senate to suspend consideration of the SALT II Treaty and announced a package of retaliatory measures, ranging from the symbolic to the substantive. The president also issued the Carter Doctrine, making the pivot to an invigorated Cold War strategy, the parameters of which were largely predefined. Admitting the indispensability of the Persian Gulf to the West—"it contains more than two-thirds of the world's exportable oil"—Carter committed the United States to repel assaults on the region by "outside" powers—read the Soviet Union. In the administration's geopolitical imagination, the Soviet invasion of Afghanistan revealed a coherent, far-reaching Soviet design on the Persian Gulf. Soviet motives were in fact more defensive than aggrandizing: some Kremlin leaders hoped to preempt the rise of Islamist influence; others worried about Afghanistan's defection from the East Bloc. The Carter administration, Brzezinski in particular, nonetheless cleaved to a maximalist interpretation of Soviet goals and seized the opportunity to implement its regional security framework.[65]

The Soviet invasion of Afghanistan smoothed the way for a regional acceptance of a US military protectorate. Brzezinski visited Saudi Arabia and Pakistan in February to conduct talks on security cooperation. On Brzezinski's return, Carter surmised that "the Saudis want us to play the lead role in the protection of the Persian Gulf." The development of a "major forward base" structure in Saudi Arabia proceeded fast. It involved the construction of facilities for American warplanes, fuel-storage depots, and anti-aircraft defense batteries. The outbreak of war between Iran and Iraq in September 1980 exacerbated regional uncertainties and further eased local acceptance of US military protection. Saudi Arabia agreed to host American AWACS early warning and control planes, resulting in a landmark deployment of US military forces to the kingdom. Obstacles endured, but the flurry of activity around the Persian Gulf in 1980 revealed a purposeful reframing of strategic priorities. "Soviet domination of Middle East oil," Brzezinski insisted, was a threat that had to be confronted. Policy choices in the region, he continued, would have to be "determined by the interaction of oil, Islamic nationalism, and Soviet political expansionism." The arc of crisis had become a strategic hinge.[66]

American decision-makers chose in 1979–80 to define the Persian Gulf as "the third strategic zone after Europe and East Asia for U.S. security." Having made this choice, they collaborated with Saudi Arabia and the mujahideen who were battling the Soviet occupiers in Afghanistan. As chastening as the 1979 Iranian Revolution had been, US officials now presumed that the Islamic forces would serve as a bulwark against an "atheistic" Soviet Union. These officials were, however, operating in circumstances that constrained, restricted, and molded their choices: the failures of energy policy, which left the industrialized countries dependent on the Persian Gulf's oil; and the fall of the shah, which foreclosed on the Nixon Doctrine, forcing US officials to devise alternative strategies for regional security. Doing nothing seemed improbable, even reckless: the oil crisis of 1979–80 revealed that there was little—if any—slack left in the global oil markets and that the effects of another supply shock would be disastrous for the industrialized democracies.[67]

In their own self-conception, American decision-makers acted on behalf of the Free World. This did not mean that their choices enjoyed the wholehearted support of US allies. Instead, Carter's reversion to Cold War rhetoric, his retaliatory measures after the Soviet invasion of Afghanistan, and his administration's elaboration of a security framework for the Middle East divided the West. Accustomed to the stability (and opportunities for trade) that détente had achieved, West European leaders—with the exception of Margaret Thatcher— looked warily upon the resurgence of Cold War thinking in Washington. French and German leaders indicated that they preferred "to get the Soviets out of Afghanistan through diplomacy," and met with Brezhnev, to the chagrin of US officials. Despite Germany's support for the US-led boycott of the 1980 Moscow Olympics, Carter complained that his allies expected "us to provide the stick" while competing "with one another about providing the biggest carrot." The EEC distanced itself from Carter's Middle East policy, issuing a declaration in favor of Palestinian statehood in June 1979. Unlike in the 1940s, the sharpening of Cold War tensions in 1980 appeared to divide the West, not unite it. The festering hostage crisis in Iran did not help, especially when an April bid to rescue the hostages in a military mission failed, prompting Cyrus Vance to resign. As West European leaders chaffed against Washington's impetuous behavior, US officials lamented their allies' disinclination to join them in embargoing Iran's oil exports.[68]

Fearing "disarray in the West," Carter campaigned for a NATO summit to restore common purpose. Rebuffed, he settled instead for an Anglo-German proposal "to discuss political and security issues" at the forthcoming G-7 summit in Venice. Fusing geopolitics and economics, the Venice summit proved to be successful, despite a bitter row between Carter and Schmidt on its eve. This success owed, in part, to quiet collusion among American, British, French and German diplomats, who had met weeks beforehand and drafted language condemning the Soviet invasion, to be issued with the final Venice communiqué. The tough-worded supplement to the summit's main communiqué signaled the West's unity, declaring the Soviet occupation of Afghanistan "unacceptable" and proclaiming the G-7's support for the Afghans' "courageous resistance." This was an apex of common purpose; although it did not restore the unity of the high Cold War years, the Venice summit papered over the cracks in the West. Carter appeared satisfied. "The basic themes I've been describing all this year," he noted in his diary, "were adopted by the others."[69]

Geopolitics overshadowed but did not supplant the summit's economic purposes. Here the conversation corroborated the discussion at Tokyo in 1979, confirming the obsolescence of the international Keynesianism that Carter had embraced in 1977–78. As at Tokyo, Carter "agreed upon the need for tight monetary measures and tight and prudent fiscal measures." The others concurred. The summit communiqué called inflation the G-7's "immediate top priority" and proscribed general adherence to a "policy of restraint." This new international consensus endorsed disciplinary solutions, but discipline would have to be implemented at the national scale—as Volcker was doing in the United States and Thatcher was doing in Great Britain. The contrast with Bonn's multilateral Keynesianism was striking, and it indicated the distance that the G-7 had traveled in the tumultuous context of the second oil crisis.[70]

If the imperative of self-discipline was the consensus of the summit, energy was its centerpiece. The summiteers would have to figure out how "to break the link between oil imports and growth," as Valéry Giscard d'Estaing put it. Carter led the way, elaborating a tripartite energy concept that involved setting quantitative targets for reducing oil imports, the collaborative promotion of alternative energies, and international assistance for the non-oil-exporting Third World countries. Giscard was supportive, but the British and the Germans were wary of international economic managerialism, preferring to rely on the market. The most that the G-7 countries could do was agree that they had to import less oil and commit to reduce oil's share of their collective energy use from 53 percent in 1980 to 40 percent in 1990. This was positive for Carter, who had assured Saudi Arabia that the G-7 would act to reduce demand for oil, and for Brzezinski, who made oil conservation a central pillar of his Persian Gulf security framework.[71]

In practice, the West's demand for oil would contract in the early 1980s—not as a result of higher oil prices but as a consequence of the recession that austerity policies triggered. This was not foreseen at Venice. The summit nonetheless accomplished what Henry Kissinger had defined as summitry's overarching strategic purpose, which was to restore unity amid division. Venice affirmed that the industrialized countries were in the same boat—or, as Japan's Saburo Okita put it, that "the free democratic nations were traveling in the same gondola." This was true—up to a point. None of the G-7 could avoid the thick economic interdependencies that now entwined the advanced industrial countries, rendering them dependent on each other and on the oil of the Middle East. Having tried—and failed—to restore economic growth through macroeconomic coordination, they embraced austerity as a shared commitment and last resort. Yet the disagreements that manifested themselves in the first months of 1980—over the Soviet Union, the Cold War, and the Arab-Israeli conflict—would recur, bringing into question not the future of "the West" so much as its coherence as a category in international politics.[72]

∽∾∽

By the summer of 1980, the Carter administration had retooled its strategic assumptions to confront what decision-makers took as a threat of resurgent Soviet power. Still, what unfolded during 1979–80 was not a sharp pivot so much as a diffusion of the administration's initial focus on post–Cold War priorities and an assimilation of Cold War commitments centered on Brzezinski's "arc of crisis" into world order priorities. The administration retooled its theory to accommodate reality, achieving what Brzezinski called a "complex foreign policy" that was not reducible "to a single and simplistic slogan." Inverting Kissinger's pivot toward interdependence issues in 1973–74, the Carter administration in 1979–80 reprioritized anti-Soviet containment. In both cases, strategic reevaluation and adjustment followed the failure of initial strategic concepts to encompass realities more vexing and diffuse than early strategic designs permitted.[73]

Carter's strategic reevaluation entailed policy departures that would become identified with his successor, Ronald Reagan. The continuities between Carter and Reagan would be clear in economic policy, where the dollar-rescue package of 1978 and the Volcker shift of 1979 prefigured the dogged pursuit in the early 1980s of price stability at the expense of other goals. Continuities would also be apparent in defense policy, where Carter initiated an increase in military spending that reversed Nixon's efforts to tame the Cold War's costs.

The White House in the winter of 1979–80 pushed Congress to increase defense appropriations, and it elaborated a five-year plan for modernizing America's nuclear and conventional forces. Supplemental appropriations would increase military spending for 1981 beyond the levels that Carter proposed, but it was Carter who initiated the return to elevated levels of defense spending, marking the end of détente's fiscal dividend (see figure 9.4). Besides increasing expenditures, the Carter administration elaborated military doctrines that antic- ipated its successor's new Cold War posture. In July 1980, Carter signed PD-59, directing the elaboration of specific plans for waging and winning a limited nuclear war. While the directive was less radical than its critics presumed, public disclosure of the PD-59 exercise confirmed the remilitarization of the Cold War, stirring fear and debate. Jimmy Carter's early hopes that he and Brezhnev would negotiate unprecedented cuts in the size of their nuclear arsenals and roll back a thirty-year-old strategic arms race now seemed distant.[74]

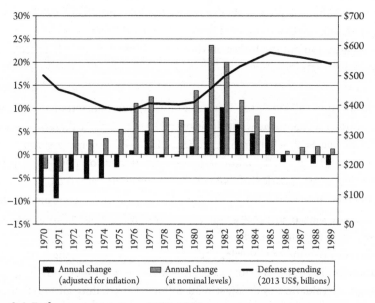

Figure 9.4 Defense appropriations, 1970–1990
Source: US Department of Defense, *National Defense Budget* (2013).

Afghanistan became the cockpit of the resurgent Cold War. US aid to the mujahideen in fact antedated the Red Army's invasion, but Carter escalated US involvement in December 1979, channeling military assistance to the anti-Soviet guerillas. The consequences of the new Cold War reverberated elsewhere in the Third World, including in Central America. Having indulged a leftist regime in Nicaragua, the Carter administration threw its support behind the right-wing junta that seized power in neighboring El Salvador in October 1979. This was a turning point in Carter's Latin American policy, away from human rights and toward anti-Communism. Even the junta's murder of Archbishop Óscar Romero, a reformer who had appealed to Carter to withhold "military equipment and advisors" from the regime, did not shake Washington's support for the El Salvadorian junta. Cold War purposes had trumped the administration's bid to recenter American foreign policy on human rights.[75]

Adopting tough-minded Cold War policies did not rescue Carter's political fortunes. The failure of an April 1980 attempt to rescue the hostages from Iran was a significant setback for the administration, and the spectacle of their captivity throughout the election campaign made Carter look hapless. The economy also counted against the president, who bore the brunt of voters' frustrations with inflation, while divisions within the Democratic Party hurt the president. Ted Kennedy challenged Carter for the nomination, promising to restore détente and the political economy of the New Deal. "The dream will never die," Kennedy promised, and the progressives cheered. It was easier to invoke the spirits of the past than to adjust policies to circumstances of constraint. Carter had made pragmatic choices in office, reevaluating his priorities as circumstances evolved, but to little political avail. Injured in the primaries by a nostalgist of the left, Carter lost November's election to a fantasist of the right. Americans, it seemed, preferred to declaim against limits than accomodate them.[76]

∽∾

Events after the election suggested the extent to which the 1970s had changed the Cold War order. The Polish crisis of 1980–81 was yet another in a series of eruptions within the East Bloc, but it revealed how global shocks—especially shocks borne of economic change—could reverberate across the Cold War's frontiers. The 1970s were difficult for Eastern Europe: productivity waned, growth slumped, and surging oil prices made it costlier for Communist governments to appease their citizens with imported goods, forcing them to borrow from the West. Poland experienced major riots in 1976 after the government raised consumer prices in an effort to tame its deficits. Officials quickly backed down, instead borrowing even more from abroad.[77]

Ideological currents also blew from afar. A handful of Czech activists and intellectuals drafted Charter 77 in the winter of 1976/7, calling on their government to honor the human rights commitments it made when it signed the

Helsinki Final Act and the UN Human Rights Covenants. They made contact with the Polish Workers Defense Committee, a group that had emerged after the 1976 protests. The election of a Polish pope emboldened the dissidents. When John Paul II visited his homeland in June 1979, he invoked the Universal Declaration of Human Rights and challenged the Communist Party to permit Poles to speak freely on matters of morality and conscience. Massive crowds fêted the new pope.[78]

It was, nonetheless, economics that brought Poland to its breaking point. Surging world oil prices, which waning Soviet oil production exacerbated, forced East European leaders to tighten their belts. On July 1, 1980, the Polish government again hiked up food prices, sparking massive strikes, which gave birth to Solidarity, an independent labor movement, in August. Within months, Solidarity's membership numbered millions. Its ascent was stunning, as was the Communist Party's apparent acquiescence to it. The flourishing of an indepen-dent labor organization devoted to "self-government, democracy, and plural-ism" challenged Communist rule and raised the question of a possible Soviet response. Would Moscow send in the tanks, as it had done in 1968? In the last months of 1980, the Soviet Union mobilized its forces.[79]

The Carter administration's policy toward Eastern Europe aimed from the outset to encourage centripetal forces—an approach reflecting Brzezinski's con-viction that the East Bloc was politically fragile and prone to fragmentation. The Polish crisis hinted at this fragmentation, which made Soviet military action an outcome the administration was determined to deter. "We've got to do all we can do," Carter noted, "to keep them from invading." During the fall, the administra-tion urged the Polish leadership to reform, worked to build a common front with its NATO allies, encouraged the AFL-CIO to finance Solidarity, and extended millions of dollars in export credits to Poland. The NSC devised a set of retalia-tory measures that the United States and its allies would implement if the Soviet Union invaded Poland, and Carter in a December 3 statement warned Moscow against military action. Superpower relations, Carter vowed, "would be directly and very adversely affected."[80]

When an East Bloc summit decided to defer military intervention, US offi-cials declared a quiet victory. The "reason for the postponement," Brzezinski explained, "was the effectiveness of the Western counter propaganda campaign." This did not mean that Poland's crisis would be resolved peacefully: having lost control, the Warsaw government would declare martial law one year later, turn-ing its tanks on its own people. By recoiling from invasion, the Soviet leader-ship nonetheless retreated from the implications of the Brezhnev Doctrine, according to which the Soviet Union reserved the right to intervene with force to reverse "the development of some socialist country toward capitalism." The costs of further aggravating East-West estrangement, which a Soviet invasion of

Poland would have done, looked at the end of the 1970s to outweigh the benefits of maintaining discipline within the bloc.[81]

For America's Polish-born national security advisor, forestalling a Soviet invasion hinted at vindication. The crisis in Poland implied, as one aide wrote, that "the dissolution of the Soviet Empire is not a wholly fanciful prediction for later in this century" and that "US policy should set its sight on that strategic goal," as Brzezinski had long argued. Events in Poland sharpened Cold War tensions, but they also augured the Cold War's resolution on the terms that Brzezinski predicted: not in a military confrontation but with the Soviet Union's assimilation to an integrating world order, to Brzezinski's technetronic age. This was more or less how things turned out in the 1980s. Carter's misfortune, it would appear in retrospect, was his timing; the moment for a post–Cold War foreign policy had in the late 1970s not yet arrived.[82]

The demise of the Cold War order in the late 1980s would create opportunities to pursue strategic purposes that were akin to those that the Carter administration had defined at the outset and toward which the departing president still harkened. In his farewell address, Carter returned to his initial purposes, exalting the control of nuclear weapons and the elevation of human rights as goals for the United States in the world. He also offered the American people a historical irony. "The same rocket technology that delivers nuclear warheads has also taken us peacefully into space," he explained. "From that perspective, we see our Earth as it really is—a small and fragile and beautiful blue globe." The paradox recalled Carter's earliest foreign policy commitments, but it also helps to explain the accomplishments and travails of his foreign policy. Caught between an emerging global order and an enduring Cold War, Carter struggled to articulate, follow, and sustain a singular, overarching concept for American power in what he called "a time of transition, an uneasy era." The problem was not the absence of strategic thinking but that strategy itself proved, in the end, to be unequal to the innate complexity of a tumultuous and transformative decade.[83]

Conclusion

> Even the most powerful nations and even the wisest planners of the
> future remain themselves creatures as well as creators of the historical
> process.
>
> Reinhold Niebuhr, *The Irony of American History* (1952)

"All great world-historical facts and personages occur twice," Karl Marx wrote.
"Once as tragedy, and again as farce." Reagan for Truman, Brezhnev for Stalin,
Afghanistan for Korea, and Poland for Poland; events and personalities at the
end of the 1970s looked to confirm Marx's point. After Afghanistan, Jimmy
Carter situated US foreign policy on an invigorated Cold War footing; Carter's
successor launched an anti-Soviet revival. "They are the focus of evil in the
modern world," Ronald Reagan proclaimed in 1983. The rhetoric recalled
the early Cold War—and so did the risks. As millions of people took part in
antinuclear protests on the streets of Bonn, London, and New York, new inci-
dents brought the superpowers to the brink of conflict. The Soviet Union in
September 1983 shot down a Boeing 747 operated by Korean Air Lines, claiming 269 victims, including a US Congressman. Two months later, Soviet leaders
misconstrued a NATO exercise, Able Archer 83, as a preemptive nuclear attack
and initiated preparations for retaliation. Cooler heads prevailed, but the Cold
War was back.[1]

The resurgence of fear in the early 1980s recalled the high Cold War that climaxed in the Cuban missile crisis. Still, it did not follow that the intervening
years had been a mere respite, an interlude of stasis. Rather, the late 1960s initiated a phase of disruption, decay, and change—for the international order and
for the American superpower. Indeed, the resolution of the Cold War, after its
re-escalation in the early 1980s, would reveal just how consequential the 1970s
had been. The rise of human rights, the remaking of national and international
economic orders, and the ascent of globalization transformed America's superpower role and contributed to the Cold War ending as it did—with the USSR's

implosion and America's presumption of victory. In other respects, however, the legacies of the seventies were far from serendipitous. The unmaking of the postwar order inaugurated a phase of prolonged instability, not a new and durable international settlement. The United States benefited from globalization in diverse ways, but the superpower also became increasingly dependent on transnational resources and prone to imperial overstretch.

∞

The remaking of American foreign relations occurred in diverse international arenas—across realms of geopolitical rivalry, economic interaction, and ideological contestation—all of which were in flux as the stirrings of globalization destabilized the postwar settlement. To grasp the transformations in America's superpower role that turned on the 1970s thus requires situating the United States in the dynamic global context of which it was part.

Begin with the breakdown of the postwar economic order, a legacy of the Great Depression and an achievement of US-led efforts to reconcile globalization with the welfare state. The postwar order depended on a containment of finance, which the Bretton Woods institutions consecrated. It also depended on the United States: the dollar was the bedrock of postwar international monetary stability, and Washington disbursed economic resources to its Cold War allies and clients, fostering their recovery and growth. In the 1960s, this postwar order fractured. Globalization undid the postwar containment of finance, while the decline of US economic power destabilized an international order organized around the dollar. Governments managed in 1971 to devise a new matrix of fixed exchange rates, but they did not reconcile monetary stability to financial globalization. Instead, they accepted floating currencies in 1973, ceding power over exchange rates to foreign exchange markets, and began to abolish capital controls. Still, what ensued after Bretton Woods was not a new international order keyed to neoliberal purposes but a prolonged phase of improvisation amid disorder.

In the absence of authoritative reform, globalization flourished. As oil prices rose, financial markets recycled petrodollar revenues, confirming globalization's ascent. The consequences became the stuff of debate—and fascination. "It is the international system of currency," exclaimed Ned Beatty's fictional businessman in the 1976 Oscar-winning film *Network*, "which determines the totality of life on this planet." Governments would reform the IMF Articles of Agreement in 1976 to formalize floating exchange rates, validating market-led globalization, but governments also cooperated to assert their collective authority over markets. Collaborative governance was the Trilateral Commission's solution to interdependence, and it enjoyed broad support among the capitalist countries in the mid-1970s. Multilateral governance orchestrated via the G-7 summits nonetheless failed to restore price stability and stable growth, and this failure led to the adoption of new solutions. For the United States, it was the Volcker shift of 1979 that marked the policy arena's reorientation toward the market.[2]

In October 1979, Paul Volcker's Federal Reserve adopted a new system of monetary targeting intended to control the money supply, restore price stability, and bolster the dollar. Doing so subjected the United States to meaningful monetary discipline for the first time since 1971, when Nixon abandoned the gold standard. Volcker did not act eagerly, but he saw few alternatives if inflation were to be quashed and the dollar's global role sustained. The consequences would include the severest recession and worst unemployment since the Great Depression. Governments elsewhere made similar choices. Margaret Thatcher embraced monetary discipline with missionary zeal, while France, in 1983–84, undertook a reluctant tournant to the market under a socialist president. Such choices were dramatic, but the retreat of managed capitalism in the 1970s owed to complex causes, some of which were endogenous to the old order. Managed capitalism faltered in the late 1960s, as productivity growth slowed and inflation mounted. Globalization also proved to be powerfully disruptive. Interdependence loosened the control of governments over their economies, which inhibited the management of national economies and prompted decision-makers, after experimenting with collaborative coordination, to submit instead to the discipline of integrating markets.[3]

For the United States, the seventies closed an era of hegemonic responsibility during which Washington had disbursed resources and upheld the international economic order, often prioritizing systemic stability over national economic interests. The collapse of the old order in 1971–73 released the dollar from the discipline of the gold standard, but the United States continued to enjoy the privileges that the dollar's leading international role conferred, not least being able to borrow in its own currency. Indeed, the sharp increase in dollar interest rates that Volcker initiated attracted floods of capital to the United States in the early 1980s, enabling Carter's successors to cut taxes and increase spending. Volcker's choice for discipline thus served, ironically, to release the United States from fiscal constraints, providing an ad hoc solution to the deficits that had bedeviled the US balance of payments since the 1960s. The United States became a net international debtor in the mid-1980s, and its international investment position declined thereafter (see figure C.1). No longer a creditor to the world, as it had been since the First World War, the United States became an importer of capital as well as goods, dependent on inflows to sustain its global military role and its citizens' consumption habits. Globalization benefited the United States, nurturing growth as it had done in the late nineteenth century, but globalization's bounty came at the costs of international indebtedness, dependence, and vulnerability.[4]

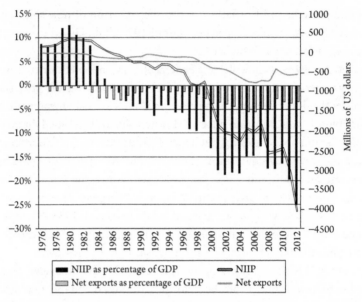

Figure C.1 US net exports and net international investment position, 1976–2012
Source: U.S. Bureau of Economic Analysis, International Economics Accounts.

Similar changes proceeded in the energy arena. Thanks to buoyant US production and a worldwide production glut, oil prices declined between the 1940s and late 1960s. Cheap oil sustained energy-intensive growth in the West, bolstering the Pax Americana. But the oil markets turned in the 1970s. The United States had produced 52 percent of the world's oil in 1950, but its share slumped to 34 percent in 1960 and 21 percent in 1970. By 1980, the United States ranked third among world oil producers, behind the Soviet Union and Saudi Arabia. As US production declined, OPEC acquired the capacity to determine prices—and did so. The price of a barrel of Dubai light crude surged, in real terms, from $10 to $101 over the decade. In the 1970s Americans nonetheless became dependent on oil imports. Amid recurrent oil crises, governments in the industrialized world collaborated to promote energy conservation and alternative fuels, but they could not reduce the West's dependence on imported oil. In energy as in finance, a striking transformation occurred in the relationship of the United States to the global economy—a shift from abundance and autonomy to dependence and vulnerability. The consequences afflicted the entire world and reverberated into the 1980s and beyond.[5]

Among the legacies of the seventies energy tumult was the reorientation of American foreign policy toward the Middle East. Despite prior US entanglements in the region, it was not until the late 1970s that the United States assumed a permanent military role in the Persian Gulf. In the context of the Iranian Revolution, the Carter administration deployed forces to the Gulf. Beyond defense commitments, regional political entanglements also turned on the 1970s. Here, few developments proved more consequential than Washington's alliance with Egypt, a defector from Moscow's Cold War bloc. American diplomats worked after 1973 to build a bilateral peace between Egypt and Israel, but they did not achieve a regional settlement capable of standing on its own. Instead, the political stability as well as the military security of the Middle East came in the late twentieth century to depend upon the United States. Washington's engagement benefited the industrialized world, which depended on Middle East oil, but it embroiled the superpower in a tumultuous region, with far-reaching consequences.

China's reorientation toward the United States was, if anything, even more consequential than Egypt's. While the Sino-Soviet split had begun much earlier, it was in the 1970s that the high Cold War order fractured amid a diplomatic revolution among the world's three greatest powers. The Sino-American opening of 1972 led to a normalization of US-China relations, which heralded China's reintegration into the liberal world economy and the formation of a tacit Sino-American alliance. The results of this anti-Soviet entente would include intelligence sharing, limited US military sales to China, and the establishment of joint intelligence facilities in western China to monitor Soviet military operations. Meanwhile, China's brief war against Vietnam in 1979 demonstrated Moscow's inability to protect its Southeast Asian ally against a resurgent China. Beijing and Washington's tacit alliance would wither into contentiousness, and the Soviet Union and China would mend their relations in the second half of the 1980s. But, for a crucial phase in the early 1980s, Sino-American rapprochement inverted the geopolitical alignments of the high Cold War, compounding the containment of the Soviet Union that American leaders had pursued since the late 1940s.[6]

As the geopolitical ice fragmented, the makers of US foreign policy embraced new ideological purposes. During the high Cold War, leaders had generally accepted ideological pluralism as a consequence of the world's geopolitical division, even as a prerequisite for peace. During the 1970s, however, the promotion of political change within the East Bloc became an avowed priority for the West, although not initially for US decision-makers. Rather, it was nongovernmental organizations, civil society activists, Soviet dissidents, and sympathetic Congressmen who led the crusade for human rights, while European diplomats championed the inclusion of human rights provisions within the Helsinki Final Act of 1975. Keyed to globalization, the human rights mobilization of the seventies transcended the Cold War. Some proponents offered human rights as the basis for a post–Cold War foreign policy; others worked to hold Washington's illiberal Cold War allies to account. The consequences of human rights mobilization for the Cold War would nonetheless prove dramatic. American zeal for human rights, once decision-makers embraced them, and the ensuing Soviet umbrage destabilized a stable Cold War settlement in the late 1970s, confirming the reemergence in US foreign policy of an ideological, crusading style that would endure beyond the Cold War.

The Cold War was back at the end of the 1970s, but the American superpower and the international system were transformed. The crumbling in the 1970s of the postwar economic order led not to a new order but to the ascendancy of market-oriented globalization. Formerly a benefactor to its allies, the United States ceased to be a disseminator of resources to the world and became, in the 1980s, dependent on the savings of foreigners. Whereas the United States ceded hegemonic responsibility for the world economic order, there occurred no parallel retrenchment in its global military role, beyond extrication from Vietnam. The United States instead acquired new military burdens in the Middle East, where it undertook to assure the security of oil supplies flowing through the Persian Gulf. What ensued in the 1970s was not a retreat from the world, such as Nixon feared, but a superpower recasting whereby the United States came to depend upon resources that globalization furnished, and American decision-makers came to identify US interests with globalization's advance. What cohered in the 1970s was a post–Cold War superpower role, distinct in crucial respects from the postwar Pax Americana. Having assumed a superpower's burdens when nationalism and decolonization were in their historical ascendancies, the United States adapted itself to the emergence of a new era that the eclipse of collectivism and the ascent of globalization and human rights would define.

༼ঔ༽

The consequences of developments that unfolded during the 1970s manifested themselves in the 1980s and after. For the United States and its allies, the breakdown of the postwar economic order was disruptive: growth slowed as globalization and crisis wrecked the capitalist world. During the 1980s, the West nonetheless resurged, as capitalist economies adapted to the challenges of a globalizing era and postindustrial growth compensated for the ongoing decline of manufacturing industries. For the Soviet Union, the patterns of these decades were different. Insulated from the shock of globalization, the Soviet Union experienced the 1970s as years of stasis, not crisis. What ensued in the 1980s was a reversal of fortune that owed as much to deep-rooted economic changes as to geopolitical developments adverse to the USSR.

East and West in the era of the high Cold War experienced comparable rates of growth (see figure C.2). Like the capitalist world, the Soviet Union flourished as an industrial economy, oriented to heavy and extractive industries: coal, steel, manufacturing, and so on. Across the blocs, the returns on heavy industrialization were by the late 1960s diminishing. Inputs that sustained postwar growth—industrial technologies, surplus labor, and cheap energy—dwindled,

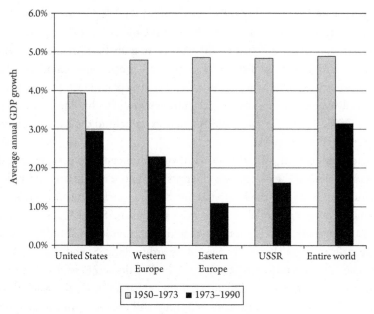

Figure C.2 Growth in two eras, 1950–1973 and 1973–1990
Source: Angus Maddison, WEHS.

and economic growth slowed. Globalization encouraged the offshoring of steel, textiles, and other old industries from the United States in the 1970s, but firms oriented to new technologies, such as the microprocessor chip that Intel debuted in 1971, were also being born. Bill Gates quit Harvard and launched Microsoft in 1975; Steve Jobs founded Apple in 1976. The Soviet Union experienced no such creative destruction. Instead, natural endowments compensated for faltering growth. As oil prices surged in 1973–74, the USSR surpassed the United States to become the world's largest oil producer. Revenues from oil exports enabled the USSR to import food, consumer durables, and high technology from the West. At home, the USSR's hydrocarbon bounty thwarted reform. Flush with energy, which inefficient state-owned enterprises devoured, Soviet leaders in the 1970s had little incentive to undertake far-reaching reforms. Instead, the planned economy creaked on into the 1980s.[7]

During the 1980s, world oil markets took a dramatic turn. Supply outstripped demand as a consequence of conservation efforts, the expansion of non-OPEC production, and world-wide economic recession. As prices fell, in real terms, from $101 per barrel in 1980 to $51 in mid-1985, the members of OPEC bickered. Saudi Arabia in late 1985 increased production in a bid to expand its market share, but doing so exerted further downward pressure on prices. Oil reached $12 per barrel in 1988—cheaper, in real terms, than at any time since 1974. For the USSR, falling world prices combined with waning production to produce a crisis no less serious than the oil shocks that hit the West in the 1970s. Beyond the loss of export earnings it caused, the Soviet Union's oil crisis exposed failures of development. The capitalist world adapted to globalization in the 1970s, but the Soviet Union remained stuck in an outmoded economic paradigm, dependent on energy exports, heavy industry, and central planning. Some Soviet technocrats advocated reform, stressing the imperatives of technological innovation, but the USSR had by the early 1980s fallen so far behind the capitalist world as to make catch-up improbable.[8]

Soviet leaders in the 1980s thus confronted unfavorable economic realities at the same time as they waged an ulcerous war in the mountains and valleys of Afghanistan. China and the United States both supported the anti-Soviet mujahideen in Afghanistan, collaborating with Pakistan and Saudi Arabia to equip the Islamist insurgents with equipment ranging from mules to shoulder-launched anti-aircraft missiles. When a new, outward-looking Soviet leader, Mikhail Gorbachev, came to power in March 1985, ending the war in Afghanistan ranked among the most urgent and difficult challenges that he faced, alongside the reinvigoration of a sclerotic command economy and escape from the geopolitical encirclement in which the Soviet Union increasingly found itself.

The transnational circulation of ideas and culture exacerbated the Soviet Union's predicament. Building on the Helsinki Final Act, Western NGOs and governments aided proponents of human rights in the East Bloc and elsewhere. The Reagan administration in 1983 created the National Endowment for Democracy, a quasi-official NGO that assisted civil society organizations including Poland's Solidarity. Human rights and democracy advanced globally in the 1980s, as authoritarian regimes from Argentina and Chile to South Korea and the Philippines crumbled. The number of countries that Freedom House categorized as "wholly free" increased from fifty-one (or 32 percent of the world's countries) at the end of the 1970s to sixty-one (or 37 percent) at the end of the 1980s. This incremental march of democratization challenged the Soviet leaders to respond.[9]

The Soviet Union and its allies encountered transnational pressures in the 1980s beyond the ideological challenges of democratization and human rights. When East Europeans looked at the West, they could not conclude that they were inhabiting the world of tomorrow. Instead, many of them envied the West's commodities, its modernity, and its popular culture—from the art rock of Frank Zappa, who inspired Czechoslovakia's Plastic People of the Universe, to the blues rock of the Rolling Stones, which circulated via *samizdat* vinyl. Cognizant of the westward yearnings of its youth, the East German Communist regime invited Bruce Springsteen to play in East Berlin in 1988, presuming that the concert would allow youthful frustrations to ventilate. An audience of 300,000 greeted Springsteen; millions more watched him on state television. In faltering

German, Springsteen told his audience: "I've come to play rock and roll for you in the hope that one day all the barriers will be torn down." Ronald Reagan in 1987 had called on the Soviet Union to raze the Berlin Wall, but Bruce Springsteen beamed that message into the East Bloc's heart. Within eighteen months, East Berliners would be rallying at the Berlin Wall, some armed with axes and shovels, to tear down the barrier that separated them from the West.[10]

Globalization exacerbated—and in some ways defined—the challenges that Mikhail Gorbachev faced on installation as General Secretary of the Communist Party. A superpower in an era of coal and steel, central planning, and workers solidarity, the USSR struggled to adapt to an era of microprocessors, financial globalization, and Amnesty International. Gorbachev grasped that the Soviet Union was slipping relative to the West. "We can't go on living like this," he told his wife. An idealist who yearned to make Communism modern while retaining its egalitarian commitments, Gorbachev moved cautiously at first. He loosened the party's grip on society, and in December 1986 he released Andrei Sakharov from internal exile. A slew of reforms followed, including the 1988 establishment of a democratic legislature, to which Sakharov won election. Gorbachev's economic reforms proved less successful: the transition from planning to markets proved insurmountable, and the Soviet Union struggled to absorb the effects of tumbling oil prices. Gorbachev nonetheless cleaved to a strategy of integration, convinced that saving the Soviet Union depended on opening it to a globalizing world. Working with Reagan, he built an unprecedented rapprochement—a relationship aimed not at Cold War stabilization, as Nixon's détente had been, but at the Cold War's transcendence and resolution, along the lines that Andrei Sakharov had advocated at the end of the 1960s.[11]

Gorbachev's embrace of globalization plunged the Soviet Union into crisis, but it healed what Zbigniew Brzezinski once called "the doctrinal abyss dividing mankind." When Eastern Europe's Communist regimes faltered in 1988–89, Gorbachev did not intervene. His renunciation of the Soviet Union's dominant role in Eastern Europe instead permitted a reintegration of Europe, undoing the schism that had made the Cold War in the first place. Two years later, the Soviet Union collapsed after a failed coup d'état by Communist hard-liners. Was this a victory for the United States, as many Americans would claim? The United States had, after all, orchestrated a difficult geopolitical environment for Moscow: Washington allied itself with China, aided Afghanistan's insurgents, and built up its own military forces. Tough-minded US policies, which Carter initiated, prompted the Soviet Union to increase military spending, increasing the strains on its economy. Reagan initially took a still-tougher line, envisioning an antimissile shield that would establish US nuclear superiority over the Soviet Union. It was nonetheless Reagan's retreat from belligerence that was his greatest contribution to resolving the Cold War. Defying the objections of self-identified realists, including Richard Nixon, Reagan in his second term extended to Gorbachev an open hand of friendship, encouraging the Soviet leader's bid for reintegration with the world.[12]

Still, American choices offer only partial explanation for the Cold War's resolution. Instead, the terms on which the Cold War ended reveal the divergent impacts of structural changes on its two superpowers. The USSR struggled to adapt to the march of globalization, the rise of a universal human rights movement, and the remaking of capitalist economies. The United States absorbed globalization's shock in the 1970s and drew thereafter on transnational resources to sustain its superpower role. Borrowed funds allowed the Reagan administration to increase military spending to levels not seen since the Korean War even as it slashed taxes, stimulating growth. While global finance underwrote US deficits, the transnational reach of ideas, culture, and aspirations served Cold War purposes. Even rock and roll became a strategic asset—an ironic fate for a musical form that had cohered in the counterculture of the 1960s. It was also ironic that the United States aligned itself with a human rights movement that had mobilized in the early 1970s against Nixon's Cold War pragmatism. Thereafter, human rights provided both an ideological wedge against Communist rule in the 1980s and a strategic rationale for US foreign policy, which indicated the diverse benefits that the American superpower derived from globalization.[13]

After the Cold War, American leaders considered globalization "the central reality of our time," as President Bill Clinton put it, and aligned their interests with its promotion. Human rights became a priority, being for Clinton both an ethical concomitant to globalization and the prerogative of a post–Cold War superpower. While Clinton did little to stop the genocide that ravaged Rwanda in 1994, failure in Africa emboldened the administration in the Balkans. At Washington's urging, NATO in 1995 deployed airpower to bring the ethnic cleansing of Bosnia's Muslims to an end. Four years later, Clinton bombed Serbia to secure Kosovo's secession, citing the "moral imperative" of protecting a "defenseless people." After Kosovo, Clinton's British ally Tony Blair, a fervent interventionist, hailed the obsolescence of old distinctions between interests and values in foreign policy. Using force to "establish and spread the values of liberty, the rule of law, human rights, and an open society is in our national interests," Blair insisted. At this, Henry Kissinger took umbrage. Humanitarian interventionism deserved "to be questioned," Kissinger wrote, "on both political and moral grounds." The conflict between pragmatism and idealism that enveloped détente in the 1970s still endured, but after the Cold War, it was the champions of morality in foreign policy who predominated, and the realists who grumbled on the sidelines.[14]

Al Qaeda's attacks on New York and Washington on September 11, 2001, confirmed the far-reaching consequences of developments that turned on the

1970s. Osama bin Laden, Al Qaeda's kingpin, was a Saudi veteran of the Afghan wars whose family fortune derived from petrodollars and whose grievances with the United States owed, he claimed, to the presence of US forces in Saudi Arabia. For the United States, Al Qaeda's attacks demonstrated just how deadly transnational threats could be. Americans struggled after 9/11 to respond. Some emphasized the need for energy conservation to reduce America's dependence on the Middle East—echoing Ford, Kissinger, and Carter. The neoconservatives who surrounded President Bush favored militarized democratization, which Bush framed in the language of human rights. Proclaiming a crusade against "terrorists and tyrants," Bush invaded Iraq, determined to remake the Middle East. Iraq instead became a quagmire that diverted resources from the parallel campaign Bush waged to eradicate Al Qaeda (and its Taliban hosts) from Afghanistan. The public at first rallied behind Bush, but the American people tired of open-ended commitments, much as they had in the 1960s, and the election of 2008 prefigured both strategic retrenchment and a rebirth of realism in American foreign policy.[15]

As George W. Bush's ideological foreign policy faltered, the benefits of economic globalization began to look more doubtful than American leaders had long assumed. Embracing globalization, the Clinton administration in the 1990s promoted trade liberalization, deregulated domestic banking, and improvised to stabilize the global financial system. At home, Clinton was a prudent fiscal manager: he raised taxes, trimmed military spending, curbed the welfare state, and set the United States on a course to pay down the Reagan deficits. Bush abandoned Clinton's caution: he slashed taxes, financed wars, and extended new healthcare benefits to senior citizens. As in the 1980s, foreign capital underwrote the Republican Party's deficits. Ordinary Americans also borrowed—to purchase homes and to compensate for salaries that had dwindled, in real terms, since the 1980s, as more and more of the nation's income accrued to its wealthiest citizens. In 2007–8, America's debt bubble burst, thrusting the world economy into a downturn more severe than any since the Great Depression. The stability and future of market-led globalization became the subject of intense debate. As critics railed against neoliberalism, globalization's proponents asked whether an integrated world economy could be stable without collaborative governance of the kind that American leaders had pursued, for a brief interlude, in the mid-1970s.[16]

Verdicts remain difficult. Did the 1970s revitalize the American superpower, prefiguring the Cold War's resolution, or did the 1970s leave the United States vulnerable to financial crises and susceptible to imperial overreach? The decade's paradox is that it left the superpower both empowered and diminished. Globalization showered foreign capital on the United States, but market-led globalization was also prone to crisis. After benefiting from a long debt-fueled boom, the United States in 2007–8 succumbed to a financial bust that recalled the financial crises that had afflicted many developing countries in the 1980s and 1990s. The fracturing of the postwar geopolitical order, meanwhile, yielded costs as well as benefits. China's defection shifted the Cold War balance against the USSR, but China's rise in time became a strategic challenge for the United States. The Islamist mobilization that had embroiled the Soviet Union in Afghanistan, meanwhile, spawned Al Qaeda and 9/11. The mujahideen had been allies of convenience, but even allies of conviction could prove fickle. The transnational human rights mobilization of the 1970s aligned with US Cold War purposes, but it also encouraged American leaders to conflate ideals and interests, much as Henry Kissinger feared, and then turned on them when US actions violated human rights strictures as they did during George W. Bush's War on Terror. Forces that bolstered American power in some contexts could—and did—inhibit American power in other circumstances.

∞

What, though, of the decision-makers who inhabit this book? Were they architects of transformation, who perceived opportunity amid turmoil and acted to mold a new era of American ascendancy? Or were they captives of circumstances, who flailed amid changes too vast to be comprehended, much less corralled? The answers reside between these positions. Decision-makers in the 1970s inhabited a decaying international order. Within faltering structures, inherited from the past, they sought to remake world politics and to secure the future of the American superpower. They followed self-conscious designs—or strategies—but these rarely yielded the outcomes their architects sought. The Nixon, Ford, and Carter administrations participated in the remaking of America's superpower role in the 1970s, but decision-makers did not remake world politics according to their own designs. Instead, the consequences of choices turned out, for the most part, to be different from what these leaders had intended.

Richard Nixon pursued a coherent strategy, but his assumptions remained those of the Cold War. Nixon's tactics, which aimed to substitute geopolitical maneuvering for waning material strength, were more original than his purpose, which was to preserve the Pax Americana. Engaging China and triangulating the Cold War was Nixon's boldest move. The China opening facilitated détente, which stabilized the East-West balance of military power and gave the United States a respite in a time of upheaval. Yet, for all his achievements, Nixon did not make a new international order. Instead, he bolstered America's position within a stable conception of Cold War politics. Strategic conservatism constrained Nixon's policies toward the Third World and his response to the stirrings of transnational humanitarianism, which he viewed, for the most part, as an irritant, not an opportunity. In foreign economic policy, similarly, the Nixon administration's choices during 1971–73 revealed not a bold choice for globalization but a disinclination to permit economic crises to intrude on the administration's overriding strategic purpose, which was to invigorate America's superpower position within the Cold War order.

The oil crisis of 1973–74 exposed the limitations of Nixon's Cold War–centric outlook. Thereafter, decision-makers diversified their priorities, and Henry Kissinger emerged as the dominant shaper of American foreign policy. Aware that transnational relationships and novel interdependencies were destabilizing the international order, Kissinger sought stability via accommodation with globalization. "Economics, technology, and the sweep of human values impose a recognition of our interdependence," he intuited. Thus directed, US foreign policy began to transcend its long-standing Soviet-centrism, even as Kissinger defended the achievements of Soviet-American détente. The Ford administration collaborated with European governments and Japan to manage an integrating world economy and to mitigate the West's dependence on imported oil. Kissinger also attempted to engage a mobilized Third World, but he struggled to assimilate human rights into his new strategic synthesis. This omission contributed to a domestic backlash that challenged the philosophical premises of his foreign policy. The United States, Kissinger's opponents argued, should redeem the international order, not stabilize it. Yet redemption was not Kissinger's goal. What he sought was a balance of stability that hinged not only on geopolitical maneuvering but also on engaging with the transnational forces, especially globalization, that were destabilizing the old order.[17]

After Kissinger, the Carter administration envisaged the "shaping of a new international system," confident that it could master "global problems never before faced by mankind." This agenda proceeded from the administration's belief that the postwar order had crumbled and its conviction that the United States could now orchestrate a new order for a new historical era. Unlike its predecessor, the Carter administration embraced human rights, presuming that the convergence of human aspirations in a globalizing world made universal rights—and even a modicum of social justice—a prerequisite for legitimate international order. The concept was bold, but Carter's bid for a new order faltered. Whereas Kissinger mastered complexity by improvising—"acrobatics" as Brzezinski put it—the Carter administration devised an architectural concept for a new "world order politics." Carter's attempt to build anew nonetheless failed to transcend the Cold War. Instead, Carter's neglect of détente and his exertions on behalf of human rights in the Soviet Union exacerbated East-West tensions, overwhelming his bid for a new American foreign policy. As the Cold War resurged, the Carter administration modified its priorities so as to reconcile anti-Soviet containment with world order objectives, achieving in the process a new strategic synthesis.[18]

Frustrated by complexity and surprised by events, American leaders in the 1970s recurrently redefined their strategic purposes. Whereas Kissinger shifted away from a strategic concept centered on the Cold War, the Carter administration refocused on the containment of Soviet power. These reorientations speak to the difficulties of making strategy in an international system manifesting plural and simultaneous challenges: policymakers in the 1970s encountered the challenges of an emerging post–Cold War era even as the Cold War endured. Still, if policymakers flailed between competing imperatives, it does not follow that their choices were without consequences. Rather, decision-makers' efforts to command outcomes at the systemic level brought ironic results. Nixon's efforts to sustain the Pax Americana exacerbated the challenges that globalization posed. Kissinger's bid to improvise a complex stabilization faltered amid a resurgence of foreign-policy idealism, which his own policies had provoked. Carter's fixation on global challenges yielded to a resurgence of geopolitical rivalries, which the Carter administration's fractious East-West diplomacy exacerbated. Actions wrought consequences, but the effects were seldom those that American decision-makers sought to achieve.

The experiences of American decision-makers in the 1970s corroborated an insight that Reinhold Niebuhr offered a generation earlier. "Even the most powerful nations and even the wisest planners of the future," Niebuhr wrote, "remain themselves creatures as well as creators of the historical process." So it remained in the 1970s. Concerned with world order and its sustenance, American decision-makers devised strategies for upholding US influence and for remaking the international order that the United States superintended. Through the strategies they devised, decision-makers imparted coherence to complex historical processes in order to comprehend and manage historical change. They aimed to subject history to clear-sighted strategies but more often than not found themselves confounded. The historical transformations in which they participated resulted from the frustration of their concepts, not the achievement of their designs. Their legacies were, as a result, neither tragic nor heroic so much as ironic: the United States in the 1970s neither imposed on the world a new empire of exploitation nor liberated it for globalization and human rights. Instead, American decision-makers experimented and faltered, under circumstances they did not fully comprehend, with consequences they could not foresee. Theirs, in the end, were stories not of great power and vast agency, inscribed upon history in the realization of bold and purposeful designs, but of frustration, adaptation, and constraint.[19]

NOTES

Abbreviations Used in Sources

AI USA	Amnesty International USA Archives
APP	American Presidency Project
ASM	Anthony Solomon Materials
BIS	Bank for International Settlements
CBP	Carter-Brezhnev Project
CHRRD	Center for Human Rights Research and Documentation (Columbia University)
CEA	Council of Economic Advisors
CenF	Central Files
CIA	Central Intelligency Agency
CFR	Council on Foreign Relations
ChronF	Chronological File
ConF	Confidential File
COS	Chief of Staff
CouF	Country Files
CVP	Cyrus Vance Papers
DBPO	*Documents on British Policy Overseas*
DC	Declassification Computer
DDRS	Declassified Documents Reference System
DNSA	Digital National Security Archive
DOD	US Department of Defense
DOS	US Department of State
FOIA	Freedom of Information Act
DPMP	Daniel P. Moynihan Papers
EBB	Electronic Briefing Book
ERP	*Economic Report of the President*
FCO	Foreign and Commonwealth Office
FO	Foreign Affairs (in WHCF and WHSF)
FRASER	Federal Reserve Archival System for Economic Research
FRUS	*Foreign Relations of the United States*
GFD	Global Financial Data
GFPL	Gerald Ford Presidential Library
HHM	Hendrik Hertzberg Materials
HIA	Hoover Institution Archive
IMF	International Monetary Fund
IMP	Ivan Morris Papers

IT	International Organizations (in WHCF and WHSF)
JCPL	Jimmy Carter Presidential Library
KSM	Kissinger Staff Meetings
KTC	Kissinger Telephone Conversations
LAT	*Los Angeles Times*
LOC	Library of Congress
MemCon	Memorandum of Conversation
MLP	Mudd Library, Princeton
MRDP	Michael Raoul-Duval Papers
MRS	Mandatory Review Series
MTA	Margaret Thatcher Archive
NARA	National Archives and Records Administration
NATO	North Atlantic Treaty Organization
NBCHP	Nigeria-Biafra Clearing House papers
NPMP	Nixon Presidential Materials Project
NSA	National Security Adviser
NSC	National Security Council
NSC-IF	National Security Council, Institutional Files
NSDM	National Security Decision Memorandum (Nixon/Ford)
NYPL	New York Public Library
NYT	*The New York Times*
PFCC	President Ford Campaign Committee
PHF	President's Handwriting File
POF	President's Office File
PPC	Policy Planning Council (also known as Policy Planning Staff and S/P)
PPF	President's Personal File
RGS	Records of George Shultz
SCPC	Swarthmore College Peace Collection
SSF	Staff Secretary's File
SuF	Subject Files
TCPS	*Twentieth Century Petroleum Statistics*
TeleCon	Telephone Conversation
UKNA	United Kingdom National Archives
UNCTAD	United Nations Conference on Trade and Development
WEHS	*The World Economy: Historical Statistics*
WHCF	White House Central Files
WHSF	White House Special Files
WNSR	Weekly National Security Report
WP	*Washington Post*
YMA	Yale Manuscripts and Archives
ZBM	Zbigniew Brzezinski Materials

Introduction

1. Fox, *Super-Powers* ("super powers"); Spykman, *America's Strategy in World Politics*. Dahl, "Concept of Power," defines power as agency over outcomes; Paul Kennedy, *Rise and Fall*, emphasizes tangible resources. Others—including Cox, *Power, Production, and World Order*, and Lukes, *Power*—emphasize control over social arenas, including the international arena. On power's specificity to context, see Nye, *Bound to Lead*, esp. chap. 6.

2. Truman, "Remarks in Chicago," July 19, 1949, APP ("God Almighty"). For an assessment of the US position at the war's end, see D. White, "Nature of World Power"; and, more broadly, Leffler, *Preponderance of Power*. On the Soviet Union, see Mastny, *Cold War and Soviet Insecurity*.

3. Peterson, "Emerging Global Economy" ("self-sufficiency"). Maier, *Among Empires*, highlights the transition from an "empire of production" to an "empire of consumption." Ferguson,

Colossus, esp. chap. 8; and P. Kennedy, *Rise and Fall,* critique, respectively, US dependence on foreign investment and imperial overstretch.

4. The pivotal importance of the 1970s for US-China relations is well established. See Cohen, *America's Response to China,* chap. 8; Kissinger, *On China;* Mann, *About Face,* chaps. 2–5; and Tudda, *Cold War Turning Point.* On U.S. foreign policy's embrace of human rights in the 1970s and after, see Keys, *Reclaiming American Virtue;* Peck, *Ideal Illusions;* Sellars, *Rise and Rise of Human* Rights; and Vogelsgang, *American Dream, Global Nightmare.*

5. *FRUS 1969–1976,* vol. 38, no. 46 ("efforts that failed").

6. Fritz Stern, "The End of the Postwar Era," *Commentary,* April 1, 1974, pp. 27–35 ("postwar era"). On the historical evolution of international order, see Bobbitt, *Shield of Achilles,* chaps. 14–27; Bull, *Anarchical Society;* Ikenberry, *After Victory;* Kennedy, *Parliament of Man;* and Mazower, *Governing the World.* Hoffman, *American Umpire* explores US participation in the making of international order; while Hendrickson, *Union, Nation, or Empire,* locates a distinctive American approach to international order in the domestic federal order. On the settlement of 1815, Kissinger, *World Restored,* stresses the balance of power, while Schroeder, *Transformation of European Politics,* emphasizes shared ideological commitments. For Kissinger's reflections on Bismarck, see "White Revolutionary." For Mazzini's internationalism, see Mazower, *Governing the World,* esp. pp. 48–54; and Mazzini, *Cosmopolitanism of Nations,* esp. chaps. 7–8.

7. On the European settlement of the 1920s, see Cohrs, *Unfinished Peace;* and Steiner, *Lights That Failed.* On its disintegration, see Steiner, *Triumph of the Dark.* For the socioeconomic foundations of stability, see Maier, *Recasting Bourgeois Europe.* On the 1919 settlement in the non-European world, see Manela, *Wilsonian Moment.*

8. For the origins of the postwar international order, see Borgwardt, *New Deal for the World;* Hoffman, *American Umpire,* esp. chaps. 8–10; Latham, *Liberal Moment;* McCormick, *America's Half Century,* esp. chaps. 1–4; and Schurmann, *Logic of World Power.* On the Cold War and the international order, see Cronin, *World the Cold War Made,* esp. chaps. 1–3; and Gaddis, "Long Peace." On US policy in the early Cold War, see Leffler, *Preponderance of Power;* Maier, *Among Empires,* chaps 4–5; Spalding, *First Cold Warrior;* and Steel, *Pax Americana.*

9. Nixon, "Second Annual Report to the Congress on U.S. Foreign Policy," February 21, 1971, APP ("postwar order"); "The 1980s Project," March 7, 1975, MLP, CFR, 1980s Project, conferences, box 312 ("deluge"); Huntington and Manshel, "Why Foreign Policy?" ("an era").

10. Seabury, *Rise and Decline of the Cold War,* p. 148 ("classic"); Kissinger, *American Foreign Policy,* pp. 53–58 ("superpowers"); Edward M. Kennedy, "Address at the University of California, Berkeley," April 11, 1975, JCPL, 1976 Campaign Files, Issues Office, box 16 ("relic of the past"); Kennan, "After the Cold War" ("fixations and rigidities"); Peterson, "Emerging Global Economy," ("obsolete").

11. For broad and narrow definitions of globalization, see, respectively, Bayly, "'Archaic' and 'Modern' Globalization"; and Spence, "Impact of Globalization." Also see Keohane and Nye, *Transnational Relations,* pp. 8–11 ("reciprocal effects"); and Barnet and Müller, *Global Reach,* p. 302 ("stability"). Statistics on finance are from UNCTAD, *World Investment Report* (1994), p. 130; and, on trade, from UNCTAD, UNCTADStat. Ball is quoted in Oliveiro, "Politics of Globalization," p. 15. The scholarship on globalization is vast, but Held et. al. *Global Transformations* remains a useful introduction.

12. For a view from the late 1960s, see Cooper, *Economics of Interdependence.* For more recent perspectives, see James, *Roman Predicament;* Kahler and Lake, *Governance in a Global Economy;* Rodrik, *Globalization Paradox;* Slaughter, *New World Order;* Stiglitz, *Making Globalization Work;* Strange, *Casino Capitalism* and *Retreat of the State;* Tabb, *Economic Governance;* and Webb, *Political Economy of Policy Coordination.* Statistics on trade are from UNCTADStat.

13. James Callaghan, "Leader's Speech, Blackpool," September 28, 1976, British Political Speech online, http://www.britishpoliticalspeech.org ("candor"). Polanyi, *Great Transformation;* and Keynes, *General Theory,* remain essential guides to the public mobilization of the 1930s and 1940s. For overviews, see Freiden, *Global Capitalism;* and Pomfret, *Age of Equality.*

14. "Desired Characteristics of an International Order of the 1980s," April 5, 1974, MLP, CFR, 1980s Project, box 301 ("long view"). On the ideological content of human rights, see Moyn, *Last Utopia.*

15. Brzezinski, "Deceptive Structure of Peace" ("global political process"). Minutes of Cabinet Meeting, January 8, 1975, GFPL, NSA Files, MemCon, box 8 ("historic opportunity"); and "Foreign Policy Priorities," YMA, CVP, Series II, Foreign Policy Articles, box 9 ("no choice"). The late twentieth-century travails of the nation-state attract much discussion in the historical sociology on the nation-state and the international system. See, inter alia, Bobbitt, *Shield of Achilles*; Buzan and Little, *International Systems in World History*; van Creveld, *Rise and Decline of the State*; Cooper, *Breaking of Nations*; Maier, "Consigning the Twentieth Century to History"; Rosecrance, *Rise of the Trading State*; Sassen, *Territory, Authority, Rights*; and Watson, *The Evolution of International Society*.

16. The scholarship on strategy is substantial. Among recent overviews, Freedman, *Strategy*, emphasizes the concept's elasticity; while Luttwak, *Strategy* adheres closer to the association with military affairs that Lidell Hart establishes in his classic *Strategy*. Legro, *Rethinking the World* stresses the importance of strategic ideas in world politics.

17. WNSR #25, August 26, 1977, JCPL, ZBM, SuF, Weekly Reports ("one piece").

18. WNSR #25, August 26, 1977, JCPL, ZBM, SuF, Weekly Reports ("rationale"); and Kissinger, *White House Years*, p. xxii ("purposes").

19. The scholarship on the Cold War is too vast to summarize here, but notable interpretations of the 1970s that proceed within a Cold War paradigm include Garthoff, *Détente and Confrontation*; and Hyland, *Mortal Rivals*. On the diplomacy of détente, Nelson, *Making Détente* stresses the proximate origins; while Loth, *Overcoming the Cold War* sees détente as a long-running counterpoint to confrontation. Hanhimäki, *Rise and Fall of Détente*, locates the seeds of the Cold War's resolution in the détente years, as does Soutou, *La guerre de Cinquante Ans*. Westad, *Global Cold War*, stresses, by contrast, the Cold War's diffusion into the Third World. On US Cold War strategy, revisionist historians often stress the continuities, as do Bacevich, *American Empire*; Layne, *Peace of Illusions*; and McCormick, *America's Half-Century*. Conversely, Gaddis, *Strategies of Containment* argues that US policymakers followed a diversity of containment strategies, a point that Sestanovich, *Maximalist*, echoes. Others look beyond the Cold War. Connelly, *Diplomatic Revolution*, rethinks the Cold War's relationship to the history of the postwar world; while Suri, *Power and Protest* shows how developments far removed from the Cold War intruded on it.

20. On the seventies, Borstelmann, *The 1970s*, stresses the advance of egalitarianism and the retreat of the market as the decade's key themes; Chassaigne, *Les anées 1970s*, locates "the origins of our modernity." Ferguson et. al., eds., *Shock of the Global* collects diverse perspectives around the theme of a transformative 1970s. Histories that stress the resurgence of globalization include Osterhammel and Petersson, *Globalization*; and Eckes and Zeiler, *United States and Globalization*. Iriye, *Global Community*; and Mazlish, *New Global History*, both stress the rise of transnational forces and actors. The historiography on the US domestic experience in the 1970s is, for historians of US foreign relations, a source of rich insight. Rodgers, *Age of Fracture*, prioritizes intellectual and shifts; Schulman, *The Seventies*, emphasizes political and political-economic realignments. On the remaking of American capitalism in the 1970s, see, Hamilton, *Trucking Country*; Krippner, *Capitalizing on Crisis*; Lichtenstein, *Retail Revolution*; Moreton, *To Serve God and Wal-Mart*; and LaFeber, *New Global Capitalism*. On deindustrialization and its consequences, see Cowie, *Stayin' Alive*; and Stein, *Pivotal Decade*. On human rights, see Moyn, *Last Utopia*.

21. Contrast with Zanchetta, *Transformation of American International Power*, another recent history of US foreign relations in the 1970s, but one framed within the Cold War paradigm. For an approach similar to this book's—but focused on the years immediately preceding it—see Gavin and Lawrence, eds., *Beyond the Cold War*. Alternative approaches to late twentieth-century globalization that stress the self-conscious agency of US decision-makers, include Gowan, *Global Gamble*; Harvey, *New Imperialism*; and Schurmann, *Foreign Politics of Richard Nixon*. Also see McDougall, "President Nixon's Historical Legacy"; and Friedman, "A Nixon Legacy Devalued by a Cold War Standard," *NYT*, May 1, 1994, p. E4.

22. The scholarship on Nixon's foreign policy is substantial. The Vietnam War and Cold War détente remain its central themes, as Bundy, *Tangled Webb*; and Dallek, *Nixon and Kissinger*, exemplify. Declassification since the 1990s has made new evidence available, prompting reevaluations of familiar episodes, but earlier scholarship remains a useful guide to strategic

purposes. Schurmann, *Foreign Politics of Richard Nixon* argues that the United States lost its postwar hegemonic position during the Nixon years but achieved a new "centrality" at "the heart and core" of a new global order; unlike this author, he sees this transition as the achievement of design. Litwak, *Détente and the Nixon Doctrine*, is a useful guide to two central concepts.

23. Kissinger fascinates historians, but much of the Kissinger scholarship is fixated on the Nixon years, to the exclusion of his late career. For examples, see Dallek, *Nixon and Kissinger*; Del Pero, *Eccentric Realist*; Hanhimäki, *Flawed Architect*; and Suri, *Henry Kissinger and the American Century*. There are, however, differences of interpretation. Del Pero and Hanhimäki stress Kissinger's deference to Cold War habits; Suri emphasizes his adaptability, as does this book. While the new departures in foreign policy in the Ford years remain a neglected theme, historians of US domestic politics increasingly see the Ford years as a novel phase, as do Kalman, *Right Star Rising*; and Mieczkowski, *Gerald Ford*.

24. Scholarship on the Carter administration is less developed than is the literature on Carter's immediate predecessors. Smith, *Morality, Reason, and Power* is classic, but Glad, *Outsider in the White House* updates it. Both emphasize tensions between the Carter's secretary of state, Cyrus Vance, and his national security adviser, Zbigniew Brzezinski, a point that this book downplays. Kaufman, *Plans Unraveled*, is an innovative critique that faults Carter's failures of management. For more positive appraisals, see Rosati, *Carter Administration's Quest*, and Strong, *Working in the World*. Insider accounts remain vital, especially Brzezinski, *Power and Principle*; Carter, *White House Diary*; and Vance, *Hard Choices*.

Chapter 1

1. Walter Lippmann, "The American Destiny," *Life*, June 5, 1939, pp. 47, 72–73 ("What Rome was"); Henry Luce, "The American Century," *Life*, February 17, 1941, pp. 61–65 ("ideals of civilization"); and Charles Beard, *Giddy Minds*, 12, 87 ("Rome or Britain").

2. Roosevelt Fireside Chat, radio addresss, December 29, 1940, APP ("their liberty"). On FDR's strategic thought, see Dallek, *Franklin D. Roosevelt*; Gaddis, *Surprise, Security*, esp. pp. 35–58; and Reynolds, *Munich to Pearl Harbor*. On ideology and the Pacific War, see Iriye, *Power and Culture*.

3. Statistics are from Maddison, WEHS. For Truman, see "Radio Report to the American People," August 9, 1945, APP ("most powerful"). On US capabilities, see Kennedy, *Rise and Fall*, pp. 357–72; and White, *American Century*, pp. 47–64.

4. Luce, "American Century." ("What internationalism"). On the resurgence of internationalism, see Divine, *Second Chance*. May, *"Lessons" of the Past* stresses the influence of history on the remaking of international order. Others emphasize liberal ideological commitments, including Borgwardt, *New Deal*; Latham, *Liberal Moment*; and Ikenberry, *After Victory*. Others relate ideological commitments to US economic interests, as do McCormick, *America's Half-Century*; Kolko and Kolko, *Limits of Power*; Schurmann, *Logic of World Power*; and Williams, *Tragedy*.

5. Steel, *Pax Americana*. On the imperial dimensions of Washington's role, also see, inter alia, Aron, *Imperial Republic*; Ikenberry, "Rethinking the Origins of American Hegemony"; Lundestad, "Empire by Invitation"; and Maier, *Among Empires*, chaps. 4–5.

6. Keynes, *General Theory*; and Skidelsky, *Keynes*, vol. 2. On economic nationalism, see Frieden, *Global Capitalism*, chaps. 9–10; Pomfret, *Age of Equality*, esp. chap. 4; and, on Europe, Berman, *Primacy of Politics*; and Eichengreen, *European Economy*, chaps. 3–4.

7. Statistics are from Office of Management and the Budget, *Budget of the US Government*. Roosevelt, "State of the Union Address," January 11, 1944, APP ("dictatorships"). On the remaking of the US political economy, see Borgwardt, *New Deal*; Katznelson, *Fear Itself*; and Sparrow, *Warfare State*. I learned much on this topic from Barnett, "Anglo-American Social Liberalism."

8. For similar interpretations, see Eckes, *Search for Solvency*; Eichengreen, *Globalizing Capital*, esp. chap. 4; Freiden, *Global Capitalism*, esp. chap. 11; James, *Monetary Cooperation*, esp. chap. 2; and Ruggie, "International Regimes." For a view stressing US commitments to self-interest, not systemic stability, see Block, *International Economic Disorder*.

9. The gold standard was in practice more complex than the discussion here permits. For a much fuller account, see Gallarotti, *Monetary Regime*. For overviews, see Eichengreen and Flandreau, *Gold Standard*; and Bordo and Schwartz, *Classical Gold Standard*. On the late nineteenth-century economy more generally, see Frieden, *Global Capitalism*, chaps. 1–5.

10. Bryan, *Cross of Gold* ("crucify"); Keynes, *Monetary Reform*, p. 172 ("barbarous"); and Polanyi, *Great Transformation*. The argument here follows the gold standard's critics—above all Eichengreen, *Golden Fetters*; and Temin, *Great Depression*. For alternative views emphasizing failures of political leadership and monetary policy, see Kindleberger, *World in Depression*; and Friedman and Schwartz, *Monetary History*, chap. 7.

11. Gardner, *Sterling-Dollar Diplomacy*, and Steil, *Battle of Bretton Woods* both emphasize Anglo-American disagreements at Bretton Woods. Eckes, *Search for Solvency*; and Ruggie, "International Regimes," downplay the discord, emphasizing instead shared commitments to the containment of finance.

12. Truman, "Address on Foreign Economic Policy," March 6, 1947, APP ("giant"). On the Anglo-American hegemonic transition, see Arrighi, *Long Twentieth Century*, pp. 269–99; Keohane, *After Hegemony*, esp. pp. 33–46; Ikenberry, "Rethinking the Origins of American Hegemony;" and Kindleberger, *World in Depression*. For US expectations of Soviet participation in Bretton Woods, see Eckes, *Search for Solvency*, esp. pp. 103–5; and Gaddis, *Origins of the Cold War*, pp. 22–23.

13. Lippmann, *Cold War*.

14. Truman, "Navy Day Address," October 27, 1945, APP ("improvement").

15. On the USSR and Bretton Woods, see H. James and M. James, "Origins of the Cold War" ("non-participation"); and H. James, *Monetary Cooperation*, pp. 70–71. On Kennan, see Gaddis, *George F. Kennan*, pp. 215–22, and *Origins of the Cold War*, chap. 9.

16. Truman, "Special Message to the Congress on Greece and Turkey," March 12, 1947, APP ("free peoples"). The scholarship on Truman and the Cold War is vast, but Leffler, *Preponderance of Power*, remains definitive.

17. NATO Military Committee 48 (final), "The Most Effective Pattern of NATO Military Strength," November 22, 1954, NATO Archive ("defend Europe"). Also see Freedman, *Nuclear Strategy*; and Trachtenberg, *Constructed Peace*, esp. chap. 5. On nuclear weapons and world politics, see, inter alia, Herz, *Atomic Age*; Jervis, *Nuclear Revolution*; and Liddell-Hart, *Revolution in Warfare*.

18. Hogan, *Marshall Plan*, emphasizes the significance of US assistance, while Milward, *Reconstruction of Western Europe* stresses the indigenous sources of Europe's recovery.

19. On the European resistance to integration, see Milward, *Rescue of the Nation State*; and Moravcsik, *Choice for Europe*. On US assistance, see Ellwood, *Rebuilding Europe*; Lundestad,*"Empire" by Integration*; and Maier, "Politics of Productivity."

20. On the Korean War's consequences for Japan, see LaFeber, *The Clash*, esp. pp. 293–5; and Guthrie-Shimizu, "Japan." For the origins of the Cold War in Northeast Asia, see Iriye, *Cold War in Asia*; and Schaller, *American Occupation of Japan*. On the Korean War, see Cumings, *Origins of the Korean War*; and Stueck, *Rethinking the Korean War*, esp. chaps. 1–3.

21. On containment and its evolution, Gaddis, *Strategies*, remains definitive. On the NSC 68 memorandum, see May, *Interpreting NSC 68*. On South Korea, see Brazinsky, *Nation Building in South Korea*.

22. See Hogan, *Cross of Iron*; and, for a contrasting view, Freidberg, *Garrison State*. For a broader context, see Sherry, *Shadow of War*.

23. Eisenhower, "Farewell Address," January 17, 1961, APP ("undue").

24. Tilly, *Coercion, Capital*, makes war the dynamic of state formation; others emphasize the effects of modernization, as do Gellner, *Nations and Nationalism*; and Hobsbawm, *Nations and Nationalism*. Still others see the state as an ideological construction, i.e., Anderson, *Imagined Communities*; and Chatterjee, *Nationalist Thought*. Statistics are based on the Correlates of War Project and Maddison, WEHS.

25. *FRUS 1941: General, Soviet Union*, pp. 367–69 ("sovereign rights"; and *FRUS 1943: The Conferences*, pp. 717–20. On FDR's anticolonialism, see Pollock and Kimball, "Monsters to Destroy"; and Kimball, *Churchill and Roosevelt*, pp. 400–404. Also see Hoopes and Brinkley, *Creation of the U.N*, esp. chaps. 3–4; and Reynolds, *Anglo-American Alliance*, chap. 10.

26. Mazower, *No Enchanted Palace*. For decolonization, see Abernethy, *Global Dominance*, chaps. 14–15; Betts, *Decolonization*; Holland, *European Decolonization*; and Philpott, *Revolutions in Sovereignty*, chaps. 8–12.

27. Political scientist James Fearon counts 820 distinct ethnocultural groups. See "Ethnic Structure and Cultural Diversity."

28. FDR, "Annual Message to Congress," January 6, 1941, APP ("four essential"). On the wartime origins of human rights, see Burgers, "Road to San Francisco"; Humphrey, *Human Rights and the United Nations*, esp. pp. 10–13; Lauren, *Evolution of International Human Rights*, esp. chap. 5; Ishay, *History of Human Rights*, pp. 211–25; and Robertson, *Crimes against Humanity*, chap. 1. On the Universal Declaration, see Glendon, *World Made New*; Lauren, *Evolution of International Human Rights*, esp. chap. 7 ("Magna Carta"); and Morsink, *Universal Declaration* ("all members"). For Humphrey, see *Edge of Greatness*, vol. 1, p. 105 ("revolutionary") and "International Protection of Human Rights." ("supranational").

29. Holman's objections are in "International Bill of Rights" and "International Proposals" ("so-called"). Also see Kaufman, *Human Rights Treaties*, esp. pp. 16–36; and Evans, *US Hegemony*, esp. pp. 105–18. The UN Charter is at http://www.un.org/en/documents/charter/ ("Nothing"). The disappointment of human rights advocates evokes the uncertain predicament of human rights in the late 1940s. See Humphrey, *Human Rights and the United Nations*, pp. 74–75; and Lauterpacht, *International Law and Human Rights*. Some historians are more optimistic, as are Bradley, "Ambiguities of Sovereignty"; and Burke, *Decolonization and Human Rights*.

30. Generally, see Karabell, *Architects of Intervention*; and Westad, *Global Cold War*. On Vietnam, see Lawrence, *Assuming the Burden*; and Logevall, *Embers of War*.

31. See Amsden, *Escape from Empire*, esp. chaps. 1–3; Ekbladh, *Great American Mission*; Gilman, *Mandarins of the Future*; and Latham, *Right Kind of Revolution*.

32. JFK, "Commencement Address," June 10, 1963, APP ("real peace"). On the missile crisis, see Frankel, *High Noon*; Dobbs, *Minute to Midnight*; and Fursenko and Naftali, *One Hell of a Gamble*. On Kennedy's policy after Cuba, see Clarke, *JFK's Last Hundred Days*; and Sachs, *To Move the World*. Dallek, *Unfinished Life*, chap. 18, offers a more cautious assessment.

33. For Khrushchev's motives, see Haslam, *Russia's Cold War*, pp. 199–204; and Taubman, *Khrushchev*, esp. pp. 529–46. On Soviet policy after Cuba, see Zubok, *Failed Empire*, pp. 143–45; and Nelson, *Making of Détente*, pp. 45–53.

34. Ellsworth, "Notes on Anecdotes and Personalities," July 12, 1967, Richard M. Nixon Presidential Library, Wilderness Years Collection, Trip Files, box 11 ("Old Testament"). For MAD, see DeGroot, *The Bomb*, chap. 7; Freedman, *Nuclear Strategy*, pp. 245–56; and, stressing its varieties, Jervis, *Nuclear Revolution*, chap. 3.

35. Treaty on the Non-Proliferation of Nuclear Weapons, July 1, 1968, IAEA. http://www.iaea.org/Publications/Documents/Treaties/npt.html; and Gavin, "Nuclear Proliferation and Non-Proliferation."

36. CIA, "Prospects for the Nonproliferation Treaty," November 27, 1968, DDRS ("partnership"); *FRUS 1964–68*, vol. 11, no. 259; *FRUS 1964–1968*, vol. 13, no. 239 ("complicity"). For NATO's security dilemmas, see Haftendorn, *NATO and the Nuclear Revolution*; Kissinger, *Troubled Partnership*; and Steel, *End of Alliance*. For LBJ, see Costigliola, "Lyndon B. Johnson"; and Schwartz, *Lyndon Johnson and Europe*. Also see *FRUS 1964–1968*, vol. 17, no. 15 ("bridge-building").

37. On de Gaulle's bid to transcend the Cold War, see Bozo, *Two Strategies for Europe*; Lundestad, *United States and Western Europe*, chap. 4; Nuenlist et. al., *Globalizing de Gaulle*; Suri, *Power and Protest*, chap. 2; and Vaïsse, *La Grandeur*. For de Gaulle and China, see Martin, "Playing the China Card?"

38. Haftendorn, *Coming of Age*, chap. 5; and Niedhart, "Ostpolitik." On Ostpolitik's origins, Hoffman, *Emergence of Détente* emphasizes the Federal Republic of Germany's exasperation with Washington, while Sarotte, *Dealing with the Devil* stresses the German Democratic Republic's desire for independence from Moscow. On its accomplishments, Garton Ash, *In Europe's Name*, is critical, while Loth, *Overcoming the Cold War* is positive.

39. On British policy, see Dockrill, *Britain's Retreat*; and Reynolds, *Britannia Overruled*. For US perspectives, see Steel, *Pax Americana*, p. 120 ("leader and protector"); Kissinger, *American Foreign Policy*, pp. 65–78 ("political multipolarity").

40. On the Prague Spring, see Bischof et. al., *Prague Spring*; and Navrátil, *Prague Spring*, pp. 152–55) "new policy." For Soviet policy, Nelson, *Making of Détente*, pp. 63–68; and Ouimet, *Rise and Fall of the Brezhnev Doctrine*, pp. 66–72.

41. On the Sino-Soviet split, Luthi, *Sino-Soviet Split*, emphasizes ideological differences; Radchenko, *Two Suns in the Heavens*, material ones. For views on the Cold War's fading, see Seabury, *Rise and Decline of the Cold War*; Shulman, *Beyond the Cold War* ("tired wrestlers"); and Steel, *Pax Americana*.

42. UNCTAD, UNCTADStat and Maddison, WEHS.

43. See Block, *International Economic Disorder*, esp. chaps. 5–7; Eichengreen, *Globalizing Capital*, chap. 4; Frieden, *Global Capitalism*, chap. 12; Gavin, *Gold, Dollars, and Power*; James, *Monetary Cooperation*, chap. 6; and Solomon, *International Monetary System*, chaps. 2–3; and Strange, *International Monetary Relations*.

44. Triffin, *Gold and the Dollar Crisis*; and US Congress, Joint Economic Committee, hearing, *Current Economic Situation*, pp. 175–207.

45. For US policy, see Eichengreen, "Benign Neglect"; Gavin, *Gold, Dollars, and Power*; and Sargent, "Lyndon Johnson." For German policy, see Treverton, "*Dollar Drain.*" On the Franco-American controversy, see Hirsch and Rueff, "Role and Rule of Gold."

46. On foreign-exchange interventions, see Coombs, *Arena of International Finance*. On SDRs, see Wilkie, *Special Drawing Rights*.

47. Aronson, *Money and Power*, esp. pp. 71–78; Hawley, *Dollars and Borders*; Helleiner, *Global Finance*, chap. 4; and Webb, *Policy Coordination*, chaps. 3–4.

48. See Clendenning, *Eurodollar Market*; Helleiner, *Global Finance*, chap. 4; Kane, *Eurodollar Market*; and Strange, *Monetary Relations*, chap. 6. On London's role, see Burn, "State, the City and the Euromarkets." Statistics are from BIS, *Annual Report*.

49. Andrew Brimmer, "Eurodollars," *Euromoney* vol. 1, no. 7 (1969), 13-22 ("complicated"); and Strange, *Monetary Relations*, chap. 6.

50. Collins, "Economic Crisis of 1968"; and Gavin, *Gold, Dollars, and Power*, chap. 7. Also Fowler to LBJ, "Gold Problems," March 4, 1968, DDRS. On the influence of private capital, see Krause, "Private International Finance"; and Hawley, *Dollars and Borders*, pp. 117–20.

51. Cooper, *Economics of Interdependence*, esp. 59–147 ("horizons").

52. Cooper, *Economics of Interdependence* ("freedom"); and Vernon, "Economic Sovereignty at Bay" ("two systems").

53. CIA, "Restless Youth," September 1968; and DOS, "Dissident Youth," September 1968, both DDRS. For contemporary views, see Brzezinski, *Between Two Ages*, pp. 236–54; Rostow, *Diffusion of Power*, chap. 32; and Wills, *Nixon Agonistes*. For historical perspectives, see Isserman and Kazin, *American Divided*; and, especially, Suri, *Power and Protest*. On Reagan, see Hayward, *Age of Reagan*, vol. 1, esp. pp. 3–104. Borstelmann, *The 1970s* evokes the convergence of left and right around "a revitalized individualism."

54. Statistics on incomes are from Maddison, WEHS. Statistics on aid are from U.S. Agency for International Development, "Overseas Grants and Loans." On US policy in the Third World, see Rakove, *Kennedy, Johnson*; and Schmitz, *Right-Wing Dictatorships*, esp. pp. 36–71.

55. Benenson, "The Forgotten Prisoners," May 28, 1961, *Observer* (UK), p. 21 ("feelings of disgust"). On Amnesty, see Clark, *Diplomacy of Conscience*; Ennals, "Amnesty International"; Hopgood, *Keepers of the Flame*; Power, *Against Oblivion*, esp. 17–34, and *Water on Stone*. On human rights NGOs more broadly, see Korey, *NGOs*, p. 85 ("odious").

56. Iriye, *Global Community*, chap. 4 ("civil society"); and Brzezinski, *Between Two Ages*, pp. 19–22 ("moral immunity").

57. Prices are from "Hammarskjold, "High-Capacity Jets." Also see Eckes and Zeiler, *United States and Globalization*, chap. 7; Osterhammel and Petersson. *Globalization*, chap. 6. On Telstar, see Mickelson, "Communications by Satellite." For containerization, see Cudahy, *Box Boats*; and Levinson, *The Box*.

58. McLuhan, *Guttenberg Galaxy*. Pope John XXIII's "Pacem In Terris," April 11, 1963, is online at the Vatican website, http://www.vatican.va/ ("common good"). Also see Brown, *World Without Borders*; Boulding, "Coming Spaceship Earth"; and Fuller, *Operating Manual*.

59. Nixon, "America in the World City," September 12, 1967, HIA, Richard Allen Papers, box 22 ("one great city").

Chapter 2

1. Nixon, "Inaugural Address," January 1, 1969, APP ("far perspective"). Nixon quoted MacLeish; the poet's words were published in "A Reflection," *NYT*, December 25, 1968, p. 1. Also see Poole, *Earthrise*; and Zimmerman, *Genesis*, pp. 343–47.

2. Nixon, "Inaugural Address," January 1, 1969, APP ("moments of beginning"); "Overview of the World Situation," July 7, 1969, NPMP, NSC Files, SuF, Strategic Overview, box 397 ("transitional period"); Kissinger, Background Briefing, June 26, 1970, NPMP, WHCF, SuF, FO, box 2 ("watershed"); and Hoffman, "Policy for the 70s," *Life*, March 21, 1969 ("irrelevant concepts"). Nixon read and circulated Hoffman's essay. See Brown to Haldeman, April 16, 1969, NPMP, WHCF, FO, box 1.

3. Haldeman, *Haldeman Diaries*, pp. 73–74 ("drain"); "Modern World," September 29, 1969, NPMP, NSC Files, SuF, Strategic Overview, box 397 ("reluctant giant"); Acheson to Kissinger, December 22, 1960, YMA, Dean Acheson Papers, box 17 ("processes"); Nixon-Kissinger TeleCon, NPMP, KTC, box 7 ("sands"); and *FRUS 1969–1976*, vol. 1, no. 27 ("terror").

4. Nixon used the phrase "structure of peace" in his inaugural address and returned to it thereafter. See, for example, *FRUS 1969–1976*, vol. 1, nos. 10, 37, 73, 78, 104, 108, 123.

5. Nixon, "Remarks on Departure," August 9, 1974, APP ("common"); and "Memorandum for Haldeman," March 13, 1972, NPMP, PPF, Memoranda from the President, box 3 ("stamina"). The most insightful biographies include Ambrose, *Education of a Politician* and *Triumph of a Politician*; Greenberg, *Nixon's Shadow*; and Reeves, *President Nixon*. Also see Nixon, *Memoirs*.

6. For Nixon's war, see Ambrose, *Education of a Politician*, pp. 105–16. On Hiss, see Haynes and Klehr, *VENONA*; Haynes et. al., *Spies*, pp. 1–32; Jacoby, *Alger Hiss*; and Weinstein, *Perjury*. On Nixon's 1950 campaign, see Mitchell, *Tricky Dick* ("pink lady").

7. "Hiss Holds Nixon Was Opportunist," *NYT*, November 12, 1972, p. 1 ("obituary"); Nixon, *Six Crises*, chap. 6, and *Memoirs*, pp. 214–27, and 244–47 ("kick around").

8. Brandon, *Retreat of American Power*, p. 25 ("frozen"). The scholarship on Kissinger is substantial. Early efforts include Graubard, *Kissinger*; and Mazlish, *Kissinger*. The most up-to-date biographies are Isaacson, *Kissinger*; Hanhimäki, *Flawed Architect*; and Suri, *Henry Kissinger*. Kissinger's memoirs *White House Years*, *Years of Upheaval*, and *Years of Renewal* are essential.

9. White, *Making of the President, 1968*, p. 171 ("domestically"); and Wills, *Nixon Agonistes*, p. 422 ("makes foreign policy"). Also see Nixon to Haldeman et. al., March 2, 1970, NPMP, PPF, box 2; and Bundy, *Tangled Web*, esp. p. 209.

10. Morris, *Uncertain Greatness*, pp. 47, 77–90 ("existing exclusion"). For Kissinger's plan, see *FRUS 1969–1976*, vol. 2, nos. 1 ("current crises"), pp. 10–11; and US Senate, Committee on Government Operations, *The National Security Council*. For analyses, see Allison and Peter Szanton, *Remaking Foreign Policy*; Andrianopoulos, *Kissinger and Brzezinski*; and Rothkopf, *Running the World*, chap. 6.

11. On Kissinger's exclusion from Middle East policy, see Nixon to Rogers and Kissinger, February 22, 1969, and Nixon to Haldeman, March 2, 1970, both in NPMP, PPF, Memoranda from the President, boxes 1–2; and Haldeman, *Diaries*, p. 132. Also see Suri, *Henry Kissinger*, pp. 207–11. For the decline of the State Department, see "Decision Power Ebbing," *NYT*, January 18, 1971, p. 1 ("in charge"); and Kissinger to Nixon, "Symington Allegations," March 2, 1971, NPMP, NSC Files, Kissinger Office Files, Domestic Agency Files, box 148 ("fundamental premise").

12. "History of the U.S. Department of State," http://www.state.gov/. For the US-Soviet back channel, see *FRUS 1969–1976*, vol. 12, no. 13; Dobrynin, *In Confidence*, pp. 199–201;

Hanhimäki, *Flawed Architect*, pp. 34–35; and Kissinger, *White House Years*, pp. 138–44 ("Dobrynin and me"). Also see *FRUS 1969–1976*, vol. 2, nos. 19 (on Kissinger's receiving foreign ambassadors) and 68 ("back-channel games").

13. For assessments of secrecy's efficacy, see Bundy, *Tangled Web*, pp. 193–97; Garthoff, *Détente and Confrontation*, pp. 87–94; and Kurizaki, "Efficient Secrecy."

14. Kissinger, "Taking Stock after Eight Months," Fall 1969, NPMP, NSC Files, SuF, Strategic Overview, box 397 ("deterioration"); Nixon-Kissinger TeleCon, December 13, 1969 ("revolutionary") and October 12, 1970 ("Civil War"), both NPMP, KTC, ChronF, boxes 3, 7; *FRUS 1969–1976*, vol. 1, no. 43 ("destroy ourselves"); Memorandum for Kissinger, February 10, 1970, NPMP, PPF, Memoranda from the President, box 2 ("freedom and peace"); and Wills, *Nixon Agonistes*, p. 20 ("good things").

15. Wills, *Nixon Agonistes*, p. 20 ("greatest"); and Reeves, *President Nixon*, pp. 341–43 ("If we retreat," etc.) Kissinger presents Wilson and Nixon as antipodes in *Diplomacy*, pp. 704–5.

16. Kissinger, *White House Years*, pp. 228–29 ("tolerance"); for Kissinger on Metternich, see *World Restored*, and on Bismarck, "White Revolutionary"; Nixon-Kissinger TeleCon, December 3, 1970, NPMP, KTC, ChonF, box 8 ("second-rate").

17. Connelly, "Taking Off the Cold War Lens" and *Diplomatic Revolution*, esp. pp. 276–88. *FRUS 1969–1976*, vol. 1, no. 41 ("direct influence").

18. US casualty figures are available at http://www.archives.gov/research/vietnam-war/casualty-statistics.html. The number of Vietnamese war deaths remains a contested subject, but see Hirschman et. al., "Vietnamese Casualties."

19. *FRUS 1969–1976*, vol. 1, no. 42 ("real point"); Kissinger," Viet Nam Negotiations"; Kissinger, *White House Years*, p. 969 ("utterly convinced"); *FRUS 1969–1976*, vol. 6, no. 135 ("yield"); Nixon, "Address to the Nation," November 3, 1969, APP ("in the Middle East"); Nixon-Sato MemCon, January 31, 1973, GFPL, NSA Files, MemCon, box 1 ("undependable"); and *FRUS 1969–1986*, vol. 6, no. 137 ("at stake").

20. See Collins, "Economic Crisis of 1968"; and Opinion Research Corporation, "Public Opinion in Late 1967," GFPL, Robert Teeter Papers, Lukens' Working File, box 132.

21. See "Laird Voices Hope of More Cutbacks," *NYT*, June 10, 1969, p. 1; and *FRUS 1969–1976*, vol. 6, nos. 38 and 117 ("to end the war"). For troop numbers, see DOD, "Military Personnel Historical Reports."

22. *FRUS 1969–1976*, vol. 6, nos. 117 ("reasonably successful") and 120 ("Saigon political war"). The scholarship on the Vietnam War is vast. For overviews, see Herring, *America's Longest War*; Lawrence, *Vietnam War*; Schulzinger, *Time for War*; and Young, *Vietnam Wars*. On Nixon's Vietnam War, see Berman, *No Peace, No Honor*; and Kimball, *Nixon's Vietnam War*.

23. See Garthoff, *Détente and Confrontation*, pp. 77–78 and 279–94. For the diplomats' perspectives, see Dobrynin, *In Confidence*, pp. 239–50; and Kissinger, *White House Years*, p. 144. For the development of the linkage strategy, see Kissinger-Ellsworth TeleCon, January 22, 1969, and Dobrynin TeleCon, February 22, 19, 1969, both in NPMP, KTC, ChronF, box 1. Also, see Kissinger and Dobrynin MemCon, April 15, 1969; and Kissinger, Nixon, and Dobrynin MemCon, October 1969, both DNSA. For Nixon and Kissinger's efforts to enlist Chinese assistance, see *FRUS 1969–1976*, vol. 17, nos. 139–40, 196, and 199. Dobrynin attests to the USSR's limited capacity to influence Hanoi in *In Confidence*, p. 248. For Nixon and Kissinger's efforts to evade linkage, see *FRUS 1969–1976*, vol. 17, no. 60; Nixon-Kissinger TelecCon, January 14, 1970, NPMP, KTC, box 3 ("no bearing"); and Kimball, *Nixon's Vietnam War*, pp. 315–17. For analysis, see Nguyen, *Hanoi's War*, esp. pp. 194–95, 213–19, 223–27, and 231–56.

24. See Nixon-Kissinger TeleCon, October 20, 1969, NPMP, KTC, box 3 ("out of control"); and Haldeman, *Ends of Power*, pp. 82–83. Aslo see Burr and Kimball, "Nixon's Secret Nuclear Alert"; and Sagan and Suri, "Madman Nuclear Alert." On the consequences for Cambodia, Shawcross, *Sideshow*, is devastating.

25. See Taylor, *Nuremberg and Vietnam*; and "Human Rights in the Vietnam War," New York Public Library, International League for the Rights of Man, Accession C, Vietnam, box 48 ("systematic terror"). For Vance, see "Evolution of American Foreign Policy," November

1981, YMA, CVP, box 27 ("television"). For the media's self-censoring, see Hallin, *Uncensored War*. For Calley, see Belknap, *Vietnam War on Trial.*

26. Nixon, "Address to the Nation on the War in Vietnam," November 3, 1969, APP ("silent majority"); Nixon-Kissinger TeleCon, May 8, 1970 ("hate us"); Kissinger-Richardson TeleCon, May 18, 1970 ("our establishment"); and Kissinger-Shakespeare TeleCon, June 2, 1970 ("destroy the society"), NPMP, KTC, boxes 3 and 5. Finally, "Memorandum to Haldeman," May 15, 1972, NPMP, PPF, Memoranda from the President ("PR effort").

27. Historians diverge in their interpretations of Nixon's motives. Kimball, *Vietnam's War* argues that the pursuit of peace was a fig leaf covering Nixon's abandonment of South Vietnam, while Berman, *No Peace, No Honor*, argues that Nixon intended to defend South Vietnam after Paris. Asselin, *Bitter Peace*, and Nguyen, *Hanoi's War*, question whether durable peace was possible. John Negroponte is cited in Young, *Vietnam Wars*, p. 279 ("we bombed the North").

28. Nixon, "Informal Remarks in Guam," July 25, 1969, APP ("Asian nations"); Nixon, "Address to the Nation on the War," November 3, 1969, APP; and "Report to the Congress on U.S. Foreign Policy," February 18, 1970, APP ("treaty commitments" etc.) Also see Nixon, *Memoirs*, pp. 394–95; and Kissinger, *White House Years*, pp. 222–25. For analyses, see Kimball, "Nixon Doctrine"; Litwak, *Détente and the Nixon Doctrine*; and Ravenal, *Foreign Policy Change.*

29. "How Nixon Doctrine Works," *WP*, July 12, 1970, p. 51 ("retreat"). Nixon's views are expressed in "Memorandum for Kissinger," February 2, 1970, NPMP, PPF, Memoranda from the President, box 2 ("a device"); Nixon-Richardson-Joint Chiefs MemCon, February 15, 1973, GFPL, NSA Files, MemCon, box 1 ("maintain our forces"); and Haldeman, *Diaries*, p. 84. For TASS, see "Foreign Radio and Press Reaction," February 26, 1970, NPMP, NSC-IF, NSSM-80, box H-165.

30. For Nixon on isolationism, see *FRUS 1969–1976*, vol. 1, no. 2 ("new spirit"); Nixon-Kissinger TeleCon, January 15, 1972 ("out of the world"), NPMP, KTC, box 12; and *FRUS 1969–1976*, vol. 1, no. 27 ("new isolationists") and no. 41 ("widespread feeling"). For Nixon on NATO, see *FRUS 1969–1986*, vol. 1, no. 19; and on anti-Americanism, Nixon-Helms MemCon, Early February, 1973, GFPL, NSA Files, MemCons, box 1. Also see Laqueur, *Neo-Isolationism*; and Tucker, *New Isolationism.*

31. For Nixon as domestic progressive, see Greenberg, *Nixon's Shadow*, chap. 8; and Hoff, *Nixon Reconsidered*, esp. 115–144. On defense spending and the balance of payments, see Mayo to Nixon, August 8, 1969, NPMP, NSC Files, SuF, Balance of Payments, box 309; and Nixon to Haldeman, June 16, 1969, NPMP, PPF, Memoranda from the President, box 1.

32. *FRUS 1969–1976*, vol. 34, nos. 2 ("military posture"), 32, and 34; and "First Meeting of Political Subgroup," March 4, 1969, DNSA.

33. *FRUS 1969–1976*, vol. 34, nos. 45, 47, 49, 51, 56; "HAK Talking Points," September 10, 1969, DNSA; and Nixon, "Report to Congress on U.S. Foreign Policy," February 18, 1970, APP ("general purpose forces").

34. "HAK Talking Points," September 10, 1969, DNSA ("simultaneous defense"); *FRUS 1969–1976*, vol. 34, no. 45 ("Soviet-Chinese attack"); and Kissinger, *White House Years*, p. 215 ("the cuts").

35. *FRUS 1969–1976*, vol. 2, no. 110 ("light of its implications"); *FRUS 1969–1976*, vol. 34, no. 55.

36. *FRUS 1969–1976*, vol. 34, no. 56 ("five year").

37. Also see Kissinger-Ehrlichman TeleCon, January 14, 1970 ("nickeled and dimed," etc.); and Kissinger-Packard TeleCon, both NPMP, KTC, box 3. For Nixon's decision, see "FY 1971–1976 Interim Guidance on U.S. Deployments," October 27, 1970, NPMP, NSC-IF, Meeting Files, Defense Program Review Committee, box H-98 ("no withdrawal"). Bergsten is in "Memorandum for Dr. Kissinger," December 3, 1970, NPMP, NSC Files, SuF, Balance of Payments, box 309 ("signal"). For Nixon, see Memorandum, March 10, 1973, NPMP, PPF, box 4 ("success or failure").

38. On aid, see Office of Management and the Budget, *Budget of the U.S. Government*. "The Organization of Security Assistance" (U/SM 78), October 28, 1970, NPMP, NSC-IF, Committee Memorandums, box H-255 ("self-sufficiency"). For adjustments to the

budgetary process see "NSSM 8," October 8, 1969; and "NSDM-112," June 10, 1971, NPMP, NSC Files, SuF, boxes 364–65. For Nixon's reforms, see "Message to Congress," September 15, 1970, APP. Also see "NSC Issues Paper: Related to Recommendations of the Peterson Task Force" (U/SM 59), March 26, 1970, NPMP, NSC-IF, Committee Memorandums, box H-254. Also see "Report on the Progress of the Overseas Private Investment Corporation," March 27, 1971, NPMP, NSC Files, SuF, OPIC, box 368. For the scuffle over the FY 1972 budget, see *FRUS 1969–1976*, vol. 4, nos. 87, 89, 91.

39. On Mansfield, see Oberdorfer, *Senator Mansfield*, pp. 387–91; and Valeo, *Mike Mansfield*, p. 274. For the administration's view, see "Talking Points for 9 a.m. Meeting," May 11, 1971 ("unacceptable"); "How the Mansfield Amendment Imperils the National Security," May 13, 1971 ("dismay," etc.), both in NPMP, NSC Files, Names File, Mansfield Amendment, box 824. For Kissinger's perspective, see *White House Years*, pp. 938–49. On public support for NATO, see "The AFL-CIO and World Affairs," Washington DC: 1971; and "Keeping U.S. Troops in Europe," March 1971, both in NPMP, NSC Files, Names File, Mansfield Amendment, box 824. For financial globalization and Mansfield's campaign, see "Eurodollar Crisis and U.S. Forces," May 12, 1971, NPMP, NSC Files, Names File, Mansfield Amendment, box 824.

40. For the administration's response, see "Legislative Interdepartmental Group Meeting," May 12, 1971; "Your Meeting with National Leaders," May 13, 1971; "Talking Points for Noon Meeting," May 14, 1971, all in NPMP, NSC Files, Names File, Mansfield Amendment, box 824. For Acheson's role, see "The Acheson Exercise," May 14, 1971; and "Memorandum for the Record," May 24, 1971 ("never disagreed on NATO"), both in NPMP, NSC Files, Names File, Mansfield Amendment, box 824; and Nixon to Acheson, May 20, 1971; and Acheson to Nixon, May 24, 1971 ("second battle"), both in YMA, Dean Acheson Papers, box 23.

41. Sakharov, *Progress, Coexistence,* and *Memoirs,* pp. 281–94 ("foolish"). Also see Holloway, *Stalin and the Bomb,* pp. 312–19. For the US reception, see, for example, "Outspoken Soviet Scientist," *NYT,* July 22, 1968, p. 16; and "A Russian Physicist's Passionate Plea," *Time,* August 2, 1968. For the debate on convergence, see Galbraith, *New Industrial State;* Levy, *Modernization and the Structure of Societies;* and Weinberg, "Problem of Convergence." For Soviet perspectives, see Kelley, "The Soviet Debate on the Convergence."

42. Kissinger, *American Foreign Policy,* esp. pp. 88–89.

43. Statistics are from National Resources Defense Council, Archive of Nuclear Data. For analyses, see Garthoff, *Détente and Confrontation,* pp. 19–26; CIA, "U.S.-USSR Offensive Strategic Force Balance," November 1976, JCPL, DC, NLC-7-29-5-5-3; and Kissinger, *White House Years,* chap. 7. On Soviet naval power, see CIA, "Trends and Prospects in Soviet Maritime Activities," NIE 11-10-69, at CIA, FOIA Reading Room. For perspectives, see Buchanan to Nixon with attachment "The Soviet Union Moves Ahead," September 8, 1970, NPMP, POF, PHF, box 7; Nixon, "Report to the Congress on U.S. Foreign Policy," February 25, 1971, APP; "Our Superpower Era Wanes," *NYT,* June 6, 1971, p. E15; Laqueur, "The World of the 1970s," November 18, 1972, in NPMP, WHCF, FO, box 4; *FRUS 1969–1976,* vol. 1, no. 20; and *FRUS 1969–1976,* vol. 12, no. 211. For McCloy, see McCloy to Nixon, December 1, 1970, NPMP, NSC Files, SuF, Names File, box 812. For the Zumwalt-Kissinger controversy, see Zumwalt, *On Watch,* p. 319; "Zumwalt," *NYT,* March 13, 1976, p. 6; and "I Never Said That!" *NYT,* April 5, 1976, p. 31.

44. Kissinger, *American Foreign Policy,* pp. 59–90 ("bipolar militarily").

45. For Nixon's views of the USSR, see Nixon-Tasca MemCon, March 28, 1974 ("subvert"), GFPL, NSA Files, MemCons, boxes 3. Also see Bull to Kehrli, September 11, 1972, NPMP, POF, PHF, box 18. Kissinger is in "Comments on Sulzberger's Thesis," October 27, 1970, NPMP, WHSF, ConF, FO box 29 ("fundamental weakness").

46. Nixon-Schlesinger MemCon, June 6, 1974, GFPL, NSA Files, MemCon, boxes 4 ("our interests").

47. *FRUS 1969–1976,* vol. 12, nos. 6, 10, and 18 ("limited adversary"). For SALT, see Garthoff, *Détente and Confrontation,* pp. 146–223.

48. See Garthoff, *Détente and Confrontation,* pp. 211–13 ("to match"), and 325–59. For the administration's assessment, see "Report to the Congress on U.S. Foreign Policy," May 3, 1973, APP ("momentum" and "advantageous").

49. See "Basic Principles of Relations," May 29, 1972, APP ("sovereignty"); and "Report to the Congress on U.S. Foreign Policy," May 3, 1973, APP ("mutual respect"). On Soviet obejctives, see Garthoff, *Détente and Confrontation*, pp. 326–38; and Zubok, *Failed Empire*, chap. 7.

50. *FRUS 1969–1976*, vol. 1, no. 10 ("benefits"). For linkage, see Kissinger, *White House Years*, pp. 129–30.

51. Kissinger, *White House Years*, p. 746 ("inherent"); and Nixon, "Asia After Viet Nam," ("outside"). *FRUS 1969–1976*, vol. 1, no. 21 ("live forever"). On tensions between State and the White House, see Nixon-Kissinger TeleCon, January 19, 1970, NPMP, KTC, box 3. Tellingly, the NSC's first wholesale review of U.S.-China relations began with "Sino-Soviet difficulties." See *FRUS 1969–1976*, vol. 17, no. 40. For Nixon and Kissinger, see Nixon-Kissinger TeleCon, January 19, 1970, NPMP, KTC, box 3 ("two enemies"); and *FRUS 1969–1976*, vol. 1, no. 24 ("antagonistic partners").

52. Kissinger, "My Talks with Chou Enlai," July 18, 1971, DNSA ("deeply worried"); for follow-up visits, see *FRUS 1969–1976*, vol. 17, nos. 164 ("Russian manners") and 222. Also see Kissinger, *White House Years*, pp. 763–70. Also see Kissinger, *On China*, chap. 8; Macmillan, *Nixon and Mao*; and Tudda, *Cold War Turning Point*.

53. "Report to the Congress on U.S. Foreign Policy," February 18, 1970, APP ("concrete" and "authentic"); "Report to the Congress on U.S. Foreign Policy," February 25, 1971, APP ("incentives").

54. Ehlichman to Shultz and Kissinger, January 16, 1971, NPMP, NSC Files, Names File, Ehrlichman, box 813 ("fetish"); and Kissinger, "East-West Trade," December 22, 1970, NPMP, NSC Files, SuF, Trade, box 401 ("nonsense"). For early advocacy of liberalization see, for example, Stans to Nixon, November 17, 1970, NPMP, NSC Files, SuF, Trade, box 401. In 1971, the Nixon administration lent tacit support to Senator Mondale's efforts to eliminate the Fino Amendment, which would permit the Export-Import Bank to finance East-West trade. See Bergsten to Kissinger, February 1, 1971; and Kissinger to MacGregor, July 27, 1971, both NPMP, NSC Files, SuF, Export-Import Bank, box 323.

55. In July 1972, the president delegated to the Secretary of Commerce authority to negotiate a U.S.-Soviet trade agreement, and, in September, Nixon decided to conclude trade negotiations "at the earliest feasible date." See NSDM 181, "Commercial Commission Negotiations," July 20, 1972, and NSDM 191, "Commercial and Related Negotiations," September 20, 1972, both in NPMP, NSC Files, SuF, NSDM, box 364. Brezhnev is in *FRUS 1969–1976*, vol. 14, no. 259 ("vast territory"). For the Shultz mission, see Kissinger-Shultz TeleCon, March 2, 1973, NPMP, NSC Files, TeleCon, box 19; and "Shultz in Soviet Union For Trade Talks," *NYT*, March 12, 1973, p. 9.

56. Brzezinski to Hertzberg, November 7, 1973, JCPL, ZBM, Trilateral Commission File, box 1.

57. For the Doomsday Clock, see http://www.thebulletin.org/minutes-to- midnight/. For Nixon, see Minutes of Cabinet Meeting, February 21, 1974, GFPL, NSA Files, MemCons, box 3 ("avert"); and Kissinger, *White House Years*, p. 764 ("thermonuclear"). On this point, to which chapter 8 returns, see Kuklick, *Blind Oracles*, pp.182–96. For Kissinger's assessment of domestic politics see *Diplomacy*, p. 703 ("civil war"). *FRUS 1969–1976*, vol. 8, no. 131 ("entirely Communist").

58. See Littwack, *Détente and the Nixon Doctrine*, p. 83; and "Report to the Congress on U.S. Foreign Policy," February 9, 1972, APP ("new dimension").

59. "Recollections of My Visit to the Lincoln Memorial," May 13, 1970, NPMP, WHSF, Memoranda from the President, box 2 ("25 years"); and Richardson, "A Cause Bigger," NPMP, NSC Files, SuF, President's Annual Review, box 325 ("missing").

Chapter 3

1. On democracy's recession, see Huntington, *Third Wave*, pp. 19–21. On authoritarian development, see Finer, *Man on Horseback*; and O'Donnell, *Modernization and Bureaucratic Authoritarianism*.

2. On US involvement in the Third World, Westad, *Global Cold War*, is vital, while the essays in McMahon, ed., *Cold War in the Third World* survey the field. On Guatemala, Gleijies, *Shattered Hope*; LaFeber, *Inevitable Revolutions*; and Schlesinger and Kinzer, *Bitter Fruit*, all

emphasize United Fruit's influence. Immerman, *CIA in Guatemala* stresses anti-Communist commitments. On South Korea, see Brazinsky, *Nation Building in South Korea*; and on South Vietnam, Jacobs, *America's Mircale Man*; and Miller, *Misalliance*. On Brazil's coup, see Leacock, *Requiem for Revolution*; and Black, *Penetration of Brazil*. On Indonesia, see Simpson, *Economists with Guns*.

3. Nixon-Moynihan TeleCon, October 7, 1971, NPMP, White House Tapes, Conv. No. 10-116, Cassettes 1049-50 ("not any good"); and Nixon-Scali MemCon, February 13, 1973, GFPL, NSA, MemCons, box 1 ("our concern").

4. Keylor, *Twentieth Century World*, a standard history, mentions South Asia in passing and omits Biafra entirely; Reynolds, *One World Divisible*,is atypical in its attentiveness to both episodes.

5. For the death toll, see Falola and Heaton, *History of Nigeria*, 178. On Biafra and the history of humanitarianism, see Barnett, *Empire of Humanity*, esp. pp. 134–45; Rieff, *Bed for the Night*; and Smith, *Genocide and the Europeans*, pp. 65–104. For Kouchner, see Allen and Styan, "Right to Interfere"; Kouchner and Bettati, *Le devoir de l'ingérence*; and Redfield, *Life in Crisis*, esp. pp. 53–57. Historians of US foreign relations have had less to say: neither Dallek's *Partners in Power* nor Hanhimäki's *Flawed Architect* even mentions Biafra. On Biafra in the international arena, Cronjé, *World and Nigeria*, and Jacobs, *Brutality of Nations*, critique international indifference. Stremlau, *International Politics* is more balanced. Thompson, *American Policy and African Famine* addresses US relief policy. On the civil war, see de St. Jorre, *Nigerian Civil War*; Gould, *Biafran War*; and the historical documents collected in Kirk-Greene, *Crisis and Conflict in Nigeria*.

6. *FRUS 1964–1968*, vol. 24, nos. 395 and 396.

7. "Agony in Biafra," *Time*, August 2, 1968 ("sad"). For the Red Cross's predicament, see Barnett, *Empire of Humanity*, pp. 135–38; and Forsythe, *Humanitarian Politics*, pp. 181–93.

8. For Catholic groups, see Stremlau, *International Politics*, pp. 118–20; and Wiseberg, "Christian Churches." The Vatican's statement is in Kirk-Greene, *Crisis and Conflict in Nigeria*, vol. 2, pp. 201–2. For the *Life* cover story, see "Biafra: A War of Extinction and Starvation," *Life*, July 12, 1968, pp. 20–29. On television, see Jacobs, *Brutality of Nations*, p. 74. The debates in the British Parliament are in *Hansard*, HC Debates, vol. 768, columns 39–44 and columns 1665–68, and vol. 769 columns 50–110. For Wilson, see *Labour Government*, p. 557 ("moral control"). On French opinion, see Stremlau, *International Politics*, p. 227.

9. Byrne, *Airlift to Biafra*; and Lloyd et. al., *Nordchurchaid Airlift* ("Jesus Christ Airlines," preface). For Joint Church Aid, see Press Release, October 17, 1969, SCPC, NBCHP, box 2. The analogy to Berlin is in Stremlau, *International Politics*, pp. 238–52 ("ward").

10. Connett to Frankfurt, September 13, 1968, SCPC, NBCHP, box 10 ("our opinion"). For the Clearing House, see Brad Lynch to Staff, December 18, 1968, SCPC, NBCHP, box 1; and Phillips to Congressmen, May 23, 1969, SCPC, NBCHP, box 6. For transnational advocacy networks, see Keck and Sikkink, *Activists Beyond Borders*, esp. 16–21.

11. See, generally, Davis, *Interpreters for Nigeria*. For Biafran PR, see "Catalogue of Actions," SCPC, NBCHP, box 7; and Cronjé, *World and Nigeria*, 210–24. Gowon is cited in Mok, *Biafra Journal*, p. 62 ("monster"). For reactions, see *FRUS 1969–1976*, vol. E-5, Part 1, no. 25 ("brilliant"); and "One Nigeria," the *Economist*, September 14, 1969, pp. 20–21 ("dunce"). For Nigerian propaganda, see "Understanding the Nigerian Crisis," the *Economist*, July 7, 1968, pp. 82–88. For perspectives on Nigeria's campaign, see "Nigerians Buy an Ad," *NYT*, July 6, 1968, p. 3; "Hunger as a Political Weapon," *NYT*, July 7, 1968, p. E3; and *FRUS 1969–1976*, vol. E-5, Part 1, no. 25. The Biafran turn to the global realm was not an original move. For similar tactics, see Connelly, *Diplomatic Revolution*, on the Algerian National Liberation Front; and Chamberlin, *Global Offensive*, on the Palestinian Liberation Organization.

12. UN Genocide Convention, December 9, 1948, at http://www.un.org/millennium/law/iv-1.htm ("intent"). For Biafran allegations, see Kirk-Greene, *Crisis and Conflict in Nigeria*, pp. 153–55, 192–99, and 247–72 ("palpable"); and "Pogrom," in SCPC, NBCHP, box 7.

13. For Tanzania, see *Crisis and Conflict in Nigeria*, pp. 206–11 ("Jews"). The Hitler advertisement is in SCPC, NBCHP, box 9. For the American Committee to Keep Biafra Alive, see Connett to Frankfurt, September 13, 1968, SCPC, NBCHP, box 10 ("tribesman").

14. For LBJ's policy, see FRUS 1964–1968, vol. 24, no. 398 ("constantly"); and Morris, *Uncertain Greatness*, p. 42 ("babies"). Also see U.S. Agency for International Development, Emergency Report, January 15, 1969, SCPC, NBCHP, box 5. For UN policy, see "Statement by the Secretary-General," September 13, 1968, SCPC, NBCHP, box 8. On nonintervention, see Gurtov, *Against the Third World*; Vincent, *Nonintervention and International Order*; and, on the OAU, Wallerstein, *Politics of Unity*.

15. For de Gaulle, see "Press Conference Held by General de Gaulle," September 9, 1968, SCPC, NBCHP, box 9 ("practical"); *FRUS 1969–1976*, vol. E-5, Part 1, no. 48; and Cronjé, *World and Nigeria*, pp. 197–204. For Tanzania's view, see "Case for the Recognition of Biafra," April 13, 1968, SCPC, NBCHP, box 7 ("inherited"); and for the confederation concept, see "The Philosophy of the Biafran Revolution," January 9, 1969, SCPC, NBHC, box 7.

16. For US views of Nigerian attitudes, see Matthews to Rusk, December 27, 1968, NPMP, NSC Files, CouF, Africa, box 741; and *FRUS 1969–1976*, vol. E-5, Part 1, no. 27 ("aid and comfort"). For LBJ's policy, see FRUS 1964–1968, vol. 24, nos. 401 and 402 ("Globemasters"); and *FRUS 1969–1976*, vol. E-5, Part 1, no. 25 ("outraged").

17. For Nixon, see Campaign Statement, September 10, 1968, NPMP, WHCF, HU-4, box 38 ("doomed"); Dick Allen re. Biafra, August 30, 1968, HIA, Richard Allen Papers, box 24; and Thompson, *American Policy*, p. 83. Historians disagree as to why Nixon dashed the hopes that the pro-Biafra community invested in him. Obiozor, *An American Dilemma* points to British pressure, while Cronjé, *World and Nigeria* and Jacobs, *The Brutality of Nations* speculate that Nixon sought access to Nigerian oil. On the State Department's and the sovereignty norm, see Cronjé, *World and Nigeria*, esp. pp. 197–204; Morris, *Uncertain Greatness*; and *FRUS 1969–1976*, vol. E-5, Part 1, no. 48 ("now exist"). For public opinion, see Gallup Poll #779, Gallup Brain.

18. *FRUS 1969–1976*, vol. E-5, Part 1, no. 27; and "Red Cross Grounds Its Biafran Airlift," January 9, 1969, *NYT*, p. 11. For pro-Biafran appeals, see "President Nixon," January 21, 1969, *NYT*, pp. 33; and "Biafran Problem." January 27, 1969, *NYT*, p. 10. For Congress, see US Congress, House, *Report of Special Fact Finding Mission to Nigeria*; and NSCIG/AF-69-1, Appendix, NPMP, NSC-IF, Study Memorandums, box H-133. Nixon is in "52 Senators Ask U.S. Aid," February 23, 1969, NPMP, NSC Files, CouF, Africa, box 741 ("more action"). For Fulton Lewis, the conservative radio host, see SCPC, NBCHP, box 9. For the American Jewish Commitee, see Newsletter, vol. 4, no. 4, August-October 1968 in SCPC, NBCHP, box 2 ("first time"). Nixon's special assistant for civil rights is in NPMP, NSC Files, CouF, Africa, box 741 ("strictly international").

19. Staff Secretary to Kissinger, January 23, 1969, Nixon Materials, NSC-IF, Study Memorandums, H-133 ("program"); and *FRUS 1969–1976*, vol. E-5, Part 1, nos. 25–26, 41–42, 44, and 46 ("two track" etc.).

20. For developments in the spring, see Situation Report, March 13, 1969, March 27, and June 6, 1969, all in NPMP, NSC Files, CouF, Africa, box 741; and *FRUS 1969–1976*, vol. E-5, Part 1, nos. 69, 70 ("illegal"), 71, 73 ("Nigeria's sovereignty"). For Nixon, *FRUS 1969–1976*, vol. E-5, Part 1, no. 65 ("I hope").

21. *FRUS 1969–1976*, vol. E-5, Part 1, no. 60 ("chorus"); and "CBS Show on Nigeria/Biafra," Undated, SCPC, NBCHP, box 10. Fifteen gubernatorial proclamations, including the ones cited here, can be found in SCPC, NBCHP, box 6 ("genocide" etc.)

22. *FRUS 1969–1976*, vol. E-5, Part 1, nos. 86 ("only man," etc.) and 90. Also see Morris to Nixon, July 17, 1969, NPMP, NSC Files, CouF, Africa, box 741. On French policy, see Butterfield to Kissinger, July 21, 1969, NPMP, NSC Files, CouF, Africa, box 741. For US peace efforts, see *FRUS 1969–1976*, vol. E-5, Part 1, nos. 101, 102 ("serious efforts"), 105, 107, 110, 112, 115, 118, 122, 125, and 132; and Nixon to Kissinger, September 22, 1969, NPMP, WHCF, CO 113-1, box 56. On DOS-NSC tensions, see *FRUS 1969–1976*, vol, E-5, Part I, nos. 111 ("guerrilla war"), 126, 130, 133, 137, and 140; Watts to Eliot, September 9, 1969; and Morris to Kissinger, September 30, 1969, both in NPMP, NSC Files, CouF, Africa, box 741.

23. *FRUS 1969–1976*, vol. E-5, Part 1, nos. 138, 143 ("disengagement"); Jacobs, *Brutality of Nations*, p. 238 ("averaging"); and Adler, "Letter from Biafra," the *New Yorker*, October 4, 1969, pp. 47–113 ("die in isolation"). For Ferguson's survey, see, US Congress, Senate, Committee on the Judiciary, *Relief Problems in Nigeria-Biafra: Part II*; and *FRUS 1969–1976*, vol. E-5, Part 1, nos. 170 and 174.

24. On the war's end, see Kirk-Greene, *Crisis and Conflict in Nigeria*, pp. 449–50, 457–61 ("sustained the rebellion"); "Nigeria Says Troops Have Cut Biafra into 3 Parts," January 3, 1970, *NYT*, p. 2; and "Ojukwu Leaves Enclave," January 11, 1970, *NYT*, p. 1. For Roger Morris's fears of genocide, see *FRUS 1969–1976*, vol. E-5, Part 1, no. 153.

25. Brown to Kissinger, January 16, 1970, NPMP, WHCF, CO 113-1, box 56 ("further tragedy"). For US policy on famine relief after the Federal Military Governments victory, see *FRUS 1969–1976*, vol. E-5, Part 1, nos. 157–158, 161–64, 16–17, 178–79, 181, 189, and 195–96; Kissinger to Nixon, "Your Meeting," January 20, 1970 ("political push"); and Laird to Kissinger, "Nigerian Relief," January 24, 1970, both in NPMP, NSC-IF, Study Memorandums, NSSM 11, box H-133.

26. Byrne, *Airlift to Biafra*, 127 ("Nigerians are the Nazis"); and Ojukwu, *Biafra*, pp. 339. On this point, consider the measured views in Destexhe, *Rwanda and Genocide*, esp. pp. 16–17.

27. Falola and Heaton, *History of Nigeria*, p. 178. For evaluations of aid deliveries, see "Nigerian Relief," February 18, 1970, NPMP, NSC-IF, Study Memorandums, NSSM 11, box H-133; and Davis, "Audits of International Relief." For Nigerian responses to US policies, see *FRUS 1969–1976*, vol. E-5, Part 1, nos. 87, 128 ("all but an enemy," etc.), 194 ("secessionists") and 206 ("suspicions").

28. Barnett, *Empire of Humanity*, p, 133 ("international response"). On Burundi, see Lemarchand, "Burundi Genocide."

29. Kissinger, *White House Years*, p. 417 ("humane side").

30. *FRUS 1969–1976*, vol. 11, no. 30 ("like Biafra"). For comparative perspectives on India and Pakistan, see Jalal, *Democracy and Authoritarianism*; and on the political influence of Pakistan's military, see Jalal, *State of Martial Rule*. On Pakistan's creation, Shaikh, *Community and Consensus*, stresses the socio-religious roots, while Jalal, *Sole Spokesman* emphasizes the historical contingencies. On relations between Pakistan's wings, see Sisson and Rose, *War and Secession*, pp. 8–9; and Jackson, *South Asian Crisis*, p. 21. On the South Asian crisis of 1971, Jackson, *South Asian Crisis* has long been standard, but Raghavan, *1971* offers expanded perspective, emphasizing the contingency of outcomes. On US policy, Bass, *Blood Telegram* offers a sharp critique, at odds with the sympathetic Sisson and Rose, *War and Secession*, but expanding upon Van Hollen, "Tilt Policy Revisited."

31. See *FRUS 1969–1976*, vol. 11, no. 2 (Mujib's Six Points); and *FRUS 1969–1976*, vol. E-7, nos. 101 and 104.

32. See *FRUS 1969–1976*, vol. 11, nos. 2, 6 ("blood bath"), and 9; *FRUS 1969–1976*, vol. E-7, no. 118; and "In Pakistan, Some Flee to the East," March 18, 1971, *NYT*, p. 2.

33. For Washington's perspective, see *FRUS 1969–1976*, vol. 11, no. 10 and 13 ("full horror"); and *FRUS 1969–1976*, vol. E-7, nos. 125–27. For press accounts, see "Pakistan Asserts Control," March 26, 1971, *NYT*, p. 1; "Army Expels 35 Foreign Newsmen," March 28, 1971, *NYT*, p. 3; "Tanks Crush Revolt in Pakistan," March 30, 1971, the *Telegraph*, p. 1 ("students dead"); and "Political Tidal Wave," May 2, 1971, *NYT*, p. SM24 ("bloodiest slaughters").

34. For the China connection, see *FRUS 1969–1976*, vol. E-7, nos. 31 and 90; and Kissinger, *White House Years*, p. 854. For Nixon's prejudices see, for example, Kissinger, *White House Years*, p. 849 ("bluff"); and *FRUS 1969–1976*, vol. 11, nos. 23 ("special feeling") and 121. For US Cold War policy in South Asia, see, inter alia, Kux, *United States and Pakistan*; and McMahon, *Cold War on the Periphery*.

35. For early arms transfer policy, see *FRUS 1969–1976*, vol. E-7, nos. 31, 42, and 62–64. Haldeman is in *FRUS 1969–1976*, vol. E-7, no. 10 ("humanitarian"). For criticism of the kind that Haldeman feared, see "Pakistan's Problem," November 26, 1970, *NYT*, p. 30; and "Passing By on the Other Side," *WP*, November 27, 1970, p. A26.

36. *FRUS 1969–1976*, vol. 11, nos. 10 ("our relationship"), 11, 14 ("wish him well"), and 15 ("don't like it").

37. *FRUS 1969–1976*, vol. 11, no. 19 ("Our government"). The State Department refused to share the telegram with Congress. See US Congress, Committee on Foreign Relations, *Suspension of Military Assistance to Pakistan*, p. 12. For fears of leaks, see *FRUS 1969–1976*, vol. 11, no. 20.

38. *FRUS 1969–1976*, vol. 11, no. 19 ("genocide"). For Mascerenhas, see "Genocide," June 13, 1971, *Sunday Times*, p. 1; and Mascerenhas, *Rape of Bangla Desh*.

39. "Genocide," *Sunday Times*, June 13, 1971 ("their sabotage"); and "Report of the World Bank Mission," in US Congress, Senate, Committee on the Judiciary, *Relief Problems in East Pakistan, Part I*, pp. 211–26 ("food problem," etc.). For NGO testimony, see US Congress, Senate, Committee on the Judiciary, *Relief Problems in East Pakistan, Part II*, esp. pp. 242–51 and 360–361. On Harrison and the Concert for Bangladesh, see Raghavan, *1971*, pp. 142–45.

40. For US policy, see *FRUS 1969–1976*, vol. E-7, no. 132 ("dead"); and *FRUS 1969–1976*, vol. 11, nos. 27, 32, 33, 35, 36 ("death-dealing" and "squeeze"), and 42 ("missionaries").

41. For the refugee flows, see "Refugees Worry Indian Officials," April 25, 1971, *NYT*, p. 10; and "Many Accept India Count of 9.4 Million," October 25, 1971, *NYT*, p. 3.

42. For Indian policy, see Gandhi, *India and Bangla Desh*, pp. 13–14 ("genocide"), and 20–23 ("internal problem") and *FRUS 1969–1976*, vol. 11, no. 46 ("millions of people"). US officials acknowledged the strain that the refugee influx imposed on India. See, for example, *FRUS 1969–1976*, vol. 11, nos. 57, 144, 162, and 248. Also see "Three Million Links in a Chain of Misery," May 23, 1971, *NYT*, p. E3, ("massive diplomatic").

43. *FRUS 1969–1976*, vol. 11, no. 56 ("constant intervention"). Also see the documents that Islamabad produced to support its case, in *Pakistan Horizon*, vol. 24, no. 2. For international responses, see Jackson, *South Asian Crisis*, pp. 38–39 ("national unity"). On the Red Cross, see *FRUS 1969–1976*, vol. 11, no. 35. For Indian assistance to the Bangla Desh movement, see Sisson and Rose, *War and Secession*, chap. 9. For Nixon, see *FRUS 1969–1976*, vol. 11, nos. 41 ("internationalization") and 121 ("Jefferson Davis").

44. For the media backlash, see, for example, "U.S. Acknowledges Sales of Ammunition," *NYT*, April 14, 1971, p. 13; "Senate Unit Asks Pakistan Arms Cutoff," *NYT*, May 7, 1971, p. 15; "U.S. Military Goods Sent to Pakistan," *NYT*, June 22 1971, p. 1; "Why Aid Pakistan," *NYT*, June 30, 1971, p. 40 ("policies of repression"); and "Abetting Repression," *NYT*, June 23, 1971, p. 44. For the debate between State and the White House, see *FRUS 1969–1976*, vol. 11, nos. 78, 111 ("our business"), 112, 131, 138, and 144. Also see Kissinger, *White House Years*, pp. 864–66; and Van Hollen, "Tilt Policy Revisited." ("to a person").

45. See, in particular, US Congress, Senate, Committee on the Judiciary, *Relief Problems in East Pakistan and India, Part I* ("moral sensibilities" and "shipment"); *Relief Problems in East Pakistan and India, Part II*; and *Relief Problems in East Pakistan and India, Part III*. For Kennedy's trip to West Bengal, see US Congress, *Crisis in South Asia*. Also see US Congress, Senate, Committee on Foreign Relations, report, *Suspension of Military Assistance to Pakistan*; and for White House reactions, see FRUS *1969–1976*, vol. 11, nos. 44 ("our ability"), 48, 78, 104, and 173.

46. *FRUS 1969–1976*, vol. 11, nos. 121 ("raising hell") and 124 ("never yielded"); and NSC Meeting Minutes, July 16, 1971, NPMP, NSC-IF, NSC Meeting Minutes, box H-110 ("world opinion"). Van Hollen, "Tilt Policy Revisited" offers a critical take on the White House efforts to separate the political and humanitarian issues. Also see Kissinger, *White House Years*, 875.

47. For the 1971 war, see Jackson, *South Asian Crisis*; Raghavan, *1971*, pp. 205–63; and Sisson and Rose, *War and Secession*, pp. 206–55. For US policy, see *FRUS 1969–1976*, vol. 11, nos. 159, 181, 183 ("weak position"), 186, 235, 246, and 248.

48. *FRUS 1969–1976*, vol. 11, nos. 228 ("power play") and 237; and *FRUS 1969–1976*, vol. E-7, no. 168 ("agony")

49. *FRUS 1969–1976*, vol. E-7, nos. 146 ("autonomy"), 165 ("scare off"), and 189 ("cannibalize"); For White House entreaties to Yahya, see *FRUS 1969–1976*, vol. 11, no. 259.

50. For the US decision to go to the UN, see *FRUS 1969–1976*, vol. 11, no. 218. For the UN debates, see UNSCOR, 1606th Meeting, December 4, 1971 ("refugee aggression"); and UNSCOR 1608th Meeting, December 6, 1971; UN General Assembly Resolution 2793, December 7, 1971; and *FRUS 1969–1976*, vol. 11, no. 260. Kissinger is in *White House Years*, p. 899 ("weird"). Also see Franck and Rodley, "After Bangladesh"; Kuper, *Prevention of Genocide*, pp. 84; and Wheeler, *Saving Strangers*, pp. 60–65.

51. Yahya solicits weapons in *FRUS 1969–1976*, vol. 11, no. 222. The administration's efforts to fulfill his request are in *FRUS 1969–1976*, vol. 11, nos. 223, 235, and 250; and *FRUS 1969–1976*, vol. E-7, nos. 165 ("done worse") and 172.

52. For Nixon's and Kissinger's assessments of the Cold War stakes, see *FRUS 1969–1976*, vol. 11, nos. 228–29, 231, 237, 269; and FRUS *1969–1969*, vol. E-7, nos. 165, 166, 169, 171, 173 and 177. Kissinger and Huang Hua are in *FRUS 1969–1976*, vol. 11, no. 274 ("maximum intimidation"). For Kissinger's perspective, see *White House Years*, pp. 842–918. Also see Dallek, *Nixon and Kissinger*, pp. 340–49; and Raghavan, *1971*, pp. 240–51.

53. Kissinger, *White House Years*, p. 911 ("reluctant decision"). Contrast with van Hollen, "Tilt Policy Revisited," p. 356. For Anderson, see Gupta, *Anderson Papers*. For the *NYT's* assessment see "South Asian Irony," January 12, 1971, p. 42 ("slippery slope"). Historians are, in general, no less critical. See, for example, Bundy, *Tangled Web*, pp. 269–92; Dallek, *Partners in Power*, esp. p. 621; Garthoff, *Détente and Confrontation*, chap. 8; Hanhimäki, *Flawed Architect*, chap. 8; McMahon, "Danger of Geopolitical Fantasies"; and Morris, *Uncertain Greatness*, chap. 5.

54. See Haldeman, *Diaries*, pp. 386–387; Kissinger, *White House Years*, p. 918 ("twist"); and US Congress, House, *Human Rights in the World Community*, p. 9 ("interdependent world").

55. *FRUS 1969–1976*, vol. E-5, Part 1, nos. 1 ("irrelevant"), 7, 53, and 194; and Lagos Embassy to State Department, March 10, 1969, NPMP, NSC Files, CouF, Africa, box 741.

56. Other scholars have noted Nixon and Kissinger's tendency to impose Cold War assumptions upon Third World conflicts. See, inter alia, Bundy, *Tangled Web*; and Dallek, *Partners in Power*.

57. Forsyth is in Gould, *Biafran War*, p. 15 ("images"). For civil rights in an international frame, see Borstelmann, *Cold War and the Color Line*; and Dudziak, *Cold War Civil Rights*.

58. For the campaign against the slave trade, see Hochschild, *Bury the Chains*; for humanitarianism and foreign policy in the nineteenth century, see Bass, *Freedom's Battle*. On the Mexican-American War, see Greenberg, *Wicked War*.

59. *FRUS 1969–1976*, vol. E-5, Part 1, no. 166 ("leadership"); *FRUS 1969–1976*, vol. E-7, no. 177 ("crap"); and FRUS *1969–1976*, vol. 11, nos. 100, 103 ("world opinion"), 123, 223 ("jerks"), 225, and 237.

60. See Kissinger, *White House Years*, p. 915 ("shortsighted"); and *FRUS 1969–1976*, vol. E-5, no. 48 ("their sovereignty"). Also see Fonteyne, "Forcible Self-Help by States."

61. Foreign reactions to allegations of genocide in Biafra are discussed in Smith, *Genocide and the Europeans*, esp. 65–88. Gould, *Biafran War*, pp. 198–99 is balanced but doubts the claims. The claim that events in East Pakistan met the criteria for genocide meets with broader approval. See Akmam, "Atrocities against Humanity"; Goldhagen, *Worse Than War*; Jahan, "Genocide in Bangladesh"; Jones, *Genocide*, pp. 340–45; Kiernan, *Blood and Soil*, pp. 574–78. The International Commission of Jurist's conclusions are in *Events in East Pakistan*. For a contrary view, see Bose, *Dead Reckoning*.

62. See Lauterpacht, *International Law*, p. 154 ("conscience"). Lillich, ed., *Humanitarian Intervention and the United Nations* collects the proceedings of a landmark conference on humanitarian intervention. Between 1950 and 1965, major journals of international law (as indexed by HeinOnline) published ten articles, notes, and comments addressing the issue. Between 1965 and 1975, sixty-one such pieces appeared, including: Franck and Rodley, "After Bangladesh"; Lillich, "Intervention to Protect Human Rights"; Nanda, "A Critique of the United Nations Inaction"; and Samuels, "Humanitarian Relief in Man-Made Disasters."

63. Moyn, *Last Utopia*, p. 219; Lillich, "Intervention to Protect Human Rights"; Riesman, "Humanitarian Intervention to Protect the Ibos"; International Commission of Jurists, *Events in East Pakistan*; and "Telegram from Lt. Col. Ojukwu," December 7, 1968, in "First International Conference on Biafra," December 7–8, 1968, SCPC, NBCHP, box 12.

64. *FRUS 1969–1976*, vol. E-7, no. 177 ("morality").

65. Collier and Sater, *History of Chile*, pp. 330–58. For a contemporary view, see Horne, *Small Earthquake*.

66. For Nixon and Kissinger's policy toward Allende, see Brands, *Latin America's Cold War*, pp. 111–20; Gustafson, *Hostile Intent*; Harmer, *Allende's Chile*; Haslam, *Death of Allende's Chile*; and Kornbluh, *Pinochet File*, pp. 119 ("potential leaders"). While Gustafson downplays US involvement in Chilean politics, Haslam emphasizes it. Brands and Harmer are more balanced, stressing both the US role in Chile's destabilization and the primacy of local agents.

67. The domestic backlash after Brazil's coup is documented in Green, *We Cannot Remain Silent*. On Chile as turning point, see Cmiel, "Emergence of Human Rights Politics"; Eckel, "International Human Rights Campaign against Chile"; Keck and Sikkink, *Activists beyond Borders*, pp. 88–92; Kelly, "1973 Chilean Coup" and "Human Rights Activism in Latin America's Southern Cone"; Sikkink, *Mixed Signals*, pp. 66–68.

68. US Congress, House, Committee on Foreign Affairs, *Human Rights in Chile*, p. 6 ("taken over the government")

69. "Chile: An Amnesty International Report," September 1974, CHRRD, IMP, Miscellaneous Files, Amnesty International, box 6.

70. For a precise definition of human rights, which makes "the move from the politics of the state to the morality of the globe" the foundational innovation, see Moyn, *Last Utopia*, p. 43.

71. For example, Wells, *Rights of Man*; and Roosevelt, "Annual Message to Congress," January 6, 1941, APP. On Tehran, see Burke, *Evolution of International Human Rights*, chap. 4 ("hegemony"); Moskowitz, *International Concern with Human Rights*, chap. 2; and Wilkins, "Implementing Human Rights," April 24, 1968, in *DOS Bulletin*, May 20, 1968, pp. 661–67 ("revolution" and "no state"). On the connections between globalization and human rights, see Brysk, ed., *Globalization and Human Rights*; Ishay, *History of Human Rights*, pp. 246–311; and Sargent, "Oasis in the Desert." On the continuities and discontinuities between domestic civil rights and human rights abroad—until recently an underdeveloped theme—Keys, *Reclaiming American Virtue*, esp. chap. 2, makes significant contributions.

72. On the covenants of the 1960s, see Ishay, *History of Human Rights*, pp. 238–47; and Lauren, *Evolution of International Human Rights*, pp. 233–34. On the historiography of human rights, orthodox approaches emphasize the depth and cosmopolitanism of the human rights idea, as do Ishay, *History of Human Rights*; Hunt, *Inventing Human Rights*; Lauren, *Evolution of International Human Rights*; and Neier, *International Human Rights Movement*. Borgwardt, *New Deal for the World*, sees the 1940s as the moment of genesis. Revisionists, by contrast, situate the breakthrough in the 1970s. For this approach, see Cmiel, "Emergence of Human Rights Politics"; Eckel and Moyn, ed., *Breakthrough*; Hoffman, ed., *Human Rights in the Twentieth Century*; Keys, *Reclaiming American Virtue*; and Moyn, *Last Utopia*.

Chapter 4

1. Peterson, *Education of an American Dreamer*, pp. 96–100, 136 ("Henry" etc.). For the origins of the Council on International Economic Policy, see "Foreign Policy," January 20, 1971, *NYT*, p. 1; "Council on International Economic Policy," *DOS Bulletin*, February 8, 1971, pp. 167–72 ("consistency"); "Organization for Foreign Economic Affairs," August 17, 1970, NPMP, WHCF, FO, Box 2; and *FRUS 1969–1976*, vol. 2, nos. 370 ("25 years") and 373.

2. Peterson, *Education of an American Dreamer*, pp. 144–48 ("strong action"); and NPMP, White House Tapes, Oval Office, April 3, 1971, Conv. no. 488-15 ("Ninety-one percent").

3. Peterson, *United States in the Changing World Economy*, vols. 1–2 ("services").

4. "Remarks to Midwestern News Media Executives," July 6, 1971, APP ("number one," etc.)

5. Scholarship on the end of the postwar international monetary order is substantial. Interpretations that emphasize the waning of US economic power include Block, *Origins of International Economic Disorder*; and Calleo and Rowland, *America and the World Political Economy*. Alfred Eckes, *Search for Solvency*, likewise emphasizes US relative decline but also stresses, as this chapter does, the effects of financial globalization. Eichengreen, *Globalizing Capital*, esp. chaps. 4–5; and Webb, *Political Economy of Policy Coordination* also emphasize the disruptive effects of financial globalization. Studies of US decision-making, including Bergsten, *Dilemmas of the Dollar*; Gowa, *Closing the Gold Window*; and, focusing on the Federal Reserve, Meltzer, *History of the Federal Reserve*, vol. 2, book 2, esp. 731–58. All concur that Nixon prioritized national interests over systemic stability. Odell, *U.S. International Monetary Policy* argues, by contrast, that neoliberal ideas eroded the commitment of US policymakers to regime maintenance, an interpretation that Leeson, *Ideology and the International Economy* also develops. Taking a different approach, Harvey, *New Imperialism* characterizes US policy as a purposeful bid to achieve "a radical restructuring of international capitalism"

in order to "impose neoliberal practices upon much of the world"—an interpretation that is difficult to reconcile with the historical evidence.

6. "NSSM #7," January 21, 1969, NPMP, NSC-IF, Meeting Files, box H-207; and *FRUS 1969–1976*, vol. 3, no. 119 ("NATO offset" and "suspension of convertibility"). Also see Bergsten, *Dilemmas of the Dollar*; Calleo, *Imperious Economy*; Gowa, *Closing the Gold Window*; and Odell, *U.S. International Monetary Policy*. For the international context, see James, *Monetary Cooperation*; and Strange, *International Monetary Relations*. Matusow, *Nixon's Economy*, situates foreign economic policy under Nixon in relation to domestic policy. On Volcker's role, see Volcker and Gyohten, *Changing Fortunes*, esp. pp. 61–73; and Silber, *Volcker*, esp. pp. 53–122.

7. *FRUS 1969–1976*, vol. 3, nos. 116, 120; "Relaxation of Balance-of-Payments Controls," March 28, 1969, NPMP, WHCF, FO-4, box 30; and "Statement on the Balance of Payments," April 4, 1969, APP. NSC officials warned that relaxing LBJ-era controls would exacerbate the strain on the payments balance. See "Relaxation of Balance of Payments Controls," April 1, 1969; and "Relaxation of Balance of Payments Controls," April 11, 1969, both in NPMP, NSC, SuF, Balance of Payments, box 309.

8. *FRUS 1969–1976*, vol. 3, no. 123 ("highly sensitive") and 126 ("accomplished fact"). On German policy, see Strange, *International Monetary Relations*, pp. 327–28.

9. *FRUS 1969-1976*, vol. 3, no. 129 ("renewed crises"). For the June 1969 meeting, see *FRUS 1969-1976*. vol. 3, nos. 130–31; and Silber, *Volcker*, pp., 62–67.

10. "Basic Options in International Monetary Affairs," June 23, 1969, quoted in Gowa, *Closing the Gold Window*, p., 69 ("constraints"). On the Nixon administration's dismantling of controls, see Odell, *International Monetary Policy*, pp., 195–96; "Further Liberalization of Exchange Controls," November 11, 1969 ("unpopular"); and "Balance of Payments Program for 1970," both in NPMP, NSC, SuF, Balance of Payments, box 309.

11. Strange, *International Monetary Relations*, pp. 323–32; "Hot Money, Cool Handshakes," the *Economist*, September 27, 1969, pp. 22–24 ; and "The Eurodollar Market in Times of Crisis," *Euromoney* vol. 1, no. 6 (1969): 12–14 ("avalanche"). On the West German Deutschmark policy, see Gray, "Floating the System" ("grand experiment").

12. Pompidou is quoted in James, *Monetary Cooperation*, p. 212 ("fixed").

13. For administration perspectives on trade legislation, see "Pending Trade Legislation," July 2, 1970 ("replicate"); and "Possible Crisis in Trade Policy," July 8, 1970 ("trade war") NPMP, NSC, SuF, Trade, box 401.

14. See Reston, *Lone Star*, p. 382 ("virtually nothing'); Safire, *Before the Fall*, pp., 496–97 ("love"). For Nixon on Connally, see *FRUS 1969–1976*, vol. 3, nos. 158 and 159 ("lead man"); and Nixon to Haldeman, March 2, 1970, NPMP, PPF, Memoranda from the President, box 2.

15. For Connally's views, see Connally to Peterson, March 29, 1971. DDRS; Connally to Peterson, May 26, 1971, NPMP, WHCF, IT 50-3, ox 13 ("Nixon Doctrine"); and Odell, *International Monetary Policy*, p. 263 ("screw").

16. See Morris and Little, "Eurodollar Market"; Bernstein, "Eurodollars" ("inflow"); Roosa, "United States Balance of Payments and the Dollar," *Euromoney* vol. 2, no. 1 (1970): 20–25; and Klopstock, "Use of Eurodollars." Balance of payments figures are from White House, *ERP* (1974). Interest rates are from IMF, *International Financial Statistics*. Little, *Euro-Dollars* remains a useful introduction. For a historical view, see Kane, *Eurodollar Market*, esp. chaps. 4–5.

17. *FRUS 1969-1976*, vol. 3, no. 1. On Burns, Nixon, and monetary loosening at home, see Matusow, *Nixon's Economy*, pp., 98–104; and Wells, *Economist in An Uncertain World*, pp. 54–55. On the exodus from the dollar in 1970–71, see "Flight from the Dollar," *Euromoney* vol. 2, no. 3 (1970): 8–11; and "International Capital Market," *Euromoney* vol. 2, no.5 (1970): 20–22 ("uncertainties"). For IMF views, see "Fourth-Quarter U.S. Balance of Payments Data," February 19, 1970; "U.S. Economy," June 4, 1970; "Recent U.S. Monetary Developments"; and "United States: Balance of Payments," March 31, 1971, IMF Archive, CouF, U.S.A, box 164 ("striking").

18. For administration perspectives, see "U.S. Balance of Payments," May 14, 1971, NPMP, WHCF, FO 4-1, box 30; "The Recent International Monetary Disturbances," May 17, 1971,

NPMP, POF, PHF, box 1 ("tidal wave"); and "International Monetary Developments," May 5, 1971, NPMP, NSC, SuF, Balance of Payments, box 309 ("tremendous").

19. For external perspectives, see Ottmar Emminger, "Short Term Capital Flows," *Euromoney* vol. 2, no. 12 (1971): 6–8 ("undermining"); and "The Eurodollar Crisis and US Forces," attached to Eliot to Kissinger, May 12, 1971, NPMP, NSC, Name Files, Mansfield Amendment, box 824.

20. Obstfeld et. al., "Trilemma in History." Obstfeld and others build on Robert Mundell's groundbreaking work on optimal currency areas. See Mundell, "Theory of Optimum Currency Areas"; and "Capital Mobility and Stabilization Policy."

21. *FRUS 1969–1976*, vol. 3, no. 156 ("route of revaluation"); and Connally, "Address to the International Meeting of the ABA," May 28, 1971, *DOS Bulletin*, vol. 65, July 12, 1971, pp., 42–46.

22. "Monetary Inquiry Urged," May 13, 1971, *NYT*, p. 75 ("investigation"); and US Congress, Joint Economic Committee, hearing, *Action Now to Strengthen the U.S. Dollar* ("huge size," etc.). Although Reuss favored keeping fixed exchange rates, he was prepared to tolerate a temporary float on the German model as a means to adjust parities. See "Shift in Monetary Set-Up," June 4, 1971, *NYT*, p. 45.

23. *FRUS 1969–1976*, vol. 3, no. 156 ("no controls"); and Connally, "Address to the International Meeting of the ABA," May 28, 1971, in *DOS Bulletin*, vol. 65, July 12, 1971, pp. 42–46 ("enormous").

24. Safire, *Before the Fall*, p. 509 ("historic nature"); and Reeves, *President Nixon*, p. 343 ("1933"). The archives reveal no formal record of the August 13 Camp David meeting. But see Safire, *Before the Fall*, pp. 508–28; and Burns, *Inside the Nixon Administration*, pp. 48–54. Also see Matusow, *Nixon's Economy*, chap. 6; and Reeves, *President Nixon*, pp. 355–63.

25. Safire, *Before the Fall*, p. 521 ("brutal"); Nixon, "Address to the Nation Outlining a New Economic Policy," August 15, 1971, APP; and, for the comparison to China, Nixon-Kissinger TeleCon, August 16, 1971, NPMP, NSC, KTC, box 11.

26. For US perspectives on the British request for "cover," see Nixon, *Memoirs*, p. 518; and Volcker and Gyohten, *Changing Fortunes*, p. 77. For a British counterpoint, see Douglas-Home to UK Embassy, August 19, 1971, UKNA, FCO 59/660. Also see Nixon-Kissinger TeleCon, August 14, 1971 ("shake"); and Nixon-Kissinger TeleCon, August 16, 1971, both in NPMP, NSC, KTC, box 11 ("big wheel").

27. *FRUS 1969–1976*, vol. 3, no.167 ("implications").

28. For overseas reactions, see "Information Memorandum," August 16, 1971, NPMP, NSC, SuF, President's Economic Program, box 376; and "Morning News Summary," August 18, 1971, NPMP, NSC, SuF, Morning News Summary, box 348 ("big stick"). The British appraisal is in "President Nixon's Announcement", August 16, 1971, UKNA, FCO 59/650 ("designed to shock"). For realistic US appraisals, see Kissinger-Peterson TeleCon, August 18, 1971, NPMP, KTC, box 11; and *FRUS 1969–1976*, vol. 3, no.174 ("bargaining lever"). Nixon is in Nixon-Kissinger TeleCon, August 16, 1971, NPMP, KTC, box 11 ("a few things").

29. Interpretations that present the NEP as a retreat from internationalism include Gowa, *Gold Window*; Kunz, *Butter and Guns*; and Matusow, *Nixon's Economy*. But see "Trade Policy Options for the U.S.," December 8, 1970, NPMP, NSC, SuF, Common Market, box 322 ("free trade"); and, reaffirming core military commitments, "FY 1971–1976 Interim Guidance on U.S. Deployments," October 27, 1970, NPMP, NSC-IF, Meeting Files, Defense Program Review Committee, box H-098.

30. See *FRUS 1969–1976*, vol. 1, no. 206 ("bothered"); and *FRUS 1969–1976*, vol. 3, no. 131 ("constraints").

31. "Remarks of John Connally before the Council on Foreign Relations," March 15, 1972, MLP, CFR, Meetings, box 475 ("plead guilty").

32. The Chamber of Commerce urged the immediate termination of all controls on international investment. See "Chamber of Commerce Proposals," June 15, 1970, NPMP, WHCF, FO 4-1, box 30. Milton Friedman made the case for floating exchange rates back in 1953. See "The Case for Flexible Exchange Rates." George Shultz pressed the case within the administration. See Memorandum to the CIEP, March 2, 1971, NPMP, WHCF, FO 4-1: Balance of Payments, box 30. McCracken is in *FRUS 1969–1976*, vol. 3, no. 157 ("rigidly fixed").

33. Nixon to Friedman, October 3, 1968, HIA, Milton Friedman Papers, box 167 ("arbitrary controls"); and *FRUS 1969–1976*, vol. 3, nos. 158 ("vigorous"). Interpretations that emphasize neoliberal influences on policy include Leeson, *Ideology and the International Economy* and Odell, *International Monetary Policy*.

34. Peter Peterson told one researcher that he was responsible for getting Kissinger to "persuade Nixon to overrule Connally." See Aronson, *Money and Power*, p. 145. Others emphasize Kissinger's role, including Shultz and Dam, *Economic Policy Beyond the Headlines*, p. 12. For Kissinger's perspective, see *White House Years*, pp. 949–67.

35. *FRUS 1969–1976*, vol. 3, nos. 170 ("fundamental strengthening") and 171 ("basic principle"), 175–76, 182, and 189. For Volcker's role, see Silber, *Volcker*, pp., 97–103

36. *FRUS 1969–1976*, vol. 3, nos. 188 ("deterimental"); Kissinger-Peterson TeleCon, November 5, 1971 ("take on"); Kissinger-McCloy TeleCon, November 11, 1971 ("counter"); and Kissinger-Haldeman TeleCon, November 13, 1971, all in NPMP, KTC, box 12 and *FRUS 1969–1976*, vol. 3, no. 201 ("inflexible position").

37. *FRUS 1969–1976*, vol. 3, nos. 203 and 236 ("convinced"); Kissinger-Kraft TeleCon, November 29, 1971, NPMP, KTC, box 12 ("basics"); and Kissiger, *White House Years*, p. 962 ("extraordinary").

38. On the substance of the agreements, see "Proposed Modification of Par Value of Dollar," February 1972, NPMP, NSC, SuF, Balance of Payments, box 309. For analyses, see Eichengreen, *Globalizing Capital*, p. 133; James, *Monetary Cooperation*, pp. 238–39; Solomon, *International Monetary System*, pp., 204–11; and Strange, *International Monetary Relations*, pp. 342–44.

39. "Remarks Announcing a Monetary Agreement," December 18, 1971, APP ("greatest").

40. On the role of capital movements forces in the December 1971 adjustment, see Volcker and Gyohten, *Changing Fortunes*, p. 83; Strange, *International Monetary Relations*, p. 342; and Shultz and Dam, *Economic Policy beyond the Headlines*, p. 115 ("alliance").

41. "Alternative Possibilities for Coordinating Balance of Payments Improvement," January 19, 1972, DDRS ("trade policies" etc.); and "Proposed Modification of Par Value of Dollar," February 1972, NPMP, NSC, SuF, Balance of Payments, box 309. The removal of foreign barriers to U.S. exports was already a well-defined objective. See "Trade Policy Options," December 8, 1970, NPMP, NSC, SuF, Common Market, box 322. For the liberalizers, see "A Start Toward Negotiating International Monetary Reform," February 22, 1972, DDRS.

42. Odell, *International Monetary Policy*, pp. 306–9; and Volcker and Gyohten, *Changing Fortunes*, p. 82 ("new basis"), and pp. 114–18.

43. *FRUS 1969–1976*, vol. 3, nos. 230 ("facilitated") and 239. For Volcker's perspective, see Volcker and Gyohten, *Changing Fortunes*, pp. 118–20; and Silber, *Volcker* pp. 111–13.

44. *FRUS 1969–1976*, vol. 3, no. 230 ("fewer restraints"); and, for analyses, Aronson, *Money and Power*, chap. 5; Odell, *International Monetary Policy*, chap. 5; and Solomon, *International Monetary System*, chap. 13.

45. "International Monetary Situation," August 2, 1972, NPMP, NSC, SuF, Monetary Matters, box 356.

46. Under the Smithsonian Agreement, actual currency values could move up or down against their stated parity by 2.25 percent, permitting fluctuation of up to 4.5 percent between two currencies. BIS, *Annual Report* (1972–73), pp. 21–22; and Solomon, *International Monetary System*, p. 218 ("snake"). On early European monetary integration, see Mourlon-Droul, *Europe Made of Money*; and Tsoukalis, *European Monetary Integration*.

47. On the sterling crisis, *FRUS 1969-1976*, vol. 3, no. 232 ("technical position"); "Real Worries about Sterling," *Euromoney*, vol. 4, no. 2 (1972): 3–5; and Solomon, *International Monetary System*, pp. 221–24. On the role of short-term capital, see "Report on Monetary Situation," June 27, 1972, NPMP, NSC, SuF, European Common Market, box 322 ("culprit"); and Aronson, *Money and Power*, p. 104. For Nixon, see *FRUS 1969-1976*, vol. 3, no. 233 ("latest episode").

48. *FRUS 1969-1976*, vol. 3, nos. 234 and 235 ("internal effect"); Erb to Flanigan, July 7, 1972, NPMP, WHCF, IT, box 3; and Solomon, *International Monetary System*, p. 223 ("massive flows").

49. *FRUS 1969-1976*, vol. 3, no. 236 ("too doctrinaire"); Shultz to Nixon, undated, NARA, RG-56, RGS, Memorandums to the President, box 5; and Hormats to Kissinger, August 22, 1972, NPMP, NSC, SuF, Monetary Matters, box 356 ("tranquility"). On foreign exchange operations and their abandonment, see Coombs, *International Finance*, pp., 226–27 ("operations").

50. Volcker and Gyohten, *Changing Fortunes*, p. 104–5 ("lead"); Transcript of a Meeting between Nixon and Haldeman, June 23, 1972, NARA, RG-460, Conversation Transcripts ("lira"); and *FRUS 1969-1976*, vol. 3, no. 236 ("blow up").

51. *FRUS 1969-1976*, vol. 1, no. 121 ("unfair")

52. See *FRUS 1969-1976*, vol. 3, no. 236 ("brutal"); and *FRUS 1969-1976*, vol. 1, no. 122 ("new balance").

53. Coombs, *International Finance*, chap. 12; and Gold, *International Capital Movements*, 35–36. Volcker was "personally disappointed" that the United States. did not negotiate a transition to a new Bretton Woods system, but he acknowledges that his views were "not widely shared." See Volcker and Gyohten, *Changing Fortunes*, p. 123. On the failures of monetary reform, see James, *International Monetary Cooperation*, chap. 9; and Williamson, *Failure of World Monetary Reform*.

54. "Text of Shultz Talk," September 27, 1972, *NYT*, p. 70 ("fixed point"); Volcker and Gyohten, *Changing Fortunes*, p. 121 ("relief"); and *FRUS 1969-1976*, vol. 3, no. 243 ("resume"). For US opposition to capital controls, see Helleiner, *Global Finance*, chap. 5. For the dollar's strengthening in late 1972, see BIS, *Annual Report* (1972–73), p. 23.

55. Nixon, "Special Message to the Congress," January 11, 1973, APP; Volcker and Gyohten, *Changing Fortunes*, p. 106 ("signal"); "U.S. Foreign Trade Deficit," *NYT*, January 25, 1973, p. 1 ("soared"); and "'72 Trade Deficit Tripled," *WSJ*, January 26, 1973, p. 3; BIS, *Annual Report* (1972–73), p., 23 ("to check"); Coombs, *International Finance*, p., 229; and "Monetary Storm Clouds Threaten," February 4, 1973, *NYT*, p. 145

56. BIS, *Annual Report*, (1972–73), p. 20 ("unfinished") and 161 (for Eurodollar deposits); White House, *ERP*, 1974; US Congress, Senate, Committee on Finance, *International Financial Crisis* (1973), p. 132 ("major contributor"); and Nixon-Shultz-Soames MemCon, February 16, 1973, GFPL, NSA Files, MemCons, box 1 ("aid recipients").

57. Silber, *Volcker*, pp., 113–18; Solomon, *International Monetary System*, pp. 229–31; Volcker and Gyohten, *Changing Fortunes*, 106–11. For the foreign plaudits, see "Common Market Chiefs Praise Action," *NYT*, February 15, 1973, 72; and Anthony Barber speech, February 22, UKNA, FCO 59/854.

58. See Shultz to Nixon, February 12, 1973, NPMP, WHCF, FO, box 4; Shultz, "Statement on Foreign Economic Policy," February 12, 1973, U.S. Department of the Treasury, *U.S. National Economy, 1916-2001: Unpublished Documentary Collections*, Part 5; and *FRUS 1969-1976*, vol. 31, no. 3. For European views, see UK Embassy Brussels to Foreign Office, March 8, 1973, UKNA, FCO 59/855 ("ordered relationships"); and Report of OECD, Working Party Three, February 19, 1973, UKNA, FCO 59/854.

59. Odell, *International Monetary Policy*, pp. 313–15 ("destabilizing"); "Dollar Declines to Low in Europe," *NYT*, March 1, 1973, p. 57 ("permissible"); "Brandt and Heath Meet on Dollar Influx," *NYT*, March 2, 1973, p. 47; "Monetary Crisis Flares Up Again," *NYT*, March 2, 1973, p. 1 ("lack of faith"); and Volcker and Gyohten, *Changing Fortunes*, p. 102 ("artistry").

60. See "Common Market Weighs Joint Step," *NYT*, March 4, 1973, p. 1 ("dollar peril"); and "EEC to Suggest U.S. Dollar Action," *NYT*, March 9, 1973, p. 49. For Brandt's Letter, see *FRUS 1969-1976*, vol. 31, nos. 6, and 18. For a British analysis, see Cromer to Foreign Office, March 4, 1973, FCO 59/857.

61. See Nixon-Kissinger TeleCon, March 3, 1973, NPMP, NSC, KTC, box 19; Kissinger-Shultz TeleCon, March 1, 1973, NPMP, NSC, KTC, box 19 ("thrashing"); and *FRUS 1969-1976*, vol. 31, nos. 16–17, 24 ("murder"), and 25 ("do anything"). On the shutdown of the New York Fed's swap network, see Coombs, *International Finance*, pp. 227–30.

62. Kissinger-Simon TeleCon, March 14, 1973, NPMP, NSC, KTC, box 19 ("basic view").

63. "Press Communiqué of the Ministerial Meeting of the Group of Ten and the EEC," March 16, 1973, U.S. Department of the Treasury, *U.S. National Economy, 1916-2001: Unpublished Documentary Collections*, Part 5. On the US removal of capital controls, see "The U.S. Market after

Controls," *Euromoney* vol. 5, no. 9 (1974): 4–7. Also see Kissinger-Simon MemCons, March 15 ("create conditions") and March 16 ("what we wanted"), both in NPMP, NSC, KTC, box 19.

64. Shultz and Dam, *Economic Policy Beyond the Headlines*, p. 128 ("improvement"); Remarks by Paul Volcker at Princeton University, March 29, 1973, U.S. Department of the Treasury. *U.S. National Economy 1916–2001: Unpublished Documentary Collections*, Part 5 ("more conducive"); and Volcker and Gyohten, *Changing Fortunes*, p. 124 ("resort").

65. "Speculators vs. Governments," *NYT*, February 18, 1973, p. 203; US Congress, Senate, Committee on Finance, *Implications of Multinational Firms*, p. 43 ("panoply"); and "Have the Markets Got It Wrong?" *Euromoney*, vol. 5, no. 3 (1973): 3 ("proletariat"). Also see Warf, "Telecommunications and the Globalization of Financial Services."

66. Zweig, *Wriston*, p. 371 ("key step").

67. The point that sustenance of Bretton Woods would have required the expansion of policy coordination is made well in Makin, "Eurocurrencies and the Evolution of the International Monetary System." Also see, more generally, Cooper, *Economics of Interdependence*; and Webb, *Political Economy of Policy Coordination*.

68. Rockefeller's proposals are attached to McCracken to Nixon, September 13, 1971, NPMP, POF, PHF, box 13. Also see Zweig, *Wriston*, p. 391 ("Chicken Little"); and Volcker and Gyohten, *Changing Fortunes*, p. 103 ("come apart"). For concurring views, see Aronson, *Money and Power* and Odell, *International Monetary Policy*—and note Arthur Burns's March 1973 insistence that bankers opposed floating, in *FRUS 1969-1976*, vol. 31, no. 16.

69. Flanigan to Shultz, March 27, 1974, NARA, RG-56, RGS, box 2 ("significant"); Flanigan to Shultz, April 5, 1974, NARA, RG-56, RGS, box 7 ("interference"); and "U.S. Policy and Objectives on International Investment," April 29, 1974, NPMP, POF, PHF, box 1 ("maximum reliance").

Chapter 5

1. "Iran: The Show of Shows," *Time*, October 25, 1971 ("equal"), pp. 34–38; and "Persian Night," *NYT*, October 15, 1971, p. 43.

2. For the sniffing, see "Royal To-Do Over Undignified Festivities," the *Guardian* (UK) August 15, 2001.

3. See Mitchell, *Carbon Democracy*; and Yergin, *The Prize*, chap. 27. Statistics on oil are from DeGolyer and MacNaughton, *TCPS* and U.S. Energy Information Administration; and, on automobiles, Flink, *Automobile Age*, esp. pp. 377–403. On oil and the Pax Americana, see Bromley *American Hegemony and World Oil*; and Painter, *Oil and the American Century*, and "International Oil and National Security." On postwar growth more generally, see Eichengreen, *European Economy*, pp. 15–51.

4. Bruce Springsteen, "Born to Run," *Born to Run* (Columbia Records); Bob Dylan, "Slow Train," *Slow Train Coming* (Sony Records).

5. On the 1953 coup, see Gasiorowski and Byrne, eds., *Mohammad Mosaddeq and the 1953 Coup*; and Kinzer, *All the Shah's Men*. Bayandor, *Iran and the CIA* downplays the role of external actors. On the 50/50 split, see Yergin, *The Prize*, chap. 22.

6. On OPEC, see Seymour, *OPEC: Instrument of Change*; Terzian, *OPEC: The Inside Story*, and Venn, *Oil Diplomacy*.

7. For contrasting perspectives on the Six-Day War, see Oren, *Six Days of War*; and Segev, *1967*. On the 1967 embargo, see Yergin, *The Prize*, pp. 554–58.

8. See *FRUS 1964–1968*, vol. 22, no. 231 ("ridiculous"); and *FRUS 1964-68*, vol. 34, no. 242.

9. Hubbert, *Nuclear Energy and the Fossil Fuels*; Prindle, *Petroleum Politics*, p. 96; and Yergin, *The Prize*, chap. 28.

10. See Vietor, *Energy Policy in America*, pp. 119–45; Yergin, *The Prize*, p. 535–40; and DeGolyer and MacNaughton, *TCPS*.

11. "Oil Import Controls," December 31, 1969; "Oil Import Meeting with Flanigan and Harlow," January 12, 1970; "Oil Imports," February 4, 1970; and "Presidential Statement on Oil Imports," February 12, 1970, all in NPMP, NSC Files, SuF, Oil, box 367. Also see Nixon,

"Statement about the Report of the Cabinet Task Force," February 20, 1970, APP. For the task force recommendations, see Cabinet Task Force, *The Oil Import Question.*

12. NSSM 114, "World Oil Situation," January 24, 1971, NPMP, NSC-IF, Study Memorandums, box H-180; and "The U.S. and the Impending Energy Crisis," November 1972, NPMP, WHSF, Staff Member and Office Files, Energy Policy Office, box 27 ("contribution").

13. On Qaddafi's coup, see Vandewalle, *History of Modern Libya*, pp.,77–83. Whether Libya ranked third or fourth among OPEC producers depends on which statistics are used. Compare DeGolyer and MacNaughton, *TCPS*, p. 3; and Yergin, *The Prize*, p. 529. For the analogy to Iraq, see *FRUS 1969–1976*, vol. E-5, Part 1, no. 39.

14. See Parra, *Oil Politics*, chap. 6; and Yergin, *The Prize*, esp. chap. 28. Also see, "Lordly Demands," January 2, 1971, the *Economist*, p. 53. For Washington perspectives, see "Status of Current OPEC Oil Negotiations," January 25, 1971; and "World Oil Situation," March 9, 1971, both in NPMP, NSC Files, SuF, Oil, box 367.

15. Levy, "Oil Power"; "Mastery over World Oil Supply Shifts," April 16, 1973, *NYT*, p. 77 ("very rich"); and Parra, *Oil Politics*, p. 114 ("most important"). For US perspectives, see Irwin to McCracken, April 10, 1971, NPMP, NSC-IF, Under Secretaries Study Memorandums, box H-261; and NSSM 114, "World Oil Situation," January 15, 1971, NPMP, NSC-IF, Meeting Files, box H-207.

16. See "The Place of the Oil Producers in the International Monetary System," September 8, 1972, UKNA, FCO 59/913; Akins, "Oil Crisis," p. 480 ("Croesus"); and UK Embassy Jeddah to FCO, March 17, 1973, UKNA, FCO 59/913 ("sinking").

17. *FRUS 1969–1976*, vol. 36, nos. 175 and 1980 ("wives"); Parsons to Wright, February 13, 1973, UKNA, FOC, 59/913; Shell Corp., "The Impact on the World Economy," May 1973, UKNA, FCO, 59/920; "How the Arabs Plan to Spend Their Riches," May 5, 1973, the *Economist*, p. 39; and Study Paper by the Working Party on the Vast Surpluses of the Oil Producers (VSOP), June 5, 1973, UKNA, FCO 59/920 ("in the ground").

18. "That Arab Oil Wealth," *NYT*, June 10, 1973, p. 174. The OECD proposed the $25 billion figure; US officials considered it a "reasonable working approximation." See "Balance of Payments with the Oil-Producers," March 10, 1973, UKNA, FCO 59/913 and "Record of Meeting at U.S. Treasury," July 6, 1973, UKNA, FCO 59/920.

19. "Balance of Payments with the Oil-Producers," March 10, 1973, UKNA, FCO 59/913 ("short-term money"). Walter Levy argued for financial liberalization as a means to finance oil deficits even before the final breakdown of Bretton Woods. See Address by Walter Levy to the American Petroleum Institute, November 14, 1972, UKNA, FCO 59/919.

20. "The U.S. and the Impending Energy Crisis," November 1972, NPMP, WHSF, Staff Member and Office Files, Energy Policy Office, box 27; Akins, "The Wolf is Here" ("extend"). For Treasury's perspective, see "Energy Policy," February 23, 1973, NARA, RG-56, RGS, Energy, box 4 ("primary causes"). For Nixon's energy policy, see "Special Message to the Congress on Energy Policy," April 18, 1973, APP. Shultz's position on quotas is in see DiBona to Ehrlichman et. al., March 30, 1973, NPMP, WHSF, Staff Member and Office Files, Energy Policy Office, box 26.

21. NSSM 174, "National Security and U.S. Energy Policy," NPMP, NSC-IF, Study Memorandums, box H-197 ("main causes").

22. *FRUS, 1947* vol. 5, 511–21 ("primary responsibility"). On Britain's post-1945 imperial consolidation, see Louis, *British Empire in the Middle East*; and, with particular attention to oil, Galpern, *Money, Oil, and Empire in the Middle East*. For the larger inter-imperial competition for the Middle East, see Fieldhouse, *Western Imperialism in the Middle East*; and, with a view to the present, Khalidi, *Resurrecting Empire*. On US involvement in Saudi Arabia, see, Vitalis, *America's Kingdom.*

23. *FRUS 1964-1968*, vol. 12, no. 289 ("damaging"); and "Future U.S. Policy in the Persian Gulf," NPMP, NSC-IF, Study Memorandums, box H-157 ("system"); and *FRUS 1969-1976*, vol. 24, no. 75. On Britain's retreat, see Dumbrell, "The Johnson Administration"; and Fielding, "Coping with Decline." Dockrill, *Britain's Retreat from East of Suez* sees a purposeful retrenchment, not a panicked retreat.

24. Saunders to Kissinger, April 24, 1970, NPMP, CouF, Iran, box 601; "Future U.S. Policy in the Persian Gulf," NPMP, NSC-IF, Study Memorandums, box H-157 ("significant role"); and *FRUS 1969-1976*, vol. 36, no. 38 ("interdiction").

25. For the differences between Rogers's approach and Kissinger's, see "NSC Meeting: The Middle East," December 10, 1969, NPMP, NSC-IF, NSC Meeting Minutes, box H-109. For Kissinger's critique of State's approach, see "Taking Stock after Eight Months," NPMP, NSC Files, SuF, Strategic Overview, box 397; and Kissinger, WHY, pp. 363–79. For a counterpoint, see Salim Yaqub, "Weight of Conquest."

26. The NSSM 66 exercise orchestrated a formal review of US policy in the Persian Gulf in 1969. See NSSM 66, July 12, 1969, NPMP, NSC-IF, SuF, NSSMs, box H-207. For the State Department's response, see "Future U.S. Policy in the Persian Gulf," NPMP, NSC-IF, Study Memorandums, box H-157; and NSDM 92, "U.S. Policy Towards the Persian Gulf," November 7, 1970, NPMP, NSC Files, SuF, NSDMs, box 363. Also see Alvandi, "Nixon, Kissinger, and the Shah"; Bill, *Eagle and the Lion*; Gasiorowski, *U.S. Foreign Policy and the Shah*; and Miglietta, *American Alliance Policy in the Middle East*.

27. Early histories of the White Revolution emphasized its fragility, as do Halliday, *Iran: Dictatorship and Development*; and Keddie and Yann, *Roots of Revolution*. More recent accounts credit Pahlavi with building an effective—if brutal—modernizing state, as do Abrahamian, *History of Modern Iran*; and Afkhami, *Life and Times of the Shah*. On Iranian dissent, see *FRUS 1969-1976*, vol. E-4, nos. 116, 169, 174, 203, 217, and 230.

28. Klare, *American Arms Supermarket*, p. 40 ("most rapid"). Also see US Congress, House, *U.S. Arms Policies in the Persian Gulf*; and Pryor, "Arms and the Shah." For a register of international arms transfers, see Stockholm International Peace Research Institute, Arms Transfers Database. Pahlavi's hovercraft are referenced in "A Napoleonic Vision of Iran," *NYT*, May 26, 1974, p. 205.

29. *FRUS 1969-1976*, vol. E-4, nos. 8, 20, 24, 29, 30, 52, 56, 73, 80, and 189. Also see Tehran Embassy to Secretary of State, February 26, 1970, "Military Sales Credit for Iran," April 16, 1970; "Iranian Credit Package," April 15, 1970; Tehran Embassy to Secretary of State, April 1, 1970, all in NARA, MPMP, NSC Files, CouF, Iran, box 601.

30. *FRUS 1969-1976*, vol. E-4, nos. 201, 204, and 214.

31. For introductions, see Al-Rasheed, *History of Saudi Arabia*; and Vasil'ev, *History of Saudi Arabia*. For US policy, *FRUS 1969-1976*, vo. 24, no. 140 ("middle class"); and NSSM 174, "National Security and U.S. Energy Policy," NPMP, NSC-IF, Study Memorandums, box H-197 (for production estimates).

32. For Saudi-Egyptian rivalries, see Kerr, *Arab Cold War*. On Saudi Arabia, oil, and Islam, see Al-Rasheed, *Saudi Arabia*, pp. 130–34; Aslan, *No God But God*, pp. 245–58; and Kepel, *Jihad*, pp. 69–75.

33. For US-Saudi Relations, see "President's Meeting with Prince Sultan," June 10, 1972 ("traditional friends"); "Closer Cooperation between the Kingdom of Saudi Arabia and the United States of America," Undated paper; MemCon of Nixon meeting with Prince Sultan, June 10, 1972, all in NPMP, MRS, CouF, Middle East, Saudi Arabia, 1971–1973, box 3; and US Congress, House, *U.S. Arms Policies in the Persian Gulf*, p. 7 ("key countries"). US policy is affirmed in NSDM 92 and NSDM 186, in NPMP, NSC Files, SuF, NSDMs, boxes 363-4. Also see *FRUS 1969-1976*, vol. 24, nos. 96, 160, and 161.

34. "Background Briefing," June 26, 1970, NPMP, WHCF, FO box 2 ("study it").

35. Interpretations that stress the Cold War's influence on US-Israel relations include Schoenbaum, *United States and the State of Israel*; and Spiegel, *Other Arab-Israeli Conflict*. On Stalin, see Zubok, *A Failed Empire*, pp. 56–57.

36. On US policy in the 1960s, Bass, *Support Any Friend* emphasizes the influence of Cold War beliefs. Goldman, "Ties That Bind," stresses JFK's affinity for Israel. For LBJ's policy, also see Cohen, "Balancing American Interests in the Middle East." On Soviet policy, see Golan, *Soviet Policies in the Middle East*, esp. 58–81; and Yaacov Ro'I and Boris Morozov, eds., *Soviet Union and the June 1967 Six Day War*, esp. 1–42.

37. See Kissinger, *White House Years*, p. 370 ("ambivalences"). Also see "New Tapes Reveal Depth of Nixon's Anti-Semitism," *WP*, October 6, 1999, A31; Dallek, *Partners in Power*, pp. 169–71; and Schoenbaum, *United States and Israel*, p. 169. For Nixon's views, see

Memorandum for Kissinger, March 17, 1970, NPMP, WHSF, PPF, box 2 ("pro-freedom"); and Nixon-Kissinger TeleCon, July 7, 1970, NPMP, NSC Files, KTC, box 6. For the Black September Crisis, see Kissinger, *White House Years*, chap. 15.

38. Saudi officials express their views on Israel in "President's Meeting with Prince Fahd," September 17, 1971; "President's Conversation with Prince Fahd," September 30, 1971; Jidda Embassy to Secretary of State, December 18, 1972 ("aggressiveness"); and Jidda Embassy to Secretary of State, December 19, 1972 ("effected"); and Faisal to Nixon, March 22, 1972, all in NPMP, MRS, NSC Files, CouF, Middle East, Saudi Arabia, box 3. For Iran's relationship with Israel, see Parsi, *Treacherous Alliance*; Sobhani, *Pragmatic Entente*; and *FRUS 1969-1976*, vol. E-4, no. 269.

39. On oil, see *FRUS 1969-1976*, vol. 24, no. 96 ("flow"); and *DBPO*, Series 3, vol. 4, no.111. Sulzberger is in "Our Superpower Era Wanes," *NYT*, June 6, 1971, p. 15 ("sympathies"). Policymakers' confidence in Israeli military superiority is evident in see NSC Meeting Minutes, December 10, 1969, NPMP, NSC-IF, NSC Meeting Minutes, box H-109; and NSC Meeting Minutes, July 16, 1971, NPMP, NSC-IF, NSC Meeting Minutes, box H-110.

40. See "Egypt's Interim Leader," *NYT*, September 30, 1970, p. 16 ("impulsive"); Bergus to State Department, December 28, 1970, ASA ("business"); and *FRUS 1969-1976*, vol. 26, no. 177 ("unfairly").

41. For Sadat's entreaties to Washington, see Cairo to Washington, April 1, 1971, ASA ("pressure"). For Sadat's moves in 1972–73, see *FRUS 1969-1976*, vol. 24, no. 153, and vol. 25, no. 14. For US and Israeli nonchalance, see *FRUS 1969-1976*, vol. 25, nos. 50, 52, 55, 59, and 67. For Sadat's purposes, see Kissinger, *Years of Upheaval*, p. 460 ("a crisis"). Also see Asher, *Egyptian Strategy for the Yom Kippur War*, pp. 58–62; Fernández-Armesto, *Sadat and His Statecraft*, pp. 143–44; and Sadat, *In Search of Identity*, pp. 230–31.

42. Israeli appeals for US support are in *FRUS 1969-1976*, vol. 25, nos. 134, 141, 166, 168, and 196. For Kissinger's views, see *FRUS 1969-1976*, vol. 25, nos. 142, and 144. For Kissinger's entreaties to the Saudis, see DNSA, EBB, October War, nos. 29a and 29b. Accounts of US policy are abundant. For Kissinger's recollections, see *Years of Renewal*, pp. 450–613. For historical analyses, see Dallek, *Partners in Power*, pp. 520–33; Garthoff, *Détente and Confrontation*, pp. 404–57; Hanhimäki, *Flawed Architect*, pp. 302–17; Isaacson, *Kissingeri*, pp. 517–24; and Quandt, *Peace Process*, pp. 105–29. Also invaluable are the collections of documents assembled in *FRUS 1969-1976*, vol. 25, and DNSA, EBB, "October War."

43. *FRUS 1969-1976*, vol. 25, no. 230.

44. Situation Reports, October 22 and 23, 1973, NPMP, NSC Files, Middle East War, Box 1175; *FRUS 1969-1976*, vol. 25, no. 246 ("decisive measures"), 267 ("act jointly"), and 269. Also see DNSA, EBB, "October War," no. 72. On the efficacy of the US alert, contrast Kissinger, *Years of Renewal*, pp. 583–84 and Israelyan, *Inside the Kremlin*.

45. For Kissinger on Nixon's intervention—"the crazy bastard really made a mess with the Russians"—see *FRUS 1969-1976*, vol 25, no. 285. For Nixon on resignation, see Nixon-Kissinger TeleCon, June 10, 1973, NPMP, NSC Files, KTC, Box 20. For Kissinger's views on Watergate's effects on foreign policy, see Nixon-Garment TeleCon, April 21, 1973; and Nixon-Shultz TeleCon, June 24, 1973, both NPMP, NSC Files, KTC, box 19-20; and *FRUS 1969-1976*, vol. 38, no. 15 Also see Dallek, *Partners in Power*, pp. 505–8; and Isaacson, *Kissinger*, pp. 502–3.

46. *FRUS 1969-1976*, vol. 25, nos. 218 ("galaxy"), 220 ("shocked"), and 250. For Kissinger on Kissinger's Middle Eastern strategy, see, *WHY*, pp. 579–82; *Years of Upheaval*, pp. 940–44, 1033–36; and *Years of Renewal*, pp. 353–55.

47. DNSA, EBB, "October War," no. 60 ("thing").

48. *FRUS 1969-1976*, vol. 36, no. 127 ("shift"). For Faisal's threats, see Jiddah Embassy to State Department, December 18, 1972 and December 19, 1972, in NPMP, MRS, NSC Files, CouF, Middle East, Saudi Arabia, box 3, both summarized in *FRUS 1969-1976*, vol. 24, no. 170; and "Faisal Warns US on Israel," July 6, 1973, *WP*, p. 1. Also see Sadat, *In Search of Identity*, pp. 327–29; and *FRUS 1969-1976*, ol. 36, nos. 183, 190, 191, 193.

49. On Pahlavi and prices, see Cooper, *Oil Kings*, esp. chap. 5. For the talks that preceded the embargo, see Terzian, *OPEC: The Inside Story*, pp. 169–75. For the rolling embargo and Faisal's threat, see *FRUS 1969-1976*, vol. 36, nos. 210, 218, 223; "WSAG Meeting," October

6, 1973, NPMP, NSC-IF, box H-94; DNSA, EBB, "October War," no. 26; and Situation Report, October 15, 1973, NPMP, NSC Files, Middle East War, box 1174. For Kissinger's response, see *FRUS 1969-1976*, vol. 36, nos. 217. Nixon's appropriation request is in "Special Message to the Congress," October 19, 1973, APP. For Faisal's response, see DNSA, EBB, "October War," no. 45b ("jihad").

50. The embargo included the Netherlands and Portugal, which Faisal adjudged to have supported Israel. For US assessments of the prospects for a broader embargo see *FRUS 1969-1976*, vol. 36, nos. 185, 206, and 215. For prices, see DeGolyer and MacNaughton, *TCPS*, p. 13; and Yergin, *The Prize*, p., 625. For Pahlavi, see "Arab Oil: Has Gone Up," *NYT*, December 30, 1973, p. 97 ("finished").

51. For energy, see International Energy Agency, *Key World Energy Statistics*. The Dow Jones Industrial Average was 948.84 on October 1, 1973. A year later, it was just 604.82. See Yahoo Finance, http://finance.yahoo.com/. Also see "1929 and All That," the *Economist*, December 1, 1973, p. 108; and "The Approaching Depression," the *Economist*, June 1, 1974, p. 69. For the effects on the capitalist countries, see Lieber, *Oil Decade*; and Vernon, *Oil Crisis*. More broadly, see Eckes and Zeiler, *United States and Globalization*, chap. 8; Stein, *Pivotal Decade*, chap. 5; and Yergin, *The Prize*.

52. "Into the Dark," the *Economist*, December 1, 1973, p. 13 ("simultaneous"); "Energy Meeting," September 8, 1973, NPMP, NSC Files, SuF, Energy Crisis, box 321 ("much damage"). Also see *FRUS 1969-1976*, vol. 36, nos. 219 and 239.

53. See *FRUS 1969-1976*, vol. 36, nos. 229 ("solution"), 247, 250, and 314 ("plan for grabbing"); and *DBPO*, Series 3, vol. 4, nos. 434 ("world war") and 490. US officials believed that their European counterparts opposed military intervention, as *FRUS 1969-1976*, vol. 36, nos. 244 and 262 indicate. For doubts about the readiness of military bases, see Secretary's Staff Meeting, January 7, 1974, NARA, RG-59, HAK Staff Meetings, box 6 ("protect access"). To explore the issue, Kissinger initiated NSSM 196, "Overseas Military Base Structure," February 25, 1974, NPMP, NSC-IF, box H-207. In January 1974, the US government proposed upgrading base facilities at Diego Garcia. See UKNA, FCO 82/460. On the prospect of Faisal's overthrow, see Kissinger-Ford MemCon, May 5, 1975, GFPL, NSA Files, MemCons, box 11. For public speculation as to the likelihood of military action, see "U.S. Might Seize Oil Fields," *LAT*, January 11, 1974; and "A Word to the Arabs," January 12, 1974, *NYT*, p. 3.

54. *FRUS 1969-1976*, vol. 36, nos. 363 ("savages); and Secretary's Staff Meeting, January 7, 1974, NARA, RG-59, HAK Staff Meetings, box 6 ("ransom").

55. Journalist Jack Anderson alleged that Kissinger had approved the December 1973 price hike. See "Kissinger Cleared Iran's Oil Gouge," *WP*, December 5, 1979, a claim that Cooper, *Oil Kings*, p. 145 repeats. Sheikh Yamani made a similar claim two decades later. See "Saudi Dove in the Oil Slick," the *Guardian* (UK), January 14, 2001. For an extreme version of this argument, see Engdahl, *Century of War*, pp. 130–38. More judicious is Walter Isaacson, who summarizes the debate in *Kissinger*, pp. 563–64. Reasoning from the available evidence, this author concludes US officials believed that *some* increase in the price of oil would serve US interests but that they were not prepared for the fourfold increase that late 1973 brought.

56. See *FRUS 1969-1976*, vol. 1, no. 41 ("condominium"). Kissinger struggled to reassure allies, as in *DBPO*, Series 3, vol. 4, nos. 119, 232, 363, 447, 513, 521, 568; and "Conversation between Kissinger and Douglas-Home," December 12, 1973, in UKNA, FCO 82/309. For a systematic assessment, see "NSSM 164: U.S. Relations With Europe," December 18, 1972, NPMP, NSC-IF, Study Memorandums, H-194 ("transitional").

57. Kissinger, "The Year of Europe," April 23, 1973 in *DOS Bulletin*, May 14, 1973, pp. 593–98 ("comprehensive"). Also see, "U.S.-EC Declaration," October 26, 1973, NPMP, NSC Files, SuF, EC, box 322, and *DBPO*, Series 3, vol. 4, no. 227; and Kissinger, *Years of Upheaval*, pp. 128–94, 700–29.

58. Douglas-Home to UK Embassies worldwide, October 15, 1973, UKNA, FCO 59/916 ("say nothing"); Kissinger Staff Meeting, October 16, 1973, NARA, RG-59, Staff Meetings, box 1; and Quandt, *Peace Process*, p. 163. For Kissinger's reaction, see *FRUS 1969–1976*, vol. 25, nos. 250 ("disgrace") and 261. For the EEC's declaration, see *DBPO*, Series 3, vol. 4, no. 375. British officials tried to reassure the US ambassador that the UK government was defying

not only Washington but also a "large majority of [pro-Israel] British public opinion." See DNSA, EBB "October War" no. 39. And *DBPO*, Series 3, vol. 4, np. 404 ("melancholy").

59. On the economic impact, see *FRUS 1969–1976*, vol. 36, nos. 223, 232, 235, 261, 262, 277. For the rush to bilateral deals, see *FRUS 1969–1976*, vol. 36, nos. 262, 299, and 345. Also see Douglas-Home to UK Missions worldwide, January 11, 1974, UKNA, FCO 59/1164 ("irresponsible"); and *FRUS 1969–1976*, vol. 36, no. 262 ("alternative").

60. Nixon, "Address to the Nation," November 7, 1973, APP ("energy needs"). For critiques, see "Mr. Nixon's Energy Program," *WP*, November 27, 1973p. 23; and "A Fortress America?" December 3, 1973, *NYT*, p. 39. Also see Nye, "Independence and Interdependence," *Foreign Policy* No. 22 (1976), pp. 130–61; and Keohane and Nye, *Power and Interdependence*, esp. 239.

61. *FRUS 1969-1976*, vol. 36, nos. 256 ("energy front"), 295, 305 ("autarky concept"), and 311.

62. Kissinger, "The United States and Europe," December 12, 1973, in *DOS Bulletin*, vol. 77, December 31, 1973, pp. 777–82 ("erosion").

63. On Kissinger's emerging energy policy, see *FRUS 1969-1976*, vol. 36, nos. 116 ("domestic action") 229 ("political benefits"), and 247; and "The Energy Problem," December 6, 1973, NARA, RG-59, PPC, Director's Files, box 346. For the Washington Conference, see Kissinger, *Years of Upheaval*, 722–29; Kissinger's Staff Meeting, January 8, 1974, NARA, RG-59, KSM, box 2; Nixon to Heads of Government, January 9, 1974, NPMP, WHCF, IT 50-3, box 13; and "President Nixon's Letters," January 11, 1974, UKNA, FCO 59/1164.

64. On Sadat and peace, see *FRUS 1969-1976*, vol. 25, nos. 118, 138, 160, 189, 190, 214, 256, and 349. On the disengagement agreement, see Kissinger, *Years of Upheaval*, pp. 799–853; and Quandt, *Peace Process*, pp. 130–43. Also useful are Kissinger's presentations to congressional leaders on January 21, 1974, and Nixon's cabinet on January 23, 1974 ("moral force"), in GFPL, NSA Files, MemCons, box 3; and the transcript of Kissinger's January 21 staff meeting in NARA, RG-59, KSM, box 2. Also see *FRUS 1969-1976*, vol. 25, nos. 303, 311, 312, 316, 317, 323, 324, 327, 329, 333, 335, 337, 341, 343, 344, 347, 349, 361, and 362.

65. On the conference itself, see "Major Oil Consuming Countries Meet at Washington," *DOS Bulletin*, vol. 70, no. 1810, pp. 201–35 ("explosion of demand," etc.); Kissinger, *Years of Upheaval*, pp. 896–925; "Briefing Notes," February 9, 1974, NPMP, NSC Files, SuF, Energy Crisis, box 321; and *FRUS 1969-1976*, vol. 36, nos. 299, 305–6, 314–15, and 319.

66. On the International Energy Agency, see Kapstein, *Insecure Alliance*, 177–84; Keohane, "International Energy Agency"; Lantzke, "OECD and Its International Energy Agency"; Scott, *History of the International Energy Agency*, esp. vol. 2; Yergin, *The Quest*, 269–75; and Willrich and Conant, "International Energy Agency." On French policy, see *DBPO*, Series 3, vol. 4, nos. 499, 501, 505, 544, 547, 549, and 550. On British policy, see *DBPO*, Series 3, vol. 4, no. 503, 516, 519, 536, 539, 542, 553 ("the Americans are right") 555, and 557. London's decision to side with the Washington owed to calculations of interest, not the pull of sentiment. On this point, see Hamilton, "Britain, France, and America's Year of Europe"; and Robb, "The Power of Oil." Kissinger is in *FRUS 1969-1976*, vol. 36, no. 314 ("Atlantic").

67. *FRUS 1969-1976*, vol. 36, no. 314 ("Band-Aid"). Kissinger envisaged a dual-track approach early on. "If they will not work multilaterally," he decided, "we will force them by going bilateral ourselves." See Staff Meeting, January 8, 1974, NARA, RG-59, KSM, box 2. For Kissinger in Saudi Arabia, see *FRUS 1969-1976*, vol. 36, nos. 330–32 ("military field"). On his return, he initiated NSSM 198, "Joint U.S.-Saudi Economic, Military, and Technological Cooperation," March 12, 1974, NPMP, NSC Files, SuF, NSSMs, box 365. Also see Bronson, *Thicker Than Oil*, pp. 126–29; Kissinger, *Years of Upheaval*, pp. 974–976; Lippman, *Inside the Mirage*, pp. 167–78; and Spiro, *Hidden Hand*, pp. 88–91. Kissinger tries to reconcile bilateralism and multilateralism in *FRUS 1969-1976*, vol. 36, no. 315. On U.S.-Iranian cooperation, see "Initial Study Report on U.S.-Iran Cooperation," April 27, 1974, NPMP, NSC-IF, Study Memorandums, box H-204.

68. On the evolution of Saudi Arabia's terms for lifting the embargo and US efforts to redefine them, see *FRUS 1969-1976*, vol. 36, nos. 298, 302, 303, 304, 307, 309, 312, 325, 327, 332, and 341 ("disengagement"). On the agreement itself, see Kissinger, *Years of Upheaval*, pp. 1032–110; and "Dr. Kissinger's Cabinet Briefing," May 31, 1974, GFPL, NSA Files, MemCons, box 4. Also see Stein, *Heroic Diplomacy*, pp. 153–62; and Quandt, *Peace Process*, pp. 148–52.

69. "Middle East Briefing," May 31, 1974, GFPL, NSA Files, MemCon, box 4 ("moving"). Also see Kissinger, *Years of Upheaval*, pp. 1033–36. For Kissinger's speech, see "The Challenge of Interdependence," April 15, 1974, *DOS Bulletin*, vol. 70, no. 477, May 6, 1974, pp. 477–83; and Secretary's Staff Meeting, March 15, 1974, NARA, RG-59, KSM, box 3.
70. Keohane, *After Hegemony*, pp. 217–40.

Chapter 6

1. "Interdependence Day," *NYT*, July 4, 1976, p. 10 ("on this day"); and "Too Old for a Birthday Party," the *Economist*, July 3, 1976, pp. 29–30.
2. Commager is in Myers and Barber, *Interdependence Handbook*, pp. 98–100 ("new era"). Also see Cleveland, "Diplomacy of Interdependence." Buchanan is in "Maybe One Declaration Is Enough," *Chicago Tribune*, June 6, 1976, A6 ("mush-headed"). On Minnesota, see Humphrey to Carter, January 25, 1977, JCPL, WHCF, HU-4, box 4.
3. Nye, "American Power and Foreign Policy," *NYT*, July 7, 1976, p. 25; and Nye, "Independence and Interdependence." For public opinion, see "American Public Opinion and U.S. Foreign Policy," in JCPL, 1976 Campaign Files, Issues Office, Foreign Policy, box 46. Also see Mandelbaum and Schneider, "New Internationalisms."
4. On food, population, and national security, see "NSSM 200: Implications of Worldwide Population Growth for U.S. Security," August 7, 1974, NPMP, NSC-IF, Under Secretaries Study Memorandums, box H-268.
5. Raymond Garthoff's verdict in *Détente and Confrontation* that the transition from Nixon to Ford was marked by "substantial consistency" (p. 263) remains the dominant view, restated, most recently, in Zanchetta, *Transformation of American International Power*. An exception is Mieczkowski, *Gerald Ford and the Challenges of the 1970s*, which acknowledges Ford's departures in foreign policy but emphasizes his domestic accomplishments. King, "U.S. Foreign Policy Decision-Making under Ford and Kissinger, 1974-77" is a creative effort to reorient scholarship to new perspectives.
6. See Cooper, *Economics of Interdependence*; Kindleberger, *Power and Money* ("idiosyncratic," p. 195); and Vernon, *Sovereignty at Bay*. Also see Kaiser, "Transnational Politics: Toward a Theory"; and, more broadly, Keohane and Nye, eds., *Transnational Relations and World Politics*.
7. Brown, *World without Borders*. For the State Department's use of Brown, see Lord to Laise, March 8, 1974, NARA, RG-59, PPC, Director's Files, box 345. For Toffler, see *Future Shock*; and Connelly, "Future Shock."
8. See Club of Rome, *Limits to Growth*; and Ehrlich, *Population Bomb*. For a useful critique of the Club's method, see James, *Monetary Cooperation*, pp. 252–53.
9. Alfred Sauvy, *Zero Growth?*
10. Keohane and Nye, "Transnational Relations and World Politics," ("inadequate basis"); and *Power and Interdependence*. For context, see Keohane and Nye, "Globalization"; Keohane, "Old IPE and the New"; Nye, "Studying World Politics"; and Keohane, "A Personal and Intellectual History." Also see Cohen, *International Political Economy*, esp. pp. 95–103.
11. For Brzezinski on Eastern Europe, see *Soviet Bloc*. On the "technetronic age," see "American Transition."
12. Brzezinski, *Between Two Ages* ("global city"); and *Fragile Blossom*. Also see "Japan's Global Engagement." On the origins of the Trilateral Commission, see Rockefeller, "Trilateral Commission at 25" ("International Commission"); and Rockefeller, *Memoirs*, pp. 416–18. This paragraph also draws on author interview with Zbigniew Brzezinski, June 24, 2009.
13. "Meeting on Proposed Trilateral Commission" ("drift aimlessly"); "Trilateral Commission," October 16, 1973 ("trilateral basis"); Franklin to Planning Group, December 19, 1972; and "Trilateral Policy Program," August 20, 1973 ("global political process"), all in JCPL, ZBM, Trilateral Commission File, boxes 1 and 3. Also see Gill, *American Hegemony*, esp. pp. 132–42; and Sklar, ed., *Trilateralism*, esp. pp. 76–82.
14. Kaji et. al., *Towards a Renovated World Monetary System*; and Duchene et. al., *Crisis of International Cooperation* ("growing interdependence").

15. Brzezinski to Kissinger, October 13, 1973; Brzezinski to Jackson, November 30, 1973; MemCon, April 16, 1973; and Summary of Meeting of the Board of Trustees, February 8, 1975, all in JCPL, ZBM, Trilateral Commission File, box 1; and author interview with President Carter, August 2, 2009 ("profoundly").

16. Conducting an Internet search for the words "Trilateral Commission" will illuminate the point. For an example of the conspiracy genre, see Marrs, *Rule by Secrecy.* For analysis of the phenomenon, see Barkun, *A Culture of Conspiracy,* esp. chap. 4. For the critique from the right, see Kristol, " 'New Cold War'," *WSJ,* July 17, 1975, p. 18; from the left, see Barraclough, "Wealth and Power," *New York Review of Books,* August 7, 1975 ("rich man's").

17. For the 1975 report, see Huntington et. al., *Crisis of Democracy* ("parochialism"). For the critique, see "The Ruling Class," *WP,* November 26, 1976, D5. Also see Kaiser, "Transnational Relations as a Threat to the Democratic Process."

18. Here I have learned much from Peterman, "Will to Respond in Common."

19. For the CFR and US policy, see Schulzinger, *Wise Men of Foreign Affairs;* and Wala, *Council on Foreign Relations.* Shoup and Minter, *Imperial Brain Trust* exaggerates the CFR's influence. Grose, *Continuing the Inquiry* is a useful official history. On Armstrong, see Roberts, "Council Has Been Your Creation."

20. "The Council and the World of the 1980s," September 10, 1973 ("traditional," etc.); Press Release, December 14, 1975, both in MLP, CFR, Projects, 1980s, box 301; and "The 1980s Project," March 7, 1975, MLP, CFR, Projects, 1980s, box 312. The 1980s Project built on an earlier CFR initiative that Miriam Camps led, which presented its conclusions in Camps, *Management of Interdependence.* Scholarship on the 1980s Project is limited, but Schulzinger addresses it in *Wise Men of Foreign Affairs,* pp. 227–35.

21. See "Report of Seminar on Economic Interdependence and the Nation's Future," NARA, RG-56, RGS, Economic Interdependence, box 3 ("major changes," etc.).

22. "Address to the General Assembly," September 18, 1974, APP ("new approaches").

23. For the Cold War in the past tense, see *FRUS 1969-1976,* vol. 25, no. 201, and vol. 31, no. 187. For the crisis of the mid-1970s, see Bundy, ed., *World Economic Crisis;* and Gardner, "World Food and Energy Crisis." For the Trilateral Commission, see Resolution, December 9–10, 1974, Rockefeller Archive Center, Trilateral Commission Records, Series I, box 5 ("drastic"). Barraclough is in "Great World Crisis I," *New York Review of Books,* January 23, 1975. For Kissinger, see *FRUS 1969-1976,* vol. 38, no. 46.

24. For Brzezinski's critique, see "Recognizing the Crisis."

25. For Prebisch, see Dosman, *Raúl Prebisch,* esp. pp. 378–441 and 473–76. Also see Mazower, *Governing the World,* pp. 299–304.

26. Statistics are from Maddison, WEHS; UN Food and Agriculture Organization, FAOSTAT; and "World Commodity Prices," the *Economist,* October 19, 1974, p.115. Also see "World Food Crisis," *NYT,* November 5, 1974, p.1. On the effects of the oil crisis, see Huntington, *Third Wave,* esp. pp. 51–54; and, on Portugal, Campbell, "Mediterranean Crisis"; and Maxwell, *Making of Portuguese Democracy,* pp. 55 and 139–42.

27. Boumedienne is in Ahmia, *Group of 77,* 3:185–204 ("decisive," etc.). For dependency theory, see Chilcote and Edelstein, eds., *Struggle with Dependency and Beyond.*

28. The Charter is UN A/RES/3281(XXIX). The NIEO sparked produced a flurry of analysis, to which Cox, "Ideologies and the New International Economic Order" and Nawaz, *New International Economic Order* are reliable guides. The historiography is more limited, but Hart, *New International Economic Order;* and Krasner, *Structural Conflict,* offer analysis, while Haq, *Poverty Curtain,* provides firsthand perspective.

29. "Challenge of Interdependence," April 15, 1974, *DOS Bulletin,* May 6, 1974, pp. 477–83 ("notion"). For the reaction, see "Kissinger at UN," *NYT,* April 16, 1974, p.1; "Resources for Mankind," *NYT,* April 16, 1974, p.38; and "Turning Towards Global Problems," *WP,* May 1, 1974, p. A24.

30. See *FRUS 1969-1976,* vol. 31, no. 292 ("confront"), and no. 299 ("theology"). On US reactions to the NIEO, see Ferguson, "Politics of the New International Economic Order"; and Olson, *U.S. Foreign Policy.* Contrast with Hudson, *Global Fracture,* a sharp critique.

31. On Washington's tolerance for diversity in the early Cold War, see Amsden, *Escape from Empire,* esp. chaps 3–6. On the rise of neoliberal ideas, see Mirowski and Plehwe, eds.,

Road from Mont Pèlerin; Stedman Jones, *Masters of the Universe*; and Yergin and Stanislaw, *Commanding Heights*. More attuned to the roles of politics and policy choices are Burgin, *Great Persuasion*; Krippner, *Capitalizing on Crisis*; and Kim Phillips-Fein, *Invisible Hands*. On Rand and Greenspan, see Burns, *Goddess of the Market*, esp. 149–51; and Greenspan, *Age of Turbulence*, pp. 40–41, 51–53. On Simon, see *Time for Truth*, p. 230 ("orthodoxy"). On tensions within the Ford administration, see Porter, *Presidential Decision Making*, pp. 49–54.

32. Statistics are from UN Food and Agriculture Organization, FAOSTAT; and *FRUS 1969-1976*, vol. 31, no.252 ("suffer").

33. "Address by Secretary Kissinger," November 5, 1974, in *DOS Bulletin*, November 9, 1974, pp. 821–29 ("cooperation"); and *FRUS 1969-1976*, vol. 31, no. 266 ("damn").

34. Destler, "United States Food Policy" ("If Henry needs it"). On the 1972 deal, see Kissinger, *White House Years*, pp. 1269–71; and Trager, *Great Grain Robbery*. For Nixon's export controls, see "Address to the Nation Announcing Price Control Measures," June 13, 1973, APP. For the backlash within the administration see *FRUS 1969-1976*, vol. 31, nos. 170–76, 180, 245; and Matusow, *Nixon's Economy*, pp. 238–40. For internal disagreements on food aid, *see* *FRUS 1969-1976*, vol. 31, nos. 253, 256, 263–67, 270, 272, 275–76. For the development of Kissinger's food concept, see *FRUS 1969-1976*, vol. 31, nos. 272 ("isolated"), 273–74 and 278.

35. Butz, "An Emerging, Market-Oriented Food and Agricultural Policy." For all Butz's genuflections to the market, subsidies continued, and set asides soon resumed. See Orden et. al., *Policy Reform in American Agriculture*, pp. 67–72. For perspective, see Gardner, *American Agriculture in the Twentieth Century*, esp. pp. 213–21; and Cochrane, *Development of American Agriculture*, esp. chap. 15. Critics often identify Butz's embrace of agribusiness as a key historical turning point. See Bittman, *Food Matters*, pp. 42–43; Pollan, *Omnivore's Dilemma*, pp. 51–53; and Roberts, *End of Food*, pp. 120–22. For Kissinger, see "Address by Secretary Kissinger," November 5, 1974, in *DOS Bulletin*, November 9, 1974, pp. 821–29 ("restrictions"). For the food reserve concept, see *FRUS 1969-1976*, vol. 31, nos. 280, 286, and 288; and Kissinger, "Strengthening the World Economic Structure," May 13, 1975, *DOS Bulletin*, June 2, 1975 ("special provision").

36. *FRUS 1969-1976*, vol. 31, no. 290 ("compromising"). On the Lomé Convention, see "The Nine and the 46," the *Economist*, February 8, 1975, pp. 12–13; and Gruhn, "Lomé Convention." Some argued that Lomé was likelier to exacerbate inequalities than resolve them. For this view, see Dolan, "Lomé Convention"; and Mytelka, "Lomé Convention." For Kissinger's defense of his policy, see *FRUS 1969-1976*, vol. 31, no. 292.

37. For Kissinger, see *FRUS 1969-1976*, vol 31, nos. 292 ("not reliable"), 293–94, 295 ("basic strategy"); and *Years of Renewal*, pp. 697–700 ("brethren"). For Moynihan's perspective, see Moynihan and Weaver, *Dangerous Place*, pp. 120–24.

38. "Global Challenge and International Cooperation," July 14, 1975, *DOS Bulletin*, August 4, 1976, pp. 149–60 ("concrete"); and "Global Consensus and Economic Development," September 1, 1975, *DOS Bulletin*, September 22, 1975, pp. 425–41 ("case by case"). Pat Moynihan read the September speech, Kissinger having been called away to finalize the Sinai II agreement. Also see *FRUS 1969-1976*, vol. 31, nos. 296–99; and Kissinger, *Years of Renewal*, pp. 698–700.

39. On the North-South dialogue, see Amuzegar, "North-South Dialogue"; Bergsten, "Interdependence and the Reform of International Institutions"; and US Congress, House, Committee on International Relations, *North-South Dialogue*. For Nairobi and the IRB initiative, see "Expanding Cooperation for Global Economic Development," May 6, 1976, *DOS Bulletin*, May 31, 1976, pp. 657–72. "Report on Secretary Kissinger's Trip," May 12, 1976, GFPL, NSA Files, MemCons, box 19; "Rich Man, Poor Man," the *Economist*, May 1, 1976, pp.81–82, and "Henry's Good Intentions," the *Economist*, May 8, 1976, pp. 95–96; and *FRUS 1969-1976*, vol. 31, nos. 304–5. Kissinger discusses his larger strategic purposes in *FRUS 1969-1976*, vol. 31, nos. 292–95, and 297.

40. "Monitoring the Crisis of the West," *WP*, July 30, 1974, p. A18 ("deepening"); Schmidt, "Struggle for the World Product" ("fragility"); William Bundy, ed., *World Economic Crisis*,

for analogies to 1930s; and "The Real Economic Threat," *NYT*, September 22, 1974, p. 10 ("catastrophe").

41. *FRUS 1969-1976*, vol. 31, no. 292 ("trick").

42. On the dilemma, see *FRUS 1969-1976*, vol. 36, no. 277, 353, and 356; and Pollack, "Economic Consequences of the Energy Crisis"; and Yergin, *The Prize*, chap. 31. For estimates of the costs, see "Implications of the Exploding World Oil Crisis,"January 1, 1974, UKNA, FCO 59/1164; "Notes on Balance of Payment Consequences of Higher Oil Prices,"January 8, 1974, IMF Archive, CenF, Economic Subject Files, S180 Oil Facility, box 468; and OECD, "Financing the Oil Deficits," April 6, 1974, UKNA, FCO 59/1173. For Witteveen, see "Recycling the Oil Billions," May 6, 1974, IMF Archive, CenF, Economic Subject Files, S180 Oil Facility, box 468.

43. Saudi enthusiasm for an IMF facility is documented in "Discussion with Mr. Anwar Ali," January 16, 1974, and "Anwar Ali Plan," April 3, both in IMF Archive, CenF, Economic Subject Files, S180 Oil Facility, box 468; and "Note for the Record," April 10, 1974, UKNA, FCO 59/1168. For the West's reorientation to market-based methods, see Report of HM Treasury Working Party, March 8, 1974, UKNA, FCO 59/1172 ("mechanisms"); and "Washington Energy Conference," March 28, 1974, UKNA, FCO 59/1168. For US opposition to IMF-based recycling, see "New Oil Facility," February 14, 1974; and "Discussion with Secretary Shultz," March 11, 1974, both in IMF Archive, CenF, Economic Subject Files, S180 Oil Facility, box 468; and *FRUS 1969-1976*, vol. 36, no. 286. For the IMF facility, see "Introduction by the Fund of an Oil Facility," January 8, 1974; "A Facility to Assist Members," February 19, 1974; "Financing Oil," March 1974; Executive Board Meeting 74/27, April 1, 1974; and "Decision on Facility," May 31, 1974, all in IMF Archive, CenF, Economic Subject Files, S180 Oil Facility, box 468. On the consequences, see BIS, *Annual Report* (1975), pp.129–47, and (1976), pp.75–95; and James, *Monetary Cooperation*, pp. 316–22.

44. Ford-Leone-Moro MemCon, September 26, 1974, GFPL, NSA Files, MemCons, box 6 ("most serious").

45. *FRUS 1969-1976*, vol. 26, no. 189 ("130 million"). On the relationship of oil to the Arab-Israeli peace process, see *FRUS 1969-1976*, vol. 26, nos. 95, 110, 111, 112, 116, 174, 189; and Cabinet Meeting Minutes, February 21, 1974, GFPL, NSA Files, MemCons, box 3. Also see Spiegel, *Other Arab-Israeli Conflict*, pp. 226–27. The historiography on the post-1973 peace process is ample. See Miller, *Much Too Promised Land*; Spiegel, *Other-Arab-Israeli Conflict*, chap. 7; Stein, *Heroic Diplomacy*; Touval, *Peace Brokers*, chap. 9; and Quandt, *Peace Process*, chap. 5. For Kissinger's role, see *Years of Renewal*, chaps. 12–14.

46. For critiques of the step-by-step approach, see Ball, *Diplomacy for a Crowded World*, pp. 133–52; and Hoffmann, *Primacy or World Order*, pp. 74–76. Kissinger mulled the adoption of a "comprehensive" approach in March 1975, but what he most likely intended was to induce Israeli flexibility, not to reevaluate strategic purposes. See *FRUS 1969-1976*, nos. 159, 164, 166, and 169. Kissinger brushes over the episode in *Years of Renewal*, chap. 14; it receives fuller treatment in Spiegel, *Other Arab-Israeli Conflict*, pp. 294–97. For Javits, see *FRUS 1969-1976*, vol. 26, no. 201 ("American Jews"). Kissinger's frustration with Israel's US supporters is evident, even poignant, in *FRUS 1969-1976*, vol. 26, nos. 197; and Ford-Kissinger MemCons, December 17, 1974 and June 23, 1975, GFPL, NSA Files, MemCons, boxes 8 and 13.

47. *FRUS 1969-1976*, vol. 26, no. 95 ("take oil fields"). Public speculation peaked in early 1975, after Kissinger told *Business Week* that force might be appropriate "where there is some actual strangulation of the industrialized world." See *DOS Bulletin*, January 27, 1975, pp. 97–107; "Armed Intervention over Oil Eyed," *WP*, November 8, 1974, p. D19; "Kissinger Won't Rule Out Force,"*Chicago Tribune*, January 3, 1975, p. 1; "Oil Field Seizure Is Not Ruled Out," *LAT*, January 3, 1975, p. A1; "An Invasion of the Oil Fields?" *Chicago Tribune*, January 5, 1975, p. A4; "Arabs Urged to Plan against U.S. Invasion," *LAT*, January 6, 1975, p. 5; "Showdown Urged with Oil Producers," *WP*, January 6, 1975, p. D11; "Why Did Mr. Kissinger Say That?" *NYT*, January 19, 1975, p. 183; and "Saudis Warn against Using Force," *WP*, May 22, 1975, p. A1. For the internal debate, see *FRUS 1969-1976*, vol. 37, nos 7, 32 ("Abu Dhabi") 36, 52, 57, and 79. Talk of military action disturbed US allies in Europe, prompting Kissinger to disavow it. See *FRUS 1969-1976*, vol. 37, nos. 9, 42, and 88. Kissinger argued that military threats engendered OPEC flexibility on prices. See *FRUS 1969-1976*, vol. 37, no. 39;

and Kissinger, *Years of Renewal*, pp. 689–90. For the US-Saudi Joint Commission, see *FRUS 1969-1976*, vol. 37, nos. 47. On the pursuit of a bilateral deal with Iran, see *FRUS 1969-1976*, vol. 26, no. 184; *FRUS 1969-1976*, vol. 37, nos. 27, 56, 67, 77 ("major crack"), 95, 96; Ford-Kissinger MemCon, March 4, 1975, GFPL, NSA Files, MemCons, box 9.

48. See "The United States and Oil Prices," September 18, 1974, UKNA, FCO 59/1161 ("velvet glove"). On Doha, see "Strategy for Preventing Oil Price Increase," November 2, 1976; "Meeting with Venezuelan Ambassador," December 1, 1976, and "Meeting with Iranian Ambassador," December 7, 1976, all in GFPL, NSA Files, International Economic Affairs, box 1; Ford-Schmidt MemCon, November 23, 1976; and Ford-Zahedi MemCon, December 7, 1976, both in GFPL, NSA Files, MemCons, box 21; and *FRUS 1969-1976*, vol. 37, nos. 106, 109, 111, 113 ("split decision"), and 114. Kissinger is in "The Energy Crisis," November 14, 1974, *DOS Bulletin*, December 2, 1974, pp. 749–56 ("objective conditions"). For analysis, see Cooper, "Showdown at Doha." On Saudi Arabian motives, see Skeet, *OPEC*, pp. 142–43.

49. For the Camp David talks of September 28-29, see *FRUS 1969-1976*, vol. 37, no. 9 ("oil prices must come down"); Ford-Kissinger MemCon, September 29, 1974, GFPL, NSA Files, MemCons, box 6. For background, "Strategies for the Oil Crisis," September 21, 1974; and "Memorandum for the Secretary," September 27, 1974, both in NARA, RG59, PPC, Director's Files, Winston Lord, box 349. British reticence is evident in "Dr. Kissinger and Oil Prices" (undated); and "Oil Prices" (undated), both in UKNA, FCO59/1161. On emergency sharing procedures, see *FRUS 1969-1976*, vol. 37, no. 6. For Kissinger, see "The Energy Crisis," November 14, 1974, *DOS Bulletin*, December 2, 1974, pp. 749–56 ("lasting creativity"); and *FRUS 1969-1976*, vol. 37, no. 18.

50. For the differences between Kissinger and Giscard, see *FRUS 1969-1976*, vol. 37, no. 10, 12 ("French sabotage"), 15, and 16. For London's reorientation towards Washington, see *FRUS 1969-1976*, vol. 37, no. 14; "International Energy Questions," November 7, 1974, UKNA, FCO 82/465. And, for the Martinique compromise, *FRUS 1969-1976*, vol. 37, nos. 22, and 24 ("parallel paths"); "Communiqué Following Discussions," December 16, 1974, APP; Kissinger to Callaghan, December 16, 1974, UKNA, FCO 82/465.

51. *FRUS 1969-1976*, vol. 37, no. 24 ("disintegration"). On Kronberg, see Shultz, "Report on Private Group of Five Meeting," February 2-3, 1975; and Ford-Kissinger-Shultz MemCon, February 7, 1975, both in GFPL, NSA Files, MemCons, box 9. For Schmidt's proposal that technical experts meet "for a further exchange of views" and Ford's enthusiastic response, see "Schmidt Invitation," March 11, 1975, GFPL, NSA Files, International Economic Affairs, box 1.

52. For the domestic implications of Kissinger's concept, see *FRUS 1969-1976*, vol. 37, nos. 39, 42, 46, 56, and 65. For Ford's policy, see "Address Reporting on the State of the Union," January 15, 1975, APP ("fee"); and "Address to the Nation on Energy Problems," May 27, 1975, APP ("nothing positive"). Also see Mieczkowski, *Gerald Ford and the Challenges of the 1970s*, chaps. 12–15; and Simon, *Time for Truth*, pp. 45–85.

53. Campbell et. al., *Energy: A Strategy for International Action* ("face the truth"). Kissinger disparaged the Trilateral Commission's advocacy of producer-consumer talks, arguing its members were putting their individual interests, which included investments in the OPEC countries, ahead of the national interest. See *FRUS 1969-1976*, vol. 37, no. 23.

54. *FRUS 1969-1976*, vo. 37, nos. 99, 102 ("sorry state"), 104.

55. For financial liberalization under Nixon, see "International Money and Capital Markets," March 27, 19774; and "Meeting of the Executive Committee of the CIEP," April 10, 1974, both in NARA, RG-56, RGS, CIEP, boxes 2–3; and "International Investment Reform," NPMP, POF, PHF, box 26. Differences within the US government are revealed in *FRUS 1969-1976*, vol. 31, nos. 16 and 17. On the C-20, see Dam, *Rules of the Game*, pp. 213–21; de Vries, *International Monetary Fund, 1972-1978*, vol. 2, pp. 123–71; James, *Monetary Cooperation*, pp. 245–59; IMF, *International Monetary Reform*; and Williamson, *Failure of World Monetary Reform*.

56. The gold controversy is documented in *FRUS 1969-1976*, vol. 31, nos. 39–40, 43, 57, 60–63, 66–67, 70, 72, 75, 78, 80–81, 86–88, 90, 97–100, 127.

57. *FRUS 1969-1976*, vol. 31, no. 80 ("perfectly useless").

58. The origins of the summit antedated the Ford administration: Schmidt urged international meetings after the collapse of fixed exchange rates and during the oil crisis. See *FRUS 1969-1976*, vol. 31, nos. 34, 94, 95; "Schmidt Invitation,"March 11, 1975; and Ford-Schmidt MemCon, May 29, 1975, GFPL, NSA Files, MemCons, box 12. On Schmidt, also see von Karczewski, "*Weltwirtschaft Ist Unser Schicksal*"; Schmidt, *Men and Powers*, esp. pp. 173–75; and Soell, *Helmut Schmidt*, vol. 2, esp. pp. 415–60. For Giscard's proposal, see *FRUS 1969-1976*, vol. 31, nos. 91 ("deteriorating") and 93. Helmut Schmidt lends Giscard's initiative his strong support in *FRUS 1969-1976*, vol. 31, nos. 94 and 95 ("concrete steps").
59. For Flanigan, see "Your UN Speech," April 5, 1974, NARA, RG-56, RGS, State, box 7 ("basic philosophy"). For U.S. reactions to the summit proposal, see *FRUS 1969-1976*, vol. 31, no. 93, 96, 104, 112, 114, and 116 ("stimulation is not").
60. For Shultz's report, see *FRUS 1969-1976*, vol. 31, no. 102. Ford and Kissinger express their preference for an unofficial preparatory process and their concerns over the rigidity of US officials in "Sommet Monétaire," July 31, 1975, MTA.
61. *FRUS 1969-1976*, vol. 31, nos. 114 ("theology"), 116 ("purely economic" and 118 ("other senior people").
62. On Eurocommunism, see Brown, *Communism*, pp. 464–68; Pons, "Rise and Fall of Eurocommunism"; and Schwab, *Eurocommunism*. Carrillo, *Eurocommunism and the State* was in its time an influential manifesto.
63. For US responses to events in Portugal, see Del Pero, "Kissinger and the Portuguese Revolution"; and Szulc, "Lisbon and Washington." Fears of Eurocommunism and of ideological contagion from Portugal were persistent themes in US discussions of Europe in 1974–76. See Ford-Kissinger MemCon, September 25, 1974; Ford-Leone MemCon, September 25, 1974, both in GFPL, NSA Files, MemCons, box 6; Secretary's Staff Meeting, January 12, 1975, NARA, RG-59, Staff Meetings, box 6; Ford-Kissinger MemCon, April 17, 1975, Ford-Kissinger MemCon, May 1, 1975, and Ford-den Uly MemCon, May 14, 1975, all in GFPL, NSA Files, MemCons, box 11; Kissinger-Schmidt MemCon, May 21, 1975, DNSA; Ford-Kissinger MemCon, May 24, 1975, GFPL, NSA Files, MemCons, box 12; Secretary's Staff Meeting, July 1, 1976, NARA, RG-59, Staff Meetings, box 10; and Kissinger-Ford Meeting with Portuguese officials, May 29, 1975, GFPL, NSA Files, MemCons, box 12. The historiography on US responses to Eurocommunism remains limited, but see Barnet, *Alliance*, pp. 350–56; Garthoff, *Détente and Confrontation*, pp. 538–42; and Weisbrode, *Atlantic Century*, pp. 258–63. For the response to French Eurocommunism, see Heurtebizé, "Union of the Left in France, 1971-1981." John Gaddis, among others, interprets Kissinger's response to Eurocommunism as an overreaction borne of a homogenizing Cold War worldview. See *Strategies of Containment*, p. 331. But see Giscard's encouragement in Ford-Giscard MemCon, May 17, 1976, GFPL, NSA Files, MemCons, box 19 ("threat"). Schmidt is in *FRUS 1969-1976*, vol. 31, no. 94 ("strong leadership").
64. On the preparations, see Ford-Kissinger-Schmidt MemCon, October 3, 1975, GFPL, NSA Files, MemCons, box 15; "Economic Summit," October 8, 1975; "Initiatives for International Summit," October 7, 1975; "International Economic Summit Preparation," all in GFPL, NSA Files, International Economic Affairs, Rambouillet, box 4; and *FRUS 1969-1976*, vol. 31, nos. 102, 104–6, 110–20, 121 ("intimate and serious").
65. *FRUS 1969-1976*, vol. 31, no. 121 ("political framework"). Kissinger's Pittsburg speech is "The Industrial Democracies and the Future," November 11, 1975, in *DOS Bulletin*, vol. 73, December 1, 1975, pp.757–64.
66. For Rambouillet's logistics, see "Pre-Advance Report," October 23, 1975, GFPL, NSA Files, International Economic Affairs, Rambouillet (box 4) ("intensive seminar"). For transcripts of the summit's sessions, see *FRUS 1969-1976*, vol. 31, nos. 122–25 ("message," etc.) but compare the British versions, available from MTA. Kissinger's recollections are in *Years of Renewal*, pp. 692–97 ("Miki").
67. For Rambouillet's results, see "Declaration of Rambouillet," November 17, 1975, MTA. For a sampling of underwhelmed press reactions, see "Summit Substance," *NYT*, November 18, 1975, p.36; "Summit at Rambouillet," *WP*, November 23, 1975, B17; and "The Rambouillet Economic Parley," *NYT*, November 28, p. 20. For Kissinger's verdict, see "Press Conference of Kissinger and Simon," November 17, 1975, GFPL, NSA Files, International Economic

Affairs, box 4 ("isolated solutions"). The historiography on the summits remains thin. But see de Menil and Solomon, *Economic Summitry*; Putman and Bayne, *Hanging Together*, pp. 36–42; and Webb, *Political Economy of Policy Coordination*, pp. 176–79.

68. US officials defined resolution of the monetary debate as their primary objective for Rambouillet. See "Strengthened Coordination of Economic and Monetary Policies," GFPL, NSA Files, International Economic Affairs, Rambouillet (box 4). On negotiations, see *FRUS 1969-1976*, vol. 31, nos. 107–8, 126–27, 128 ("sweeping"), and 129. Also see de Vries, *International Monetary Fund, 1972-1978*, vol. 2, p. 761 ("embodiment").

69. For the fall 1975 colloquium, see "Brainstorming on Global Economics," October 11, 1975, GFPL, NSA Files, International Economic Affairs, Rambouillet, box 4 ("uncontrolled"). The phrase "non-system" is Harold James's; see *International Monetary Cooperation*, chap. 9.

70. *FRUS 1969-1976*, vol. 31, nos. 130–32, 133 ("sick countries"), 134–36; Ford-Giscard MemCon, May 17, 1976, GFPL, NSA Files, MemCons, box 19; "Your Meeting with George Shultz on Economic Summit" (with attachments), May 24, 1976; and Hormats, "Preparatory Meeting for Puerto Rico Summit," June 16, 1976, both in GFPL, NSA Files, International Economic Affairs, Puerto Rico, box 3.

71. *FRUS 1969-1976*, vol. 31, nos. 137–39, 140 ("SOBs"), 141–43, 144 ("moral foundation"), 145.

72. *FRUS 1969-1976*, vol. 31, nos. 147 ("common efforts"), 148 ("inflationary climate"), 149. For Ford and Kissinger's verdicts, see MemCon, June 29, 1976, GFPL, NSA Files, International Economic Affairs, Puerto Rico, box 4.

73. "Britain at the Brink," *NYT*, October 14, 1976, p. 49 ("doesn't work"); and Callaghan, Speech to Labour Party, September 28, 1976, at http://www.britishpoliticalspeech.org ("borrowed"). Yields on ten-year British Treasury bill increased from 12.3 percent in April 1976 to 15.1 percent in October, statistics from GFD. For the evolution of US policy on the British crisis, see "Call from Prime Minister Callaghan," (undated); Callaghan to Ford, September 30, 1976; Hormats to Scowcroft, October 27, 1976; Hormats to Scowcroft, November 2, 1976; Hormats to Scowcroft, "UK Economic Difficulties," November 12, 1976; Callaghan to Ford, November 12, 1976, all in GFPL, NSC Files, International Economic Affairs, United Kingdom, box 3. For Britain's "IMF Crisis" more broadly, see Burk and Cairncross, *Goodbye, Great Britain*; and Wass, *Decline to Fall*.

74. On the politics of adjustment, see James, *International Monetary Cooperation*, pp. 277–85. For the argument that the key turning points antedated the IMF's conditions, see Ludlam, "Gnomes of Washington."

75. *FRUS 1969-1976*, vol. 31, no. 144.

Chapter 7

1. Moynihan, "United States in Opposition," *Commentary*, March 1975, pp. 31–44 ("libertarian ideology"); and "Bilateral Traditions and Multilateral Realities," August 14, 1975, LOC, DPMP, United Nations File, box 338. On Moynihan in India, see Hodgson, *Gentleman from New York*, chap. 9.

2. For the appointment, see Kissinger-Moynihan TeleCons, February 24 and 26, 1975, DOS, FOIA Reading Room, Ford-Kissinger MemCon, March 26, 1975 and Ford-Kissinger-Moynihan MemCon, March 26, 1975, both in GFPL, NSA Files, MemCons, box 10. For the mood of early 1975, see Kissinger-Schlesinger MemCon, February 8, 1975, GFPL, NSA Files, MemCons, box 9. On Kissinger's "heartland" speeches, see Hanhimäki, *Flawed Architect*, pp. 434–36; and Worthen, *Man on Whom Nothing Was Lost*, pp. 117–24. For Moynihan on human rights, see Memorandum for the Secretary, September 9, 1975 ("claims"); and Moynihan to Rogers, February 9, 1976 ("secret weapon") LOC, DPMP, United Nations File, boxes 337 and 342; and Daniel P. Moynihan, "Was Woodrow Wilson Right?" *Commentary*, vol. 57, no. 5 (May 1974), pp. 25–30.

3. Speech by Idi Amin, October 1, 1975. LOC, DPMP, United Nations File, box 334; and Moynihan, *Dangerous Place*, pp. 158–66 ("murderer").

4. See UN A/RES/3379, "Elimination of All Forms of Racial Discrimination," November 12, 1975. For Moynihan's campaign against the Zionism Resolution, see *Dangerous Place*, pp. 169–99 ("damage"); and Troy, *Moynihan's Moment*. For Freedom House's involvement, see "Background for Ambassador Moynihan's United Nations Speech," November 13, 1975 ("challenged"); Sussman to Moynihan, November 14, 1975, LOC, DPMP, United Nations File, box 335; and Sussman's December 4, 1975 testimony in US Congress, Senate, Committee on Foreign Relations, hearing, *Foreign Assistance Authorization, Arms Sales* (1975), pp. 487–98. Moynihan's speech is in LOC, DPMP, United Nations File, box 335 ("selective morality"). Also see Moynihan, *Dangerous Place*, chap. 10; and Troy, *Moynihan's Moment*, esp. pp. 109–57.

5. See Ford-Kissinger MemCons, October 25, 1975; November 11, 1975 ("130 dictators"); and December 18, 1975 ("disaster"), in GFPL, NSA Files, MemCons, boxes 16-7. Also see Kissinger-Moynihan TeleCons, September 20, 1975, and December 18, 1975, in DOS, FOIA Reading Room. For Moynihan's views on the Igor Richard affair, see *Dangerous Place*, pp. 200–223. For Moynihan's resignation, see Moynihan, MemCon, January 27, 1976, LOC, DPMP, United Nations File, box 342; and Ford-Kissinger MemCon, January 29, 1976, GFPL, NSA Files, MemCons, box 17. The circumstances of the resignation are examined in "Moynihan's Resignation," *NYT*, February 16, 1976, p. 6; "What about Moynihan?" *NYT*, January 30, 1976, p. 25; and Stacks, *Scotty*, p. 332. For Moynihan's view, see *Dangerous Place*, chap. 12.

6. On human rights in US foreign policy, see Apodaca, *Understanding U.S. Human Rights Policy*; Sellars, *Rise and Rise of Human Rights*; Vogelgesang, *American Dream, Global Nightmare*; and, most recently, Keys, *Reclaiming American Virtue*.

7. Moynihan, "Three Structural Problems in American Foreign Policy," February 19, 1976, LOC, DPMP, United Nations File, box 350 ("accommodation"); and *FRUS 1969-1976*, vol. 26, no. 18 ("quieted down"). On the ethics of détente, see "Moral Foundations of Foreign Policy," July 15, 1975 in *DOS Bulletin*, August 4, 1975, pp. 161–68 ("moral imperative"); and "Permanent Challenge of Peace," February 3, 1976 in *DOS Bulletin*, February 23, 1976, pp. 201–12 ("historic obligation").

8. For Kissinger's distinction between status quo and revolutionary powers, see *World Restored*, pp. 1–3 ("framework"). Historians debate whether détente reconciled Soviet leaders to the status quo. Zubok, *Failed Empire* suggests that it did, esp. pp. 215–16. Focusing not on the Kremlin but on the KGB and the Communist Party's International Bureau, Andrew and Mitrokhin, *World Was Going Our Way*, suggests that it did not. Garthoff, *Détente and Confrontation* emphasizes the dissonance between Soviet and American conceptions of stability.

9. Brandon, *Retreat of American Power*, pp. 140–53 ("spearhead"). Some echo Brandon, as do Bundy, *Tangled Web*, 383–99; and Hanhimäki, *Flawed Architect*, esp. chap. 15. On the new internationalists, see Johnson, *Congress and the Cold War*, esp. chap. 6. On MCPL, see MCPL to Nixon, June 26, 1972, NPMP, WHCF, IT-64, box 16; and Heritage Foundation Research Staff, "Members of Congress for Peace through Law," April 1977, Heritage Foundation at http://www.heritage.org.

10. US Congress, House, Committee on Foreign Affairs, *International Protection of Human Rights* ("millions"). Also see Snyder, "Call for U.S. Leadership."

11. Fraser's report was published as US Congress, Committee on Foreign Affairs, *Human Rights in the World Community*. For the view from the State Department, see Secretary's Staff Meeting, June 12, 1974, NARA, RG-59, KSM, box 3 ("lone Indian")

12. For Congress and South Korea, see US Congress, House, Committee on Foreign Affairs, *Human Rights in South Korea*. For Congress and Greece, see US Congress, report, *Infringement of Human Rights in Greece*. For a State Department view on congressional activism, see "U.S. Policies on Human Rights," attached to Lord to Olmsted, December 21, 1974, NARA, RG-59, PPC, Director's Files, box 348.

13. For Amnesty reports on the three regimes discussed here, see "Human Rights in Greece 1973" in CHRRD, AI USA, Executive Director Files, National Section Memos, box 9; and "Chile: An Amnesty International Report" and "Report of Commission to South Korea," both in CHRRD, IMP, Miscellaneous Files, box 6.

14. "U.S. Policies on Human Rights," p. 3, attached to Lord to Olmsted, December 21, 1974, NARA, RG-59, PPC, Director's Files, box 348. Kissinger is in Kissinger-Pinochet MemCon, June 8, 1976, DNSA ("domestic problems").

15. See Apodaca, *Human Rights Policy*; and Forsythe, *Human Rights*, pp. 51–79. Also see Foreign Assistance Act of 1973, Public Law 93-189, December 17, 1973 ("deny"); International Development and Food Assistance Act of 1975, Public Law 94-161, December 20, 1975 ("no assistance"); Public Law 93-559, Part II, chapter 1, sec. 502B, December 30, 1974; and International Security Assistance and Arms Export Control Act of 1976, Public Law 94-329, June 30, 1976 ("exceptional").

16. Fraser, "Human Rights and U.S. Foreign Policy" ("best thing"). For the State Department's response, see Wilson, "Diplomatic Theology," GFPL, JWP, box 1. Much scholarship adopts a favorable view of congressional human rights legislation, as, for example, does Sikkink, *Mixed Signals*, p. 70. For a more critical approach, see Keys, "Congress, Kissinger, and the Origins of Human Rights Diplomacy."

17. Falk, *Legal Order in a Violent World*, p. 75 ("world level"); and US Congress, House, Committee on International Relations, hearing, *Human Rights in the International Community*, p. 246 ("peoples elsewhere"); and Brzezinski, "Search for Focus" ("planetary humanists"). Gardner is in "U.S. Foreign Policy and Human Rights," July 18, 1977, JCPL, ZBM, SuF, box 23.

18. Kennedy, "Address at the University of California, Berkeley," April 11, 1975, JCPL, 1976 Campaign Files, Issues Office, Foreign Policy, box 16 ("our heritage"); and US Congress, House, Committee on Foreign Affairs, *Human Rights in the World Community*, p. 9 ("fundamental").

19. On the movement, see Ehrman, *Rise of Neoconservatism*; Halper and Clarke, *America Alone*; and Vaïsse, *Neoconservatism*. Also see Podhoretz to Moynihan, September 2, 1975, LOC, DPMP, United Nations File, box 339 ("sovereign individuals" and "individual").

20. Kissinger, "Nature of the National Dialogue on Foreign Policy" ("sovereign countries"). For Kissinger's views, see Secretary's Staff Meetings, October 22, 1974 ("What I believe"); and January 5, 1975 ("name of human rights"), in NARA, RG-59, KSM, boxes 3, 5, and 7; and Ford-Kissinger MemCon, December 3, 1974, GFPL, NSA Files, MemCons, box 7.

21. For the quantitative assessment of Kissinger's speeches, see Arnold, "Henry Kissinger and Human Rights." For Kissinger, see "Building International Order", September 22, 1975, in *DOS Bulletin*, October 13, 1975, pp. 545–53 ("global community").

22. On the Policy Planning Staff under Kissinger, see "The Role of the Policy Planning Staff," February 8, 1975, NARA, RG-59, PPC, Director's Files, box 349. For the 1974 study, see "U.S. Policies on Human Rights," attached to Lord to Olmsted, December 21, 1974, NARA, RG-59, PPC, Director's Files, box 348 ("violations" etc.).

23. "U.S. Policies on Human Rights," attached to Lord Olmsted ("proper subject of concern").

24. "U.S. Policies on Human Rights," attached to Lord to Olmsted ("few countries").

25. For Wilson's perspective, see "Diplomatic Theology," GFPL, James M. Wilson Papers, box 1. For an interpretation of this phase emphasizing Kissinger's reticence, see Keys, "Congress, Kissinger."

26. For Kissinger's efforts to mollify Fraser see MemCons, December 17, 1974 and January 28, 1975, DNSA. For his defenses of his policies, see Staff meeting, December 3, 1974, NARA, RG-59, KSM, box 5 ("very good").

27. Ford-Kissinger MemCon, June 15, 1976, GFPL, NSA Files, MemCons, box 19 ("doctrine of intervention").

28. For AI USA's Ivan Morris on the bias question, see Morris to Grant, December 6, 1974, CHRRD, IMP, Miscellaneous Files, Amnesty International, box 5. On the AI USA resolution, see "Draft Resolution on Impartiality," March 13, 1975 ("areas of neglect"); and "Report and Decisions of the 8th International Council Meeting," September 12, 1975, in CHRRD, IMP, Miscellaneous Files, Amnesty International, box 5. Also see Grant to Morris, November 6, 1974 ("political and cultural differences"); and Turchin, "What Is Impartiality," both in CHRRD, IMP, Misc. Files, AI, box 5; and Hawk, "Balance Question," CHRRD, AI USA, Executive Director Files, David Hawk, box 1. For a critique of Amnesty's "left wing bias," see George Nash, "Ordeal of Amnesty International," *National Review*, December 6, 1974, pp. 1407–11.

29. Kissinger's argument that the insertion of human rights into détente was a self-conscious act is developed in *Years of Renewal*, esp. pp. 635–63. For a rejoinder, see Kagan, "Revisionist," *New Republic*, June 21, 1999, pp. 38–48. For the consequences of human rights in the 1980s, see Foot, "Cold War and Human Rights"; Gaddis, *Cold War*, esp. pp. 179–203; Garthoff, *Détente and Confrontation*, esp. pp. 673–78; Leffler, *For the Soul of Mankind*, esp. pp. 234–37; Snyder, *End of the Cold War*; and Thomas, *Helsinki Effect*.

30. Nixon, Radio and Television Address, May 28, 1972, APP ("new road"). For Sakharov's, see *Sakharov Speaks*, pp. 194–207 ("rapprochement," etc.); and *Memoirs*, pp. 385–86.

31. On the dissident movement's early history, see Chalidze, *To Defend These Rights*, pp. 50–66; Gilligan, *Defending Human Rights in Russia*, pp. 24–34; Grigorenko, *Memoirs*, pp. 327–90; Lourie, *Sakharov*, pp. 185–242; Reddaway, *Uncensored Russia*, pp.150–70; and Rubenstein, *Soviet Dissidents*, pp. 97–152. On the *Chronicle* and the Moscow Committee, see Reddaway, *Uncensored Russia*, pp. 53–59; and Sakharov, *Memoirs*, pp. 315–21. For the 1972 crackdown, see "Hard Times for the Dissenters," *NYT*, August 27, 1972, p. E3. On Chalidze, see *Chronicle of Human Rights in the USSR*, no. 1, November 1972–March 1973, pp. 50–55; and on Sakharov, see Rubenstein and Gribanov, *KGB File of Andrei Sakharov*, pp. 100–239; and Rubenstein, *Soviet Dissidents*, pp. 141–49.

32. See Rubenstein and Gribanov, *KGB File of Andrei Sakharov*, pp. 133–34 ("clandestine"); on the League, see Press Release, June 29, 1971, New York Public Library, International League for the Rights of Man, Accession D, Part 1, box 61; on Amnesty, Blane to Morris, January 31, 1974, CHRRD, AI USA, BDF, Board Meetings, box 1; and Sakharov, *Memoirs*, pp. 448–49. For Solzhenitsyn, see *Warning to the West*, p. 48 ("interfere").

33. See Slezkine, *Jewish Century*, pp. 329–48. Contrast to Wistrich, *Lethal Obsession*, esp. pp. 129–53. Heroic accounts of the *refusenik* phenomenon also stress the severity of late Soviet anti-Semitism, as do Beckerman, *When They Come for Us*, pp. 92–95; Reddaway, *Uncensored Russia*, pp. 298–318; and Rubenstein, *Soviet Dissidents*, pp. 153–85.

34. For the US mobilization, see Altshuler, *From Exodus to Freedom*; and Lazin, *The Struggle for Soviet Jewry*. Also see DeBow to Geller, "Interfaith Task Force," October 18, 1971; Graubart to Geller, "Task Force," November 19, 1971; and "Report on National Interreligious Consultation," March 19–20, 1972, all available from American Jewish Committee Online Archive. For MLK, see Schneier, *Shared Dreams*, pp. 118–19 ("genocide"). For Weiss, see US Congress, House, Committee on Foreign Relations, *Soviet Jewry* (1971), pp. 80–85.

35. Kissinger to Moynihan, September 26, 1969, NPMP, WHCF, IT-65, box 15 ("Soviet Jewry").

36. On Jackson-Vanik, see Kochavi, "Insights Abandoned, Flexibility Lost." For Kissinger's perspective, see *Years of Upheaval*, pp. 985–97. For Sakharov, see *Sakharov Speaks*, pp. 159–63, and 211–215; *Memoirs*, pp. 342–44, 394, and 403, and *My Country and the World*, pp. 51–61.

37. See Sakharov, *Sakharov Speaks*, pp. 211–15 ("defense"); Nixon, Address at the US Naval Academy, June 5, 1974, APP ("gear"). For administration perspectives more generally, see *FRUS 1969-1976*, vol. 31, nos. 178, 186–87, 191, 195, 200, 211, 216; and "U.S. Statements Warning of Dangers of Linking U.S.-Soviet Economic Relations to Emigration," January 31, 1975, GFPL, NSA Files, Europe, Canada, and Ocean Affairs Staff, USSR, box 37. For the dialogue with Jackson, see *FRUS 1969-1976*, vol. 15, nos. 14–16, 22, 26, 31–35, 52, 58–60, 61 ("benchmark"); *FRUS 1969-1976*, vol. 31, nos. 207, 210–11, 213, 215, 217, 219–22; and Kissinger, *Years of Renewal*, pp. 255–60 ("great victory"). For US-Soviet diplomacy, see *FRUS 1969-1976*, vol. 15, no. 40, 64 ("angry"), 65–66, 74–76, 78 ("pressure tactics")

38. Kissinger, *Years of Upheaval*, p. 983. For a similar view from the time, see Ford-Kissinger MemCon, January 8, 1975, GFPL, NSA Files, MemCons, box 8.

39. On Vladivostok, see Kissinger, *Years of Renewal*, pp. 251–55 and 277–302.

40. See Kissinger-Ford MemCon, December 13, 1974 ("military-industrial"); and January 6, 1975 ("so easy"), GFPL, NSA Files, MemCons, boxes 7-8.

41. For Soviet expectations, see "East European Attitudes to the CSCE," March 20, 1972, *DBPO*, Series 3, vol. 2, no. 5 ("results"); and "Soviet Expectations of A European Security Conference," October 1972, CIA, FOIA Reading Room. For early US views, see "Current

Issues of European Security," August 12, 1970, NPMP, NSC-IF, box H-166; and *DPBO*, Series 3, vol. 2, nos. 6 and 12. For CSCE and MBFR, see *FRUS 1969-1976*, vol. 39, nos. 69, 75, 89, 112, and 162; and Laird to Nixon, "MBFR," October 19, 1971; Haig to Laird, "U.S. Position on MBFR and CES," October 22, 1971; and "MBFR and CSCE," March 30, 1972, all DNSA. For a British perspective on US policy, see *DPBO*, Series 3, vol. 2, nos. 13 and 100.

42. *DBPO*, Series 3, vol. 2, nos. 11 ("contagion") 57 ("division"), and 58.

43. On the CSCE negotiations, see Kavass et. al., *Human Rights, European Politics*; Maresca, *To Helsinki*; Mastny, *Helsinki, Human Rights, and European Security*; Stefan, "Drafting of the Helsinki Final Act." For analysis, see Thomas, *Helsinki Effect*; and Morgan, "Origins of the Helsinki Final Act." For the origins of the "baskets" format, see *DPBO*, Series III, vol. II, no. 20. For the controversy over Basket I, see Stefan, "Helsinki Final Act"; and *DPBO*, Series III, vol. II, no. 21.

44. This interpretation of Kissinger's motives is at odds with *Years of Renewal*, esp. pp. 635–63, but it aligns with what other historians have argued. See Hanhimäki, "They Can Write It in Swahili"; and Morgan, "United States and the Making of the Helsinki Final Act." For quotations, see Ford-Kissinger MemCon, August 15, 1974, DNSA ("never wanted" and "hang up"); *FRUS 1969-1976*, vol. 39, nos. 177 ("nothing" and "euchred") and 196 ("cabaret"); Nixon-Kissinger-Kriesky MemCon, June 11, GFPL, NSA Files, MemCons, box 4 (*"New York Times"*).

45. See *FRUS 1969-1976*, vol. 35, no. 196 ("rubbish"); and *DBPO*, Series 3, vol. 2, no. 94 ("intergovernmental").

46. Ford-Kissinger MemCon, October 8, 1974, GFPL, NSA Files, MemCons, box 6 ("jeopardize"). For Hartman and Lord's warning, see "CSCE," February 7, 1974, NARA, RG-59, PPC, Director's Files, box 345 ("sharp resentment"). Also see "Issues Paper on CSCE" and "CSCE: State of Play," both January 14, 1975, GFPL, NSA Files, NSC Files, Europe, Canada, and Ocean Affairs, box 44.

47. *DBPO*, Series 3, vol. 2, nos. 91 ("dispiriting"); and 98 ("raped"). Also see "Geneva Trip Report," April 19, 1975 ("asset"); and Reports from U.S. Delegation dated April 1 and April 29, 1975, all in GFPL, NSA Files, NSC Files, Europe, Canada, and Ocean Affairs, box 44. The NSC's recommendation is in *FRUS 1969-1976*, vol. 39, no. 282 ("impress").

48. Stefan, "Helsinki Final Act" emphasizes Kissinger's shifting mood. *FRUS 1969-1976*, vol. 16, no. 147 ("overthrown"); Kissinger, "Challenges of Peace," May 12, 1975 in *DOS Bulletin*, June 2, 1975, pp. 705–12 ("mortgage").

49. *FRUS 1969-1976*, vol. 39, nos. 284 ("new one" etc.) and 286.

50. On the final phase of negotiations, see "CSCE: Soviet Flexibility on Basket 3," May 29, 1975, GFPL, NSA Files, Europe, Canada, and Ocean Affairs, box 44 ("significant concessions"); "The Development of Basket Three—As Told By Ambassador Sherer," November 26, 1975, LOC, DPMP, United Nations File, box 336 ("bad one"); and, from a British perspective, *DPBO*, Series III, vol. II, no. 136. For the backlash, see "Road To Helsinki," *NYT*, July 21, 1975, p. 3 ("goals"). For Safire, see "Super Yalta," *NYT*, July 29, 1975, p. 21. On the domestic politics, see Ford-Kissinger MemCon, July 5, 1975, GFPL, NSA Files, MemCons, box 13 ("ethnics"). Finally, "Jerry, Don't Go," *WSJ*, July 23, 1975, p. 14; and Synder, "'Jerry, Don't Go.'"

51. Ford, "Address in Helsinki," August 1, 1975, APP ("deep devotion"). For the backstory, see Hartmann, *Palace Politics*, pp. 342–45; and Ford, *Time to Heal*, pp. 303–6.

52. Cabinet Meeting, February 21, 1974, GFPL, NSA Files, MemCons, box 3 ("nuclear conflict").

53. For views on the Helsinki Commission, see "HR 10193," November 12, 1975; and "Enrolled Bill S. 2679," May 28, 1976 both in GFPL, NSA Files, Europe, Canada, and Ocean Affairs, box 44; Ford-Kissinger MemCon, July 26, 1976, GFPL, NSA Files, MemCons, box 20 ("constitutionality"). On Helsinki and the Cold War's end, see Snyder, *Human Rights Activism* and Thomas, *Helsinki Effect*.

54. "President Carter's Assessment," February 10, 1977, US Congress, House, Committee on House Administration, *The Presidential Campaign*, vol. 1, Part 2, pp. 1126–27 ("overriding").

55. On the Cold War and Angola, see Garthoff, *Détente and Confrontation*, pp. 556–93; Gleijeses, *Conflicting Missions*, pp. 246–394; Hanhimäki, *Flawed* Architect, pp. 403–26; and Westad, *Global Cold War*, pp. 207–49. Kissinger's account, which blames Congress for US inaction and Neto's triumph, is in *Years of Renewal*, pp. 791–833. Also see Kissinger-Ford MemCons, July 7, July 17, and July 18 ("lose southern Africa"), 1975, all in GFPL, NSA Files, MemCons, box 13; and NSC Meeting Minutes, June 27, DDRS.

56. See Kissinger, *Years of Renewal*, p. 810 ("Soviet effort"). On tensions within State, see Davis, "The Angola Decision"; and "DCI Briefing for June 27 Meeting," DDRS. For the Clark Amendment, see Johnson, "Unintended Consequences of Congressional Reform." Finally, Ford-Kissinger MemCon, December 18, 1975, GFPL, NSA Files, MemCons, box 17 ("nihilistic").

57. See Garthoff, *Détente and Confrontation*; and "Kissinger Moscow Trip, January 21-23" GFPL, NSA Files, MemCons, USSR, China, Middle East, box 1.

58. See Kissinger, *Years of Renewal* p. 35 ("withdraw"); and Dobrynin, *In Confidence*, esp. pp. 360–73.

59. For public opinion, see Watts and Free, "Nationalism, Not Isolationism" ("weakening"); and "Public Opinion and U.S. Foreign Policy, 1975," JCPL, 1976 Campaign Files, Issues Office, Foreign Policy, box 46 ("blurred"); and "New Yeast in the Old Internationalism," *NYT*, September 19, 1975, p. 35 ("interrelated").

60. Garment is in "Human Rights / General Assembly," July 9, 1976, GFPL, MRDP, Human Rights, box 15. Also see Garment Statement to the American Jewish Committee, April 1, 1976 and note to Moynihan, December 5, 1977, in LOC, DPMP, United Nations File, SuF, boxes 336 and 350. For Moynihan's perspective, see *Dangerous Place*, pp. 105–10, 280. On détente, see Teeter to Cheney, November 12, 1975, GFPL, Robert Teeter Papers, 1976 Campaign, box 63.

61. "Report of the AI Washington Committee," September 20, 1976, CHRRD, AI USA, Executive Director Files, David Hawk Files, box 5 ("co-option"); "Preliminary Discussion of Issues," September 7, 1976; and "Role of Washington Office," September 16, 1976, both in CHRRD, AI USA, Executive Director Files, David Hawk Files, box 5. For the work of the Washington Office, see, for example, "Activities for Week of September 13"; "AI's Role in the 502B Process," October 7, 1976; "Week in Review—October 4th," October 8, 1976; and "Areas of Work Undertaken," October 15, 1976, all in CHRRD, AI USA, Executive Director Files, David Hawk Files, box 5. Also see Weissbrodt, "Report of the Washington Committee," October 22, 1976, CHRRD, AI USA, Executive Director Files, David Hawk Files, box 5 ("world"). For the International Secretariat's skeptical views on AI USA's collaborations with the US government, see Carroll to Weissbrodt, October 12, 1977, CHRRD, AI USA, Executive Director Files, David Hawk Files, box 5.

62. For Amnesty's concerns, see "Background Paper for Working Party #2," March 1977, CHRRD, AI USA, Board of Directors' Files, Board Meetings, box 1 ("Western cause"). For Ullman, see "A Note on Basic Assumptions," April 1974, MLP, CFR, 1980s Project, box 312. For Podhoretz, see Podhoretz to Moynihan, September 2, 1975, LOC, DPMP, United Nations File, box 339 and discussion in note 4, above.

63. See Kissinger, "Moral Promise and Practical Needs," November 15, 1976, DOS, *Bulletin*, November 15, 1976, pp. 597–605 ("150"). On public opinion, see Watts and Free, "Nationalism, Not Isolationism" ("seriously wrong"). Also see "Wary Public Endorses Détente," January 19, 1976, GFPL, PFCC Files, box H48, and "Kissinger's Popularity Down," January 29, 1976, GFPL, Rogers Morton Papers, box 1.

64. For Reagan's views, see compilation of statements dated February 1976 in GFPL, Rogers Morton Papers, box 1 ("appeasement"). For Kissinger, see *FRUS 1969-1976*, vol. 15, no. 273 ("bum rap").

65. "Reagan Jabs At Kissinger," *NYT*, May 14, 1976 ("foremost symbol") and Drew, *American Journal*, p. 48 ("Pepsi"). For the campaign's polling figures, see "Data on Détente," March 11, 1976, GFPL, Rogers Morton Papers, box 1. The view from State can be inferred from "The Reagan Speech and the Facts," April 1, 1976, GFPL, PFCC Files, box G16; and Kissinger-Eagleburger MemCon, March 26, 1976, DOS, FOIA Reading Room. On the

language of détente, see UPI press clippings in GFPL, PFCC Files, Press Clippings, Kissinger, box G16; and Nessen Press Conference, March 2, 1976, GFPL, Ron Nessen Papers, box 94. For the Morton-Kissinger controversy, see Nessen Press Conferences, April 5, 1976, and April 8, 1976, in GRPL, NRP, box 95. Also see Bon Tempo, "Human Rights and the U.S. Republican Party."

66. See Kissinger, *Years of Renewal*, pp. 919–84 ("race war," etc.); and "United States Policy on Southern Africa," April 27, 1976. *DOS Bulletin*, May 31, 1976, pp. 672–84.

67. See Ford-Kissinger MemCon, August 30, 1976, GFPL, NSA Files, MemCons, box 20 ("son-of-a-bitch"); Kissinger, *Years of Renewal*, p. 919 ("collapse"); Ford-Kissinger MemCon, April 21, 1976, GFPL, NSA Files, MemCons, box 19 ("with the whites"); and "Reagan on Troops to Rhodesia," June 2, 1976, GFPL, Ron Nessen Papers, Ronald Reagan, box 39. For US public opinion on Rhodesia, see Harris Survey, June 28, 1976, GFPL, Agnes Waldron Files, Kissinger Poll Results, box 20. On Rhodesia and the Texas primary, see Drew, *American Journal*, 236.

68. See Duval to Cheney, August 17, 1976. GFPL, MRDP, Republican Party Platform, box 28 ("tyranny"); "Secretary Kissinger," June 8, 1976, GFPL, MRDP, box 15; and Kissinger, "Moral Promise and Practical Needs," November 15, 1976, *DOS Bulletin*, November 15, 1976, pp. 597–605 ("imperative").

69. For public opinion on Kissinger's performance, see data collected in GFPL, Agnes Waldron Files, Kissinger Poll Results, box 20. The point about Kissinger's negative ratings in 1976 is based on American National Election Survey, Time Series Study 1976. I am grateful to Sam Abrams for interpreting this data.

70. For Carter on détente, see Drew, *American Journal*, pp. 90–91, 270; compilations of Carter quotes and speeches in GFPL, PFCC Files, Carter Quotes—Détente, box H24 ("second"). For Carter on Kissinger, see quotes compiled in GFPL, PFCC Files, Carter Quotes—Kissinger, box H28; and Transcript of Carter Interview with Harry Reasoner, July 1976, GFPL,WHSF, Ford-Carter Debate, box 1 ("ranger"). For the NGO outreach, see Robinson to AI USA, June 21, 1976, CHRRD, AI USA, Executive Director Files, David Hawk Files, box 1 ("strong concern"). Carter's worldview is expressed in "Our Nation's Past and Future," July 15, 1976, APP ("framework of peace"). On Trilateralism and human rights, see "Relations between World's Democracies," June 23, 1976, in US Congress, House, Committee on House Administration, *The Presidential Campaign 1976*, vol. 1, Part 1, pp. 266–75 ("We and our allies"). Kissinger is in Ford-Kissinger MemCon, October 3, 1976, GFPL, NSA Files, MemCons, box 21 ("world as it is").

71. Carter, "Addressing B'nai B'rith," September 8, 1976, US Congress, House, Committee on House Administration, *The Presidential Campaign 1976*, vol. 1, Part 2, pp. 709–14 ("conscience"). For the October 6, 1976 debate, see APP. For Ford on the controversy, see Ford, *Time to Heal*, pp. 422–26. Ford's notes make clear that his intent was contrary to his effect. These are in GFPL, WHST, Carter-Ford Debates, box 2. For analyses of the impact, see "The Public's Response . . . " May 1977, GFPL, Robert Teeter Papers, box 62; and President's Daily News Summary, October 7, 1976, GFPL, MRDP, box 28. Dick Cheney is more measured in "The 1976 Presidential Debates," October 1977, GFPL, Robert Teeter Papers, Post-Election Analyses, box 62. Moderator Max Frankel raised the prospect of a "new Ford Foreign Policy" in the October 6 debate.

Chapter 8

1. Truman, "Inaugural Address," January 20, 1949 ("false"); Eisenhower, "Inaugural Address," January 20, 1953 ("slavery"); Kennedy, "Inaugural Address," January 20, 1961 ("burden"); Carter, "Inaugural Address," January 20, 1977 ("clear-cut" etc.), all APP; and Warnke, "Friends, Enemies, and Others," YMA, CVP, Series II, Foreign Policy Articles, box 9 ("years ago").

2. Carter, *Keeping Faith*, p. 19; and *White House Diary*, p. 10 ("imperial status"). On the imperial presidency, see Schlesinger, *Imperial Presidency*; and Wills, *Bomb Power*.

3. Carter, "Inaugural Address," January 20, 1977, APP ("new spirit," etc.).

4. "U.S. Foreign Policy Remarks to People of Other Nations," January 20, 1977, APP.

5. Gardner, "To Make the World Safe for Interdependence," undated, JCPL, 1976 Campaign Files, Issues Office, Foreign Policy, box 17; Carter, "Our Foreign Relations," March 15, 1976, in US Congress, House, Committee on House Administration, *The Presidential Campaign 1976*, vol. 1, Part 1, pp. 109–19; and Ullman, "Trilateralism" ("consensus position").

6. This interpretation diverges from historians who emphasize the strategic continuities between Carter and his predecessors, as do Gaddis, *Strategies of Containment*, esp. pp. 343–49; Glad, *Outside in the White House*; Mitchell, "Cold War and Jimmy Carter"; and Thornton, *Carter Years*. In contrast, Strong, *Working in the World* emphasizes Carter's commitment to post–Cold War policies, as does Rosati, *Carter Administration's Quest*. Sneh, *Future Almost Arrived*, follows a similar line but disagrees on some key points, including the role of Zbigniew Brzezinski, whom Sneh presents as a Cold Warrior. Others see Carter's priorities as evolving over time, as do Garthoff, *Détente and Confrontation*, esp. chaps. 17–21 and 27; Kaufman, *Plans Unraveled*; and Zanchetta, *Transformation of American International Power*, esp. chaps. 8–12.

7. See Carter, *Hour before Daylight*; Godbold, *Jimmy and Rosalynn Carter*. Carter discussed Truman's example in author interview, August 2, 2009, Plains, GA.

8. Godbold, *Jimmy and Rosalynn Carter*, chap. 19; and Carter to Brzezinski, December 15, 1973, JCPL, ZBM, Trilateral Commission File, box 5 ("trilateral").

9. Jordan to Carter, untitled memorandum, November 4, 1972, JCPL, 1976 Campaign Files, Hamilton Jordan File, box 199 ("knowledge and experience"). On the 1976 campaign, see Elizabeth Drew, *American Journal*; and Witcover, *Marathon*.

10. Joe Klein, "The Whizz Kids," *Rolling Stone*, May 19, 1977, pp. 60–71 ("backwoods"). On the Trilateral Commission, see "Carter and Key Advisers," *NYT*, January 1, 1977, p. 41; "But What Are They?" *WP*, January 16, 1977; and Shoup, "Jimmy Carter and the Trilateralists." On the formulation of Carter's strategic concepts, see Stevens, "Jimmy Carter's Presidential Campaign."

11. See Gardner, "To Make the World Safe for Interdependence," undated, in JCPL, 1976 Campaign Files, Issues Office–Eizenstat, Foreign Policy, box 17; Gardner to Hunter, September 20, 1976, JCPL, 1976 Campaign Files, Issues Office–Rubenstein, box 45; and Owen, *Next Phase in U.S. Foreign Policy*, p. 4 ("nation-state"). For foreign policy during the campaign, see "Canvas of views," undated, and "Foreign Policy Briefing Book," October 6, 1976, both in JCPL Campaign Files, 1976, Issues Office–Rubenstein, box 45. Finally, "Foreign Policy Priorities of the First Six Months," in YMA, CVP, Series II, Foreign Policy Articles, box 9 ("cooperation or fragmentation").

12. "Our Foreign Relations," March 15, 1976 ("monopolies"); and "Nuclear Energy and World Order," May 13, 1976 ("world order"), both in US Congress, House, Committee on House Administration, *The Presidential Campaign 1976*, vol. 1, Part 1, pp. 109–18, 183–94; and "Foreign Policy Priorities of the First Six Months," in YMA, CVP, Series II, Foreign Policy Articles, box 9 ("new phase").

13. "Press Briefing by Zbigniew Brzezinski," December 20, 1977, in JCPL, HHM, SuF, Foreign Policy, box 38 ("awakening"); and "Foreign Policy Priorities of the First Six Months," in YMA, CVP, Series II, Foreign Policy Articles, box 9 ("entire").

14. See Carter, *Keeping Faith*, esp. pp. 212–18 ("mad race"); "Foreign Policy Briefing book," October 6, 1976, JCPL, 1976 Campaign Files, Issues Office–Rubenstein, box 45; and "Address Announcing Candidacy," December 12, 1974, "Address Accepting the Presidential Nomination," July 15, 1976, and "Inaugural Address," January 20, 1977, all APP. For the transition team's prioritization of disarmament, see "Foreign Policy Priorities of the First Six Months," in YMA, CVP, Series II, Foreign Policy Articles, box 9 ("major"). Sorenson is in "U.S. Foreign Policy Over the Next 4-8 Years," November 1, 1976, YMA, CVP, Series II, Foreign Policy Articles, box 9.

15. See Holbrooke draft of Carter speech, September 1-2, 1976, JCPL, 1976 Campaign Files, Issues Office–Eizenstat, box 20 ("special"); Tuchman to Aaron, "Human Rights Background Policy," March 17, 1977, JCPL, WHCF, HU, box 1 ("feelings"); and Fallows to Snider, July 13, 1977, JCPL, HHM, Speech Files, Human Rights, box 2 ("complicated").

16. Carter is quoted in Stevens, "Jimmy Carter's Presidential Campaign," esp. pp. 42–43 ("forced on us"). For Vance, see "Human Rights and Foreign Policy," April 30, 1977 in *DOS Bulletin*, May 23, 1977, pp. 505–8 ("challenge for all countries"). On Carter and Niebuhr, see Morris, *Jimmy Carter, American Moralist*, pp. 159–62. Preston, *Sword of the Spirit, Shield of Faith*, esp. pp. 575–79, downplays the influence of Carter's religious belief on his human rights policy. For an opposing (but less persuasive) view, see Berggren and Rae, "Jimmy Carter and George W. Bush."

17. Interpretations that present Carter's human rights policy as a quest for absolution include Keys, *Reclaiming American Virtue*; and Moyn, *Last Utopia*, esp. pp. 154–61.

18. Interview with Zbigniew Brzezinski, June 24, 2009, Washington, DC ("embedded"); Brzezinski, "Remarks to Trilateral Commission," October 25, 1977 ("basic rights"); and "Press Briefing by Zbigniew Brzezinski," December 20, 1977 ("inevitability of our time"), in JCPL, HHM, SuF, Foreign Policy, box 38. For Brzezinski and Amnesty, see "Minutes of Board of Directors' Meeting," November 18, 1971, CHRRD, AI USA, Board of Directors Files, Board Meetings, box 1; and Freedom House, see Brzezinski to Sussman, December 20, 1976; and Brzezinski to van Slyck, February 5, 1977, both in MLP, Freedom House Papers, Correspondence, Brzezinski, box 11.

19. WNSR #3, March 5, 1977, JCPL, ZBM, SuF, Weekly Reports, box 42 ("grand strategy"); and Carter to Fallows, April 26, 1977, JCPL, SSF, PHF, box 20.

20. "Address at Notre Dame," May 22, 1977, APP ("unifying threat").

21. "Comments on President's Notre Dame Speech," May 22, 1977, JCPL, NSA Files, SuF, Human Rights, box 28 (for overseas press reactions); and "A 'New' Foreign Policy," *NYT*, May 30, 1977, p. 14.

22. Carter, "The Worst Record Since the Depression," September 15, 1976, in US Congress, House, Committee on House Administration, *The Presidential Campaign 1976*, vol. 1, Part 2, pp. 746–50. For economic performance (including statistics), see CEA, *ERP*, 1977, esp. pp. 58–99.

23. Cooper et. al., "Towards a Renovated International System".

24. On labor productivity in the mid-1970s, see White House, *ERP*, 1977, esp. 45–57. For context, see Brenner, *Economics of Global Turbulence*; Eichengreen, *European Economy Since 1945*, esp. pp. 253–56; and Maier, " 'Malaise': The Crisis of Capitalism in the 1970s."

25. See Collins, *More*; and Maier, "Politics of Productivity."

26. For the preoccupation with planning in the mid-1970s, see Gruchy, "Institutionalism, Planning"; Heilbroner, "American Plan," *NYT*, January 25, 1976, Magazine, p. 9, 35–40; and Leontief, "National Economic Planning." Also see Stein, *Pivotal Decade*.

27. For the Trilateralist critique, see Cooper et. al., *Towards a Renovated International System* ("threaten the systems"). For the Carter administration, see Biven, *Jimmy Carter's Economy*, pp. 61–93; and Campagna, *Economic Policy in the Carter Administration*, esp. 34–43. Also see Bergsten and Fried, "U.S. Foreign Economic Policy," April 1974, JCPL, 1976 Campaign Files, Issues Office—Eizenstat, Foreign Policy, box 16; and "Carter on Economic Issues," Undated, GFPL, WHSF, Ford-Carter Debate File, box 1. On the domestic stimulus, see Schultze to Burns, January 26, 1977, in JCPL, CEA, SuF, box 8; and Schultze, "Payoff of the Economic Stimulus," February 19, 1977, JCPL, SSF, PHF, box 6.

28. For Giscard, "Evening Report," December 8, 1976, GFPL, NSA Files, International Economic Affairs, Puerto Rico, box 4 ("developing division"). Also see *FRUS 1969-1976*, vol. 31, no. 152. For the Brookings report, see Basevi et al., *Economic Prospects and Policies*. Also see Putman and Bayne, *Hanging Together*, pp. 63–66.

29. For the march to the summit, see Carter-Callaghan TeleCon, January 13, 1977, MTA; Mondale-Callaghan Meeting, January 27, 1977, MTA. For West German priorities, see Schmidt to Carter, March 8, 1977, JCPL, NSA Files, President's Correspondence with Foreign Leaders, Germany, box 6 ("concerted").

30. For the strategic underpinnings, see "U.S. Foreign Economic Policy," April 1974, JCPL, 1976 Campaign Files, Issues Office–Eizenstat, Foreign Policy, box 16 ("fact of international life"); "An Early Economic Summit," in YMA, CVP, Series II, Carter Presidency Transition, box 8 ("bleak economic prospects"); and WNSR #4, March 11, 1977, in JCPL, ZBM, SuF, Weekly Reports, box 41 ("most important").

31. For US objectives, see "Strategy in Preparation for the Summit," March 22, 1977; "Downing Street Summit," April 1977; "Summit Preparations: A Progress Report," April 15, 1977; "Comments on Draft Declaration," April 19, 1977, all DDRS; Carter to Schmidt, April 29, 1977, JCPL, NSA Files, President's Correspondence with Foreign Leaders, Germany, box 6; and "Summary of a Joint Economic Committee Report," May 5, 1975, JCPL, SSF, PHF, box 23. For German positions, see Schmidt to Carter, March 8, 1977; and Schmidt to Carter, March 30, 1977, both in JCPL, NSA Files, Correspondence, Germany, box 6. Also see US Congress, Joint Economic Committee, hearing, *Issues at the Summit*.

32. Brzezinski, "Meeting April 25," April 23, 1977 ("leadership and purpose," etc.); and Carter, *White House Diary*, p. 47 ("great desire").

33. On Carter's about-turn, see "Economic Stimulus Package Remarks," April 14, 1977, APP; and Biven, *Carter's Economy*, pp. 75–79. For Carter's explanation, see *Keeping Faith*, pp. 76–78, and *White House Diary*, p. 39. For the summit, see "London Summit (Session 1), May 5, 1977, MTA ("step backwards"); "Declaration," May 8, 1977, in Hajnal, ed., *Seven Power Summit*, pp. 33–42; "Leaders in London Meet Accord," *NYT*, May 8, 1977, p. 1; and Putman and Bayne, *Hanging Together*, pp. 63–72.

34. "London Summit (Session 2), May 7, 1977, MTA ("discrimination"); and Putman and Bayne, *Hanging Together*, pp. 63–72. On human rights, also see "Note by the Prime Minister of a Meeting at 10 Downing Street," May 9, 1977, MTA.

35. Carter, *White House Diary*, pp. 49–50 ("productive"); and Owen to Carter, May 20, 1977, JCPL, WHCF, FO 6-2. box 43 ("institution").

36. Schultze to Carter, "International Economic Conditions," August 31, 1977; Solomon to Blumenthal, "Summit Follow-Up," September 12, 1977 ("numerical target," etc.); and "G-5 Discussions on the World Economy," September 22, 1977, all in JCPL, ASM, ChronF, box 2; and White House, *ERP* (1978), pp. 103–8.

37. For balance of payments policy, see Blumenthal, "U.S. Trade Balance," July 1, 1977 ("differential"); Eizenstat and Ginsburg, "Trade Deficit," August 12, 1977; Eizenstat and Ginsburg, "Call to Chairman Burns," August 12, 1977; Schultze, "Secretary Blumenthal's Memo," November 15, 1977; Eizenstat, "Balance of Payments," December 17, 1977; and "Notes on the Dollar Strategy," January 17, 1978, all in JCPL, CEA, SuF, boxes 38–39, 52, and 68; and Blumenthal, "International Financial Issues," December 20, 1977, JCPL, ASM, ChronF, box 3. For the German view, see Schmidt to Carter, December 23, 1977, JCPL, NSA Files, President's Correspondence with Foreign Leaders, Germany, box 6.

38. "The President's News Conference," January 12, 1978, APP ("heavy dependence").

39. Statistics are from EIA. Brzezinski is in WNSR #5, March 18, 1977, JCPL, ZBM, SuF, Weekly Reports, box 41 ("significant effect").

40. For Carter's views, see "Nuclear Energy and World Order," May 13, 1976, in US Congress, House, Committee on House Administration, *The Presidential Campaign 1976*, vol. 1, Part 1, pp. 183–94; and Carter, *Keeping Faith*, pp. 91–124. For nonproliferation and US-Japan relations, see WNSR #2, February 26, 1977; and WNSR #5, March 18, 1977, both in JCPL, ZBM, SuF, Weekly Reports, box 41; and Mansfield to State Department, July 23, 1977; Brzezinski, "Japanese Nuclear Reprocessing," August 15, 1977; and "Tokai Decision," August 23, 1977; all in JCPL, NSA Files, CouF, Japan, box 40. On this issue, I have learned much from Shih, "Tokai Reprocessing Issue." Also see Oberdorfer, *Senator Mansfield*, pp. 461–66 ("life or death").

41. Carter, "Address to the Nation on Energy," April 18, 1977 ("moral equivalent"), and "National Energy Plan," April 20, 1977, both APP. For Carter's energy policy, see *Keeping Faith*, pp. 91–124; Barrow, "Age of Limits"; and Bourne, *Jimmy Carter*, pp. 375–77. Also see *FRUS 1969-1976*, vol. 27, no. 122; and "Briefing Materials on National Energy Plan," October 19, 1977, JCPL, SSF, PHF, box 55.

42. Carter, *White House Diary*, p. 110 ("influence").

43. Brzezinski, WNSR #35, November 4, 1977, JCPL, ZBM, SuF, Weekly Reports, box 42 ("very little"); Blumenthal, "Inflation, Energy, and the Dollar," March 24, 1978, JCPL, SSF, PHF, box 78; and Carter, *Keeping Faith*, p. 103 ("embarrassment").

44. Carter to Blumenthal and Schultze, January 13, 1978, in JCPL, ASM, ChronF, box 3 ("informed").

45. For the administration's approach, see "Talking Points for Remarks by the Honorable Michael Blumenthal," February 7, 1978, JCPL, ASM, ChronF, box 3. On the risks of the falling dollar, see "Saudi Concerns about the Dollar and Inflation," February 3, 1978, JCPL, ASM, ChronF, box 3; and "Talking Points" April 4, 1978, JCPL, CEA, SuF, Memos to President, box 53 ("financial crisis" and "national security"). For US-German actions, see "Stepping In," January 5, 1978, *WSJ*, p. 1; "Minutes of the Cabinet Meeting," March 13, 1978, JCPL, CEA, SuF, box 20; and "Plan is Announced," *NYT*, March 14, 1978, p. 73. Callaghan's proposals are in letter to Carter, March 16, 1978, MTA. For Blumenthal's response, see "Callaghan's Forthcoming Visit," March 21, 1978, JCPL, SSF, PHF, box 77 ("road back"). For the administration's strategy, see Carter to Schmidt, February 9, 1978, JCPL, NSA Files, President's Correspondence with Foreign Leaders, Germany, box 6; "WP-3 Issues," February 14, 1978, JCPL, CEA, SuF, box 20; and MemCon, Callaghan and Carter, March 23, 1978, MTA. Also see Bevin, *Carter's Economy*, pp. 113–21 ("talking down"); Moffitt, *World's Money*, pp. 145–46; and Solomon, *International Monetary System*, pp. 344–50.
46. Callaghan to Carter, March 16, 1978 ("new act"); and "International Action on Growth, Currency Stability, Energy, and Other Matters," March 16, 1978, both MTA.
47. Callaghan to Carter, March 16, 1978 ("further action"); Carter Meeting with Callaghan, March 23, 1978; and Carter to Schmidt, March 27, 1978, all MTA. For Owen, see Owen to Mondale, February 2, 1978, DDRS. Also, Putman and Bayne, *Hanging Together*, pp. 79–82.
48. For the making of US summit, policy, see Owen to Carter, "Chancellor Schmidt's Messages," April 8, 1978; and Hunt note on "Bonn Summit," June 30, 1978, both in MTA; Schultze to Blumenthal et al., May 15, 1978; "Breakfast with Schmidt," May 28, 1978; and "Meeting of the OECD Economic Policy Committee," June 6, 1978, all JCPL, CEA, SuF, Bonn Summit, box 6; and Owen, "Our Summit Goals," June 23, 1978, DDRS ("three-way deal"). For US-German diplomacy, see Carter to Schmidt, March 27, 1978, April 11, and May 15, 1978, both in JCPL, NSA Files, President's Correspondence with Foreign Leaders, Germany, box 6; and Schultze to Carter, June 27, 1978, JCPL, SSF, PHF, box 93. On energy and the summit, see *FRUS 1969-1976*, vol. 37, nos. 149, 153 ("forceful action"), 154, and 156; Renner, "The Summit and Energy," July 6, 1978, JCPL, WHCF, FO 6-5, box 44; and Owen to Carter, "Summit and Energy," July 11, 1978, in JCPL, CEA, SuF, Bonn Summit, box 6. US goals for the summit are summarized in "Summit Briefing," July 15, 1978, DDRS. For analysis of the administration's two-level tactics, see Putman and Bayne, *Hanging Together*, pp. 82–84.
49. Carter to Strauss, Powell, and Owen, June 28, 1978, JCPL, WHCF, FO 6-5, box 44 ("boxed in"), and Carter, *White House Diary*, pp. 205–6 ("fraternity"). For the media's verdict, see "Leadership without Greatness," *WP*, July 16, 1978, B7; and "What They Achieved in Bonn," *WP*, July 18, 1978, p. A10.
50. For transcripts of the summit sessions, see Records of Bonn Summit, Sessions 1-4, July 16-17, MTA ("age of uncertainty"). Carter's annotated briefing notes are in JCPL, SSF, PHF, box 95. For the summit declaration, see Hajnal, ed., *Seven Power Summits*, pp. 47–57 ("quantitatively substantial").
51. See US Congress, Senate, Committee on Foreign Relations, *Oversight of International Economic Issues*, pp. 139–49 ("substantial advantage"). On oil decontrol, see "Crude Oil Pricing," March 18, 1979, JCPL, WHCF, CM-11, box 7. For Carter, see "New Approach to Foreign Policy," May 28, 1975, in US Congress, House, Committee on House Administration, *The Presidential Campaign 1976*, vol. 1, Part 1, pp. 66–70 ("sacrifice").
52. On the historiography of the summit, the major treatments are Putman and Bayne, *Hanging Together*; and Webb, *Political Economy of Policy Coordination*, both of which salute summitry's accomplishments. With exceptions, including Barnet, *Alliance*, summitry remains an understated theme in the scholarship on US foreign policy in the 1970s.
53. Record of Bonn Summit, Sessions 1 ("closely interdependent"), 3 and 4. Statistics are from UNCTAD, UNCTADStat.
54. Record of Bonn Summit, Sessions 1, 3 and 4 ("rich industrialized"), July 16–17, 1978; and Bonn Summit Declaration in Hajnal, ed., *Seven Power Summits*, pp. 47–57 ("shared"). On North-South trade disputes, see Winham, *International Trade and the Tokyo Round*, esp. pp. 274–80.

55. For Brzeziniski, see WNSR #7," April 1, 1977 ("political consciousness" and "comprehensive"); WNSR #14, May 26, 1977; WNSR #15, June 3, 1977; and WNSR #23, July 29, 1977, all in JCPL, ZBM, SuF, Weekly Reports, box 41; Brzezinski-Genscher MemCon, March 14, 1977, JCPL, NSA Files, SuF, Brzezinski MemCons, box 33 ("long-run"); and "Press Briefing," December 20, 1977, JCPL, HHM, SuF, Foreign Policy, box 38 ("social justice"). For administration perspectives, see "Overview of Foreign Policy Issues and Positions," October 24, 1976, YMA, CVP, Series II, Carter Campaign, box 9 ("single"); and "North-South History," December 5, 1980, JCPL, ZBM, SuF, NSC Accomplishments, box 34 ("whose time").

56. "A Human Rights Strategy," February 28, 1977, JCPL, ZBM, SuF, Human Rights, box 28 ("embarked"); and Carter, "Address to the General Assembly," March 17, 1977, APP. Historians disagree as to the centrality of human rights to Carter's foreign policy. Schmitz and Walker, "Jimmy Carter and the Foreign Policy of Human Rights" puts human rights at the center and salutes the accomplishment, as does Strong, *Working in the World*, esp. pp. 71–97. Kaufman, *Plans Unraveled*, esp. pp. 29–41, affirms the centrality of human rights to Carter's initial outlook but is more skeptical about the results. Vogelgesang, *American Dream, Global Nightmare* emphasizes the inconsistences of application and the disruptive consequences. Others see human rights as more an anti-Soviet ruse than a conceptual innovation. For this approach, see Glad, *Outsider in the White House*, esp. pp. 69–76.

57. UN, "Universal Declaration of Human Rights" ("including"). For Carter's view, see Carter to Eizenstat and Fallows, March 28, 1977, JCPL, HHM, Speech Files, box 1 ("broadest"); and for Brzezinski's, see WNSR #9, April 16, 1977, JCPL, ZBM, SuF, Weekly Reports, box 41 ("universal"). Vance is in "Human Rights and Foreign Policy," April 30, 1977, in *DOS Bulletin*, May 23, 1977, pp. 505–8 ("our policy").

58. On the covenants, see Lauren, *Evolution of International Human Rights*, pp. 234–47; and Ishay, *History of Human Rights*, pp. 223–24. For Carter's policy, see Lipshutz, "Four International Human Rights Treaties and Covenants," February 9, 1977, JCPL, WHCF, HU, box 1; Lipshutz, "Four International Human Rights Treaties and Covenants," February 9, 1977, JCPL, WHCF, HU, box 1; "United Nations Remarks," October 5, 1977, APP; and "Message on Human Rights Covenants," February 23, 1978, APP. Carter committed to seek ratification during the campaign. See speech to B'nai B'raith, September 1, 1976, in JCPL, 1976 Campaign Files, Issues Office–Eizenstat, Foreign Policy, box 20. For the NGOs, see Letter to President Carter, December 1, 1978, JCPL, Hertzberg Materials, Speech Files, box 3. Amnesty's commitment to ratification is further discussed in "Report to the Membership and Board," CHRRD, AI USA, Executive Director Files, David Hawk, box 4; and "Fulfilling Our Promises," CHRRD, AI USA, Executive Director Files, Gerhard Elston, box 5. For Henkin, see "The Case for Ratification," *NYT*, April 1, 1977, p. 20. Also see Louis Sohn's letter to Senator Jackson, January 21, 1977, in University of Washington, Henry M. Jackson Papers, Accession no. 3560-006: F/Pol. and Defense, box 36. For officials' reflections, see PRM-28, "Human Rights"; and "The Human Rights Policy: An Interim Assessment," January 16, 1978, JCPL, WHCF, HU, box 1.

59. For the bureaucratic reorganization, see Brzezinski, *Power and Principle*, pp. 124–25 ("cut across"); Maynard, "Bureaucracy and Implementation of U.S. Human Rights Policy"; and Warshawsky, "Department of State and Human Rights Policy." For policy, Bloomfield, "The Carter Human Rights Policy," January 1, 1981, JCPL, ZBM, SuF, NSC Accomplishments, box 34 ("frank").

60. On the Christopher Committee, see Brzezinski to Vance, April 1, 1977; Pisano to Aaron, "Interagency Group," May 6, 1977 ("uneasy"); and Mathews to Brzezinski, "Human Rights and OPIC," June 27, 1978 ("making"), all in JCPL, NSA Files, SuF, Human Rights, box 28.

61. Tuchman and Pisano, "Proposed Administration Position on Human Rights Amendments," April 13, 1977; and Vance, "International Financial Institutions Authorization Bill," April 15, 1977, both in JCPL, Counsel's Office, Human Rights, box 14; Brzezinski, "Administration Strategy on Human Rights Amendments," April 16, 1977, JCPL, SSF, PHF, box 18; Blumenthal, "IFI Authorization Bill," JCPL, CEA, SuF, Hutcheson, box 39; Solomon, "Items for Friday," September 22, 1977, JCPL, ASM, ChronF, box 2; Brzezinski, "Human Rights," December 3, 1977, JCPL, HHM, SuF, Human Rights, box 2; and Bloomfield, "Carter Human Rights Policy." Also see Volgelsgang, *American Dream*, pp. 137–40.

62. Christopher, "PRM on Human Rights," July 7, 1977, JCPL, Counsel's Office, Human Rights, box 14 ("carrot"); and Bloomfield, "Carter Human Rights Policy."

63. PRM-28, "Human Rights," May 20, 1977 ("basic economic"); and PD-30, "Human Rights," February 27, 1978 ("full range"), both JCPL, PRM/PD. Carter's annotations are in in JCPL, SSF, PHF, box 72. For an analysis of the PRM/PD process, Schmitz and Walter, "Jimmy Carter and the Foreign Policy of Human Rights."

64. Brzezinski to Carter, "Human Rights," February 10, 1978, including attachment, "Draft PD," in JCPL, SSF, PHF, box 72 ("positive inducements"); PD-30, "Human Rights," February 27, 1978 ("primary emphasis"); and Carter, "Address to the General Assembly," March 17, 1977, APP ("own ideals")

65. Fraser to Carter, March 23, 1977, JCPL, NSA Files, SuF, Human Rights, box 28; and Fraser to Carter, April 1, 1977, JCPL, WHCF, HU-1, box 1 ("interference"). For the May 1977 poll, see Rosapepe to Hawk (and attachment), July 13, 1977, CHRRD, AI USA, Executive Director Files, Gerhard Elston Files, box 11 ("striking"). For Caddell, see Memo to Carter, October 21, 1977, JCPL, COS, SuF, Pat Caddell, box 33. For overseas opinion, see Brzezinski to Carter, May 3, 1977, JCPL, NSA Files, SuF, Human Rights, box 28. Lake's verdict is in "The Human Rights Policy," January 16, 1978, JCPL, WHCF, HU, box 1 ("best thing").

66. On Latin America in the Cold War, Brands, *Latin America's Cold War* emphasizes the local sources of political violence; while Grandin, *Empire's Workshop* and *Last Colonial Massacre*; Rabe, *Killing Zone*; Schoultz, *Beneath the United States*; and Smith *Talons of the Eagle* stress US interventionism. On Condor, see Dinges, *Condor Years*. On US human rights policy in Latin America, see Schoultz, *Human Rights and United States Policy*. On transnational human rights activism, see, Kelly, "'Magic Words'"; and Sikkink, *Mixed Signals*. Contrast to Skiba, "Shifting Sites of Argentine Advocacy," emphasizing the national origins of human rights in Argentina.

67. The administration's first Presidential Review Memorandum dealt with Panama; Carter transformed it into a "broad review of our policy toward Latin America." See PRM/NSC-1, January 21, 1977, and PRM/NSC-17, January 26, 1977, both JCPL, PRM/PD. For Carter's Latin America policy, see "Review of U.S. Policy Toward Latin America," March 12, 1977, JCPL, DC, NLC-17-26-1-1-3; "PRC Meeting on Latin America," March 14, 1977 ("imperialistic legacy"); and "Minutes of PRC Meeting on Latin America, March 23, 1977," March 31, 1977, both in JCPL, ZBM, SuF, PRC Meetings, box 24; Brzezinski, WNSR #7, April 1, 1977, JCPL, ZBM, SuF, Weekly Reports, box 41; and "NSC Contributions to the Carter Administration's Policy on Latin America," January 18, 1981, JCPL, ZBM, SuF, NSC Accomplishments, box 34. For Carter's reflections, see *White House Diary*, p. 86 and 90 ("cheated"). Also see Glad, *Outsider in the White House*, esp. pp. 88–106; and Strong, *Working in the World*, pp.153–82. For Carter's on sovereignty, see "Address before the Organization of American States," April 14, 1977, APP ("high regard"). The administration grasped Latin American mistrust of its policy, as in Brzezinski to Carter, "Report on the Impact of Human Rights Policy," May 19, 1977, JCPL, WHCF, HU, box 1.

68. For Amnesty's role see "Report of an Amnesty International Mission," November 6–15, 1976, Amnesty International Online Library.

69. For the Grenada OAS meeting, see "The OAS General Assembly and the Human Rights Issue," June 28, 1977, JCPL, DC, NLC-24-50-1-4-5 ("battleground"); and Schoultz, *Human Rights and United States Policy*, pp. 132–33. On Latin American reactions, see "Impact of the U.S. Stand on Human Rights," June 6, 1977, JCPL, WHCF, HU, box 1; and "Human Rights Ferment in Latin America," June 5, 1977, JCPL, DC, NLC-7-15-1-3-4. On arms transfers, see Stockholm International Peace Research Institute, Arms Transfers Database; and Schoultz, *Human Rights and United States Policy*, p. 362. The fullest account of Carter's human rights policy in Argentina is Schmidli, *Fate of Freedom Elsewhere*.

70. For the CIA's assessment, see "Human Rights Performance: January 1977-July 1978," JCPL, DC, NLC-28-17-15-9-8 ("encouraging"). For the State Department's, see "Human Rights Improvements," May 11, 1977, JCPL, NSA Files, SuF, HR, box 28. Lake's comments are in "The Human Rights Policy," JCPL, WHCF, HU, box 1 ("cannot know"). Also see Schoultz, see *Human Rights and United States Policy*, pp. 346–64.

71. Brazinsky, *Nation Building in South Korea*, p. 226 ("growing conflict"). Also see "Report of the Mission to the Republic of Korea," March 27–April 9, 1975, in CHDR, AI USA, Executive Director Files, David Hawk, box 4; and US Congress, House, Committee on International Relations, *Human Rights in South Korea and the Philippines*.

72. For Carter's policy, see Bloomfield, "Carter Human Rights Policy." On its effects, see CIA, "Human Rights Performance: January 1977-July 1978." For Carter and Park, see "Notes on Private Meeting with Park," June 30, 1979 ("extreme"); "Private Meeting with President Park," July 1, 1970; and MemCon, July 5, 1979, all in JCPL, Susan Clough/Plains File, President's Personal Foreign Affairs File, Korea, box 2.

73. Bloomfield, "Carter Human Rights Policy" ("most difficult"). For NGO engagement, see ICJ, "Human Rights and the Legal System in Iran," CHRD, IMP, Miscellaneous Files, box 6; and the testimony in US Congress, House, *Human Rights in Iran*. For newspaper accounts, see "Iran Secret Police," *WP*, May 29, 1976, p. A9; "Torture, Terror, in Iran," *WP*, May 29, 1976, p. B11; "Iran Secret Police," *Chicago Tribune*, May 29, 1976, p. 16; "Torture and Denials of Rights," *NYT*, May 29, 1976, p. 51; "SAVAK," *WP*, May 9, 1977, p. A1; "U.S. Is Said to Aid Shah's Secret Police," *WP*, August 20, 1977, p. B11; and "Iran Accused of Frequent Torture," *NYT*, Nov. 29, 1977, p. A8. Baraheni's testimony is in US Congress, House, *Human Rights in Iran* ("exceptional cases"), but also see *Crowned Cannibals*, published to acclaim in 1977.

74. "PRM on Human Rights," July 8, 1977, JCPL, Counsel's Office, Human Rights PRM, box 14 ("immune").

75. On Pahlavi, see Afkhami, *Life and Times of the Shah*, pp. 446–52; and Bill, *Eagle and the Lion*, pp. 219–22. For the quiet entreaties, see ICJ to Pahlavi, June 17, 1977, University of Washington, Henry M. Jackson Papers, Accession no. 3560-6, box 36. For the administration's efforts, see Bloomfield, "Carter Human Rights Policy" ("derelictions"). For Vance's visit, see Vance, *Hard Choices*, pp. 318–19; and "The Secretary's Meeting with the Shah," May 13, 1977, DNSA. For the debate on AWACS, see US Congress, House, Committee on International Relations. *Prospective Sale of Airborne Warning and Control System (AWACS) Aircraft*; and US Congress, Senate, *Sale of AWACS to Iran*. For Carter's meeting with Pahlavi, see *Keeping Faith*, 436–37 ("combat"); and *White House Diary*, pp. 135–37.

76. See Brzezinski, "Information Items," November 14, 1977, JCPL, DC, NLC-1-4-4-29-1; Tuchman, "Assessment of Human Rights Accomplishments," January 5, 1978, JCPL, WHCF, HU, box 1; Lake, "The Human Rights Policy," January 16, 1978, JCPL, WHCF, HU, box 1; and "Human Rights Performance: January 1977-July 1978," JCPL, DC, NLC-28-17-15-9-8 ("forced on the Shah").

77. On the Iranian Revolution, Kurzman, *Unthinkable Revolution*, focuses on the 1977–79 phase; Halliday, *Dictatorship and Development*, emphasizes the disruptive effects of oil-related economic dislocations in the 1970s; and Hooglund, *Land and Revolution in Iran* stresses the legacies of the Shah's reforms. Axworthy, *Revolutionary Iran* provides an accessible overview. On Khomeini's use of cassette tapes, see Sreberny and Mohammadi, *Small Media, Big Revolution*.

78. US policy is amply documented. Brzezinski, *Power and Principle*, chap. 10; and Vance, *Hard Choices*, chaps. 14–15, acknowledge the disagreements. Bill, *Eagle and the Lion*, chap. 7; Rubin, *Paved with Good Intentions*; Sick, *All Fall Down*; and Sullivan, *Mission to Iran* offer context. For Carter, see *White House Diary*, pp. 257–58. ("strong leader").

79. Kissinger is in "Henry Kissinger," *Trialogue* no. 19, available at http://www.trilateral.org ("vocal"). On the influence of Carter's human rights policy, see Bill, *Eagle and the Lion*, chap. 7. Pahlavi's views are in *Answer to History*. For Ravenal, see Fallows to Brzezinski, January 16, 1978, "Human Rights Policy," JCPL, HHM, SuF, Foreign Policy, box 38 ("nasty").

80. Hawk's evaluation is in "Human Rights at Half Time," April 7, 1977, JCPL, HHM, SuF, Foreign Policy, box 38 ("more aware"); the League's is in Bloomfield, "Carter Human Rights Policy" ("focus for discussion").

81. WNSR #1, January 22, 1977, JCPL, ZBM, SuF, Weekly Reports, box 41 ("all nations"). On East Timor, see Simpson, "Denying the 'First Right.'" On Cambodia, see Clymer, "Human Rights, and Cambodia." Carter is in "Remarks Commemorating the 30th Anniversary of the Universal Declaration," December 5, 1978, APP ("soul").

Chapter 9

1. "State of the Union Address," January 23, 1980, APP ("most serious threat").
2. See Carter, "Address to the Nation on the Soviet Invasion," January 4, 1980, APP; and *White House Diary*, p. 388 ("use in the mountains"). For administration views, see "Reflections on Soviet Invasion," December 26, 1979; "Possible Steps in Reaction to Soviet Intervention," January 2, 1980, both in JCPL, ZBM, Geographic File, Southwest Asia/Persian Gulf, box 17; "Our Response to Soviet Intervention," December 29, 1979; "Strategic Reaction to the Afghanistan Problem," January 3, 1980; and "A Long-Term Strategy for Coping," January 9, 1980, all DDRS; and Minutes of SCC Meeting, January 17, 1980, JCPL, ZBM, SuF, Meetings–SCC, box 32. Vance's views are in *Hard Choices*, p. 388. For Carter, see "The Chill of a New Cold War," *Newsweek*, January 14, 1980 ("opinion"). Carter's State of the Union Address is consecrated as official line in "The U.S. Response to Afghanistan," February 12, 1980 JCPL, CEA, SuF, NSC, box 58.
3. Brzezinski modeled Carter's Doctrine on Truman's, invoking one of the predecessors whom Carter most admired. See *Power and Principle*, pp. 444–45. For reactions, see Hoffman, "Toward a Foreign Policy," *NYT*, January 25, 1980, p. A23 ("useful"); Kennan, "Talk of War," *NYT*, February 3, 1980, p. 3 ("bizarre"); and Kennedy, "Sometimes a Party Must Sail against the Wind," *WP*, January 29, 1980, p. A4 ("militarism").
4. Historians have, in general, hailed Carter's hawkish shift as a significant turning point, although explanations for it vary. Glad, *Outsider in the White House*, and Smith, *Morality, Reason, and Power*, emphasize conflict between Vance and Brzezinski; Kalman, *Right Star Rising*; and Zelizer, *Arsenal of Democracy*, stress the influence of broader political currents. Skidmore, *Reversing Course*, sees Carter's reversal as a result of his failure to gain legitimacy for his early policy, while Nichols, "Carter and the Soviets" sees the shift as a direct response to Soviet behavior. Auten, *Carter's Conversion*, argues that what changed was not so much Soviet behavior as Carter's perceptions of it. On the continuities between Carter and Reagan, see Halliday, *Second Cold War*; and Njølstad, "Carter Legacy."
5. "Memorandum on Foreign Policy Priorities," YMA, CVP, Series II, Foreign Policy Articles, box 9 ("new phase"); and Brzezinski "Remarks to the Trilateral Commission" October 25, 1977, JCPL, HHM, SuF, box 3 ("complex foreign policy").
6. "Address at Commencement Exercises," May 22, 1977, APP ("inordinate fear"); and Minutes of Cabinet Meeting, November 21, 1977, JCPL, CEA, SuF, Cabinet Meeting Minutes, box 9 ("glue").
7. See WNSR #24, August 19, 1977, JCPL, ZBM, SuF, Weekly Reports, box 41 ("dominated everything"); "Détente," October 6, 1976, YMA, CVP, Series II, Carter Presidency Transition, box 8 ("Other priorities"); "The New U.S. Challenge to Russia," *U.S. News and World Report*, May 30, 1977, p. 35 ("historically irrelevant"); "Remarks to the Trilateral Commission," October 25, 1977, ("to assimilate"); "Foreign Policy Priorities; and *Power and Principle*, p. 177 ("historically optimistic"). Carter's approach resembled the Trilateral Commission's, as presented in Azrael et. al., *Overview of East-West Relations.*
8. On Vladivostok, see Kissinger-Carter MemCon, November 20, 1976, YMA, CVP, Series II, Carter Presidency Transition, box 8; and Garthoff, *Détente and Confrontation*, pp. 494–505. For Carter's views, see "Address to the UN General Assembly," March 17, 1977, APP ("deep reduction"); and *Keeping Faith*, pp. 212–17. On human rights, see Speech to B'nai B'rith, September 8, 1976, US Congress, House, Committee on House Administration, *The Presidential Campaign 1976*, vol. 1, Part 2, pp. 709–14 ("deprivation"). For the outreach to Soviet dissidents, see WNSR #1, February 19, 1977; and WNSR #3, March 5, 1977, both JCPL, ZBM, SuF, Weekly Reports, box 41; Bloomfield, "Carter Human Rights Policy," pp. 22–23; and Garthoff, *Détente and Confrontation*, pp. 627–30. On Sakharov, see Bergman, *Meeting the Demands of Reason*, pp. 256–59; and Sakharov, *Memoirs*, pp. 464–66. Anatoly Dobrynin later confirmed that Carter's correspondence with Sakharov was, from a Soviet perspective, "very offensive." See "SALT II and the Growth of Mistrust," pp. 56–57, DNSA, CBP, and Dobrynin, *In Confidence*, pp. 383–92. Finally, Brezhnev to Carter, February 26, 1977, DNSA, CBP ("like that").

9. For Brezhnev, see Garthoff, *Détente and Confrontation*, p. 647 ("certain trust"); WNSR #2, February 26, 1977, JCPL, ZBM, SuF, Weekly Reports, box 41; and Brezhnev to Carter, February 4, 1977, DNSA, CBP, ("equality," etc.). The "comprehensive and reciprocal" formula was Brzezinski's, as he explains in *Power and Principle*, pp. 147–150. The State Department managed to excise the language from Carter's Notre Dame speech as comparison of the penultimate draft (in JCPL, OSS, PHF, box 30) with the version delivered on May 22, 1977 (APP) indicates. See, finally, Carter, *White House Diary*, p. 20 ("cooperate").

10. On the military balance, see "U.S.-USSR Offensive Strategic Force Balance," in JCPL, NSA Files, SuF, Human Rights, box 28. Also see Garthoff, *Détente and Confrontation*, pp. 865–77; and Vance, *Hard Choices*, chap. 3. On the SS-20, see Jackson, "Memorandum for the President," February 15, 1977, University of Washington, Henry M. Jackson Papers, Accession no. 3560-5, box 5; and, for a more measured view, Burt, "The SS-20 and the Eurostrategic Balance," *The World Today* (1977), pp. 43–51. Schmidt's speech is "The 1977 Alastair Buchan Memorial Lecture" in *Survival* (Jan.–Feb.1978), pp. 1–10. Also see Brzezinski, *Power and Principle*, pp. 290–91; Garthoff, *Détente and Confrontation*, pp. 941–42; Vance, *Hard Choices*, p. 64.

11. "Soviet Strategic Objectives: An Alternative View," December 1976, DNSA, CBP ("maximum possible"). Contrast with NIE 11-3/8-76, "Soviet Forces for Intercontinental Conflict," DNSA, CBP. For a sense of the debate, see "New CIA Estimate," *NYT*, December 26, 1976, p. 1; and Pipes, "Why the Soviet Union Thinks It Could Fight and Win a Nuclear War," *Commentary*, vol. 64, no. 1 (1977): 21–34. On the episode, see Cahn and Prados, "Team B"; Vaïsse, *Neoconservatism*, pp. 153–57; and Walsh, *Military Balance in the Cold War*, pp. 180–83. For Carter, see "U.S. News Interview," May 24, 1976, in US Congress, House, Committee on House Administration, *The Presidential Campaign 1976*, vol. 1, Part 1, pp. 199–205 ("second best").

12. On the CPD, see Dalby, *Creating the Second Cold War*; and Sanders, *Peddlers of Crisis*. For Vance on détente, see *Hard Choices*, chap. 3 ("main problem"), and on human rights, see "Minutes of Cabinet Meeting," February 7, 1977, JCPL, CEA, SuF, Cabinet Meetings, box 8. Contrast with Brzezinski in WNSR #7, April 1, 1977, JCPL, ZBM, SuF, Weekly Reports, box 41. For Vance on arms control, see Vance to Carter, July 31, 1976, YMA, CVP, Series II, Carter Presidential Campaign, box 8. For Carter's views, see Carter- Dobrynin MemCon, February 1, 1977, JCPL, NSA Files, SuF, President MemCons, box 34; "Address to the UN General Assembly," March 17, 1977, APP; *White House Diary*, p. 35; and *Keeping Faith*, pp. 215–20. For a summary of the options, see WNSR #4, March 11, 1977, JCPL, ZBM, SuF, Weekly Reports, box 41.

13. For a sampling of the domestic criticism, see "Kennan on Carter's Diplomacy," *NYT*, April 2, 1977, p. 49; "Mr. Carter's 'Open Mouth' Diplomacy," *WSJ*, April 22, 1977, p. 16; and "Behind the Moscow SALT Setback," *WP*, April 26, 1977, p. B13. Also see Garthoff, *Détente and Confrontation*, pp. 883–94; Talbott, *Endgame*, pp. 38–75; and Vance, *Hard Choices*, chap. 3. For a Soviet view, see Dobrynin, *In Confidence*, pp. 390–94.

14. "PRM/NSC-10: Comprehensive Net Assessment and Military Force Posture Review," February 18, 1977 ("trends"); "PRM/NSC-10: Military Strategy and Force Posture Review," June 5, 1977 ("to prevail"); and "PD/NSC-18: U.S. National Strategy," August 24, 1977 all JCPL, PRM/PD; and Brzezinski, *Power and Principle*, pp. 177–78 ("optimistic").

15. For the NATO summit, see Owen to Carter, "Summit Preparations," April 15, 1977, DDRS; and "Note by the Prime Minister on a Meeting," May 9, 1977, MTA.

16. Meeting with Dobrynin, February 1, 1977, JCPL, NSA Files, SuF, MemCons, box 34 ("intention"). For Soviet reactions, see Dobrynin, *In Confidence*, pp. 386–90; Garthoff, *Détente and Confrontation*, pp. 628–35; and Leffler, *For the Soul of Mankind*, pp. 263–70. Soviet vexation was clear to US officials at the time. See Brezhnev to Carter, February 26, 1977, DNSA, CBP ("pseudo-humane"); "Soviet Objectives and Tactics," May 1977, JCPL, DC; "Impact of the U.S. Stand on Human Rights," June 6, 1977, JCPL, WHCF, HU, box 1; and Carter-Gromyko MemCon, September 23, 1977, DNSA, CBP. For US statements and actions, see "U.S. Government Initiatives," April 17, 1980, JCPL, ZB, SuF, Human Rights, box 29. On Shcharansky, see Beckerman, *When They Come for Us*, pp. 311–47; and Shcharansky and Hoffman, *Fear No Evil*. On Soviet antidissident campaigns, see Moscow

Embassy to Secretary of State, February 13, 1977, JCPL, ZBM, SuF, Human Rights, box 28; and "Origins of Soviet Campaign Against Dissidents" July 19, 1977, JCPL, DC. Brzezinski is in WNSR #32, October 14, 1977; and WNSR #33, October 21, 1977, both JCPL, ZBM, SuF, Weekly Reports, box 41.

17. On US policy toward the CSCE, see Brzezinski-Fascell MemCon, April 5, 1977, JCPL, ZBM, SuF, MemCons, box 33; and PRC Minutes, August 23, 1977, JCPL, ZBM, SuF, Meetings–PRC, box 24. For a positive appraisal of Goldberg's accomplishments, see Snyder, *Human Rights Activism*, pp. 100–11. More critical are Sherer, "Breakdown at Belgrade"; and Sherer, "Goldberg's Variation." Dorothy Goldberg, Arthur's wife, offers a useful narrative in "Personal Journal: Helsinki Negotiations for Human Rights," in LOC, Arthur Goldberg Papers, Part I, box 173. For the official US report, see US Congress, House, Commission on Security and Cooperation in Europe, *The Belgrade Followup Meeting*. On the diplomatic frictions, see Fascell, "Did Human Rights Survive Belgrade?" For the NGO connection, see Brzezinski to Sussman, February 28, 1977, JCPL, WHCF, HU, box 1; and Freedom House, "An Advisory for the Administration," April 12, 1977, JCPL, WHCF, IT, box 5; and McRae to Yeo et. al., October 9, 1977, CHRRD, AI USA, Executive Director Files, David Hawk Files, box 5 ("degenerated").

18. "Interview with the Nation's Health," in US Congress, House, Committee on House Administration, *The Presidential Campaign, 1976*, vol. 1, Part 2, pp. 797–99 ("chess game"). Also see "Business Week Interview," September 26, 1976, in US Congress, House, Committee on House Administration, *The Presidential Campaign, 1976*, vol. 1, Part 2, pp.790–96; and "Foreign Policy Priorities."

19. See, generally, Saunders and Onslow, "Southern Africa in the Cold War." On US policy and the Horn, see Brzezinski; *Power and Principle*, pp. 178–90; Glad, *Alone in the White House*, chap. 7; Jackson, *Jimmy Carter and the Horn of Africa*; and Vance, *Hard Choices*, pp. 72–75, 84–88. On the Horn crisis more broadly, see Garthoff, *Détente and Confrontation*, pp. 695–719; Tareke, "Ethiopia-Somalia War of 1977"; and Westad, *Global Cold War*, chap. 7. For an interpretation of Soviet motives emphasizing opportunism and ideology, see Patman, *Soviet Union in the Horn of Africa*. Brzezinski's views are in WNSR #46, February 9, 1978, JCPL, ZBM, SuF, Weekly Reports, box 41 ("strategic deterioration"); "Minutes of Cabinet Meeting," February 27, 1978, JCPL, CEA, SuF, Cabinet Meetings, box 9; and "The Soviet Union and Ethiopia," March 3, 1978, JCPL, ZBM, SuF, Meetings–SCC, box 28 ("some deterrent").

20. Vance, *Hard Choices*, pp. 84, 101–2 ("targets" and "new Cold War"). For Brzezinski, see WNSR #46, February 9. 1978, and WNSR #55, April 21, 1978 ("China card"), both JCPL, ZB, SuF, Weekly Reports, box 41; and Brzezinski, *Power and Principle*, pp. 203–6. The key decisions on the Horn are in Minutes of SCC Meeting, March 16, 1978; Brzezinski to Carter, March 27, 1978, and Minutes of SCC Meeting, April 7, 1978, all in JCPL, ZB, SuF, Meetings–SCC, box 28.

21. The best account of the Naval Academy speech is Strong, *Working in the World*, chap. 4. The source of the stapling legend is Fallows, "The Passionless Presidency," *Atlantic*, May 1, 1979. Carter's handwritten notes are in JCPL, SSF, PHF, box 89. Also see Vance to Carter, June 2, 1978; and Doolittle and Hertzberg to Carter, June 2, 1978, both in JCPL, HHM, SuF, box 5; Fallows to Carter, "Naval Academy Speech," May 23, 1978; and Brzezinski to Carter, June 2, 1978, both in JCPL, SSF, PHF, box 89. For the speech itself, "Address at the Commencement Exercises," June 7, 1978, APP ("totalitarian").

22. Brzezinski, *Power and Principle*, pp. 519–20 ("two alternative").

23. Brzezinski, *Between Two Ages* ("technetronic"); and Press Briefing, December 20, 1977, JCPL, HHM, SuF, Foreign Policy, box 38 ("awakening"). For Carter, see *White House Diary*, pp. 123 ("ogres").

24. "Politburo Session of the Central Committee of the CPSU," June 8, 1978, DNSA, CBP ("deterioration"); and "The President's News Conference," June 26, 1978, APP ("peace").

25. For differences over human rights, see *Pravda*, "On the Present Policy of the U.S. Government," June 17, 1978 ("same designs"), cited in Garthoff, *Détente and Confrontation*, p. 673; and "Operation Human Rights," June 2, 1978, in JCPL, HHM, SuF, Human Rights, box 2. For the sharpening of US policy, see "Human Rights," July 7, 1978, JCPL, WHCF, HU, box 2; "U.S. Government Initiatives," April 17, 1980, JCPL, NSA Files, SuF, box 29;

and Garthoff, *Détente and Confrontation*, pp. 673–78. For differences over the Third World, see Carter-Gromyko MemCon, May 27, 1978, DNSA, CBP; and "The President's News Conference," May 25, 1978, APP. Also see Gleijeses, "Truth or Credibility"; and Garthoff, *Détente and Confrontation*, pp. 687–95. On Camp David, Brzezinski recognized that Egyptian-Israeli peace would undermine Soviet hopes for "greater U.S.-Soviet parallelism in that region." See WNSR #39, December 9, 1977, JCPL, ZBM, SuF, Weekly Reports, box 41.

26. For the early policy, see Brzezinski, *Power and Principle*, pp. 196–202; and Vance, *Hard Choices*, pp. 77–83. For Vance's 1977 trip, see "Secretary Vance's PRC Trip," August 29, 1977, JCPL, COS, SuF, China, box 34A. On Deng's policy, Ezra Vogel emphasizes the discontinuities in *Deng Xiaoping and the Transformation of China*, esp. pp. 311–48; while Li Lanqing, a reformist official, presents Deng's "opening-up" as a realization, not a repudiation, of Mao's purposes in *Breaking Through*, esp. pp. 4–72.

27. Brzezinski, *Power and Principle*, pp. 206 ("badgered"). Also see WNSR #42, January 13, 1978; WNSR #46, February 9, 1978, both in JCPL, ZBM, SuF, Weekly Reports, box 41; and "The Soviet Union and Ethiopia," March 3, 1978, JCPL, ZBM, SuF, Meetings–SCC, box 28. For Brzezinski's 1978 trip, see WNSR #60, May 26, 1978 ("hearty agreement"); Brzezinski, *Power and Principle*, pp. 209–19; "Polar Bear Tamer," *Newsweek*, June 5, 1978 ("oppose the Russians"); and *FRUS 1977-1980*, vol. 13, nos. 108–10. For assessments of the geopolitical dividends, see WNSR #63, June 16, 1978; and WNSR #71, September 9, 1978, both in JCPL, ZBM, SuF, Weekly Reports, box 41. For Chinese economic ventures, see "Memorandum for Dr. Brzezinski," September 23, 1978, JCPL, DC, NLC-1-7-9-26-6.

28. For Deng's visit, see Carter, *White House Diary*, pp. 283–84 ("oppose the Soviet Union"); and *FRUS 1977-1980*, vol. 13, esp. nos. 196, 202 ("Cuba of the East"), 203–9. Also see Brzezinski, *Power and Principle*, pp. 403–14; Carter, *Keeping Faith*, pp. 202–11; Kissinger, *On China*, 359–66; and "An Interview with Teng Hsiao-p'ing," *Time*, February 5, 1979, pp. 32–35 ("polar bear"). On Vietnam and humanitarian intervention, see Wheeler, *Saving Strangers*, pp. 78–110; and Quinn-Judge, "Fraternal Aid, Self-Defense, or Self Interest?"

29. On Cambodia, see Carter, "Human Rights Violations in Cambodia," April 21, 1978, APP ("worst"); Clymer, "Human Rights and Cambodia"; and Kiernan, *Blood and Soil*, pp. 546–54 Vance offers a frank analysis in *Hard Choices*, pp. 124–27. On human rights in China, see Buckley, see "On Rights for the Chinese," November 5-6, 1977, in LOC, AGP, Part I, box 143; Simon Leys, "Human Rights in China" *National Review*, December 8, 1978, pp. 1537–541, 1544–544, 1559; and Shirk, "Human Rights: What about China?" Contrast with Barnett, "Make an Issue of Rights in China?" *NYT*, April 2, 1978, p. E19. For the administration's rationalizations, see "PRM on Human Rights," JCPL, Counsel's Office, Human Rights PRM, box 14 ("other considerations"); and *FRUS 1977-1980*, vol. 13, no. 145. For the NGO view, see AI-USA draft resolution on impartiality, March 3, 1975, in CHRRD, IMP, Miscellaneous Files, AI, box 5. For Tiananmen Square, see "Marchers in Peking Demand Democracy," January 8, 1979, *NYT*, p. A5.

30. Carter, "Remarks at the Annual Convention of the American Newspaper Publishers Association," April 25, 1979, APP ("mutual annihilation"). On SALT II, see Garthoff, *Détente and Confrontation*, pp. 883–912; Talbott, *Endgame*; and Vance, *Hard Choices*, pp. 133–39. More critical is Glynn, *Closing Pandora's box*, pp. 277–305. On the ratification debate is Caldwell, *Dynamics of Domestic Politics*.

31. Carter, "Some thoughts jotted down at Camp David," JCPL, OSS, PHF, box 100.

32. Carter-Schmidt MemCon, July 7, 1978, MTA, "monetary stability"; and Blumenthal, "Steering in Crowded Waters" ("underlying"). On post-1973 international monetary relations, see de Vries, *International Monetary Fund, 1972-78*, vol. 2, pp. 801–68; James, *Monetary Cooperation*, pp. 261–346; Solomon, *Monetary System*, chap. 18; and Strange *Casino Capitalism*, esp. pp. 8–11. On the EMS, see Mourlon-Druol, *Europe Made of Money*; and for a contrasting interpretation stressing the primacy of economic motives, Moravcsik, *Choice for Europe*, pp. 241–91. On Carter and the EMS, see Basosi, "Changing International Monetary System."

33. "A Reserve Currency," *WSJ*, August 21, 1978, p. 8 ("wrecking"). Exchange rates are from BIS Statistics. For analyses, see BIS, *Annual Report* (1979), pp. 3–5, 134–44; "Who's to Blame for the Dollar," the *Economist*, August 19, 1978, pp. 53–54; and White House, *ERP* (1979), pp. 153–56. For Carter, see Notes on NSC Meeting, August 15, 1978, SSF, PHF, box 100.

For Blumenthal, see "Attitudes at IMF/IBRD Meeting," October 4, 1978, JCPL, CEA, SuF, box 42 ("serious doubts"). On the IMF meeting, also see de Vries, *International Monetary Fund, 1972-1978*, vol. 2, pp. 858–62.

34. On inflation, see Samuelson, *Great Inflation and Its Aftermath;* and, stressing both the interplay of politics and economics and the diversity of national experiences, Lindberg and Maier, eds., *Politics of Inflation and Economic Stagnation.* For a monetarist view, see Meltzer, *History of the Federal Reserve,* vol. 2, book 2, esp. chap. 7. Contrast with the CEA's perspective in White House, *ERP* (1979), which points the finger at businesses and unions ("corrosive effects" and "full employment"). For Carter's policy, see Biven, *Carter's Economy,* chaps. 6, 9–10; and "Address to the Nation," October 24, 1978, APP.

35. Solomon, "Report," October 26, 1978, JCPL, ASM, ChronF, box 5 ("depreciated sharply"); and "Dollar Hits Lowest Levels Since WW II," *LAT,* October 26, 1976, p. D12 ("woefully inadequate"). For Carter's response, see "Remarks Announcing Measures to Strengthen the Dollar," November 1, 1978, APP. On the November 1 package, see Biven, *Carter's Economy,* pp. 165–71; Moffitt, *World's Money,* pp. 162–66; and Solomon, *International Monetary System,* pp. 348–51; White House, *ERP* (1979), pp. 153–56; and Blumenthal's in US Congress, Joint Economic Committee, hearing, *Dollar Rescue Operations,* pp. 8–20. For the effects, see Solomon, "Report," November 2, 1978, JCPL, ASM, ChronF, box 5.

36. Meltzer, *History of the Federal Reserve,* vol. 2, book 2, p. 934 ("international concerns").

37. On the effects of financial globalization, see Moffitt, *World's Money,* esp. pp. 133–64. For Blumenthal, see US Congress, Senate, Committee on Foreign Relations, *Oversight of International Economic Issues* (1979), esp. pp. 17–18 ("technology"). The administration's disinclination to impose capital controls is discussed in Helleiner, *Global Finance,* chap. 6; and affirmed in Blumenthal to Carter, "Contingency Planning with Respect to the Dollar," January 19, 1978, JCPL, SSF, PHF, box 72; and Solomon to Byrd, August 11, 1978, JCPL, ASM, ChronF, box 4.

38. For the 1979–80 oil crisis, see Alnasrawi, *OPEC in a Changing World Economy,* p. 109–12; Parra, *Oil Politics,* chap. 11; Schneider, *Oil Price Revolution,* chap. 13; Seymour, *OPEC: Instrument of Change,* chap. 8; Skeet, *OPEC: Twenty-Five Years,* chap. 8; and Yergin, *The Prize,* chap. 33. These interpretations resemble this book's. For an alternative view implicating horizontal conspiracy among the oil companies, see Sherrill, *Oil Follies of 1970-1980,* esp. pp. 433–39. Production statistics are from DeGolyer and MacNaughton, *TCPS;* prices are for Dubai Light Crude from GFD.

39. For OPEC's hikes, see *FRUS 1969-1976,* vol. 37, nos. 160–61, 178–80; "OPEC Raises its Prices," *LAT,* March 28, 1979, p. SD1; "U.S. Critical of Move," *NYT,* March 29, 1970, p. A1 ("justifiable"); and "OPEC's Move to More Flexible Pricing," *WSJ,* March 30, 1979, p. 7.

40. On price controls, see Vietor, *Energy Policy in America,* chap. 10. For Carter's policy, see Barrow, "Age of Limits"; Biven, *Carter's Economy,* pp. 171–77; and Carter, *Keeping Faith,* pp. 91–124.

41. See Carter, "Energy Address to the Nation," April 5, 1979, APP ("economic shock"). Statistics are from EIA.

42. Saudi Arabia lifted its production ceiling from 8.5m to 9.5m barrels per day to compensate for Iran's shortfall but re-imposed the 8.5m ceiling in April before raising it again in July. See *FRUS 1969-1976,* vol. 37, nos. 180, 182, 188, 202.

43. *FRUS 1969-1976,* vol. 37, no. 225 ("success"); Carter, *White House Diary,* pp. 335–36 ("worst days" and "problems"); and "Declaration: Tokyo Summit Conference," June 28–29, MTA. On the summit, see Putman and Bayne, *Hanging Together,* pp. 110–18.

44. For the summit, see "The Economic Summit Meeting in Tokyo," June 28–29, Sessions 1-4, MTA (all quotes). For US policy, see *FRUS 1969-1976,* vol. 37, no. 218–19; and Owen, "The Tokyo Summit," June 22, 1979, MTA.

45. For the discussion on import ceilings after Tokyo, see *FRUS 1969-1976,* vol. 37, nos. 226, 235, 250, 251, 256, and 273.

46. See "Text of Eizenstat's Memo," July 8, 1979, *NYT,* p.32 ("Since you left"). For opinion polls, see APP. For Rosalynn Carter see *First Lady from Plains,* p. 302 ("Nobody"). For Carter's perspective, see *White House Diary,* pp. 334–41 ("broader"). Eizenstat elaborates the context in "Interview with Stuart Eizenstat," January 29–30, Miller Center, University of Virginia,

Carter Presidency Project. Also see Bourne, *Jimmy Carter*, esp. pp. 441–55; Kalman, *Right Star Rising*, pp. 324–29; Mattson, *Mr. President*; and Strong, "Recapturing Leadership."

47. Bourne, *Jimmy Carter* ("sweeping"), p. 442; and Caddell, "Of Crisis and Opportunity," April 23, 1979, JCPL, Jody Powell Files, Memoranda, box 40 ("crisis of confidence" etc.).

48. Carter's notes are in JCPL, Susan Clough/Plains File, Camp David Summit, box 19. For Carter's account, see *White House Diary*, pp. 340–44 ("Great Society"). The speech is "Address to the Nation on Energy and National Goals," July 15, 1979, APP. For the public response, see Carter, *White House Diary*, p. 344; and Mattson, *Mr. President*, pp. 7–9.

49. "Economic Strategy—Alternative Courses," June 20, 1979, JCPL, CEA, SuF, box 38 ("core"); and Owen, "Theme for Speech and Policy," July 12, 1979, JCPL, SSF, PHF, box 138. And, of course, Sex Pistols, God Save the Queen, Never Mind the bollocks, ©1977, 1977 by Warner Brothers, Compact Disc.

50. Some scholars who celebrate Volcker's achievements but take a low view of Carter's present Volcker's appointment as reluctant and/or unwitting on Carter's part. For this approach, see Greider, *Secrets of the Temple*, p. 46; and Samuelson, *Great Inflation*, pp. 118–20. Others give Carter more credit, including Biven, *Carter's Economy*, pp. 237–40; and Meltzer, *History of the Federal Reserve*, vol. 2, book, 2, p. 1009. Carter corroborates the impression of purposeful choice in *White House Diary*, p. 347 ("committed" and "strongest"), as do Volcker's recollections in Silber, *Volcker*, pp. 145–46. For Lance's objections, see Bourne, *Jimmy Carter*, p. 448 ("mortgaging").

51. "Statement by Paul A. Volcker," September 5, 1979, ("most pressing"), FRASER. Also see Greider, *Secrets of the Temple*, chap. 3; Kettl, *Leadership at the Fed*, pp. 173–76; Meltzer, *History of the Federal Reserve*, vol. 2, book 2, pp. 1008–33; Moffitt, *World's Money*, pp. 165–76; and Silber, *Volcker*, pp. 147–77.

52. "Meeting of Federal Open Market Committee," October 6, 1979, FRASER ("problem").

53. Volcker's reflections on "inflationary psychology" are quoted in Silber, *Volcker*, p. 155.

54. "Meeting of FOMC," October 6, 1979, FRASER. For Volcker's explanations of the October 6 package, see, *inter alia*, "Transcript of Press Conference with Paul Volcker," October 6, 1979; Volcker, "A Time of Testing," October 9, 1979; and "The New Federal Reserve Technical Procedures," all from FRASER.

55. Many scholars hail the Volcker shift of 1979 as a major turning point, comparable in significance to Nixon's 1971 abandonment of gold-dollar convertibility. For a critical interpretation emphasizing the prioritization of international over domestic objectives, see Stein, *Pivotal Decade*, pp. 227–31. Krippner, *Capitalizing on Crisis*, presents the "Volcker Shock" as a turning point in the "financialization" of the US political economy, esp. pp. 116–20. Others echo Krippner's conclusions, including Morgan, "Monetary Metamorphosis." Marxist scholarship goes further still: Arrighi, "World Economy and the Cold War" frames the Volcker shift as a bid to attract capital from the developing world, while Brenner, *Economics of Global Turbulence*, sees in Volcker's choice the hinge of a transition from a Keynesian order toward "a more or less permanent anti-inflationary approach" (p. 170). Panitch and Gindin, *Making of Global Capitalism*, concludes that "the Volcker shock was not so much about finding the right monetary policy as shifting the balance of class forces in American society," esp. pp. 167–72. Others are more restrained. Meltzer sees the restoration of the Fed's credibility as Volcker's major accomplishment in *History of the Federal Reserve*, vol. 2, book 2, esp. pp. 1008–31. Still others, including the present author, see the Volcker shift as the product of constraint more than choice—a bid for stability amid rampant inflation and international monetary instability. For example: Johnson, *Government of Money*, pp. 176–82; Silber, *Volcker*, esp. pp. 163–64; and Solomon, *International Monetary System*, pp. 352–54.

56. Statistics are from BLS. On Carter and the end of the Keynesian era, see Shulman, "Slouching Toward the Supply Side"; and Judith Stein, *Pivotal Decade*.

57. "Address at Wake Forest University," March 17, 1978, APP ("depend").

58. See *FRUS 1969-1976*, vol. 37, no. 230 ("heavy and alarming" etc.); and "Schlesinger in Farewell, Demands Balance with Russians," August 16, 1979, *NYT*, p. A8 ("Allah"). Also see Yergin, *The Prize*, p. 680.

59. See "Foreign Policy Priorities for the First Six Months," November 3, 1976; and "Overview of Foreign Policy Issues and Positions," October 24, 1976, both YMA, CVP, Series II,

Foreign Policy Articles, box 9; and WNSR #42, JCPL, ZBM, SuF, Weekly Reports, box 41. On the administration's peace diplomacy see Brzezinski, *Power and Principle*, pp. 234–88 ("new phase"); Carter, *Keeping Faith*, pp. 269–429; and Quandt, *Camp David*, esp. pp. 291–319. Carter acknowledged at Tokyo that Saudi reactions to the Egyptian-Israeli Treaty were adverse. See *FRUS 1969-1976*, vol. 37, no. 202.

60. "Consultative Security Framework for the Middle East," February 28, 1979, JCPL, ZBM, Geographic File, Southwest Asia/Persian Gulf, box 15 ("greatest vulnerability" etc.); and WNSR #81, December 2, 1978, JCPL, ZBM, SuF, Weekly Reports, box 42. The theory's public debut came in a speech to the Foreign Policy Association. See "Brzezinki Says Soviet Arms Pact Will Not Weaken U.S.," December 21, 1978, *NYT*, p. A3. For the subsequent development of a concept also framed as the "arc of instability," see WNSR #83, December 28, 1978; WNSR #86; January 26, 1979; and WNSR #87, February 2, 1979, all JCPL, ZBM, SuF, Weekly Reports, box 42. An early formulation that identifies the historian Hugh Seton-Watson's *Nations and States* as a source for the "arc of crisis" theory is in *FRUS 1977-1980*, vol. 13, no. 101.

61. Carter, *White House Diary*, pp. 293–94 ("closer relationship"). For the development of Middle East policy, see WNSR #91, March 23, 1979; WNSR #96, May 12, 1979; WNSR #101, June 22, 1979; WNSR #103, July 20, 1979; WNSR #106, August 10, 1979, all JCPL, ZBM, SuF, Weekly Reports, box 42; Minutes of SCC Meeting, May 11, 1979. For the differences between State's and DOD/NSC's approaches, see Sick and Ermart, "PRCs on Middle East/Persian Gulf," June 19, 1979, JCPL, ZBM, Geographical File, Southwest Asia/Persian Gulf, box 15 ("just and comprehensive"). Also see William Odom's comments in "Afghanistan and the Fall of Détente," DNSA, CBP, esp. pp. 60–64.

62. The 1977 proposal is in PD/NSC-18, "U.S. National Strategy," August 26, 1977, JCPL, PRM/PD ("deployment force"). For it rehabilitation, see Brzezinski, "Persian Gulf Contingency Forces," July 9, 1979; Brzezinski, "U.S. Capability to Respond to Limited Contingencies," August 17, 1979; and Aaron, "JCS Briefing on the RDF," December 27, 1979, all JCPL, ZBM, Geographic File, Southwest Asia/Persian Gulf, box 15. On the transition from the Rapid Deployment Force to CENTCOM, see Stork and Wenger, "U.S. in the Persian Gulf." On Oman, see Brezinzki Memo, December 5, 1979, JCPL, ZBM, Geographic File, Southwest Asia/Persian Gulf, box 15; and Zakheim, "Of Allies and Access." On military assistance to Saudi Arabia, see *FRUS 1969-1976*, vol. 37, no. 253 ("Riyadh"). On Egypt, see Minutes of PRC Meeting, September 20, 1979, JCPL, ZBM, SuF, Meetings–PRC, box 25; WNSR #110, September 21, 1979, JCPL, ZBM, SuF, Weekly Reports, box 42; Brzezinski, "Military Assistance Program for Egypt," JCPL, OSS, PHF, box 149 ("major"); and Carter, *White House Diary*, p. 371 ("two-pronged").

63. "Consultative Security Framework," February 28, 1979, JCPL, ZBM, Geographic File, Southwest Asia/Persian Gulf, box 15 ("Instability"); and WNSR #96, May 12, 1979, JCPL, ZBM, SuF, Weekly Reports, box 42 ("par with Europe"). NSC officials Fritz Ermart and Gary Sick were more restrained, situating the Persian Gulf "barely behind Northeast Asia and Europe in strategic importance." See "PRCs on Middle East/Persian Gulf," June 19, 1979.

64. The scholarship on the hostage crisis is substantial. For a view from Washington, see Brzezinski, *Power and Principle*, pp. 470–509; Carter, *Keeping Faith*, pp. pp. 433–571; and Vance, *Hard Choices*, pp. 368–413. Among the histories of the episode, Farber, *Taken Hostage* stands out for its rigor. On the seizure of the Grand Mosque, see Trofimov, *Siege of Mecca*. For the burning of the Islamabad Embassy, see Coll, *Ghost Wars*, pp. 21–37. Khomeini's statement is in "Captives Will be Slain" November 22, 1979, *Chicago Tribune*, p. 1. On Islamism popular accounts often emphasize the intellectual genealogies, as does Wright, *Looming Tower*. Others prioritize the proximate causes, including the petrodollar influx of the 1970s, as does Kepel, *Jihad*, and downplay the popular appeal, as does Roy, *Failure of Political Islam*. For Brzezinski's summary of the NSC's research, see WNSR #87, February 2, 1979, JCPL, ZBM, SuF, Weekly Reports, box 42 ("revivalist movements"). For a contrary view from a NSC consultant, see Griffith, "Revival of Islamic Fundamentalism."

65. "State of the Union Address," January 23, 1980, APP ("oil"). For the subsequent development of Brzezinski's Persian Gulf security framework, see WNSR #141, May 16, 1979; JCPL,

ZBM, SuF, Weekly Reports, box 42; "Persian Gulf Security Framework," June 3, 1980; "Status Report on the Security Framework," August 29, 1980; untitled memo dated September 26, 1980; and "Talking Points on the Security Framework," October 8, 1980, all JCPL, ZBM, Geographic File, Southwest Asia/Persian Gulf, boxes 15-16. For historians' assessments of Soviet motives, see Haslam, *Russia's Cold War*, pp. 319–27; Jones, *In the Graveyard of Empires*, chap. 1; Njølstad, "Collapse of Superpower Détente"; Westad, "Road to Kabul"; and Zubok, *Failed Empire*, pp. 259–64.

66. Carter, *White House Diary*, p. 398 ("the Saudis"); "Foreign Policy: Coherence and Sense of Direction," March 25, 1980, JCPL, ZBM, SuF, Meetings–SCC, box 32 ("oriented"); and "Arc of Crisis," May 23, 1980, MTA ("forward base"). On assistance to Saudi Arabia, see Carter to Giscard, Undated (September 1980); and "Assistance to Saudi Arabia," October 4, 1980, both in JCPL, ZBM, Geographic File, Southwest Asia/Persian Gulf, box 16. Also see Long, *United States and Saudi Arabia*, pp. 59–66. The reorientation of American power toward the Persian Gulf in 1979-80 remains an understated theme in the historiography on Carter's foreign policy, although Brzezinski claims the credit in *Power and Principle*, pp. 445–50. The best accounts are Njølstad, "Shifting Priorities;" and Palmer, *Guardians of the Gulf*, esp. pp. 103–11 Also see Bromley, *American Hegemony*, pp. 221–25; Halliday, "Arc of Crisis and the New Cold War"; and Sidaway, "What Is in A Gulf?"

67. "Persian Gulf–South West Asia Region," April 29, 1980, JCPL, ZBM, Geographic File, Persian Gulf/Southwest Asia, box 15 ("third strategic zone"); and "Address to the Nation on the Soviet Invasion," January 4, 1980, APP ("atheistic"). Mahmood Mamdani, among others, sees US assistance to the mujahideen as a catalyst of Al-Qaeda's rise. See *Good Muslim, Bad Muslim*, esp. 119–77.

68. WNSR #140, May 9, 1980, JCPL, ZBM, SuF, Weekly Reports, box 42 ("through diplomacy"); and Carter, *White House Diary*, p. 407 ("carrot"). On the intra-alliance relations in 1980, see Barnet, *Alliance*, pp. 399–410; Goldman, "President Carter, Western Europe, and Afghanistan in 1980"; Lundestad, *United States and Western Europe since 1945*, pp. 208–11; Kaufman, *Plans Unraveled*, pp. 213–15; Moore, *Margaret Thatcher*, pp. 561–65; and Schmidt, *Men and Powers*, pp. 193–211.

69. Carter advocates a summit in "Messages to Schmidt and Thatcher," March 27, 1980 ("disarray"); Thatcher and Schmidt deliberate in "Record of Discussion," March 28, 1980; Carter accepts their proposal in message to Thatcher, April 7, 1980, all in MTA. Also see Thatcher to Carter, April 10, MTA ("issues at Venice"). The Carter-Schmidt row is in Carter-Schmidt MemCon, June 21, 1980, JCPL, Susan Clough/Plains File, President's Personal Foreign Affairs File, Summit Meetings, box 4. For the pre-summit talks, see Memorandum of Quadripartite Meeting, Vienna, May 16, 1980; and "Political Discussion at the Venice Summit," June 6, 1980, both MTA. For the discussion, see "Second Session of Economic Summit," June 22, 1980, MTA; and for the declaration, see "Political Topics," June 22, 1980 in Hajnal, ed., *Seven-Power Summit*, pp. 93–95. For Carter, *White House Diary*, p. 442 ("adopted").

70. See "Record of the First Session of the Venice Economic Summit," June 22, 1980 ("tight monetary measures" etc.); and "Revised Draft Declaration of the Venice Summit," June 22–23, 1980 ("top priority"), both MTA.

71. "Record of the First Session of the Venice Economic Sumit," June 22, 1980, MTA ("break the link" etc.). For Carter's assurances to Fahd, see *FRUS 1969-76*, vol. 37, no. 274.

72. For assessments of the Venice Summit, see Carter, *White House Diary*, pp. 439–42; Garavoglia, "From Rambouillet to Williamsburg"; and Putman and Bayne, *Hanging Together*, pp. 118–26. For the State Department's view, see *FRUS 1969-76*, vol. 37, no. 276.

73. Brzezinski, "Priorities of U.S. Foreign Policy" ("complex") and "Remarks to the Trilateral Commission," October 25, 1977 ("slogan"), both in JCPL, HHM, SuF, box 3. Also see Brzezinski's response to Donovan and his critique of Reagan's "one-dimensional" focus on the USSR in WNSSR #149 and WNSR #150, both JCPL, ZBM, SuF, Weekly Reports, box 42.

74. For PD-59, a host of supporting documents, and an extensive analysis, see DNSA, EBB no. 390. Also see Brzezinski, *Power and Principle*, pp. 454–59; Garthoff, *Détente and*

Confrontation, pp. 869–71; Glad, *Outsider*, pp. 219–29; and Kaufman, *Plans Unraveled*, p. 215–17

75. On Carter's soft-pedaling with Argentina in 1980, see Kaufman, *Plans Unraveled*, pp. 212–13; and Schmidli, "Institutionalizing Human Rights." For Nicaragua and El Salvador, see Coatsworth "Cold War in Central America"; Glad, *Outsider in the White House*, pp. 250–57; and LeoGrande *Our Own Back Yard*, esp. pp. 11–64. Kirkpatrick is in "Dictatorship and Double Standards." For Romero's letter to Carter, see DNSA, EBB no. 399, Doc. no. 4.

76. Kennedy, "Address to the Democratic National Convention," August 12, 1980. Available at <http://tedkennedy.org>.

77. On the Polish crisis, see Brown, *Rise and Fall of Communism*, chap. 21; Garton Ash, *Polish Revolution*; and Judt, *Postwar*, pp. 585–90. On John Paul II, see Caryl, *Strange Rebels*, pp. 197–209. On the socialist system's economic difficulties, see Berend, *From the Soviet Bloc to the European Union*, esp. chap. 1; and Kotkin, "East Bloc Goes Borrowing."

78. For contacts between Charter 77 and the Polish Workers Defense Committee, see DNSA, EBB no. 213, Section III, docs. 6-8.

79. For Solidarity, see "Solidarity's Program," October 16, 1981 in Stokes, ed., *From Stalinism to Pluralism*, pp. 209–13 ("self-government").

80. For Carter's policy toward Eastern Europe in general, see "Four Year Goals," JCPL, ZBM, SuF, box 23; and WNSR #42, JCPL, ZBM, SuF, Weekly Reports, box 41. For overviews of US policy toward Poland in 1980, see Brzezinski, *Power and Principle*, pp. 463–68; Carter, *Keeping Faith*, pp. 583–85; Glad, *Outsider in the White House*, pp. 240–41; and Kaufman, *Plans Unraveled*, pp. 227–29. Also see WNSR #151, August 29, 1980; WNSR #152, September 5, 1979; WNSR #160, December 12, 1980; and WNSR #161, December 19, 1980 ("postponement"), all JCPL, ZBM, SuF, Weekly Reports, box 42; Carter, *White House Diary*, p. 491 ("invading"); and "East European Chronology," December 18, 1980, JCPL, ZBM, SuF, NSC Accomplishments, box 34. The NSC debates retaliatory measures in "SCC Meeting," October 23, 1980, JCPL, ZBM, SuF, box 33. Carter announces them in "Situation in Poland," December 3, 1980, APP ("adversely affected").

81. On Soviet foreign policy and the implications for the Brezhnev Doctrine, see Loth, "Moscow, Prague and Warsaw" ("the development"); Ouimet, *Rise and Fall of the Brezhnev Doctrine*, pp. 131–242; and Zubok, *Failed Empire*, pp. 265–70.

82. WNSR #152, September 5, 1979, JCPL, ZBM, SuF, Weekly Reports, box 42 ("dissolution").

83. "Farewell Address," January 14, 1981, APP ("rocket technology").

Conclusion

1. Marx, "Eighteenth Brumaire of Louis Napoleon" in Tucker, ed., *Marx-Engels Reader*, pp. 594–617 ("occur twice"); Reagan, "Remarks at the Annual Convention of the National Association of Evangelicals," March 8, 1983, APP. On the Cold War's escalation, see Halliday, *Second Cold War*; and Soutou, *La guerre de Cinquante Ans*, pp. 631–61. On the antinuclear movement, see Wittner, *Toward Nuclear Abolition*, pp. 130–252.

2. Chayefsky, Paddy, *Network*. Directed by Sidney Lumet. Los Angeles: Metro-Goldwyn-Mayer, 1976.

3. Generally, Helleiner, *States and the Reemergence of Global Finance*, chap. 6.

4. On the crisis of US hegemony, see Arrighi, *Long Twentieth Century*; Calleo, *Imperious Economy*; Gilpin, *Political Economy of International Relations*; and Keohane, *After Hegemony*. Rauchway, *Blessed among Nations*, esp. 170–73, suggests the parallels with nineteenth-century globalization.

5. Statistics on oil are from DeGolyer and MacNaughton, *TCPS*.

6. On Sino-US cooperation in the late Cold War see Chen Jian, "China and the Cold War After Mao"; Mann, *About Face*, esp. chap. 5; Ross, *Negotiating Cooperation*, pp. 120–245; and Vogel, *Deng Xiaoping and the Transformation of China*, pp. 523–40. For a different view, stressing the origins of Sino-Soviet rapprochement, see Radchenko, *Unwanted Visionaries*.

7. On Soviet industrialization, see Allen, *Farm to Factory*; and, for a more skeptical view, Nove, *Economic History of the USSR*. On the USSR and oil in the 1970s, see Kotkin, *Armaggedon Averted*, esp. chap. 1. On the stagnation of the Soviet economy more broadly, see Hanson,

Rise and Fall of the Soviet Economy. On Eastern Europe, see Berend, *From the Soviet Bloc to the European Union*; and Kotkin, "East Bloc Goes Borrowing."

8. Oil prices are from GFD and are in 2010 US dollars. For Soviet difficulties in the 1980s, see Gaidar, *Collapse of an Empire*; and Kotkin, *Armageddon Averted*. Observers in the West in the 1970s, in contrast, detected the stirrings of a postindustrial revolution, as did Bell, *Coming of Post-Industrial Society*; and Brzezinski, *Between Two Ages*. On capitalism and creative destruction, see Schumpeter, *Capitalism, Socialism, and Democracy*, esp. chap. 7. For a fuller account of the literature on economic change and the Cold War's end, see Sargent, "Cold War and the International Political Economy."

9. On human rights and the end of the Cold War, see Snyder, *Human Rights Activism*; and Thomas, *Helsinki Effect*. On Reagan's support for human rights and democratization, see Smith, *America's Mission*, chap. 10; and, from a more critical vantage, Peck, *Ideal Illusions*, chap 3. On democratization in the 1980s, see Huntington, *Third Wave*; and Teorell, *Determinants of Democratization*. Data is from Freedom House, "Freedom in the World."

10. On rock music in the USSR, see Ryback, *Rock around the Bloc*; and Zhuk, *Rock'n'Roll in the Rocket City*. On Springsteen, see Kirschbaum, *Rocking the Wall* ("all the barriers").

11. For Gorbachev, see Brown, *Gorbachev Factor*; Gorbachev, *Memoirs*; and Volkogonov, *Rise and Fall of the Soviet Empire*, chap. 7 ("living like this," p. 445).

12. On Reagan, Gorbachev, and the diplomacy of the Cold War's resolution, see Fischer, *Reagan Reversal*; Mann, *Rebellion of Ronald Reagan*; and Wilson, *Triumph of Improvisation*.

13. On globalization and the end of the Cold War, see Brooks and Wohlforth, "Power, Globalization, and the End of the Cold War"; and Lockwood, *Destruction of the Soviet Union*.

14. See Clinton, "Address to Congress," January 27, 2000 ("reality"), and "Address to the Nation on Airstrikes against Serbian Targets," March 24, 1999, both APP; Blair, "Doctrine of the International Community," April 24, 1999, available at http://www.britishpoliticalspeech. org ("national interests"); and Kissinger, "New World Disorder," *Newsweek*, May 31, 1999, pp. 41–44 ("moral and political"). On Clinton's foreign policy, see Bacevich, *American Empire*; and Chollet, *America between the Wars*.

15. White House, "National Security Strategy of the United States" ("terrorists and tyrants"). On Bin Laden, see Coll, *Bin Ladens*; National Commission on Terrorist Attacks, *9/11 Commission Report*, esp. chap. 2; and Wright, *Looming Tower*. On Bush and Iraq, see Mann, *Rise of the Vulcans*; Packer, *Assassin's Gate*; and Wawro, *Quicksand*, chap. 17. Sestanovich, *Maximalist*, chap. 12 suggests parallels between Obama's predicament and Nixon's.

16. On the financial crisis, see Blinder, *After the Music Stopped*; Chinn and Frieden, *Lost Decades*. For the post-2008 debate on governance, see, inter alia, Minsky, *Stabilizing an Unstable Economy*—published in the 1980s but rediscovered after 2008, Rodrik, *Globalization Paradox*; Temin and Vines, *Leaderless Economy*; and Wolf, *Fixing Global Finance*.

17. Kissinger, "Challenge of Interdependence," April 15, 1974 ("our interdependence").

18. "Four-Year Foreign Policy Objectives," JCPL, ZBN, SF, Four-Year Goals, box 23 ("new international system" etc.)

19. Niebuhr, *Irony of American History*, p. 134.

SOURCES

Archive Collections

Center for Human Rights Research and Documentation, Columbia University Libraries and Information Services, New York, NY
Amnesty International USA Archives
Ivan Morris Papers

Gerald Ford Presidential Library, Ann Arbor, MI.
Agnes Waldron Files
James M. Wilson Papers
Michael Raoul-Duval Papers
National Security Adviser Files
President Ford Campaign Committee Files
Robert Teeter Papers
Rogers Morton Papers
Ron Nessen Papers
White House Special Files

Hoover Institution Archive, Stanford University, Stanford, CA
Milton Friedman Papers
Richard Allen Papers

International Monetary Fund Archive, Washington, DC
Central Files
Country Files

Jimmy Carter Presidential Library, Atlanta, GA
Anthony Solomon Materials
1976 Campaign Files
Chief of Staff Files
Council of Economic Advisors Files
Declassification Computer
Hendrik Hertzberg Materials
Jody Powell (Press Office) Files
National Security Adviser Files
Presidential Review Memoranda and Presidential Directives
Staff Secretary's Files
Susan Clough/Plains File
White House Counsel (Lipshutz) File
White House Central Files
Zbigniew Brzezinski Materials

Library of Congress, Manuscript Division, Washington, DC
Arthur Goldberg Papers
Daniel P. Moynihan Papers

Mudd Library, Princeton University, Princeton, NJ
Council on Foreign Relations Records
Freedom House Papers

National Archives and Records Administration, College Park, MD
Record Group 56, Records of the Department of the Treasury
    Records of George Shultz, Secretary of the Treasury
Record Group 59, Records of the Department of State
    Henry A. Kissinger Staff Meetings
    Records of the Policy Planning Council (S/P)
Record Group 460, Records of the Watergate Special Prosecution Force
Richard M. Nixon Presidential Materials Project
    Henry A. Kissinger Telephone Conversations
    Mandatory Review Series
    National Security Council Files
    National Security Council Institutional Files
    President's Personal File
    President's Office File
    White House Central Files
    White House Special Files
    White House Tapes

New York Public Library, Manuscripts and Archives Division, New York, NY
International League for the Rights of Man Papers

Richard M. Nixon Presidential Library, Yorba Linda, CA
Wilderness Years Collection

Rockefeller Archive Center, Pocantico Hills, NY
Trilateral Commission Papers

Swarthmore College Peace Collection, Swarthmore, PA
Papers of the Nigeria-Biafra Clearing House

United Kingdom National Archives, Kew, London
Foreign and Commonwealth Office

University of Washington Library, Seattle, Washington
Henry M. Jackson Papers

Yale Manuscripts and Archives, Yale University, New Haven, CT
Cyrus Vance Papers
Dean Acheson Papers

ONLINE AND PUBLISHED DOCUMENTS

American Jewish Committee Online Archives. http://www.ajcarchives.org.
American Presidency Project. http://www.presidency.ucsb.edu.
Amnesty International Online Library. http://www.amnesty.org/en/library/.
Anwar Sadat Archives. http://sadat.umd.edu/archives/.

Bank for International Settlements, *Annual Report*. Various years. http://www.bis.org/publ/arpdf/archive/index.htm

Central Intelligence Agency, FOIA Reading Room. http://www.foia.cia.gov.

Declassified Documents Reference System. http://infotrac.galegroup.com/

Department of State, FOIA Reading Room. http://foia.state.gov.

Documents on British Policy Overseas. London: HMSO.

Federal Reserve Archival System for Economic Research. http://fraser.stlouisfed.org.

Digital National Security Archive. http://nsarchive.chadwyck.com/.

Hansard, *House of Commons Debates*. http://hansard.millbanksystems.com.

NATO Archives. http://www.nato.int/archives.

Margaret Thatcher Archive. http://www.margaretthatcher.org/archive/.

United Nations Security Council Official Records (UNSCOR).

U.S. Department of State, *Bulletin*.

U.S. Department of State. *Foreign Relations of the United States*. Washington, DC: U.S. GPO. http://history.state.gov/historicaldocuments.

U.S. Department of the Treasury. *U.S. National Economy, 1916–2001: Unpublished Documentary Collections*. Lexis Nexis, Microfilm.

Periodicals

The Atlantic
Chicago Tribune
Commentary
The Economist (United Kingdom)
Euromoney
The Guardian (United Kingdom)
Life
Los Angeles Times
The New York Times
The National Review
The New Republic
The New Yorker
The New York Review of Books
Newsweek
The Observer (United Kingdom)
Pakistan Horizon (Pakistan)
Rolling Stone
The Sunday Times (United Kingdom)
Survival
The Telegraph (United Kingdom)
Time
Trialogue. http://www.trilateral.org
U.S. News and World Report
The Washington Post
The World Today

Statistics

Angus Maddison. *The World Economy: Historical Statistics*. http://www.ggdc.net/maddison/oriindex.htm.

American National Election Studies. 1976 Time Series Study. http://www.electionstudies.org/.

Bank for International Settlements. Statistics. http://www.bis.org/statistics/eer/.

Correlates of War Project. http://www.correlatesofwar.org.

DeGolyer and MacNaughton, *Twentieth Century Petroleum Statistics* (*TCPS*). 2009.

Federal Reserve System, Historical Data. http://www.federalreserve.gov/econresdata/.

Freedom House, Freedom in the World. http://www.freedomhouse.org/.

Gallup Brain. http://institution.gallup.com/.

Global Financial Data. http://www.globalfinancialdata.com.

International Energy Agency, *Key World Energy Statistics* (2010). http://www.iea.org/ publications.

International Monetary Fund (IMF), International Financial Statistics. http://elibrary-data.imf. org.

National Resources Defense Council, Archive of Nuclear Data. http://www.nrdc.org/nuclear/ nudb/datainx.asp.

OECD, iLibrary. http://www.oecd-ilibrary.org/statistics.

Stockholm International Peace Research Institute, Arms Transfers Database. http://armstrade. sipri.org.

US Agency for International Development. *Overseas Grants and Loans* ("Greenbook"). http:// gbk.eads.usaidallnet.gov.

US Bureau of Economic Analysis, International Economics Accounts. http://www.bea.gov/inter national/index.htm.

US Bureau of the Census, Foreign Trade Statistics. http://www.census.gov/foreign-trade/ statistics/historical/.

US Department of Defense. National Defense Budget. 2013. http://comptroller.defense.gov/.

US Department of Defense. Military Personnel Historical Reports. http://siadapp.dmdc.osd.mil/ index.html.

US Department of Labor, Bureau of Labor Statistics. http://www.bls.gov/data/.

US Energy Information Administration. http://www.eia.gov/totalenergy/data.

US Office of Management and the Budget. *Budget of the U.S. Government*. http://www.white house.gov/omb/budget.

UN Food and Agriculture Organization, FAOSTAT. http://faostat.fao.org

UNCTAD. UNCTADStat. http://unctadstat.unctad.org/.

UNCTAD. *World Investment Report*, various years.

White House. *Economic Report of the President*, various years.

United States Government Publications

EXECUTIVE BRANCH

Cabinet Task Force on Oil Import Control. *The Oil Import Question*. Washington, DC: U.S. GPO, 1970.

White House. *National Security Strategy of the United States*. Washington, DC: U.S. GPO, 2002.

U.S. CONGRESS

Congressional Research Service Reports

Infringement of Human Rights in Greece and the Response of the United States and the United Nations. CRS Report. 93rd Cong., 2nd Sess. Washington, DC: U.S. GPO.

Joint Committees

Joint Economic Committee. Hearing. *Current Economic Situation and Short-Run Outlook*. 86th Cong., 2nd sess., December 7 and 8, 1960. Washington, DC: U.S. GPO, 1961.

Joint Economic Committee. Hearing. *Issues at the Summit*. 95th Cong., 1st sess., April 20–22, 1977. Washington, DC: U.S. GPO, 1977.

Joint Economic Committee. Subcommittee on International Exchange and Payments. Hearing. *Action Now to Strengthen the U.S. Dollar*. 92nd Cong., 1st sess., August 1971. Washington, DC: U.S. GPO, 1971.

Joint Economic Committee. Subcommittee on International Economics. Hearing. *The Dollar Rescue Operations and Their Domestic Implications*. 95th Cong., 2nd. sess., December 14–15, 1978. Washington, DC: U.S. GPO, 1979.

House of Representatives

Committee on Foreign Affairs. *Report of Special Fact Finding Mission to Nigeria, Feb. 7–20, 1969, by Reps. Charles C. Diggs, Jr., and J. Herbert Burke.* 91st Cong., 1st sess., March 12, 1969. Washington, DC: U.S. GPO, 1969.

Committee on Foreign Affairs. Subcommittees on Asian and Pacific Affairs and on International Organizations and Movements. Hearing. *Human Rights in South Korea: Implications for U.S. Policy.* 93rd Cong., 2nd sess., July 30, August 5, and December 20, 1974. Washington, DC: U.S. GPO, 1974.

Committee on Foreign Affairs. Subcommittee on Europe. Hearing. *Soviet Jewry,* 92nd Cong., 1st sess., November 9–10, 1971. Washington, DC: U.S. GPO, 1971.

Committee on Foreign Affairs. Subcommittee on International Organizations and Movements. Hearing. *Human Rights in the World Community: A Call for U.S. Leadership.* 93rd Cong., 2nd sess., August-December 1973. Washington, DC: U.S. GPO, 1974.

Committee on Foreign Affairs. Subcommittee on International Organizations and Movements. Hearing. *International Protection of Human Rights: The Work of International Organizations and the Role of U.S. Foreign Policy.* 93rd Cong., 1st sess., August-December 1973. Washington DC: U.S. GPO, 1973.

Committee on Foreign Affairs. Subcommittee on International Organizations and Movements. Hearing. *Human Rights in Chile.* 93rd Cong., 1st sess., December 9, 1973. Washington DC: U.S. GPO, 1973.

Committee on House Administration. *The Presidential Campaign 1976.* 2 vols. 95th Cong., 2nd sess. Washington, DC: U.S. GPO, 1978.

Committee on International Relations. Hearing. *Human Rights in Iran.* 94th Cong., 2nd sess., August-September 1976. Washington, DC: U.S. GPO, 1976.

Committee on International Relations. Hearing. *North-South Dialogue: Report of a Staff Study Mission to the Conference on International Economic Cooperation held in Paris, Dec. 16–19, 1975.* 94th Cong., 2nd sess., February 9, 1976. Washington, DC: U.S. GPO, 1976.

Committee on International Relations. Hearing. *Prospective Sale of Airborne Warning and Control System (AWACS) Aircraft to Iran.* 95th Cong., 1st sess., June 29, July 19 and 21 1977. Washington, DC: U.S. GPO, 1977.

Committee on International Relations. Hearing. *U.S. Arms Policies in the Persian Gulf and Red Sea Areas: Past, Present, and Future.* 95th Cong., 1st sess., December 1977. Washington, DC: U.S. GPO 1977.

Committee on International Relations. Commission on Security and Cooperation in Europe. Committee Print. *The Belgrade Followup Meeting to the Conference on Security and Cooperation in Europe.* 95th Cong., 2nd sess., May 17, 1978. Washington, DC: U.S. GPO, 1978.

Committee on International Relations. Subcommittee on International Organizations. Hearing. *Human Rights in the International Community and in U.S. Foreign Policy, 1945–76.* 95th Cong., 1st sess., July 24, 1977. Washington, DC: U.S. GPO, 1977.

Committee on International Relations. Subcommittee on International Organizations and Movements. Hearing. *Human Rights in South Korea and the Philippines: Implications for U.S. Policy.* 94th Cong., 1st sess., May-June 1975. Washington DC: U.S. GPO, 1975.

U.S. Senate

Committee on Finance. Subcommittee on International Finance and Resources. Hearing. *The International Financial Crisis.* 93rd Cong., 1st sess., May 30, June 1, 5, 1973. Washington, DC: U.S. GPO, 1973.

Committee on Finance. Subcommittee on International Trade. Hearing. *Implications of Multinational Firms for World Trade and Investment and for U.S. Trade and Labor.* 93rd Cong., 1st sess., February 1973. Washington, DC: U.S. GPO, 1973.

Committee on Foreign Relations. Hearing. *Foreign Assistance Authorization, Arms Sales Issues,* 94th Cong., 1st sess., June 17–18, November 19, 21, December 4–5, 1975. Washington, DC: U.S. GPO, 1975.

Committee on Foreign Relations. Hearing. *Sale of AWACS to Iran.* 95th Cong., 1st sess., July 18, 22, 25, 27 and September 19, 1977. Washington, DC: U.S. GPO, 1977.

Committee on Foreign Relations. Report. *Suspension of Military Assistance to Pakistan.* May 13, 1971, 92nd Cong., 1st Sess. Washington, DC: U.S. GPO, 1971.

Committee on Foreign Relations. Subcommittee on International Economic Policy. Hearing. *Oversight of International Economic Issues.* 96th Cong., 1st sess., May 22–24, 1979. Washington, DC: U.S. GPO, 1979.

Committee on Government Operations. Subcommittee on National Security and International Operations. Committee Prints. *The National Security Council: New Role and Structure.* Washington, DC: U.S. GPO, 1969.

Committee on the Judiciary. Hearing. *Relief Problems in East Pakistan and India, Part I,* June 28, 1971. 92nd Cong., 1st sess. Washington, DC: U.S. GPO, 1971.

Committee on the Judiciary. Hearing. *Relief Problems in East Pakistan and India, Part II,* September 30, 1971. 92nd Cong., 1st sess. Washington, DC: U.S. GPO, 1971.

Committee on the Judiciary. Hearing. *Relief Problems in East Pakistan and India, Part III,* October 4, 1971. 92nd Cong., 1st sess. Washington, DC: U.S. GPO, 1971.

Committee on the Judiciary. Hearing. *Relief Problems in Nigeria-Biafra, Part 2.* 91st Cong., 2nd sess., January 21–22, 1970. Washington, DC: U.S. GPO, 1970.

Bibliography

Abernethy, David B. *The Dynamics of Global Dominance: European Overseas Empires, 1415–1980.* New Haven, CT: Yale University Press, 2000.

Abrahamian, Ervand. *A History of Modern Iran.* New York: Cambridge University Press, 2008.

Afkhami, Gholam R. *The Life and Times of the Shah.* Berkeley: University of California Press, 2009.

Ahmia, Mourad. *The Group of 77 at the United Nations: The Collected Documents of the Group of 77.* 4 vols. New York: Oxford University Press, 2006.

Akins, James E. "The Oil Crisis: This Time the Wolf Is Here." *Foreign Affairs* 51, no. 3 (April 1973): 462–90.

Akmam, Wardatul. "Atrocities against Humanity during the Liberation War in Bangladesh: A Case of Genocide." *Journal of Genocide Research* 4, no. 4 (2002): 543–59.

Allen, Robert C. *Farm to Factory: A Reinterpretation of the Soviet Industrial Revolution.* Princeton University Press, 2003.

Allen, T., and D. Styan. "A Right to Interfere? Bernard Kouchner and the New Humanitarianism." *Journal of International Development* 12 (2000): 825–42.

Allison, Graham, and Peter Szanton. *Remaking Foreign Policy: The Organizational Connection.* New York: Basic Books, 1976.

Alnasrawi, Abbas. *OPEC in a Changing World Economy.* Baltimore, MD: John Hopkins University Press, 1985.

Al-Rasheed, Madawi. *A History of Saudi Arabia.* New York: Cambridge University Press, 2002.

Altshuler, Stuart. *From Exodus to Freedom: A History of the Soviet Jewry Movement.* Lanham, MD: Rowman & Littlefield, 2005.

Alvandi, Roham. "Nixon, Kissinger, and the Shah: The Origins of Iranian Primacy in the Persian Gulf." *Diplomatic History* 36, no. 2 (2012): 337–72.

Ambrose, Stephen. *Nixon: The Education of a Politician, 1913–1962.* New York: Simon and Schuster, 1987.

Ambrose, Stephen. *Nixon: The Triumph of a Politician, 1962–1972.* New York: Simon and Schuster, 1989.

Amsden, Alice H. *Escape from Empire: The Developing World's Journey through Heaven and Hell.* Cambridge, MA: MIT Press, 2007.

Amuzegar, Jahangir. "The North-South Dialogue: From Conflict to Compromise." *Foreign Affairs* 54, no. 3 (1976): 547–62.

Anderson, Benedict R. *Imagined Communities: Reflections on the Origin and Spread of Nationalism.* New York: Verso, 2006.

Andrew, Christopher, and Vasili Mitrokhin. *The World Was Going Our Way: The KGB and the Battle for the Third World.* New York: Basic Books, 2005.

Andrianopoulos, Gerry. *Kissinger and Brzezinski: The NSC and the Struggle for Control of U.S. National Security Policy.* London: Macmillan, 1991.

Apodaca, Claire. *Understanding U.S. Human Rights Policy: A Paradoxical Legacy*. New York: Routledge, 2006.

Arnold, Hugh M. "Henry Kissinger and Human Rights." *Universal Human Rights* 2, no. 4 (1980): 57–71.

Aron, Raymond. *The Imperial Republic: The United States and the World, 1945–1973*. Cambridge, MA: Winthrop Publishers, 1974.

Aronson, Jonathan. *Money and Power: Banks and the World Monetary System*. Beverly Hills, CA: Sage Publications, 1977.

Arrighi, Giovanni. *The Long Twentieth Century: Money, Power and the Origins of Our Times*. New York: Verso, 2010.

Arrighi, Giovanni. "The World Economy and the Cold War." In *The Cambridge History of the Cold War*, edited by Melvyn P. Leffler and Odd Arne Westad, 3:23–44. New York: Cambridge University Press, 2010.

Asher, Daniel. *The Egyptian Strategy for the Yom Kippur War: An Analysis*. Jefferson, NC: McFarland, 2009.

Aslan, Reza. *No God but God: The Origins, Evolution, and Future of Islam*. New York: Random House, 2005.

Asselin, Pierre. *A Bitter Peace: Washington, Hanoi, and the Making of the Paris Agreement*. Chapel Hill: University of North Carolina Press, 2002.

Auten, Brian. *Carter's Conversion: The Hardening of American Defense Policy*. Columbia: University of Missouri Press, 2008.

Axworthy, Michael. *Revolutionary Iran: A History of the Islamic Republic*. New York: Oxford University Press, 2013.

Azrael, Jeremy, Richard Löwenthal, and Tohru Nakagawa. *An Overview of East-West Relations*. Triangle Papers 15. New York: Trilateral Commission, 1978.

Bacevich, Andrew J. *American Empire: The Realities and Consequences of U.S. Diplomacy*. Cambridge, MA: Harvard University Press, 2002.

Ball, George W. *Diplomacy for a Crowded World: An American Foreign Policy*. Boston: Little, Brown, 1976.

Baraheni, Reza. *The Crowned Cannibals: Writings on Repression in Iran*. New York: Vintage, 1977.

Barkun, Michael. *A Culture of Conspiracy: Apocalyptic Visions in Contemporary America*. Berkeley: University of California Press, 2003.

Barnet, Richard J. *The Alliance: America, Europe, Japan: Makers of the Postwar World*. New York: Simon and Schuster, 1985.

Barnet, Richard J., and Ronald E. Müller. *Global Reach: The Power of the Multinational Corporations*. New York: Simon and Schuster, 1974.

Barnett, Alex. "Allies in the Slaying of Five Giants: William Beveridge, His Historic Report, and the Age of Anglo-American Social Liberalism, 1931–1946." BA thesis, Department of History, University of California, Berkeley, May 2010.

Barnett, Michael N. *Empire of Humanity: A History of Humanitarianism*. Ithaca, NY: Cornell University Press, 2011.

Barrow, John. "An Age of Limits." In *The Carter Presidency: Policy Choices in the Post–New Deal Era*, edited by John Barrow and Gary Fink, 158–78. Lawrence: University of Kansas Press, 1998.

Basevi, Giorgio, and the Brookings Institutiion. *Economic Prospects and Policies in the Industrial Countries: A Tripartite Report*. Washington, DC: Brookings Institution, 1977.

Basosi, Duccio. "The U.S., Western Europe, and a Changing International Monetary System." In *Europe in the International Arena during the 1970s*, edited by Antonio Varsori and Guia Migani, 99–116. New York: Peter Lang, 2011.

Bass, Gary J. *The Blood Telegram: Nixon, Kissinger, and a Forgotten Genocide*. New York: Alfred A. Knopf, 2013.

Bass, Gary J. *Freedom's Battle: The Origins of Humanitarian Intervention*. New York: Random House, 2008.

Bass, Warren. *Support Any Friend: Kennedy's Middle East and the Making of the U.S.-Israel Alliance*. New York: Oxford University Press, 2003.

Bayandor, Darioush. *Iran and the CIA: The Fall of Mosaddeq Revisited*. New York: Palgrave Macmillan, 2010.

Bayly, C. A. "'Archaic' and 'Modern' Globalization." In *Globalization in World History* edited by A. G. Hopkins, 45–72. London: Pimlico, 2002.

Beard, Charles. *Giddy Minds and Foreign Quarrels: An Estimate of American Foreign Policy.* New York: The Macmillan Company, 1939.

Beckerman, Gal. *When They Come for Us, We'll Be Gone: The Epic Struggle to Save Soviet Jewry.* Boston: Houghton Mifflin Harcourt, 2010.

Belknap, Michal R. *The Vietnam War on Trial: The My Lai Massacre and the Court-Martial of Lieutenant Calley.* Lawrence: University Press of Kansas, 2002.

Bell, Daniel. *The Coming of Post-Industrial Society: A Venture in Social Forecasting.* New York: Basic Books, 1973.

Berend, Ivan T. *From the Soviet Bloc to the European Union: The Economic and Social Transformation of Central and Eastern Europe since 1973.* New York: Cambridge University Press, 2009.

Berggren, D. Jason, and Nicol C. Rae. "Jimmy Carter and George W. Bush: Faith, Foreign Policy, and an Evangelical Presidential Style." *Presidential Studies Quarterly* 36, no. 4 (2006): 606–32.

Bergman, Jay. *Meeting the Demands of Reason: The Life and Thought of Andrei Sakharov.* Ithaca, NY: Cornell University Press, 2009.

Bergsten, C. Fred. *The Dilemmas of the Dollar: The Economics and Politics of United States International Monetary Policy.* New York: New York University Press, 1975.

Bergsten, C. Fred. "Interdependence and the Reform of International Institutions." *International Organization* 30, no. 2 (1976): 361–72.

Berman, Larry. *No Peace, No Honor: Nixon, Kissinger, and Betrayal in Vietnam.* New York: Free Press, 2001.

Berman, Sheri. *The Primacy of Politics: Social Democracy and the Making of Europe's Twentieth Century.* New York: Cambridge University Press, 2006.

Bernstein, Edward M. "Eurodollars: Capital Flows and the U.S. Balance of Payments." In *The Eurodollar,* edited by Herbert Prochnow and Edward M. Bernstein, 122–47. Chicago: Rand McNally & Co., 1970.

Betts, Raymond. *Decolonization.* London: Taylor & Francis, 2007.

Bill, James A. *The Eagle and the Lion: The Tragedy of American-Iranian Relations.* New Haven, CT: Yale University Press, 1988.

Bischof, Günter, and Stefan Karner, eds. *The Prague Spring and the Warsaw Pact Invasion of Czechoslovakia in 1968.* New York: Lexington, 2010.

Bittman, Mark. *Food Matters.* New York: Simon and Schuster, 2009.

Biven, W. Carl. *Jimmy Carter's Economy: Policy in an Age of Limits.* Chapel Hill, NC: University of North Carolina Press, 2002.

Black, Jan Knippers. *United States Penetration of Brazil.* Philadelphia: University of Pennsylvania Press, 1977.

Blinder, Alan S. *After the Music Stopped: The Financial Crisis, the Response, and the Work Ahead.* New York: Penguin, 2013.

Block, Fred L. *The Origins of International Economic Disorder: A Study of United States International Monetary Policy from World War 2 to the Present.* Berkeley: University of California Press, 1977.

Blumenthal, W. Michael. "Steering in Crowded Waters." *Foreign Affairs* 56, no. 4 (July 1978): 728–39.

Bobbitt, Philip. *The Shield of Achilles: War, Peace, and the Course of History.* New York: Alfred A. Knopf, 2002.

Bon Tempo, Carl J. "Human Rights and the U.S. Republican Party in the Late 1970s." In *The Breakthrough: Human Rights in the 1970s,* edited by Jan Eckel and Samuel Moyn, 146–65. Philadelphia: University of Pennsylvania Press, 2013.

Bordo, Michael D., and Anna Jacobson Schwartz, eds. *A Retrospective on the Classical Gold Standard, 1821–1931.* Chicago: University of Chicago Press, 1984.

Borgwardt, Elizabeth. *A New Deal for the World: America's Vision for Human Rights.* Cambridge, MA: Harvard University Press, 2005.

Borstelmann, Thomas. *The Cold War and the Color Line: American Race Relations in the Global Arena.* Cambridge MA: Harvard University Press, 2001.

Borstelmann, Thomas. *The 1970s: A New Global History from Civil Rights to Economic Inequality.* Princeton, NJ: Princeton University Press, 2012.

Bose, Sarmila. *Dead Reckoning: Memories of the 1971 Bangladesh War.* New York: Columbia University Press, 2011.

Boulding, Kenneth. "The Economics of the Coming Spaceship Earth." In *Environmental Quality in a Growing Economy,* edited by Henry Jarrett, 3–14. Baltimore, MD: Johns Hopkins University Press, 1966.

Bourne, Peter G. *Jimmy Carter: A Comprehensive Biography from Plains to Post-Presidency.* New York: Scribner, 1997.

Bozo, Frédéric. *Two Strategies for Europe: De Gaulle, the United States, and the Atlantic Alliance.* Lanham, MD: Rowman & Littlefield, 2001.

Bradley, Mark. "The Ambiguities of Sovereignty: The United States and the Global Rights Cases of the 1940s." In *The State of Sovereignty: Territories, Laws, Populations,* edited by Douglas Howland and Luise White, 124–47. Bloomington: University of Indiana Press, 2009.

Brandon, Henry. *The Retreat of American Power.* New York: Dell, 1973.

Brands, Hal. *Latin America's Cold War.* Cambridge, MA: Harvard University Press, 2010.

Brazinsky, Gregg. *Nation Building in South Korea: Koreans, Americans, and the Making of a Democracy.* Chapel Hill: University of North Carolina Press, 2007.

Brenner, Robert. *The Economics of Global Turbulence: The Advanced Capitalist Economies from Long Boom to Long Downturn, 1945–2005.* New York: Verso, 2006.

Bromley, Simon. *American Hegemony and World Oil: The Industry, the State System, and the World Economy.* University Park: Pennsylvania State University Press, 1991.

Bronson, Rachel. *Thicker Than Oil: America's Uneasy Partnership with Saudi Arabia.* New York: Oxford University Press, 2006.

Brooks, Stephen G., and William C. Wohlforth. "Power, Globalization, and the End of the Cold War: Reevaluating a Landmark Case for Ideas." *International Security* 25, no. 3 (2001): 5–53.

Brown, Archie. *The Gorbachev Factor.* New York: Oxford University Press, 1996.

Brown, Archie. *The Rise and Fall of Communism.* New York: Ecco, 2009.

Brown, Lester. *World without Borders.* New York: Random House, 1972.

Bryan, William Jennings. *The Cross of Gold: Speech Delivered before the National Democratic Convention at Chicago, July 9, 1896.* Lincoln: University of Nebraska Press, 1996.

Brysk, Alison. *Globalization and Human Rights.* Berkeley: University of California Press, 2002.

Brzezinski, Zbigniew. "The American Transition." *New Republic* 157, no. 26 (1967): 18–21.

Brzezinski, Zbigniew. *Between Two Ages: America's Role in the Technetronic Era.* New York: Penguin Books, 1970.

Brzezinski, Zbigniew. "The Deceptive Structure of Peace." *Foreign Policy* 14 (1974): 35–55.

Brzezinski, Zbigniew. *The Fragile Blossom: Crisis and Change in Japan.* New York: Harper and Row, 1972.

Brzezinski, Zbigniew. "Japan's Global Engagement." *Foreign Affairs* 50, no. 1 (January 1972): 270–70.

Brzezinski, Zbigniew. *Power and Principle: Memoirs of the National Security Adviser, 1977–1981.* New York: Farrar, Straus and Giroux, 1983.

Brzezinski, Zbigniew. "Recognizing the Crisis." *Foreign Policy* 17 (1974): 63–74.

Brzezinski, Zbigniew. *The Soviet Bloc: Unity and Conflict.* Cambridge, MA: Harvard University Press, 1960.

Brzezinski, Zbigniew. "U.S. Foreign Policy: The Search for Focus." *Foreign Affairs* 51, no. 4 (July 1973): 708–27.

Bull, Hedley. *The Anarchical Society: A Study of Order in World Politics.* New York: Columbia University Press, 1977.

Bundy, William P., ed. *The World Economic Crisis.* New York: W. W. Norton, 1975.

Bundy, William. *A Tangled Web: The Making of Foreign Policy in the Nixon Presidency.* New York: Hill and Wang, 1998.

Burgers, Jan H. "The Road to San Francisco: The Revival of the Human Rights Idea in the Twentieth Century." *Human Rights Quarterly* 14, no. 4 (1992): 447–77.

Burgin, Angus. *The Great Persuasion: Reinventing Free Markets Since the Depression.* Cambridge, MA: Harvard University Press, 2012.

Burk, Kathleen, and Alec Cairncross. *Goodbye, Great Britain: The 1976 IMF Crisis*. New Haven, CT: Yale University Press, 1992.

Burke, Roland. *Decolonization and the Evolution of International Human Rights*. Philadelphia: University of Pennsylvania Press, 2010.

Burn, Gary. "The State, the City and the Euromarkets." *Review of International Political Economy* 6, no. 2 (1999): 225–61.

Burns, Arthur F., and Robert H. Ferrell. *Inside the Nixon Administration: The Secret Diary of Arthur Burns, 1969–1974*. Lawrence: University Press of Kansas, 2010.

Burns, Jennifer. *Goddess of the Market: Ayn Rand and the American Right*. New York: Oxford University Press, 2009.

Burr, William, and Jeffrey Kimball. "Nixon's Secret Nuclear Alert: Vietnam War Diplomacy and the Joint Chiefs of Staff Readiness Test, October 1969." *Cold War History* 3, no. 2 (2003): 113–56.

Butz, Earl L. "An Emerging, Market-Oriented Food and Agricultural Policy." *Public Administration Review* 36, no. 2 (1976): 137–42.

Buzan, Barry, and Richard Little. *International Systems in World History: Remaking the Study of International Relations*. New York: Oxford University Press, 2000.

Byrne, Tony. *Airlift to Biafra: Breaching the Blockade*. Dublin: Columba Press, 1997.

Cahn, Anne Hessing, and John Prados, "Team B: The Trillion-Dollar Experiment," *Bulletin of the Atomic Scientists* 49, no. 3 (1993): 22, 24–27.

Caldwell, Dan. *The Dynamics of Domestic Politics and Arms Control: The SALT II Treaty Ratification Debate*. Columbia: University of South Carolina Press, 1991.

Calleo, David P. *The Imperious Economy*. Cambridge, MA: Harvard University Press, 1982.

Calleo, David P., and Benjamin M. Rowland. *America and the World Political Economy: Atlantic Dreams and National Realities*. Bloomington: Indiana University Press, 1973.

Campagna, Anthony. *Economic Policy in the Carter Administration*. Westport, CT: Greenwood Press, 1995.

Campbell, John C. "The Mediterranean Crisis." *Foreign Affairs* 53, no. 4 (1975): 605–24.

Campbell, John, Guy de Carmoy, and Sinichi Kondo. *Energy: A Strategy for International Action*. Triangle Papers 6. New York: Trilateral Commission, 1974.

Camps, Miriam. *The Management of Interdependence: A Preliminary View*. New York: Council on Foreign Relations, 1974.

Carrillo, Santiago. *Eurocommunism and the State*. Westport, CT: Lawrence Hill, 1978.

Carter, Jimmy. *An Hour before Daylight: Memories of a Rural Boyhood*. New York: Simon and Schuster, 2001.

Carter, Jimmy. *Keeping Faith: Memoirs of a President*. New York: Bantam Books, 1982.

Carter, Jimmy. *White House Diary*. New York: Farrar, Straus and Giroux, 2010.

Carter, Rosalynn. *First Lady from Plains*. Fayetteville: University of Arkansas Press, 1994.

Caryl, Christian. *Strange Rebels: 1979 and the Birth of the 21st Century*. New York: Basic Books, 2013.

Chalidze, Valerii. *To Defend These Rights: Human Rights and the Soviet Union*. New York: Random House, 1975.

Chamberlin, Paul Thomas. *The Global Offensive: The United States, the Palestine Liberation Organization, and the Making of the Post–Cold War Order*. New York: Oxford University Press, 2012.

Chassaigne, Philippe. *Les années 1970: Fin d'un monde et origine de notre modernité*. Paris: Armand Colin, 2012.

Chatterjee, Partha. *Nationalist Thought and the Colonial World*. Minneapolis: University of Minnesota Press, 1993.

Chen, Jian. "China and the Cold War after Mao." In *The Cambridge History of the Cold War*, edited by Melvyn P. Leffler and Odd Arne Westad, 3:181–200. New York: Cambridge University Press, 2010.

Chilcote, Ronald H., and Joel C. Edelstein, eds. *Latin America: The Struggle with Dependency and Beyond*. New York: Halsted Press, 1974.

Chinn, Menzie D., and Jeffry A. Frieden. *Lost Decades: The Making of America's Debt Crisis and the Long Recovery*. New York: W. W. Norton, 2001.

Chollet, Derek. *America between the Wars: From 11/9 to 9/11: The Misunderstood Years between the Fall of the Berlin Wall and the Start of the War on Terror.* New York: Public Affairs, 2008.

Clark, Ann Marie. *Diplomacy of Conscience: Amnesty International and Changing Human Rights Norms.* Princeton, NJ: Princeton University Press, 2001.

Clarke, Thurston. *JFK's Last Hundred Days: The Transformation of a Man and the Emergence of a Great President.* New York: Penguin, 2013.

Clendenning, E. Wayne. *The Eurodollar Market.* New York: Oxford University Press, 1970.

Cleveland, Harlan. "The Diplomacy of Interdependence." *Public Administration Review* 37, no. 1 (1977): 80–82.

Club of Rome. *The Limits to Growth: A Report for the Club of Rome's Project on the Predicament of Mankind.* New York: Universe Books, 1972.

Clymer, Kenton. "Jimmy Carter, Human Rights, and Cambodia." *Diplomatic History* 27, no. 2 (2003): 245–78.

Cmiel, Kenneth. "The Emergence of Human Rights Politics in the United States." *Journal of American History* 86, no. 3 (1999): 1231–50.

Coatsworth, John. "The Cold War in Central America, 1975–1991." In *The Cambridge History of the Cold War*, vol. 3, edited by Melvyn P. Leffler and Odd Arne Westad, 3:201–21. New York: Cambridge University Press, 2010.

Cochrane, Willard Wesley. *The Development of American Agriculture: A Historical Analysis.* Minneapolis: University of Minnesota Press, 1979.

Cohen, Benjamin J. *International Political Economy: An Intellectual History.* Princeton, NJ: Princeton University Press, 2008.

Cohen, Warren I. *America's Response to China: A History of Sino-American Relations.* New York: Columbia University Press, 2010.

Cohen, Warren. "Balancing American Interests in the Middle East." In *Lyndon Johnson Confronts the World*, edited by Nancy Bernkopf Tucker and Warren Cohen, 279–310. New York: Oxford University Press, 1994.

Cohrs, Patrick O. *The Unfinished Peace after World War I: America, Britain and the Stabilisation of Europe, 1919–1932.* New York: Cambridge University Press, 2008.

Coll, Steve. *The Bin Ladens: An Arabian Family in the American Century.* New York: Penguin, 2008.

Coll, Steve. *Ghost Wars: The Secret History of the CIA, Afghanistan, and Bin Laden, from the Soviet Invasion to September 10, 2001.* New York: Penguin, 2004.

Collier, Simon, and William F. Sater. *A History of Chile, 1808–2002.* 2nd ed. Cambridge University Press, 2004.

Collins, Robert M. "The Economic Crisis of 1968 and the Waning of the 'American Century.'" *American Historical Review* 101, no. 2 (1996): 396–422.

Collins, Robert M. *More: The Politics of Economic Growth in Postwar America.* New York: Oxford University Press, 2000.

Connelly, Matthew. *A Diplomatic Revolution: Algeria's Fight for Independence and the Origins of the Post–Cold War Era.* New York: Oxford University Press, 2002.

Connelly, Matthew. "Future Shock: The End of the World as They Knew It." In *The Shock of the Global*, edited by Niall Ferguson, Charles S. Maier, Erez Manela, and Daniel J. Sargent, 337–50. Cambridge, MA: Harvard University Press, 2010.

Connelly, Matthew. "Taking Off the Cold War Lens: Visions of North-South Conflict During the Algerian War for Independence." *American Historical Review* 105, no. 3 (2000): 739–69.

Coombs, Charles. *The Arena of International Finance.* New York: John Wiley, 1976.

Cooper, Andrew Scott. *The Oil Kings: How the U.S., Iran, and Saudi Arabia Changed the Balance of Power in the Middle East.* New York: Simon and Schuster, 2011.

Cooper, Andrew Scott. "Showdown at Doha: The Secret Oil Deal That Helped Sink the Shah of Iran." *Middle East Journal* 62, no. 4 (2008): 567–91.

Cooper, Richard N. *The Economics of Interdependence: Economic Policy in the Atlantic Community.* New York: Council on Foreign Relations, 1968.

Cooper, Richard N., Karl Kaiser, and Masataka Kosaka. *Towards a Renovated International System.* Triangle Papers 14. New York: Trilateral Commission, 1977.

Cooper, Robert. *The Breaking of Nations: Order and Chaos in the Twenty-First Century.* London: Atlantic Books, 2003.

Costigliola, Frank. "Lyndon B. Johnson, Germany, and the 'End of the Cold War.'" In *Lyndon Johnson Confronts the World: American Foreign Policy, 1963–1968*, edited by Warren Cohen, 173–210. New York: Cambridge University Press, 1994.

Cowie, Jefferson. *Stayin' Alive: The 1970s and the Last Days of the Working Class*. New York: New Press, 2010.

Cox, Robert W. "Ideologies and the New International Economic Order: Reflections on Some Recent Literature." *International Organization* 33, no. 02 (1979): 257–302.

Cox, Robert. *Production, Power and World Order: Social Forces in the Making of History*. New York: Columbia University Press, 1987.

Cronin, James E. *The World the Cold War Made: Order, Chaos and the Return of History*. New York: Routledge, 1996.

Cronjé, Suzanne. *The World and Nigeria: The Diplomatic History of the Biafran War, 1967–1970*. London: Sigwick & Jackson, 1972.

Cudahy, Brian. *Box Boats: How Container Ships Changed the World*. New York: Fordham University Press, 2006.

Cumings, Bruce. *The Origins of the Korean War*. 2 vols. Princeton, NJ: Princeton University Press, 1981, 1990.

Dahl, Robert A. "The Concept of Power." *Behavior Science* 2, no. 3 (1957): 201–15.

Dalby, Simon. *Creating the Second Cold War: The Discourse of Politics*. New York: Guilford Press, 1990.

Dallek, Robert. *Franklin D. Roosevelt and American Foreign Policy, 1932–1945*. New York: Oxford University Press, 1995.

Dallek, Robert. *Nixon and Kissinger: Partners in Power*. New York: HarperCollins, 2007.

Dallek, Robert. *An Unfinished Life: John F. Kennedy, 1917–1963*. New York: Hachette, 2003.

Dam, Kenneth W. *The Rules of the Game: Reform and Evolution in the International Monetary System*. Chicago: University of Chicago Press, 1982.

Davis, Morris. "Audits of International Relief in the Nigerian Civil War: Some Political Perspectives." *International Organization* 29, no. 2 (1975): 501–12.

Davis, Morris. *Interpreters for Nigeria: The Third World and International Public Relations*. University of Illinois Press, Urbana, 1977.

Davis, Nathaniel. "The Angola Decision of 1975: A Personal Memoir." *Foreign Affairs* 57, no. 1 (1978): 109–24.

Degroot, Gerard. *The Bomb: A Life*. Random House, 2011.

Del Pero, Mario. *The Eccentric Realist: Henry Kissinger And The Shaping Of American Foreign Policy*. Ithaca, NY: Cornell University Press, 2010.

Del Pero, Mario. "Which Chile, Allende? Henry Kissinger and the Portuguese Revolution." *Cold War History* 11, no. 4 (2011): 625–57.

de Menil, Georges, and Anthony Solomon. *Economic Summitry*. New York: Council on Foreign Relations, 1983.

de St. Jorre, John. *The Nigerian Civil War*. London: Hodder and Stoughton, 1972.

Destexhe, Alain. *Rwanda and Genocide in the Twentieth Century*. New York: New York University Press, 1995.

Destler, Ivan M. "United States Food Policy 1972–1976: Reconciling Domestic and International Objectives." *International Organization* 32, no. 3 (1978): 617–653.

de Vries, Margaret G. *The International Monetary Fund, 1972–1978: Cooperation on Trial*. 3 vols. Washington DC: International Monetary Fund, 1985.

Dinges, John. *The Condor Year: How Pinochet and His Allies Brought Terrorism to Three Continents*. New York: New Press, 2004.

Divine, Robert A. *Second Chance: The Triumph of Internationalism in America During World War II*. New York: Atheneum, 1967.

Dobbs, Michael. *One Minute to Midnight: Kennedy, Khrushchev, and Castro on the Brink of Nuclear War*. Alfred A. Knopf, 2008.

Dobrynin, Anatolii. *In Confidence: Moscow's Ambassador to Six Cold War Presidents*. Seattle: University of Washington Press, 1995.

Dockrill, Saki. *Britain's Retreat from East of Suez: The Choice between Europe and the World?* New York: Palgrave Macmillan, 2002.

Dolan, Michael B. "The Lomé Convention and Europe's Relationship with the Third World: A Critical Analysis." *Journal of European Integration* 1, no. 3 (1978): 369–94.

Dosman, Edgar J. *The Life and Times of Raul Prebisch, 1901–1986.* Montreal: McGill-Queen's University Press, 2008.

Drew, Elizabeth. *American Journal: The Events of 1976.* New York: Vintage, 1978.

Duchene, Francois, Kinhide Mushakoji, and Henry D. Owen. *The Crisis of International Cooperation: A Report of the Trilateral Political Task Force to the Executive Committee of the Trilateral Commission, Tokyo, October 22–23, 1973.* Triangle Papers 2. New York: Trilateral Commission, 1974.

Dudziak, Mary L. *Cold War Civil Rights: Race and the Image of American Democracy.* Princeton, NJ: Princeton University Press, 2011.

Dumbrell, John "The Johnson Administration and the British Labour Government: Vietnam, the Pound and East of Suez." *Journal of American Studies* 30, no. 2 (1996): 211–31.

Eckel, Jan, and Samuel Moyn, eds. *The Breakthrough: Human Rights in the 1970s.* University of Pennsylvania Press, 2014.

Eckel, Jan. "'Under a Magnifying Glass': The International Human Rights Campaign against Chile in the Seventies." In *Human Rights in the Twentieth Century*, edited by Stefan-Ludwig Hoffmann, 321–41. New York: Cambridge University Press, 2011.

Eckes, Alfred E. *A Search for Solvency: Bretton Woods and the International Monetary System, 1941–1971.* Austin: University of Texas Press, 1975.

Eckes, Alfred E., and Thomas W. Zeiler. *Globalization and the American Century.* New York: Cambridge University Press, 2003.

Ehrlich, Paul R. *The Population Bomb.* New York: Ballantine Books, 1968.

Ehrman, John. *The Rise of Neoconservatism: Intellectuals and Foreign Affairs.* New Haven, CT: Yale University Press, 1995.

Eichengreen, Barry. *The European Economy since 1945: Coordinated Capitalism and Beyond.* Princeton, NJ: Princeton University Press, 2008.

Eichengreen, Barry. "From Benign Neglect to Malignant Preoccupation: U.S. Balance-of-Payments Policy in the 1960s." National Bureau of Economic Research Working Paper Series, no. 7630 (2000). http://www.nber.org/papers/w7630.

Eichengreen, Barry. *Globalizing Capital: A History of the International Monetary System.* Princeton, NJ: Princeton University Press, 1996.

Eichengreen, Barry. *Golden Fetters: The Gold Standard and the Great Depression.* New York: Oxford University Press, 1992.

Eichengreen, Barry J., and Marc Flandreau, eds. *The Gold Standard in Theory and History.* New York: Routledge: 1997.

Ekbladh, David. *The Great American Mission: Modernization and the Construction of an American World Order.* Princeton, NJ: Princeton University Press, 2010.

Ellwood, David W. *Rebuilding Europe: Western Europe, America, and Postwar Reconstruction.* London: Longman, 1992.

Engdahl, William. *A Century of War: Anglo-American Oil Politics and the New World Order.* Ann Arbor, MI: Pluto Press, 2004.

Ennals, Martin. "Amnesty International and Human Rights." In *Pressure Groups in the Global System*, edited by Peter Willets, 63–83. London: Pinter, 1982.

Evans, Tony. *U.S. Hegemony and the Project of Universal Human Rights.* New York: St. Martin's, 1996.

Falk, Richard A. *Legal Order in a Violent World.* Princeton, NJ: Princeton University Press, 1968.

Falola, Toyin, and Matthew M. Heaton. *A History of Nigeria.* New York: Cambridge University Press, 2008.

Farber, David R. *Taken Hostage: The Iran Hostage Crisis and America's First Encounter with Radical Islam.* Princeton, NJ: Princeton University Press, 2005.

Fascell, Dante, "Did Human Rights Survive Belgrade?" *Foreign Policy*, no. 38 (Summer 1978): 104–18.

Fearon, James. "Ethnic Structure and Cultural Diversity around the World: A Cross-National Data Set on Ethnic Groups." Working Paper, Stanford University, 2003. www.stanford.edu/group/ethnic/workingpapers/egroups.pdf.

Ferguson, C. Clyde. "The Politics of the New International Economic Order." *Proceedings of the Academy of Political Science* 32, no. 4 (1977): 142–58.

Ferguson, Niall. *Colossus: The Price of America's Empire*. New York: Penguin, 2004.

Ferguson, Niall, and Charles S. Maier, Erez Manela, and Daniel J. Sargent, eds. *The Shock of the Global: The 1970s in Perspective*. Cambridge, MA: Harvard University Press, 2010.

Fernández-Armesto, Felipe. *Sadat and His Statecraft*. London: Kensal Press, 1982.

Fieldhouse, David K. *Western Imperialism in the Middle East 1914–1958*. Oxford: Oxford University Press, 2006.

Fielding, Jeremy. "Coping with Decline: U.S. Policy Toward the British Defense." *Diplomatic History* 23, no. 4 (1999): 633–56.

Finer, Samuel. *The Man on Horseback: The Role of the Military in Politics*. New Brunswick, NJ: Transaction, 2002.

Fischer, Beth A. *The Reagan Reversal: Foreign Policy and the End of the Cold War*. Columbia: University of Missouri Press, 2000.

Flink, James. *The Automobile Age*. Cambridge, MA: MIT Press, 1988.

Fonteyne, Jean-Pierre L. "Forcible Self-Help by States to Protect Human Rights." In *Humanitarian Intervention and the United Nations*, edited by Richard Lillich, 197–221. Charlottesville: University of Virginia Press: 1973.

Foot, Rosemary. "The Cold War and Human Rights." In *The Cambridge History of the Cold War*, edited by Melvyn P. Leffler and Odd Arne Westad, 3:445–65. New York: Cambridge University Press, 2010.

Ford, Gerald R. *A Time to Heal: The Autobiography of Gerald R. Ford*. Norwalk, CT: Easton Press, 1987.

Forsythe, David. *Humanitarian Politics: The International Committee of the Red Cross*. Baltimore, MD: Johns Hopkins University Press, 1977.

Forsythe, David. *Human Rights and U.S. Foreign Policy: Congress Reconsidered*. Gainesville: University of Florida Press, 1988.

Fox, William T. R. *The Super-Powers: The United States, Britain, and the Soviet Union; Their Responsibility for Peace*. New York: Harcourt, Brace and Co., 1944.

Franck, Thomas, and Nigel Rodley. "After Bangladesh: The Law of Humanitarian Intervention by Military Force." *American Journal of International Law* 67, no. 2 (April 1973): 275–305.

Frankel, Max. *High Noon in the Cold War: Kennedy, Khrushchev, and the Cuban Missile Crisis*. New York: Random House, 2004.

Fraser, Donald. "Human Rights and U.S. Foreign Policy: Some Basic Questions Regarding Principle and Practice." *International Studies Quarterly* 23, no. 2 (1979): 174–85.

Freedman, Lawrence. *The Evolution of Nuclear Strategy*. New York: St. Martin's Press, 1983.

Freedman, Lawrence. *Strategy: A History*. Oxford University Press, 2013.

Friedberg, Aaron L. *In the Shadow of the Garrison State: America's Anti-Statism and Its Cold War Grand Strategy*. Princeton, NJ: Princeton University Press, 2000.

Frieden, Jeffry A. *Global Capitalism: Its Fall and Rise in the Twentieth Century*. New York: W. W. Norton, 2006.

Friedman, Milton. "The Case for Flexible Exchange Rates." In *Essays in Positive Economics*, 157–203. Chicago: University of Chicago Press, 1953.

Friedman, Milton, and Anna Schwartz. *A Monetary History of the United States, 1867–1960*. Princeton, NJ: Princeton University Press, 1963.

Fuller, Buckminster. *Operating Manual for Spaceship Earth*. Carbondale: Southern Illinois University Press, 1969.

Fursenko, Aleksandr, and Timothy J. Naftali. *One Hell of a Gamble: Khrushchev, Castro, and Kennedy, 1958–1964*. New York: W. W. Norton, 1997.

Gaddis, John Lewis. *The Cold War: A New History*. New York: Penguin, 2005.

Gaddis, John Lewis. *George F. Kennan: An American Life*. New York: Penguin, 2011.

Gaddis, John Lewis. "The Long Peace: Elements of Stability in the Postwar International System." *International Security* 10, no. 4 (1986): 99–142.

Gaddis, John Lewis. *Strategies of Containment: A Critical Appraisal of Postwar American National Security Policy*. New York: Oxford University Press, 1982.

Gaddis, John Lewis. *Surprise, Security, and the American Experience*. Cambridge, MA: Harvard University Press, 2004.

Gaddis, John Lewis. *The United States and the Origins of the Cold War, 1941–1947*. Columbia Studies in Contemporary American History. New York: Columbia University Press, 1972.

Gaidar, Yegor. *Collapse of an Empire: Lessons for Modern Russia*. Washington, DC: Brookings Institution Press, 2010.

Galbraith, John Kenneth. *The New Industrial State*. Boston: Houghton Mifflin, 1967.

Gallarotti, Giulio M. *The Anatomy of an International Monetary Regime: The Classical Gold Standard, 1880–1914*. New York: Oxford University Press, 1995.

Galpern, Steven G. *Money, Oil, and Empire in the Middle East: Sterling and Postwar Imperialism, 1944–1971*. New York: Cambridge University Press, 2009.

Gandhi, Indira. *India and Bangla Desh: Selected Speeches and Statements, March to December 1971*. New Delhi: Orient Longman, 1972.

Garavoglia, Guido. "From Rambouillet to Williamsburg." In *Economic Summits and Western Decision-Making*, edited by Cesare Merlini, 1–42. New York: Palgrave Macmillan, 1984.

Gardner, Bruce L. *American Agriculture in the Twentieth Century: How It Flourished and What It Cost*. Cambridge, MA: Harvard University Press, 2002.

Gardner, Richard N. *Sterling-Dollar Diplomacy: The Origins and Prospects of Our International Economic Order*. New York: Oxford University Press, 1956.

Gardner, Richard N. "*The World Food and Energy Crisis: The Role of International Organizations*." Rensselaerville, NY: Institute on Man and Science, 1974.

Garthoff, Raymond L. *Détente and Confrontation: American-Soviet Relations from Nixon to Reagan*. Washington, DC: Brookings Institution, 1994.

Garton Ash, Timothy. *In Europe's Name: Germany and the Divided Continent*. New York: Vintage, 1994.

Garton Ash, Timothy. *The Polish Revolution: Solidarity*. New York: Scribner, 1984.

Gasiorowski, Mark J. *U.S. Foreign Policy and the Shah: Building a Client State in Iran*. Ithaca, NY: Cornell University Press, 1991.

Gasiorowski, Mark J., and Malcolm Byrne, eds. *Mohammad Mosaddeq and the 1953 Coup in Iran*. Syracuse, NY: Syracuse University Press, 2004.

Gavin, Francis J. "Nuclear Proliferation and Non-Proliferation during the Cold War." In *The Cambridge History of the Cold War*, edited by Melvyn P. Leffler and Odd Arne Westad, 2:395–416. New York: Cambridge University Press, 2010.

Gavin, Francis J. *Gold, Dollars, and Power: The Politics of International Monetary Relations, 1958–1971*. Chapel Hill: University of North Carolina Press, 2004.

Gavin, Francis J., and Mark Atwood Lawrence, eds. *Beyond the Cold War: Lyndon Johnson and the New Global Challenges of the 1960s*. New York: Oxford University Press, 2014.

Gellner, Ernest. *Nations and Nationalism*. Ithaca, NY: Cornell University Press, 2008.

Gill, Stephen. *American Hegemony and the Trilateral Commission*. New York: Cambridge University Press, 1990.

Gilligan, Emma. *Defending Human Rights in Russia*. New York: RoutledgeCurzon, 2004.

Gilman, Nils. *Mandarins of the Future: Modernization Theory in Cold War America*. Baltimore, MD: Johns Hopkins University Press, 2007.

Gilpin, Robert. *The Political Economy of International Relations*. Princeton, NJ: Princeton University Press, 1987.

Glad, Betty. *An Outsider in the White House: Jimmy Carter, His Advisors, and the Making of American Foreign Policy*. Ithaca, NY: Cornell University Press, 2009.

Gleijeses, Piero. *Conflicting Missions: Havana, Washington, and Africa, 1959–1976*. Chapel Hill: University of North Carolina Press, 2002.

Gleijeses, Piero. *Shattered Hope: The Guatemalan Revolution and the United States, 1944–1954*. Princeton, NJ: Princeton University Press, 1991.

Gleijeses, Piero. "Truth or Credibility: Castro, Carter, and the Invasions of Shaba." *International History Review* 18, no. 1 (1996): 70–103.

Glendon, Mary Ann. *A World Made New: Eleanor Roosevelt and the Universal Declaration of Human Rights*. New York: Random House, 2001.

Glynn, Patrick. *Closing Pandora's Box: Arms Races, Arms Control, and the History of the Cold War.* New York: Basic Books, 1992.

Godbold, E. Stanly. *Jimmy and Rosalynn Carter: The Georgia Years, 1924–1974.* New York: Oxford University Press, 2010.

Golan, Galia. *Soviet Policies in the Middle East: From World War Two to Gorbachev.* New York: Cambridge University Press, 1990.

Gold, Joseph. *International Capital Movements under the Law of the IMF.* Washington, DC: International Monetary Fund, 1977.

Goldhagen, Daniel Jonah. *Worse Than War: Genocide, Eliminationism, and the Ongoing Assault on Humanity.* New York: Public Affairs, 2009.

Goldman, Minton F. "President Carter, Western Europe, and Afghanistan in 1980: Inter-Allied Differences over Policy toward the Soviet Invasion." In *Jimmy Carter: Foreign Policy and Post-Presidential Years*, edited by Herbert D. Rosenbaum and Alexej Ugrinsky, 19–34. Westport, CT: Greenwood, 1993.

Goldman, Zachary K. "Ties That Bind: John F. Kennedy and the Foundations of the American-Israeli Alliance." *Cold War History* 9, no. 1 (2009): 23–58.

Gorbachev, Mikhail S. *Memoirs.* New York: Doubleday, 1996.

Gould, Michael. *The Biafran War: The Struggle for Modern Nigeria.* New York: I. B. Tauris, 2013.

Gowa, Joanne. *Closing the Gold Window: Domestic Politics and the End of Bretton Woods.* Ithaca, NY: Cornell University Press, 1983.

Gowan, Peter. *The Global Gamble: Washington's Faustian Bid for World Dominance.* New York: Verso, 1999.

Grandin, Greg. *Empire's Workshop: Latin America, the United States, and the Rise of the New Imperialism.* New York: Metropolitan Books, 2006.

Grandin, Greg. *The Last Colonial Massacre: Latin America in the Cold War.* Chicago: University of Chicago Press, 2011.

Graubard, Stephen R. *Kissinger: Portrait of a Mind.* New York: W.W. Norton, 1974.

Gray, William G. "Floating the System: Germany, the United States, and the Breakdown of Bretton Woods, 1969–1973." *Diplomatic History* 31, no. 2 (2007) 295–323.

Green, James Naylor. *We Cannot Remain Silent: Opposition to the Brazilian Military Dictatorship in the United States.* Durham, NC: Duke University Press, 2010.

Greenberg, Amy S. *A Wicked War: Polk, Clay, Lincoln, and the 1846 U.S. Invasion of Mexico.* New York: Alfred A. Knopf, 2012.

Greenberg, David. *Nixon's Shadow: The History of an Image.* New York: W. W. Norton, 2003.

Greenspan, Alan. *The Age of Turbulence: Adventures in a New World.* New York: Penguin, 2008.

Greider, William. *Secrets of the Temple: How the Federal Reserve Runs the Country.* New York: Simon and Schuster, 1989.

Griffith, William E. "The Revival of Islamic Fundamentalism: The Case of Iran." *International Security* 4, no. 1 (1979): 132–38.

Grigorenko, Petro. *Memoirs.* New York: W. W. Norton, 1982.

Grose, Peter. *Continuing the Inquiry: The Council on Foreign Relations from 1921 to 1996.* New York: Council on Foreign Relations, 1996.

Gruchy, Allan G. "Institutionalism, Planning, and the Current Crisis." *Journal of Economic Issues* (1977): 431–48.

Gruhn, Isebill. "The Lomé Convention: Inching towards Interdependence." *International Organization* 30, no. 2 (1976): 241–62.

Gupta, Vinod. *The Anderson Papers: A Study of Nixon's Blackmail of India.* New Delhi: ISSD, 1972.

Gurtov, Melvin. *The United States against the Third World: Antinationalism and Intervention.* New York: Praeger, 1974.

Gustafson, Kristian. *Hostile Intent: U.S. Covert Operations in Chile, 1964–1974.* Washington, DC: Potomac Books, 2007.

Guthrie-Shimizu, Sayuri. "Japan, the United States, and the Cold War, 1945–1960." In *The Cambridge History of the Cold War*, edited by Melvyn P. Leffler and Odd Arne Westad, 1:244–65. New York: Cambridge University Press, 2010.

Haftendorn, Helga. *Coming of Age: German Foreign Policy since 1945.* Lantham, MD: Rowman & Littlefield, 2006.

Haftendorn, Helga. *NATO and the Nuclear Revolution: A Crisis of Credibility, 1966-1967.* Oxford: Oxford University Press, 1996.

Hajnal, Peter I., ed. *The Ends of Power.* New York: Times Books, 1978.

Hajnal, Peter I., ed. *The Seven-Power Summit: Documents from the Summits of Industrialized Countries, 1975-1989.* White Plains, NY: Kraus International Publications, 1989.

Haldeman, H. R. *The Haldeman Diaries: Inside the Nixon White House.* New York: G. P. Putnam's, 1994.

Halliday, Fred. "The Arc of Crisis and the New Cold War." *MERIP Reports,* no. 100/101 (October–December 1981): 14–25.

Halliday, Fred. *Iran: Dictatorship and Development.* New York: Penguin, 1978.

Halliday, Fred. *The Making of the Second Cold War.* London: Verso, 1986.

Hallin, Daniel C. *The Uncensored War: The Media and Vietnam.* Berkeley: University of California Press, 1986.

Halper, Stefan, and Jonathan Clarke. *America Alone: The Neo-Conservatives and the Global Order.* New York: Cambridge University Press, 2004.

Hamilton, Keith. "Britain, France, and America's Year of Europe, 1973." *Diplomacy and Statecraft* 17, no. 4 (2006): 871–95.

Hamilton, Shane. *Trucking Country: The Road to America's Wal-Mart Economy.* Princeton, NJ: Princeton University Press, 2008.

Hammarskjold, Knut. "Economic Implications of High-Capacity Jets and Supersonic Aircraft." *Financial Analysts Journal* 23, no. 2 (1967): 67–82.

Hanhimäki, Jussi. *The Flawed Architect: Henry Kissinger and American Foreign Policy.* New York: Oxford University Press, 2004.

Hanhimäki, Jussi. *The Rise and Fall of Détente: American Foreign Policy and the Transformation of the Cold War.* Washington, DC: Potomac Books, 2013.

Hanhimäki, Jussi. "'They Can Still Write It in Swahili': Kissinger, the Soviets and the Helsinki Accords, 1973–75." *Journal of Transatlantic Studies* 1, no. 1 (2003): 37–58.

Hanson, Philip. *The Rise and Fall of the Soviet Economy: An Economic History of the USSR from 1945.* New York: Longman, 2003.

Haq, Mahbub ul. *The Poverty Curtain: Choices or the Third World.* New York: Columbia University Press, 1976.

Harmer, Tanya. *Allende's Chile and the Inter-American Cold War.* Chapel Hill: University of North Carolina Press, 2011.

Hart, Jeffrey A. *The New International Economic Order: Conflict and Cooperation in North-South Economic Relations, 1974–77.* New York: St. Martin's Press, 1983.

Hartmann, Robert Trowbridge. *Palace Politics: An Inside Account of the Ford Years.* New York: McGraw-Hill, 1980.

Harvey, David. *The New Imperialism.* New York: Oxford University Press, 2003.

Haslam, Jonathan. *The Nixon Administration and the Death of Allende's Chile: A Case of Assisted Suicide.* London; New York: Verso, 2005.

Haslam, Jonathan. *Russia's Cold War: From the October Revolution to the Fall of the Wall.* New Haven, CT: Yale University Press, 2011.

Hawley, James P. *Dollars and Borders: U.S. Government Attempts to Restrict Capital Flows, 1960–1980.* Armonk, NY: M. E. Sharpe, 1987.

Haynes, John E., and Harvey Klehr. *VENONA: Decoding Soviet Espionage in America.* New Haven, CT: Yale University Press, 1999.

Haynes, John Earl, Harvey Klehr, and Alexander Vassiliev. *Spies: The Rise and Fall of the KGB in America.* New Haven, CT: Yale University Press, 2009.

Hayward, Steven F. *The Age of Reagan: The Fall of the Old Liberal Order: 1964–1980.* New York: Random House, 2009.

Held, David, Anthony McGrew, David Goldblatt, and Jonathan Perraton. *Global Transformations: Politics, Economics, and Culture.* Palo Alto, CA: Stanford University Press, 1999.

Helleiner, Eric. *States and the Reemergence of Global Finance: From Bretton Woods to the 1990s.* Ithaca, NY: Cornell University Press, 1994.

Hendrickson, David C. *Union, Nation, or Empire: The American Debate over International Relations, 1789–1941*. Lawrence: University of Kansas Press, 2009.

Herring, George C. *America's Longest War: The United States and Vietnam, 1950–1975*. Boston: McGraw-Hill, 2002.

Herz, John H. *International Politics in the Atomic Age*. New York: Columbia University Press, 1958.

Heurtebizé, Frédéric. "The Union of the Left in France, 1971–1981: A Threat to NATO? The View from Washington." *Journal of Transatlantic Studies* 9, no. 3 (2011): 244–56.

Hirschman, Charles, Samuel Preston, and Vu Manh Loi. "Vietnamese Casualties during the American War: A New Estimate." *Population and Development Review* 21, no. 4 (1995): 783–812.

Hobsbawm, Eric J. *Nations and Nationalism since 1780*. New York: Cambridge University Press, 1992.

Hochschild, Adam. *Bury the Chains: Prophets and Rebels in the Fight to Free an Empire's Slaves*. Boston: Houghton Mifflin, 2006.

Hodgson, Godfrey. *The Gentleman from New York: Daniel Patrick Moynihan; a Biography*. Boston: Houghton Mifflin, 2000.

Hoff, Joan. *Nixon Reconsidered*. New York: Basic Books, 1995.

Hoffman, Elizabeth Cobbs. *American Umpire*. Cambridge, MA: Harvard University Press, 2013.

Hoffmann, Stanley. *Primacy or World Order: American Foreign Policy since the Cold War*. New York: McGraw-Hill, 1978.

Hoffmann, Stefan-Ludwig, ed. *Human Rights in the Twentieth Century*. Cambridge: Cambridge University Press, 2010.

Hofmann, Arne. *The Emergence of Détente in Europe: Brandt, Kennedy and the Formation of Ostpolitik*. London: Routledge, 2007.

Hogan, Michael J. *A Cross of Iron: Harry S. Truman and the Origins of the National Security State*. New York: Cambridge University Press, 1998.

Hogan, Michael J. *The Marshall Plan: America, Britain, and the Reconstruction of Western Europe, 1947–1952*. New York: Cambridge University Press, 1987.

Holland, R. *European Decolonization, 1918–1981: An Introductory Survey*. New York: St. Martin's Press, 1985.

Holloway, David. *Stalin and the Bomb: The Soviet Union and Atomic Energy, 1939–56*. New Haven, CT: Yale University Press, 1994.

Holman, Frank. "An 'International Bill of Rights': Proposals Have Dangerous Implications for U.S." *Journal of the American Bar Association* 34 (November 1948): 984–86, 1078–81.

Holman, Frank. "International Proposals Affecting So-Called Human Rights." *Law and Contemporary Problems* 14, no. 3 (1949): 479–89.

Hooglund, Eric J. *Land and Revolution in Iran, 1960–1980*. Austin: University of Texas Press, 2012.

Hoopes, Townsend, and Douglas Brinkley. *FDR and the Creation of the U.N.* New Haven, CT: Yale University Press, 1997.

Hopgood, Stephen. *Keepers of the Flame: Understanding Amnesty International*. Ithaca, NY: Cornell University Press, 2006.

Horne, Alistair. *Small Earthquake in Chile*. London: Viking, 1973.

Hubbert, M. K. *Nuclear Energy and the Fossil Fuels: American Petroleum Institute Drilling and Production Practice Proceedings*. Houston, TX: Shell Development Co, 1956.

Hudson, Michael. *Global Fracture: The New International Economic Order*. Ann Arbor, MI: Pluto Press, 2005.

Humphrey, John P. *Human Rights and the United Nations: A Great Adventure*. Dobbs Ferry, NY: Transnational Publishers, 1984.

Humphrey, John P. "International Protection of Human Rights." *Annals of the American Academy of Political and Social Science* 255 (January 1948): 15–21.

Humphrey, John P. *On the Edge of Greatness: The Diaries of John Humphrey, First Director of the United Nations Division of Human Rights*, edited by A. John Hobbins. 4 vols. Montreal: McGill-Queens University Press, 1994-2000.

Hunt, Lynn Avery. *Inventing Human Rights: A History*. New York: W. W. Norton, 2007.

Huntington, Samuel P. *The Third Wave: Democratization in the Late Twentieth Century*. Norman: University of Oklahoma Press, 1991.

Huntington, Samuel P., Michel Crozier, and Joji Watanuki. *The Crisis of Democracy: A Report on the Governability of Democracies to the Trilateral Commission.* New York: New York University Press, 1975.

Huntington, Samuel P., and Warren D. Manshel. "Why 'Foreign Policy'?" *Foreign Policy* 1, no. 1 (1970): 3–5.

Hyland, William G. *Mortal Rivals: Superpower Relations from Nixon to Reagan.* New York: Random House, 1987.

Ikenberry, G. John. *After Victory: Institutions, Strategic Restraint, and the Rebuilding of Order after Major Wars.* Princeton, NJ: Princeton University Press, 2001.

Ikenberry, G. John. "Rethinking the Origins of American Hegemony." *Political Science Quarterly* 104, no. 3 (1989): 375–400.

Immerman, Richard H. *The CIA in Guatemala: The Foreign Policy of Intervention.* Austin: University of Texas Press, 1982.

International Commission of Jurists. *The Events in East Pakistan, 1971: A Legal Study.* Geneva: International Commission of Jurists, 1972.

International Monetary Fund. *International Monetary Reform: Documents of the Committee of Twenty.* Washington, DC: IMF, 1974.

Iriye, Akira. *The Cold War in Asia: A Historical Introduction.* Englewood Cliffs, NJ: Prentice-Hall, 1974.

Iriye, Akira. *Global Community: The Role of International Organizations in the Making of the Contemporary World.* Berkeley: University of California Press, 2002.

Iriye, Akira. *Power and Culture: The Japanese-American War, 1941–1945.* Cambridge, MA: Harvard University Press, 1981.

Isaacson, Walter. *Kissinger: A Biography.* New York: Simon and Schuster, 1992.

Ishay, Micheline. *The History of Human Rights: From Ancient Times to the Globalization Era.* Berkeley: University of California Press, 2004.

Israelyan, Victor. *Inside the Kremlin during the Yom Kippur War.* University Park: Pennsylvania State University Press, 1995.

Isserman, Maurice, and Michael Kazin. *America Divided: The Civil War of the 1960s.* New York: Oxford University Press, 2000.

Jackson, Donna R. *Jimmy Carter and the Horn of Africa: Cold War Policy in Ethiopia and Somalia.* Jefferson, NC: McFarland & Co., 2007.

Jackson, Robert. *South Asian Crisis: India, Pakistan and Bangladesh.* New York: Praeger, 1975.

Jacobs, Dan. *The Brutality of Nations.* New York: Alfred A. Knopf, 1987.

Jacobs, Seth. *America's Miracle Man in Vietnam: Ngo Dinh Diem, Religion, Race, and U.S. Intervention in Southeast Asia.* Durham, NC: Duke University Press, 2005.

Jacoby, Susan. *Alger Hiss and the Battle for History.* New Haven, CT: Yale University Press, 2009.

Jahan, Rounaq. "Genocide in Bangladesh." In *Century of Genocide: Critical Essays and Eyewitness Accounts,* 3rd. ed., edited by Samuel Totten and William S. Parsons, 245–66. New York: Routledge, 2008.

Jalal, Ayesha. *Democracy and Authoritarianism in South Asia: A Comparative and Historical Perspective.* New York: Cambridge University Press, 1995.

Jalal, Ayesha. *The Sole Spokesman: Jinnah, the Muslim League and the Demand for Pakistan.* Cambridge: Cambridge University Press, 1985.

Jalal, Ayesha. *The State of Martial Rule: The Origins of Pakistan's Political Economy of Defense.* New York: Cambridge University Press, 1990.

James, Harold. *International Monetary Cooperation since Bretton Woods.* New York: Oxford University Press, 1996.

James, Harold. *The Roman Predicament: How the Rules of International Order Create the Politics of Empire.* Princeton, NJ: Princeton University Press, 2008.

James, Harold, and Marzenna James, "The Origins of the Cold War: Some New Documents." *Historical Journal* 37, no. 3 (1994), 620–22.

Jervis, Robert. *The Meaning of the Nuclear Revolution: Statecraft and the Prospects of Armageddon.* Ithaca, NY: Cornell University Press, 1989.

Johnson, Peter A. *The Government of Money: Monetarism in Germany and the United States.* Ithaca, NY: Cornell University Press, 1998.

Johnson, Robert D. *Congress and the Cold War*. New York: Cambridge University Press, 2005.

Johnson, Robert D. "The Unintended Consequences of Congressional Reform: The Clark and Tunney Amendments and U.S. Policy Toward Angola." *Diplomatic History* 27, no. 2 (2003): 215–43.

Jones, Adam. *Genocide: A Comprehensive Introduction*. 2nd ed. New York: Routledge, 2010.

Jones, Seth G. *In the Graveyard of Empires: America's War in Afghanistan*. New York: W. W. Norton, 2009.

Judt, Tony. *Postwar: A History of Europe Since 1945*. New York: Penguin, 2005.

Kahler, Miles, and David A. Lake, eds. *Governance in a Global Economy: Political Authority in Transition*. Princeton, NJ: Princeton University Press, 2003.

Kaiser, Karl. "Transnational Politics: Toward a Theory of Multinational Politics." *International Organization* 25, no. 4 (1971): 790–817.

Kaiser, Karl. "Transnational Relations as a Threat to the Democratic Process." *International Organization* 25, no. 3 (1971): 706–20.

Kaji, Motoo, Richard Cooper, and Claudio Segré. *Towards a Renovated World Monetary System: A Report of the Trilateral Monetary Task Force to the Executive Committee of the Trilateral Commission, Tokyo, October 22–23, 1973*. The Triangle Papers 1. New York: Trilateral Commission, 1973.

Kalman, Laura. *Right Star Rising: A New Politics, 1974–1980*. New York: W. W. Norton, 2010.

Kane, Daniel. *The Eurodollar Market and the Years of Crisis*. London: Croom Helm, 1983.

Kapstein, Ethan. *The Insecure Alliance: Energy Crises and Western Politics since 1944*. New York: Oxford University Press, 1990.

Karabell, Zachary. *Architects of Intervention: The United States, the Third World, and the Cold War, 1946–1962*. Baton Rouge: Louisiana State University Press, 1999.

Katznelson, Ira. *Fear Itself: The New Deal and the Origins of Our Time*. New York: W. W. Norton, 2013.

Kaufman, Natalie H. *Human Rights Treaties and the Senate: A History of Opposition*. Chapel Hill: University of North Carolina Press, 1990.

Kaufman, Scott. *Plans Unraveled: The Foreign Policy oof the Carter Administration*. DeKalb: Northern Illinois University Press, 2008.

Kavass, Igor, ed. *Human Rights, European Politics, and the Helsinki Accord: The Documentary Evolution of the Conference on Security and Cooperation in Europe, 1973–1975*. Buffalo, NY: William S. Hein, 1981.

Keck, Margaret, and Kathryn Sikkink. *Activists beyond Borders: Advocacy Networks in International Politics*. Ithaca, NY: Cornell University Press, 1998.

Keddie, Nikki R., and Richard Yann. *Roots of Revolution: An Interpretive History of Modern Iran*. New Haven, CT: Yale University Press, 1981.

Kelley, Donald. "The Soviet Debate on the Convergence of the American and Soviet Systems." *Polity* 6, no. 2 (1973): 174–96.

Kelly, Patrick William. "'Magic Words': The Advent of Transnational Human Rights Activism in Latin America's Southern Cone in the Long 1970s." In *The Breakthrough: Human Rights in the 1970s*, edited by Jan Eckel and Samuel Moyn, 88–106. Philadelphia: University of Pennsylvania Press, 2013.

Kelly, Patrick William. "The 1973 Chilean Coup and the Origins of Transnational Human Rights Activism." *Journal of Global History* 8, no. 1 (2013): 165–86.

Kennan, George S. "After the Cold War." *Foreign Affairs* 51, no. 1 (1972): 210–27.

Kennedy, Paul. *The Parliament of Man: The Past, Present, and Future of the United Nations*. New York: Random House, 2006.

Kennedy, Paul. *The Rise and Fall of the Great Powers: Economic Change and Military Conflict from 1500 to 2000*. New York: Random House, 1987.

Keohane, Robert O, *After Hegemony: Cooperation and Discord in the World Political Economy*. Princeton, NJ: Princeton University Press, 1984.

Keohane, Robert O. "The International Energy Agency: State Influence and Transgovernmental Politics." *International Organization* 32, no. 4 (1978): 929–51.

Keohane, Robert O. "The Old IPE and the New." *Review of International Political Economy* 16, no. 1 (2009): 34–46.

Keohane, Robert O. "A Personal and Intellectual History." In *Journeys through World Politics: Autobiographical Reflections of Thirty-Four Academic Travelers*, edited by Joseph Kruzel and James Rosenau, 403–15. Lexington, MA: Lexington Books, 1989.

Keohane, Robert O., and Joseph S. Nye. "Globalization: What's New? What's Not? (and So What?)." *Foreign Policy*, no. 118 (2000): 104–19.

Keohane, Robert, and Joseph Nye. *Power and Interdependence: World Politics in Transition*. Boston, MA: Little, Brown, 1977.

Keohane, Robert, and Joseph Nye, eds. *Transnational Relations and World Politics*. Cambridge, MA: Harvard University Press, 1972.

Keohane, Robert O., and Joseph S. Nye. "Transnational Relations and World Politics: A Conclusion." *International Organization* 25, no. 3 (1971): 721–48.

Kepel, Gilles. *Jihad: The Trail of Political Islam*. Cambridge, MA: Harvard University Press, 2002.

Kerr, Malcolm H. *The Arab Cold War: Gamal Abd Al-Nasir and His Rivals, 1958–1970*. London: Oxford University Press, 1971.

Kettl, Donald F. *Leadership at the Fed*. New Haven, CT: Yale University Press, 1986.

Keylor, William R. *The Twentieth-Century World and Beyond: An International History Since 1900*. New York: Oxford University Press, 2011.

Keynes, John Maynard. *The General Theory of Employment, Interest, and Money*. San Diego, CA: Harcourt, 1964.

Keynes, John Maynard. *A Tract on Monetary Reform*. Amherst, NY: Prometheus Books, 2000.

Keys, Barbara. "Congress, Kissinger, and the Origins of Human Rights Diplomacy." *Diplomatic History* 34, no. 5 (2010): 823–51.

Keys, Barbara. *Reclaiming American Virtue: The Human Rights Revolution of the 1970s*. Cambridge, MA: Harvard University Press, 2014.

Khalidi, Rashid. *Resurrecting Empire: Western Footprints and America's Perilous Path in the Middle East*. Boston: Beacon Press, 2005.

Kiernan, Ben. *Blood and Soil: A World History of Genocide and Extermination from Sparta to Darfur*. New Haven, CT: Yale University Press, 2007.

Kimball Warren F. *Churchill and Roosevelt: The Complete Correspondence*. Princeton, NJ: Princeton University Press, 1984.

Kimball, Jeffrey. "The Nixon Doctrine: A Saga of Misunderstanding." *Presidential Studies Quarterly* 36, no. 1 (2006): 59–74.

Kimball, Jeffrey. *Nixon's Vietnam War*. Lawrence: University of Kansas Press, 1998.

Kindleberger, Charles P. *Power and Money: The Economics of International Politics and the Politics of International Economics*. New York: Basic Books, 1970.

Kindleberger, Charles P. *The World in Depression, 1929–1939*. Berkeley: University of California Press, 1973.

King, Robert G. "U.S. Foreign Policy Decision-making under Ford and Kissinger, 1974–77." Master's thesis, University of Cambridge, 2011.

Kinzer, Stephen. *All the Shah's Men: An American Coup and the Roots of Middle East Terror*. Hoboken, NJ: John Wiley & Sons, 2008.

Kirk-Greene, A. H. M. *Crisis and Conflict in Nigeria: A Documentary Sourcebook*. 2 vols. London: Oxford University Press, 1971.

Kirkpatrick, Jeane. "Dictatorship and Double Standards." *Commentary* 68 (1979): 34–45.

Kirschbaum, Erik. *Rocking The Wall: Bruce Springsteen: The Untold Story of a Concert in East Berlin That Changed the World*. New York: Berlinica Publishing, 2013.

Kissinger, Henry. *American Foreign Policy: Three Essays*. New York: W. W. Norton, 1969.

Kissinger, Henry. *Diplomacy*. New York: Touchstone, 1994.

Kissinger, Henry. "The Nature of the National Dialogue on Foreign Policy," in *The Nixon-Kissinger Foreign Policy*, edited by Fred Warner Neal and Mary Kersey Harvey, 6–17. Santa Barbara, CA: Center for the Study of Democratic Institutions, 1974.

Kissinger, Henry. *On China*. New York: Penguin Books, 2012.

Kissinger, Henry. *The Troubled Partnership: A Reappraisal of the Atlantic Alliance*. New York: McGraw-Hill, 1965.

Kissinger, Henry. "The Viet Nam Negotiations." *Foreign Affairs* 49, no. 2 (1969): 211–34.

Kissinger, Henry. *White House Years*. Boston: Little Brown, 1979.

Kissinger, Henry. "The White Revolutionary: Reflections on Bismarck." *Daedalus* 97, no. 3 (summer 1968): 888–924.

Kissinger, Henry. *A World Restored: Metternich, Castlereagh and the Problems of Peace, 1812–22.* Boston: Houghton Mifflin, 1957.

Kissinger, Henry. *Years of Renewal.* New York: Simon and Schuster, 1999.

Kissinger, Henry. *Years of Upheaval.* Boston: Little Brown, 1982.

Klare, Michael. *American Arms Supermarket.* Austin: University of Texas Press, 1984.

Klopstock, Fred H. "Use of Eurodollars by U.S. Banks." In *The Eurodollar*, edited by Edward M. Bernstein and Herbert Prochnow, 69–83. Chicago: Rand McNally & Co., 1970.

Kochavi, Noam. "Insights Abandoned, Flexibility Lost: Kissinger, Soviet Jewish Emigration, and the Demise of Détente." *Diplomatic History* 29, no. 3 (2005): 503–30.

Kolko, Gabriel, and Joyce Kolko. *The Limits of Power: The World and United States Foreign Policy.* New York: Harper & Row, 1972.

Korey, William. *NGOs and the Universal Declaration of Human Rights: "A Curious Grapevine."* Basingstoke, UK: Macmillan, 1998.

Kornbluh, Peter. *The Pinochet File: A Declassified Dossier on Atrocity and Accountability*, 2003. New York: New Press.

Kotkin, Stephen. "The Kiss of Debt: The East Bloc Goes Borrowing." In *The Shock of the Global*, edited by Niall Ferguson, Charles S. Maier, Erez Manela, and Daniel J. Sargent, 80–93. Cambridge, MA: Harvard University Press, 2010.

Kotkin, Stephen. *Armageddon Averted: The Soviet Collapse, 1970–2000.* New York: Oxford University Press, 2001.

Kouchner, Bernard, and Mario Bettati. *Le Devoir de l'ingerence: peut-on les laisser mourir?* Paris: Denoel, 1987.

Krasner, Stephen D. *Structural Conflict: The Third World against Global Liberalism.* Berkeley: University of California Press, 1985.

Krause, Lawrence. "Private International Finance." In *Transnational Relations and World Politics*, edited by Robert Keohane and Joseph Nye, 173–90. Cambridge, MA: Harvard University Press, 1972.

Krippner, Greta R. *Capitalizing on Crisis: The Political Origins of the Rise of Finance.* Cambridge, MA: Harvard University Press, 2011.

Kunz, Diane. *Butter and Guns: America's Cold War Economic Diplomacy.* New York: Free Press, 1997.

Kuper, Leo. *The Prevention of Genocide.* New Haven, CT: Yale University Press, 1985.

Kurizaki, Shuhei. "Efficient Secrecy: Public versus Private Threats in Crisis Diplomacy." *American Political Science Review* 101, no. 3 (2007): 543–58.

Kurzman, Charles. *The Unthinkable Revolution in Iran.* Cambridge, MA: Harvard University Press, 2004.

Kux, Dennis. *The United States and Pakistan, 1947–2000: Disenchanted Allies.* Baltimore, MD: Johns Hopkins University Press, 2001.

LaFeber, Walter. *The Clash: U.S.-Japan Relations throughout History.* New York: W. W. Norton, 1997.

LaFeber, Walter. *Inevitable Revolutions: The United States in Central America.* New York: Norton, 1983.

LaFeber, Walter. *Michael Jordan and the New Global Capitalism.* New York: W. W. Norton, 1999.

Lantzke, Ulf. "The OECD and Its International Energy Agency." *Daedalus* 104, no. 4, The Oil Crisis: In Perspective (Fall 1975), 217–27.

Laqueur, Walter. *Neo-Isolationism and the World of the Seventies.* New York: Library Press, 1972.

Latham, Michael E. *The Right Kind of Revolution: Modernization, Development, and U.S. Foreign Policy from the Cold War to the Present.* Ithaca, NY: Cornell University Press, 2011.

Latham, Robert. *The Liberal Moment: Modernity, Security, and the Making of Postwar International Order.* New York: Columbia University Press, 1997.

Lauren, Paul Gordon. *The Evolution of International Human Rights: Visions Seen.* 2nd ed. Philadelphia: University of Pennsylvania Press, 2003.

Lauterpacht, Hersch. *International Law and Human Rights.* New York: F. A. Praeger, 1950.

Lawrence, Mark Atwood. *Assuming the Burden: Europe and the American Commitment to War in Vietnam*. Berkeley: University of California Press, 2005.

Lawrence, Mark Atwood. *The Vietnam War: A Concise International History*. New York: Oxford University Press, 2008.

Layne, Christopher. *The Peace of Illusions: American Grand Strategy from 1940 to the Present*. Ithaca, NY: Cornell University Press, 2007.

Lazin, Fred A. *The Struggle for Soviet Jewry in American Politics: Israel versus the American Jewish Establishment*. Lanham, MD: Lexington Books, 2005.

Leacock, Ruth. *Requiem for Revolution: The United States and Brazil, 1961–1969*. Kent, OH: Kent State University Press, 1990.

Leeson, Robert. *Ideology and the International Economy: The Decline and Fall of Bretton Woods*. New York: Palgrave Macmillan, 2003.

Leffler, Melvyn P. *For the Soul of Mankind: The United States, the Soviet Union, and the Cold War*. New York: Hill and Wang, 2007.

Leffler, Melvyn P. *A Preponderance of Power: National Security, the Truman Administration, and the Cold War*. Palo Alto, CA: Stanford University Press, 1992.

Legro, Jeffrey. *Rethinking the World: Great Power Strategies and International Order*. Ithaca, NY: Cornell University Press, 2005.

Lemarchand, René. "The Burundi Genocide." In *Century of Genocide*, edited by Samuel Totten and William Parsons, 321–37. New York: Routledge, 2004.

LeoGrande, William M. *Our Own Back Yard: The United States in Central America, 1977–1992*. Chapel Hill: University of North Carolina Press, 1998.

Leontief, Wassily. "National Economic Planning: Methods and Problems." *Challenge* 19, no. 3 (1976): 6–11.

Levinson, Marc. *The Box: How the Shipping Container Made the World Smaller and the World Economy Bigger*. Princeton, NJ: Princeton University Press, 2006.

Levy, Marion, Jr. *Modernization and the Structure of Societies: A Setting for International Affairs*. Princeton, NJ: Princeton University Press, 1966.

Levy, Walter. "Oil Power." *Foreign Affairs* 49, no. 4 (1971): 652–68.

Li, Lanqing. *Breaking Through: The Birth of China's Opening-up Policy*. New York: Oxford University Press, 2009.

Lichtenstein, Nelson. *The Retail Revolution: How Wal-Mart Created a Brave New World of Business*. New York: Picador, 2010.

Lillich, Richard. B. "Intervention to Protect Human Rights." *Michigan Law Journal* 15, no. 2 (1970): 205–19.

Liddell Hart, Basil. *The Revolution in Warfare*. Westport, CT: Greenwood Press, 1980.

Liddell Hart, Basil. *Strategy*. 2nd ed. New York: Meridian Books, 1991.

Lieber, Robert J. *The Oil Decade: Conflict and Cooperation in the West*. New York: Praeger, 1983.

Lillich, Richard. B. *Humanitarian Intervention and the United Nations*. Charlottesville: University of Virginia Press, 1973.

Lindberg, Leon N., and Charles S. Maier, eds. *The Politics of Inflation and Economic Stagnation: Theoretical Approaches and International Case Studies*. Washington, DC: Brookings Institution, 1985.

Lippman, Thomas W. *Inside the Mirage: America's Fragile Partnership with Saudi Arabia*. Boulder, CO: Westview, 2005.

Lippmann, Walter, *The Cold War: A Study in U.S. Foreign Policy*. New York: Harper & Row, 1972.

Little, Jane S. *Euro-Dollars*. New York: HarperCollins, 1975.

Litwak, Robert S. *Détente and the Nixon Doctrine: American Foreign Policy and the Pursuit of Stability*. New York: Cambridge University Press, 1985.

Lloyd, H. G., M. L. Mollerup, and C. A. Bratved. *The Nordchurchaid Airlift to Biafra, 1968–1970: An Operations Report*. Copenhagen: Folkekirkens Nödhjælp, Eksp., 1972.

Lockwood, David. *The Destruction of the Soviet Union: A Study in Globalization*. New York: St. Martin's Press, 2000.

Logevall, Fredrik. *Embers of War: The Fall of an Empire and the Making of America's Vietnam*. New York: Random House, 2012.

Long, David E. *The United States and Saudi Arabia: Ambivalent Allies*. Boulder, CO: Westview Press, 1985.

Loth, Wilfried. "Moscow, Prague and Warsaw: Overcoming the Brezhnev Doctrine." *Cold War History* 1, no. 2 (2001): 103–18.

Loth, Wilfried. *Overcoming the Cold War: A History of Détente, 1950–1991*. New York: Palgrave, 2002.

Louis, William Roger. *The British Empire in the Middle East, 1945–1951: Arab Nationalism, the United States, and Postwar Imperialism*. New York: Oxford University Press, 1984.

Lourie, Richard. *Sakharov: A Biography*. Hanover, NH: University Press of New England, 2002.

Ludlam, Steve. "The Gnomes of Washington: Four Myths of the 1976 IMF Crisis." *Political Studies* 40, no. 4 (1992): 713–27.

Lukes, Steven. *Power: A Radical View*. 2nd ed. London: Palgrave Macmillan, 2005.

Lundestad, Geir. *"Empire" by Integration: The United States and European Integration, 1945–1997*. New York: Oxford University Press, 1998.

Lundestad, Geir. "Empire by Invitation? The United States and Western Europe, 1945–1952." *Society for Historians of American Foreign Relations Newsletter*, vol. 15, September 1984, 1–21.

Lundestad, Geir. *The United States and Western Europe Since 1945: From "Empire" by Invitation to Transatlantic Drift*. New York: Oxford University Press, 2005.

Luthi, Lorenz M. *The Sino-Soviet Split: Cold War in the Communist World*. Princeton, NJ: Princeton University Press, 2008.

Luttwak, Edward Nicolae. *Strategy: The Logic of War and Peace*. Cambridge, MA: Harvard University Press, 2001.

Macmillan, Margaret. *Nixon and Mao: The Week That Changed the World*. New York: Random House, 2006.

Maier, Charles S. *Among Empires: American Ascendancy and Its Predecessors*. Cambridge, MA: Harvard University Press, 2006.

Maier, Charles S. "Consigning the Twentieth Century to History." *American Historical Review* 105, no. 3 (2000): 807–31.

Maier, Charles S. "'Malaise': The Crisis of Capitalism in the 1970s." In *The Shock of the Global*, edited by Niall Ferguson, Charles S. Maier, Erez Manela, and Daniel J. Sargent, 25–48. Cambridge, MA: Harvard University Press 2010.

Maier, Charles S. "The Politics of Productivity: Foundations of American International Economic Policy after World War II." *International Organization* 31, no. 4 (1977): 607–33.

Maier, Charles S. *Recasting Bourgeois Europe*. Princeton, NJ: Princeton University Press, 1988.

Makin, John H. "Eurocurrencies and the Evolution of the International Monetary System." In *Eurocurrencies and the International Monetary System*, edited by Carl H. Stem, John H. Makin, and Dennis E. Logue, 17–53. Washington, DC: American Enterprise Institute, 1976.

Mamdani, Mahmood. *Good Muslim, Bad Muslim: America, the Cold War, and the Roots of Terror*. New York: Pantheon Books, 2004.

Mandelbaum, Michael, and William Schneider. "The New Internationalisms." In *Eagle Entangled: U.S. Foreign Policy in a Complex World*, edited by Kenneth Oye, Donald Rothschild, and Robert J. Lieber, 34–88. New York: Prentice Hall, 1979.

Manela, Erez. *The Wilsonian Moment: Self-Determination and the International Origins of Anticolonial Nationalism*. New York: Oxford University Press, 2007.

Mann, James. *About Face: A History of America's Curious Relationship with China from Nixon to Clinton*. New York: Alfred A. Knopf, 1999.

Mann, James. *The Rebellion of Ronald Reagan: A History of the End of the Cold War*. New York: Viking, 2009.

Mann, James. *Rise of the Vulcans: The History of Bush's War Cabinet*. New York: Penguin, 2004.

Maresca, John J. *To Helsinki: The Conference on Security and Cooperation in Europe*. Durham, NC: Duke University Press, 1985.

Marrs, Jim. *Rule by Secrecy: The Hidden History That Connects the Trilateral Commission, the Freemasons, and the Great Pyramids*. New York: HarperCollins, 2001.

Martin, Garrett. "Playing the China Card? Revisiting France's Recognition of Communist China, 1963–1964." *Journal of Cold War Studies* 10, no. 1 (2008): 52–80.

Mascarenhas, Anthony. *The Rape of Bangla Desh*. New Delhi: Vikas Publications, 1971.

Mastny, Vojtech. *The Cold War and Soviet Insecurity.* New York: Oxford University Press, 1996.

Mastny, Vojtech. *Helsinki, Human Rights, and European Security: Analysis and Documentation.* Durham, NC: Duke University Press, 1986.

Mattson, Kevin. *"What the Heck Are You Up To, Mr. President?": Jimmy Carter, America's "Malaise," and the Speech That Should Have Changed the Country.* New York: Bloomsbury, 2009.

Matusow, Allen J. *Nixon's Economy: Booms, Busts, Dollars, and Votes.* Lawrence: University of Kansas Press, 1998.

Maxwell, Kenneth. *The Making of Portuguese Democracy.* New York: Cambridge University Press, 1997.

May, Ernest R. *American Cold War Strategy: Interpreting NSC 68.* Boston: Bedford / St. Martin's Press, 1993.

May, Ernest R. *"Lessons" of the Past: The Use and Misuse of History in American Foreign Policy.* New York: Oxford University Press, 1973.

Maynard, Edwin S. "The Bureaucracy and Implementation of U.S. Human Rights Policy." *Human Rights Quarterly* 11, no. 2 (1989): 175–248.

Mazlish, Bruce. *Kissinger: The European Mind in American Policy.* New York: BasicBooks, 1976.

Mazlish, Bruce. *The New Global History.* New York: Routledge, 2006.

Mazower, Mark. *Governing the World: The History of an Idea.* New York: Penguin, 2012.

Mazower, Mark. *No Enchanted Palace: The End of Empire and the Ideological Origins of the United Nations.* Lawrence Stone Lectures. Princeton, NJ: Princeton University Press, 2009.

Mazzini, Giuseppe. *A Cosmopolitanism of Nations: Giuseppe Mazzini's Writings on Democracy, Nation Building, and International Relations.* Princetin, NJ: Princeton University Press, 2009.

McCormick, Thomas J. *America's Half-Century: United States Foreign Policy in the Cold War and After.* Baltimore, MD: Johns Hopkins University Press, 1995.

McDougall, Walter. A. "President Nixon's Historical Legacy." Speech, Yorba Linda, CA, August 5, 2004. In *Watch on the West: A Newsletter of FPRI's Center for the Study of America and the West* 5, no. 6 (2004).

McLuhan, Marshall. *The Gutenberg Galaxy: The Making of Typographic Man.* Toronto: University of Toronto Press, 1962.

McMahon, Robert J., ed. *The Cold War in the Third World.* New York: Oxford University Press, 2013.

McMahon, Robert J. *The Cold War on the Periphery: The United States, India, and Pakistan.* New York: Columbia University Press, 1994.

McMahon, Robert J. "The Danger of Geopolitical Fantasies: Nixon, Kissinger, and the South Asia Crisis of 1971." In *Nixon and the World: American Foreign Relations, 1969–1977,* edited by Andrew Preston and Fredrik Logevall, 249–68. New York: Oxford University Press.

Meltzer, Allan H. *A History of the Federal Reserve.* 2 vols. Chicago: University of Chicago Press, 2003–10.

Mickelson, Sid. "Communications by Satellite." *Foreign Affairs* 48, no. 1 (1969): 67–79.

Mieczkowski, Yanek. *Gerald Ford and the Challenges of the 1970s.* Lexington: University of Kentucky Press, 2005.

Miglietta, John P. *American Alliance Policy in the Middle East, 1945–1992.* Lanham, MD: Lexington Books, 2002.

Miller, Aaron David. *The Much Too Promised Land: America's Elusive Search for Arab-Israeli Peace.* New York: Bantam, 2008.

Miller, Edward Garvey. *Misalliance: Ngo Dinh Diem, the United States, and the Fate of South Vietnam.* Cambridge, MA: Harvard University Press, 2013.

Milward, Alan S. *The European Rescue of the Nation-State.* New York: Routledge, 2000.

Milward, Alan S. *The Reconstruction of Western Europe, 1945–1951.* Berkeley: University of California Press, 1984.

Minsky, Hyman. *Stabilizing an Unstable Economy.* New York: McGraw Hill, 2008.

Mirowski, Philip, and Dieter Plehwe. *The Road from Mont Pèlerin: The Making of the Neoliberal Thought Collective.* Cambridge, MA: Harvard University Press, 2009.

Mitchell, Greg. *Tricky Dick and the Pink Lady: Sexual Politics and the Red Scare.* New York: Random House, 1998.

Mitchell, Nancy. "The Cold War and Jimmy Carter." In *The Cambridge History of the Cold War*, edited by Melvyn P. Leffler and Odd Arne Westad, 3:66–88. New York: Cambridge University Press, 2010.

Mitchell, Timothy. *Carbon Democracy: Political Power in the Age of Oil*. London: Verso, 2013.

Moffitt, Michael. *The World's Money: International Banking from Bretton Woods to the Brink of Insolvency*. New York: Simon and Schuster, 1984.

Mok, Michael. *Biafra Journal*. New York: Time-Life Books, 1969.

Moore, Charles. *Margaret Thatcher: The Authorized Biography; from Grantham to the Falklands*. New York: Alfred A. Knopf, 2013.

Moravcsik, A. *The Choice for Europe: Social Purpose and State Power from Messina to Maastricht*. Ithaca, NY: Cornell University Press, 1998.

Moreton, Bethany. *To Serve God and Wal-Mart: The Making of Christian Free Enterprise*. Cambridge, MA: Harvard University Press, 2009.

Morgan, Iwan. "Monetary Metamorphosis: The Volcker Fed and Inflation." *Journal of Policy History* 24, no. 4 (2012): 545–71.

Morgan, Michael. "*The Origins of the Helsinki Final Act*." PhD diss., Yale University, 2010.

Morgan, Michael. "The United States and the Making of the Helsinki Final Act." In *Nixon in the World: American Foreign Relations, 1969–1977*, edited by Fredrik Logevall and Andrew Preston, 164–83. New York: Oxford University Press, 2007.

Morris, Frank E., and Jane S. Little. "The Eurodollar Market Today: Size, Scope, and Participants." In *The Eurodollar*, edited by Herbert Prochnow and Edward M. Bernstein. 42–67. Chicago: Rand McNally & Co., 1970.

Morris, Kenneth E. *Jimmy Carter, American Moralist*. Athens: University Of Georgia Press, 1997.

Morris, Roger. *Uncertain Greatness: Henry Kissinger and American Foreign Policy*. New York: Harper & Row, 1977.

Morsink, Johannes. *The Universal Declaration of Human Rights: Origins, Drafting, and Intent*. Philadelphia: University of Pennsylvania Press, 1999.

Moskowitz, Moses. *International Concern with Human Rights*. Dobbs Ferry, NY: Oceana Publications, 1974.

Mourlon-Druol, Emmanuel. *A Europe Made of Money: The Emergence of the European Monetary System*. Ithaca, NY: Cornell University Press, 2012.

Moyn, Samuel. *The Last Utopia: Human Rights in History*. Cambridge, MA: Belknap Press, 2010.

Moynihan, Daniel P., and Suzanne Weaver. *A Dangerous Place*. Boston: Little, Brown, 1978.

Mundell, Robert A. "Capital Mobility and Stabilization Policy under Fixed and Flexible Exchange Rates." *Canadian Journal of Economics and Political Science/Revue Canadienne d'Economique et de Science Politique* 29, no. 4 (1963): 475–85.

Mundell, Robert A. "A Theory of Optimum Currency Areas." *American Economic Review* 51, no. 4 (1961): 657–65.

Myers, Sondra, and Benjamin R. Barber. *The Interdependence Handbook: Looking Back, Living the Present, Choosing the Future*. New York: Central European University Press, 2004.

Mytelka, Lynn. "The Lomé Convention and a New International Division of Labour." *Journal of European Integration* 1, no. 1 (1977): 63–76.

Nanda, V. P. "A Critique of the United Nations Inaction in the Bangladesh Crisis." *Denver Law Journal* 49 (1972–73): 53–68.

National Commission on Terrorist Attacks. *The 9/11 Commission Report: Final Report of the National Commission on Terrorist Attacks upon the United States*. W. W. Norton, 2004.

Navrátil, Jaromír, ed. *The Prague Spring 1968*. New York: Central European University Press, 2006.

Nawaz, Tawfique. *The New International Economic Order: A Bibliography*. Westport, CT: Greenwood Press, 1980.

Neier, Aryeh. *The International Human Rights Movement: A History*. Princeton, NJ: Princeton University Press, 2012.

Nelson, Keith. *The Making of Détente: Soviet-American Relations in the Shadow of Vietnam*. Baltimore, MD: Johns Hopkins University Press, 1995.

Nguyen, Lien-Hang T. *Hanoi's War: An International History of the War for Peace in Vietnam*. Chapel Hill: University of North Carolina Press, 2012.

Nichols, Thomas M. "Carter and the Soviets: The Origins of the U.S. Return to a Strategy of Confrontation." *Diplomacy and Statecraft* 13, no. 2 (2002): 21–42.

Niebuhr, Reinhold. *The Irony of American History.* Chicago: University of Chicago Press, 2008.

Niedhart, Gottfried. "Ostpolitik: Phases, Short-Term Objectives, and Grand Design." *German Historical Institute Bulletin,* supplement 1 (2003): 118–36.

Nixon, Richard. "Asia after Vietnam." *Foreign Affairs* 46, no. 1 (1967): 111–25.

Nixon, Richard M. *The Memoirs of Richard Nixon.* New York: Touchstone, 1978.

Nixon, Richard M. *Six Crises.* Garden City, NY: Doubleday, 1962.

Njølstad, Olav. "The Carter Legacy." In *The Last Decade of the Cold War,* edited by Olav Njølstad, 196–225. New York: Routledge, 2004.

Njølstad, Olav. "The Collapse of Superpower Détente." In *The Cambridge History of the Cold War,* edited by Melvyn P. Leffler and Odd Arne Westad, 3:135–55. New York: Cambridge University Press, 2010.

Njølstad, Olav. "Shifting Priorities: The Persian Gulf in U.S. Strategic Planning in the Carter Years." *Cold War History* 4, no. 3 (2004): 21–55.

Nove, Alec. *An Economic History of the USSR, 1917–1991.* London: Penguin, 1992.

Nuenlist, Christian, Anna Locher, and Garret Martin, eds. *Globalizing de Gaulle: International Perspectives on French Foreign Policies, 1958–1969.* Lanham, MD: Lexington Books, 2010.

Nye, Joseph S. "Studying World Politics." In *Journeys through World Politics: Autobiographical Reflections of Thirty-Four Academic Travelers,* edited by Joseph Kruzel and James Rosenau, 119–212. Lexington, MA: Lexington Books, 1989.

Nye, Joseph S. *Bound to Lead: The Changing Nature of American Power.* New York: Basic Books, 1990.

Nye, Joseph. "Independence and Interdependence." *Foreign Policy,* no. 22 (1976): 130–61.

O'Donnell, Guillermo. *Modernization and Bureaucratic Authoritarianism: Studies in South American Politics.* Berkeley: University of California Press, 1973.

Oberdorfer, Don. *Senator Mansfield: The Extraordinary Life of a Great Statesman and Diplomat.* Washington, DC: Smithsonian, 2003.

Obiozor, George A. *The United States and the Nigerian Civil War: An American Dilemma in Africa, 1966–1970.* Lagos: Nigerian Institute of International Affairs, 1993.

Obstfeld, Maurice, Jay C. Shambaugh, and Alan M. Taylor. "The Trilemma in History: Tradeoffs among Exchange Rates, Monetary Policies, and Capital Mobility." *Review of Economics and Statistics* 87, no. 3 (2005): 423–38.

Odell, John S. *U.S. International Monetary Policy: Markets, Power, and Ideas as Sources of Change.* Princeton, NJ: Princeton University Press, 1982.

Ojukwu, Chukwuemeka Odumegwu. *Biafra: Selected Speeches and Random Thoughts.* New York: Harper & Row, 1969.

Oliveiro, Vernie Alison. "The United States, Multinational Corporations, and the Politics of Globalization." PhD diss., Harvard University, 2010.

Olson, Robert K. *U.S. Foreign Policy and the New International Economic Order: Negotiating Global Problems, 1974–1981.* Boulder, CO: Westview Press, 1981.

Orden, David, Robert L. Paarlberg, and Terry L. Roe. *Policy Reform in American Agriculture: Analysis and Prognosis.* Chicago: University of Chicago Press, 1999.

Oren, Michael. *Six Days of War.* New York: Oxford University Press, 2002.

Osterhämmel, Jurgen, and Niels Petersson. *Globalization: A Short History.* Princeton, NJ: Princeton University Press, 2005.

Ouimet, Matthew J. *The Rise and Fall of the Brezhnev Doctrine in Soviet Foreign Policy.* Chapel Hill: University of North Carolina Press, 2003.

Owen, Henry. *The Next Phase in Foreign Policy.* Washington, DC: Brookings Institution, 1973.

Packer, George. *The Assassins' Gate: America in Iraq.* New York: Farrar, Straus and Giroux, 2005.

Pahlavi, Mohammad Reza. *Answer to History.* New York: Stein and Day, 1980.

Painter, David S. "International Oil and National Security." *Daedalus* 120, no. 4 (1991): 183–206.

Painter, David S. *Oil and the American Century: The Political Economy of U.S. Foreign Oil Policy, 1941–1954.* Baltimore, MD: Johns Hopkins University Press, 1986.

Palmer, Michael A. *Guardians of the Gulf: A History of America's Expanding Role in the Persian Gulf, 1833–1992.* New York: Simon and Schuster, 1992.

Panitch, Leo, and Sam Gindin. *The Making of Global Capitalism: The Political Economy of American Empire*. London: Verso, 2012.

Parra, Francisco R. *Oil Politics: A Modern History of Petroleum*. New York: I. B. Tauris, 2010.

Parsi, Trita. *Treacherous Alliance: The Secret Dealings of Israel, Iran, and the United States*. New Haven, CT: Yale University Press, 2007.

Patman, Robert G. *The Soviet Union in the Horn of Africa: The Diplomacy of Intervention and Disengagement*. New York: Cambridge University Press, 1990.

Peck, James. *Ideal Illusions: How the U.S. Government Co-opted Human Rights*. New York: Metropolitan Books, 2011.

Peterman, Kelly. "*The Will to Respond in Common: Elite Networks and the Formulation of Interdependence*," Paper presented at the Berkeley International and Global History Conference, March 4–5, 2011, Berkeley, CA.

Peterson, Peter G. *The Education of an American Dreamer: How a Son of Greek Immigrants Learned His Way from a Nebraska Diner to Washington, Wall Street, and Beyond*. New York: Hachette, 2009.

Peterson, Peter. "The New Politics of the Emerging Global Economy." In *American Foreign Policy in the Age of Interdependence*, edited by Fred Warner Neal and Mary Kersey Harvey, 3–22. Santa Barbara, CA: Center for the Study of Democratic Institutions.

Peterson, Peter. *The United States in the Changing World Economy*. 2 vols. Washington, DC: US Government Printing Office, 1971.

Phillips-Fein, Kim. *Invisible Hands: The Businessmen's Crusade against the New Deal*. New York: W. W. Norton, 2010.

Philpott, Daniel. *Revolutions in Sovereignty: How Ideas Shaped Modern International Relations*. Princeton, NJ: Princeton University Press, 2001.

Polanyi, Karl. *The Great Transformation: The Political and Economic Origins of Our Time*. Boston: Beacon Press, 2001.

Pollack, Gerald A. "The Economic Consequences of the Energy Crisis." *Foreign Affairs* 52, no. 3 (April 1974): 452–71.

Pollan, Michael. *The Omnivore's Dilemma*. New York: Penguin, 2007.

Pollock, Fred E., and Warren Kimball. "'In Search of Monsters to Destroy': Roosevelt and Colonialism." In Warren Kimball, *The Juggler: Franklin Roosevelt as Wartime Statesman*, 127–57. Princeton, NJ: Princeton University Press, 1991.

Pomfret, Richard W T. *The Age of Equality: The Twentieth Century in Economic Perspective*. Cambridge, MA: Harvard University Press, 2011.

Pons, Silvio. "The Rise and Fall of Eurocommunism." In *The Cambridge History of the Cold War*, edited by Melvyn P. Leffler and Odd Arne Westad, 3:45–65. New York: Cambridge University Press, 2010.

Poole, Robert. *Earthrise: How Man First Saw the Earth*. New Haven, CT: Yale University Press, 2008.

Porter, Roger. *Presidential Decision Making: The Economic Policy Board*. New York: Cambridge University Press, 1980.

Power, Jonathan. *Against Oblivion: Amnesty International's Fight for Human Rights*. London: Fotana, 1981.

Power, Jonathan. *Like Water on Stone: The Story of Amnesty International*. Boston: Northeastern University Press, 2001.

Preston, Andrew. *Sword of the Spirit, Shield of Faith Religion in American War and Diplomacy*. New York: Random House, 2012.

Prindle, David F. *Petroleum Politics and the Texas Railroad Commission*. Austin: University of Texas Press, 1984.

Pryor, Leslie M. "Arms and the Shah." *Foreign Policy*, no. 31 (1978): 56–71.

Putman, Robert, and Nicholas Bayne. *Hanging Together: The Seven Power Summits*. Cambridge, MA: Harvard University Press, 1984.

Quandt, William B. *Camp David: Peacemaking and Politics*. Washington, DC: Brookings Institution, 1986.

Quandt, William B. *Peace Process: American Diplomacy and the Arab-Israeli Conflict Since 1967*. Berkeley: University of California Press, 2005.

Quinn-Judge, Sophie. "Fraternal Aid, Self-Defense, or Self Interest?" In *Humanitarian Intervention*, edited by Brendan Simms and D. J. B. Trim, 343–62. New York: Cambridge University Press, 2011.

Rabe, Stephen G. *The Killing Zone: The United States Wages Cold War in Latin America*. New York: Oxford University Press, 2012.

Radchenko, Sergey. *Two Suns in the Heavens: The Sino-Soviet Struggle for Supremacy, 1962–1967*. Washington, DC: Woodrow Wilson Center, 2009.

Radchenko, Sergey. *Unwanted Visionaries: The Soviet Failure in Asia at the End of the Cold War*. New York: Oxford University Press, 2014.

Raghavan, Srinath. *1971: A Global History of the Creation of Bangladesh*. Cambridge, MA: Harvard University Press, 2013.

Rakove, Robert B. *Kennedy, Johnson, and the Nonaligned World*. Cambridge: Cambridge University Press, 2012.

Rarchie, Timothy W. *Rock Around the Bloc: A History of Rock Music in Eastern Europe and the Soviet Union*. New York: Oxford University Press, 1990.

Rauchway, Eric. *Blessed among Nations: How the World Made America*. New York: Hill & Wang, 2006.

Ravenal, Earl C. *Large-Scale Foreign Policy Change: The Nixon Doctrine as History and Portent*. Berkeley: Institute of International Studies, University of California, 1989.

Reddaway, Peter. *Uncensored Russia: Protest and Dissent in the Soviet Union*. New York: American Heritage Press, 1972.

Redfield, Peter. *Life in Crisis: The Ethical Journey of Doctors without Borders*. Berkeley: University of California Press, 2013.

Reeves, Richard. *President Nixon: Alone in the White House*. New York: Touchstone, 2001.

Reston, James. *The Lone Star: The Life of John Connally*. New York: Harper & Row, 1989.

Reynolds, David J. *Britannia Overruled: British Policy and World Power in the Twentieth Century*. New York: Longman, 2000.

Reynolds, David J. *From Munich to Pearl Harbor: Roosevelt's America and the Origins of the Second World War*. Chicago: Ivan R. Dee, 2001.

Reynolds, David J. *One World Divisible: A Global History since 1945*. London: Penguin, 2000.

Riesman, Michael. "Humanitarian Intervention to Protect the Ibos." In *Humanitarian Intervention: A History*, edited by Richard Lillich, 67–195. Charlottesville: University of Virginia Press, 1973.

Ro'i, Yaacov, and Boris Morozov. *The Soviet Union and the June 1967 Six Day War*. Palo Alto, CA: Stanford University Press, 2008.

Robb, Thomas. "The Power of Oil: Edward Heath, the Year of Europe and the Anglo-American Special Relationship." *Contemporary British History* 26, no. 1 (2011): 73–96.

Roberts, Paul. *The End of Food*. Boston: Mariner Books, 2009.

Roberts, Priscilla. "The Council Has Been Your Creation': Hamilton Fish Armstrong, Paradigm of the American Foreign Policy Establishment?" *Journal of American Studies* 35, no. 1 (2001): 65–94.

Robertson, Geoffrey. *Crimes against Humanity: The Struggle for Global Justice*. London: Allen Lane, 1999.

Rockefeller, David. "*The Trilateral Commission at 25*." Unpublished paper. http://www.trilateral.org/download/file/speeches_25_anniversary.pdf.

Rockefeller, David. *Memoirs*. New York: Random House, 2003.

Rodgers, Daniel T. *Age of Fracture*. Cambridge, MA: Harvard University Press, 2010.

Rodrik, Dani. *The Globalization Paradox: Democracy and the Future of the World Economy*. New York: W. W. Norton, 2011.

Rosati, Jerel A. *The Carter Administration's Quest for Global Community: Beliefs and Their Impact on Behavior*. Columbia: University of South Carolina Press, 1987.

Rosecrance, Richard N. *The Rise of the Trading State: Commerce and Conquest in the Modern World*. New York: Basic Books, 1986.

Ross, Robert S. *Negotiating Cooperation: The United States and China, 1969–1989*. Palo Alto, CA: Stanford University Press, 1995.

Rostow, Walter W. *The Diffusion of Power: An Essay in Recent History*. New York: Macmillan, 1972.

Rothkopf, David. *Running the World: The Inside Story of the National Security Council.* New York: PublicAffairs, 2005.

Roy, Olivier. *The Failure of Political Islam.* Cambridge, MA: Harvard University Press, 1994.

Rubenstein, Joshua, and Alexander Gribanov. *The KGB File of Andrei Sakharov.* New Haven, CT: Yale University Press, 2005.

Rubenstein, Joshua. *Soviet Dissidents: Their Struggle for Human Rights.* Boston: Beacon Press, 1985.

Rubin, Barry M. *Paved with Good Intentions: The American Experience and Iran.* New York: Oxford University Press, 1980.

Rueff, Jacques, and Fred Hirsch. "The Role and Rule of Gold: An Argument." *Princeton Essays in International Finance,* no. 47 (1965).

Ruggie, John G. "International Regimes, Transactions, and Change: Embedded Liberalism in the Postwar Economic Order." *International Organization* 36, no. 2 (1982): 379–415.

Sachs, Jeffrey. *To Move the World: JFK's Quest for Peace.* New York: Random House, 2013.

Sadat, Anwar. *In Search of Identity: An Autobiography.* New York: Harper & Row, 1978.

Safire, William. *Before the Fall: An Inside View of the Pre-Watergate White House.* New York: Ballantine Books, 1977.

Sagan, Scott D., and Jeremi Suri. "The Madman Nuclear Alert: Secrecy, Signaling, and Safety in October 1969." *International Security* 27, no. 4 (2003): 150–83.

Sakharov, Andrei. *Memoirs.* New York: Alfred A. Knopf, 1990.

Sakharov, Andrei. *My Country and the World.* New York: Alfred A.Knopf, 1975.

Sakharov, Andrei. *Progress, Coexistence, and Intellectual Freedom.* New York: W. W. Norton, 1968.

Sakharov, Andrei. *Sakharov Speaks.* London: Collins & Harvill, 1974.

Samuels, J. W. "Humanitarian Relief in Man-Made Disasters: International Law, Government Policy and the Nigerian Experience." *Canadian Yearbook of International Law* 10 (1972): 3–39.

Samuelson, Robert J. *The Great Inflation and Its Aftermath: The Past and Future of American Affluence.* New York: Random House, 2008.

Sanders, Jerry Wayne. *Peddlers of Crisis: The Committee on the Present Danger and the Politics of Containment.* Boston: South End Press, 1983.

Sargent, Daniel J. "The Cold War and the International Political Economy in the 1970s." *Cold War History.* Vol. 13, no. 3 (2013): 393–425.

Sargent, Daniel J. "Lyndon Johnson and the Challenge of Economic Globalization." In *Lyndon B. Johnson and the Dawn of the Post–Cold War Era,* edited by Mark Atwood Lawrence and Francis J. Gavin, 3–29. New York: Oxford University Press, 2013.

Sargent, Daniel J. "Oasis in the Desert? America's Human Rights Rediscovery." In *The Breakthrough: Human Rights in the 1970s,* edited by Jan Eckel and Samuel Moyn, 124–45. Philadelphia: University of Pennsylvania Press, 2014.

Sarotte, Mary E. *Dealing With the Devil: East Germany, Détente, and Ostpolitik, 1969–1973.* Chapel Hill: University of North Carolina Press, 2001.

Sassen, Saskia. *Territory, Authority, Rights: From Medieval to Modern Assemblages.* Princeton, NJ: Princeton University Press, 2006.

Saunders, Chris, and Sue Onslow. "Southern Africa in the Cold War 1976–1990." In *The Cambridge History of the Cold War,* edited by Melvyn P. Leffler and Odd Arne Westad, 3:222–43. New York: Cambridge University Press 2010.

Sauvy, Alfred. *Zero Growth?* New York: Praeger, 1976.

Schaller, Michael. *The American Occupation of Japan: The Origins of the Cold War in Asia.* New York: Oxford University Press, 1987.

Schlesinger, Arthur, Jr. *The Imperial Presidency.* Boston: Houghton Mifflin, 1973.

Schlesinger, Stephen C., and Stephen Kinzer. *Bitter Fruit: The Story of the American Coup in Guatemala.* 2nd ed. Cambridge, MA: Harvard University Press.

Schmidli, William Michael. *The Fate of Freedom Elsewhere: Human Rights and U.S. Cold War Policy Toward Argentina.* Ithaca, NY: Cornell University Press, 2013.

Schmidli, William Michael. "Institutionalizing Human Rights in US Foreign Policy: US-Argentine Relations, 1976–1980." *Diplomatic History* 35, no. 2 (2011): 351–77.

Schmidt, Helmut. *Men and Powers: A Political Retrospective.* New York: Random House, 1989.

Schmidt, Helmut. "The Struggle for the World Product: Politics between Power and Morals." *Foreign Affairs* 52, no. 3 (April 1974): 437–51.

Schmitz, David F. *The United States and Right-Wing Dictatorships, 1965–1989.* Cambridge: Cambridge University Press, 2006.

Schmitz, David F., and Vanessa Walker. "Jimmy Carter and the Foreign Policy of Human Rights: The Development of a Post–Cold War Foreign Policy." *Diplomatic History* 28, no. 1 (2004): 113–43.

Schneider, Stephen A. *The Oil Price Revolution.* Baltimore, MD: Johns Hopkins University Press, 1983.

Schneier, Marc. *Shared Dreams: Martin Luther King, Jr. and the Jewish Community.* Woodstock, VT: Jewish Lights Publishing, 1999.

Schoenbaum, David. *The United States and the State of Israel.* New York: Oxford University Press, 1993.

Schoultz, Lars. *Beneath the United States: A History of U.S. Policy Toward Latin America.* Cambridge, MA: Harvard University Press, 1998.

Schoultz, Lars. *Human Rights and United States Policy Toward Latin America.* Princeton, NJ: Princeton University Press, 1981.

Schroeder, Paul W. *The Transformation of European Politics, 1763–1848.* Oxford: Oxford University Press, 1994.

Schulman, Bruce J. *The Seventies: The Great Shift in American Culture, Society, and Politics.* New York: Free Press, 2001.

Schulzinger, Robert D. *A Time for War: The United States and Vietnam, 1941–1975.* Oxford: Oxford University Press, 1997.

Schulzinger, Robert D. *The Wise Men of Foreign Affairs: The History of the Council on Foreign Relations.* New York: Columbia University Press, 1984.

Schumpeter, Joseph Alois. *Capitalism, Socialism, and Democracy.* New York: Harper, 2008.

Schurmann, Franz. *The Foreign Politics of Richard Nixon: The Grand Design.* Berkeley: Institute of International and Area Studies, University of California, 1987.

Schurmann, Franz. *The Logic of World Power: An Inquiry into the Origins, Currents, and Contradictions of World Politics.* New York: Pantheon, 1974.

Schwab, George, ed. *Eurocommunism: The Ideological and Political-Theoretical Foundations.* Westport, CT: Greenwood Press, 1981.

Schwartz, Thomas A. *Lyndon Johnson and Europe: In the Shadow of Vietnam.* Cambridge, MA: Harvard University Press, 2003.

Scott, Richard. *The History of the International Energy Agency.* Vol. 2. Paris: OECD, 1995.

Seabury, Paul. *The Rise and Decline of the Cold War.* New York: Basic Books, 1967.

Segev, Tom. *1967: Israel, the War, and the Year That Transformed the Middle East.* New York: Macmillan, 2007.

Sellars, Kirsten. *The Rise and Rise of Human Rights.* Stroud, UK: Sutton, 2002.

Sestanovich, Stephen. *Maximalist: America in the World from Truman to Obama.* New York: Random House, 2014.

Seton-Watson, Hugh. *Nations and States: An Enquiry into the Origins of Nations and the Politics of Nationalism.* London: Methuen, 1977.

Seymour, Ian. *OPEC: Instrument of Change.* New York: St. Martin's Press, 1981.

Shaikh, Farzana. *Community and Consensus in Islam: Muslim Representation in Colonial India, 1860–1947.* Cambridge: Cambridge University Press, 1989.

Shawcross, William. *Sideshow: Kissinger, Nixon, and the Destruction of Cambodia.* London: Andre Deutsch, 1979.

Shcharansky, Anatoly, and Stefani Hoffman. *Fear No Evil: The Classic Memoir of One Man's Triumph over a Police State.* New York: Public Affairs, 1998.

Sherer, Albert. "Goldberg's Variation." *Foreign Policy,* no. 39 (Summer 1980): 154–59.

Sherer, Caroll. "Breakdown at Belgrade." *Washington Quarterly* 1, no. 4 (1978): 79–85.

Sherrill, Robert. *The Oil Follies of 1970–1980: How the Petroleum Industry Stole the Show (and Much More Besides).* Garden City, NY: Anchor/Doubleday, 1983.

Sherry, Michael. *In the Shadow of War: The United States since the 1930s.* New Haven, CT: Yale University Press, 1995.

Shih, Ashanti. "The Tokai Reprocessing Issue." BA thesis. University of California, Berkeley, May 2011.

Shirk, Susan. "Human Rights: What about China?" *Foreign Policy*, no. 29 (Winter 1977–78): 109–27.

Shoup, Laurence. "Jimmy Carter and the Trilateralists." In *Trilateralism: The Trilateral Commission and Elite Planning for World Management*, edited by Holly Sklar, 199–211. Boston: South End Press, 1980.

Shoup, Laurence H., and William Minter. *Imperial Brain Trust: The Council on Foreign Relations and United States Foreign Policy*. New York: Monthly Review Press, 1977.

Shulman, Bruce. "Slouching Toward the Supply Side." In *The Carter Presidency*, edited by Gary M. Fink and Hugh Davis Graham, 51–71. Lawrence: University Press of Kansas, 2008.

Shulman, Marshal. *Beyond the Cold War*. New Haven, CT: Yale University Press, 1966.

Shultz, George P., and Kenneth W. Dam. *Economic Policy beyond the Headlines*. Stanford, CA: Stanford Alumni Association, 1977.

Sick, Gray. *All Fall Down: America's Fateful Encounter with Iran*. New York: I. B.Tauris, 1985.

Sidaway, James Derrick. "What Is in a Gulf? From the Arc of Crisis to the Gulf War." In *Rethinking Geopolitics*, edited by Gearóid Ó Tuathail and Simon Dalby, 224–39. New York: Routledge, 1998.

Sikkink, Kathryn. *Mixed Signals: U.S. Human Rights Policy and Latin America*. Ithaca, NY: Cornell University Press, 2004.

Silber, William L. *Volcker: The Triumph of Persistence*. New York: Bloomsbury, 2012.

Simon, William. *A Time for Truth*. New York: McGraw-Hill, 1980.

Simpson, Bradley R. "Denying the First Right: The United States, Indonesia, and the Ranking of Human Rights by the Carter Administration, 1976–1980." *International History Review* 31, no. 4 (2009): 798–826.

Simpson, Bradley. *Economists with Guns: Authoritarian Development and U.S.-Indonesian Relations*. Palo Alto, CA: Stanford University Press.

Sisson, Richard, and Leo Rose. *War and Secession: Pakistan, India, and the Creation of Bangladesh*. Berkeley: University of California Press, 1990.

Skeet, Ian. *OPEC: Twenty-Five Years of Prices and Politics*. New York: Cambridge University Press, 1988.

Skiba, Lynsay. "Shifting Sites of Argentine Advocacy and the Shape of 1970s Human Rights Debates." In *The Breakthrough: Human Rights in the 1970s*, edited by Jan Eckel and Samuel Moyn, 107–24. Philadelphia: University of Pennsylvania Press, 2013.

Skidelsky, Robert. *John Maynard Keynes: A Biography*. Vol. 2, *The Economist as Savior*. New York: Penguin, 1995.

Skidmore, David. *Reversing Course: Carter's Foreign Policy, Domestic Politics, and the Failure of Reform*. Nashville, TN: Vanderbilt University Press, 1996.

Sklar, Holly. *Trilateralism: The Trilateral Commission and Elite Planning for World Management*. Boston: South End Press, 1980.

Slaughter, Anne-Marie. *A New World Order*. Princeton, NJ: Princeton University Press, 2005.

Slezkine, Yuri. *The Jewish Century*. Princeton, NJ: Princeton University Press, 2004.

Smith, Gaddis. *Morality, Reason, and Power: American Diplomacy in the Carter Years*. New York: Hill & Wang, 1986.

Smith, Karen Elizabeth. *Genocide and the Europeans*. New York: Cambridge University Press, 2010.

Smith, Peter. *Talons of the Eagle: Latin America, the United States, and the World*. New York: Oxford University Press, 2007.

Smith, Tony. *America's Mission*. Princeton, NJ: Princeton University Press, 1995.

Sneh, Itai Nartzizenfield. *The Future Almost Arrived: How Jimmy Carter Failed to Change U.S. Foreign Policy*. New York: Peter Lang, 2008.

Snyder, Sarah B. "'A Call for U.S. Leadership': Congressional Activism on Human Rights." *Diplomatic History* 37, no. 2 (April 2013): 372–97.

Snyder, Sarah B. "'Jerry, Don't Go': Domestic Opposition to the 1975 Helsinki Final Act." *Journal of American Studies* 44, no. 1 (2010): 67–81.

Snyder, Sarah B. *Human Rights Activism and the End of the Cold War: A Transnational History of the Helsinki Network*. New York: Cambridge University Press, 2011.

Sobhani, Sohrab. *The Pragmatic Entente: Israeli-Iranian Relations, 1948–1988*. New York: Praeger, 1989.

Soell, Hartmut. *Helmut Schmidt.* 2 vols. Munich, Germany: Deutsche Verlags-Anstalt, 2003.

Solomon, Robert. *The International Monetary System, 1945–1981.* New York: Harper & Row, 1982.

Solzhenitsyn, Aleksandr Isaevich. *Warning to the West.* New York: Farrar, Straus and Giroux, 1976.

Soutou, Georges-Henri. *La guerre de cinquante ans: les relations Est-Ouest, 1943–1990.* Paris: Fayard, 2001.

Spalding, Elizabeth Edwards. *The First Cold Warrior Harry Truman, Containment, and the Remaking of Liberal Internationalism.* Lexington: University Press of Kentucky, 2006.

Sparrow, James T. *Warfare State: World War II Americans and the Age of Big Government.* New York: Oxford University Press, 2011.

Spence, Michael. "The Impact of Globalization on Income and Employment." *Foreign Affairs* 90, no. 4 (2011): 28–41.

Spiegel, Steven L. *The Other Arab-Israeli Conflict: Making America's Middle East Policy, from Truman to Reagan.* Chicago: University of Chicago Press, 1986.

Spiro, David. *The Hidden Hand of American Hegemony: Petrodollar Recycling and International Markets.* Ithaca, NY: Cornell University Press, 1999.

Spykman, Nicholas J. *America's Strategy in World Politics: The United States and the Balance of Power.* New York: Harcourt, Brace and Co., 1942.

Sreberny, Annabelle, and Ali Mohammadi. *Small Media, Big Revolution: Communication, Culture, and the Iranian Revolution.* Minneapolis: University of Minnesota Press, 1994.

Stacks, John F. *Scotty: James B. Reston and the Rise and Fall of American Journalism.* Boston: Little, Brown, 2003.

Stedman Jones, Daniel. *Masters of the Universe: Hayek, Friedman, and the Birth of Neoliberal Politics.* Princeton, NJ: Princeton University Press, 2012.

Steel, Ronald. *Pax Americana.* New York: Viking, 1967.

Steel, Ronald. *The End of Alliance: America and the Future of Europe.* New York: Viking, 1964.

Stefan, Charles G. "The Drafting of the Helsinki Final Act: A Personal View of the CSCE's Geneva Phase (September 1973 until July 1975)." *Society for Historians of American Foreign Relations Newsletter* 31, no. 2 (2000): 1–10.

Steil, Benn. *The Battle of Bretton Woods: John Maynard Keynes, Harry Dexter White, and the Making of a New World Order.* Princeton, NJ: Princeton University Press, 2013.

Stein, Judith. *Pivotal Decade: How the United States Traded Factories for Finance in the Seventies.* New Haven, CT: Yale University Press, 2011.

Stein, Kenneth W. *Heroic Diplomacy Sadat, Kissinger, Carter, Begin, and the Quest for Arab-Israeli Peace.* New York: Routledge, 1999.

Steiner, Zara S. *The Lights That Failed: European International History, 1919–1933.* New York: Oxford University Press, 2005.

Steiner, Zara S. *The Triumph of the Dark: European International History 1933–1939.* New York: Oxford University Press, 2011.

Stevens, Simon. "Jimmy Carter's Presidential Campaign and the Search for a New American Foreign Policy, 1972–1977." MPhil thesis, Cambridge University, 2008.

Stiglitz, Joseph E. *Making Globalization Work.* W. W. Norton, 2007.

Stokes, Gale. *From Stalinism to Pluralism: A Documentary History of Eastern Europe Since 1945.* New York: Oxford University Press, 1996.

Stork, Joe, and Martha Wenger. "The U.S. in the Persian Gulf: From Rapid Deployment to Massive Deployment." *Middle East Report,* no. 168 (1991): 22–26.

Strange, Susan. *Casino Capitalism.* Oxford: Basil Blackwell, 1986.

Strange, Susan. *International Monetary Relations, 1959–1971.* New York: Oxford University Press, 1976.

Strange, Susan. *The Retreat of the State: The Diffusion of Power in the World Economy.* New York: Camridge University Press, 1996.

Stremlau, John J. *The International Politics of the Nigerian Civil War, 1967–1970.* Princeton, NJ: Princeton University Press, 1977.

Strong, Robert A. "Recapturing Leadership: The Carter Administration and the Crisis of Confidence." *Presidential Studies Quarterly* 16, no. 4 (Fall 1986): 636–50.

Strong, Robert A. *Working in the World: Jimmy Carter and the Making of American Foreign Policy.* Baton Rouge: Louisiana State University Press, 2000.

Stueck, William. *Rethinking the Korean War: A New Diplomatic and Strategic History.* Princeton, NJ: Princeton University Press, 2004.

Sullivan, William H. *Mission to Iran.* New York: W. W. Norton, 1981.

Suri, Jeremi. *Henry Kissinger and the American Century.* Cambridge, MA: Harvard University Press, 2007.

Suri, Jeremi. *Power and Protest: Global Revolution and the Rise of Detente.* Cambridge, MA: Harvard University Press, 2003.

Szulc, Tad. "Lisbon and Washington: Behind the Portuguese Revolution." *Foreign Policy,* no. 21 (1975): 3–62.

Tabb, William K. *Economic Governance in the Age of Globalization.* New York: Columbia University Press, 2004.

Talbott, Strobe. *Endgame: The Inside Story of SALT II.* New York: Harper & Row, 1980.

Tareke, Gebru. "The Ethiopia-Somalia War of 1977 Revisited." *International Journal of African Historical Studies* 33, no. 3 (2000): 635–67.

Taubman, William. *Khrushchev: The Man, His Era.* London: Free Press, 2003.

Taylor, Telford. *Nuremberg and Vietnam: An American Tragedy.* Chicago: Quadrangle Books, 1970.

Temin, Peter, and David Vines. *The Leaderless Economy: Why the World Economic System Fell Apart and How to Fix It.* Princeton, NJ: Princeton University Press, 2013.

Temin, Peter. *Lessons from the Great Depression.* Cambridge, MA: MIT Press, 1989.

Teorell, Jan. *Determinants of Democratization: Explaining Regime Change in the World, 1972–2006.* New York: Cambridge University Press, 2010.

Terzian, Pierre. *OPEC: The Inside Story.* Avon, UK: Zed, 1985.

Thomas, Daniel C. *The Helsinki Effect: International Norms, Human Rights, and the Demise of Communism.* Princeton, NJ: Princeton University Press, 2001.

Thompson, Joseph E. *American Policy and African Famine: The Nigeria-Biafra War, 1966–1970.* Westport, CT: Greenwood Press, 1990.

Thornton, Richard C. *The Carter Years: Towards A New Global Order.* New York: Paragon House, 1982.

Tilly, Charles. *Coercion, Capital, and European States, AD 990–1990.* Cambridge, MA: Basil Blackwell, 1990.

Toffler, Alvin. *Future Shock.* New York, N.Y: Random House, 1970.

Touval, Saadia. *The Peace Brokers: Mediators in ihe Arab-Israeli Conflict, 1948–1979.* Princeton, NJ: Princeton University Press, 1982.

Trachtenberg, Marc. *A Constructed Peace: The Making of the European Settlement.* Princeton, NJ: Princeton University Press, 1999.

Trager, James. *The Great Grain Robbery.* New York: Ballantine Books, 1975.

Treverton, Gregory F. *The "Dollar Drain" and American Forces in Germany: Managing the Political Economies of Alliance.* Athens: University of Ohio Press, 1978.

Triffin, Robert. *Gold and the Dollar Crisis: The Future of Convertibility.* New Haven, CT: Yale University Press, 1961.

Trofimov, Yaroslav. *The Siege of Mecca: The Forgotten Uprising in Islam's Holiest Shrine.* London: Penguin, 2008.

Troy, Gil. *Moynihan's Moment: America's Fight against Zionism as Racism.* New York: Oxford University Press, 2013.

Tsoukalis, Loukas. *The Politics and Economics of European Monetary Integration.* London: Allen & Unwin, 1977.

Tucker, Robert C., ed. *The Marx-Engels Reader.* New York: W. W. Norton, 1989.

Tucker, Robert W. *A New Isolationism: Threat or Promise?* New York: Universe Books, 1972.

Tudda, Chris. *A Cold War Turning Point: Nixon and China, 1969–1972.* Baton Rouge: Louisiana State University Press, 2012.

Ullman, Richard. "Trilateralism: Partnership for What?" *Foreign Affairs* 55, no. 1 (October 1976): 1–19.

Vaïsse, Justin. *Neoconservatism: The Biography of a Movement.* Cambridge, MA: Harvard University Press, 2010.

Valeo, Francis R. *Mike Mansfield, Majority Leader: A Different Kind of Senate, 1961–1976*. Armonk, NY: M. E. Sharpe, 1999.

van Creveld, Martin L. *The Rise and Decline of the State*. New York: Cambridge University Press, 1999.

Van Hollen, C. "The Tilt Policy Revisited: Nixon-Kissinger Geopolitics and South Asia." *Asian Survey* 20, no. 4 (1980).

Vance, Cyrus R. *Hard Choices: Critical Years in America's Foreign Policy*. New York: Simon and Schuster, 1983.

Vandewalle, Dirk J. *A History of Modern Libya*. New York: Cambridge University Press, 2006.

Vasil'ev, Aleksej. *The History of Saudi Arabia*. London: Saqi Books, 2000.

Venn, Fiona. *Oil Diplomacy in the Twentieth Century*. New York: Macmillan, 1986.

Vernon, Raymond, ed. *The Oil Crisis in Perspective*. New York: W. W. Norton, 1976.

Vernon, Raymond. "Economic Sovereignty at Bay." *Foreign Affairs* 47 (1968): 110–22.

Vernon, Raymond. *Sovereignty at Bay*. New York: Basic Books, 1971.

Vietor, Richard H. K. *Energy Policy in America Since 1945: A Study of Business-Government Relations*. New York: Cambridge University Press, 1987.

Vincent, R. J. *Nonintervention and International Order*. Princeton, NJ: Princeton University Press, 1974.

Vitalis, Robert. *America's Kingdom: Mythmaking on the Saudi Oil Frontier*. Palo Alto, CA: Stanford University Press, 2007.

Vogel, Ezra F. *Deng Xiaoping and the Transformation of China*. Cambridge, MA: Harvard University Press, 2011.

Vogelgesang, Sandy. *American Dream, Global Nightmare: The Dilemma of U.S. Human Rights Policy*. New York: W. W. Norton, 1980.

Volcker, Paul, and Toyoo Gyohten. *Changing Fortunes: The World's Money and the Threat to American Leadership*. New York: Times Books, 1992.

Volkogonov, Dmitri. *The Rise and Fall of the Soviet Empire: Political Leaders from Lenin to Gorbachev*. New York: HarperCollins, 1999.

von Karczewski, Johannes. *"Weltwirtschaft Ist Unser Schicksal": Helmut Schmidt Und Die Schaffung Der Weltwirtschaftsgipfel*. Bonn, Germany: J. H. W. Dietz, 2008.

Wala, Michael. *The Council on Foreign Relations and American Foreign Policy in the Early Cold War*. Providence, RI: Berghahn Books, 1994.

Wallerstein, Emmanuel. *Africa: The Politics of Unity*. London: Pall Mall Press, 1967.

Walsh, David. *The Military Balance in the Cold War: U.S. Perceptions and Policy, 1976–85*. New York: Routledge, 2008.

Warf, Barney. "Telecommunications and the Globalization of Financial Services." *Professional Geographer* 41, no. 3 (1989): 257–71.

Warshawsky, Howard. "The Department of State and Human Rights Policy: A Case Study of the Human Rights Bureau." *World Affairs* 142, no. 3 (1980): 188–215.

Wass, Douglas. *Decline to Fall: The Making of British Macro-Economic Policy and the 1976 IMF Crisis*. New York: Oxford University Press, 2008.

Watson, Adam. *The Evolution of International Society: A Comparative Historical Analysis*. New York: Routledge, 1992.

Watts, William, and Lloyd A. Free. "A New National Survey: Nationalism, Not Isolationism." *Foreign Policy*, no. 24 (October 1, 1976): 3–26.

Wawro, Geoffrey. *Quicksand: America's Pursuit of Power in the Middle East*. New York: Penguin, 2010.

Webb, Michael C. *The Political Economy of Policy Coordination: International Adjustment Since 1945*. Ithaca, NY: Cornell University Press, 1995.

Weinberg, Ian. "The Problem of the Convergence of Industrial Societies: A Critical Look at the State of a Theory." *Comparative Studies in Society and History* 11, no. 1 (1969): 1–15.

Weinstein, Allen. *Perjury: The Hiss-Chambers Case*. New York: Random House, 1997.

Weisbrode, Kenneth. *The Atlantic Century: Four Generations of Extraordinary Diplomats Who Forged America's Vital Alliance with Europe*. New York: Da Capo Press, 2009.

Wells, H. G. *The Rights of Man, or What Are We Fighting For?* Harmondsworth, England: Penguin, 1940.

Wells, Wyatt C. *Economist in an Uncertain World: Arthur F. Burns and the Federal Reserve, 1970–1978*. New York: Columbia University Press, 1994.

Westad, Odd Arne. "The Road to Kabul." In *The Fall of Détente*, edited by Odd Arne Westad, 118–48. Ann Arbor: University of Michigan Press, 1997.

Westad, Odd Arne. *The Global Cold War: Third World Interventions and the Making of Our Times*. New York: Cambridge University Press, 2005.

Wheeler, Nicholas J. *Saving Strangers*. New York: Oxford University Press, 2000.

White, Donald. *The American Century: The Rise and Decline of the United States as a World Power*. New Haven, CT: Yale University Press, 1996.

White, Donald W. "The Nature of World Power in American History: An Evaluation at the End of World War II." *Diplomatic History* 11, no. 3 (1987): 181–202.

White, Theodore. *The Making of the President, 1968*. New York: Athaneum, 1969.

Wilkie, Christopher. *Special Drawing Rights (SDRs): The First International Money*. Oxford: Oxford University Press, 2011.

Williams, William A. *The Tragedy of American Diplomacy*. New York: W. W. Norton, 1972.

Williamson, John. *The Failure of World Monetary Reform, 1971–74*. New York: New York University Press, 1977.

Willrich, Mason, and Melvin A. Conant. "The International Energy Agency: An Interpretation and Assessment." *American Journal of International Law* 71, no. 2 (1977): 199–223.

Wills, Garry. *Bomb Power: The Modern Presidency and the National Security State*. New York: Penguin, 2010.

Wills, Garry. *Nixon Agonistes: The Crisis of the Self-Made Man*. Boston: Houghton Mifflin, 1970.

Wilson, Harold. *The Labour Government, 1964–70: A Personal Record*. London: Penguin, 1971.

Wilson, James Graham. *The Triumph of Improvisation: Gorbachev's Adaptability, Reagan's Engagement, and the End of the Cold War*. Ithaca, NY: Cornell University Press, 2014.

Winham, Gilbert R. *International Trade and the Tokyo Round Negotiation*. Princeton, NJ: Princeton University Press, 1986.

Wiseberg, Laurie. "Christian Churches and the Nigerian Civil War." *Journal of African Studies* 2, no. 3 (1975): 315–31.

Wistrich, Robert S. *A Lethal Obsession: Anti-Semitism from Antiquity to the Global Jihad*. Random House, 2010.

Witcover, Jules. *Marathon: The Pursuit of the Presidency, 1972–1976*. New York: Viking, 1977.

Wittner, Lawrence S. *Toward Nuclear Abolition: A History of the World Nuclear Disarmament Movement, 1971–Present*. Palo Alto, CA: Stanford University Press, 2003.

Wolf, Martin. *Fixing Global Finance*. Baltimore, MD: Johns Hopkins University Press, 2010.

Worthen, Molly. *The Man on Whom Nothing Was Lost: The Grand Strategy of Charles Hill*. New York: Mariner Books, 2007.

Wright, Lawrence. *The Looming Tower: Al-Qaeda and the Road to 9/11*. New York: Vintage, 2007.

Yaqub, Salim. "The Weight of Conquest: Henry Kissinger and the Arab-Israeli Conflict." In *Nixon in the World*, edited by Fredrik Logevall and Andrew Preston, 227–48. New York: Oxford University Press, 2008.

Yergin, Daniel. *The Prize: The Epic Quest for Oil, Money, and Power*. New York: Free Press, 1993.

Yergin, Daniel. *The Quest: Energy, Security and the Remaking of the Modern World*. New York: Penguin Press, 2011.

Yergin, Daniel, and Joseph Stanislaw. *The Commanding Heights: The Battle for the World Economy*. New York: Touchstone, 2002.

Young, Marilyn B. *The Vietnam Wars*. New York: HarperCollins, 1991.

Vaïsse, Maurice. *La Grandeur: Politique étrangère du Général de Gaulle, 1958–1969*. Paris: Fayard, 1998.

Zakheim, Dov S. "Of Allies and Access." *Washington Quarterly* 4, no. 1 (1981): 87–96.

Zanchetta, Barbara. *The Transformation of American International Power in the 1970s*. New York: Cambridge University Press, 2013.

Zelizer, Julian E. *Arsenal of Democracy: The Politics of National Security: From World War II to the War on Terrorism*. New York: Basic Books, 2010.

Zhuk, Sergei. *Rock and Roll in the Rocket City: The West, Identity, and Ideology in Soviet Dniepropetrovsk, 1960–1985*. Baltimore, MD: Johns Hopkins University Press, 2010.

Zimmerman, Robert. *Genesis: The Story of Apollo VIII, the First Manned Flight to Another World.* New York: Four Walls Eight Windows, 1998.

Zubok, Vladislav. *A Failed Empire: The Soviet Union in the Cold War from Stalin to Gorbachev.* Chapel Hill: University of North Carolina Press, 2009.

Zumwalt, Elmo. *On Watch: A Memoir.* New York: New York Times Book Company, 1976.

Zweig, Phillip L. *Wriston: Walter Wriston, Citibank, and the Rise and Fall of American Financial Supremacy.* New York: Crown, 1995.

INDEX

CPSIA information can be obtained
at www.ICGtesting.com
Printed in the USA
BVOW08s2311120217
475725BV00006B/1/P